BATH PLANNING

BATH PLANNING

Guidelines, Codes, Standards

Second Edition

KATHLEEN PARROTT PH.D., CKE

JULIA BEAMISH PH.D, CKE

JOANN EMMEL PH.D.

MARY JO PETERSON, CKD, CBD, CAPS, CAASH

Cover image: left: Design by Yuko Matsumoto, CKD, CBD Photograph by Douglas Johnson Photography
right: Design by Elizabeth A. Rosensteel; codesigner Meredith Comfort Photograph by Robert Reck
Cover design: Anne-Michele Abbott

This book is printed on acid-free paper. ♾

National Kitchen & Bath Association
687 Willow Grove Street
Hackettstown, NJ 07840
Phone: 800-THE-NKBA (800-843-6522)
Fax: 908-852-1695
Website: NKBA.org

Published by John Wiley & Sons, Inc., Hoboken, New Jersey.

Published simultaneously in Canada.

Library of Congress Cataloging-in-Publication Data

Parrott, Kathleen R. (Kathleen Rose), 1950-
Bath planning: guidelines, codes, standards/Kathleen Parrott, Ph.D., CKE, Julia Beamish, Ph.D., CKE, JoAnn Emmel, Ph.D., Mary Jo Peterson, CKD, CBD, CAPS.—Second Edition.
pages cm
Includes index.
ISBN 978-1-118-36248-8 (cloth); 978-1-118-40449-2 (ebk.); 978-1-118-40450-8 (ebk.); 978-1-118-40451-5 (ebk.); 978-1-118-40452-2 (ebk.); 978-1-118-43865-7 (ebk.)
1. Bathrooms. I. Beamish, Julia. II. Emmel, JoAnn. III. Peterson, Mary Jo. IV. Title.
TH6485.P37 2013
690'.42—dc23

2012026249

Printed in the United States of America

SKY10022562_111320

Sponsors

The National Kitchen and Bath Association recognizes, with gratitude, the following companies whose generous contributions supported the development of this second edition of *Bath Planning*:

PLATINUM PLUS SPONSOR

Buy it for looks. Buy it for life.®

WWW.MOEN.COM

PLATINUM SPONSOR

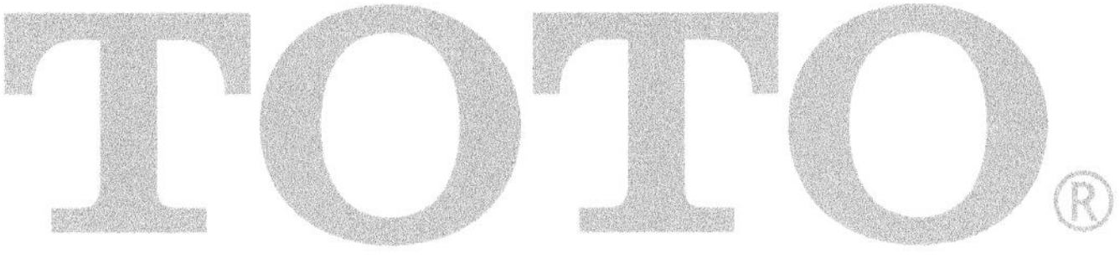

WWW.TOTOUSA.COM

GOLD SPONSORS

Delta Faucet Co.

Dornbracht

About The National Kitchen & Bath Association

The National Kitchen & Bath Association (NKBA) is the only non-profit trade association dedicated exclusively to the kitchen and bath industry and is the leading source of information and education for professionals in the field. Fifty years after its inception, the NKBA has a membership of more than 50,000 and is the proud owner of the Kitchen & Bath Industry Show (KBIS).

The NKBA's mission is to enhance member success and excellence, promote professionalism and ethical business practices, and provide leadership and direction for the kitchen and bath industry worldwide.

The NKBA has pioneered innovative industry research, developed effective business management tools, and set groundbreaking design standards for safe, functional, and comfortable kitchens and baths.

Recognized as the kitchen and bath industry's leader in learning and professional development, the NKBA offers professionals of all levels of experience essential reference materials, conferences, virtual learning opportunities, marketing assistance, design competitions, consumer referrals, internships, and opportunities to serve in leadership positions.

The NKBA's internationally recognized certification program provides professionals the opportunity to demonstrate knowledge and excellence as Associate Kitchen & Bath Designer (AKBD), Certified Kitchen Designer (CKD), Certified Bath Designer (CBD), Certified Master Kitchen & Bath Designer (CMKBD) and Certified Kitchen & Bath Professional (CKBP).

For students entering the industry, the NKBA offers Accredited and Supported Programs, which provide NKBA-approved curriculum at more than 50 learning institutions throughout the United States and Canada.

For consumers, the NKBA showcases award winning designs and provides information on remodeling, green design, safety, and more at NKBA.org. The NKBA Pro Search tool helps consumers locate kitchen and bath professionals in their area.

The NKBA offers membership in 11 different industry segments: dealers, designers, manufacturers and suppliers, multi-branch retailers and home centers, decorative plumbing and hardware, manufacturer's representatives, builders and remodelers, installers, fabricators, cabinet shops, and distributors. For more information, visit NKBA.org.

Table of Contents

Preface

Bathrooms in the home continue to change as new products are introduced to the market, new standards have an impact on energy and water consumption, and people change in their abilities, preferences, and desires. Therefore this book needs to be updated periodically and that is what the National Kitchen and Bath Association has undertaken in conjunction with John Wiley and Sons. Some of the changes include expanded information on sustainability and environmental issues and more information about universal design, including applications for a variety of users. To put the subject of bathroom planning into perspective, in chapter 1 we included information on historical and consumer trends, and research on bath design and planning. In chapter 2 we continued with information on the infrastructure of the home, in order to point out things to consider before the design process begins. The expanded chapter 3 on environmental concerns includes new information on building "green" and conserving water.

We next approached the design of the bathroom with the understanding that a key component to any designed space is the user, so in chapter 4 we discuss universal design and ergonomics. Gathering information about the client and their home is a key first step to pulling things together and planning a great bathroom. This is presented in chapter 5, with sample needs assessment forms provided to assist in that process.

Chapter 6 covers bathroom planning principles and presents each of the NKBA Bathroom Planning Guidelines within the context of a step-by-step consideration of the tasks and activities that occur in the various centers of the bathroom. Diagrams and illustrations help explain these basics. Chapter 7, on mechanical planning, continues to highlight some of the technical planning requirements related to systems in the bathroom.

An expanded Chapter 8 on universal design and accessible design provides an in-depth look at the NKBA Bathroom Access Standards and discusses how they can be incorporated into designs, when required by the client. In chapter 9 we provided ideas for designing spaces related to bathrooms, such as closets, laundries, exercise areas and home spas. Finally, in chapter 10 we walk through the process of developing the bathroom plan, based on client needs and planning guidelines.

We organized and presented this book as if we were talking to a new bathroom designer, just starting a career. At the same time, we offered information, ideas, suggestions and tips of use to the more experienced designer. We firmly believe we can all learn something new—as we certainly did in revising this book! We assumed our readers have little knowledge of, or background in, bathroom design.

We have included many drawings, diagrams and dimensioned plans to aid you in understanding the concepts presented. We have added and updated photographs to show how the content is integrated into "real life" settings and to spark ideas of your own.

There are many worksheets and checklists to use in your work and with your clients. Feel free to use them as is or to adapt them to be useful to you.

Our goal and hope continues to be that this book will help you to be a better designer—more creative and more knowledgeable. This is not the type of book that you read cover to cover. It is a book to be used!

We hope that we find this book on a shelf near your drawing board or computer. We hope this book will be in your studio, office or showroom—wherever you are at your creative best. We envision a book that gets worn from your use, with your comments written in the margin and "sticky notes" coming out in all directions.

Enjoy design and making people comfortable and safe in their homes!

Acknowledgments

The NKBA gratefully acknowledges the following Peer Reviewers of this book:

Becky Sue Becker, CKD, CBD
Leonard Casey
Carolyn Cheetham, CMKBD
Dee David, CKD, CBD
Denise Dick, CMKBD
Kathleen Donohue, CMKBD
Pietro A. Giorgi, Sr., CMKBD
Mark Karas, CMKBD
Martha Kerr, CMKBD
Corey Klassen, AKBD
David Newton, CMKBD
Michael Palkowitsch, CMKBD
Al Pattison, CMKBD
John Petrie, CMKBD
Les Petrie, CMKBD
Betty Ravnik, CMKBD
Klaudia Spivey, CMKBD
Thomas D. Trzcinski, CMKBD
Deleigh Van Deursen, CKD, CBD
Lilley Yee, CKD, CBD

Bathroom History, Research, and Trends

Although the bathroom has changed throughout history, it has always reflected the prevailing cultural attitudes toward hygiene, cleanliness, privacy, relaxation, socializing, and even morality and religion. The development of our modern bath has also been dependent upon evolution in public infrastructure, technology, codes, and other policies.

Today the bathroom is not only the center for personal hygiene, but also a place for relaxation. Research continues to contribute important knowledge related to designing bathrooms for function and safety. Since many bathrooms are being downsized because homes are shrinking in size, the efficient use of space becomes more important than ever. Today's bathrooms emphasize quality and function, and they make use of a variety of materials and designs to produce a unique and personalized room for a household.

The changing demographic makeup of North American households will continue to alter the way our bathrooms look and how they serve users, especially in light of the growing number of older people in our population. This chapter examines the history of the bath, reviews important research in bathroom design, and provides an overview of key demographic and psychographic trends that are now affecting bathroom design.

Learning Objective 1: Describe how evolving lifestyles and technologies have impacted bathroom trends over time.

Learning Objective 2: Describe new trends in present-day bathroom design.

A BRIEF HISTORY OF THE BATHROOM

The typical North American bathroom, as we know it today, has a relatively short history. The early "bath room" or "bath house" was strictly for bathing. It was not until the mid-nineteenth century that one room in the home included all personal hygiene activities in one place. However, some of the activities and rituals currently enjoyed in our baths had their origins centuries ago.

Early Civilizations and the Bath

Although evidence indicates that ancient Egyptians and the residents of Crete had bathing facilities, the bath was taken to new levels by early Greek, Minoan, and Roman civilizations, which embraced it as a way to escape the stresses of everyday life. Most people found the experience so soothing that they typically bathed daily in public bath houses. The baths were not just for cleaning but were a way of life, and in many societies the baths were enjoyed by all social classes of people.

The Greeks developed the "gymnasium," which means "the naked place." After working up a sweat while exercising, the Greek participants would then take a very brief splash of water to cool down but did not really experience what we would consider a thorough cleaning.

The Romans were more serious about their bathing. The early Roman bath houses were often highly decorated with paintings, statues, and elaborate architectural details to add to the pleasure. Because aqueducts could deliver large amounts of water to cities, numerous and large public baths appeared. In addition to both hot and cold tubs, filled from pipes or aqueducts, these ancient bath houses may have included steam chambers, showers, and rooms with dry heat. These efficient systems would not be matched for another 1500 years. The Roman bathing ritual involved many steps. After soaking, bathers were covered with ointments and oils. The ointments and oils were then scraped off of the bather's skin and along with them came the dirt.

The public bath house was also the center of social activities and a form of recreation (see Figure 1.1). For example, baths in the Roman City of Herculaneum included courts for playing ball and a gymnasium. Other baths incorporated libraries, shops, tennis courts, and snack bars. Because of the bath house's significance in society, these cultures found no need to incorporate baths into private homes.

FIGURE 1.1 The Roman bath was a place frequented by Romans of all classes. The baths were often large and ornately decorated, such as the Great Bath in Bath, England.
Steve Cadman on Flickr

In addition to making bathing an enjoyable experience and a prominent part of their lives, the Greeks' and Romans' understanding and practice of good sanitation were extraordinary for the time. The Greek and Roman concept of the "bath" and their belief in the power of water has come full circle to the pools, hot tubs, soaking tubs, mineral baths, and spas we enjoy today.

Public baths were a part of other cultures as well. The "Turkish bath," a steam bath that is followed by a shower and massage, developed when Roman bathing customs were combined with those of nomadic people such as the Byzantines. The early Japanese culture also embraced communal public baths.

Latrines

Just as baths were public facilities in early Roman and Greek civilizations, so were latrines. Although, some early evidence of the home chamber pot was also recorded, Roman water closets and latrines were actually flushed by water. In addition to a public water supply achieved through aqueducts, the Roman Empire also established quite sophisticated sewer systems, which did not appear again until the nineteenth century.

The Middle Ages

With the fall of the Roman Empire, the bath was no longer an important part of daily life and disappeared for centuries. Through the Middle Ages, the fifth to fifteenth centuries, bathing was not a common activity and little attention was given to personal hygiene. Much of the decline was due to physicians who thought bathing was harmful to health, and clerics—in particular the Puritans—who thought nakedness and bathing to be indecent and sinful. The spread of diseases and the tightening of church doctrine eventually closed down communal baths in Europe.

Sanitation in general suffered during the Middle Ages. Few, if any, advances were made in devices to collect waste. Without a sewer system or other disposal methods, chamber pots were usually emptied out the windows. Sometimes that meant pouring waste onto the streets below and often onto people using the streets. Water for home use was drawn from the closest water supply, which could easily be contaminated by free-flowing waste. During the Middle Ages, there was an awareness of the link between sanitation and disease, but no real effort was made to improve the conditions.

Seventeenth and Eighteenth Centuries

The European immigrants brought similar beliefs about indecency and the harmful effects of bathing to America. During the seventeenth and much of the eighteenth centuries in America, little attention was given to body care. Pioneers who desired to bathe did so infrequently because it was so difficult. They first needed to find a container large enough to bathe in, and then carry in water and heat it. These obstacles also meant that clothes were washed infrequently.

The Bathtub

Bathing for the middle class during this time usually involved a portable bathtub placed in the kitchen (see Figure 1.2)—typically the warmest room in the house with a nearby heat source for water. The fireplace used to cook the family meals also heated water for the bath. Eventually fireplaces were built with a water reservoir, making hot water more accessible. Once the bathtub was filled, it usually served the entire family, with the dirtiest family member going last. These tubs were also used for other purposes such as laundry.

Bathing in private was very limited at this time. Wealthy households, who generally used servants to carry water for the bath and dispose of it afterward, had the luxury of locating bathtubs in the privacy of their bedroom. Over time, bathtubs changed in size, shape, and materials. The earliest tubs were basically wooden barrels and then became wooden boxes lined with metal. Later tubs were made of all metal, porcelain crockery, and cast iron with porcelain enamel. More elaborate bathtubs in the bedroom incorporated a hinged cover that helped keep the warmth in the tub.

FIGURE 1.2 The kitchen of early colonial homes was multifunctional, including a space for the family bathtub near the fireplace, the source of heat and hot water.
JoJan/CC-BY-SA-3.0

For families who did not have the luxury of a bathtub in the home, or if someone wanted to freshen up between infrequent baths, a bowl was used for a sponge bath that could take place in the privacy of the bedroom. The idea of incorporating a bathtub of any type into the home evolved very slowly. Even in seventeenth- and eighteenth-century Europe, these facilities were only present in homes of royalty and the very wealthy.

Hot Water

The task of supplying hot water to the bath became easier with new innovations, one of which was the cast iron stove. A water vat was located at the back of the stove. As the family baked and prepared meals, the stove heated water for baths and other uses.

Heaters were eventually attached to the portable tub so that hot water did not need to be carried. They were later attached to the permanently installed tub, and eventually the hot water came from a single source in the home, the water heating system most homes use today.

The Privy

Facilities for toileting have also changed over time. The seventeenth- and eighteenth-century American homes made use of the privy (an English word derived from the Latin word *privatus*, meaning secret, not publicly known) or outhouse installed outside the house. Indoors, the chamber

FIGURE 1.3 The chamber pot was used for indoor toileting and was often very decorative, especially if it was to be visible in the room. *Peter Reed*

pot (see Figure 1.3) was used during bad weather or at night, and the waste was disposed of as quickly as possible. Made of ceramic or metal, the small pot could be stored under a bed, in a cabinet, or in a stool often called a commode. To be more discrete, the chamber pot was later designed into a piece of furniture like a chair called a *closestool*, or night chair, which had the bottom enclosed to hide the pot. Other chamber pots were allowed to sit out in the room, and these were usually highly decorated.

Sanitation

Colonial America also did not have the luxury of a public water supply or sewer system, so the disposal of waste was as primitive as it had been for centuries. Outdoor privies were built over large pits. In some cases, the pit was deep enough to reach the water table, which allowed waste to gradually dissolve and wash away, possibly into a stream or the well next door. Other families emptied their chamber pots into the backyard. When the accumulation became large enough, it needed to be hauled away. As in earlier times, for some lazier households in cities, the streets became the collection area.

Water Closet

The first modern water closets in America most likely came from England. The term "water closet" developed as water was used in the waste disposal process. Although there is evidence of some type of built-in water closet existing in the palaces of Crete, the first attempt at the modern water closet was made by Sir John Harington, around 1596 in England, who designed the device for his home and also installed one in the home of his godmother, Queen Elizabeth I. The device did not live up to expectations, so the idea was deemed too undependable to duplicate. Although a patent was filed in 1617 for a newer version of the water closet, a more successful flushing water closet appeared in 1775.

The American Bathroom Takes Shape—Nineteenth Century and Beyond

As American cities became more congested and as the number of backyard privies near water supplies increased, the issue of sanitation grew more acute. Yellow fever epidemics erupted in the United States, particularly in New York, in the mid-nineteenth century, prompting physicians to declare publicly that unsanitary conditions were the root of the disease, and they asked that taxes be levied to develop a sewer system to remedy the problem. Many larger U.S. cities began to look into developing safe water supplies and disposal systems. As a result of this awareness, the nineteenth century brought many changes in how people viewed personal hygiene, as well as changes in the infrastructure and technologies that made the home bathroom a reality for the masses. One important step toward improving personal hygiene was primarily due to the medical profession. The medical field now supported the idea of hydrotherapy and also publicized the importance of personal and public hygiene, especially as cities grew larger and more congested. Increased awareness of the germ theory in the 1880s, and the connection between disease, germs, and personal hygiene, led to a preoccupation with personal cleanliness and sanitation. "Housewives" began to take this task very seriously and became hygiene experts.

Water and Sewer Systems

To deliver the necessary fresh water for personal hygiene in the home, a safe and reliable water supply had to be developed. Prompted by a series of cholera epidemics, city officials took a closer look at public sanitation. As cholera was linked to drinking water, officials now realized the entire population was at risk, not just those living in less sanitary neighborhoods. This realization had a dramatic impact on the establishment of sewer systems and the sanitation movement began.

The prison system was actually a pioneer in the provision of toilet facilities. However, the idea of a permanent water closet indoors was slow in coming to most homes. People were accustomed to using the outdoor privy, and they were well aware of the odors produced there and did not want them inside the house. There was also the issue of where the water closet could be placed in the home. In addition, the development of the indoor toilet was dependent on the advances made in public water supply and sewer systems, which were slow in coming to many areas.

The earliest indoor water closets were disguised as furniture, much like the chamber pot. They were located in a separate unvented room or "closet" without running water, which was often located at the end of the hall, under the stairs, or on the stair landing. Thomas Jefferson is said to have had the first indoor privies with a vent to remove unwanted odors. These privies were not high tech, however, as waste fell into a pit that was emptied by slaves. For the first flushing privies, water had to be carried to the water closet for the flushing. One variation of the water closet was the "earth closet," but it too required much work and added waste materials to the backyard.

Earth Closet

The earth closet was like a water closet, but instead of washing waste away, dry soil was added after each use to absorb moisture and cover offensive odors. Periodically the contents were removed and the soil with the decomposing organic matter was used as compost. The earth closet, popular in the 1860s because of the undependable water supplies, was quite labor intensive. It was not widely used unless the household had servants to haul soil in and out of the home.

City sanitation began with moving the waste out of neighborhoods. Improvements in sanitation began as some cities incorporated drainage systems that carried waste through canals or pipes to the nearest river or stream. Although these systems cleaned up the neighborhoods to some extent, they basically just moved the problem from one place to another. Chicago built its first sewer system around 1856. In about 1880, municipalities began to pay more attention to city plumbing problems, and health departments in New York City, Washington, DC, and Brooklyn, New York established some of the first plumbing codes.

Sanitation problems continued to increase as populations grew larger and more concentrated in metropolitan areas. City officials recommended that a standard of at least one water closet per family be in place before the end of the nineteenth century. This goal was not met, however. An 1893 Bureau of Labor report stated that only 2.83 percent of the people in some parts of New York City and Chicago had bathroom facilities. Running water and disposal facilities were limited to the middle class and wealthy.

Improvements to the water supply continued at a slow pace. Modern plumbing, including fresh water supplies and effective sewer systems, did not become widely used until the late nineteenth century. One improvement was replacing wooden pipes with lead pipes.

Indoor Plumbing

The bathroom did not become common in the average home until there was a reliable supply of running water and the availability of inexpensive metal pipe and ceramic fixtures that were made possible through mass production during the Industrial Revolution. Early commodes were scarce because of the high cost to produce them by hand, so many households continued to use the outdoor privies. Before public water supplies, households used a faucet or hand pump that drew water from a cistern in the attic. Water was collected from the rain or pumped up from water sources below. The introduction of running water made it both practical and economical to bring personal hygiene activities all into the same space. With the water supply in the attic, it made sense to locate the home's bathroom on the second floor, although many were also on the first floor next to the kitchen. The second floor location also provided the privacy that many people desired.

With running water available, the next generation of water closets was a "washout" or "wash down" design that used a tremendous amount of water to flush waste away completely. The water closet that incorporated running water was the first application of indoor plumbing for the middle class (see Figure 1.4). In 1895, a siphon action water closet was developed that used vacuum action

The Legend of Thomas Crapper

Although different accounts exist, perhaps the most familiar name associated with the modern toilet is Thomas Crapper. Crapper was born in England in 1836, and operated a successful plumbing business from 1861 to 1904. Although he had a number of plumbing-related patents, there is no evidence that Thomas Crapper actually invented the toilet, as many people think. Just how Crapper became so closely associated with the device is not clear. One theory is that he bought the patent for the toilet and marketed it with his name. Then, World War I doughboys passing through England brought together Crapper's name and the toilet, thus establishing the slang name "the crapper."

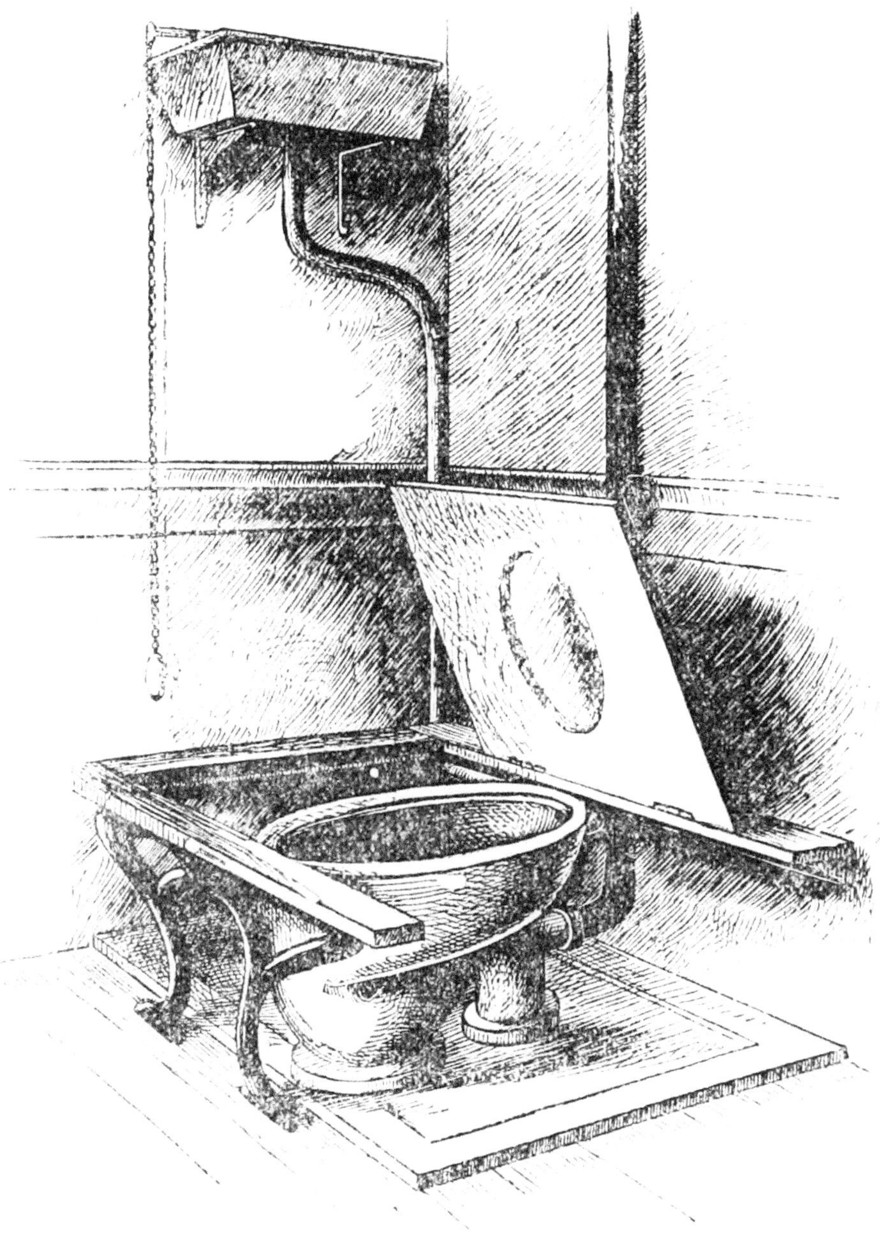

FIGURE 1.4 Early flush toilets used an overhead tank to hold the water that would be used for the flush.
Source: Popular Science Monthly vol. 34.

to more efficiently flush away the waste with less water. This siphonic action is used by most modern toilets. The water closet or toilet, as we know it today, did not become a common household fixture in American homes until the early twentieth century.

Bathing

Bathing methods also changed with the availability of running water. A concern about hygiene prompted people to question how someone could become clean while sitting in a tub of water that became increasingly dirty as one bathed. Such concerns led to an interest in the vapor or steam bath and the shower as superior alternatives to the tub bath.

The shower became possible when a method was found to pump hot water up a pipe for the overhead spray. The modern concept of the shower evolved from military barracks and gyms commonly used by men. It was increasingly recommended as a preferred bathing method over the bathtub in both private homes and public baths of the working class. The first shower was a simple device that used a hand pump to move water up a pipe over a portable or outdoor tub. Eventually, public water supplies included enough pressure to force the water to the showerhead.

Because of their invigorating water action, the first home showers were considered to have therapeutic value. The state-of-the-art shower at the time was a needle spray, which had a series of sprays placed around the body for various needs. It included a kidney spray, a spinal spray, a bidet spray, and so forth, each with a separate control. A crude valve for mixing hot and cold water often left the bather either scalding or chilled. At the time, the idea of water spraying the bather was considered too vigorous for the "gentle sex." For women, it was not uncommon to contact a physician before undertaking a shower.

Most likely the last fixture to be plumbed was the lavatory. The new fixture was designed much like the former wash basin and stand, emerging as a bowl-shaped basin on a pedestal base with a drain in the middle (see Figure 1.5) It turned a china bowl *on* a marble stand into a china bowl *in* a marble stand. The first faucet used a hand pump to draw water, and later a faucet with hot and cold water controls was attached. Soon the pedestal lavatories disappeared as cabinetry entered the bathroom, and sinks were installed into vanities that contained the much desired and needed built-in storage. This design became common by the 1950s.

A Real Bathroom

Older homes did not have an extra space that could be devoted to a complete bathroom. It was relatively easy to add a small toilet or a lavatory, but including a bathtub required a significant amount of space. Bathrooms might be fitted into a bedroom or dressing room, but because they were thought of as a functional space, it was considered a waste to devote too much room to them.

The earliest complete bathrooms belonged to the wealthy, who usually converted a spare bedroom into a bathroom. By the mid-nineteenth century, finer homes were built with a separate bathroom. Although it was possible to have hot and cold running water by the late 1800s and early 1900s, it was still considered a luxury and only incorporated into the homes of the wealthy. The finest luxury bathrooms of the time often included a sitz bath, foot bath, bidet, pedestal lavatory, siphon-action water closet, enameled tub, and shower bath with receptor. Smaller, more functional bathrooms had fixtures crowded together for efficiency and were welcomed because servants were no longer around to carry the water and perform other duties.

During the late nineteenth and early twentieth centuries, people who did convert a room to a bathroom were not quite sure how it should appear, so the earliest bathrooms were unique in design and layout. Many styles emerged during this era, including wood encased bathrooms, with a wooden toilet tank, seat, and a wood-trimmed tub that were massive and imposing. Some luxury rooms were heavily draped, elaborately wallpapered, and carpeted. They included marble, glass, and glazed tiles.

For the middle class, however, the stark, simple, hygienic bathroom with plaster walls and hardwood floors eventually became the standard. Early in the twentieth century, the compact sanitary

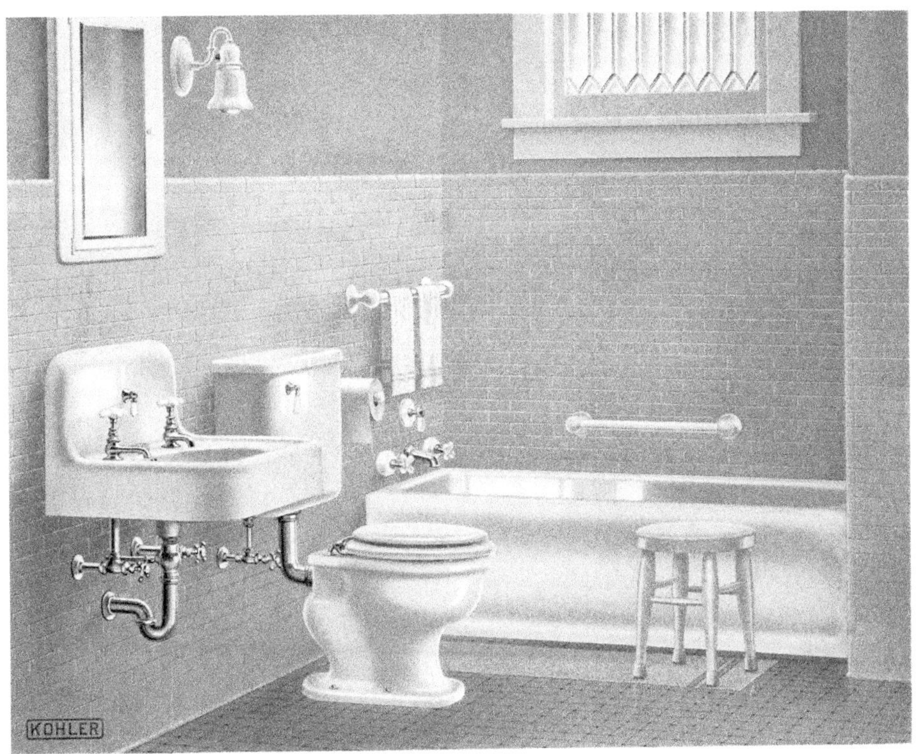

Bath Room FH

F-17-R 5 foot "Viceroy" Bath Tub with F-1785 supply and waste fixture.
F-332-UO 18x24 inch "Emmet" Lavatory fitted with F-2156 faucets, F-2175 ⅜ inch supply pipes, F-2271 lift waste with china *lever* handle, F-2220 1¼ inch "P" trap.
F-1349 Closet Combination.
F-1968 Built in Cabinet.
F-1998 18 inch Hand Rail.
F-2004 24 inch Towel Rack.
F-2031 Bath Room Stool.
F-2071 Toilet Paper Holder.

Size of room 6x8½ feet.

17

FIGURE 1.5 White was the only choice for early bathrooms, which lacked space and storage. Rectangular bathtubs included controls and spout mounted vertically on the wall.
Courtesy of Kohler Company

bathroom with its white walls and fixtures became the model of the modern bathroom and an American symbol. Pipes were left exposed, partly to show the shiny, sanitary fixtures, but also because many people still feared the dangers of trapped gas.

The early bathroom was minimal in size and contained three standard fixtures—a toilet, a lavatory, and a bathtub/shower. The popularity of the bathroom increased, and more households found ways to convert space to accommodate a bathroom. As bathrooms became required by codes, floor plans for new homes replaced a closet or pantry with a bathroom.

To overcome space limitations, R. Buckminster Fuller designed a prefab bathroom in the 1930s that only needed assembly. In 1948, Add-a-Bath offered an already assembled bathroom ready to simply add onto the house.

Plumbing Codes

With an increasing number of bathrooms, more regulations were necessary, which led Secretary of Commerce, Herbert Hoover, to establish the 1924 Bureau of Standards for basic plumbing. Although these codes were not enforceable, they were effective and provided a technical solution to the plumbing aspects of safety and sanitation. Almost 20 years later, the 1940 Housing Census found that still only 50.9 percent of all U.S. houses were in good condition with a bath and flush toilet.

The plumbing situation improved by 1950 with more than 85 percent of urban homes having hot and cold running water, 92 percent a flush toilet, and 89 percent a bathtub or shower. In rural areas, however, more than half of farm homes lacked a bathroom. In 1951, the Department of Commerce established a National Plumbing Code, and in 1955, the American Standards Association distributed a list of basic plumbing principles that served as recommendations to municipalities.

Today, technological solutions, as well as strict plumbing codes, have made a safe water supply and sanitary disposal system available to all except a very small portion of the American population. As new innovations emerge, care is taken to make sure they continue to meet the sanitation standards necessary for good health.

Today's Bathrooms

The bathrooms of today contain many of the basic elements of earlier bathrooms, but new technologies, materials, and lifestyles have made the bathroom into a more inviting, relaxing, and comfortable room to enjoy. Awareness of the need for universal and **accessible design** has been growing since the end of World War II, with the requirements of disabled veterans, polio patients, and the aging population becoming more important.

Today the bathroom is undergoing a reinvention similar to the kitchen. No longer just a place to cleanse the body, the bathroom is also serving as a place to relax and become revitalized, a place to awaken the senses to a pleasurable experience. Much like the baths of the early Greeks and Romans, the bath is a place to relax and shower or soak away the stresses of the day.

BATHROOM-RELATED RESEARCH

Bathroom design today has also benefited from key research on anthropometrics, ergonomic design, and universal design. Designers now have a better understanding of the human body, the design and space requirements to accommodate it, and the interface between humans and their interior space. The result has been fixtures and spaces that are more convenient, easier to use, and more versatile. Following is a summary of some major research that has impacted bathroom design.

Center for Housing and Environmental Studies

Perhaps the first extensive research into bathroom use began in 1958 by Alexander Kira at the Center for Housing and Environmental Studies located at Cornell University in Ithaca, New York. The research was sponsored jointly by the Cornell University Agricultural Experiment Station and the Plumbing and Heating Division of the American Radiator and Standard Sanitary Corporation.

The aim of the research was to thoroughly investigate what was then the unexplored area of personal hygiene, and establish basic criteria and parameters for design of facilities to accommodate these activities. The study included a laboratory investigation of the problems and needs posed by the principal personal hygiene activities.

The report covered such topics as the purpose of personal hygiene and the concept of dirt, attitudes about body cleaning, the anatomy and physiology of cleaning, and design considerations related to personal hygiene activities. The report described each activity in much detail, including the motion and position of the body before and after, as well as during, the activity. It was this study that developed a rationalization for ergonomic design in bathrooms.

Space Standards for Household Activities

Another study, conducted from 1956 to 1957 by the University of Illinois Agriculture Experiment Station, in cooperation with four other state Experiment Stations, involved taking and recording basic body measurements, as well as the human measurements for body activities. The primary objective was to determine the floor space needed by people to perform various activities in the home. Measurements were taken to establish clearances needed for activities, as well as the basic movements involved in fundamental activities, such as reaching and bending, that are a part of many other activities. This study set some very basic parameters for human space needs in the home.

Human Engineering

In the field of human engineering, which is the application of knowledge about human beings to design, Henry Dreyfuss and Associates are pioneers. This group was perhaps the first to take anthropometric measurements gathered through military and civilian studies and transform them into a form that could be used by designers. The first documents presenting these ideas were the innovative work of Alvin Tilley, *Measures of Man* (1960) and *Humanscale* (1974 and 1981); these were followed by a more recent book, *The Measure of Man and Woman: Human Factors in Design*, published in 1993.

This most recent book presents human body dimensions from birth to adulthood. For adult dimensions, it applies the concept of the percentile person to provide not only average body dimensions, but also the extremes. Sections of the book address the needs of the elderly and people with mobility aids, as well as space requirements for the home and other locations.

The Human Body and Interior Spaces

The next major work that impacted bathroom design was assembled by Julius Panero and Martin Zelnik into a sourcebook titled, *Human Dimension & Interior Space: A Source Book of Design Reference Standards*, published in 1979. The purpose of their book was to focus on the anthropometric aspects of ergonomic fit, or *ergofitting*, and applying the data to the design of interior spaces where people work, play, or live.

Early in their study of the relationships between the user and his or her space, the authors realized that most references for professionals dealt with general planning and design criteria. They found that very little information addressed the physical fit between the human body and the different components of interior space.

In their search for anthropometric data, the measuring of humans and their relationship to objects and spaces, they discovered that most of the previous human engineering had taken place in industry and the military sectors. An enormous boost to the database came during World War II, when the need arose to match human capabilities with new technologically advanced equipment such as airplanes. These sectors continue to generate anthropometric research today. One important civilian study prepared by the U.S. Department of Health, Education and Welfare contributed to their database as well.

In their sourcebook, the authors presented numerous diagrams for human structural and functional dimensions. Structural dimensions are the static dimensions of the head, torso, and limbs in a standing or seated position. The functional dimension is the measurement of a working position or the movement associated with a task. As they continued their research, the authors found that it continually reinforced the need to use anthropometric data in the design process. This meant bath designers would now have a basis for design considerations related to fixture and storage use.

A 1995 version of this work by DeChiara, Panero, and Zelnik titled *Time-Saver Standards for Housing and Residential Development*, includes much of the same anthropometric measures and information as the earlier document, with additional planning guidelines, including dimensions for such spaces as exercise areas and hydrotherapy pools. This reference remains perhaps the most comprehensive and primary reference for anthropometric measures.

Additional Human Factors Research

Human factors research is also being conducted at other universities, but with the focus on universal design and accessible design related to specific populations. Three major programs conducting research in these areas include the Center for Inclusive Design and Environmental Access (IDeA) at the State University of New York (SUNY) Buffalo, the Trace Research and Development Center at the University of Wisconsin–Madison, and the North Carolina State University Center for Universal Design. All three have conducted extensive research in the areas of universal design and are involved with projects specifically addressing accessible design. Major funding for these programs comes through the Department of Education and the National Institute on Disability and Rehabilitation Research (NIDRR).

The mission of the IDeA Center in the Buffalo School of Architecture and Planning program at SUNY Buffalo, which started in 1984 and received major NIDRR funding in 1999, is twofold:

- To use research, product development, and information dissemination to create new resources for universal design practice
- To facilitate a dialogue on the practice and delivery of universal design in order to build a national and international universal design community

Three projects they have undertaken specifically addressed accessible design in the bathroom. The first was a Prototype Anthropometric Database project that gathered anthropometric measurements of 500 wheelchair users. Information from this study was used to develop a prototype database specifically for bathrooms and bathing facilities. The second was the Visit-ability Project, which examined how to make homes more visit-able for people with disabilities, including bathroom entry and access. The third involved assessing the bathing needs and preferences of older persons with disabilities who lived at home. Data from this study was also used to design bathing facilities.

The Trace Research and Development Center, part of the College of Engineering at the University of Wisconsin–Madison, was started in 1971 and has primarily focused on finding ways to make information technologies and telecommunications systems more accessible and usable by people with disabilities. An additional research program was designed to gain an understanding of why and how companies adopt universal design, what factors are most important in making this decision, and what factors discourage or impede the adoption and successful practice of universal design.

Research activities at The Center for Universal Design in the College of Design at North Carolina State University began in 1989 and include applied research studies on human factors and user needs, usability of accessible and universally designed products and environments, and the impact of universal design. The bathroom is an important focus in this research.

As changes take place in bathroom use and products, ongoing research is needed to ensure the bathroom is a comfortable, safe, and efficient space. Universities and other institutions will continue to contribute to the body of knowledge that can assist bathroom designers.

Further explanation and application of the research findings from these various sources is examined in chapter 4, "Human Factors and Universal Design Foundation."

MAJOR BATHROOM TRENDS

After becoming an integral part of the home early in the twentieth century, the bathroom has undergone many changes and experienced many design trends. Some reflect changes in lifestyles, while others came about with the development of new materials, products, and processes. Knowledge of these trends would be useful when renovating a bathroom in an older/historic home where keeping to the period design is important. Following is a summary, by decade, of select bathroom design trends.

Bathroom Design Trends by Decade

Early 1900s

- Bathroom design was moving away from the lavish toward the convenient, family-style bathroom.
- A concern for sanitation and hygiene was paramount in bathroom design.
- An emphasis on maintenance and safety emerged, with consumers demanding products and materials that were easy to clean.
- Everything came in white, presenting the "antiseptic" look.
- Cabinetry was not popular because exposed pipes were considered more sanitary and easier to repair.
- A claw-foot tub (see Figure 1.6), pedestal lavatory, and water closet with an elevated tank made up the standard three-piece bathroom.

THE SATURDAY EVENING POST 55

"Colonna" Bath, Plate No. K-64

This trade-mark appears on every piece of KOHLER enameled plumbing ware. It is incorporated in faint blue in the enamel, at the points indicated by the arrows, and corresponds in size to the name "KOHLER" shown in the illustration.

"Bretton" Lavatory, Plate No. K-580

KOHLER OF KOHLER

And the permanent trade-mark incorporated in the easy-to-clean enamel

You prospective builders—you who contemplate remodeling—you who are building homes and apartments—have the opportunity to select enameled plumbing ware which bears the permanent trade-mark KOHLER as a guarantee of its superior quality.

It is your right to be able to identify Kohler Enameled Ware

We have adopted this permanent trade-mark for KOHLER easy-to-clean enameled plumbing ware, so that you will always be able to identify it. The word "KOHLER" in faint blue is permanently incorporated in the enamel of every KOHLER bathtub, lavatory, sink or other easy-to-clean enameled fixture.

This trade-mark is inconspicuous, but is easily found.

It is your guarantee of superior quality and evidence of our confidence in the excellence of our products. You should look for it. Your plumber will show it to you, because it means as much to him as it does to you.

KOHLER is the only enameled plumbing ware that has the trade-mark incorporated permanently in the enamel.

All KOHLER fixtures are of one quality, the highest—and of uniform color.

"It's in the Kohler Enamel"

Write for our descriptive booklet — KOHLER OF KOHLER

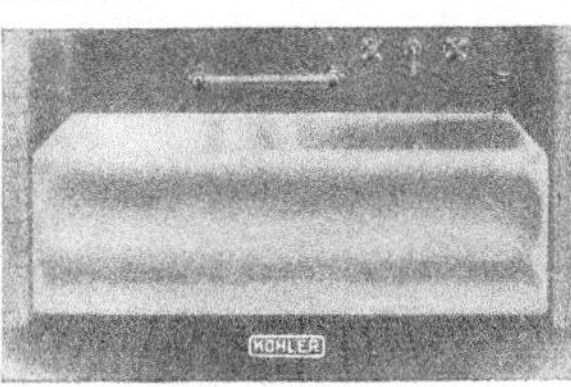

"Viceroy" ONE-PIECE Bath, Plate No. V-16-D. (Patent applied for)

Originators of ONE-PIECE construction

KOHLER CO. originated **one-piece** enameled bathtubs, lavatories and sinks. The KOHLER factory is the largest in the world devoted exclusively to the manufacture of enameled plumbing ware. KOHLER bathtubs, whether built-in or other styles, are easy-to-clean and hygienic in design.

Every Kohler design modern and artistic

No antiquated patterns are made by KOHLER. Your architect will tell you that this is a KOHLER characteristic. Your plumber is glad to install KOHLER easy-to-clean enameled plumbing ware, because it costs no more to put in than cheap, inferior fixtures, and its many superiorities satisfy his customers.

MAKERS OF
Enameled Bathtubs,
Lavatories, Sinks, Etc.

"It's in the Kohler Enamel"

KOHLER CO.
Founded 1873
Kohler, Wis. U.S.A.

BRANCHES
Boston New York Chicago
San Francisco London

FIGURE 1.6 The claw-foot tub had legs with claws on its feet to allow cleaning beneath the tub.

Courtesy of Kohler Company

- If the home had electricity, lighting most likely consisted of a shadeless, clear bulb, usually hanging from the center ceiling on a cloth-covered cord.
- The cage shower was introduced as a single shower fixture.

1920s

- Sanitary plumbing was so widespread among the middle and upper class that attention turned to aesthetic considerations.
- The shower became common in the home.
- The closed-in, rectangular porcelain tub replaced the claw-foot tub (see Figure 1.7).
- Faucets and shower controls lined up vertically under the showerhead.
- Pedestal lavatories were popular, as well as console lavatories supported by metal legs.

A FOUR-FIXTURE BATHROOM BUILT AROUND THE NEW *Cosmopolitan* BATH

One of the most interesting details of this colorful room is the new Kohler Cosmopolitan . . . the bath with flatter bottom, wider rim, lower sides, K-554-CV. Other matched fixtures which make up the foursome are the Claridge vitreous china lavatory, K-4946-F; Walcot vitreous china dental lavatory, K-5360-BA; quiet-performing siphon jet Integra closet, K-5580-A. The Kohler color is Tuscan.

The bathroom above measures 12'x11' 4". Floor and wainscot are 6"x12" glazed tile. Upper walls are sand blasted plate glass. Glass linen cabinet doors. Indirect lighting above the tub and in lavatory recess. Plaster ceiling is painted.

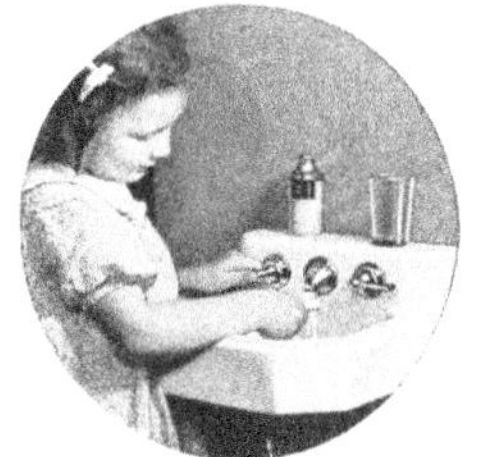

The dental lavatory should be in every home, especially one with children, as it encourages regular brushing of teeth. Relieves bathroom congestion. Shelf at back. Hot-and-cold water. K-5360-BA.

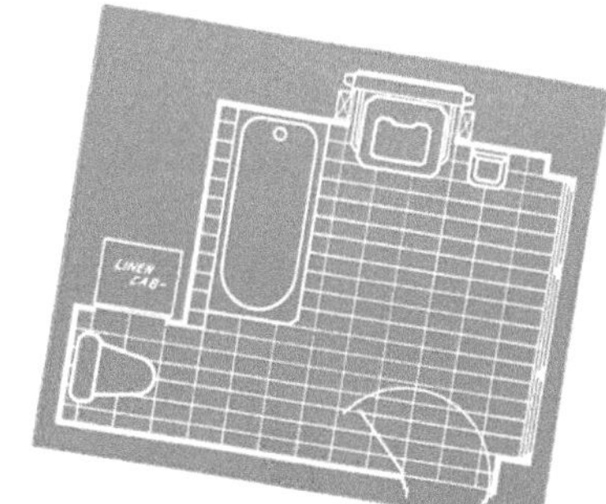

3

FIGURE 1.7 Rectangular tubs replaced the claw-foot tubs, and new colors, like this soft yellow, emerged on the market.
Courtesy of Kohler Company

- Lavatories were often made of Monel, a corrosive-resistant, light-weight, white metal containing a mix of copper and nickel.
- Nickel was used for bright work on faucets.
- Hand-painted murals, mirrors, and cloth were common surface coverings for walls.
- White was still popular, but porcelain made it possible to add color.
  - The color matching of vitreous china glazes and cast iron enamels was perfected.
  - Although black fixtures appeared, they would not be popular on the market for four decades.
  - Colors included blue, green, ivory, yellow (see Figure 1.7), brown, lavender, and gray.
- Dressing table vanities were featured as more activities moved into the bathroom space (see Figure 1.8).

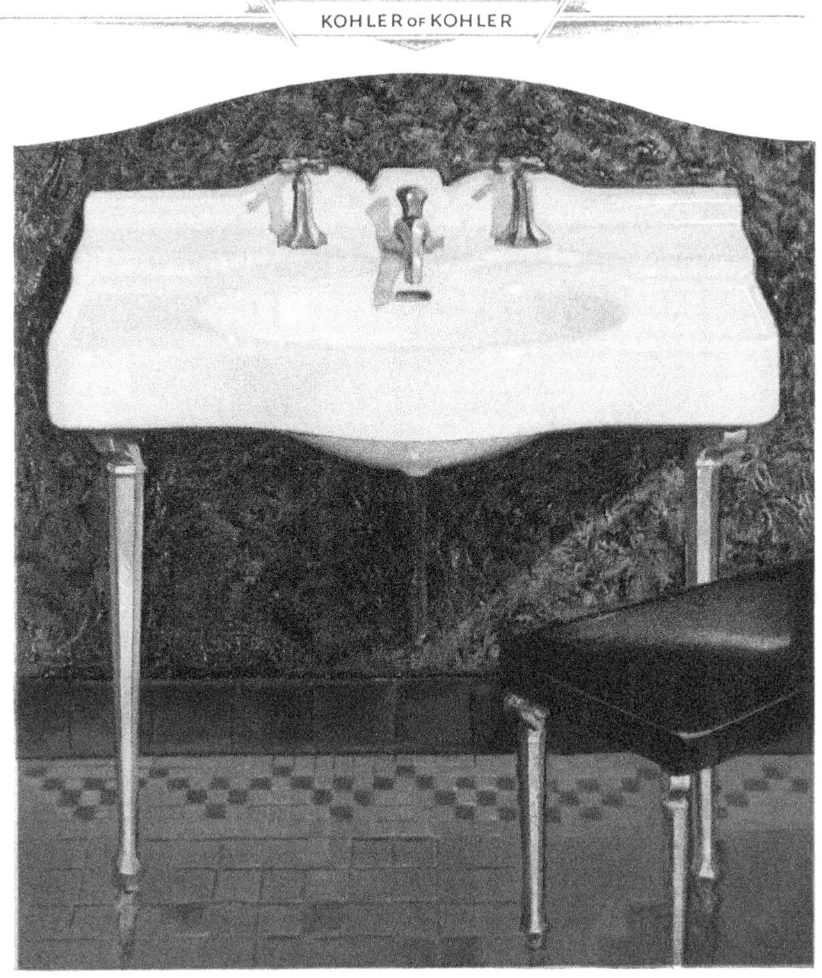

Kohler Bellaires Lavatory K-4915

AN artistic triumph in vitreous china is the Kohler Bellaires lavatory. A monument to the skill and craftsmanship of the Kohler artisans. The broad, massive slab is cast in one piece. The graceful curving back, the slightly raised shelf, the spacious tablelike end portions and generous bowl combine to give this boudoir lavatory a beauty, utility, and appeal never before approached.

The fittings, like two shining obelisks, are dainty and lovely with their coating of shining gold. Yet they are sturdy, and efficient as well.

The finely sculptured legs are cast of fine metal. They have all the grace found in fine furniture. Placed far apart, they allow the use of a dressing table bench such as is shown in the above illustration.

Prices

Fixture	Size		Chromium Plated Fittings	Gold Plated Fittings
Bellaires K-4915	20 x 36 inches	White	$540.00	$700.00
Bellaires K-4915	20 x 36 inches	Colored	630.00	790.00

29

FIGURE 1.8 This console "boudoir" lavatory, supported by two cast metal legs, included a raised shelf and room for a dressing table bench under it.
Courtesy of Kohler Company

- The bathroom continued to be viewed as a functional space, not for relaxation.
- Lighting consisted of a center ceiling lamp surrounded by milk-glass diffusers of various shapes.
- The first copper plumbing systems were installed late in the decade.

1930s

- The bathroom began to resemble the rest of the house with comfort emphasized.
- Small lavatories called dental lavatories were marketed as a means to help children practice dental hygiene.
- The four-fixture bathroom was now common—tub/shower, lavatory, dental lavatory, and toilet.
- Wall-hung lavatories were shown, along with lavatories supported by metal posts that included towel bars on the sides.
- Disappearing steps were incorporated to help children reach the lavatory.
- The leak-proof, one-piece shower was developed.
- Pedestal lavatories were common.
- Late in the decade, plumbing was hidden and fixtures were compartmentalized.
- Ads showed Americans how to design unused space (under stairs, dormer rooms, or large closets) into small bathrooms Kohler named the "lavette." (See Figure 1.9)
- Plans were available to show homeowners how to convert underused space to a bathroom.
- Although introduced in 1893, glass block was now heavily promoted for residential buildings.
- Bathrooms were lit by a single, flush-mounted ceiling fixture in the center of the room, which remained the norm until the 1970s.
- The influence of the Arts and Crafts Movement introduced more colors into the bathroom.

1940s

- New colors, such as rouge (burgundy), Tuscan (gold), and spring green (light green), as well as pink (see Figure 1.10) and bright blue, emerged.
- By the mid-1940s, the dental lavatory disappeared from ads.
- The single, mixing lever for showers was now available.
- The bench bath allowed parents to sit on the edge to watch children as they bathed (see Figure 1.11).
- Smaller bathtubs were designed for smaller bathrooms (see Figure 1.12).
- Laminates, mirrored walls, glass counters, and cork floors were trendy.
- Chromium experienced widespread use, followed by silver plate and gold plate.
- Linoleum replaced the white tile look and added color to the floor.
- Plastic appeared in fixtures.
- Glass block continued its popularity.
- Stainless steel became popular for lavatories and countertops.
- Small appliances, like hair dryers, entered the bathroom.

1950s

- Most new innovations came in the way of new materials.
- The 4 ft × 4 ft (1.2 m × 1.2 m) tub/shower became a solution for small spaces.
- Lavatory cabinets were common (see Figure 1.13).
- The term "powder room" was beginning to be used.
- New innovations in the bathroom included a telescoping towel bar; ceiling fixtures with a light, heater, and fan; adjustable showers; and an electric heated towel bar.
- The plastic tub with glass fibers was patented.
- Pink and gray were popular colors.
- Stainless steel remained popular for lavatories and countertops.

1960s

- The idea of relaxation was finally coming back to the bathroom.
- Ads portrayed hometown girls and happy moms relaxing in the bathroom.
- Bold colors emerged (see Figure 1.14), including orange, bright yellow, deep red, dark brown, and dark green, as well as the colors so distinctive of the era—avocado green and harvest gold.

Above is a section through a stairway showing how a small amount of space under it can be utilized. Plan with minimum dimensions is also shown above. Both these drawings supplement the one in color to the right.

At the end of a large bedroom a strip 3 feet wide can well be utilized, as shown by the perspective above and the plan below. In one compartment is the Lavette, in the other a dressing table and closet.

Another arrangement where a 3-foot strip is taken off a bedroom is shown in perspective above and in the plan below. The plumbing roughing-in is simpler than the scheme above, but a disadvantage is that there are three doors necessary (instead of two), and so less bedroom wall space is available.

OTHER LAVATORIES FOR THE LAVETTE

Top: THE GRAMERCY. The 4½" wide shelf at back is a "natural" for the Lavette. Holds powder puff and powder, cream and soap, and other accessories used in a first-floor washroom. Vitreous china, beautifully proportioned. Hot-and-cold water fitting is not in your way. Pop-up drain. 3" back. Trap and supplies with stops. Size 22"x18". K-4964-BA.

Center: THE NAROBOL. This lavatory is meant for small Lavettes where space is at a premium. Projects only 14" from wall and is 26" long. Back is 5½" high. Glistening enameled cast iron. Hot and cold, chromium plated faucets. Supplies and trap. Roomy basin. K-604-M.

Bottom: THE HUDSON. Its modern lines, beveled corners, and flat surfaces make this lavatory look expensive. And yet it isn't. Smooth, glossy, enamel cast iron. The compact Centra hot-and-cold water fitting leaves plenty of unobstructed space on the slab. Trap and supply pipes with stops. Metal parts are chromium plated. 6-inch high back. Size 20"x18". K-226-CA.

FOR HALL *Lavette*

"Lavette" is the Kohler term for a wash-up room, "a small indispensable room which can often take the place of an extra bathroom." In existing houses more often than not the family desires additional bathroom facilities, especially when the morning rush takes place, when "company comes," and when guests stay overnight. If there is not room for a full-fledged bathroom, determined sleuthing will usually uncover some unused or seldom-used space off the first floor hall such as is shown above. If the first floor will not yield even a cut-off ceiling space under the stair, the second floor may have a bedroom which is larger than actually need be, and can spare a strip 2½ to 3 feet wide to be taken off at one end, as shown in the two lower pairs of drawings at the left margin.

The Lavette above exhibits what can be accomplished with cramped space under a stair. The lavender of the Integra closet (K-5580-A) and the Strand lavatory (K-5320-BA with K-5471 legs) is repeated throughout the woodwork, as well as on the mirror frame. The walls are decorated with white wall paper or canvas covering, the latter having preferably a small geometric pattern in chrome orange (rather than a large sprawling design) so that the room may appear larger by contrast.

The ceiling is given warmth by being pale lemon yellow. Golden yellow complements the lavender and white by being the color of the overdrape (over a lemon yellow glass curtain), as well as in the inside of the cabinet and on the towel edging.

8

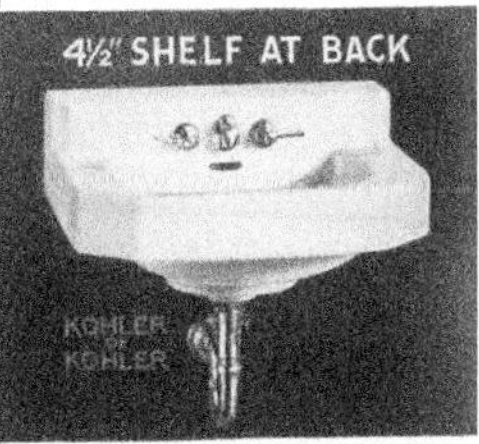

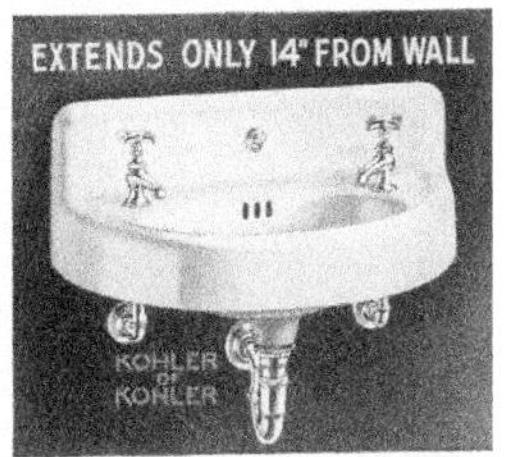

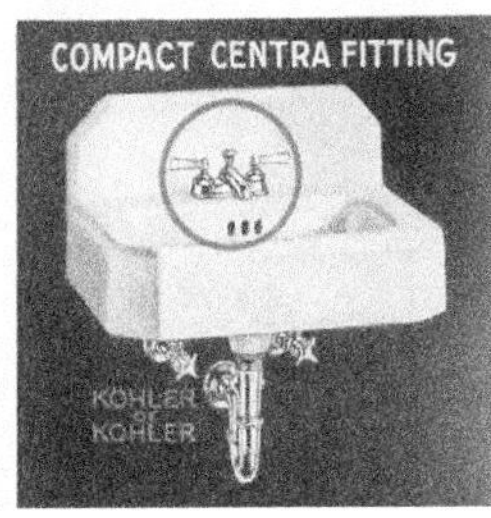

FIGURE 1.9 The "lavette," later called the powder room, was marketed by Kohler as a way to incorporate an extra bathroom by converting small spaces, such as bedroom closets and spaces under stairs, into a small bathroom. *Courtesy of Kohler Company*

- New bathrooms were more luxurious and second bathrooms were promoted.
- The new self-rimming lavatory was incorporated into the vanity.
- The California hot tub and backyard pool were popularized.
- The claw-foot tub disappeared.

1970s

- Multiperson tubs for group soaks were popular.
- Hydromassage tubs, such as the whirlpool tub, were developed.
- New colors included sand, gray, black, and pink.
- Colored fixtures were an important part of the bathroom design.
- The double lavatory became an important selling point in new homes.
- The nostalgic look reappeared in a vintage toilet with elevated tank and chain pull, the ball-and-claw-foot tub, and pedestal lavatory.

Matched Styling AT ITS BEST

Fixtures: Cosmopolitan K-526-CF recess Bench Bath; Gramercy K-1850-BA vitreous china lavatory with "neatness shelf," metal legs and Wall-free towel bars; Walcot K-2200-BA vitreous china dental lavatory; Integra K-3610-PB one-piece closet.

The problem of the two-door bathroom is here solved by grouping the fixtures closely, with all hot water outlets on the same inside wall to save on piping and protect from freezing. A Kohler Compact radiator, recessed under the window to meet cold as it enters, keeps the bathroom comfortably warm.

A true recess with dropped ceiling, lighted from above and faced with Vitrolite to ceiling height, focuses importance on the tub. Vitrolite continues around the room as a wainscot, drawing the other fixtures into the picture. Above the wainscot the walls are wallpaper, in which is repeated the Peachblow of the fixtures.

4

FIGURE 1.10 One of the popular bathroom colors in the 1940s was pink.
Courtesy of Kohler Company

- Theme designs were shown for the bathroom, including the patriotic, desert Southwest, and Caribbean motifs.
- Solid surface countertops with integral lavatory were developed in 1968, but were not introduced to the builder market until 1971. Four colors were available.
- Later in the decade, bathrooms were becoming a place of leisure with larger tubs for relaxation.
- Homeowners switched to fluorescent lamps to save energy, and to track lighting to increase the amount of light.

1980s

- Bathrooms increased greatly in size.
- Softer pastel colors returned.

Centra lavatory fitting.

BATHROOM EFFICIENCY

In a Lively Setting

• If your bathroom is Kohler-equipped, which means that the fixtures have Kohler fittings as well, your reward is a smooth-working, matched set of which you can feel proud.

In the bathroom shown, the 5′6″ Cosmopolitan Bench Bath, K-526-F, with seat at front, has a popular feature in the Triton shower and bath fitting. The dial mixer tempers the water for either the shower or the tub. After the correct temperature is obtained, raising the knob on the spout diverts the water to the shower head.

The lavatory is the K-1740-C vitreous china Chesapeake, 24 x 20″, with compact Centra fitting illustrated, and the closet indicated in the floor plan is the K-3665-EB close-coupled Bolton.

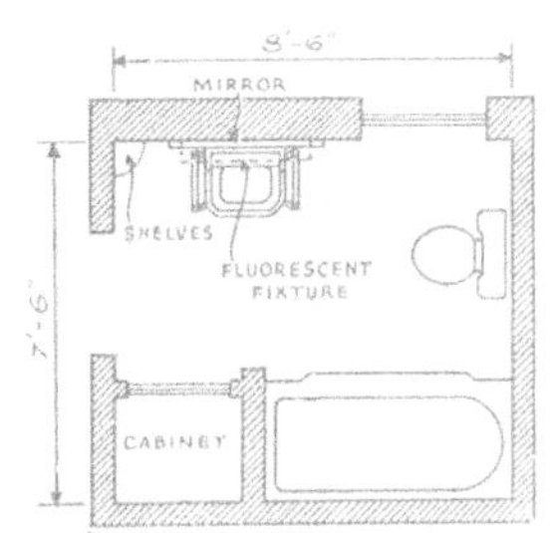

3

FIGURE 1.11 A wide side on the bathtub served as a bench where parents could sit to help children during bathing.
Courtesy of Kohler Company

- Designs appeared on the surface of bathroom fixtures.
- More high-end homes incorporated hydromassage tubs.
- Large tubs that accommodated group soaks remained popular.
- Faucets and controls moved from the lavatory to the counter.
- Pedestal lavatories (see Figure 1.15) and claw-foot tubs remained popular.
- There was a significant increase in the use of small, grooming appliances in the bathroom.
- New toilet designs included models with reduced water use.
- Glass block enjoyed a resurgence.
- Recessed down lighting was part of the lighting plan.
- In 1980, the American National Standards Institute standards were revised to include residential bathroom applications.
- In 1984, the Uniform Federal Accessibility Standards were published, providing **accessibility** guidelines for federal buildings and government-funded apartment buildings

1990s

- Sculptured fixtures added softer lines and new interest to the bathroom fixtures.
- Lavatory faucets appeared on the walls, as well as on the lavatory surface and counter.
- Many new types of vessel-style lavatories were introduced in a multitude of materials.
- Whirlpool and jetted tubs were common, especially in the higher-end market.
- Spacious bathrooms incorporated room for many activities, including meditation, exercise, and relaxation.
- Clothing storage and a dressing area were incorporated into larger bathrooms.
- Metallic finishes were added to lavatory surfaces.
- Detailed designs covered the surface of vitreous china fixtures.
- His and her spaces were beginning to emerge.
- Fine furniture was used for a vanity.
- New types of lighting were incorporated, including recessed, low voltage, and compact fluorescents.
- In 1991, Fair Housing Laws required that all new multifamily buildings have adaptable units.

FIGURE 1.12 Smaller bathrooms incorporated smaller bathtubs.
Courtesy of Kohler Company

FIGURE 1.13 Bathrooms were now being shown with cabinets along with the lavatory, providing much needed storage.
Courtesy of Kohler Company

2000s

- Larger homes of this period brought additional bathrooms and larger bathrooms.
- Energy and water conservation features are incorporated into more eco-friendly bathrooms, some of which were required such as the new U.S. federal mandate which required 1.6-gallon (6 liters) flush toilets in all new residential applications.
- Furniture pieces are taking the place of cabinetry, and contemporary styling is emerging with its clean lines and floating cabinetry (see Figure 1.16).

FIGURE 1.14 The 1960s brought many new bold colors to the bathroom.
Courtesy of Kohler Company

- More color is coming into the bathroom, including colored bathroom fixtures and the use of more ornamental design elements.
- The master bath suite becomes multipurpose, incorporating space for two users and activities such as dressing, laundry, and relaxation.
- Feng Shui and the Asian culture are influencing bathroom designs.
- Jetted tubs continue to be popular.
- Vessel lavatories are appearing in many styles, materials, and mounting configurations (see Figure 1.16).
- A heightened awareness of universal design is influencing bathroom design, materials, and styling.
- Showers are more popular than ever and are emerging as the preferred bathing method for most adults.
- The outpost or morning kitchen is added to the master suite
- Technology is an important part of the modern bathroom and is used for entertainment, relaxation, and grooming.

FIGURE 1.15 The pedestal lavatory reappears, especially in powder rooms.
Courtesy of Porcher

- The influence of nature appears in bathrooms through color, materials, and the use of large windows to bring the outside indoors.
- Height of vanity and/or bowls are adjusted up or down to vary with the user.

CURRENT DEMOGRAPHIC AND POPULATION TRENDS

With each era, new design trends emerge that incorporate the lifestyles and technologies of the time. In this new millennium, we see many factors influencing bathroom design, one of which is the changing demographics of North America. There are two major trends emerging in the population: an increasingly more diverse population and a larger number of older people. Another long-term trend affecting bath design is changing household composition, namely a large number of multigenerational households.

U.S. Population Growth

The general population of the United States continues to increase and according to the 2010 Census it now exceeds 300 million. The population increase from 2000 to 2010 was the third largest in U.S. history, adding 27.3 million people—a 9.7 percent increase. Historically, the highest increase in population was during the "baby boom" years of the 1950s when the population increased 19 percent, adding 17.5 million people.

FIGURE 1.16 The vessel sink with a wall-mounted faucet adds to the contemporary look of floating, straight-lined cabinets.
Courtesy of Duravit

Household Growth

Although the general population has increased, household growth has slowed, averaging only 1.12 million households during the 2000s, a full 17 percent below the 1990s according to the 2010 U.S. Census. The portion of young adults age 20 to 24 heading independent households has also dropped by 2.6 percent and for those ages 25 to 29 by 2.8 percent since 2007. This trend could be very different over the next 15 years, however, as immigration continues and a large percentage of the echo-boom generation (born 1986 to 2005), numbering around 80.8 million, approach young adulthood. Even with immigration at only half that rate, their numbers will grow to 86.5 million by 2020, and added to the echo boomers will produce a higher demand for apartments and smaller "starter homes" during the next 15 years.

The future of household formation is uncertain. On one hand, the recent drop in home prices and a favorable rental market may encourage more employed individuals to form households of their own. In addition, those doubling up to save expenses are typically in a temporary situation and will eventually seek their own place. On the other hand, the rate of household formation among young adults may continue to decline due to sustained unemployment, home foreclosures, delayed marriage and childbearing, the increased importance of higher education, and the rising cost of going away to college. These young adults will continue to double up or live with their parents.

Not only have the economic and housing situations in 2010 decreased household growth, they have also led to lower mobility. Between 2005 and 2008, overall mobility fell about 12.6 percent with the deepest decline among homeowners. This trend may continue as financially stressed households find it easier to stay in their current residence rather than experience a financial loss.

Household Composition

Other demographic changes that could impact the design market include changes in household composition as summarized in the 2010 U.S. Census. Households are becoming smaller. In 2010, one- and two-person households accounted for more than 63 percent of all households. The share of single-person households rose to 28 percent, with a higher percentage being 65 and older. Married couples, for the first time, represented less than 50 percent of the households (48 percent) and unrelated adults living together made up 6.2 percent. Married couples with children were fewer than 20 percent of all households. The largest change in household composition was an increase in households headed by women without husbands—up 18 percent since 2000.

One other prominent change in households is the return of the multigenerational family household as reported by the Pew Research Center in 2010. A record 49 million Americans, or 16.1 percent of the population, in 2008 lived in a household that included at least two adult generations or a grandparent. The rate was only 12 percent in 1980. Multigenerational trends include:

- In 2010, 44.7 percent of the 20 to 24 year olds who do not live on their own are living with their parents, along with 18.0 percent of the 25 to 29 year olds. Since 2005, an additional 1.6 million young adults live at home. Many reasons could account for this increase in adult children living at home, including difficulty with finding a job or launching a career, or marrying at an older age. In the 25 to 34 age group, more men than women are likely to live in multigenerational family households.
- The high rate of immigration since 1970 was dominated by Latin Americans and Asians, who are far more inclined to be part of a multigenerational household. Hispanics (22 percent), blacks (23 percent), and Asians (25 percent) are all more likely than whites (13 percent) to be a multigenerational household.
- A significant change in multigenerational composition involves older adults. Once more likely to live in such situations (57 percent of adults 65 and older in 1900), only 17 percent of older adults today live in multigenerational family households because of better health, better financial situations, and better social safety net programs. This number has been increasing some in recent years due to the availability of more grown children who are informed caregivers and recent cuts in Medicare programs. More likely to outlive their spouse, a higher percentage of women are part of this type of household.

- Some 49 million Americans live in a multigenerational family household. Of those, 47 percent are made up of two adult generations of the same family with the youngest adult at least 25 years of age, 47 percent live with three or more generations of family members, and 6 percent belong to a "skipped" generation household with a grandparent and grandchild and no parent.

Population Diversity

According to the 2010 U.S. Census and the State of the Nation's Housing 2011, a publication of the Joint Center for Housing Studies of Harvard University, we continue to see demographic changes due to changes in immigration and the minority populations. Minorities account for 92 percent of the total U.S. population growth between 2000 and 2010, and the growth of the population under the age of 18 was at 1.9 million, driven mostly by racial/ethnic minorities. Immigrants and minorities also account for a large percentage of the household growth in the past decade. The Echo Boom generation is already 42 percent minority and over the next 15 years this diverse generation, along with other minority households, will increase the demand for smaller starter homes, apartments, and remodeling projects. Statistics Canada places the percentage of visible minority residents in Canada at 16.2 percent (about 5 million people) in 2006, up from 13.4 percent in 2001.

The largest increases for the United States are among Hispanics. Since 2000, the Hispanic population in the United States has increased 43 percent and has doubled since 1990. According to the 2010 U.S. Census, there are 50 million Hispanics in the United States, or one in every six residents and about 16 percent of the population. The U.S. Asian American population increased 43 percent since 2000, but Asians still make up less than 5 percent of the total population.

Immigration also had a key role in the slowdown in household growth. During the 2000s, not only did the growth of the foreign-born population slow, but the growth of foreign-born households stalled due to the recession. Although the number of households headed by foreign-born citizens increased by about 200,000 from 2004 to 2010, the number of foreign-born noncitizen households declined by the same amount from 2007 to 2010.

An Aging Population

The 2010 U.S. Census places the 65 and older population at 38.6 million, up from 34.9 million in 2000. The U.S. population between ages 65 and 74 is expected to increase 6.5 million over the next decade, a rise as more "baby boomers" reach retirement. The 55 to 64 age group is expected to grow by 3.7 million. Over the next 20 years, the share of 65 and older will rise from 13 percent of the population to 19 percent. Estimates of the Canadian 2011 Census by Statistics Canada places their 65 and older age group at 14.1 percent of the overall 2011 population number of 34,600,346, with a large portion of the over 65 group living in more rural areas.

Increased life expectancy is credited with some of the increase in this older age group. When the United States was founded, the average American was expected to live to the age of 35, but according to the World Bank, the 2009 life expectancy of U.S. citizens is 78.1 years of age and for Canadian citizens it is 80.66 years of age.

The State of the Nation's Housing 2010 states that this increasing number of "baby boomer" retirees has dominated housing market trends for decades and will continue to have a significant impact. As they purchased their first homes and then traded up to bigger, better homes, the sheer numbers of individuals in this group has shaped the housing market. Now, as they reach retirement, many are seeking housing to meet their current needs, either by making changes to their current home or by moving to a smaller home.

The number of older homeowners able to move from their current residence has declined sharply in recent years due to the nation's financial crisis that depressed home equity and reduced retirement income. This trend will open the market for remodeling projects that allow people to "age in place." Those boomers who can relocate tend to downsize to smaller homes with fewer rooms and one-level living.

For both the remodeling market and new, smaller retirement home market, there will be an increased interest in bathrooms that are safe, comfortable, and ergonomically designed. Of course, accessible design will be critical for those aged individuals with disabilities. See chapter 8, "Accessibility in Practice," for additional characteristics of this population and design applications appropriate for them.

BATHROOM TRENDS

These changing demographic characteristics also impact how consumers use their baths, the products they demand, and the looks and styles they favor. The retail markets of today offer the consumer and designer an unlimited array of choices for bathroom design. Although certain styles may go in and out of fashion, today's selection of colors, materials, styles, sizes, and textures allows the designer to create a room to fit every preference and situation. As new trends are incorporated into the bathroom, you, as the designer, must always keep in mind that the bathroom is a very complex space to plan, and the fundamental characteristics of sanitation, ergonomics, and safety should always be considered.

In addition to population and demographic changes that may affect bathroom design, specific consumer preferences can greatly impact the bathroom projects your clients request. Surveys conducted by national trade magazines, associations, and manufacturers can give designers an idea of what consumers prefer in their bathroom. Just remember, tastes change quickly today.

Housing and Consumer Buying Trends

Design trends begin with general home trends. Surveys by the National Association of Home Builders (NAHB) and Better Homes and Gardens provide a profile of home trends and what people want in their homes. The average home size shrank to 2,480 square feet in 2009 as reported by NAHB, but the U.S. Census found the average home size to be at about 2,100 square feet. Builders expect homes to continue at this smaller size, averaging about 2,152 square feet in 2015. These smaller homes are not only desired by individuals 65 and older looking to downsize, but by the echo boomers interested in smaller, more affordable starter homes.

NAHB survey findings also show that the number of homes with three or more bathrooms declined for the first time since 1992. More builders plan to incorporate luxury features like master baths with multiple showerheads, and they will focus on energy-saving features. Many new homes of the future expected to have a master bedroom and bath on the first floor of two-story homes.

Nevertheless, surveys consistently show that bath remodeling remains one of the most popular remodeling projects. The primary goals of households who are remodeling a bathroom vary somewhat from survey to survey, but generally include updating the appearance, adding new fixtures, and often, making the bath larger if possible.

A large percentage (65 percent) of the consumers surveyed wanted an additional bedroom with bath to accommodate the multigenerational household. Consumers would rather downplay the master bedroom suite and put more money into rooms like the bathroom. Consumers are also becoming more savvy buyers, taking a lot longer researching purchases and projects. Many consumers (58 percent) are "extremely reluctant" to spend money they do not have.

As a professional designer, you will find it beneficial to stay up to date on ever-changing consumer preferences, as well as style, material, and color trends, by reading consumer and trade magazines, visiting industry-related websites, and attending trade shows.

Design Trends

Following are some of the key design trends in bathrooms today. Many of these trends are visible in both the U.S. and Canadian bathroom projects, but some specific regional trends are highlighted in later sections.

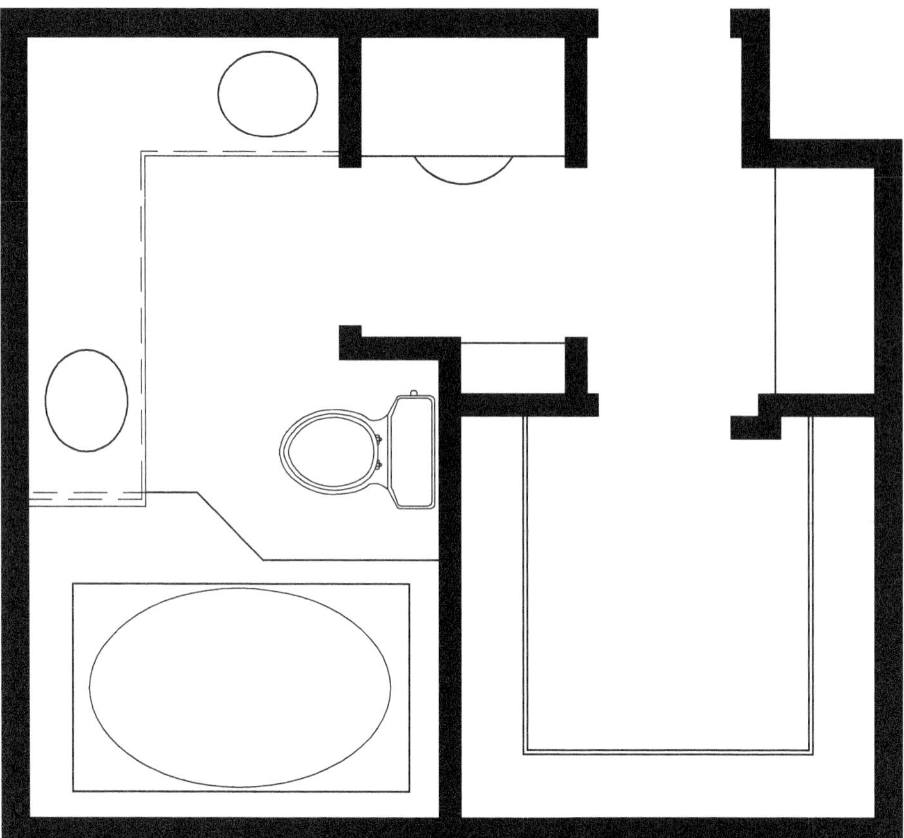

FIGURE 1.17 Closets in the bathroom area form a dressing area that is convenient to the grooming area in the bath.
NKBA

Space Use Trends

- **Open spaces.** Most bathrooms of the past were minimal in size and looked upon as very private and somewhat hidden spaces. Although some homeowners and builders are downsizing the bathroom in the current economy, consumers still desire space, and there are many ways in which designers can incorporate a feeling of openness. Designers can expand the bathroom space both visually and physically by carefully selecting the appropriate size and style of fixtures, using mirrors and large windows, and incorporating higher ceilings.
- **Outdoor access.** Today's consumers have a love for nature, the outdoors, sunshine, and fresh air, so this feeling can be created in the bathroom by physically opening the space to the outside through access to a private deck or patio and incorporating large windows.
- **Suites.** A popular idea is merging the bedroom and the bathroom or providing access through a dressing area to create the bathroom suite. Bathroom designs are moving away from the bathroom as a confined area into one that is a fluid living space.
- **Dressing.** Dressing areas and closets are moving into the bathroom (see Figure 1.17) from the actual bedroom space. The closet may include hanging and drawer space, as well as a cedar-lined compartment. You will find additional information on closet design in chapter 9, "More than a Bathroom."
- **Two users.** Designing a bathroom with two simultaneous users in mind is essential for many households. The double lavatory has been used for some time as a means of eliminating the morning wait, and it is in even higher demand today. Compartmentalized areas (see Figure 1.18) have also helped provide privacy for one individual while another is using the space.

Color and Theme Trends

- **Nature.** The natural look with colors and textures to match the surrounding outdoor environment is gaining favor among designers and consumers. The nature-inspired designs might include natural stone or warm woods for a soft natural beauty. Nature is also brought indoors through the use of large windows (see Figure 1.19).

- **Neutral colors dominate.** Whites and off-whites, beiges, and browns are the most common used colors in bathrooms.
- **Abundance of light.** Designers are not only incorporating light for general and task purposes, but are using it to add interest in other places. Products in today's market allow designers to illuminate almost everything in the bathroom including, toilets, faucets, showers, and mirrors, as well as shower, wall, and floor tiles.
- **Green bathrooms.** The "green bathroom" is not only an eco-friendly theme but also a color theme that has recently grown in popularity. Green color palettes are used by an increasing number of designers. Blues (see Figure 1.20) and warm gray neutrals are also popular colors in Canada as well as the United States, creating a relaxing and spa-like environment. Gray is the new black!
- **Utility-chic.** Some designers see a continuation of what they call "utility-chic," a mix of wood and stainless steel, exposed light bulbs, and art that references old signage.
- **Art.** Once absent from most bathrooms, artwork and art objects are finding their way into the bath, helping to create a certain theme or adding to the feeling of relaxation in the room, especially for the spa experience.
- **Traditional styling.** Traditional styling is clearly dominating U.S. bathroom projects (see Figure 1.21).
- **Contemporary.** Also popular is contemporary styling with its clean lines (see Figure 1.22). Designers emphasize this theme through floating (wall-hung) vanities and toilets, clean lines, and contemporary materials like glass. Even traditional designs are including contemporary elements like the vessel bowl lavatory and stone.

FIGURE 1.18 A compartmentalized bathroom will more easily allow multiple users at one time.
Courtesy of Porcher

FIGURE 1.19 A feel of the outdoors and nature are created with the use of stone, warm woods, and a view outdoors.
Design by NKBA member: Holly Rickert, Co-Designer: Julia Kleyman

- **Shaker styling.** A style incorporated by about one-third of the designers is the Shaker style.
- **Zen- or spa-like theme.** Designers are creating individualist and personalized spaces in bathrooms that recreate the spa or Zen-like feel. Fireplaces, music, sleek designs, and comfort-fit fixtures all help provide the homeowner with a spa-like experience at home. Glass tiles, clean lines, and floating vanities add to the feel.
- **Japanese and Asian influence.** Although Asian influences have been a part of home design schemes for some time, some designers see the Japanese influence as a major design statement in U.S. bathrooms and no longer just incorporated into a few accessories (see Figure 1.23). The feel is subtle and achieved with clean lines, open spaces and neutral colors with a bold splash of color for an accent. Japanese furniture may be used as a vanity to add to the theme.

FIGURE 1.20 This blue bathroom with traditional styling includes double vessel sinks and a grooming area.

Design by NKBA member: Kenneth Kelly, CKD, CBD, CR

Multicultural Influences

- **Multiple generations.** For many cultures, one home may accommodate many generations. Therefore, designers may need to plan spaces that will accommodate this multigenerational family. This typically means more bathrooms and perhaps separate suites with a private bath.
- **Folk and ethnic patterns.** Designers are using more folk- and ethnic-inspired patterns in their bathrooms. Incorporating hand-sewn trims on towels and the use of birds and flowers in accessories help create what they call the "folkloric" look.

Fixtures

- **Luxury bathrooms.** Despite the fact that some people are cutting out some of the extravagant features in their bathroom, people still enjoy space and luxury if they can afford it. In today's luxury bathrooms, fixtures make a statement. They can dominate, through the use of large tubs and massive stone pieces, or they can present a softened look by using sculptured fixtures with delicate lines.
- **Lavatory choices.** New trends are emerging in fixture design. The undermount lavatory dominates newly remodeled bathrooms with the vessel or bowl lavatory as a clear second. These vessels, which can be made of many different types of materials, often sit on a flat, wall-hung base with plumbing exposed below, but can be placed on a vanity cabinet as well. Counter- and wall-mounted spouts and controls are commonly used with these fixtures. Integrated, pedestal and drop-in lavatories are still popular, but were specified less often by designers.

FIGURE 1.21 The popular traditional styling of this bathroom incorporates dark woods, the look of furniture in the bookcases used for storage, and the graceful lines of the vanity area.
Design by NKBA member: J. David Ulrich, CKD

- **Reevaluating the jetted tub.** In the past number of years, more households are finding that they are not using their large whirlpool or jetted tubs, once a must in most luxury master baths. Designers report that if jetted tubs are incorporated they are becoming more therapeutic with gentler hydrotherapy bubbles, as well as integral support, lighting, sound, and scents to provide more of the spa experience.
- **Freestanding tubs.** Whether jetted or just used for soaking, large tubs that are incorporated into larger master baths are freestanding and take a central and prominent place in the room. The tub's styling may be rounded or angled, depending on the styling of the room.
- **Fewer tubs.** Whether remodeling or designing a new home, a trend among more homeowners is to install only showers in most of the home's bathrooms and perhaps have a standard tub in only one location. In general, households are using showers instead of tubs and many times a shower can be installed in a smaller space and perhaps at less expense. At least one tub may be needed in the home, however, for bathing children and for those who prefer tub bathing.
- **Large, open showers.** Although some homeowners are hanging onto tubs to preserve resale value, others are eliminating the tub altogether in the master bath and replacing it with a large shower stall, especially where space is limited and the room cannot accommodate both. For daily uses, the shower is becoming the preferred method of bathing instead of a tub for that quick morning getaway. These larger showers are often designed to accommodate more than one person and have a surround enclosure design with an open entrance (see Figure 1.24). Steam, lights, multiple showerheads and body sprays (see Figure 1.25), rain showerheads, aromatherapy, chromatherapy, and music are also becoming part of the showering experience.

FIGURE 1.22 The contemporary style with its simple lines is displayed here in the increasingly popular gray hues.

Design by NKBA member: Jan E. Regis, CMKBD

- **Universal design.** Universal design considerations are incorporated into bathroom fixture selection and placement. Vanities with knee space, single-lever plumbing fixtures, hand spray fixtures, comfort-height toilets, larger showers with illuminated thresholds and doors or a zero entry shower, eliminating the threshold all make the bathroom a place that accommodates everyone's needs. Grab bars no longer look institutional, and tubs have doors and soft, contoured seats. More information on universal design is included in chapter 4.
- **Faucet finishes.** The most popular finish for faucets in 2010 was satin nickel, with brushed nickel also being a favorite. Other popular faucet finishes are bronze and oil-rubbed bronze, polished chrome, and polished nickel.
- **White fixtures dominate.** The most common color of bathroom fixture is white. Bisque and off-white were used in far fewer projects by designers.
- **Countertops.** Quartz is gaining ground on granite as a popular bathroom vanity top material, but granite still dominates the market.
- **Tile still trendy.** Ceramic and porcelain tiles on the floor continue to dominate the projects with natural stone also proving to be popular. Variations of inlay floors are also appearing, especially in many traditional themes like those that carry a French chateau feel. Faux hardwood porcelain tiles shaped in planks give the hardwood look to the floor without actually using wood, which can be easily damaged by moisture, a major concern in a bathroom.
- **New tile trends.** Nontraditional materials are showing up in tiles for the bathroom including copper, bronze, stainless steel, and glass. Glass tiles, in particular, are being incorporated into

FIGURE 1.23 Asian influences with earthy color tones create a warm feel in this contemporary bathroom.

Design by NKBA member: Cheryl Kees Clendenon, Co-Designer: Stacy Miller

floors, backsplashes, and shower walls to create a luxury spa-like atmosphere. Many of the glass tiles are made from recycled glass. Designers are incorporating textured metallic floor and wall tiles that incorporate what they see as a "Russian" influence. The newer 3D wall tiles add texture to rooms.

- **Natural materials.** A prevalent design element is the use of natural materials. The natural or organic feel includes the use of wooden bathtubs and sinks, and rich wood grains in cabinetry. In places where water is a concern, the "wood look" tiles may be used, and they even come in "log cut" styles for the log cabin feel. New waterproof wood coverings can be used for floors or walls to create that nature-inspired room. The use of natural stone (see Figure 1.26) adds to the earthy look, but porcelain tiles laser printed with natural stone patterns are also emerging, having the added benefits of scratch resistance, durability, suitability to wet areas, cost efficiency, and no need of sealing.

FIGURE 1.24 The luxury bathroom often includes an oversized shower without a door, shown here in this neutral-colored decor.

Design by NKBA member: John Sylvestre, CKD

Furniture

- **Furniture replaces cabinetry.** Furniture is being introduced into the bathroom much as it has been in the kitchen. There is a trend toward less use of cabinetry and more furniture items, such as the console lavatory, to create a look that is unified with the bedroom.
- **Contemporary look.** Contemporary lines are echoed in the freestanding furniture pieces.
- **Floating cabinets.** Many cabinets are taking on the "floating look," whereby they are attached to a wall instead of grounded on the floor.

Sustainable Design

- **Environmentally friendly products.** Clients are continually becoming more pro-environment and looking for environmentally friendly products, including those made of recycled and renewable materials, to use in their homes.
- **Water and energy saving fixtures.** In addition to water and energy saving features, consumers want products that are low maintenance to reduce cleaning and the use of chemicals. They also want durable materials so they will not need to be replaced frequently.
- **Chemical sensitivity.** Many people are very sensitive to chemicals, so selecting products with low or no chemical emissions is important in these cases.
- **Efficient lighting.** People in general desire bright spaces and the use of daylighting is bringing in an abundance of natural light for daytime use. Energy-efficient LED lighting is also becoming the lamp of choice for many purposes. You will find more information on sustainable design in chapter 3, "Environmental and Sustainability Considerations."

FIGURE 1.25 Larger, spacious showers may incorporate multiple showerheads.
Courtesy of Danze, Inc.

Activity Trends

Grooming

Providing a place for applying makeup no longer means just an open space with a stool at the lavatory counter. Larger, more luxurious bathrooms include a special vanity area designed with adequate lighting, storage, and multiple mirrors for special grooming activities.

Relaxation

The idea of using the bathroom as a retreat for relaxation has hit new heights in American homes. The reemerging interest in health and spirituality has brought new attention to the "bath." Spurred by the popularity of the hot tub and hydrotherapy, the home spa concept (see Figure 1.27) has evolved into a spa bathroom that includes multiple ways to slow down the pace of life, relax, and soothe away the stresses of the day. Spa bathrooms might include a spa tub, whirlpool/jetted tub, sauna, and steam shower. You can find tips for designing a spa bathroom in chapter 9, "More Than a Bathroom."

FIGURE 1.26 The look of natural stone is prominent in the wall tile of this bathroom. *Design by NKBA member Victoria Shaw*

In addition to using water for relaxation, the bathroom can be an intimate and private space that has an emotional and mental feel like no other in the home. Linking the bedroom, library, and bath creates a space to relax and read. A fireplace brings back the intimate sitting room of the past, where the tub was brought into the bedroom and placed near the fireplace for warmth.

Comfort Station

In creating an inviting and relaxing space, comfort is a top priority, and new materials and technologies are used to design these elements of comfort.

- Tubs not only contour to the body, but are made of a soft, resilient material to cushion the body as the bather enjoys the relaxing hydrotherapy.
- Cushioned and heated toilet seats have been available in other parts of the world and have made a fairly recent appearance in the North American market. These high-tech toilets also warm your feet, play music, light up, and raise and lower the cover as you approach and leave.
- Additional comfort is added through heated floors so people no longer step out of the tub onto an icy, cold surface.
- Warm towels are very comforting to people as they step out of the shower, or used to warm up muscles before beginning exercise. Towel warmers and warming drawers make warm towels available.

Meditation

Meditation rooms or spaces provide a quiet place to relax and reflect. Japanese rock and sand gardens allow the user to create a peaceful setting. A space devoted to exercises like yoga, helps create a relaxing end to a busy day.

FIGURE 1.27 Larger bathrooms can turn into a spa with the inclusion of a whirlpool and deluxe shower.

Design by NKBA member: John A. Petrie, CMKBD

Health and Wellness

An interest in healthy routines and health monitoring among an aging population has made its way into the design concept of more luxury bathrooms. Designers are including massage tables for treatments at home, as well as room for a gym or exercise studio.

With the newest technologies, consumers can also use the bathroom for health monitoring. Fixture companies are marketing toilets that monitor waste for various health-related indicators. Bidet features on toilets add to the feeling of cleanliness after toilet use. A concern for health has also fostered the development of antimicrobial finishes to deter bacterial growth. Touchless or hands-free faucets and toilets increase the emphasis on hygiene.

Technology and Electronic Devices

The modern bathroom is not lacking in technology and electronic devices. Equipped with radio, CD/DVD players, televisions, and speaker systems, consumers can stay abreast of the current world news while dressing, or listen to music while relaxing in the tub or sauna. Not only are flat screen televisions incorporated into some jetted tubs and vanity mirrors (see Figure 1.28), but showers also can have a waterproof television screen blended into the tile wall, controlled by a waterproof remote, and heard on ceiling speakers.

Location Trends

Outpost Kitchen Area

As part of the master bathroom suite, many households are incorporating what might be referred to as a mini kitchen, outpost kitchen, or morning kitchen to handle food, drink, and health needs

FIGURE 1.28 No need to miss the morning news when you can have a television panel as part of your bathroom mirror.
Courtesy of Seura, Inc.

(see Figure 1.29). Households are finding these outposts a very convenient solution to the morning rush and an enhancement for evening relaxation. Often included in these kitchens are a coffeemaker, a small refrigerator or refrigerator drawers, and a small microwave oven.

Once thought of as a luxury, these auxiliary kitchens can also serve as support stations when a family member is injured or ill, or when a caregiver is involved. Medications may need to be refrigerated, or baby bottles may need to be stored and warmed for a baby in the family. The bedroom suite does not need to be extremely large to accommodate a few of these appliances.

Multipurpose Space

Just as the kitchen has evolved into the "hub" of family activities, the bathroom is now taking on a similar role in some homes, with parts of the bathroom space providing a place for family members to gather, share time together, and communicate about the day's activities. Compartmentalization provides the privacy needed, so that open spaces can be enjoyed by many.

- **Massage space.** Some luxury bathrooms are incorporating space for a massage table.
- **Exercise room.** A room devoted to exercise may adjoin some large luxury bathrooms.
- **Spa room.** Large bathrooms may have a room devoted to spa features such as a sauna, whirlpool or steam room.
- **Multiple entries.** A second bathroom with more than one entrance (see Figure 1.30) provides a means for establishing a guest suite without adding another bathroom. Examples include an entrance from one bedroom and the hall, or a bathroom between two bedrooms.

FIGURE 1.29 Coffee and a quick morning breakfast can be served up as you prepare for the day with this morning kitchen located in the master bathroom.
Courtesy of Wellborn Cabinet, Inc.

- **Laundry area.** Because most laundry is produced in bedrooms and bathrooms, designers and builders are incorporating a laundry area, or even a second laundry area, into or near the bathroom and bedroom area. Chapter 9, "More Than a Bathroom," contains more details on planning a laundry area.

Storage Trends

- **Multiple types.** Once almost devoid of storage, the bathroom now contains multiple types of storage (see Figure 1.31) to handle items for the variety of activities that take place there.
- **Clothes storage.** In larger bathrooms, there is now more clothing storage, both folded and hanging, as part of a dressing area. These dressing areas can be entire rooms, taking all clothes storage out of the bedroom space. See chapter 9, "More Than a Bathroom," for additional information on clothes storage.
- **Open storage.** In the form of open shelves, open cabinets, or poles with wire baskets attached, these provide visual appeal as well as convenience.
- **Barn door closures.** A door hanging from and sliding along a rail, much like the mechanism used on animal barns, is used as a closet door and even the door for entering the bathroom from the master suite. This type of closure allows the user to slide the door along an adjacent wall, allowing 100 percent access to the door opening.
- **Appliance storage.** An increase in the use of portable electric appliances/devices in the bathroom calls for more storage for these items, as well as consideration for utility connections. These appliances/devices require storage space not only in cabinets and drawers, but on the counter as well. Built-in appliances, such as refrigeration units, may need special circuits and electrical connections incorporated into the plan.

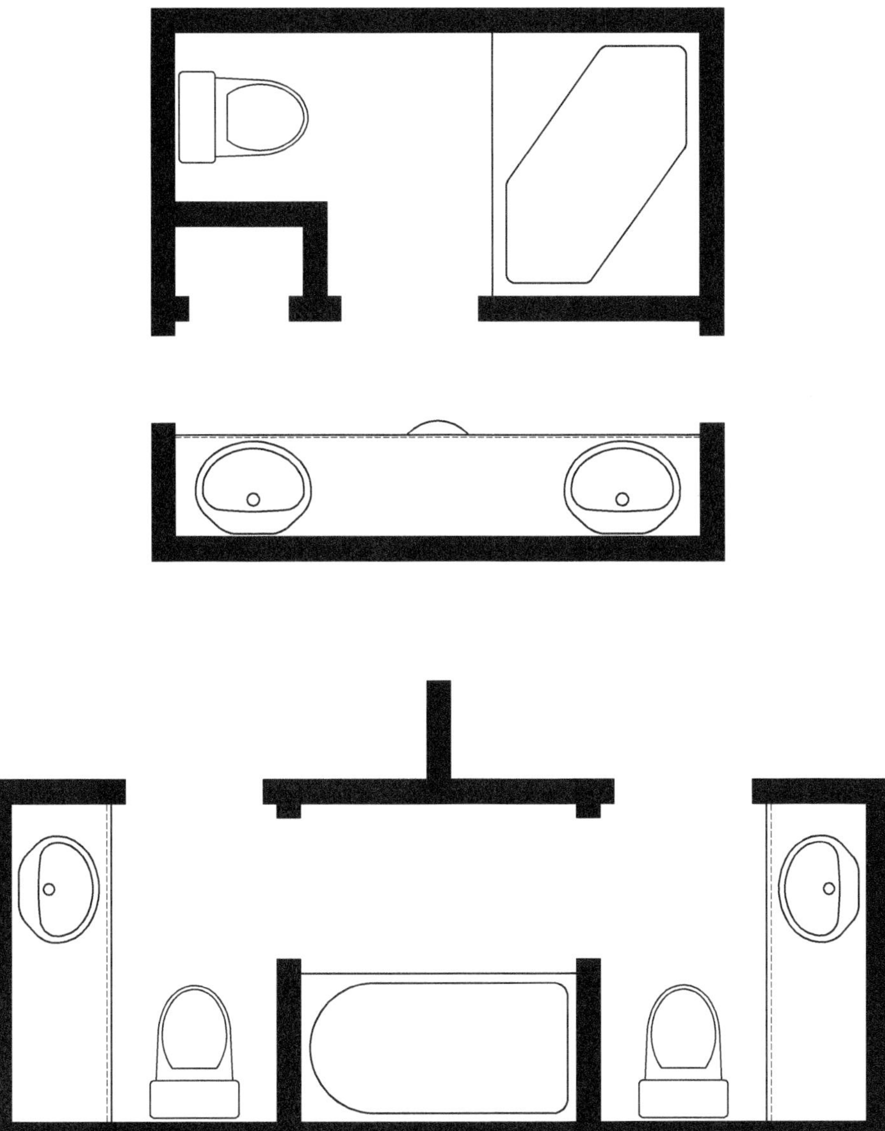

FIGURE 1.30 Double-entry bathrooms make the room available from two different areas, such as two bedrooms or a bedroom and a hall.

- **Electronics.** Designers are also providing storage for electronic equipment incorporated into the bathroom. A television, DVD equipment for the exercise room, a radio, a CD player, and speakers all need space out of the traffic pattern, yet positioned so they can easily be used during bathroom activities.

SUMMARY

The bathroom space, as we know it today, has evolved through time, starting with the early Greek and Roman bathing concepts, but taking its current shape during the seventeenth and eighteenth centuries in North America. Concern for sanitation and health, changes in lifestyles, the development of new materials and technologies, and the installation of a dependable infrastructure for water and waste have all fostered the design of today's bathroom. Lifestyle changes and technological developments continue to influence the design of our bathrooms, incorporating not only function and accessibility, but also the element of relaxation fostered by the early Greek and Roman civilizations. Designers need to stay informed about demographic and lifestyle changes as well as trends in order to design bathrooms that meet the needs and desires of their clients.

FIGURE 1.31 To assist with the ever-growing need for storage in the bathroom, this large bathroom includes a wall of cabinets.

Design by NKBA member John A. Granato II, CKD

REVIEW QUESTIONS

1. What role did bathing play in the life of early Roman civilizations and what elements of these baths do we have in modern bathrooms? (See "Early Civilizations and the Bath" pages 1–3)
2. Why did bathing disappear during the Middle Ages and what events prompted an increased awareness of sanitation in the eighteenth century? (See "The Middle Ages" page 3)
3. Describe how space used for bathroom activities has changed from Colonial times to the current day. (See "The American Bathroom Takes Shape" through "Design Trends" pages 5–27)
4. What is human factors research and how does this research benefit bathroom design for consumers? (See "Bathroom-Related Research" pages 10–12)
5. What are some current demographic trends related to household size, diversity, and composition in the United States and Canada? How do they impact bathroom design considerations? (See "Current Demographic and Population Trends" pages 24–27)
6. What are the general trends that have impacted the look and function of today's luxury bathrooms? (See "Bathroom Trends" pages 27–41)

Infrastructure Considerations

Before beginning a bathroom project, you will need to consider the infrastructure of the bathroom space and related areas in the home. In chapter 5, Form 6: Jobsite Inspection is provided to help you carefully examine the structure of the home, particularly the areas where the bathroom project will take place. No matter what type of construction project you have planned, from remodeling a bathroom to designing a new one, you must take time to carefully plan infrastructure needs and double-check your list so that nothing is forgotten. Forgetting or miscalculating some aspect of the installation may not only be difficult to change later, but most likely expensive as well.

This chapter provides an overview of the structural and plumbing infrastructure considerations that may impact your decisions while designing a bathroom project.

> *Learning Objective: Identify infrastructure needs assessment issues that can be posed by floors, walls, windows, and plumbing.*

CODES

The fundamental regulations that govern the types of materials that can be used in construction, as well as how they may be used, are called *building codes*. Although you may be working with a plumber or contractor who is very familiar with these codes, having a working knowledge of the codes will help you be more aware of restrictions or requirements that must be followed as you develop a bathroom design. Building codes are legally binding, and inspection may be required to assure compliance.

Although a new model international building code, called the International Residential Code (IRC), has been developed to form a set of consistent, correlated, comprehensive, and contemporary building code regulations for homes throughout North America, the code must be adopted by state and/or local governments. Some states and jurisdictions also adopt other codes in addition to the IRC or a more stringent version of a portion of the code. So becoming familiar with the state and local codes specific to your area is essential. A few specific items to be aware of are included in this chapter.

In addition to residential construction codes, your bathroom project may be covered by one or more codes targeted at making buildings accessible to people with disabilities. Accessibility codes and laws for the United States and Canada are discussed in chapter 4, "Human Factors and Universal Design Foundation."

Plumbing, Electrical, and Other Codes

IRC (International Residential Code) plumbing codes regulate the types of materials and structural makeup for components used in the house plumbing system and the methods for installing them. Although some codes may vary by area of the country, one water conservation code that has been mandated nationwide in the United States is the 1.6-gallon (6-liter) single flush on toilets. Be aware that some states or local jurisdictions may have adopted codes requiring even a lower water usage.

For new construction, complying with the codes is just a matter of your plumbing contractor selecting the materials and methods allowed for your area. For remodeling projects, however, it may take a little more planning to evaluate the situation, decide what is feasible, and make certain the changes reflect the current plumbing codes.

Electrical code considerations are discussed in chapter 7, "Mechanical Planning."

If you are remodeling a fairly old bathroom, you may find that codes require other updates to your bathroom materials and structure. Some other common code upgrades for safety and health require the use of a vent fan or operable window (covered in chapter 7, "Mechanical Planning"), safety glass, and scald prevention systems like pressure balanced or thermostatic shower valves. Accessibility codes are also important to make the space easy to use. These codes are covered in chapter 4, "Human Factors and Universal Design Foundation."

STRUCTURAL ISSUES

Whether you are working with new construction or a remodeling project, special structural considerations may be necessary for many different installations. Again, your building contractor may be well aware of these issues, but careful planning or a careful examination of the current structural components in the bathroom will be critical when making decisions about design options. You can begin with the original construction plans as a guide, but eventually you will need to verify that the structure is actually built as indicated on the plans. Chapter 5 has useful information, forms, and checklists to help you gather information about the existing structure. Form 6: Jobsite Inspection will be especially useful to inspect the structure.

Following are some of the structural considerations to keep in mind.

Floor Structures

Whenever the floor will be changed in some manner during your remodeling project, it is important to know more about the floor structure and what is hidden within that floor. Once you have verified the direction and size of the floor joists or floor trusses, it is essential that you know what components are already within the floor structure so that you do not damage them during the remodeling process. Concealed air ducts or plumbing may be difficult and expensive to relocate. After this inspection you will have a better idea of how to proceed with plans for new plumbing, wiring, or heating components that need to be placed in the floor. An examination of structural components will also help you determine the floor strength.

When locating a toilet in a new bathroom, floor framing must take into account the toilet placement so that the waste pipe can be properly installed between the joists in the floor (see Figure 2.1). If you are remodeling and plan to move the toilet location, the waste pipe may need to be relocated, depending on the distance it is moved. This may be a very difficult and expensive process. When only a small adjustment needs to be made in order for the toilet to line up with the waste drain, an offset flange attachment can allow you to move the toilet as much as 2 inches (51 mm), code permitting of course, in order to make use of the current waste drain. Roof venting may also need to be adjusted, so check to see what that may involve.

Damage

Check for any water damage that may have weakened the floor structure. Leaking toilets or pipes can cause structural supports to deteriorate over time, and often this damage goes undetected

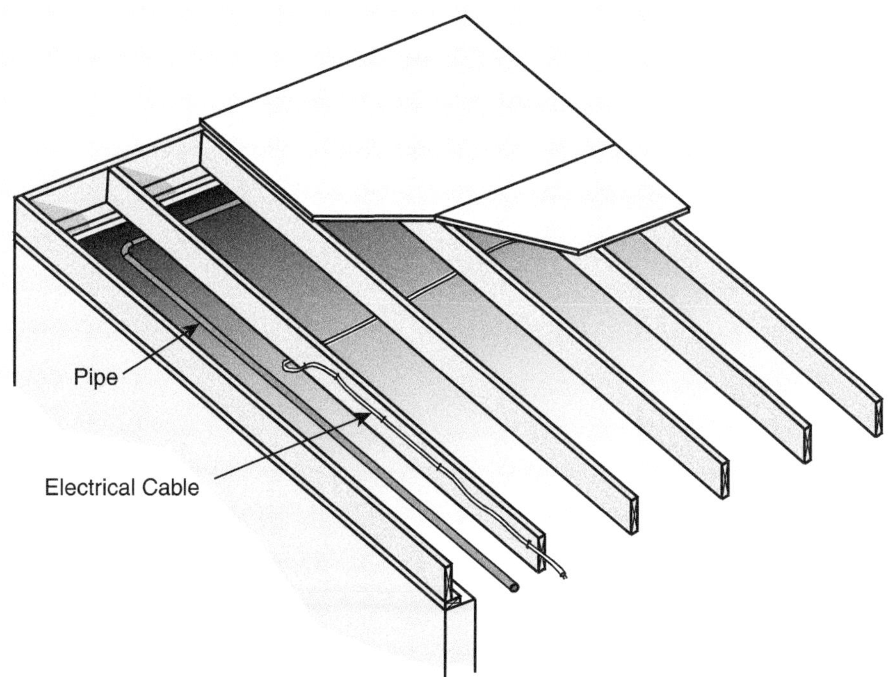

FIGURE 2.1 Check for ductwork, pipes, or electrical wiring hidden between the joists before drilling through floors or ceilings.
NKBA

because it is hidden by a floor covering. Lifting or removing the floor covering or checking for possible evidence of water damage on the ceiling directly below the bathroom will give clues to such damage.

If the damage is severe, subflooring materials or even floor joists may need to be replaced or reinforced. To prevent some of these problems in the future, seal the floors to prevent moisture from reaching the subflooring and joists. This is especially true around toilets, tubs, or showers.

The floor covering may serve as the seal if it is made of a material that water cannot penetrate and is caulked at the joints and seams. Special concrete or other poured floors may be a better choice for sealing out water as well as providing additional floor stability. Along with the structural damage, you may find mold inside the floor area where moisture was trapped. Chapter 3, "Environmental and Sustainability Considerations," discusses mold in greater detail.

Another type of damage prominent in warmer climates is termite damage. If the home has not been inspected for termites, then this would be important to recommend to your client. If the home has a history of termite infestation or if close neighbors have termites, an inspection should be completed before you begin the remodeling project. Termites can cause a tremendous amount of damage to the structure, so eliminating the threat and correcting the damage will provide a high-quality structure for your new project.

No-Threshold Showers

Clients who find it difficult to maneuver over a typical shower threshold or need to wheel into a shower will benefit from the installation of a curbless or no-threshold shower opening. If your client is considering a no-threshold or curbless shower, there are many special floor construction features that must be considered. With any shower, a major design consideration is to keep water contained so it does not seep into the subfloor and cause damage. Because no-threshold showers may not have a door, designing these showers such that water will not splash out the opening is an additional design challenge. The design components important for keeping water in the shower space include the size of the shower, the location of the handheld showerhead, the slope of the floor, and the drain location. You will find more details about no-threshold showers in chapter 8, "Accessibility in Practice." You can also reference a publication from North Carolina State University titled *Curbless Showers: An Installation Guide*, which is available on the companion website to this book (www.wiley.com/go/bathplanning) and online at www.ncsu.edu/ncsu/design/cud/pubs_p/docs/Curbless.pdf.

Oversized Tubs

A whirlpool, jetted tub, or soak tub can exert a great deal of pressure on a floor because of their weight when filled with water and people. In new construction, extra supports are fairly easy to add. In older homes, however, a careful evaluation of the floor structure is needed. Older floors were typically not built to hold these oversized tubs; therefore, reinforcing the floor is necessary (see Figure 2.2). Stripping the floor down to the joists will help clarify if the joists are large enough and spaced appropriately with enough support to hold these heavy tubs. If they are not, more support will need to be added.

Stability and Evenness

Whether poorly constructed, weakened by time, or sagging because of a settling foundation, floors can become weak or uneven. Stable and even floors are essential for many bathroom applications, one being the toilet. As someone sits on the toilet, he or she would not want it to wobble or become unstable and having a flat surface will avoid such issues. In addition, toilets are sealed at the floor with some type of seal, such as a wax ring, to prevent any water leakage from the drain. If the toilet does not fit flat on the floor, this unstable toilet could break the seal and create a major water leak.

Other bathroom installations also require a stable and flat foundation on which to rest a product. Floor tile must have a flat and nonflexible surface to prevent the tiles from breaking and grout from cracking as people walk on it. Tub and shower pans also must have a flat surface to be stable and prevent damage. Another consequence of unstable floors is squeaking. The constant squeak can not only be annoying, but make for plenty of uninvited noise in other spaces next to or below the bathroom.

Laundry

Laundry areas on the second floor, or even above a finished basement, may also have special flooring considerations. Some manufacturers of laundry equipment with drums that rotate at high revolutions per minute (rpm) recommend extra floor support to handle the added vibration that could form. With

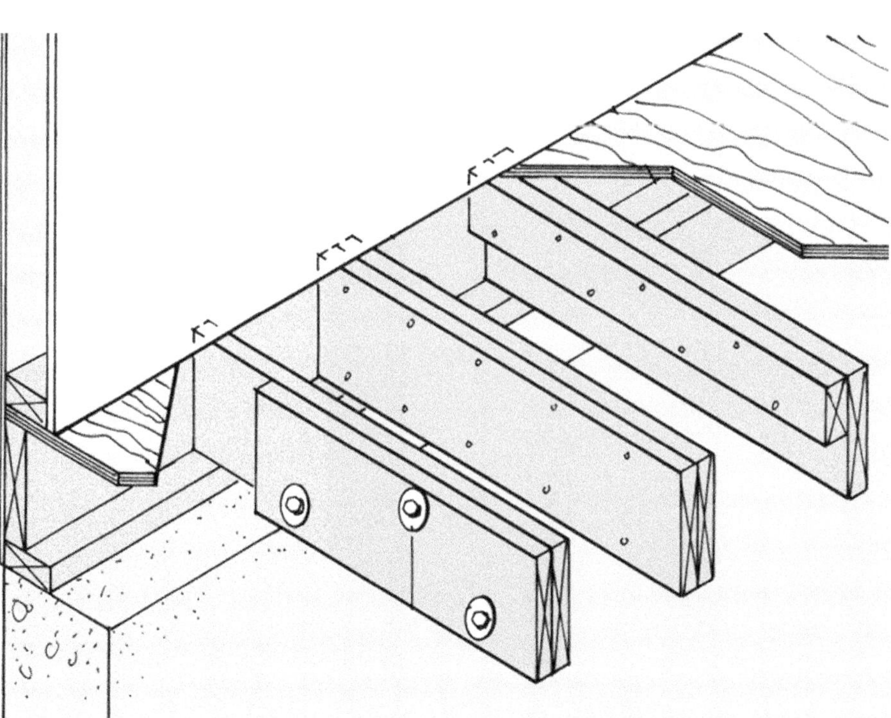

FIGURE 2.2 Extra floor supports may be needed when installing heavy bathroom fixtures.
NKBA

standard construction, joist spacing may be such that it sets up a vibration that could travel to other parts of the home, like an echo, as the laundry equipment drum rotates. As an alternative to adding extra support to the floor joists, a thicker subfloor could be placed down to stop the vibration from forming. Keep in mind that if a thicker subfloor is added, it may affect door clearances at the floor line.

The possibility of overflow from the washer should also be considered as the floor structure is evaluated. If you incorporate a floor drain in the laundry area, the floor will need to be recessed or sloped, which requires special construction techniques. A drain will also need to be installed and linked with the house's drain/waste system. This could be a fairly complicated addition. If a floor drain cannot be incorporated, a water pan of some type should be added to contain water that might overflow from the washer.

Walls

Many times, remodeling projects call for altering the wall or wall surface. Whenever walls are to be removed or exposed, do not break into them until you know what is behind them. Walls may hide wiring, plumbing, drain lines and vent pipes, and even heating, air conditioning, and air return ducts in some older homes. Any damage to these could not only be expensive, but disastrous.

Load-Bearing Walls

Walls can be either load-bearing or non-load-bearing. If you are expanding the bathroom or reconfiguring the walls, be aware of the load-bearing walls in your plan. Load-bearing walls are those that support the weight of the structure above. These make up the frame or skeleton of the house that keeps the structure standing even through wind storms and snow loads. The ends of the ceiling joists must connect to the load-bearing walls for support. If this skeleton is not strong and stable, it will shift and cause the walls to crack, floors to sag, and windows and doors to stick and not move smoothly. Over time it can cause the house to become out of square or plumb.

Removing non-load-bearing walls is usually not a problem when considering structural support of the floors above. Many times, in an effort to open up space, load-bearing walls may need to be removed. As a general rule, you can identify which walls are load-bearing by checking to see in which direction they run. Exterior walls that run perpendicular to the ceiling and floor joists are load-bearing. If you do not have ready access to the joists, you may either need to remove some molding or drill holes in the ceiling to determine where the joists are located.

If load-bearing walls need to be removed, local codes specify the type and length of header that needs to be used to span the opening for support (see Figure 2.3). Usually wood beams will be sufficient for short spans, but steel I-beams or structural beams made of laminated timbers are needed for longer spans.

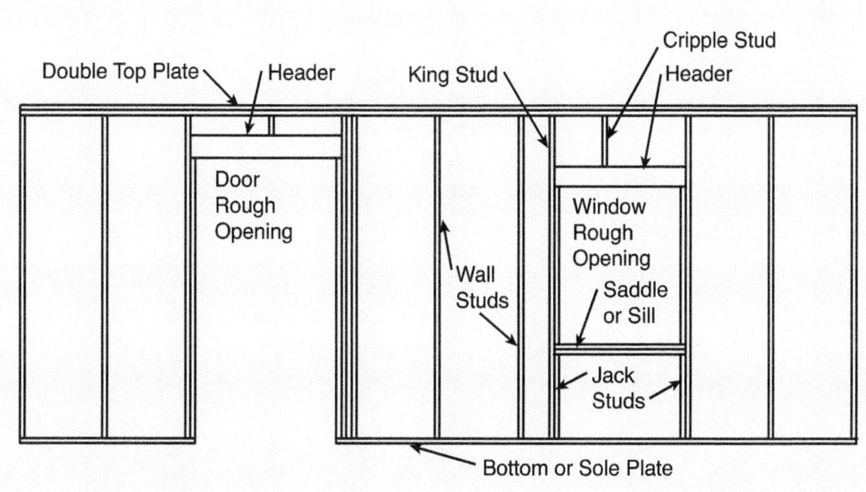

FIGURE 2.3 When openings are made in load-bearing walls, headers are needed in each opening for support.

Added Support

Many bathroom designs today are incorporating features that hang from the wall, including cabinets, sinks, toilets, bars, and doors. In order to ensure that these wall-mounted items are securely attached, additional wall supports may be necessary.

Keep in mind that when specifying wall-mounted cabinets, toilets, and sinks, not only does the mounting device need to be strong enough to support the weight of the fixture, but it must also be able to support the weight of people. Wall-mounted toilets, logically, must support a person sitting on the toilet, within certain weight limits. Although we usually do not sit on cabinets and sinks, people may have the habit of leaning, or even lightly sitting, on these fixtures and cabinets at times, which means these fixtures may also need to support additional weight.

Grab bars and some hinged shower/bathtub doors also need additional support inside the walls, often referred to as "blocking." Grab bars, usually incorporated to aid people as they move in and out of showers or tubs, or on and off toilets, must be able to support a person in the event they slip and grasp the grab bar as they fall. These grab bars must support 250 pounds (11.34 kilograms) to comply with the standard. In addition to the manner in which the bar is attached to the wall, the necessary support must come from the bar itself. Standard towel bars are not strong enough structurally to hold a person as he or she falls, and they are typically not designed to incorporate the hardware necessary to form a solid connection to the wall. Once again, keep in mind that some people may lean on standard towel bars and even use them for support. It is very important to discuss grab bar needs with your client so that the proper type of bar and mounting are incorporated. Guideline 14 provides specific information on how grab bars should be installed. More information on grab bars is located in chapter 6, "Bathroom Planning," and chapter 8, "Accessibility in Practice."

Some glass door designs for showers or tub/shower combinations have the doors hinged directly to the wall rather than to the shower frame. This application does not typically call for special mounting unless you select doors that are made of extra-heavy plate glass. This type of glass is often used with the frameless glass door style. If your client decides to use this type of glass, it will be necessary to place additional studs on the inside of the wall for support.

Uneven Walls

Uneven walls and the absence of square corners may make it difficult to properly install wall finishes, fixtures, and cabinets. This can be a problem in both new and older construction. Walls can become uneven for a number of reasons. Over time, old plaster walls crack, and in an effort to restore them, the surface is distorted. Drywall board may be damaged and not properly repaired or suffer moisture damage at some point, causing the wallboard to soften and possibly bow before drying again. Or, walls may not have been installed square when initially built.

If these walls are to be retained in the new project, problems can arise whenever this uneven surface interferes with the installation of a product. For example, if you are adding tile or stone to the wall, the pieces may not lie flat on the surface. Uneven walls will not allow a plate glass mirror to make complete contact on the wall, or the edges of a glass door to fit flush or flat. If you do not plan to replace these walls, find surface treatments, such as liners or wall panels, that will help smooth them out enough to meet your purposes. If the walls or corners are off-square, you may find that preformed showers or other fixtures may not fit well into corners, so gaps may need to be filled in. Cabinet fillers may also be needed where gaps exist as cabinets are placed against a wall. If you are adding squares of tile to an off-square wall, you will also notice that the tile lines will not be even, causing the tile sizes to vary as they are installed down the uneven wall.

Increased Wall Depth

Early in the planning process, consider where extra wall depth may be needed to accommodate items that are recessed into walls, such as medicine cabinets and plumbing and/or electrical components that accompany bathroom fixtures. A 6-inch- (152 mm) deep wall is typically needed for these items. Installation instructions for some equipment, like full-body spray showers and wall-mounted/hung toilets, specify a 2 inch by 6 inch (51 mm by 152 mm) studded wall to enclose valves and pipes.

Insulation

Wall insulation can be beneficial in the bathroom for a number of reasons. The first is auditory privacy. This means privacy for the bathroom user as well as the occupants of adjoining rooms. You will find a complete description of specific noise issues related to the bathroom and how they can be handled in the "Noise" section beginning on page 61. Insulation is also essential when it comes to controlling energy and moisture. Added insulation on the exterior walls will keep the room warmer in the winter and cooler in the summer. A warmer room is more comfortable for users, especially when they are wet, and you will need less energy for additional heating. Added insulation on the exterior also means a warmer wall. Because warm, moist air is attracted to cold surfaces, a warmer wall will attract less moisture and therefore mean fewer condensation problems. Moisture control is covered in more detail in chapter 3, "Environmental and Sustainability Considerations."

If you want to add additional insulation but do not plan to replace the wallboard on bathroom walls, you will probably need to use a foam or blown-in type insulation to fill the walls. Professional installers can do this for you. If the wallboard is being replaced or you are working with new construction, consider adding insulation in all walls that adjoin another room and extra insulation on exterior walls.

Moisture

Excess moisture is another issue associated with bathrooms. Because of all the moisture-producing activities, special measures must be taken when constructing the walls to prevent mold, mildew, and rot from forming. The shower, steam room, and tub all produce moisture that can come into contact with the walls. To prevent this moisture from making contact with the wall structure, cover all walls in these heavy moisture areas with water-impervious wallboard. If you have a steam shower, the ceiling must also be waterproof, as well as sloped or curved to allow water to drain off. Refer to chapter 3, "Environmental and Sustainability Considerations" for more information on moisture control and ventilation.

DOORS AND WINDOWS

Doors and windows are very important components of the room structure and should be planned with consideration for other aspects of the room. Use Forms 8 and 9 in chapter 5, "Assessing Needs," to gather information and measurements on existing windows and doors. For new construction, discuss with clients the type and amount of window space they desire, and the type of door that best fits their design and room configuration. For remodeling projects, examine the windows and doors carefully to decide whether they need to be replaced or just renewed.

Door Choices

When you decide to replace a door or modify the room entry, be sure the new plan fits with the other components of the room or other changes you plan to make. A new door size may mean a different-sized door swing that could interfere with the placement of fixtures.

Pocket doors are nice for opening up rooms and eliminating the door swing issue, but they require their own unique installation. First of all, pocket doors need adequate wall space to enclose the pocket free from plumbing, electrical, or HVAC (heating, ventilating, and air conditioning) components. Address this possibility when a pocket door style is being considered. Because they must move into the wall, pocket doors also may take away from the support in that wall. Historically, pocket door hardware has not been very good quality, but that has changed in recent years. If the wall contains plumbing or HVAC components that would be difficult or expensive to relocate, one alternative to the pocket door is a sliding door, sometimes called the "barn" style door (see Figure 2.4), with hardware that mounts on the outside of the wall. With this type of door, the door slides along the face of a wall, so adequate open wall space is needed.

FIGURE 2.4 One alternative to a pocket door is a sliding door with hardware that mounts on the outside of the wall, sometimes referred to as a barn-style door.
Courtesy of inFORM by Beyerle

Many times other bathroom modifications can affect the door fit. For example, some floor covering applications, such as tile or stone, or floor heating systems, may raise the floor level enough that the door will need to be trimmed in order to clear the floor.

Windows

Many times a bathroom remodeling project includes replacing the window(s). If the excess moisture in the bathroom is not adequately vented out of the room, bathroom windows can begin to have rot or mold and mildew issues before other windows of the home.

Simply replacing a window with one of the same dimensions will not usually require any changes in the wall structure. However, if you decide a window needs to be moved or increased in size, carefully examine the wall space on which the changes will be made. Be aware of any structural issues, such as studs that need to be removed or moved, vent stacks that might be present, or headers that need to be modified. Also check for any specific code requirements related to the type of window glazing to be installed.

With any type of replacement window, consider the fenestration pattern of the windows on the exterior. You want a new window to blend with the other windows of the home, especially if it faces the street. Also, if you modify the size or move the window opening, consider whether exterior surfacing materials can be repositioned or reapplied to blend in.

Selection Considerations

There are numerous window choices and considerations when selecting a bathroom window.

- **Operability.** Windows can be operable or fixed. If your client desires some natural ventilation in the bathroom, an operable window would be the choice. Place this type of window where it can be easily accessed. Locating it at the back of a counter or tub area would make it difficult for the user to reach and open.
- **Security.** Vandalism, break-ins, or theft can be a concern for any window in the home. Glass block is often used in bathrooms as a good security option. When natural ventilation and a view are not considerations, glass block can provide a large amount of natural light, an obstructed view, and a surface that cannot be easily penetrated.
- **Privacy.** If privacy is a concern, especially if the bathroom window is facing a busy street or the house next door, select a type of window glass that offers the maximum amount of privacy. For example, frosted glass does not allow a clear view through the window. Inside window treatments can also add privacy, but you need to discuss that option with your client.
- **Cost.** The cost of windows can vary tremendously. The framing materials, size, quality of construction, and energy efficiency can all factor into the cost. It is usually advisable to buy the best windows you can afford, as they will last a long time, be easier to operate, and make your home more pleasant and comfortable.
- **Exterior bathroom features.** Many times clients want to take advantage of an exterior feature outside the bathroom. This could be a wonderful view they would like to enjoy while soaking in a tub or perhaps a patio and flower garden they would like the bathroom to open up onto. Keep these features in mind as you plan the window space for the client.
- **Tempered glazing.** The code requires that glass be tempered or equal if it is located within reach (60 inches [1524 mm]) of the tub/shower floor. See "Guideline 15 - Glazing" for more information on the use of tempered glazing.

Window Style

The type, style, and size of window you choose for your bathroom will depend on the size of the bathroom, the intended use, the view, and where it will be placed. Small bathrooms may be very limited for window locations. Larger bathrooms may have multiple windows or even a sliding glass door to the outdoors. Whatever the size, windows are an important part of your design plan.

There are a number of common window styles that could be used in a bathroom (see Figure 2.5). These include:

- **Single- or double-hung windows.** Single- and double-hung windows are common window styles used in homes. In double-hung both sashes slide vertically, whereas only the bottom sash slides upward in the single-hung window. Many of these windows also have sashes that tilt inward for easy cleaning. These sliding windows generally have higher air leakage rates than hinged windows, and you usually need to be very close to the window in order to open it.
- **Casement windows.** Casement window panels are hinged at the side and crank open to a 90-degree angle, exposing almost all of the window area to the outside. This style has almost double the ventilation area compared to a double- or single-hung window, especially if there is a little breeze. Perhaps a downside to these windows is that the screen is on the inside of the window. Because the sash is closed by pressing against the frame, they have a lower air leakage rate than sliding type windows.

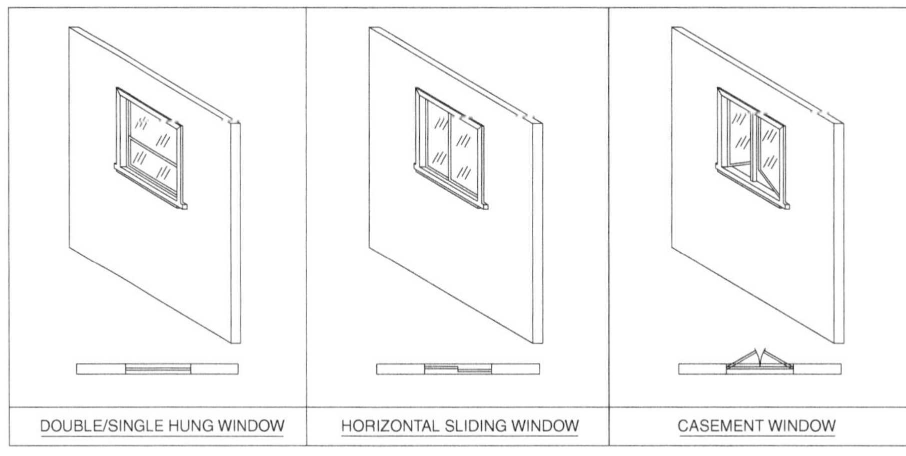

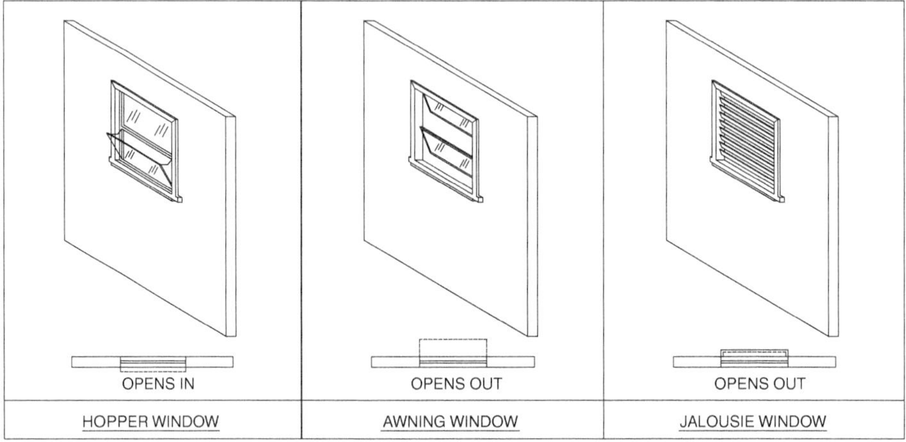

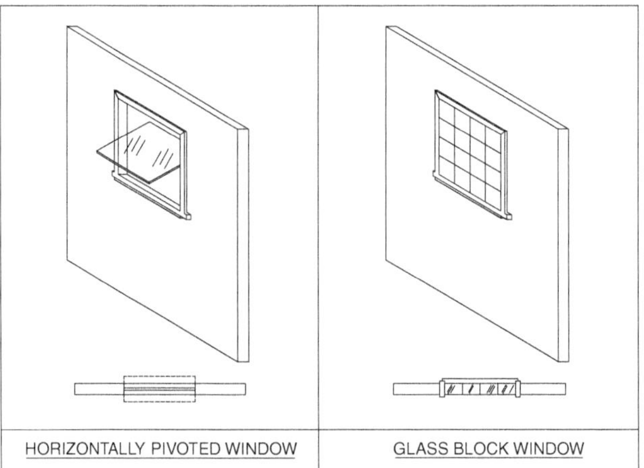

FIGURE 2.5 Common window styles.

- **Hopper and awning windows.** Hopper windows are hinged at the bottom and open inward, and awning windows are hinged at the top and open outward. In both styles the sash closes by pressing against the frame, so they generally have a lower air leakage rate than sliding windows.
- **Single- and double-sliding windows.** Both sashes slide horizontally in a double-sliding window, and only one sash slides in a single-sliding window, opening part of the window at a time. Like the single- and double-hung windows, they have a higher air leakage rate.
- **Decorative fixed windows.** A second source of light and a decorative touch to a bathroom can be added with a variety of fixed windows. These windows can be octagon, square, round, or oval in shape and can be made with plain or decorative glass, such as stained, beveled, etched, or leaded glass. They can provide good natural light because they typically are not

covered on the inside and thus reveal their decorative nature. If placed high on the bathroom wall, people on the outside would not be able to see through them. However, if these windows are placed in the direct line of view as people walk through a bathroom or are bathing, then the windows will need to be shielded on the inside so that people in the bathroom cannot be seen from the outdoors. Even etched glass may shield a direct view but the shadows of individuals might still be seen.

Energy Efficiency

The energy efficiency of the window area in the bathroom is extremely important for a number of reasons. More efficient windows will improve energy efficiency and increase comfort. Efficient windows also have less moisture accumulation on the window (those frosty windows we sometimes see on cold winter days) because warm, moist air is naturally attracted to cold surfaces like those of poorly insulated windows.

Windows in older homes can be extremely inefficient. First of all, they may have loose-fitting frames and poorly working components that allow air infiltration. Another reason for poor efficiency is the type of frame and glazing present. Uninsulated metal frames and single glazed (one pane of glass) windows will allow warmth to be conducted through the materials very easily. If the client wants to keep the current windows in place, the windows can be tightened up with caulking and weatherstripping. Adding full storm windows is another way to improve efficiency, but your client may not want to deal with storm windows every season. Windows that are energy efficient will have at least two layers of glazing (glass); a low-e coating (low-emittance) (see Figure 2.6); a good-quality, insulating frame; tight-fitting parts; and sometimes argon or another gas between the panes of glazing. One way to identify the most efficient windows on the market is to look for the Energy Star label. (Refer to chapter 3, "Environmental and Sustainability Considerations," for more information about Energy Star.)

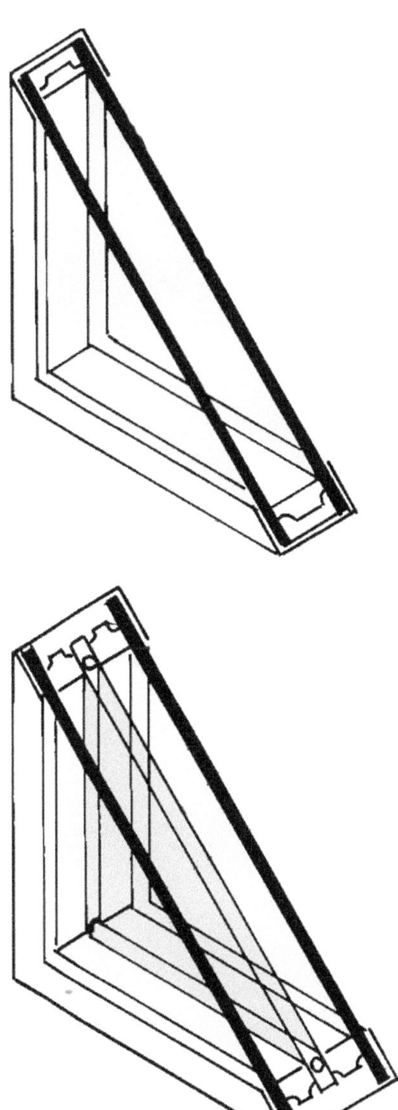

FIGURE 2.6 A low-e coated surface or low-e coated polyester films improve the energy efficiency of a window by limiting heat gain and reflecting heat back into the home.
NKBA

The National Fenestration Rating Council (NFRC) is a nationally recognized organization that has developed a rating system for windows and skylights. This rating system allows the purchaser to compare different attributes of windows related to energy performance, solar gain, visibility, air leakage, and condensation. Figure 2.7 shows an NFRC sample label.

The NFRC label contains ratings on the following factors:

- **U-factorsfor windows and skylights.** U-factor is a measurement of heat conductivity or thermal transfer. This can be heat loss or heat gain. The lower the U-factor, the more energy efficient the window. The U-factor is especially important in heating-dominated climates, but it is also beneficial in cooling-dominated climates.
- **Solar heat gain coefficient (SHGC).** SHGC is a measure of how much solar radiation passes through the glass. This is expressed as a number between 0 and 1, and the lower the number the less solar heat it transmits. The desired rating depends on the location of the window and the climate. For example, a high SHGC is desirable for passive solar heat gain in a cold climate while a low SHGC is preferred in a hot, sunny climate. West-facing windows can be an issue in most any climate, so a low SHGC is important for these windows, blocking the intense western sun.
- **Visible transmittance (VT).** VT indicates the amount of visible light transmitted through the glass. The NFRC's VT is a whole window rating and includes the impact of the frame. The VT rating varies between 0 and 1 and the higher the VT the more light transmitted, thus maximizing the amount of daylight passing through the window. Most double- and triple-pane windows are between 0.30 and 0.70.
- **Air leakage (AL).** The air leakage is the amount of heat loss or gain that occurs by infiltration through cracks and openings in the window assembly. The AL is measured in cubic feet of air through a square foot of window area (L/s/m2 or m3/h/m). The lower the AL the less air will pass through the window assembly, and this rating is optional on the NFRC label. This rating does not measure air leakage between the window assembly and the wall, after the window has been installed.
- **Condensation resistance (CR).** The CR measures how well a window resists the formation of condensation on the inside surface of the window and is expressed as a number between 1 and 100. The higher the number the better the resistance to condensation, and this is also an optional rating on the NFRC label.

National Fenestration Rating Council®

CERTIFIED

World's Best Window Co.

Millennium 2000+

Vinyl-Clad Wood Frame

Double Glazing • Argon Fill • Low E

Product Type: **Vertical Slider**

ENERGY PERFORMANCE RATINGS

U-Factor (U.S./I-P)	Solar Heat Gain Coefficient
0.30	**0.30**

ADDITIONAL PERFORMANCE RATINGS

Visible Transmittance	Air Leakage (U.S./I-P)
0.51	**0.2**

Manufacturer stipulates that these ratings conform to applicable NFRC procedures for determining whole product performance. NFRC ratings are determined for a fixed set of environmental conditions and a specific product size. NFRC does not recommend any product and does not warrant the suitability of any product for any specific use. Consult manufacturer's literature for other product performance information.
www.nfrc.org

FIGURE 2.7 NFRC sample label.
National Fenestration Rating Council

Window energy efficiency requirements may vary by climate zone, but also by jurisdiction if a variation of the IRC code is adopted.

Framing Materials

Choosing energy-efficient, durable, low-maintenance framing materials is important for windows. Following the recommendations of the Energy Star program would be a good suggestion. Energy Star–qualified windows come in a variety of framing materials as follows:

- Fiberglass frames are strong, durable, low maintenance, and provide good insulation. Fiberglass frames can be either hollow or filled with foam insulation.
- Vinyl frames are low maintenance and provide good thermal insulation. Sections may be hollow or filled with foam insulation. Wide vinyl sills may be reinforced with metal or wood.
- Aluminum frames are durable, low maintenance, recyclable, and typically have at least 15 percent recycled content. Frame design typically includes thermal breaks to reduce conductive heat loss through the metal.
- Wood frames are strong, provide good insulation, and are generally favored in historical neighborhoods. The exterior surfaces of many wood windows are clad (or covered) with aluminum or vinyl to reduce maintenance.
- Combination frames use different materials separately throughout the frame and sash to provide optimal performance. For example, the exterior half of a frame could be vinyl while the interior half could be wood.
- Composite frames are made of various materials that have been blended together through manufacturing processes to create durable, low-maintenance, well-insulated windows.

Skylights

Another way to add additional daylight to a bathroom is through the use of a skylight. They are also a good option for adding light to a windowless room or area, such as an inside dressing room or a hallway. Skylights bring in natural light, usually eliminating the need for artificial light during the daylight hours. Skylights can be Energy Star–qualified and they carry NFRC ratings as well. When selecting a skylight for a bathroom, consider many of the same factors you would for other windows. Skylights can come in two basic styles (see Figure 2.8):

- **Traditional.** A traditional skylight typically uses the same basic technologies to construct the window as a standard window. Many skylights are fixed, but some are operable to let warm air out of the house in the summer. These operable skylights can be installed horizontally, at an angle, or perpendicular to the roof joists. Another form of skylight is a plate of glass fixed to an opening in the roof and often covered by an opaque bubble to help shield the glass and add some insulating value. Traditional skylights have an opening in the ceiling that extends from the glass area on the roof through the attic to the bathroom below. The opening can remain the size of the window glass or flare out as it enters the room space to add light to a larger area.
- **Tubular.** The tubular daylight devices (TDD) are tubes that extend from the roof down through the roof /attic to the bathroom space. These devices gather light at the roof and transmit it down to a diffusing lens mounted in an interior surface, usually the ceiling. The opening for these tubes is usually smaller than a typical skylight so it is a means to add daylight to many areas of the home, including closets, bathrooms, or halls, that would not have access to sunlight.

The quality of the skylight or tube is important because skylights are usually exposed to the extremes of sun and weather for longer periods of the day than standard windows of the home, especially those that are installed horizontal to the roof. They could even be covered with snow for periods of time. Skylights have had the reputation of leaking because anytime you penetrate the roof, water leaks are a possibility. Proper installation and using high-quality products are essential to prevent such water damage.

PLUMBING

Of prime importance in any bathroom are the water delivery and drainage systems, including the water-heating equipment. Many of the activities that take place in the bathroom rely on a dependable and adequate supply of both hot and cold water, so careful consideration should be given to structuring the plumbing system to meet the needs of the client and the fixtures they have chosen. Standing all lathered in a shower and having the water turn icy cold because the hot water ran out is not the most pleasant experience for anyone.

Most water supply systems, either public or private, should not have a difficult time keeping up with the water requirements of a standard bathroom. However, when high water–demanding fixtures like large tubs and multiple-head showers are added to a system, there is a good chance demand can exceed supply, or the water pressure cannot provide the force or timely delivery expected.

Manufacturers' instructions that accompany products should provide information on water delivery requirements. If there is a problem with water volume, water pressure, or the amount of available hot water, assist your client with investigating ways to remedy these issues to improve the entire home's water system.

Water quality related to water hardness can also impact water delivery when it leads to minerals clogging the showerheads or filling the water heaters with sediment. Chapter 3, "Environmental and Sustainability Considerations," provides information on hard water and other water concerns, and how to remedy water problems in the home.

In new construction, the plumbing system can be planned with the new bathroom in mind. With today's new plumbing and connector technologies, plumbing can be placed most anywhere, so do not let it restrict your design. If you are working with a remodeling project, however, two questions must be answered early in the planning process:

FIGURE 2.8 (a) Traditional skylights also aid in venting of excess humidity from showers. (b) Cutaway view of tubular skylight application.
Images: VELUX America

1. Which fixture changes are economical to make?
2. How does the present plumbing structure affect plans for changing fixtures and fixture locations?

Fixtures

A new bathroom means selecting all new fixtures, but when a client is remodeling a bathroom they can make choices as to which fixtures they replace. If cutting costs is a goal, some of the fixtures may be able to be reused, especially if they have been replaced fairly recently. If the client chooses to keep some of the present fixtures, can they be successfully removed and relocated if the new plan called for a new location? Refer to Form 10 in chapter 5, "Assessing Needs" to collect information and measurements on existing fixtures and water-using appliances.

When new fixtures are desired, will they be able to be installed using the old plumbing or will new lines need to be added? This is discussed in more detail below. Another consideration with new fixtures is their fit in the old spaces. If the basic structure of the bathroom will stay, and the desire is to update the fixtures and look, work with your client to select fixtures that will fit in the old spaces with minimal changes. For example, find a new shower or tub to fit the previous space, or install a new lavatory into a vanity cabinet and counter the client wishes to reuse. With the use of many new finished wall materials, you may even be able to convert a tub space to a shower and vice versa. For tubs, showers, or lavatories, if you decide to relocate the water controls to the counter or wall, or offset for easier access, are there major problems with doing so? For a new or remodeled bathroom project, talk with the client about the fixtures they have in mind, and the basic water and plumbing requirements for each. As an example, keep in mind that the type and location of pedestal lavatories or above-counter vessel bowls have specific requirements for drainpipes or wall-mounted faucets. Corner designed fixtures, especially lavatories and toilets may also have special requirements (see Figure 2.9).

FIGURE 2.9 A corner lavatory or fixture may require special techniques for installing and concealing the plumbing.
Courtesy of Porcher

Another key consideration is water usage. Be sure to select low-flush toilets, low-flow showerheads, and other water-conserving WaterSense® plumbing fixtures. Using these water-efficient fixtures may solve or avoid some of the problems or concerns related to high water–demand fixtures and the client is incorporating sustainable measures as well. See chapter 3, "Environmental and Sustainability Considerations," for more information on water conservation and other water issues.

You should always discuss the implications of the client's fixture choices. Larger tubs and high-volume showers can use a tremendous amount of water, which will increase water bills. Also, in order to provide a sufficient spray for massaging showers, a specific water pressure level must be maintained, which may be an issue with some water systems.

Water Delivery

Getting water to the fixture also has to be considered. Following are some factors to keep in mind.

- Beyond standard water requirements, bathrooms that include a spa tub, whirlpool tub, or high-volume or multihead showers require not only large volumes of water and adequate water pressure, but also different-sized delivery lines. The standard 1/2-inch (12 mm) pipe used for most plumbing installations may be insufficient for large water demands. Larger tubs and whirlpools should use a 3/4-inch (20 mm) water supply line with a 3/4-inch (20 mm) iron pipe size valve and bath spout to ensure proper water delivery. If the home relies on a well or cistern for water, you may not be able to accommodate high-water-use fixtures in the design.
- To help cut costs in new construction or remodeling projects, locate the bathroom near another room with plumbing, such as the kitchen, another bathroom, or the laundry room, to take advantage of existing plumbing lines.
- In cold climates, avoid placing water supply pipes on exterior walls if possible. If that cannot be avoided, be sure to insulate the wall well. Those in extremely cold climates may need to consider a double-wall construction to make sure there is space for adequate insulation, so pipes do not freeze and burst.
- New flexible water supply lines make it possible to easily reposition fixtures, such as a sink, along a wall. Before you count on using these, check local codes to make sure they are allowed. Also remember that you also need to relocate the drain.
- It would be a good idea to have a water shut-off valve in or near each bathroom fixture for emergency shut off of water. Many times the only shut-off valve for the home water supply is located in the basement or outside the house, which is a long way to go if you are on the second floor. Some valves are also difficult to access because they are hidden behind panels or doors that are semi-permanently attached. A good location for a valve would be where the water supply enters the area.
- This access is required by IRC building codes and information on the equipment must be left with the homeowner. This requirement is stated in Bathroom Planning Guideline 19. Valves and water lines for showers or tubs that are permanently concealed behind walls or tile will require a major excavation and much expense if these lines need to be accessed. Cleverly disguised doors or removable tiles can serve as easy access as long as the consumer is aware of the panel and can easily open it (see Figure 2.10).

Drain/Waste/Vent Pipes

As you examine the plumbing in the bathroom you are remodeling, you may notice that current local code requirements for the size, type, and/or height of plumbing components may require a few structural changes. For example, codes set a minimum diameter for stack and vent pipes in relation to the number of fixtures installed. If the home is quite old, a careful examination may find that the current configuration of pipes does not meet these codes, so you must decide what it will take to make the necessary changes. There is also approximately a 5-foot (1.5-m) limit for relocating some fixtures before a new vent needs to be added.

Newer code requirements could also impact how some bathroom fixtures work with older plumbing systems. For example, if you are remodeling a bathroom in an older home, you may encounter

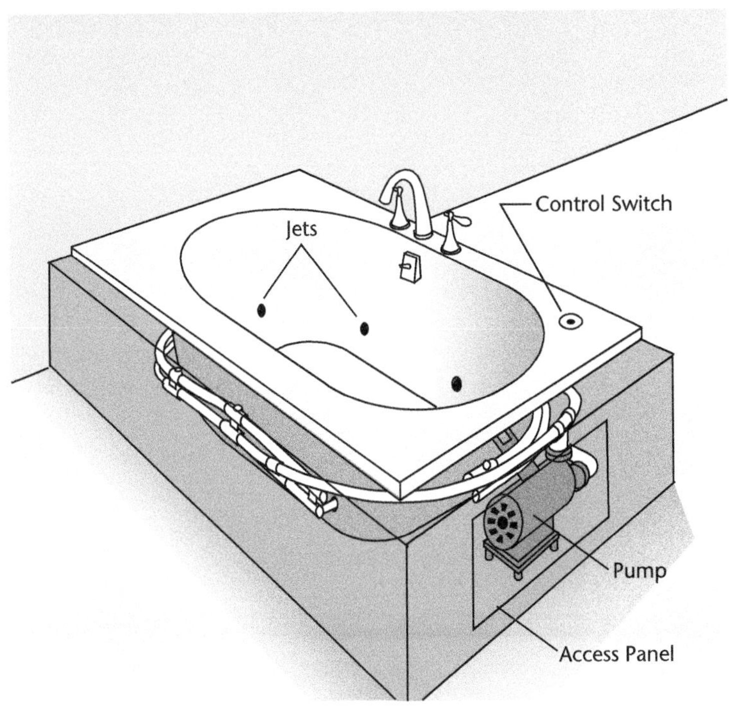

FIGURE 2.10 Conceal water shut-off valves (as well as other mechanical systems) with removable panels for easy access.
NKBA

problems with the new 1.6-gallon (6 liter) low-flush toilet fixtures. Older waste pipes may be made of cast iron, which has a rougher interior surface than the present plastic pipes, and this could lead to back-ups and clogs. In this case, a power-assisted flush may be needed if new waste pipes are not installed.

Following are other waste/vent considerations:

- If you are remodeling a bathroom, check to see if the new fixtures can make use of existing vent stacks and drains. If not, these could be costly to move because they may require major structural changes.
- High-volume showers need enlarged drain lines.
- Be aware that changes in fixtures may require changes in the drain size or location. For example, the drain line size requirement may change if you replace a tub with a shower. In other cases, fixtures may be able to share a drain line, such as two lavatories. When replacing old fixtures, it would be best if you could select a new fixture that would use the same drain location as the previous fixture to eliminate the need to relocate the drain. As an example, showers come with a drain opening at either the center or side. Select a new shower that will be compatible with the existing drain.
- When replacing an old freestanding toilet, drain location specifications on the new fixtures may be different. Many older toilets were mounted such that the distance from the center of the drain outlet to the stud wall was 10, 12, or 14 inches (250, 300 or 350 mm) . Newer toilets are mounted with the center of the drain 12 inches (300 mm) from the wall. An offset flange may be used to adjust for this difference if it is 1½ inches (37 mm) or less.
- If you are including a steam unit somewhere in the bathroom, be sure the contractor has planned a drainpipe for the steam generator.
- One other consideration in the waste/drain system, for clients who are not connected to a municipal waste system, is the septic tank. Septic tanks are sized based on the house and family size. If your client plans to install a whirlpool, full body-spray shower, or other high water–use fixtures that will place an increased amount of water into the waste system, you will need to check the capacity of the septic system to make sure it can handle the additional water. It may be that you will need to have the client add a larger septic tank, or additional septic tank, to accommodate the extra water. If too much water flows through a septic tank, the system cannot

adequately deal with the waste products, leading to a breakdown of the septic system and environmental consequences.

Below-Grade Applications

If the house is built on a slab, reconfiguring plumbing will involve additional challenges. In order to move or add new pipes, you may need to chip into the slab's concrete.

Basement Bathrooms

Basement bathroom installations can also be challenging. If the basement is not pre-plumbed for a bathroom, considerable work will be needed to add the necessary water sources and drains. You can make the installation a little easier by locating the new bathroom next to existing plumbing, but adding the waste drain lines will be the most difficult. You will first need to locate the main sewer or septic line and determine its location below ground level.

Many sewer lines are actually quite deep, and with proper excavating you may be able to form the necessary 1/4 inch per foot (6 mm per 300 mm) of slope that is required for good drainage. The sewer line depth may be recorded at the local city or county public works department. The location of septic lines may be recorded on the plan for the lot. If the records are not available, you may need to talk with an excavator who is familiar with the area or dig a test hole to locate the line.

Once the sewer line is located, you will need to compare it to the exact level of the proposed toilet installation. A plumber, contractor, or excavator can help you make this comparison. If the sewer line level is sufficiently below the level of the toilet, you can simply install a 3-inch (75 mm) drain line from the toilet to the sewer.

Ejector Toilets

When the drain for the new bathroom installation ends up below the main sewer line for the house, you cannot take advantage of gravity to remove waste and water. In this case, a sewage ejector toilet is needed to pump waste up to the main sewer line.

A typical ejector toilet has a pedestal made of polyethylene, which acts as a base for mounting the toilet. This pedestal, which is 5 to 6 inches (125 to 150 mm) high, can sit directly on the floor or be recessed into the floor. Recessing the pedestal will place the toilet level with the floor. Inside the unit is a set of impellors and a sewage ejector pump, which processes the waste and pushes it up to the main sewer line (see Figure 2.11). Tubs, showers, and lavatories can also be drained into the toilet ejector tank.

Some models of ejector toilets are designed such that the pump, vent, and pipes are located a distance behind the toilet. This makes it possible to build a wall between the toilet and the equipment, which allows for a cleaner installation and makes the pipes and equipment much less obtrusive. In some situations, a false or raised floor can be used to give space for plumbing lines if you have enough ceiling height to do so.

Composting Toilets

Another below-grade option that eliminates the need for a pump and gives the environment a boost is the composting toilet. This fully self-contained toilet requires no water inlet, no connection to the sewer, and no chemicals in order to operate, but it does need an electrical connection and a vent to the outside. The composting toilet works much like a septic tank. About 90 percent of the waste material is actually water. A small electric heating grid and fan in the unit evaporate the liquids and send the vapor up the vent pipe. The solid waste material breaks down through normal bacterial action, converting it to a soil-type residue. The residue filters down to a collection tray at the bottom, which needs to be emptied about once a year. These units can operate very efficiently if the usage isn't excessive, and odors should not be a problem if the toilet is operating properly.

Water Heaters

An adequate supply of hot water is essential for the bathroom, as well as other rooms in the home. Plan the hot water needs carefully to ensure that plenty of water will be available during peak use times, such as early in the morning, when many family members may be getting ready for the day.

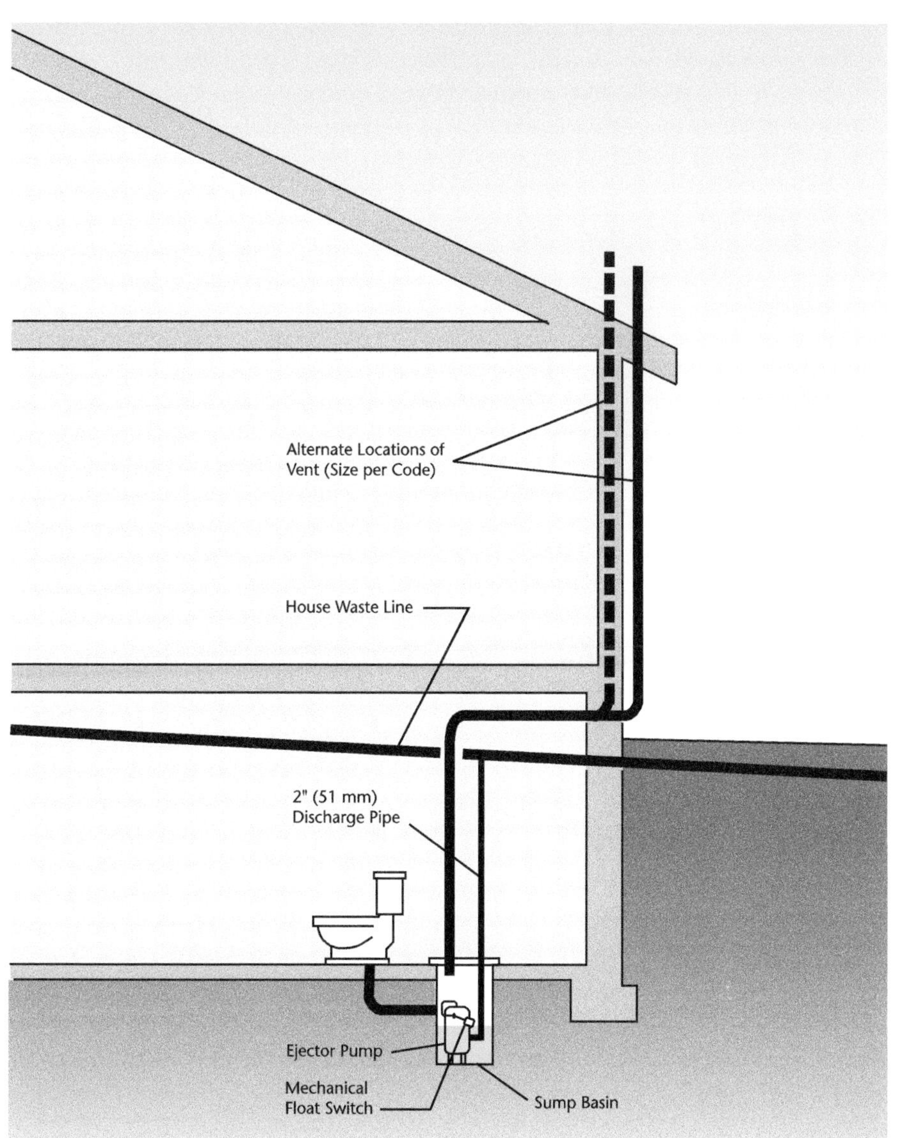

FIGURE 2.11 When toilets are installed below the waste line of the house, they must be hooked up to an ejector pump that grinds the waste into slurry and pumps it up to the waste line. The device can be mounted in a pit below the floor, as shown, or set behind the toilet if the toilet is installed on a platform above the floor.
NKBA

How quickly hot water arrives to the bathroom fixtures can vary depending on the location of the water heater in relation to the bathroom. A somewhat common home design scenario is where the bathroom ends up on the opposite end of the house from, or two stories above, the home's water heater. Not only does this make for a long time lapse before hot water reaches the bathroom fixtures, but a large amount of water is wasted while waiting for the hot water to arrive.

If this appears to be an issue, a second water heater located near the bathrooms, would be a good idea. A second water heater may also be recommended if your client wants to install a whirlpool type tub or multihead shower that require a large amount of hot water. Chapter 7, "Mechanical Planning" contains details on water heater selection.

NOISE

Bathroom noise is an issue of running water, flushing toilets, and people—well, you know what they are doing! Auditory privacy can be an important factor in designing a bathroom, especially in one that is centrally located in a home, or near the social or living areas. In addition, noises in a bathroom near a bedroom can seem especially loud and disturbing when someone is trying to sleep.

Noise is often defined as unwanted sound. Therefore, controlling noise is a matter of limiting the transfer of sound from one part of the home to another. Sound moves by vibrations, which are transmitted through both air and building materials. Soft materials, such as carpet and draperies, tend to absorb sound. Hard materials, such as the ceramic tile and stone, that are common in bathrooms, tend to reflect and/or transmit sounds. Bathroom noise is controlled, and auditory privacy provided, in several ways:

- Reducing the amount of sound or noise that is generated
- Isolating and buffering the sources of noise through space planning
- Using construction techniques to insulate and stop sound transmission

Reduce Noise Generated

Many bathroom features generate noise. Bathroom ventilation fans are necessary to control moisture, yet motors and air movement can be noisy. The importance of selecting quiet bathroom fans with a minimum sone rating is discussed in chapter 7, "Mechanical Planning," with other information about bathroom ventilation. A fan that generates too much noise simply will not get used.

Jetted tubs may offer stress-relief and rejuvenation but are not silent in operation. As tub and motor size, and the volume of water movement, increase, the potential for noise grows.

Laundry areas (discussed in chapter 9, "More Than a Bathroom") are sometimes included in the bathroom. Noise transmission, especially to the sleeping area, should be a consideration in the placement and installation of washers and dryers.

Motors, such as those used in ventilation fans, jetted tubs, and washing machines, may vary in pitch (hertz). Many people perceive lower pitch noises to be less annoying. However, it is important for your client to "test listen" to different motors to determine their reaction to the noise.

Pressure-assisted toilet flushing systems minimize the use of water while increasing flushing effectiveness, but the sudden rush of water can seem loud. Noise complaints about the mandated low-flush toilets have been frequent, but manufacturers continue to improve the product. However, toilets that use air pressure to assist the flush tend to be noisier.

Buffer the Noise

If you have the opportunity to influence the home design beyond just the bathroom space, you can help buffer the bathroom space, and reduce sound transmission. Look for ways to put sound-absorbing spaces between the bathroom and quiet areas of the home. For example, a closet between a bathroom and a bedroom is an excellent way to buffer bathroom noise and keep sleeping areas undisturbed. Other spaces that make good sound buffers are built-in cabinets, bookshelves, stairways, and utility closets.

Another sound-buffering space planning technique is to back noisy area to noisy area. For example, put the toilet on the wall that is shared with the kitchen rather than the wall that is shared with the bedroom.

Sound-Insulating Construction Techniques

In new construction, or renovations that include building new walls, sound insulating construction techniques can be used to isolate bathroom noises. The simplest approach is to use acoustical materials such as acoustical tiles, cork, carpet, and other textiles. However, these softer and absorbent materials may not be the best choices in the bathroom, where water-resistance, easy cleaning, and mold-resistance are important. Therefore, look at wall construction techniques that reduce sound transmission.

Avoid air paths between the bathroom and other spaces to minimize sound transmission. Recommend resilient, nonhardening caulk to seal around receptacles, plumbing, light fixtures, and other openings in walls and ceilings. Also, recommend sealing where the wall partition joins the floor and ceiling. If there are switches, receptacles, and other openings on opposite sides of a wall, avoid locating them in the same stud space. If possible, separate these switches and receptacles, horizontally, by at least 24 inches (610 mm).

There are several ways to construct the walls to minimize sound transmission (see Figure 2.12). A standard stud wall can be insulated with fiberglass or a similar material, to absorb sound.

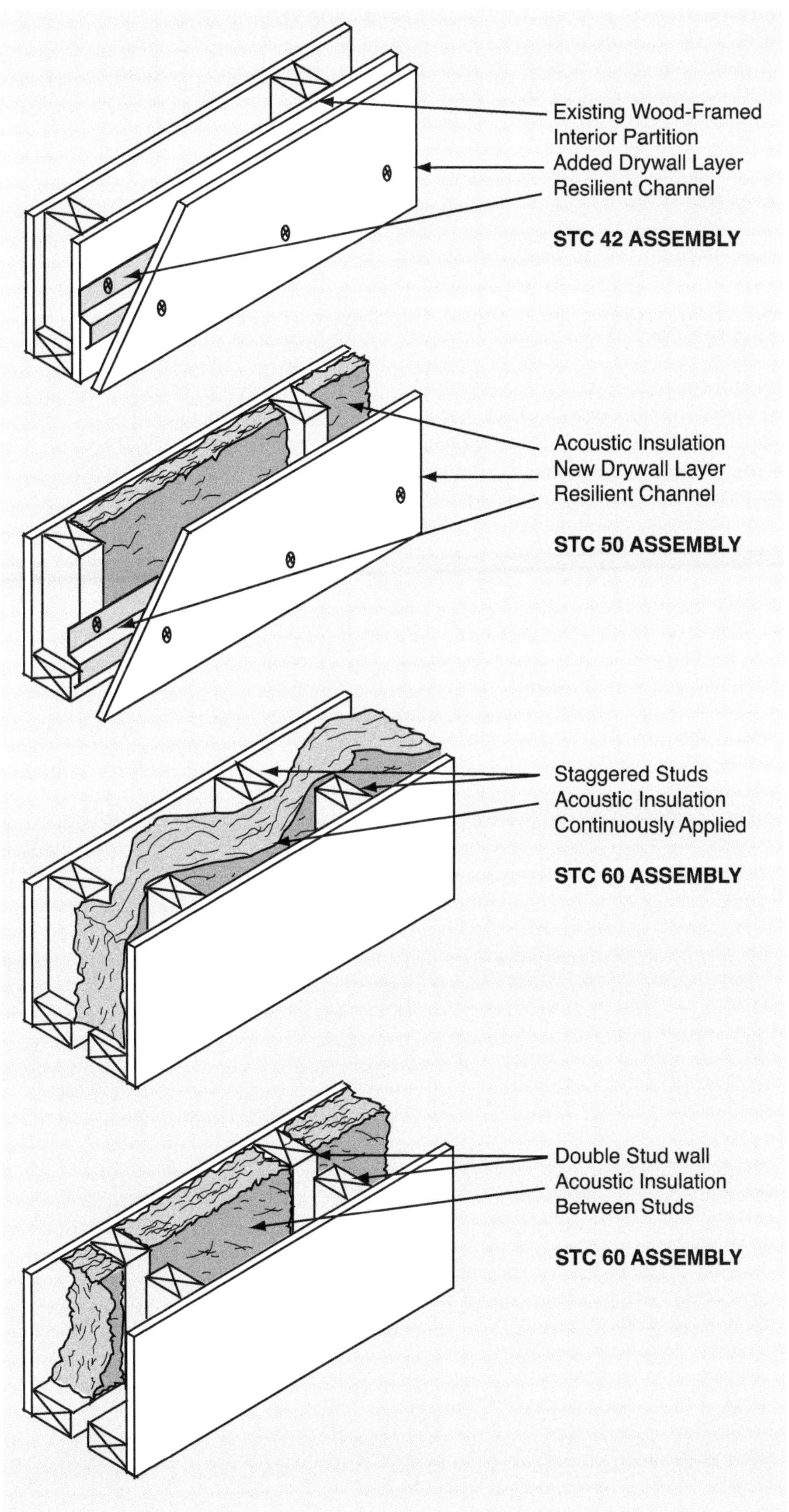

FIGURE 2.12 Different building techniques can be used to reduce sound transmission through walls, which is measured in sound transmission units, or STC.

NKBA

A sound-deadening gasket can be used between the studs and the drywall, to minimize vibration and sound transmission. A double-stud wall, with the studs on separate plates, reduces sound transmission by separating the two wall structures and limiting vibration. A staggered-stud, double-stud wall will be even more effective. Insulating material can be added to any of the special wall constructions.

Keep in mind that special sound-insulating wall constructions do have several drawbacks, and the tradeoffs need to be considered. Cost is increased for extra materials and construction time. Floor space is lost, especially with the double walls. Also, the need to run plumbing, wiring, and ducts in the walls has to be considered, especially with a staggered-stud, double wall.

SUMMARY

Whether you are helping a client plan a new bathroom or remodel their current bathroom, carefully investigate the basic infrastructure components that are essential to a successful project. Floors must be structurally sound to accommodate the fixtures that will be installed. Not only do walls need to be flat and square for cabinet, fixture, and surface finishes, but special wall supports may need to be added for some applications.

Windows are important for lighting and ventilation but should also be energy efficient to add to the comfort of the area. Carefully examine the plumbing changes and needs for the new plan. Plumbing requirements and changes may pose problems related to meeting code requirements or altering structural components.

All of these considerations involve details that must be identified and dealt with before the finishing touches are applied. The more knowledgeable you are about these issues, the fewer changes you will need later on and the more functional your plan will become.

REVIEW QUESTIONS

1. Explain why it is important to have level, stable floors and even walls when installing products in a bathroom project. (See "Stability and Evenness" page 46)
2. How can you tell if a wall is load-bearing and what special accommodations are needed if you plan to remove this wall? (See "Load-Bearing Walls" page 47)
3. What are the benefits and issues related to installing skylights and how do traditional skylights differ from tubular styles? (See "Skylights"page 55)
4. What issues might arise when considering the repositioning of bathroom fixtures during remodeling projects? (See "Fixtures" page 57)
5. What special fixture and installation considerations are often needed for below-grade bathroom installations? (See "Below-Grade Applications" page 60)
6. Explain the ways to control bathroom noise. (See "Reduce Noise Generated" page 62)

Environmental and Sustainability Considerations

Good design includes planning spaces that are environmentally friendly and healthy for the user. Good design reflects sustainable use of resources. In this chapter, we will look at important issues of energy efficiency, water quality, waste management, and air quality. We will consider these issues from the choices you, the designer, must make, as well as the impact on your client.

This chapter is a brief review of environmental and sustainability issues affecting bathroom design. If you as the designer, or your client, need further information on these issues, you can contact the U.S. Environmental Protection Agency (EPA). The website www.epa.gov is a good place to start. Other excellent resources are Natural Resources Canada (www.oee.nrcan.ga.ca) and Health Canada (www.hc-sc.gc.ca). Or contact the office of your local Cooperative Extension Service, health department, or water authority. Additional resources are included at the end of this book.

After reading this chapter, you may wish to pursue further study and learn more about sustainable and environmental issues. Many of the organizations and agencies discussed in this chapter offer educational classes and opportunities to become a certified professional with special environmental and sustainable knowledge.

Learning Objective 1: Identify and discuss sustainable products and practices for the bathroom.

Learning Objective 2: Identify and discuss energy and water efficient policies and practices in the design and construction of the bathroom.

Learning Objective 3: Identify and discuss policies and practices for healthy housing.

SUSTAINABLE DESIGN AND BUILDING

Sustainability, as applied today, has many definitions. It is being energy efficient, but much more. Most definitions of sustainability revolve around the idea of balance, thinking of the future and minimizing impact today. Sustainability issues in buildings include energy efficiency, water management, air quality, waste management, and recycling. There are sustainable practices, products, and techniques in the design and construction of a building. Sustainability is also a philosophical approach that guides design and business decisions.

Envision a Sustainable Building

The Rocky Mountain Institute (www.rmi.org) offers this description of a sustainable building:

- Makes appropriate use of land.
- Uses water, energy, lumber, and other resources efficiently.
- Enhances human health.
- Strengthens local economies and communities.
- Conserves plants, animals, endangered species, and natural habitats.
- Protects agricultural, cultural, and archeological resources.
- Is economical to build and operate.
- Is nice to live in.

In recent years, the term *green building* has come to represent policies and practices that are environmentally responsible—sustainable. Sustainable, green building practices are recognized to:

- Promote healthy places to live and work.
- Enhance and protect natural ecosystems and biodiversity.
- Improve air and water quality.
- Reduce solid waste.
- Conserve natural resources.

For the designer, there are many opportunities to implement sustainable design policies and practices. A general overview is presented in the following list. This chapter will further detail many opportunities to practice sustainability that are particularly applicable to bathroom design and construction.

- Think small, compact—minimalist. A smaller space is a more sustainable space. Fewer materials are used in the constructing of a smaller space. There is less space to heat and cool. Less energy is needed for lighting (see Figure 3.1).
- Specify environmentally healthy building and interior finish materials, including nontoxic, sustainably harvested, recycled, or renewable resource products. Look for opportunities to reuse materials through salvage or repurposing.
- Specify materials and products from local sources to minimize the energy or pollution "cost" for transportation.
- Specify products, including appliances, which are energy efficient.
- Specify plumbing fixtures and appliances that conserve water.
- Maximize the use of daylight and specify energy-efficient light sources.
- Plan window placement to maximize passive solar gain through south-facing windows. Minimize heat loss through north windows and limit heat gain though west windows.
- Plan the layout of the bathroom and auxiliary spaces to maximize the use of standard size materials and products, minimizing the amount of construction waste.
- Investigate and implement opportunities to recycle construction and demolition waste. Encourage clients to donate serviceable cabinetry, appliances, and fixtures removed in renovations to charitable organizations.

CHOOSING SUSTAINABLE PRODUCTS

Product specifications are an important part of any design project. There are many criteria that influence the best choice of materials, fixtures, appliances, lighting, or any of the many items that go into a bathroom or the auxiliary spaces that you are designing. The products must be functional

FIGURE 3.1 A New Orleans example of a compact house
Infrogrmation/ CC-BY-SA-3.0

as well as aesthetic, meet the needs of the client, follow the building code, fall within the budget, be compatible with other products being installed—and the list goes on. Add the priority of sustainability, and a complex process is now even more complex.

Evaluating a product for sustainability can be difficult because the criteria are not always clear-cut. Some sustainable practices are easier to accomplish or may be a higher priority for your client. Some sustainable practices have immediate impact, some do not.

Resource use is a basic measure of sustainability. For example, how much energy or water does this product use? Transportation costs are another measure. For example, was the product manufactured locally? However, the picture can then become more complex to evaluate. How sustainable is the manufacturing process for different product choices? Which material has the lesser impact on indoor air quality? Which product can be recycled after use?

There are a growing number of independent and reliable testing, evaluation, and certification programs that evaluate one or more sustainability criteria of products and materials used in bathrooms and auxiliary spaces. Many of these programs are discussed in this chapter and can be used to assist you and your client in developing a high-quality and effective sustainable project.

R-2000

R 2000 is a voluntary technical performance standard for energy efficiency, indoor air tightness quality, and environmental responsibility in home construction. The program is industry-endorsed and administered by Natural Resources Canada. Houses built to the R-2000 standard typically exceed the energy performance requirements of the current Canadian building codes. The standard was introduced over 25 years ago, and is continually upgraded to include new technologies as they become established in the marketplace.

R-2000 homes are tested and certified by independent, third-party evaluators.

More information is available at www.oee.nrcan.gc.ca.

GREEN BUILDING PROGRAMS

One approach to specifying sustainable products and materials is to become familiar with the criteria for one or more of the programs for certifying residential *green buildings*. The United States Green Building Council's *LEED for Homes,* the National Association of Home Builders' National Green Building Standards™, and the Natural Resources Canada R-2000 Standard are examples of programs that provide guidelines for certifying homes based on sustainability criteria. In addition, regional and local programs, such as Southface Institute's Earthcraft House, Canada's BUILT GREEN®, Earth Advantage Institute's New Homes, and Austin, Texas's Austin Energy® Green Building provide similar certification opportunities.

A program that certifies a home as a *green building* sets criteria for products, materials, and practices that are sustainable. Credit toward certification may be given for features such as water-conserving plumbing fixtures, materials with recycled content, or energy-efficient appliances. Therefore, specifying materials and products that meet national, regional, or local green building program criteria contributes to a project's sustainability.

As a designer, you may be part of a team that is seeking a green building certification of a home or building. Careful record keeping and documentation will be required. However, you can take pride in your contribution to a more sustainable world. In addition, completion of a certified green building project is a marketable accomplishment and a valuable addition to your portfolio.

LEED for Homes

LEED, or Leadership in Energy and Environmental Design, is a program of the United States Green Building Council. LEED provides building owners and operators with a framework for identifying and implementing practical and measurable green building design, construction, operations, and maintenance solutions.

LEED certification provides independent, third-party verification that a building, home, or community was designed and built using strategies aimed at achieving high performance in key areas of human and environmental health: sustainable site development, water savings, energy efficiency, materials selection, and indoor environmental quality.

LEED-certified buildings are designed to:

- Lower operating costs and increase asset value
- Reduce waste sent to landfills
- Conserve energy and water
- Be healthier and safer for occupants
- Reduce harmful greenhouse gas emissions
- Qualify for tax rebates, zoning allowances, and other incentives in many communities

LEED has multiple rating systems for different situations and buildings. LEED for Homes is targeted to residential buildings (see Figure 3.2).

The Canada Green Building Council provides a version of the LEED program that is adapted for the Canadian climate, construction practices, and regulations (www.cagbc.org).

More information about LEED is available at www.usgbc.org.

FIGURE 3.2 A house in Maine, United States, rated as LEED Platinum, the highest level of performance in LEED for Homes certification.
Peripitus/ CC-BY-SA-3.0

National Green Building Standards™

The creation of the ICC 700 *National Green Building Standard*™ was initiated by the National Association of Home Builders (NAHB) and the International Code Council (ICC) to offer a national rating system and standard definition for green building. This building standard has received approval from the American National Standards Institute (ANSI), indicating it was developed through an open, consensus-based process with representative stakeholder participation and ample opportunity for public comment. The standard defines green building for single- and multifamily homes and residential remodeling, and land development.

There are four performance point levels: bronze, silver, gold, and emerald. The threshold level (bronze) results in an energy savings approximately 15 percent above code requirements for the 2008 version of the standard. To achieve higher performance levels, the home must meet minimum performance points in each of six categories:

- Lot design, preparation, and development
- Resource efficiency
- Energy efficiency
- Water efficiency
- Indoor environmental quality
- Operation, maintenance, and building owner education

(Continued)

An updated version of the NGBS, to be released in 2013, will include a number of changes including more stringent energy efficiency requirements, as well as the ability to certify small remodeling projects, such as kitchens, bathrooms, and basements.

Homes being rated for the *National Green Building Standards*™ are evaluated by trained, independent raters at the NAHB Research Center (see Figure 3.3). NAHB provides training and information for both the building industry and homeowners on green building at www.nahbgreen.org.

(a)

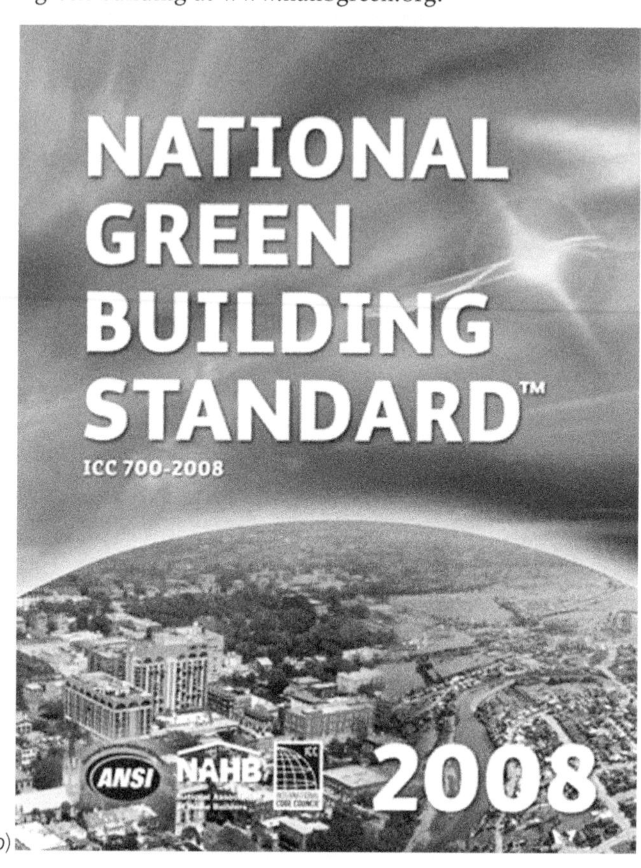

(b)

FIGURE 3.3 The NAHB Research Center certifies houses conforming to the ICC 700 National Green Building Standard™.

SUSTAINABLE CERTIFICATION PROGRAMS

Choosing sustainable products and practices can take time and require research. It will require careful reading of manufacturers' specifications and other product information. You may have to become familiar with new terminology. However, there are ways to make the process both easier and more reliable.

Look for products and materials that are *certified* by an independent organization. A valuable certification will require third-party, independent testing of the product or material to verify that the manufacturer meets the organization's standards or criteria. Certified products or materials will carry a label or logo from the certifying organization. The logo is a clear identification that the product or material meets the certification. This is different than marketing materials that may indicate the product "meets criteria" or is "qualified" but is not actually tested and certified.

Certifications are renewed on a regular basis. New models or types of materials require testing to qualify. Take care to determine what is actually being certified. For example, is the product being certified for some performance characteristic, such as energy use? Or is the manufacturing process being certified for sustainable practices?

This chapter introduces and describes a number of certifications for products and materials commonly used in bathrooms. Most certifying organizations maintain websites that describe their programs and include lists of the specific products that are certified.

Specifying Certified Products and Materials

In this section, we describe some of the major certification programs that certify materials and products with respect to sustainability. This list is not exhaustive, but it introduces you to common certifications you might encounter in product literature, marketing materials, or elsewhere. We also discuss some other certification programs throughout this chapter where they fit better with the topic.

Scientific Certification Systems

Scientific Certification Systems works with manufacturers and businesses to offer a variety of certification programs in multiple areas. Some programs are designated under Scientific Certification Systems' own programs, such as the calCOMPliant™ Certification, for compliance with California Air Resources Board requirements on formaldehyde emissions. Other certification programs are developed in conjunction with industry organizations, such as the Resilient Floor Covering Institute and the Forest Stewardship Council to offer independent, third-party testing and verification.

Scientific Certification Systems certifications evaluate many construction products of interest to the bathroom designers. In particular, their sustainable certification programs verify recycled content, biodegradability, and chemical emissions. Further information is available at www.scscertified.com.

Cradle to Cradle Certification℠

The Cradle to Cradle Certified℠ Program is a third-party ecolabel that assesses a product's safety to humans and the environment from a lifecycle perspective. The Cradle to Cradle® framework focuses on using safe materials that can later be disassembled and recycled or composted. Criteria for certification include material health, material reutilization, renewable energy use, water stewardship, and social responsibility.

A wide variety of products have achieved Cradle to Cradle certification. Product categories of particular interest to bathroom designers are countertop materials, flooring, insulation, lighting, and wall coverings. Further information is available at www.c2ccertified.org. Cradle to Cradle Certified℠ is a certification mark licensed by the Cradle to Cradle Products Innovation Institute. Cradle to Cradle® is a registered trademark of McDonough Braungart Design Chemistry, LLC (see Figure 3.4).

Ecolabel

The Ecolabel is a program of the European Union and is based on a lifecycle analysis of a product or service that is "kinder to the environment." Over 1100 licenses have been granted for products and services meeting the Ecolabel criteria that starts with the raw material and finishes with disposal.

Currently, floor coverings, light bulbs, paints, varnishes, and some appliances are qualified for the Ecolabel. Toilets, showerheads, taps (faucets), and other appliances are under evaluation. More information is available at www.ecolabel.eu.

Certifications for Wood Products

There are three different certification programs that certify woods that are used in cabinetry, flooring, and other products that you might specify in a bathroom.

- **Forest Stewardship Council (FSC).** The FSC Principles and Criteria describe how forests around the world can be managed to meet social, economic, ecological, cultural, and spiritual needs of present and future generations. The FSC offers a **Forest Management Certification** for forest operations that are managed in an environmentally appropriate manner. A **Chain of Custody Certification** verifies FSC Certified forest products through the production chain. (www.fsc.org)
- **American Tree Farm System® (ATFS).** This program targets small woodland owners. Certification requires implementation of a management plan for sustainable forest stewardship. (www.treefarmsystem.org)

FIGURE 3.4 The Cradle to Cradle logo uses two Cs to emphasize the cyclical nature of the model.

- **Programme for the Endorsement of Forest Certification (PEFC). PEFC** is an international organization dedicated to promoting sustainable forest management. PEFC promotes good practice so that forest products are produced with respect for the highest ecological, social, and ethical standards. The PEFC Ecolabel identifies products from sustainably managed forests. PEFC is an umbrella organization that has endorsed about 30 national certification systems, making it the world's largest forest certification system. PEFC programs of interest to the bathroom designer include its labeling of sustainable forest products and chain of custody certification. (www.pefc.org)

Certified Recycled—What Does That Mean?

Using fewer new resources, and maximizing the use of the resources we have is an important part of sustainability. More and more, sustainable products and materials are those that are made from recycled materials. But is it postconsumer, preconsumer, or postindustrial recycled? And is the material recyclable or compostable or biodegradable after use? (See Figure 3.5.) If sustainability is based on the full lifecycle of the product or material, and considers the impact on the future as well as the present, we need to stop and ask these questions. A few definitions are needed, courtesy of the Environmental Protection Agency and the Federal Trade Commission.

- **Recycled.** Recycling turns materials that would otherwise become waste into valuable resources. Therefore, *recycled content* is material that has been recovered or diverted from the solid waste stream. *Preconsumer* (sometimes called postindustrial) recycled content is waste from the manufacturing process that would not normally be reused by industry. *Postconsumer* recycled content is from the waste stream after consumer use. If the entire product or material is not of recycled content, qualifying words on the labeling is required (such as percentage).
- **Recyclable.** A material that is recyclable can be collected, separated, or recovered from the solid waste stream and used again or made into other useful products.
- **Degradable.** Degradable materials will break down and return to nature in a reasonable time frame after disposal. *Biodegradable* materials are broken down by naturally occurring microorganisms, such as bacteria. *Photodegradable* materials are broken down by exposure to light.
- **Salvaged or reclaimed.** There is no legal definition for these terms, but they are generally used to describe materials that are reused for a similar purpose in a building project. Often the building materials are taken from buildings, ships, or other sources that are no longer in existence in total. Salvaged or reclaimed materials are a good way to make sustainable use of existing resources as long as the item being salvaged is safe and appropriate for the new use.
- **Repurposed**. A popular term used to describe using a product, material, or item for a new purpose in a project. As with salvage, the repurposed item needs to be safe and environmentally appropriate for the new use.

ENERGY ISSUES AND BUILDING CODES

The International Residential Code (IRC) is a model code published by the International Code Council. Although this model code is considered a benchmark in the building industry, it does not have the force of law until adopted by a state or municipal code agency. In 2012, the IRC incorporated the Residential Provisions of the International Energy Conservation Code into the sections on Energy Efficiency. The IRC model code requirements represent important standards for energy efficiency in building design and construction. Although not all parts of the energy efficiency code are applicable to bathroom design, it is necessary for a designer to have an overall understanding of an energy-efficient building as represented by the IRC. This understanding prepares you for applying relevant parts of the code to your particular design project.

FIGURE 3.5 The universal symbol for recyclable or recycled products.

The 2012 IRC divides the United States and Canada into eight climate zones. Many code requirements are then specific to each climate zone, which is designated by state, province, county, and territory. The energy-efficiency section of the code emphasizes creating a building structure that has a *thermal envelope* and *air barrier* that minimizes heat loss in winter, heat gain in summer, and air leakage year-round. This is done with construction standards that are appropriate and cost effective to the climate.

Of interest to the bathroom designer are the following requirements for windows, doors, and walls:

- **U-factors** for windows, skylights, and exterior doors. U-factor is a measurement of heat conductivity or thermal transfer. The lower the U-factor, the more energy efficient the window or door.
- **Solar heat gain coefficient** (SHGC) for windows. SHGC and other window characteristics are detailed in chapter 2, "Infrastructure Considerations."
- **R-value** of insulation in floors, walls, and ceilings. R-value is a measure of the resistance to heat conductivity. The higher the R-value, the better the insulation.

The code provides detailed information about sealing the structure to limit air infiltration as well as where to locate insulation. In addition, there are requirements related to ventilation, which are further discussed in chapter 7, "Mechanical Planning." Of particular note is the requirement for whole house mechanical ventilation to provide adequate fresh air.

From the beginning of the design process, it is important to be aware of the influence of energy-efficiency codes on potential design and space solutions. Issues such as wall thickness and floor area; selection and placement of doors, windows, and lighting fixtures; placement of plumbing pipes and fixtures; and installation of venting systems are examples of design and construction decisions that can be influenced by requirements of the energy code.

WATER

A bathroom is a wet place. Water is used for many purposes, both utilitarian and luxurious. In the process of using a bathroom, people may swallow, inhale, and absorb water. For these reasons, the water used in a bathroom should be safe and healthy, as well as smell, taste, and look good. Clients need water that works well for all bathroom uses and does not contribute to maintenance problems. At the same time, water is a finite resource, and we have a responsibility to use it wisely and efficiently. The designer is an important influence in sustainable use of water in the bathroom.

Chapter 2, "Infrastructure Considerations," of this book discusses issues of an adequate water supply, water pressure, and the plumbing infrastructure necessary for a well-designed bathroom. This chapter first discusses issues of water quality—water that is safe, healthy, and functional for use in the bathroom. Next, efficient and sustainable use of water in the bathroom, especially in the choice of water-efficient fixtures, is presented.

Water Quality Standards

There are two types of water quality standards in the United States. The first type of standard is used to ensure that water is safe to drink or ingest. These standards are called *Primary Drinking Water Standards* and are enforced by law. The second type of standard is to ensure that water is functional and aesthetic for various uses such as bathing and washing. These standards are referred to as *Secondary Drinking Water Standards,* and they are voluntary.

The Environmental Protection Agency (EPA) establishes drinking water standards in the United States. State and local health departments or environmental agencies work with municipal or public water authorities to meet the required primary standards. These water authorities must regularly test and, if necessary, treat their water to ensure that they are meeting the primary standards. Individual or small private water systems (defined by the number of households connected to the water system) are not required to meet any water quality standards. However, owners of private water systems are encouraged to use the EPA standards as benchmarks for testing and treatment of their water.

Health Canada (www.hc-sc.gc.ca) is the ministry responsible for drinking water standards in Canada and for educating Canadians about the importance of safe drinking water. The Guidelines for Canadian Drinking Water Quality addresses many of the same primary and secondary contaminant issues as the EPA guidelines described earlier. Similar to the United States, Health Canada works with provincial and territorial governments to ensure that Canadian water is safe to drink as well as functional and aesthetic for household uses. Environment Canada (www.ec.gc.ca) monitors Canadian water quality and provides leadership for water management issues.

Primary Drinking Water Standards

The Primary Drinking Water Standards are based on the *Maximum Contaminant Levels* (MCLs), or highest concentration, of pollutants allowed in public drinking water. The pollutants that are regulated by the primary standards are those that are known to cause adverse health effects and for which there is information available about chronic or acute health risks. These pollutants include: disease-causing organisms, such as bacteria; toxic chemicals, such as lead and nitrates; and radioactive contaminants, such as radon.

Secondary Drinking Water Standards

Secondary Drinking Water Standards are based on the *Secondary Maximum Contaminant Levels* (SMCLs) of pollutants that affect the aesthetics and function of water. These are contaminants that impact water qualities such as appearance, taste, odor, residues, or staining. Examples of secondary standard contaminants are chloride, iron, manganese, sulfur, and altered pH. While these might not present a health threat, they can be very important to water use in the bathroom. Secondary standards are voluntary and are not required. A public water system may choose to test and treat for some of the SMCLs.

Other Water Contaminants

Two other water contaminants are not covered by the EPA standards but are a concern in bathrooms.

Hard Water

Hard water is water with a high mineral content, mostly calcium and magnesium. Hard water usually is found in groundwater sources, such as water from wells. Both private and municipal systems can use groundwater. Hard water creates problems with mineral deposits on fixtures and plumbing, which can reduce water pressure and lead to mechanical failures. The mineral deposits can also be unsightly, particularly on darker materials. Hard water also reduces the effectiveness of cleaning products, including shampoos and soaps, and increases soap scum deposits. The end result of hard water is usually reduced performance and increased maintenance.

If your client lives in a community with known hard water problems, or their water is from a groundwater source, recommend testing for water hardness. Depending on the test results, discuss water-softening treatment to extend the life and appearance of their new plumbing fixtures.

Iron Bacteria

Iron bacteria form a reddish brown slime that can clog pipes and fixtures. It is most likely to result when water is left standing. Typically, it is first noticed in the toilet tank or bowl. Iron bacteria are naturally occurring and more common with well water. They are an unpleasant nuisance and can cause staining. Cleaning products can treat iron bacteria but will not eliminate the problem.

Water Quality Testing

As part of your design preparation and household assessment (see chapter 5, "Assessing Needs"), you will want to find out if there are any water-quality concerns. If the project is a renovation, you can look in the existing bathroom(s) for evidence of water concerns such as fixture staining or hard water deposits. Check to see if the household uses water filters in the kitchen for drinking water. You may even want to draw a glass of water and evaluate how it looks and smells.

If the home is, or will be, on a municipal water system, you can assume that the water is safe for drinking, and thus for bathroom uses such as teeth brushing. If the home is on a private water system, ask your client about any testing or treatment. Regular testing is the best method to help maintain a safe water system. Most experts recommend that private water sources, such as a well, be tested annually.

More frequent tests may be recommended, depending on the water source and recent water pollution problems in the home or area. A financial institution may require water testing before money is lent for any construction or home improvements. The local or state health department is an excellent place to contact for further information about water testing.

Never have a water test done by a company that wants to sell you, or the homeowner, water treatment equipment. Contact the water testing company and describe the water problem. They can recommend the necessary tests as well as the procedure for gathering the water sample.

Solving Water Quality Problems

There are many options for solving water quality problems (see Table 3.1). Some may be as complex as having to locate a new water source, such as drilling a new well. Others may be as simple as attaching a filter to a faucet.

It is important for you, the designer, to discuss water quality problems with your client. The water in a new bathroom should not be a health threat. New fixtures and fittings need to be protected from staining, deposits, and other maintenance problems caused by water problems. Aesthetic problems with water can detract from the enjoyment of jetted tubs or luxury showers. Early in the design process, determine if water quality problems are a concern. Help your client get expert advice about water testing, and if needed, the selection of appropriate water treatment equipment.

EFFICIENT AND SUSTAINABLE USE OF WATER

A large custom shower provides space for two people. A jetted tub full of hot water gives a stress-relieving water massage. A body shower pulsates with multiple streams of water. A toilet has both a bidet and a self-cleaning wash system. These amenities in today's bathrooms, designed as private

TABLE 3.1 Common Types of Water Treatment Methods

Water Treatment Method	Typical Contaminants
Activated carbon filtration	Odors, chlorine, radon, organic chemicals
Anion exchange	Nitrate, sulfate, arsenic
Chlorination	Coliform bacteria, iron, iron bacteria, manganese
Distillation	Metals, inorganic chemicals, most contaminants
Neutralizing filtration	Low pH
Oxidizing filtration	Iron, manganese
Particle or fiber filtration	Dissolved solids, iron particles
Reverse osmosis	Metals, inorganic chemicals, most contaminants
Water softening (cation exchange)	Calcium, magnesium, iron

retreats and luxury spaces, may be desirable in the context of our busy, demanding lives. Yet, the bathroom is a place of high water use and many luxury water features may be in conflict with the desire for sustainability in housing.

Toilets, showers, and bathroom faucets are responsible for over half the water use in a typical home. Precisely because so much water is used in the bathroom, the designer needs to be aware of, and plan for, efficient water use. As populations expand, finite water resources need to be shared with more people. It is a major community—and taxpayer—investment to collect, treat, and deliver high-quality water to residents as well as to treat the resulting wastewater.

There are many benefits to efficient and sustainable use of water:

- Reduced pollution caused by excessive water in our wastewater systems
- Healthier natural wetlands
- Reduced need for communities to construct water and wastewater treatment facilities
- Fewer dams and reservoirs needed to provide a water supply
- Reduced energy use to treat both the water supply and wastewater

Efficient use of water in the bathroom means that water is not wasted, but can be used where it is most needed and most appreciated.

Hot Water

Much of the water used in a bathroom is heated. Wasting water would also be wasting the energy used to heat the water. Conserving and reducing the energy used to heat water are part of a sustainable home.

Insulating hot water pipes reduces standby heat loss. Putting a secondary water heater in or near the bathroom minimizes the water that is wasted waiting for the hot water to reach the bathroom and well as the energy lost when the hot water cools in the pipes after hot water is no longer drawn by a bathroom fixture. Installing a tankless or on-demand water heater in the home adds the additional savings in energy that is no longer used to maintain a storage tank of hot water.

In this book, installing, locating, and selecting water heaters are discussed in chapter 2, "Infrastructure Considerations," and chapter 7, "Mechanical Planning." It is also important to select a water heater that is energy efficient and sized to household needs. A too-large water heater will use extra energy and provide more hot water than is required. There are several technologies and water heater designs that offer particular advantages in energy efficiency. These technologies include high-efficiency gas, tankless (on-demand), heat pump, condensing, and solar.

If a design project will include the need to specify a new water heater, or will include water features that increase the use of hot water, you should encourage your client to consider an energy-efficient water heater. For example, an Energy Star–rated water heater would be a good choice. In addition, some local codes may specify the type or efficiency of a new water heater for remodeling, replacement, or new construction.

Energy Star®

Energy Star is an international symbol of premium energy efficiency (see Figure 3.6). In the United States, Energy Star is a program of the Environmental Protection Agency and the Department of Energy that promotes the protection of the environment through energy-efficient products and practices. Energy Star was established to:

- Reduce greenhouse gas emissions and other pollutants caused by inefficient use of energy.
- Make it easy to identify and purchase energy-efficient products without sacrificing performance, features, and comfort.

Energy Star product specifications are based on the following key guiding principles:

- Product categories contribute significant energy savings.
- Qualified products deliver the features and performance demanded by consumers as well as increased energy efficiency.
- If the energy-efficient product costs more than a less-efficient product, the purchaser recovers their increased cost through utility bill savings within a reasonable period of time.
- Energy efficiency is achieved through broadly available, nonproprietary technologies.
- Product energy consumption and performance can be measured and verified.
- Labeling effectively differentiates energy-efficient products.

FIGURE 3.6 The Energy Star logo is found on qualified products.

A wide variety of products are **certified** as energy efficient by Energy Star. Product categories of particular interest to bathroom designers include clothes washers, dehumidifiers, light bulbs and fixtures, ventilating fans, and water heaters.

Further information and lists of qualifying Energy Star products can be found at www.energystar.gov.

Toilets

In most homes, the single greatest use of water is for flushing the toilet. Older toilets may use three, five, or more gallons (liters) per flush. Toilets manufactured since the early 1990s have been federally mandated to use 1.6 gallons (6 liters) of water or less (see Figure 3.7). Some toilets on the market today use even less water per flush. Toilet manufacturers have improved the technology for toilet flushing systems to make them more efficient, effective, and quieter. An effective flushing system reduces the likelihood that a second flush will be used to remove all the waste. In addition to saving water, efficient and effective flushing systems reduce maintenance.

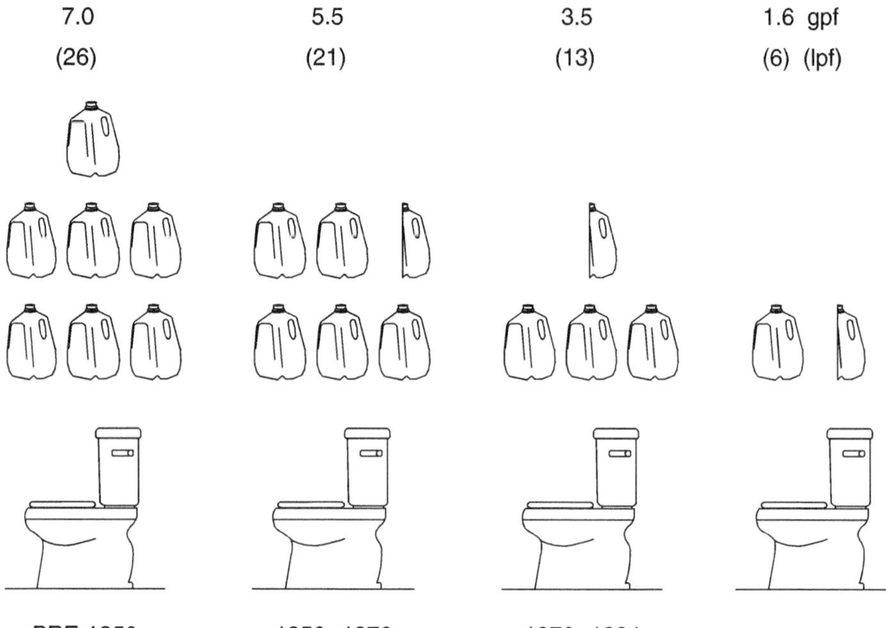

FIGURE 3.7 The number of gallons (liters) per flush has decreased as toilets became more efficient.

Norbert Lechner, *Plumbing, Electricity, Acoustics: Sustainable Design Methods for Architecture.* New York: John Wiley & Sons, 2012.

In a remodeling project, you may be replacing an older toilet that used more water in the flush. Make sure the water pressure is adequate for the new, more efficient toilet. Explain to your client that the new toilet may sound or operate differently. For example, some toilets have dual-flush systems that let the user choose the amount of water per flush. In some communities, the water authority may offer rebates for installing a more water-efficient toilet.

Showers

The early 1990s also saw new regulations limiting showers to 2.5 gallons (9.5 liters) per minute flow rate. Many fixtures offer even more efficient water-flow rates of 2.0 gallons (7.6 liters) per minute or less (see Figure 3.8).

When designing shower systems with multiple showerheads, put individual controls on each fitting. The user can then adjust showerheads to provide only the desired amount of water, reducing waste, especially of hot water. This is particularly important in two-person showers that may be used, at times, by only one person.

Bathtubs

Water use in the bathtub is largely related to the size of the tub. A tub for soaking needs to have enough water to cover most of a person's body. Sometimes smaller, but deeper, tubs may use less water. In jetted tubs, the tub must be filled over the jets for operation, so consider the height of the jets. Jets placed lower in the tub can provide an effective massage with less water.

Faucets

Aerators on faucets are important to water conservation. With an aerator, the air added to the water flow increases the pressure and makes the flow seem greater. Water use is reduced.

Often water is wasted at the bathroom lavatory faucet during a grooming activity (such as teeth brushing) because it is inconvenient to turn the water on and off. A method to control water use is to install a faucet with an electronic, motion-activator control that only turns on when a hand,

FIGURE 3.8 Danze's air injection technology uses a mix of air and water to provide a high-performance shower with lower flow rates (as low as 1.5 gpm).
Courtesy of Danze, Inc.

toothbrush, or razor is under the faucet. Additionally, foot controls could be used to make it easier to control the faucet to minimize water use.

WATERSENSE

WaterSense® is a public-private partnership program between the Environmental Protection Agency and manufacturers to provide water-efficient products. WaterSense products have been independently tested and certified. As a result of meeting the WaterSense standards, the products can bear the WaterSense logo (see Figure 3.9) in all packaging, marketing, and promotion.

Generally, products that meet the WaterSense standards are 20 percent more efficient than comparable products on the market. In addition, the products must perform their intended function without sacrificing performance, especially to conserve water. In addition, through an agreement between the Environmental Protection Agency and Environment Canada, WaterSense products will be available in Canada.

FIGURE 3.9 WaterSense makes it easy to find and select water-efficient products and ensures consumer confidence in those products with a label backed by third-party, independent, testing and certification.
U.S. Environmental Protection Agency

Choosing WaterSense products for a bathroom offers the designer an excellent opportunity to maximize the sustainable use of water in the bathroom. In fact, the majority of WaterSense products currently available are residential bathroom fixtures! The designer can choose WaterSense toilets, bathroom lavatory faucets and aerators, and showerheads. WaterSense products offer an opportunity to increase water efficiency yet still give the designer many options in creating a unique, and perhaps luxury, space.

WaterSense Toilets

The current standard for a toilet is 1.6 gallons (6 liters) per flush (gpf or lpf). The WaterSense toilet specification is 1.28 gpf (4.8 lpf). Some toilets on the market offer even more efficient water use, such as 1.0 gpf (3.8 lpf).

Manufacturers have achieved the efficient use of water for toilet flushing through the use of different technologies. This includes improving the existing flushing system or using air pressure to power the flush. With a dual-flush system, more water is used when flushing solid waste than liquid waste, but the average water use meets the WaterSense standard. Some toilets may use a pump to assist the flush, requiring an electrical connection for installation.

WaterSense toilets must also meet the minimum MaP threshold for flushing of solid waste: 350 grams of solid waste (including toilet paper) in a single flush. The MaP (Maximum Performance Testing) program creates a standard of effective performance that prevents double flushing, and thus inefficient use of water. MaP is a voluntary testing program recognized in both the United States and Canada.

WaterSense Bathroom Lavatory Faucets

The average flow rate for a bathroom lavatory faucet today is 2.2 gallons per minute (gpm) (8.3 liters per minute [lpm]). The WaterSense specification is 1.5 gpm (5.7 lpm) at a water pressure of 60 pounds per square inch (psi) (413.69 kilopascals [kPa]). Aerators and flow restrictor devices that retrofit a faucet to bring its flow rate to the WaterSense specification also qualify as a WaterSense product.

WaterSense Showerheads

The average flow rate for a showerhead today is 2.5 gpm (9.5 lpm). The WaterSense specification is a flow rate of 2.0 gpm (7.6 lpm), although some showerheads are achieving even lower flow rates, such as 1.75 gpm (6.6 lpm). Manufacturers are designing water-efficient showerheads to make the water flow feel richer, more luxurious, or more invigorating, yet use less water. A WaterSense showerhead might have a wider spray, pulsing, or a massage spray. Your client may want to see the showerhead demonstrated before making a choice, based on personal preference.

WATER LEAKS

An important factor in efficient use of water is to avoid water leaks. Toilets or faucets that drip can waste tremendous amounts of water. For example, the EPA estimates a faucet that loses one drop of water per second can waste 3000 gallons (11,356 liters) of water in a year. Talk to your client about selecting quality fixtures, fittings, and water-using appliances that will be easy to maintain and are less likely to develop leaks. This is an important water conservation measure, but it will also save money and reduce maintenance for the client.

GRAYWATER

So far, the discussion on efficient and sustainable use of water has focused on conserving water use. Another approach is to reuse or recycle water. Reusing water is a sustainable practice that has all the same benefits of using less water. *Recycling water* is the term used to describe the practice of treating wastewater, usually in a centralized location, and then using the water for a variety of purposes, including landscaping. *Graywater* describes the practice of collecting household water from drains and then reusing it onsite for landscaping irrigation or toilet flushing.

The interest in graywater is growing, particularly in the southwestern and western United States where water supplies are limited. Effective use of graywater reduces the demand for treated drinking-quality water and decreases the water going into wastewater treatment facilities.

The model 2012 International Residential Code (IRC) details the design of graywater recycling systems in the section on Sanitary Drainage. Some local codes now require new residential construction to include connections for graywater plumbing. According to the 2012 IRC, discharge water may be collected from bathtubs, showers, lavatories, clothes washers, and laundry trays for a graywater system. The water collected is then used for flushing toilets and urinals or landscape irrigation.

Including a graywater system in a bathroom design can challenge a designer. The system needs to be correctly sized. There are requirements for additional plumbing pipes. A collection reservoir or storage tank is needed. While the opportunity for implementing an important sustainable practice is exciting, advanced and careful planning is needed. Familiarity with all applicable codes and/or permits, and perhaps additional expert advice may be needed.

An innovative design for water recycling and graywater use combines a small hand-washing lavatory directly over the toilet tank (see Figure 3.10). After hand-washing, the water flows into the toilet tank, to be used for the next flush of the toilet.

AIR QUALITY

Good indoor air quality makes a space pleasant to be in—and healthy for the user. Part of the design process is to ensure that the space is pollution free.

Providing good indoor air quality is a three-step process:

1. **Source Control**—minimizing or preventing the sources of indoor air pollution in a room or building

FIGURE 3.10 This simple WaterSense® certified gray-water system is useful where space is tight. The lavatory water flows directly into the toilet tank ready to flush the bowl.

Caroma's Profile Smart by Sustainable-Solutions.com

2. **Ventilation**—providing adequate air exchange, through natural or mechanical ventilation, to dilute the concentration of indoor air pollutants and ensure that the space has a supply of fresh air
3. **Air Cleaning**—when necessary, using filters or other devices to remove potentially harmful indoor air pollutants

Source Control

In the bathroom, there are a number of sources of potential air pollution. Excess moisture is at the top of the list. Too much moisture can create a sticky space for the bathroom user and can also lead to structural damage. A high level of moisture in an enclosed space like a bathroom creates and/or fosters the growth of biological pollutants such as molds, viruses, and bacteria.

Many grooming products used in bathrooms have the potential to be air pollutants, particularly those that are in aerosol form. Perfumed products may be pleasant to one person and annoying to another. As the designer, you do not control the use of grooming products. However, you can provide effective and easy-to-use ventilation to remove potential pollutants. Refer to chapter 7, "Mechanical Planning," for more information on planning bathroom ventilation.

Indoor Air Quality and Construction

Some of the potential pollution in a bathroom can come from building and interior finish materials. New building materials such as paint, manufactured woods, varnishes, adhesives, and plastics can off-gas, or emit chemicals into the air, as the materials age or cure. This is especially true of products made from, or with, volatile organic compounds (VOCs) such as some paints, particleboards, or wood finishes. The heat and moisture in a bathroom can increase off-gassing, or evaporation into the air.

Volatile Organic Compounds—VOCs

A common hazardous substance is a *volatile organic compound,* or a VOC.

- *Volatile* means gets into the air easily during use or as it ages. *Organic* means any carbon-based compound.
- VOCs are used in many common household products. VOCs are found in wood preservatives and finishes, composite building materials, glues, adhesives, and solvents.
- VOCs have a strong smell, are easily evaporated, toxic, potentially harmful, and flammable.
- VOCs can have serious health effects.
- VOCs are *sensitizers,* which are chemicals that may lead to allergic or other serious reactions after many uses.
- Side effects of VOC use can include irritation, drowsiness, headache, nausea, depression of nervous system, or cancer.

Choose building materials that have low amounts of VOCs. Many alternatives are available, such as latex paints, water-based varnishes, and low-VOC wood products. Some building materials can be ventilated for 24 to 48 hours before installation in the new bathroom, so that most off-gassing occurs outside your client's home. Increasing ventilation during and immediately after installation of new building materials is important to good indoor air quality.

The *Greenguard Environmental Institute* (GEI) focuses on protecting human health and improving quality of life by enhancing indoor air quality. GEI conducts third-party testing to certify products for low chemical emissions, including cabinetry and shower enclosures (www.greenguard.org).

The state of California's Air Resources Board oversees stringent air quality standards. Among the consumer products evaluated for off-gassing of formaldehyde (a VOC) are composite wood products as might be used in cabinetry and construction. Products must meet these standards to be sold in California, but could be marketed as meeting these standards in other locations.

Renovation Hazards

New construction sometimes means removing old construction. Make sure your client is aware of possible air quality problems that can result from demolition. Some things to consider and discuss with the contractor and your client are:

- How will the demolition area be isolated from the rest of the home? (See Figure 3.11.)
- Will the heating or air conditioning system be blocked in the demolition area, so that dust and debris are not circulated throughout the home?
- If the home was constructed before 1978, it is important to determine if there is any lead paint in the demolition area. Although lead paint was available until 1978, it was especially common

FIGURE 3.11 Plastic sheeting is essential for isolating the workspace from the living area. *www.remodelwest.com*

in homes built before 1950. Disturbing lead paint can cause serious air pollution and health effects, especially for young children.

- Asbestos is another hazard in houses built before the late 1970s. Disturbing asbestos-containing materials can create airborne health hazards. If asbestos is a possible hazard, special removal and disposal procedures by a trained contractor may be needed.
- Sometimes demolition uncovers things like dead animals and insects in walls, attics, and other spaces. This is part of the reason it is important to isolate the demolition area from the rest of the home.
- How will demolition waste be removed and disposed? Can any of the materials be recycled or salvaged? Is any of the waste considered hazardous, such as asbestos-containing materials or preservative-treated wood? Are local regulations for disposal of construction waste being followed?

Lead: Renovation, Repair, and Painting Rule

In the United States, the Lead Renovation, Repair, and Painting Rule went into effect in 2010. It applies to all housing built in 1978 or earlier. All contractors performing renovations, repairs, or painting must be trained and certified to follow lead-safe work practices. The focus of these lead-safe work practices is:

- Contain the work area.
- Minimize dust.
- Clean up thoroughly.

The contractor must provide information on lead-safe practices to the property owner.

Lead hazards are not regulated in Canada.

More information is available at www.epa.gov/lead.

Air Cleaning

Air cleaners are often incorporated into the heating, ventilating, and/or air conditioning system of the home, where they are used to filter heated or cooled air before it is returned, through ducts, to the house. Sometimes portable, tabletop, or larger console air cleaners are used in individual rooms. Air cleaners are most likely to be used to control particulate pollutants such as dust, pollen, or tobacco smoke.

A typical air cleaner will use a fan to take air through a filtering medium, and then blow the air back into the room, or through ductwork. Because of the importance of exhaust ventilation in a bathroom, which removes moist and possibly polluted air to the outside, individual air cleaners are rarely used. In addition, the fan of the air cleaner may create objectionable noise in the small space of a bathroom.

If an air cleaner is desired, choose a filtering medium that is effective for the type of pollutant the client wants removed. Look for information that the air cleaner has been tested and rated against an efficiency standard, such as ASHRAE's (American Society of Heating, Refrigeration and Air-Conditioning Engineers) standard for in-duct cleaners or AHAM's (Association of Home Appliance Manufacturers) and ANSI's (American National Standards Institute) CADR (clean air delivery rate) standard for portable air cleaners. Finally, make sure the capacity of the air cleaner is matched to the size of the room.

MOISTURE AND INDOOR AIR QUALITY

The bathroom is a major source of moisture within a home—showering, soaking in the bathtub, running water in the lavatory, water evaporating from the toilet bowl, towels drying. In a new bathroom, many building products such as grout, joint compounds, plaster, and latex paints also contain water. These products dry and cure, and water vapor is released.

Even in a very dry climate, excess moisture inside a building structure can lead to serious problems.

Prevention of moisture problems within the bathroom is part of the designer's responsibility. The designer needs to consider problems that might occur throughout the home due to moisture generated in the bathroom. The designer's goal should be to make it as easy as possible to control moisture in the bathroom, and to minimize the potential for problems from moisture that is not controlled.

Excess moisture is a potential problem for both the building and the people who live in it. Excess moisture in building materials leads to structural problems, such as peeling paint, rusting metal, and deterioration of joists and framing. Damp building materials tend to attract dirt and therefore require more cleaning and maintenance.

Damp spaces make good environments for the growth of many biological pollutants. Bacteria and viruses thrive, as do pests from dust mites to cockroaches. Wet building materials can also harbor mold, which leads to further structural damage. Mold can be a health threat. In addition, mold growing on interior finish materials smells bad and is ugly.

Moisture Basics

Water vapor is present in the air in varying amounts, depending on the temperature. The warmer the air, the more water vapor it will hold. *Humidity* describes how much water vapor there is in air. *Relative humidity*, expressed as a percent, can be explained by the following formula:

$$\frac{\text{Amount of water vapor in the air}}{\text{Maximum amount of water vapor air can hold at that temperature}} \times 100 = \text{Relative humidity}$$

Note that the temperature of the air is important to understanding relative humidity. For example, on a winter's day, when the temperature is 20 degrees Fahrenheit (–7 degrees Celsius) and the relative humidity is 70 percent, the air will actually be much drier, and have less moisture, than on a summer's day, when the temperature is 85 degrees Fahrenheit (21 degrees Celsius) and the humidity is 70 percent.

Condensation, the opposite of evaporation, occurs when water vapor returns to a liquid state. As air cools, it can no longer hold as much water vapor, so the water condenses into a liquid. The temperature at which condensation occurs is referred to as the *dew point.* Most everyone is familiar with the experience of taking a warm shower and then finding that water has condensed onto the cooler surface of the bathroom mirror.

The cycle of water evaporating and condensing in a bathroom can lead to moisture problems. A bathroom tends to be warmer than other parts of the home, which is desirable as it increases the comfort level when someone is naked or wet. However, because they are warmer, bathrooms tend to have higher humidity.

Many bathroom activities, such as showers and baths, further increase the temperature of the air as well as the moisture level. However, materials and surfaces in the bathroom tend to be cooler

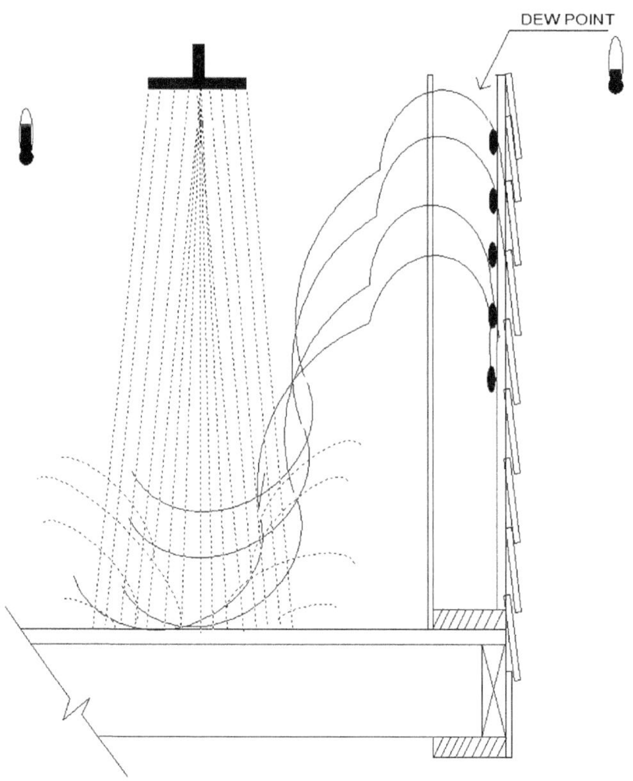

FIGURE 3.12 As warm, moist air moves through a wall, condensation will occur when the air is cooled to the dew point temperature. *Rendered in 20-20 by Michael Brgoch, CKD*

than the air—which leads to condensation. In addition, when the user finishes showering or bathing, the room tends to cool down, leading to more condensation.

Wet materials result in increased maintenance, and eventually, deterioration. This is especially true of any that are absorbent and stay damp, such as drywall and textiles.

Hidden Condensation

The air temperature inside the bathroom tends to be higher than the air temperature on the other side of the walls, floor, and ceiling. This is especially true, in winter, of exterior walls, and a ceiling with an attic above it. There is a natural tendency for warm air to move to cool air. This is nature's way of trying to maintain equilibrium. In a bathroom, warm, moist air will tend to move through walls and ceilings, moving from warm to cool.

As the air moves through the wall or ceiling, it is cooled. When the dew point temperature is reached, condensation occurs (see Figure 3.12). This hidden condensation inside walls and attics can be a particular nightmare for homeowners. As building materials get wetter, deterioration and mold growth can become extensive before the problem is noticed.

Household Humidity

Managing the humidity level in a home is a balancing act between maintaining the comfort of the occupants and protecting the structure. Excess moisture leads to many indoor air quality, structural and maintenance problems, and makes the home's occupants feel "sticky." Too little moisture dries out skin, nasal passages, and throats, as well as wood in furniture and the house's structure. Generally, a relative humidity level of about 40 to 60 percent is a good compromise. At this level, most condensation and mold growth is prevented, but people are comfortable.

One method of controlling household humidity is through exhaust ventilation of moisture-laden indoor air. However, when the outside air is warm and humid, ventilation will not solve the problem.

Mechanical air conditioning (cooling) of the air inside the home is effective in dehumidification, by condensing water vapor from the air. If the air conditioner is oversized, however, it may cool the home's air quickly but not operate long enough to provide adequate dehumidification.

Mechanical dehumidifiers may be used in the home to control humidity in moisture-prone areas. A dehumidifier operates on the same principle as an air conditioner. While dehumidifiers can be effective in controlling moisture, they do require regular maintenance, and generate heat and noise. A dehumidifier needs to be sized to the space in which it will be operating.

Molds, Moisture, and Health

Molds are fungi. There are thousands of varieties of molds, which reproduce by spores that are blown out into the air. The spores can be dormant for years. Then, given the right conditions of food and moisture, they can begin to grow.

At any given time, there are usually mold spores in the air around us. Molds are a natural part of the ecosystem and play an important role in digesting organic debris, such as dead leaves, insects, and wood. The problem occurs when there is an excess of mold growth, and the organic matter they are digesting is part of the building structure.

Molds require moisture, oxygen, and food to grow. How much of each of these elements is required depends on the mold variety. However, most will start growing at a relative humidity of 70 percent or more. Molds can make food out of almost any organic matter, including skin cells and residues from shampoo.

FIGURE 3.13 Growth of various types of mold on wood under flooring.
CC-BY-SA-3.0

Cellulosic building materials such as paper, wood, textiles, many types of insulation, carpet, wallpaper, and drywall make an excellent environment for mold growth (see Figure 3.13). The cellulosic materials absorb moisture, providing the right growth conditions, and the materials themselves provide the food.

Molds grow fast. If cellulosic building materials get wet, mold growth will begin in 24 to 48 hours. Mold growth on the surface of noncellulosic materials can start in the same time period, as long as food and moisture are present.

Molds can affect people in different ways. Some people are allergic to specific species. Molds produce chemicals that are irritants to most people, and can cause problems such as headaches, breathing difficulties, and skin irritation, as well as aggravating other health conditions such as asthma. Molds can sensitize the body so that someone becomes more susceptible to health effects from future exposures. Finally, some molds produce toxins. The likelihood of health effects increases with the amount of exposure to mold, and also depends on the sensitivity of the individual.

Preventing Moisture Problems

Good ventilation is absolutely necessary to prevent moisture problems and mold growth in the bathroom. Exhaust ventilation removes excess moisture and prevents condensation. Ventilation systems are discussed in more detail in chapter 7, "Mechanical Planning." The importance of moisture control in a laundry area that might be part of a bathroom is discussed in chapter 9, "More Than a Bathroom." Closets, dressing areas, and linen closets that might be part of or adjacent to bathrooms are also discussed in chapter 9. Good ventilation for moisture control in these areas, especially for doors, is stressed.

Ventilation Recommendations to Control Moisture

The 2012 International Residential Code (IRC) details ventilation requirements for houses. The 2012 International Energy Conservation Code, which is incorporated into the IRC, requires whole-house mechanical ventilation to provide adequate fresh air as well as moisture control. In a whole-house ventilation system, the bathroom would be an area where the air is exhausted directly to the outdoors. The code requirement is:

- 50 cubic feet per minute (24 liters per second) intermittent exhaust or
- 20 cubic feet per minute (9 liters per second) continuous exhaust

More information on ventilation systems is provided in chapter 7, "Mechanical Planning."

Finish materials can contribute to, or help prevent, moisture problems. After exposure to water and humidity, the more absorbent the materials, the longer they will stay damp. Specifying hard surface or nonabsorbent materials such as glazed tiles, solid surfacing, vitreous china, or engineered stone reduces the likelihood of moisture problems. Materials that stay damp are much more likely to support mold growth. Specifying sealers for absorbent or porous materials, such as clay tiles, marble, or grout, can also reduce moisture absorption.

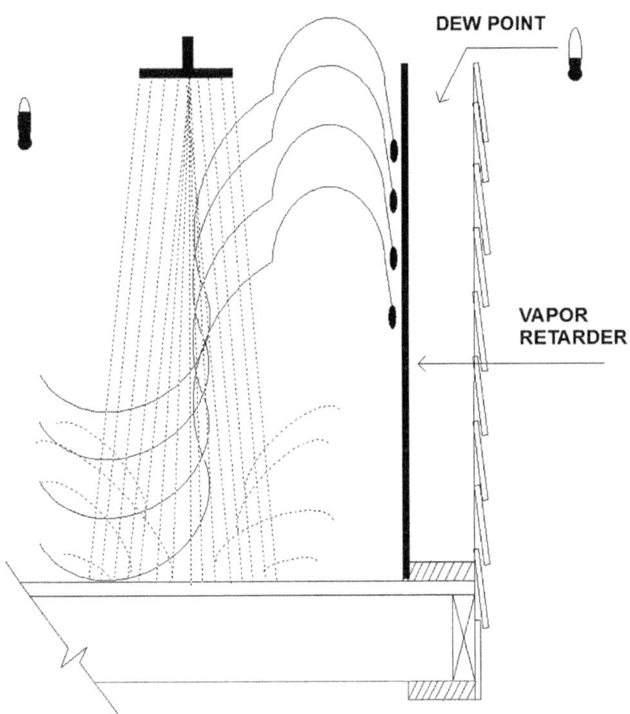

FIGURE 3.14 Place a vapor retarder material on the warm or interior side of the wall, to help prevent moisture condensation inside the wall, in climates with cold winters. In hot, humid climates, where air conditioning is used most of the year, the placement of the vapor retarder may be different.
Rendered in 20-20 by Michael Brgoch, CKD

It is especially important that wall and ceiling finishes or materials block the flow of moisture into wall cavities or attics. This can be accomplished by selecting materials that are not moisture permeable, such as glazed tiles or vinyl wall coverings. Additionally, a vapor retarder material, such as plastic sheeting, can be used in the wall construction (see Figure 3.14). There are special considerations about the placement of a vapor retarder, depending on whether the climate is dominated by heating or cooling. The vapor retarder is placed on the warm side to the wall. In a climate that is dominated by a heating season or has both heating and cooling, that is the interior side. In a hot climate that is dominated by the cooling season, the vapor retarder is usually placed on the exterior side of the wall.

Low-maintenance materials, fixtures, and fittings are also important. Materials that are kept clean are less likely to accumulate surface debris that can support mold growth. Avoid fixtures and fittings with cracks, seams, crevices, and indentations that can accumulate residue from skin, body oils, grooming products, and cleaning products—all organic materials that provide food for molds.

Antimicrobial Finishes

Some products, especially textiles, are available with various types of antimicrobial finishes or additives. Generally, an antimicrobial finish means that the material is treated with a pesticide of some sort to protect the material or product itself. For example, paints are available with fungicides to protect the paint from mold growth in the paint itself. This does not mean that mold will not grow on the paint, in a moist environment, if a food source such as skin cells or shampoo residues were to accumulate on the painted surface. Antimicrobial products may be desirable to minimize mold or bacterial problems, but will not be an adequate substitute for good maintenance and moisture control practices. There are also some concerns about the safe use of antimicrobial products that are classified as pesticides.

Towel Bars

Damp towels can be ideal environments for mold growth, which can lead to musty odors. Plan adequate towel bars, rings, and hooks for all bathroom users. Good air circulation around towels provides for quick drying. Consider placing towel bars near heat registers. Heated towel bars not only provide luxuriously warm towels after a shower or bath, but can also speed drying and thus prevent musty odors.

SUMMARY

Sustainable design benefits your client as well as the community as a whole. Sustainability is a philosophical approach that guides design and business decisions. Sustainability in the built environment encompasses energy efficiency, water management, air quality, waste management, and recycling. To be sustainable also means to provide a healthy place to live.

Sustainability can be practiced many different ways. Options include specifying products and materials or following practices that qualify for a national or local *green building program.* Alternatively, specifying products and materials that have been certified by an independent, third-party organization can be a sustainable choice. Another option is to follow the recommendations of the model International Energy Conservation Code.

The designer who makes sustainability a priority uses the various codes, standards, certifications, and guidelines to be informed and knowledgeable on products, policies, and practices. The goal is always to use resources efficiently, to think to the future, and to be concerned about the health and safety of the client.

REVIEW QUESTIONS

1. Describe three building or design practices that incorporate the goals of sustainability. (See "Sustainable Design and Building" page 65)
2. Describe a *green building program*. (See "Green Building Programs" page 68)
3. If a designer wants to specify sustainable products, how can product certifications assist the process? (See "Sustainable Certification Programs" page 71)
4. Explain how conserving water also saves energy. (See "Hot Water" page 76)
5. Summarize the requirements for a product to achieve the WaterSense certification. (See "WaterSense" page 79)
6. What are the steps to providing good indoor air quality? (See "Air Quality" page 81)
7. Explain why mold is a particular problem in the bathroom and a threat to a healthy home. (See "Molds, Moisture, and Health" page 87)
8. What types of information of use to the bathroom designer would be found in the 2012 International Residential Code? (See "Energy Issues and Building Codes" page 73)

Human Factors and Universal Design Foundation

Like most principles and elements of design, universal design is an enduring approach that draws from both science and spirit. Based solidly on human factors and, along with this quantitative information, it places equal value on the aesthetics of a space or product. Universal design responds to our growing appreciation and respect for diversity in the spaces we design, and in the stature, age, abilities, and culture of the people for whom we design. Simply defined, it is the design of products and spaces to be usable by all people, to the greatest extent possible.

The study of human dimensions and the design of spaces and products around human factors are solid steps toward good universal design. Traditionally, human factors–based design seemed to center on two extremes. It was either one size fits all for the nonexistent "average person" or totally custom design for each individual client's dimensions, abilities, and needs. Universal design moves away from these extremes and builds on anthropometry and ergonomics in different ways. It embraces as broad a range of human factors as possible. One example is the placement of a wall switch that is dictated not by the reach range of the average height person, but by overlap of the reach ranges of the shorter and the taller among us. In addition, universal design places equal emphasis on aesthetics, acknowledging the importance of beauty and comfort in design solutions.

In this chapter, you will explore anthropometric and ergonomic information, as well as human factors studies that help guide design of spaces. Also covered are the basic concepts of universal design, which have become essential to good bathroom planning. Throughout this book, universal design concepts have been incorporated where applicable. Further information on access and specific user groups will be the focus of chapter 8, "Accessibility in Practice," which focuses on both universal and access-related design considerations.

Learning Objective 1: Define and describe universal design.

Learning Objective 2: Define and describe anthropometry and its relation to universal design.

Learning Objective 3: Identify and list basic components of universal design as outlined in the Principles of Universal Design.

Learning Objective 4: Recognize some of the sources of information on access available in laws, codes, and related standards.

ANTHROPOMETRY

A basic understanding of the human body, including its limitations and capabilities, is helpful in any space planning, particularly in a room of such concentrated high activity as the bath. While you will often determine a client's particular dimensions and needs, there are general areas where standards, based on research, are useful. Anthropometry, defined as the study of human measurements such as size and proportion, and parameters such as reach range and visual range, is a good starting point. While not an exact science, anthropometry uses populations grouped according to specific criteria, such as age, gender, or ability, to collect data on bodies at rest (structural or static) and bodies in motion (functional or dynamic). Much of the information offered here on anthropometry is sourced from *Human Dimension & Interior Space* by Panero and Zelnik (1979) which is the generally accepted reference for interior space planning in the building industry.

In this chapter, we will discuss the various types of anthropometric information. In chapter 5, which focuses on needs assessment, there is information about collecting anthropometric information on your specific clients. Included in chapter 5, "Assessing Needs," you'll find Form 1: Getting to Know Your Client, which provides graphics to guide you in collecting anthropometric dimensions (Part 1.2), reach and grasp profiles (Part 1.3), and anthropometric dimensions with mobility aids (Part 1.5).

Structural Anthropometry

Also called static anthropometry, structural anthropometry includes many dimensions relating to the body at rest. Figure 4.1 illustrates those dimensions that clearly impact bathroom space planning and will be important to the design applications that will be detailed in chapter 6, "Bathroom Planning."

The dimensions presented in Figure 4.1 are defined as follows:

- Stature is the vertical distance from the floor to the top of the head. It impacts such spatial considerations as minimum height of door openings or showerhead heights.
- Eye height while standing is the vertical distance from the floor to the inner corner of the eye. It dictates and impacts such things as sight lines, or the height of wall sconces, mirrors, or wall art.
- Elbow height is the vertical distance from the floor to the depression formed at the elbow. This affects such things as comfortable counter heights, lavatory heights, and some grab bar heights.
- Sitting height is the vertical distance from the sitting surface to the top of the head when a person is sitting erect. This impacts the heights of such things as the privacy wall at a toilet or at the bath/shower area.
- Eye height while sitting is the vertical distance from the sitting surface to the inner corner of the eye with the person sitting erect. This dictates the sight lines that will influence makeup/dressing counter lighting and mirrors, or window heights.
- Mid-shoulder-height sitting is the vertical distance from the sitting surface to the point of the shoulder midway between the lower neck and the acromion (outmost point of the shoulder). It will influence the location of neck or head rests in the tub.
- Shoulder breadth (width) is the maximum horizontal distance across the deltoid muscles. It is very important in determining needed clearance between lavatory sinks, for walk aisles, or in helping to determine shower sizes.
- Elbow-to-elbow breadth is the horizontal distance with the elbows flexed and resting against the body. It is critical to the position a person might assume to groom or wash his or her hair, and influences shower width and depth, or the space between mirrors and returning walls.
- Hip breadth is the breadth of the body measured across the widest portion of the hip. It impacts bench or seat width, bathtub width, and clearance and passage.
- Elbow rest height is the height from the top of the sitting surface to the bottom of the tip of the elbow. It impacts such things as armrests, some grab bar placement, and vanity counter heights.
- Thigh clearance is the vertical distance from a sitting surface to the top of the thigh at the point where the thigh and abdomen intersect. This is important when planning full-depth knee spaces, including the apron or drawer height.
- Knee height is the vertical distance from the floor to the midpoint of the kneecap, and it is useful when planning a partial knee space.

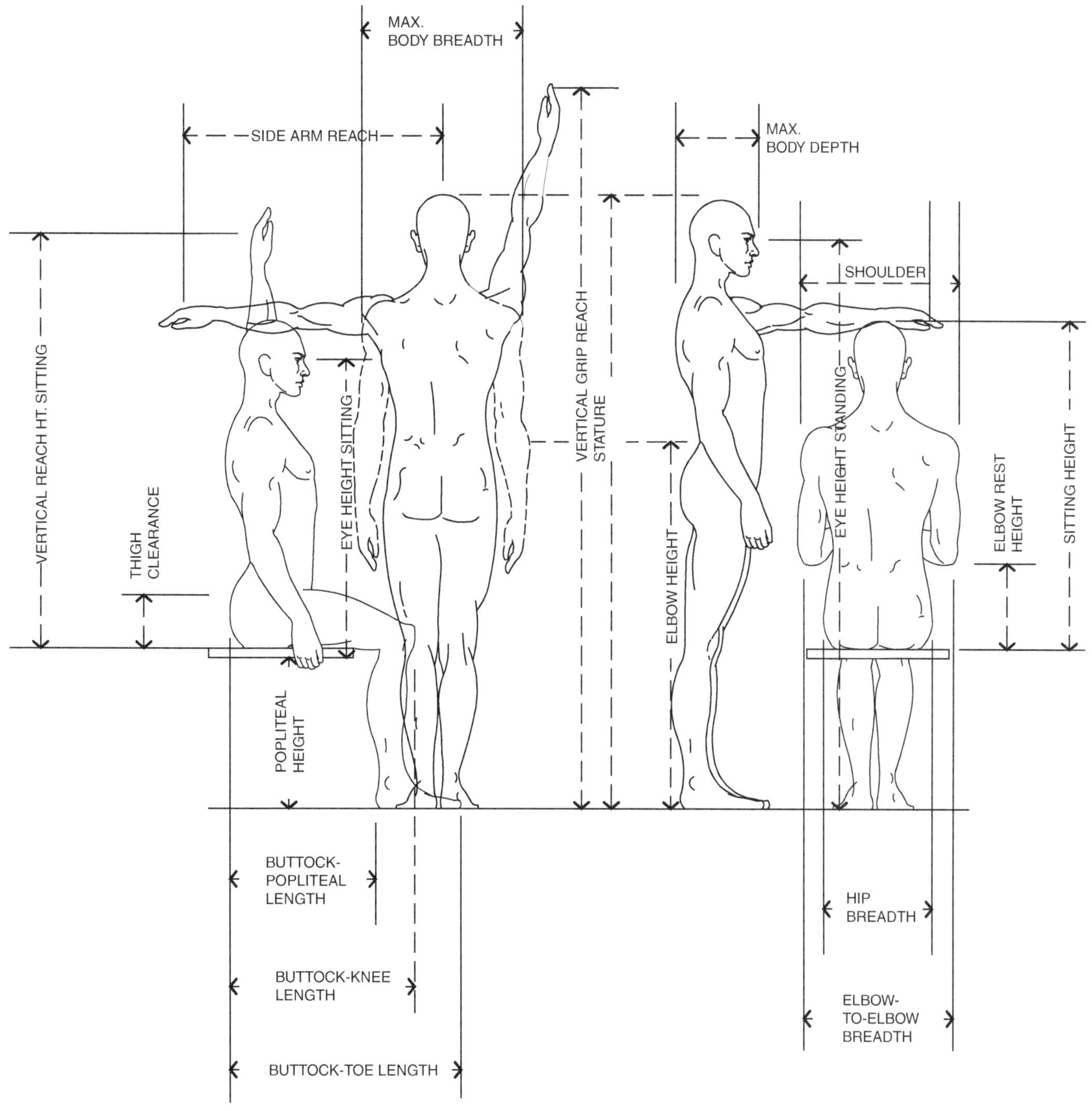

FIGURE 4.1 These are some of the body measurements that influence interior space planning. (Based on *Human Dimension & Interior Space* by Julius Panero and Martin Zelnik, 1979, Watson-Guptill Publications, p. 30)

- Popliteal height (behind knee) is the vertical distance from the floor to the underside portion of the thigh just behind the knee while a person is seated. It impacts the height of benches and seats, and should impact toilet heights.
- Buttock to popliteal length is the horizontal distance from the rearmost surface of the buttock to the back of the lower leg. It indicates the necessary depth for seats, benches, elongated or standard toilet seats, or bidets.
- Maximum body depth is the horizontal distance between the most anterior point, usually the chest or abdomen, to the most posterior point, usually found in the buttocks or shoulder. It influences shower sizes, clearance, and passage. To accommodate people who use mobility aids, this measurement must include the aid.
- Maximum body breadth is the distance, including arms, across the body. It impacts the widths of aisles, doors and doorways, as well as shower and tub sizes, and the width of vanity areas at the sink. To accommodate people who use mobility aids, this measurement must include the aid.

Functional Anthropometry

Functional anthropometry, also referred to as dynamic anthropometry, is the measurement of the body in motion. It includes movement of body parts in relationship to one another and measures of strength. Because it is more complex, it is more difficult to accurately measure. However, certain measurements are very helpful to bathroom planning, mainly the reach range and the functional space of a person using a variety of mobility aids.

- Vertical reach height sitting (see Figure 4.2) is the height above the sitting surface of the tip of the middle finger when the arm, hand, and fingers are extended vertically. It impacts general overhead, and shower and bathtub controls, as well as storage.
- Vertical grip reach (see Figure 4.3) is the distance from the floor to the top of a bar grasped in the hand, raised as high as it can without discomfort, while the subject stands erect. It is important in planning the height of bookshelves, storage shelves, or controls. Vertical grip reach from a seated position is also important in design that accommodates operating from a seated position.
- Side arm grip reach (see Figure 4.4) is the distance from the centerline of the body to the outside surface of a bar grasped in the hand, stretched horizontally without experiencing discomfort or strain, while the subject stands erect. This measurement helps determine a comfortable height for fixture controls and general storage. There seems to be more information available on this dimension for a standing person, but the data and its application involve the seated user as well.
- Forward grip reach or thumb tip reach (see Figure 4.5) is the distance to the tip of the thumb measured with the subject's shoulders against the wall, with the arm extended forward and index finger touching the tip of the thumb. This dimension influences depth and height of work counters and shelves above the counters as well as general storage.

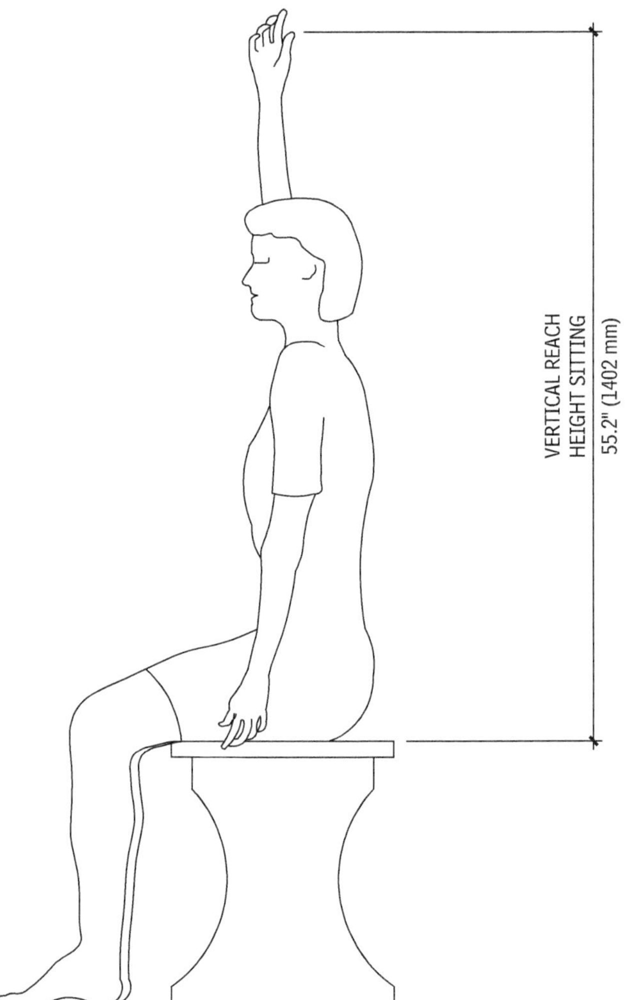

FIGURE 4.2 As a population, women are shorter than men, so we have indicated the sitting adult female vertical reach height. If a design accommodated this shorter reach, it would also include 95 percent of women and others with a taller reach. (Based on *Human Dimension & Interior Space* by Julius Panero and Martin Zelnik, 1979, Watson-Guptill Publications, p. 100.)

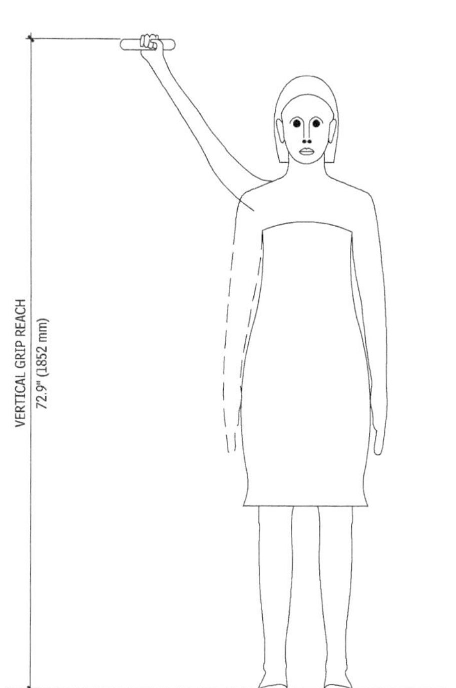

FIGURE 4.3 The vertical grip reach is useful in determining maximum height for readily accessed storage. This drawing and related measurements are based on the adult female in the 5th percentile, this time in a standing position. (Based on *Human Dimension & Interior Space* by Julius Panero and Martin Zelnik, 1979, Watson-Guptill Publications, p. 100.)

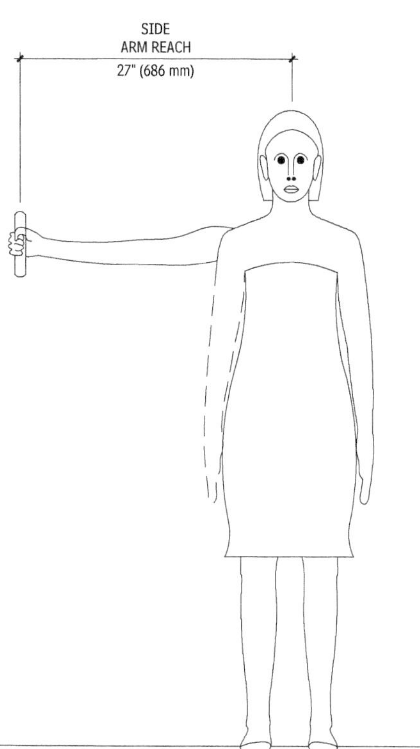

FIGURE 4.4 Whether seated or standing, the side arm grip reach will influence placement of stored items and controls. These numbers are based on a standing adult female in the 5th percentile. (Based on *Human Dimension & Interior Space* by Julius Panero and Martin Zelnik, 1979, Watson-Guptill Publications, p. 100.)

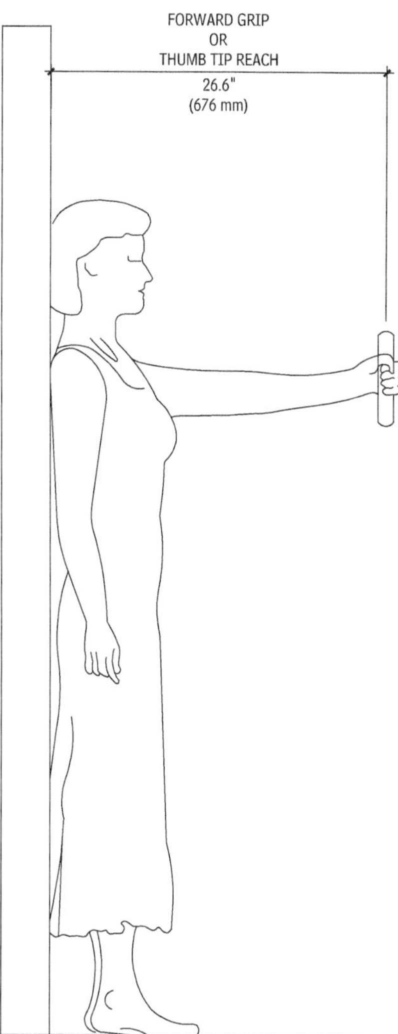

FIGURE 4.5 Using the dimension for forward grip reach based on adult females in the 5th percentile is a good basis for planning within the reach of most people. (Based on *Human Dimension & Interior Space* by Julius Panero and Martin Zelnik, 1979, Watson-Guptill Publications, p. 100.)

Height and Reach Ranges

Height and reach ranges vary according to stature, physical ability, and obstructions. The height range within a person's reach is useful for planning functional storage, fixtures, fittings, and controls in the bathroom.

- The lower end of a forward reach range is 15 inches to 24 inches (381 mm to 610 mm) off the floor, depending on a person's ability to bend. The upper length can go as high as 72 inches (1823 mm), depending on a person's stature and any obstruction, such as a counter or shelf.
- The average person who remains seated to maneuver in the bathroom has a forward reach range of 15 inches to 48 inches (381 mm to 1219 mm).
- A standing person who has difficulty bending may have a forward reach range of 24 inches to 72 inches (610 mm to 1823 mm).
- People who use crutches, walkers, or in some way needs their hands to maintain balance, have a slightly different reach range, depending on their mobility aid and physical ability.

TABLE 4.1 Working with the Functional Dimensions and Reach Ranges of a Variety of People, Universal Design Proponents Use the Universal Reach Range to Accommodate Most People

	Seated	Standing with Mobility Aid	Standing 5 foot 3 inches to 5 foot 7 inches (1600–1700 mm)	Universal
Lower Limit Bending	15 inches (381 mm)	15 inches (381 mm)	15 inches (381 mm)	15 inches (381 mm)
Lower Limit–No Bending	—	24 inches (610 mm)	24 inches (610 mm)	24 inches (610 mm)
Upper Limit	48 inches (1219 mm)	72 inches (1829 mm)	79 ½ inches (2019 mm)	48 inches (1219 mm)

Combining these reach ranges with the functional limits of reaching over a 25-inch (635-mm) -deep counter, a universal reach range of 15 inches to 48 inches (381 mm to 1219 mm) has been suggested. This range is generally accepted and used to guide placement of storage, controls, and more.

Range-of-Joint Motion

Range-of-joint motion is another aspect of human dimension that obviously impacts the design of the space and components within a bathroom. These include: movements of the hands, wrists, and fingers; movement and flexibility of the shoulders and elbows; bending or twisting at the waist or spine; and movement of the knees (see Figure 4.6). Because no joint operates in isolation, it is difficult to generate accurate and useful information regarding range of motion of joints. However, understanding the areas to consider will help in developing a space that works for a specific client. If you can observe and estimate a client's range-of-joint motion, your design and specifications can more accurately meet the client's needs.

FIGURE 4.6 A person's range of motion in the spine and shoulders can impact the appropriate size of a shower and location of its fittings. (Based on *Human Dimension & Interior Space* by Julius Panero and Martin Zelnik, 1979, Watson-Guptill Publications, p. 115.)

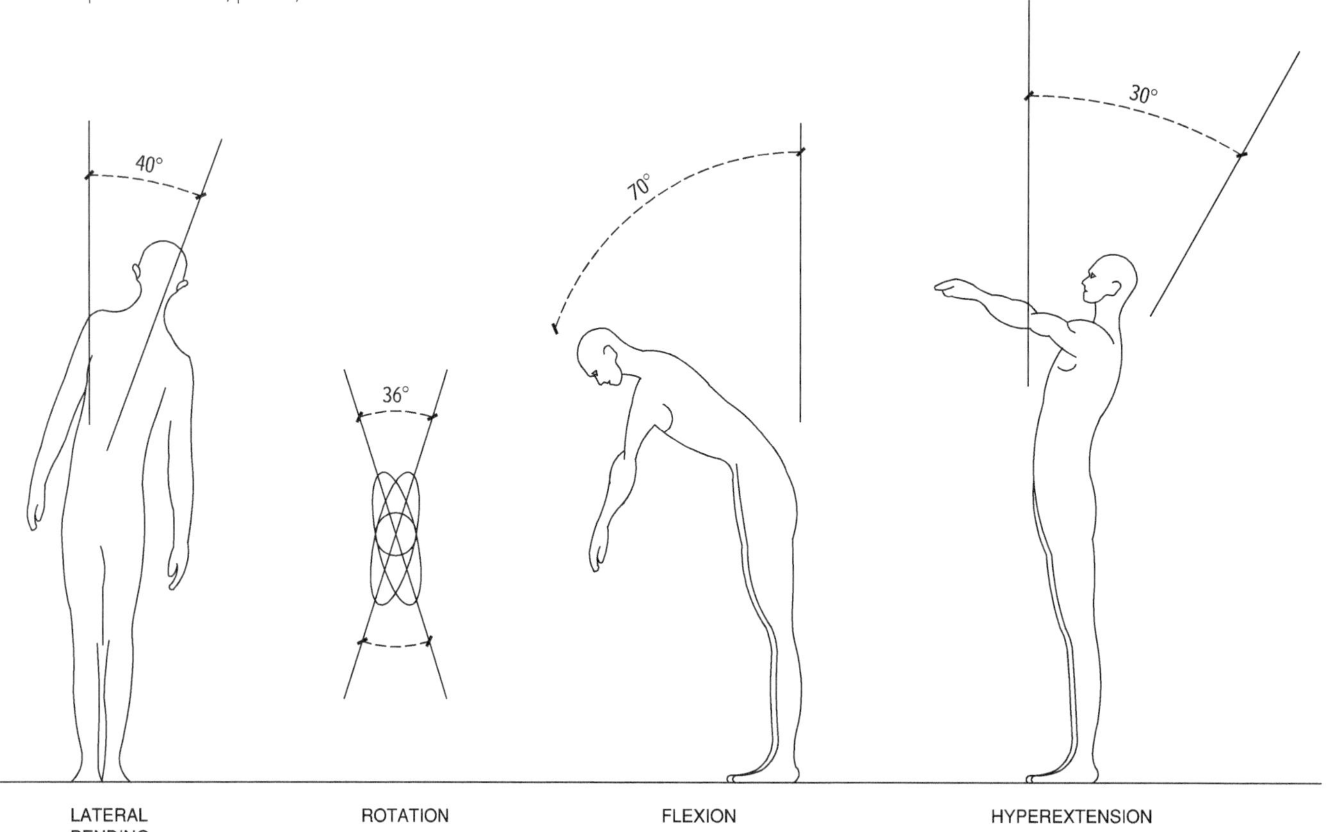

Mobility Aids

There is a growing amount of useful data related to movement and maneuvering, including information related to walking or moving with an assistive device (see Figures 4.7 to 4.10). Although this data seems less plentiful, Panero and Zelnik do offer minimal parameters. Access guidelines such as those from the American National Standards Institute (ANSI), the International Codes Council (ICC), or Uniform Federal Accessibility Standard (UFAS) can be helpful. One critical rule is to consider the person and the aid as one. Also, just as for a person who does not use a mobility aid, these figures increase when the person using an aid goes from a static position to motion.

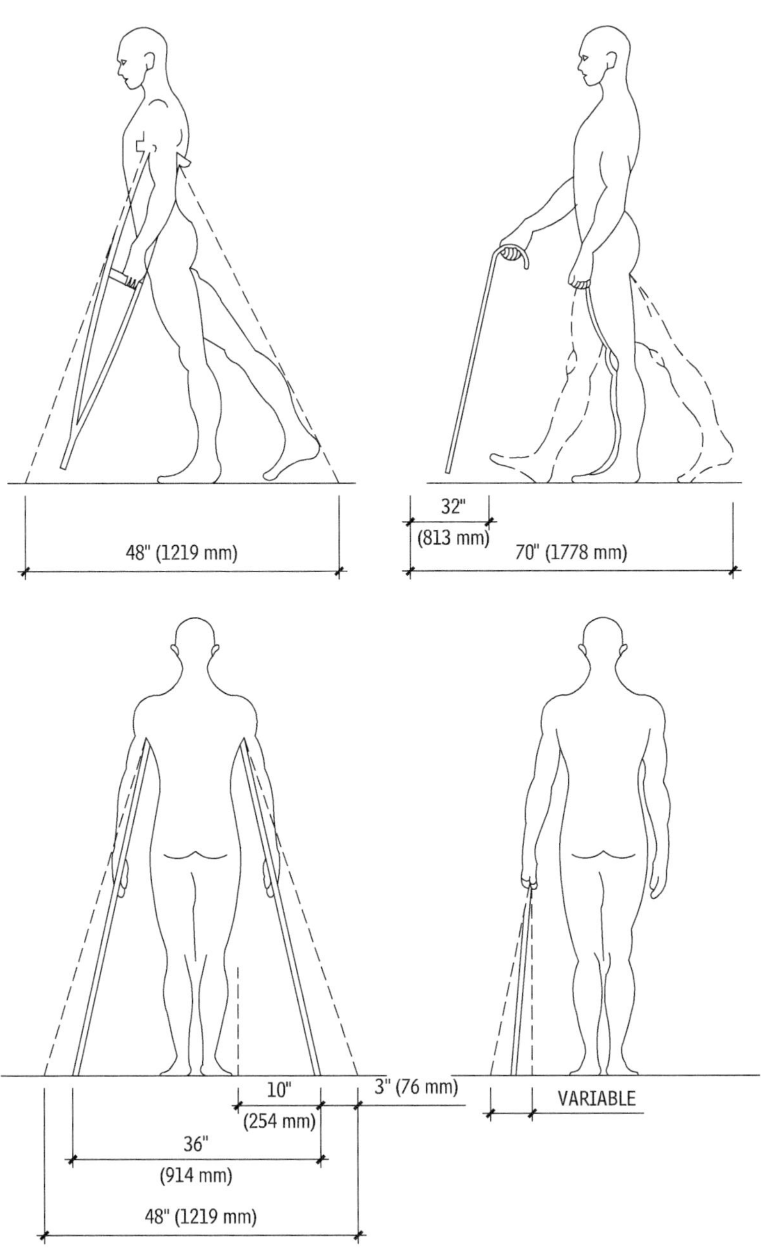

FIGURE 4.7 These minimum allowances will help in planning spatial clearance. Note that in this case, using the larger dimensions of percentile of adult males provides clearances for any human of smaller dimensions as well. (Based on *Human Dimension & Interior Space* by Julius Panero and Martin Zelnik, 1979, Watson-Guptill Publications, p. 54.)

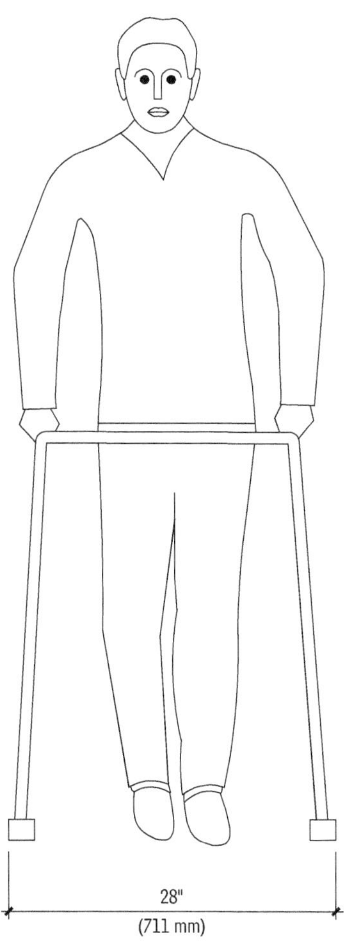

FIGURE 4.8 The width of a walker will determine the minimum clearance needed. (Based on *Human Dimension & Interior Space* by Julius Panero and Martin Zelnik, 1979, Watson-Guptill Publications, p. 54.)

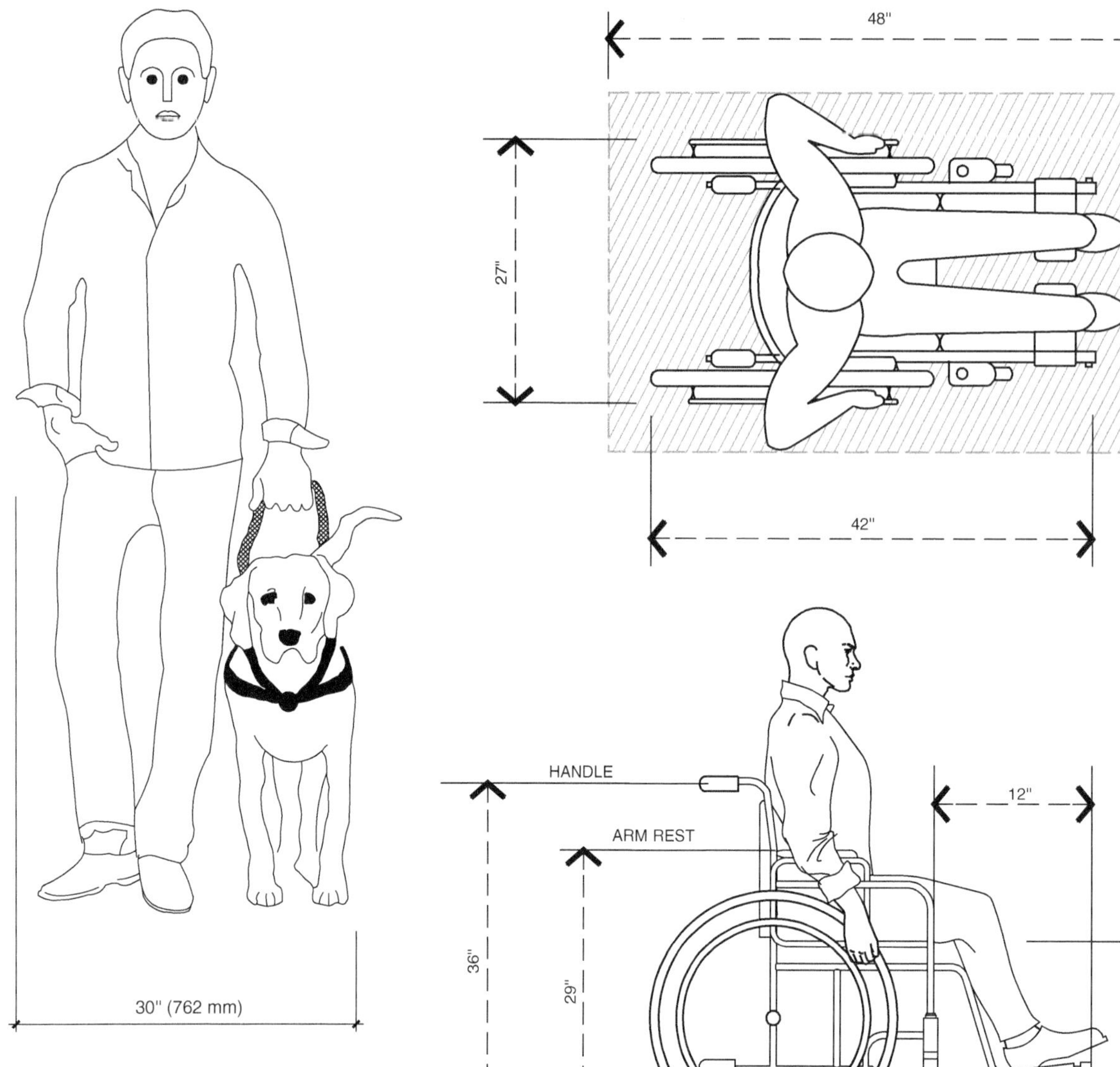

FIGURE 4.9 In this case, the clearance dimensions must be based on the actual user and dog, but the given dimension of 30 inches (762 mm) could be used as an absolute minimum. (Based on *Human Dimension & Interior Space* by Julius Panero and Martin Zelnik, 1979, Watson-Guptill Publications, p. 54.)

FIGURE 4.10 Although these standards for a person using a chair are useful in general, it is much better to measure the person in his or her chair. The variables are impacted by the person's size and ability as well as the design and fit of the chair.

Comfort Zone

Based on psychological factors, we can also identify a body buffer zone or comfort zone. We maintain this personal space between ourselves and others who are walking, talking, or just standing with us (see Figure Figure 4.11) While we maintain a greater distance with strangers, the personal or close zone will be most applicable to bathroom design.

Anthropometry of Children

Historically there has been very little anthropometric data available regarding children. However, given the growing national focus on childhood health and safety, we can expect this to change. Although functional data would be most applicable, body dimensions of children are available and can be a starting point for the design of child-oriented spaces (see Table 4.2)

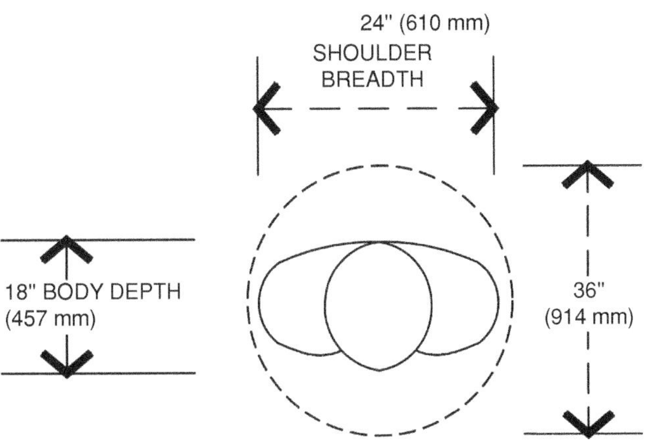

FIGURE 4.11 Based on a shoulder breadth of 24 inches (610 mm) and a body depth of 18 inches (457 mm), a minimum area of approximately 3 square feet (914 mm) per person is a guide in planning a space to be shared. (Based on *Human Dimension & Interior Space* by Julius Panero and Martin Zelnik, 1979, Watson-Guptill Publications, p. 41.)

TABLE 4.2 the Height and Breadth of Children, Both Standing and Seated, Can Be Useful Dimensions When Planning a Bathroom That Must Accommodate Them as They Grow

Stature (Height)		**6 years**	**11 years**
95th Percentile	**Boys**	50.4″ (1280 mm)	61.8″ (1570 mm)
	Girls	49.9″ (1267 mm)	62.9″ (1598 mm)
5th Percentile	**Boys**	43.6″ (1107 mm)	53″ (1346 mm)
	Girls	42.6″ (1083 mm)	53.3″ (1354 mm)
Sitting Height		**6 years**	**11 years**
95th Percentile	**Boys**	27.4″ (695 mm)	31.7″ (805 mm)
	Girls	27.1″ (688 mm)	32.8″ (833 mm)
5th Percentile	**Boys**	23.7″ (602 mm)	27.6″ (701 mm)
	Girls	23.1″ (588 mm)	27.4″ (697 mm)
Elbow-to-Elbow Breadth		**6 years**	**11 years**
95th Percentile	**Boys**	11.3″ (288 mm)	14.7″ (373 mm)
	Girls	11.1″ (281 mm)	14.7″ (373 mm)
5th Percentile	**Boys**	8.5″ (217 mm)	10.1″ (257 mm)
	Girls	8.3″ (211 mm)	9.6″ (244 mm)
Hip Breadth		6 years	11 years
95th Percentile	**Boys**	9.3″ (236 mm)	12″ (305 mm)
	Girls	9.3″ (236 mm)	13.3″ (338 mm)
5th Percentile	**Boys**	7.1″ (181mm)	8.7″ (221 mm)
	Girls	7.1″ (181 mm)	8.8″ (223 mm)
Popliteal Height (to knee from floor when sitting)		**6 years**	**11 years**
95th Percentile	**Boys**	12.8″ (325 mm)	16.3″ (414 mm)
	Girls	12.6″ (320 mm)	16.4″ (417 mm)
5th Percentile	**Boys**	10.4″ (264 mm)	13.3″ (338 mm)
	Girls	10.2″ (259 mm)	13.1″ (333 mm)
Buttock- Popliteal Length (wall to back of knee when sitting)		**6 years**	**11 years**
95th Percentile	**Boys**	14.7″ (374 mm)	19″ (483 mm)
	Girls	15.2″ (386 mm)	19.9″ (505 mm)
5th Percentile	**Boys**	11.3″ (287 mm)	14.5″ (368 mm)
	Girls	11.3″ (287 mm)	15″ (381 mm)

ERGONOMIC AND UNIVERSAL DESIGN

Based on anthropometric data and other human factors, ergonomics is the study of the relationship of people to their environment. Ergonomic design is the application of human factors data to the design of products and spaces to improve function and efficiency. Universal design builds on ergonomics to improve the use of products, spaces, and systems equally for people of a variety of size, ages, and abilities. This basis for the design guidelines and access standards, as well as applications, are detailed in chapter 6, "Bathroom Planning," and throughout this book.

This discussion should help drive home the point that universal design is much more than the misconception that it is design limited to medical solutions for access challenges.

History and State of the Art

Since the end of World War II, awareness of the need for improved access and universal design has been growing. Currently, we are experiencing unprecedented interest, worldwide, in the design of environments and products that respect the diversity of human beings. Nowhere is this more true than in the bathroom (and kitchen) encompassing activities of daily life critical to everyone.

People are living longer, largely due to healthier lifestyles, better medicine, and vaccines and sanitation, which have virtually eliminated many deadly infectious diseases. According to the U.S. Census Bureau, life expectancy is projected to be 79.5 years for those born in 2012. We are redefining retirement to encompass active adult living, and our designs must include the support that will enable active lifestyles. In addition, more people are living with disabilities and they want to live better. There is a huge population of veterans with disabilities. Antibiotics and other medical advances have enabled people to survive accidents and illnesses that were previously fatal.

According to the U.S. Census Bureau's Survey of Income and Program Participation (SIPP), in 2005, approximately 19 percent of the population had some level of disability, and approximately 12 percent had a severe disability. In addition, the National Center for Injury Prevention and Control estimates that one out of three adults 65 or over falls each year. In short, in response to our current society, universal design concepts must be applied to planning a bathroom so that it will function for, and benefit, all the residents of, and visitors to, a home.

Ron Mace, FAIA, known as the father of universal design, defined it as "the design of products and environments to be usable by all people to the greatest extent possible." From 1994 to 1997, Mace led a research and demonstration project at the Center for Universal Design at NC State University, funded by the U.S. Department of Education's National Institute on Disability and Rehabilitation Research (NIDRR), which included the development of universal design guidelines or principles.

Following is that current list of the Seven Principles of Universal Design with design applications for the bathroom. You might find these principles a good checklist to use in the design process, as additional criteria when choosing between options

1. Equitable Use

   The design is useful and marketable to people with diverse abilities. Design provides the same means of use for all users: identical whenever possible; equivalent when not. It avoids segregating or stigmatizing any users (see Figure 4.12). Provisions for privacy, security, and safety should be equally available to all users. Also, the design should be appealing to all users.

   Design applications include the visit-able guest bathroom, center-mounted lavatory faucets, grab bars, tall storage, rocker light switches, an automatically opening toilet, and motion-sensor lighting, ventilation, and water at the vanity.

2. Flexibility in Use

The design accommodates a wide range of individual preferences and abilities. It provides choice in methods of use and accommodates right- or left-handed access and use. The design facilitates the user's accuracy and precision. And it provides adaptability to the user's pace. Design applications include a removable (see Figure 4.13) or built-in tub seat and reinforcement for, or installation of, multiple grab bars to support tub or shower use by a seated or standing user. Other applications include grab bars for use in a horizontal or vertical position, or that can be folded down out of the way.

FIGURE 4.12 A common example of universal design is the lever handle. This example does not stigmatize and appeals to all users.
Courtesy of Schlage

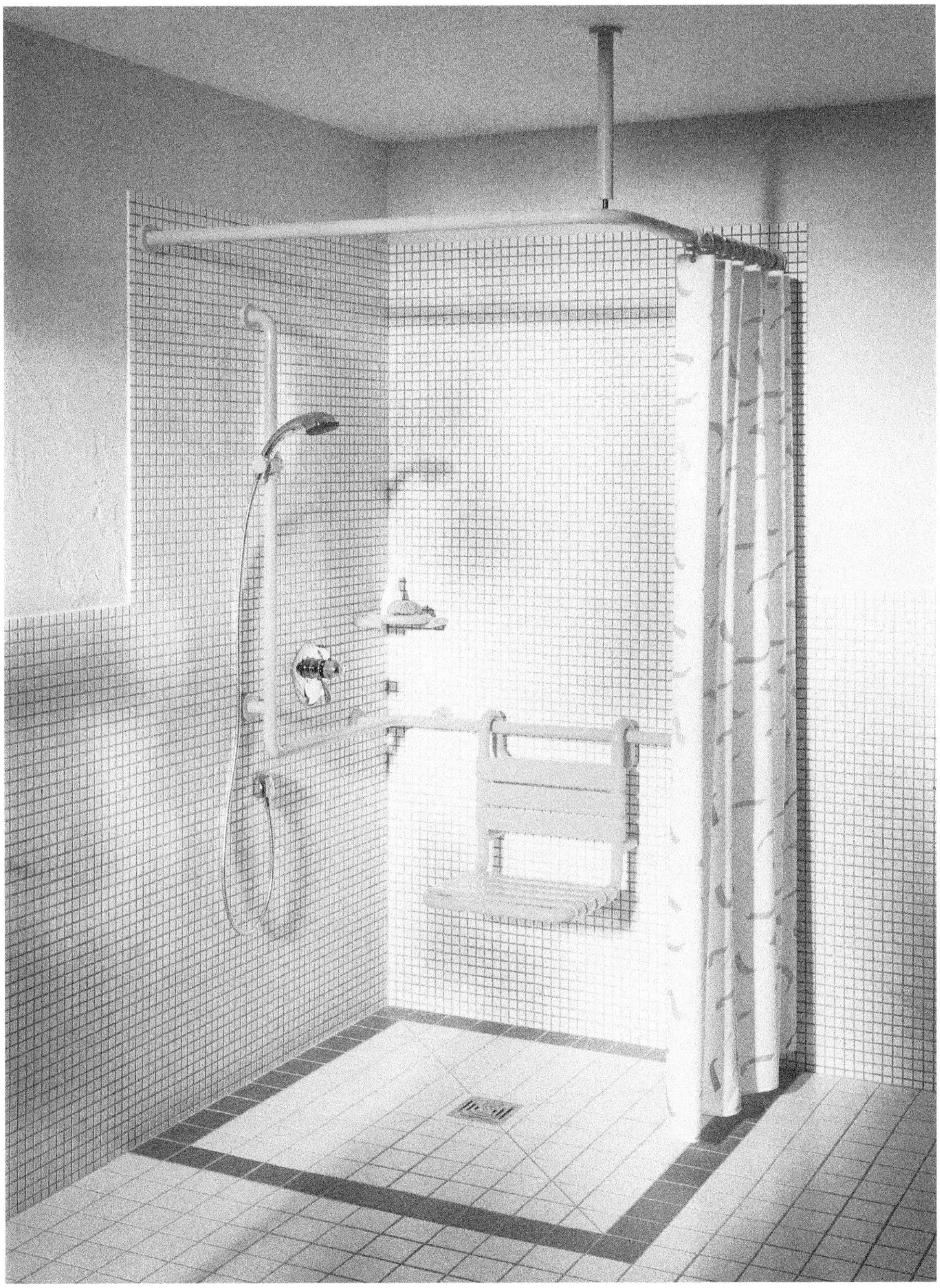

FIGURE 4.13 A removable seat offers flexibility in use, providing for a seated or standing shower.
Courtesy of Hewi by Hafele

3. Simple and Intuitive Use

The design is easy to understand, regardless of the user's experience, knowledge, language skills, or current concentration level. It eliminates unnecessary complexity and is consistent with user expectations and intuition. The design accommodates a wide range of literacy and language skills. It arranges information consistent with its importance. Also, it provides effective prompting and feedback during and after task completion.

Design applications include single-lever faucet operation that is left for hot and right for cool, or the use of red to indicate hot and blue to indicate cold (see Figure 4.14 and 4.15).

4. Perceptible Information

The design communicates necessary information effectively to the user, regardless of ambient conditions or the user's sensory abilities. It uses different modes (pictorial, verbal, tactile) for redundant presentation or redundant cuing of essential information. The design provides adequate contrast between essential information and its surroundings. It maximizes "legibility" of essential information. It differentiates elements in ways that can be described (i.e., makes it easy to give instructions or directions). Also, it is compatible with a variety of techniques or devices used by people with sensory limitations.

Design applications include open or visible storage, a digital temperature control that both makes a sound and blinks when temperature limits are reached, or lighting controls that light up in the "off" position and go dark when the light is on (see Figure 4.16).

FIGURE 4.14 This single-lever shower control has arrows to indicate hot and cold for simple and intuitive use.
Photo courtesy of Moen

FIGURE 4.15 This semiautomatic faucet displays the water temperature through LED lighting for simple and intuitive use, perceptual information, and tolerance for error.
Photo courtesy of Hansa

FIGURE 4.16 This image is a great example of universal design. It provides flexibility to choose to stand or sit at the lavatory and for anyone to use the lavatories; visual cuing at the toe kick for tolerance for error, visible tall storage for perceptual information and lighting, and the length of the mirror is appropriate for people of varying heights.

5. Tolerance for Error

The design minimizes hazards and the adverse consequences of accidental or unintended actions. It arranges elements to minimize hazards and errors, with the most-used elements being the most accessible, and hazardous elements eliminated, isolated, or shielded. The design provides warnings of hazards and errors, and fail-safe features. It discourages unconscious action in tasks that require vigilance.

Design applications include GFCI receptacles that reduce the risk of shock, temperature-limiting faucets that prevent accidental scalding, and timed automatic shut-offs on faucets, small appliances, or ventilation devices (see Figure 4.17 and Figure 4.18).

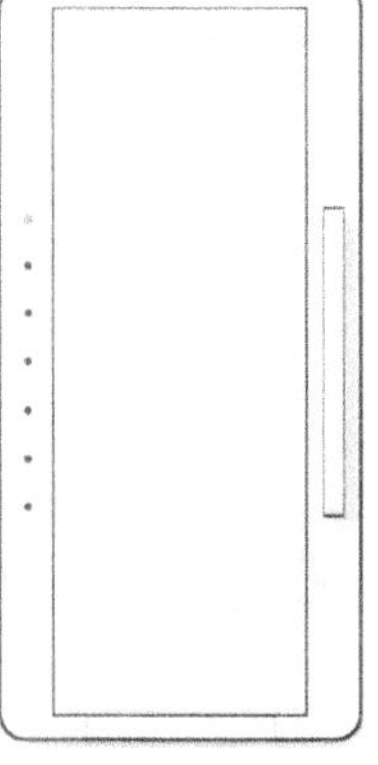

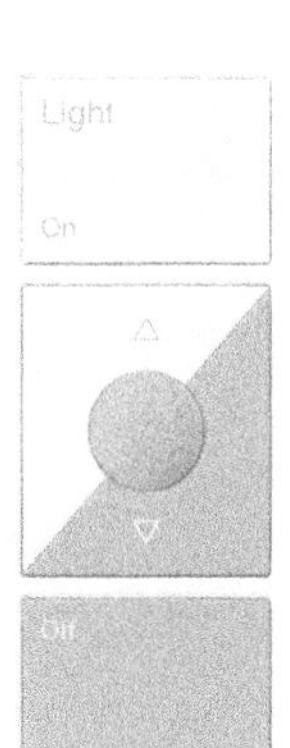

FIGURE 4.17 This automatic digital timer shuts off lights, ventilation, or whirlpools; it's an example of tolerance for error.
Courtesy of Lutron

FIGURE 4.18 This programmable shower control can be paused, turned off, or diverted with one push of a button, and the exact water temperature can be set, addressing a number of universal design principles.
Courtesy of Kohler Company

6. Low Physical Effort

The design can be used efficiently, comfortably, and with a minimum of fatigue. It allows the user to maintain a neutral body position and use reasonable operating forces. It minimizes repetitive actions and sustained physical effort.

Design applications include lever handle on cabinetry and doors, tall storage, remote controls for operating windows, and remote flushers, as well as motion-activated appliances and fittings, and conveniently located towel bars and toilet paper holders (see Figures 4.19 and 4.20).

7. Size and Space for Approach and Use

Appropriate size and space are provided for approach, reach, manipulation, and use, regardless of the user's body size, posture, or mobility. Design provides a clear line of sight to important elements for any seated or standing user. Reach to all components is comfortable for any seated or standing user. Variations in hand and grip size are accommodated. There is adequate space for the use of assistive devices or personal assistance.

FIGURE 4.19 This toilet has a remote control for the bidet seat, used for personal hygiene, a good example of features that reduce physical effort.
Photo courtesy of TOTO

FIGURE 4.20 The single-lever faucet handle can be used with low physical effort, centered on the lavatory for equitable, and simple and intuitive use.

Design by NKBA member Scott Gjesdahl, Co-Designer Sandra Gjesdahl

Design applications include full-height mirrors, movable (portable) storage, knee space (see Figure 4.21) at a the vanity and/or the lavatory, and private toilet compartments that incorporate 48 inches by 30 inches (1219 mm by 762 mm) of clear floor space.

The field of universal design represents a convergence of several threads of design practice with a focus on usefulness. To this end, the State University of New York (SUNY) at Buffalo is home to the Center for Inclusive Design and Environmental Access, the IDEA Center, an excellent source of information on the current state of universal design. Both the IDEA Center and the recently published book, *Universal Design: Creating Inclusive Environments*, are good sources of information on global and national movement in universal design.

FIGURE 4.21 An example of a knee space that provides size and space for approach and use.
Design by NKBA member Tess Giuliani, CKD

The term "universal design" is sometimes inaccurately used as the politically correct description of compliance with the Americans with Disabilities Act (ADA) and other access standards or guidelines. While access standards and guidelines are important as a minimum, universal design is a broader approach that works to incorporate the needs of all users and is not limited to any one specific group. Universal design is an ideal, a way of thinking, whereas code compliance is often simply following a dictate.

A number of terms are used that relate to universal design but have slightly different meanings.

- Lifespan design refers to the aspect of universal design that provides for the changes that may occur in the lifespan of household members, such as the birth and growth of children, or the return home after a skiing accident that resulted in a broken bone.
- Transgenerational design refers to design that acknowledges and supports the multiple generations commonly living under one roof today.

- Barrier-free design is an older term, first used to refer to solutions that removed barriers in the environment. While removing barriers is still one important aspect, in North America universal design has been embraced as a broader, more positive approach and term. Universal design seeks to eliminate building of architectural or structural barriers that will need to be removed at a later time.
- Accessible design or accessibility refers to characteristics of spaces or products that meet prescribed requirements for particular variations in ability. It is often a function of compliance with regulations or criteria that established a minimum level of design necessary to accommodate a person with a disability, that is, "wheelchair accessible."
- Adaptable design refers to features that are either adjustable or capable of being easily added or removed to "adapt" the unit to individual needs or preferences.
- Aging-in-place (design for): Design that considers the changes that occur as one ages, supporting the ability to live in one's own home and community safely, independently, and comfortably, regardless of age, income, or ability level.
- Visit-ability refers to basic accommodations that will allow people of differing abilities to visit a home. In terms of bath design, visit-ability requires at least one bath on the main floor, with a minimum 32-inch (813-mm) -wide clear passage at the door. In some jurisdictions, it includes requirements for clear floor space and reinforcement for possible addition of grab bars.
- FlexHousing is a Canadian concept in housing that incorporates the ability to make future changes easily and with minimum expense, to meet the evolving needs of its occupants. FlexHousing is simply an approach to designing and building homes based on the principles of adaptability, accessibility, affordability, and healthy housing.

  The FlexHousing concept of accessibility is user-friendly, and its features add convenience and practicality to the functions of a home. Another consideration is the reduction of potential hazards. Although the initial cost of FlexHousing is slightly more than a conventional home, FlexHousing features recover their investment over the long-term because pre-engineered features allow for easy and inexpensive change and renovation. The integration of healthy building materials and innovative housing technology or Healthy Housing protects the health of the occupants and the environment.

Dispelling Myths

There are many misconceptions regarding universal design. Let's put an end to the most common ones.

Myth 1: Universal design is nothing more than design for people in wheelchairs.

> Fact: The opposite is true. To be considered universal, a design will be accessible not only to people in wheelchairs, but also to people of most sizes, shapes, and abilities. Universal design applies to people tall or short, young or old, left-handed or right-handed, visitors to an unfamiliar city or home, parents with children, people carrying packages, and more.

Myth 2: Universal design only helps people with disabilities and older people.

> Fact: Universal design extends the benefits of functional design to many people, including short or tall people, large people, frail people, pregnant women, children, or even people traveling with much to carry or where there is a language barrier—everyone eventually.

Myth 3: Universal design costs more than traditional design.

> Fact: Many universal concepts are standard products and cost no more than traditional products. The degree of customization and quality of the products will have the greater impact on cost.

Myth 4: Universal design is stigmatizing because it looks medical.

> Fact: The best universal design is invisible. When done well, universal design enhances the appearance and personality of a space, as well as the function of that space, for a variety of users.

ACCESS CODES, LAWS, AND STANDARDS

In the United States, most existing access-related laws, building codes, and standards are intended as minimum criteria for access for people with disabilities, applicable, for the most part, in other than privately owned single-family residential spaces. While this is not universal design, the related guidelines can serve as a starting point for design parameters that support universal thinking, and in fact, the NKBA Access Standards are based on the ICC (ANSI) standard.

American National Standard for Accessible and Usable Buildings and Facilities (ICC A117.1)

The first edition of the American National Standard for Accessible and Usable Buildings and Facilities (ANSI A117.1) was issued in 1961. Since then, the standard has been updated and revised several times; the latest and current revision being the 2009 edition, now called the ICC A117.1, was developed under the International Code Council and approved by ANSI.

Since the International Code Council (ICC) is the current secretariat for the standard, it is referred to as the ICC standard and includes technical design guidelines for making buildings and sites accessible to, and usable by, people with disabilities. The ICC standard is the referenced technical standard for compliance with the accessibility requirements of the International Building Code and many other state and local codes. The 1986, 1992,1998, and 2003 editions of the ANSI A117.1 standard are also U.S. Department of Housing and Urban Development (HUD) approved "safe harbors" for compliance with the technical requirements of the Fair Housing Amendments Act of 1988 (the Act) when used with the Fair Housing Act, the regulations implementing the Act, and the Fair Housing Accessibility Guidelines. The Act is a federal mandate for accessibility in multifamily housing.

Uniform Federal Accessibility Standards (UFAS)

First published in 1984, Uniform Federal Accessibility Standards (UFAS) includes criteria for the design and construction of federally financed buildings to provide access for people with disabilities. UFAS is the technical standard referenced by three federal mandates for accessibility: the Architectural Barriers Act (ABA), Title II of the Americans with Disabilities Act (recognizes UFAS for work prior to March 15, 2012), and Section 504 of the Rehabilitation Act of 1973 (Section 504). The ABA requires access to buildings constructed, altered, leased, or financed in whole or in part by the United States federal government; and Section 504 requires that federally financed programs and activities be accessible to people with disabilities. Section 504 also requires access to federally financed newly constructed and altered buildings. The technical provisions of UFAS are largely the same as the 1980 ANSI A117.1 standard.

Fair Housing Act Accessibility Guidelines

First published in 1991, the Fair Housing Act Accessibility Guidelines (the Guidelines) provide architects, builders, developers, and others, technical guidance for compliance with the accessibility requirements of the Fair Housing Amendments Act of 1988 (the Act). The Act is a law that covers newly constructed multifamily buildings containing at least four dwellings built for first occupancy on or after March 13, 1991.

Safe Harbors

1. HUD Fair Housing Accessibility Guidelines published on March 6, 1991 and the Supplemental Notice to Fair Housing Accessibility Guidelines: Questions and Answers about the Guidelines, published on June 28, 1994
2. HUD Fair Housing Act Design Manual
3. ANSI A117.1 (1986), used with the Fair Housing Act, HUD's regulations, and the Guidelines
4. CABO/ANSI A117.1 (1992), used with the Fair Housing Act, HUD's regulations, and the Guidelines
5. ICC/ANSI A117.1 (1998), used with the Fair Housing Act, HUD's regulations, and the Guidelines
6. Code Requirements for Housing Accessibility 2000 (CRHA)

7. International Building Code 2000 as amended by the 2001 Supplement to the International Codes
8. International Building Code 2003, with one condition*
9. ICC/ANSI A117.1 (2003) used with the Fair Housing Act, HUD's regulations, and the Guidelines
10. 2006 International Building Code® (loose leaf)

Safe harbor standards constitute safe harbors only when adopted and implemented in accordance with the policy statement that HUD published in the Federal Register on March 23, 2000. That policy statement notes, for example, that if a jurisdiction adopts a model building code that HUD has determined conforms with the design and construction requirements of the Act, such as those listed above, then covered residential buildings that are constructed in accordance with plans and specifications approved during the building permitting process will be in compliance with the requirements of the Act.

If the building code official has waived one or more of those requirements, or the building code official has incorrectly interpreted or applied the building code provisions, then the buildings are not in compliance. In addition, adoption of a HUD recognized safe harbor does not change HUD's enforcement efforts, including conducting investigations when complaints are filed.

Americans with Disabilities Act Accessibility Guidelines and the 2010 Standards for Accessible Design

First produced in 1991, the Americans with Disabilities Act Guidelines (ADAAG) are guidelines for compliance with the accessibility requirements of the ADA. The ADA is a law that addresses access to the workplace (Title I), state and local government services (Title II), and places of public accommodation and commercial facilities (Title III). It also requires phone companies to provide telecommunications relay services for people who have hearing or speech impairments (Title IV) and miscellaneous instructions for federal agencies that enforce the law (Title V).

On September 15, 2010, the U.S. Department of Justice published new ADA Title II and III regulations and adopted updated design standards called the 2010 Standards for Accessible Design. On and after March 15, 2012, use of the 1990 ADA as it applied to facilities and entities covered by Titles II and III and the 1991 ADAAG (ADA Access Guidelines) standard was no longer permitted for new construction and for alterations of existing elements conducted after that date.

Canadian Policies and Practices

The National Building Code (NBC), developed by the Canadian Codes Center of the Institute for Research in Construction (a branch of the National Research Center), is the standard on which many of the provincial regulations are based. The Canadian Standards Association (CSA) developed B651, the Barrier Free Design Standards in 1975. This standard, now called B651-04 Accessible Design for the Built Environment, specifies minimum technical requirements, including a section that addresses kitchen and bathroom specifications. It has been revised many times, with the current version reaffirmed in 2010. As is true in the United States, this standard does not have the force of law unless mandated by a particular province. It is based on "average adult" dimension and to effectively use the concepts, a designer would need to consult with the end user.

Because of provincial jurisdiction, progress has been difficult in Canada in the development and enforcement of national civil rights or legislation related to housing, such as the ADA and the Fair Housing Act in the United States. In 1982, the federal government enacted the Charter of Rights and Freedoms including Section 15 prohibiting discrimination on the basis of mental or physical handicap. However, the Charter of Rights has not been as thoroughly implemented into specific enforceable legislation as the Fair Housing Act and the ADA in the United States.

---

* Effective February 28, 2005, HUD determined that the IBC 2003 is a safe harbor, conditioned upon ICC publishing and distributing a statement to jurisdictions and past and future purchasers of the 2003 IBC stating, "ICC interprets Section 1104.1, and specifically, the exception to Section 1104.1, to be read together with Section 1107.4, and that the Code requires an accessible pedestrian route from site arrival points to accessible building entrances, unless site impracticality applies. Exception 1 to Section 1107.4 is not applicable to site arrival points for any Type B dwelling units because site impracticality is addressed under Section 1107.7."

In Ontario, the building code includes specific requirements for accessible buildings, and in 2001, the Ontarians with Disabilities Act (ODA) was passed. The purpose of the ODA is to improve opportunities for people with disabilities, and to enable them to become involved in the identification, removal, and prevention of barriers faced by persons with disabilities.

Recognizing the difficulties in mandating change, the Canadian federal government, through Canada Mortgage and Housing (CMHC), has chosen to assist the development of housing through financial instruments such as grants, loans, and insurance arrangements. CMHC assistance helps low income and older Canadians, people with disabilities, and Aboriginals, with housing options and help with housing expenses.

For example, in 1986 the Residential Rehabilitation Assistance Program (RRAP-D) for Persons with Disabilities was developed to offer financial assistance to homeowners and landlords to undertake accessibility work to modify dwellings occupied, or intended for occupancy by, low-income persons with disabilities. Another example is the Home Adaptations for Seniors' Independence (HASI) program, which helps homeowners and landlords pay for minor home adaptations to extend the time low-income seniors can live in their own homes independently.

SUMMARY

There is a wealth of information available to plan bathroom spaces based on realistic human dimensions. Anthropometric studies give you basic dimensions for people of a variety of sizes and ages. Awareness of this information as you develop a plan for a client's bath will help to more accurately determine sizes and spatial relationships in each case.

In this chapter, you have also been presented with a quick summary of federal access laws, codes, and standards. While this overview provides a level of familiarity, each bathroom you design may fall under specific local regulations, and you will need to work with your local officials for guidance and technical assistance.

For more information on housing accessibility, contact the U.S. Department of Housing and Urban Development (HUD). For ADA access issues concerning public facilities, contact the U.S. Department of Justice. For issues pertaining to UFAS, ADAAG, and the 2010 Standards, contact the Access Board. To increase your awareness of local access laws, contact the building inspector and consult local homebuilder associations.

As one universal design leader noted, "It is questionable whether accessibility standards will ever encourage designers to practice universal design." However, considering the long-term demographic trends pointing to an increase in older age groups, access needs will not go away, and universal design is a broad and beautiful way to achieve improved access without mandates.

REVIEW QUESTIONS

1. Define universal design and explain who benefits from it (See "Universal Design" page 91).
2. What is anthropometry and how does it help determine bathroom planning guidelines? (See "Anthropometry" page 92)
3. What is the standard reach range of someone who remains seated to maneuver in the bathroom? (See "Height and Reach Range" page 95)
4. What is the referenced technical standard for compliance with the accessibility requirements of the International Building Code and many other state and local codes? (See "American National Standard for Accessible and Usable Buildings and Facilities" page 108)

Assessing Needs

A bathroom is a very personal and private space. People use the space in different ways and have different ideas about function, mood, and ambience. To design a bathroom, your challenge will be to move past your own assumptions and learn about your clients' personal preferences.

This chapter focuses on assessing the needs of your client in preparation for developing a design. A needs assessment is the critical first step in the design process. Without knowing what your client wants and needs, you cannot know how to design the space.

Needs assessment includes both your client and their house. It involves gathering information about your client and their use of the bathroom, as well as inspecting and measuring the jobsite.

Learning Objective 1: Identify and list the needs of a client in preparation for the development of a design plan for a bathroom.

Learning Objective 2: Describe the purpose and elements of a design program.

THE DESIGN PROCESS

The *design process* is a multistage process in which the designer moves from an idea to a completed product. As part of the design process, the designer can gather and organize information, develop visual diagrams and presentations, refine ideas and ensure accuracy, and manage the installation. In Chapter 10, "Putting It All Together," the design process is discussed in detail and an example of a formal design process is presented. To quote Chapter 10, the design process "involves a lot of going back and forth, checking and rechecking. A. . . design involves a dose of inspiration, a spark of creativity, but mostly a lot of hard work."

A necessary part of the design process is to gather information about your client and the space you will design. This information needs to be organized in a way that is useful to you throughout the design process. You will refer to this information as you develop your design, as you check the details, and as your project is constructed. This organized and documented information is the *design program.* The design program is both your guide through the design process and the inspiration to your creativity.

For a designer to complete the design process with a successful product and a satisfied client, the design programming stage is critical. The design program is built on accurate and complete information about the client, their needs and wants, and the space to be designed. This chapter, on needs assessment, is planned to facilitate design programming and lead to a successful design process.

INTERVIEWING THE CLIENT

From your first meeting with a potential client, you are gathering information. Informal conversations can help you learn more about their household, who will use the bathroom, and their goals and dreams for a new bathroom. However, you will soon want a more structured needs-assessment interview and information-gathering session with your client.

Prepare for the Interview

You may want to interview your client in your office or showroom. Alternatively, you may set an appointment and go to your client's home, which provides the opportunity to observe it firsthand. Even if your client is building a new home, a visit to their existing home can help you better understand what your client wants. Your client may feel more comfortable talking in their home, and their existing bathroom(s) may give them clues about things to tell you. Finally, you may also be able to collect initial measurements (important for a remodel) during the same appointment.

Recording the interview on audio tape gives you an accurate record of information and avoids the need to take notes while talking to the client. However, after the interview, it can be time-consuming to transcribe information from the recording. Be sure to ask permission before recording the interview.

Needs Assessment Forms

Using a prepared interview format is helpful. This assures that you gather all the information that you need, and gives you a way to record and later, to organize, the responses to the interview. In some cases, you can give your client a checklist to complete and return to you.

The authors have created ten different needs assessment forms for use when gathering information about your client, their home, and the bathroom design project. They provide an organized way to complete your interview and jobsite inspection. These needs assessment forms are discussed and included in this chapter and are also available online at: www.wiley.com/go/bathplanning

The needs assessment forms are:

- Client information forms
  - Form 1: Getting to Know Your Client
  - Form 2: Getting to Know Your Client's Home
  - Form 5: Your Client's Bathroom Preferences
- Checklists for client use
  - Form 3: Checklist for Bathroom Activities
  - Form 4: Bathroom Storage Inventory
- Jobsite and house information forms
  - Form 6: Jobsite Inspection
  - Form 7: Dimensions of Mechanical Devices
  - Form 8: Window Measurements
  - Form 9: Door Measurements
  - Form 10: Fixture Measurements

Additional forms for planning closets and exercise areas are discussed in chapter 9, "More Than a Bathroom."

National Kitchen & Bath Association Bath Design Survey Form

The National Kitchen & Bath Association (NKBA) developed a Bathroom Design Survey Form, which covers some of the same information as the forms in this book. This form is used by professional designers and students in NKBA–accredited programs. Familiarity with the NKBA survey form is necessary for Certified Bath Designer (CBD) certification.

You might want to adapt the needs assessment forms to develop an interview format that works well on a computer, and take a laptop with you to record information. The forms can be adapted as needed for your business, and used in either an electronic or printed format.

Personal Information

In order to complete a client interview, you need to ask some questions about intimate and personal activities related to the bathroom. To put your client at ease, adopt an open and frank approach. Use the correct terms for body functions and avoid euphemisms. Explain that some of the questions may seem personal, but the more information you have, the more successful your design.

During the interview, you will be asking about physical abilities. This can also be a sensitive subject. A client who is getting older may not recognize or accept the physical changes of aging. People with degenerative conditions may not be willing to yield to the impact of the disease on their bodies. Physical limitations can sometimes be hidden for short periods of time, especially with a relative stranger. Again, be open and stress the importance of fully knowing the client's physical situation, in order to develop the most supportive design. For more information on working with clients with special needs, refer to chapter 8, "Accessibility in Practice."

GETTING TO KNOW YOUR CLIENT (FORM 1)

The first thing you want to know is who uses the bathroom? Gather information about the users of the bathroom, their physical profiles, and any specialized needs they have. For instance, who are the primary users of the bathroom? How old are they? How tall are they?

You will want to collect anthropometric (human measurement) information about your individual clients. This is especially important if your clients have any physical limitations or concerns about access to bathroom activities.

Review chapter 4, "Human Factors and Universal Design Foundation," to learn more about the importance of anthropometry and ergonomic design. Form 1: Getting to Know Your Client, is a tool you can use to collect anthropometric information about your client. Form 1 is also designed to help you collect information about any of your client's special needs with respect to the bathroom space. For example, do any of the users have special physical needs or situations? Do any of them require a mobility aid, such as a wheelchair or cane?

In addition to the anthropometric information and other special needs, you need to learn a little about your client's attitudes toward bathroom use and activities. It will be important to determine issues such as: Will more than one person be using the bathroom at the same time? What are they comfortable doing in a shared bathroom space? Form 1 can assist you in gathering this information.

Form 1: Getting to Know Your Client

This form collects information about your clients. Use the parts that are appropriate to your design project. A custom design project, or a client with special needs, may require more detailed information.

1. Users of the bathroom:

   Name: ____________________ Age: ________

   Height: __________ Weight: __________ Handedness: ☐ Right ☐ Left

   Special needs or concerns: ____________________

   Name: ____________________ Age: ________

   Height: __________ Weight: __________ Handedness: ☐ Right ☐ Left

   Special needs or concerns: ____________________

   Name: ____________________ Age: ________

   Height: __________ Weight: __________ Handedness: ☐ Right ☐ Left

   Special needs or concerns: ____________________

   Name: ____________________ Age: ________

   Height: __________ Weight: __________ Handedness: ☐ Right ☐ Left

   Special needs or concerns: ____________________

   Name: ____________________ Age: ________

   Height: __________ Weight: __________ Handedness: ☐ Right ☐ Left

   Special needs or concerns: ____________________

2. Anthropometric information (See Figure 5.1)
3. Reach and grasp profile (See Figure 5.2)
4. Physical profile

   Physical characteristic(s) affecting activities in the bathroom:

   A. Sight:

      Do you wear glasses for: ☐ Reading ☐ Distance

      Are you taking medications that affect your sight?

      Are you sensitive to light?

   B. Hearing:

      What issues regarding your hearing will affect your activities in the bathroom?

   C. Tactile/touch:

      Can you feel hot and cold?

   D. Taste/smell:

      What issues regarding your sense of taste or smell will affect your activities in the bathroom?

   E. Strength and function:

      What can you lift? Carry?

      Do you have more strength on one side than the other?

(*continued*)

2. ANTHROPOMETRIC INFORMATION

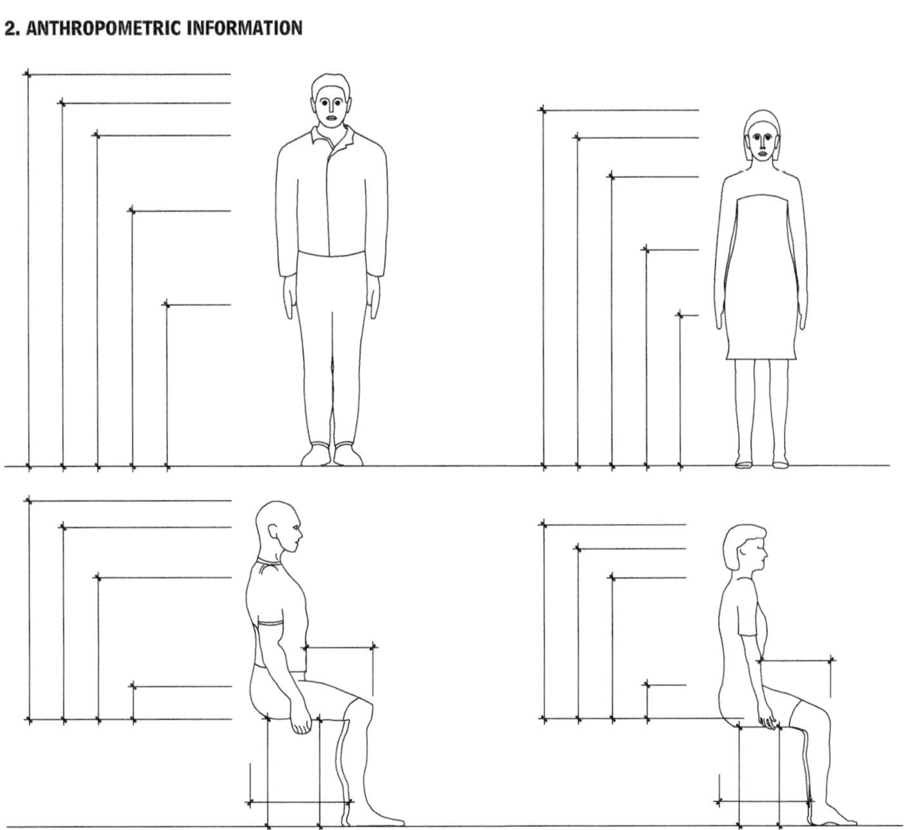

FIGURE 5.1 Use the drawings in this figure to record anthropometric information about your client.

3. REACH AND GRASP PROFILE

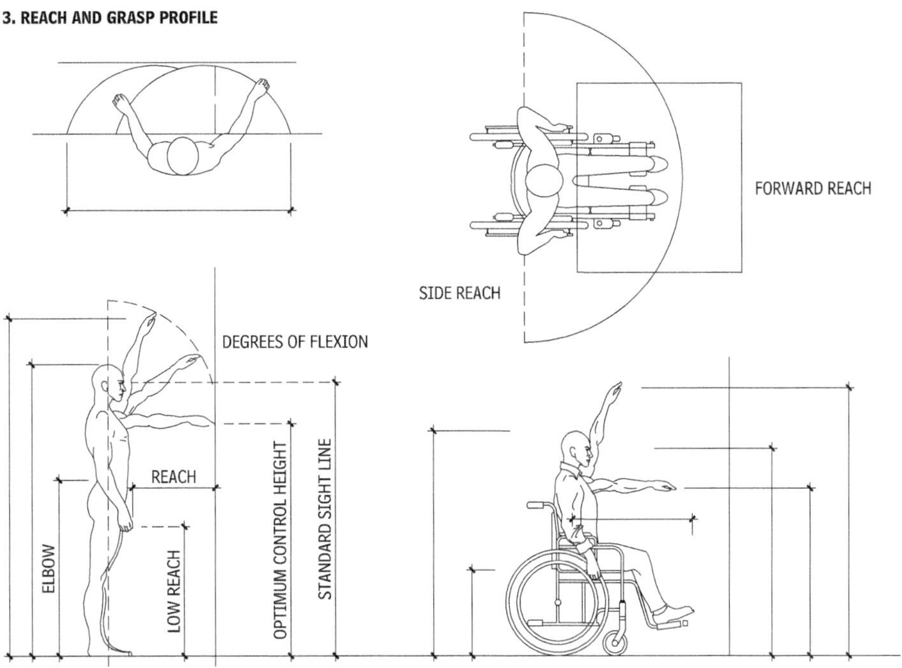

FIGURE 5.2 Use the drawings in this figure to record additional antropometric information about your client, including their ability to reach.

(continued)

Form 1: Getting to Know Your Client (*continued*)

Do you use both hands fully? Palms only?

How is your grip?

Left side? Right side?

F. Balance, mobility, and assistance:
How is your balance: Standing? Bending?

Does your mobility or balance vary by time of day?

Does an assistant help you: Sometimes? All the time?

What adaptive equipment do you use?

G. Prognosis: Is your condition stable? Is further deterioration anticipated? Is improvement anticipated?
H. Other physical concerns:
I. Special safety concerns:

5. Mobility Aids
If a mobility aid, such as wheelchair, walker, or cane is used, it is important to collect information on the size of the mobility aid, as well as anthropometrical information about the client when using the mobility aid (Figure 5.3).

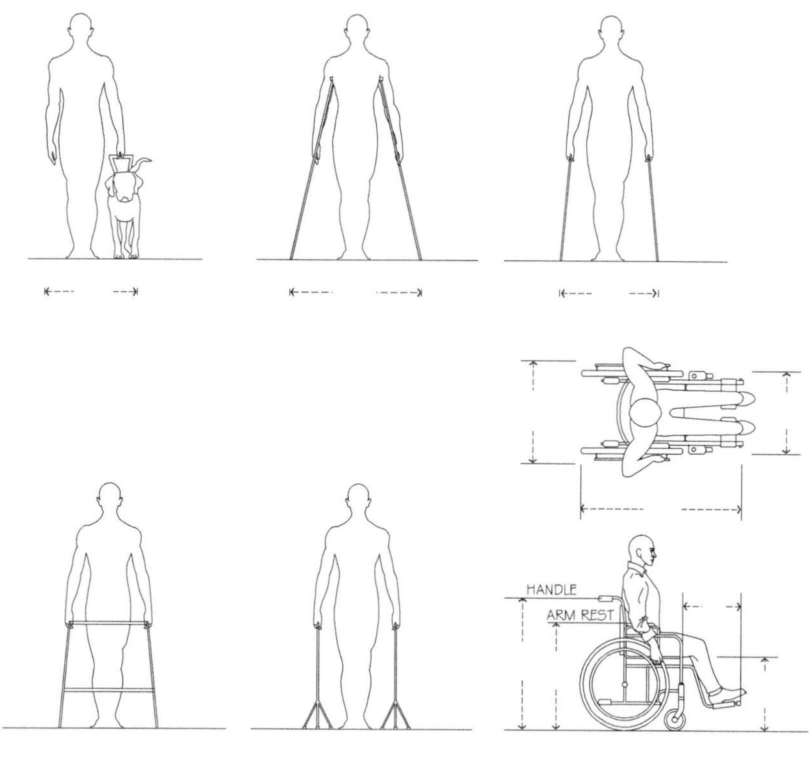

FIGURE 5.3 If appropriate to your client, use the drawings in this figure to record information about your client that includes a mobility aid.

6. Personal Information about the bathroom
- Will more than one person be using the bathroom at the same time? How often?
- What types of bathroom activities can be done in a shared bathroom space?
- What types of bathroom activities need to be done in private?
- How important is auditory privacy? Are bathroom noises a problem?

(*continued*)

7. Visit-ability
   - Will this bathroom be used by visitors to the home? Overnight or just for social occasions?
   - Will the visitors be children or adults?
   - Do any regular or frequent visitors have any physical limitations?
8. Future Plans
   - How long do you plan to live in this home?
   - Do you anticipate changes in your household size or make-up?
   - Will this affect who uses the bathroom?
   - Is resale value of the home important?

Your Client's Home: Location, Location, Location

Start with the big picture. Where is the home located? How will the location influence the design of the bathroom? Location determines climate, telling you whether there are cold winters, hot summers, or long seasons where the windows might be open to the outside air. Will there be views of the ocean, a lake, mountains, trees, or a city skyline, to be captured in the design? Or does the location determine that the bathroom needs to be more inwardly focused, sheltered from things such as traffic noise or close-by buildings?

Location of the home can also give you a clue to your client's lifestyle. A bathroom in an urban apartment, a large ranch home in a rural area, or a condominium in a resort community represent different types of homes as well as lifestyles, and thus different types of bathroom design needs.

Finally, different countries, as well as different regions of the same country, can have variation in design trends. Vernacular housing describes housing styles that are typical of, or common to, a region, and that have been influenced by factors such as climate, available building materials, and cultural heritage. Knowing something about the vernacular housing of the area of your client's home may give you some ideas about style, color, or materials to use in the bathroom design.

What Type of Home?

Most bathroom designers work on projects in single-family homes—but not always. Especially in urban areas, a designer may work on a home that is an apartment, townhouse, or other type of multifamily structure. There may be some unique concerns in this type of home. For example, in many multifamily housing communities, plans for remodeling must be approved by a group such as the homeowners' association. You may be limited in making changes affecting the home's exterior. Likewise, plumbing changes may be limited. Carefully consider any possible factors that could occur in a multifamily project.

Sometimes, single-family housing may be in a community with a homeowners' association with rules affecting renovations. In addition, sometimes there may be covenants in a property's deed that could affect a bathroom remodeling project, such as the size of an addition or the style and placement of windows.

While you are considering these special and legal situations that can affect your design for the bathroom, be sure to consider the impact of the building permit process. You, as the designer, are responsible for knowing the building codes that impact your bathroom project. Further, you need to work with the contractor/builder to see that all building permits are obtained and inspections completed. This process will be easier and more successful if you include all building codes and permits as part of your needs assessment and design planning.

GETTING TO KNOW YOUR CLIENT'S HOME (FORM 2)

Another part of the big picture is the total home. If you are working on a remodeling project, ask to take a tour of the existing home. Observe the size of the home, the number of bedrooms and other bathrooms. How will traffic flow to the bathroom you will be designing?

A tour of your client's home will also be useful to get a sense of style and color. Ask your client to describe what they like and do not like about other rooms in the home. Use this information to give you clues about design preferences.

During the home tour, note what rooms are on the other sides of the bathroom walls. This information might be useful as you think about factors such as "borrowing" space from another room, planning for sound insulation, or reconfiguring plumbing. Look for details that might give you valuable information and prevent surprises during the construction phase, such as the presence of heating or cooling ducts. You might want to make a sketch of the bathroom space, or do this as part of the jobsite inspection (see Form 6).

Take along a copy of Form 2: Getting to Know Your Client's Home, when you do a home tour. This form can be used to gather information about the "big picture" of your client's home and their bathroom.

A camera can be a useful tool during a home tour. Be sure to ask permission first. Use the camera to make visual notes of features that will be useful to remember during the design process. A digital camera is particularly helpful for this type of documentation, as pictures are easily transferred to a computer file. Also, take pictures of family members, favorite accessory items, or views from windows. Later, you may be able to incorporate these into presentation drawings for a wonderful personal touch.

The Home of the Future

Finish your understanding of the big picture by talking to your client about future plans for the home. Is this a home in which they plan to retire? Will they be likely to remodel or expand this home in the future? Form 1: Getting to Know Your Client and Form 2: Getting to Know Your Client's Home can guide you in gathering this type of information.

While you are learning about future plans for their home, you can ask about the future of their family or household. "Expanding" households are typically younger, and are at the life stage where they can expect to add new household members, such as by marriage or birth. Sometimes a new household member is an older relative. "Launching" households are more likely to be older, with children that will soon be leaving. Future changes in household size or composition can influence who uses a bathroom, as well as the activities that take place in that space.

Form 2: Getting to Know Your Client's Home

This form can be used to collect general information about your client's home to help in developing your design. Specific structural and mechanical information is collected in other forms.

Location of home: ______________________________

Type of neighborhood: ______________________________

Type of home: ☐ single-family home ☐ duplex ☐ townhouse ☐ apartment/flat ☐ other ______________

Structure of home: ☐ one-story ☐ two-story ☐ three-story ☐ ranch ☐ split-level ☐ split foyer/raised ranch ☐ high rise ☐ other

Approximate size of home: ______________________________

Number of bedrooms: ______________ Number of bathrooms: ______________

Style of home (exterior): ______________________________

Is the home historic? What time period? ______________________________

Are there historic covenants or restrictions affecting the home? ______________________________

____

____

Is the home part of a homeowner's association? ______________________________

Are there any covenants or restrictions affecting the home? ______________________________

____

____

Are there any deed restrictions? ______________________________

____

____

Style of home (interior): ______________________________

____

____

Colors? ______________________________

____

Materials? ______________________________

Furniture? ______________________________

____

Accessories? ______________________________

____

Future plans for resale or remodeling? ______________________________

____

____

ACTIVITIES IN THE BATHROOM (FORM 3)

You now know something about who is using the bathroom, so you want to gather information about what they actually do there. Major bathroom activities fall into three categories: grooming; bathing/showering; and toileting. Using these categories will help you design the bathroom centers presented in chapter 6, "Bathroom Planning." There are many different activities that fall into these three categories. In addition, there are other activities that can take place in the bathroom, such as dressing, exercise, and laundry.

Since the potential bathroom activities are numerous, you can give your clients an activity checklist to complete (Form 3). This can save time and may get you more complete information. You may want to review the checklist with them and then ask them to complete it at home. Alternatively, you can mail (or email) the checklist to them in advance and then review it during the interview. Form 3: Checklist for Bathroom Activities is written for your client to use. It also asks about location and frequency of activities—information that is very useful during the design process.

In addition to the information provided on the checklist, you may need clarification on certain activities. For instance, ask about activities that your client prefers to do while seated or standing. When is privacy important for an activity? What activities might be done in shared space? If your client has completed the checklist in advance, these issues can be discussed at the interview. Form 3 gives you space to make notes after the client has completed the checklist.

Form 3: Checklist for Bathroom Activities

Directions: Review the list of activities in each section. If it is an activity that you do or want to do in the bathroom, place a check in the first column. Then check the appropriate location and frequency column. Extra lines are left in each section for you to add activities as needed.

Grooming Activities								
✓	Activity	Location					Frequency	
		Vanity/Lavatory	Toilet	Bathtub	Shower	Other (Specify)	Often	Sometimes
	Body: apply lotion							
	Cosmetics: apply, remove							
	Face: skin care							
	Face: wash							
	First aid: treating cuts and burns							
	Hair care: blow dry, curl							
	Hair care: brush, style							
	Hair care: color							
	Hair care: cut, trim							
	Hair care: shampoo, condition							
	Hands: apply lotion							
	Hands: wash							
	Medicines/vitamins							
	Nails (finger): clip, file, polish							
	Nails (toe): clip, file, polish							
	Shave: face							
	Shave: legs, underarms							
	Teeth: brush, floss							
	Other grooming activities:							

Notes:

(continued)

Form 3: Checklist for Bathroom Activities (*continued*)

Bathing/Showering Activities								
✓	Activity	Location					Frequency	
		Vanity/Lavatory	Toilet	Bathtub	Shower	Other (Specify)	Often	Sometimes
	Bathing pets							
	Bathing in tub							
	Bathing: assisting an adult							
	Bathing children							
	Bathing: soaking, relaxing							
	Douching							
	Sauna: relaxing							
	Showering							
	Showering: assisting an adult							
	Showering with someone							
	"Sponge" bath							
	Steam showering							
	Whirlpool soaking							
	Other bathing/showering activities:							

Notes:

(*continued*)

Toileting Activities								
✓	Activity	Location					Frequency	
		Vanity/Lavatory	Toilet	Bathtub	Shower	Other (Specify)	Often	Sometimes
	Defecate							
	Diapers: change infant/child							
	Diapers: change adult							
	Diapers: rinse out							
	Personal cleansing-bidet							
	Tampons/pads: change							
	Urinate							
	Other toileting activities:							

Notes:

(continued)

Form 3: Checklist for Bathroom Activities (*continued*)

Other Bathroom Activities

✓	Activity	Location					Frequency	
		Vanity/Lavatory	Toilet	Bathtub	Shower	Other (Specify)	Often	Sometimes
	Display collections							
	Dressing: underwear, sleeping clothes							
	Dressing: "street" clothes							
	Drink beverages							
	Eat snacks							
	Exercise							
	Exercise using equipment							
	Grow plants							
	Laundry: air dry							
	Laundry: hand wash							
	Laundry: machine wash							
	Laundry: sort, fold							
	Listen to music							
	Massage							
	Meditation							
	Personal pampering							
	Polish shoes							
	Read: books, newspapers							
	Supervise children							
	Talking on telephone							
	Talking with people							
	Tanning/sunning							
	Undressing							
	Watch television							
	Other activities:							

Notes:

STORAGE IN THE BATHROOM (FORM 4)

Talking about activities in the bathroom can easily lead to discussing your client's storage needs. What does your client want to keep in the bathroom? Where will they use the different items stored in the bathroom? How frequently do they use each item? These are some examples of information that is useful to you, the designer, in planning bathroom storage.

The users of the bathroom space can complete the storage inventory checklist in Form 4: Bathroom Storage Inventory. This inventory is divided into several sections, by location of storage: near the vanity/lavatory/grooming center; near the bathtub/shower; near the toilet/bidet; and other; as well as for display only. In addition, your client is asked to identify frequency of use and type of storage. The Form 4 checklist has many common bathroom items already listed to make it easier to use. This checklist will be very helpful in the design process, so encourage your client to be thorough in completing it. Also, it is helpful if the client has completed this inventory in advance of the interview.

You will want to compare Form 3: Checklist for Bathroom Activities with Form 4: Bathroom Storage Inventory. Are there supplies needed for an activity that are not included on the storage inventory? Do some of the storage items suggest activities that are not included on the checklist? You may need to go back to the client for clarification.

If you are going to design a clothes closet adjacent to, or integrated into, the bathroom, you may need more detail than is provided in the bathroom storage inventory. Form 11: Clothes Storage Inventory for Hanging Clothes, Form 12: Clothes Storage Inventory for Folded, Rolled, and Other Types of Clothes, and Form 13: Worksheet for Folded or Rolled Clothing are available to gather specific information for designing closets. If you will be incorporating an exercise area in or near the bathroom, you may want to use Form 15: Assessment for Exercise Area to help in planning the space. These forms are provided and discussed in chapter 9, "More Than a Bathroom," along with more information about planning closets and exercise areas.

Towels

Towels need special consideration when designing a bathroom. In addition to the storage inventory information on towels, you need to consider the regular users of the bathroom, their activities, and the size towels they use, to determine how many towel bars are needed. Do not forget to ask about special towel storage features, such as heated towel bars or towel warmers.

Your client may want a linen closet in, or adjacent to, the bathroom. Refer to chapter 9 for Form 14: Linen Closet Storage Inventory for more information on planning linen closets.

Form 4: Bathroom Storage Inventory

Instructions: This inventory is divided into sections representing areas in the bathroom. Many of the typical items found in bathrooms are already listed. Check those items you want to store in the bathroom. Add any additional items needed. Complete the form, indicating how many of each item you have, how frequently you use it, and the type of storage you would like. Blank lines are included for items you have that are not listed. A space for notes is at the end of each section. Include information about special size or space requirements, items that need to be stored away from children, or other important details.

Items Stored Near the Vanity/Lavatory/Grooming Center

✓	Item to Store	How Many?	Frequency of Use		Type of Storage			
			Often	Sometimes	Cabinet	Open Shelf	Drawer	(Other Describe)
	Barrettes, pins, clips							
	Contact lens supplies							
	Curlers: electric							
	Curling iron							
	Hair brush, comb							
	Hair care products, e.g., mousse, gel							
	Hair dryer							
	First aid supplies							
	Glasses: drinking							
	Lotion							
	Make-up/cosmetics, e.g. mascara, lipstick							
	Medicines, vitamins							
	Nail clippers, files							
	Nail polish, manicure supplies							
	Perfume, cologne							
	Razor							
	Razor, electric							
	Shaving cream, after shave							
	Soap							
	Tissues							
	Toothbrush							
	Toothbrush, electric							
	Toothpaste, dental floss							
	Towels, face							
	Towels, hand							
	Tweezers							
	Additional vanity/lavatory/grooming items:							

Notes:

(*continued*)

✓	Item to Store	How Many?	Frequency of Use		Type of Storage			
			Often	Sometimes	Cabinet	Open Shelf	Drawer	(Other Describe)
	Bubble bath							
	Cleaning supplies							
	Clothes: dirty							
	Clothes: robe, pajamas or sleeping clothes							
	Clothes: underwear							
	Douching equipment							
	Lotion							
	Powder							
	Radio, CD player							
	Razor							
	Scale							
	Shampoo, conditioner							
	Shower gel							
	Soap							
	Sponges							
	Squeegee							
	Television							
	Towels, bath							
	Towels, bath sheets							
	Towels, face or hand							
	Towels, guest							
	Toys							
	Additional bathtub/shower items:							

Items Stored Near the Bathtub/Shower

Notes:

(continued)

Form 4: Bathroom Storage Inventory (*continued*)

Items Stored Near the Toilet/Bidet									
✓	Item to Store	How Many?	Frequency of Use		Type of Storage			
			Often	Sometimes	Cabinet	Open Shelf	Drawer	(Other Describe)
	Books							
	Diapers: clean							
	Diapers: soiled							
	Magazines, newspapers							
	Medicines							
	Sanitary napkins, tampons							
	Soap							
	Toilet bowl brush							
	Toilet bowl cleaners							
	Toilet paper							
	Towels							
	Wet wipes							
	Additional toilet/bidet items:							

Notes:

(*continued*)

Other Items to Store (if a separate linen or clothes closet is planned, additional information may be needed)								
✓	Item to Store	How Many?	Frequency of Use		Type of Storage			
			Often	Sometimes	Cabinet	Open Shelf	Drawer	(Other Describe)
	Accessories, e.g., scarves, belts							
	Clothes: folded clothes							
	Clothes: rod storage (specify height)							
	Clothes: rod storage (specify height)							
	Coffee maker							
	Coffee or tea supplies, e.g., cups, spoons							
	Exercise equipment							
	Household linens, miscellaneous							
	Household linens, pillows							
	Household linens, pillow cases							
	Household linens, sheets							
	Jewelry							
	Laundry products							
	Robe, pajamas, nightgown							
	Shoes, slippers							
	Additional items:							

Notes:

(*continued*)

Form 4: Bathroom Storage Inventory (*continued*)

Items For Display								
✓	Item to Store	How Many?	Frequency of Use		Type of Storage			
			Often	Sometimes	Cabinet	Open Shelf	Drawer	(Other Describe)
	Antiques							
	Baskets							
	Bottles, jars, bowls							
	Decorative items, miscellaneous							
	Pictures, artwork							
	Plants							
	Additional display items:							

Notes:

YOUR CLIENT'S BATHROOM PREFERENCES (FORM 5)

After determining bathroom activities and storage requirements, you need to ask your client what they do and do not like in a bathroom—and what is feasible for their space and budget.

Begin with their current bathroom(s), even ones they are not planning to remodel (at this time). Ask what they do not like about the space. Be very specific. Let your client volunteer information first, such as:

- There is not enough light over the vanity.
- The space feels crowded.
- There are not enough towel bars.

Then ask what they do like, such as:

- The bathtub is comfortable for soaking.
- The towel racks are convenient to the shower.

Ideas suggested by your client, positive or negative, can indicate areas of strong feeling. Remember these as you develop your design.

Next, ask your client to talk about what they want in a bathroom. Let them suggest ideas, but be sure to cover the major features. Form 5: Your Client's Bathroom Preferences can help you collect and organize this information.

Client's Preferences and Specifications

Many clients think and dream about a bathroom project before it becomes a reality. They read shelter magazines, visit showrooms, and surf the Internet. Many have a file of ideas about design, products, fixtures, materials, and other features. By asking questions about preferences—or definite specifications—you are moving from general ideas to specific decisions to be made about the design.

In some cases, your client may have a specific item from the current bathroom to be included in the new one. Or, they may have salvage items, such as cabinet or door hardware, to include in the new design. Be sure to determine if there are any pieces like this. Get detailed information such as size, and any mechanical requirements such as plumbing connections. Form 5: Your Client's Bathroom Preferences will prompt you to collect this information.

Some clients may prefer to shop for, and select, certain pieces such as a mirror or a faucet, on their own. If the client is going to provide items for the new bathroom, this information will need to be specified in your contract. You and your client will need to agree on the specifications of the items they will provide. Timing will be important as well, so that the installation of the new bathroom is not delayed waiting for a client-provided item.

Budget

At some point, you will need to discuss the project budget. Unless your client has carefully researched the issue before meeting with you, there is a good chance that their budget amount is not in the same range as their ideas. You will probably want to get an idea of the client's budget at the time you are gathering the information you need to develop the design. The farther their ideas are from their pocketbook, the more you will need to focus on priorities. Help your client think about what they really need, want, and would like to have, in their bathroom. The clearer these ideas, the easier it is to make budget decisions.

Form 5: Your Client's Bathroom Preferences

Use these questions to get general ideas about your client's preferences, and then as a check to make sure you have the specific details needed.

Features

- Are there specific materials, fixtures, cabinetry, or other features that have been preselected by the client that are to be included in the project?
- Do they want a shower or bathtub? If they want both, will they be separated or a combination?
- Do they want a toilet, a urinal, or both?
- Do they want a bidet?
- How many lavatories do they want? Do they have ideas about the style?
- Do they want luxury features, such as a jetted tub or spa, soaking tub, steam shower, or sauna?
- What about clothes storage? Will this be adjacent to or included in the bathroom space?
- Do they want a linen closet in the bathroom? Will it be used to store household linens or just towels?
- Do they want to include a laundry area? What about a washer or dryer?
- Do they want an exercise area?
- Do they want a food or drink area, such as for coffee, tea, or snacks? Will this area include appliances, such as a coffee maker, refrigerator, or microwave? Should this area include a separate sink?

Layout

- What ideas do they have about arrangement of the bathroom?
- Do they have ideas about areas that should be spacious or compact?
- What areas should be open to another?
- Do they want a compartmentalized bathroom? If so, what areas should be separate?

Windows

- Will the bathroom have windows?
- Should the window(s) be operable?
- What style of window is preferred?
- Is there a view to be considered? From where in the bathroom should the view be visible—such as the bathtub or vanity?
- What about window privacy?

Doors

- From what rooms will they enter the bathroom?
- Should the doors swing in or out? Or is a pocket or folding door preferred?
- Is a locking door preferred?

General Preferences

- Style?
- Color?
- Architectural details retained in existing space?
- Architectural details added in new bathroom design?

Cabinetry

- Door style?
- Type of wood or face material?
- Color?
- Hardware?

Fixtures—Style, Color, Material

- Lavatory?
- Bathtub?

(continued)

- Shower?
- Toilet?
- Urinal?
- Bidet?
- Other fixtures?

Fittings
- Material or color? Style?

Countertops
- Material?
- Color or pattern?
- Backsplash?
- Edge treatment?

Finish Materials
- Floors? Heated?
- Walls?
- Ceilings?
- Doors, windows?
- Moldings and trims?

Lighting
- Style?
- Control features?
- Type of light sources?
- Furniture?

Accessories
- Towel bars or warmers?
- Toilet paper holders?
- Mirror?
- Full-length mirror?
- Other items?
- Appliances?
- Other materials or fixtures to include?

Scope of the Project
- What is the potential for structural changes in the bathroom, including:
  - Can the location of the bathroom be moved?
  - Is an addition to the home being considered?
  - Is there opportunity to incorporate space from within the home, such as a closet, hall, or bedroom?
  - Is relocating the plumbing an option?
- Will there be other building or remodeling projects that will be happening at the same time as the bathroom?
- Are there specific construction parameters or limitations, such as walls or doors that cannot be moved?
- What part of the project, if any, do the clients want to do themselves?
- Is there any part of the project to be done by another professional designated by the client?
  - Contact information:
- What is the time frame of the project?
- Are there specific events that affect the project schedule?
- Is there another bathroom in the home?
- Are there specific times when the workers cannot have access to the bathroom space?

THE JOBSITE

Before you can begin the actual design, you have one more major assessment. This is of the jobsite. Structurally and mechanically, you need to know if you can make your design ideas work. Unless you are experienced in "reading" a house and understanding its systems, you may want to enlist the help of a contractor or other knowledgeable person to assist you.

New Construction

If your bathroom project is new construction or an addition, get involved in the planning before construction begins. Get a copy of all drawings that impact your bathroom design. Make sure that you have all dimensions and mechanical information that relates to the bathroom.

Study the plans for the new space. Find out what is fixed and what is flexible. For example, can an entry door be moved or a window relocated? Or, can an interior wall be increased in width to make it work as a plumbing or "wet" wall?

Although you may or may not be able to inspect the jobsite when designing for new construction, be sure to review the information in Form 6: Jobsite Inspection (discussed below). This helps you review jobsite factors that may influence your design.

Remodeling (Form 6)

If you are working on a project that is a remodeling, you need to know all the structural and mechanical information as well, but it may be harder to find. A thorough and detailed inspection of the area and surrounding rooms will be necessary. If your client has plans or drawings of the space, this will be very useful and can save you time. However, you will need to verify that the rooms were actually built as drawn. You may want to make copies of client drawings, so that you can mark them up as needed.

Prepare for your jobsite inspection by making an appointment with your client. Give them an idea of what you need to do, and make sure that you have access to all the areas of the home. You may do the jobsite inspection at the same time you do the client interview, especially if you have to travel a distance to your client's home. Wear comfortable clothes that allow you to bend and stretch. Bring a sturdy measuring tape, graph paper (four squares to the inch is recommended), pencils, and a flashlight. A camera will also be useful.

Your jobsite inspection needs to cover several areas: overall knowledge about the bathroom and its relationship to other spaces in the home; structure; mechanical systems; access; construction/installation planning; and dimensions (discussed in the next section). As with the client interview, if you use a prepared form or outline, you will be more likely to get all the information you need. You can follow Form 6: Jobsite Inspection to gain a thorough analysis of the needed information.

Form 6: Jobsite Inspection

The information on this form needs to be collected through a thorough inspection of the existing structure and/or construction documents. You are looking for detailed information! Some information may appear to repeat some of the questions on other forms, which ask for client ideas and preferences. However, use this form to verify specifics at the actual site.

Overall Bathroom

Begin with a floor plan sketch to understand the relationship of spaces and to make notes about structural and mechanical details. Use graph paper (4 squares to the inch) and sketch at a scale of 1/2" = 1' 0" or use a metric scale of mm or cm at a ratio of 1:20. See the following questions for additional information to add to your sketch.

Note the following information on your bathroom sketch:

- What rooms are above, below, and around the existing bathroom space?
- Can any of the surrounding space be incorporated into the new plan? If so, how much—exactly?
- What walls can be changed—moved, removed, or otherwise altered?
- Which windows and doors are to remain or be reused?
- What doors and windows can be changed—moved, removed, or changed in size or type?
- What fixtures are to remain? Are they to be left in the same location, or can they be moved?
- Is there cabinetry that is to be left in place or reused in the new design?
- Which way do the floor joists run? Does the floor seem sturdy and stiff?
- Are there load-bearing walls to consider?
- Where does plumbing come into the space?
- Where are the soil stack and other drain/waste/vent pipes?
- Where are existing ducts and registers located? Can these be moved?
- What is the condition of finish materials—floors, walls, and ceilings? Are any of the finish materials to remain unchanged?
- Is there a view from the bathroom? Is the view from the bathroom important? Determine the following additional information about the bathroom:
  - Bathroom is on

☐ north	☐ northeast
☐ east	☐ southeast
☐ south	☐ southwest
☐ west	☐ northwest

- If new fixtures are to be installed, are they to be put in the same location as the old fixtures?
- If the remodeled bathroom project will impact on the exterior of the home, are there any restrictions to be considered? Will existing siding or roof materials be easy to match?
- Are there any home improvements or repairs to be incorporated into the bathroom project, such as new siding or a roof replacement?
- If the home is older than 1978, could there be lead-based paint or asbestos in the existing space?

Structure

- What is the construction of the house?
- What is the condition of the existing structure? Look for sound and level floors, squareness of corners, and materials in good condition. Do floors squeak?
- Is there evidence of water leaks or pest damage?
- What size are the joists and will they be adequate support for the new fixtures?
- Are windows and doors in good repair and do they operate smoothly? Are new or replacement windows and doors to match the existing windows with respect to type, size, style, and material?
- Is the home well insulated? Are doors and windows energy-efficient?

(*continued*)

Form 6: Jobsite Inspection (*Continued*)

Mechanical Systems

- Can you relocate any plumbing pipes?
- What is the capacity of the plumbing system?
- What size are the supply pipes? Is there adequate water pressure?
- Is the water of good quality?
- Will you be able to add additional fixtures, or higher-capacity fixtures to the existing plumbing?
- Where is the water heater? What is its capacity?
- Can the soil stack and other drain/waste/vent pipes be relocated if needed?
- Where are the traps, and what type are they?
- Is the home on a municipal or private sewage system? Are there any concerns about system capacity if the amount of wastewater is increased?
- How many electrical circuits come into the space, and what is the capacity?
- Do the circuits have GFCI (ground fault circuit interrupter) protection?
- Is the wiring in good condition?
- Can existing receptacles be moved?
- If needed, are 240-volt circuits available?
- Where is the electrical service panel for the house?
- Can additional electrical circuits be added if needed?
- How is the existing space heated and cooled? Is the current HVAC (heating, ventilating, and air conditioning) equipment in good condition and adequate in size?
- If there will be an increase in the size of the bathroom, will the HVAC system be adequate?
- Is there an exhaust ventilation system? Is it adequate in size? How is make-up air provided?
- Does all or part of the ventilation system need replacement?

Access

- What size are any doors between the bathroom and the exterior of the home? Are there narrow hallways or sharp turns? Will there be any problems in removing or bringing in large, bulky, and/or heavy fixtures?
- Is this an apartment that must be accessed by an elevator? What are the size limitations of the elevator?
- Is there finished living space above or below the bathroom? Will you be able to open up floors, ceilings, or walls to get access to plumbing, electrical, and HVAC systems?

Construction/Installation Planning

- Can fixtures, cabinetry, and materials be stored at the jobsite? How much space is there? Is the storage secure and protected from the weather?
- Where will trash be collected?
- How will workers get into and out of the jobsite? Is there carpeting or furniture that needs to be protected?
- Where can workers park? Where can they take breaks or eat lunch?
- What about smoking, playing music, eating, and drinking at the jobsite? What about bathroom facilities for workers' use?
- Do community or building restrictions apply to construction projects, such as time restrictions for use of an elevator for deliveries, construction equipment access and parking, or notification of neighbors?

Dimensions (Forms 7 through 10)

Accurate dimensions of the existing space are critical for a renovation project. This is also true for any fixtures or structural elements that will remain in the newly designed space or will be reused or repurposed. Many designers make a second trip to the client's home to verify all measurements and determine the accuracy of their design.

To collect dimensions of mechanical devices, fixtures, and structural elements, you can use:

- Form 7: Dimensions of Mechanical Devices
- Form 8: Window Measurements
- Form 9: Door Measurements
- Form 10: Fixture Measurements

As a reminder, all the needs assessment forms are also available online at www.wiley.com/go/bathplanning.

Following are suggestions on how to collect accurate and complete measurements. Make your drawings at the site (client's home) on graph paper. Alternatively, take your laptop and enter the drawings directly into a computer-aided design drawing program. Date your drawings and label with the client's name and jobsite location.

- Measure each wall. Take at least two measurements, one low and one high on the wall, to help determine variations in corners.
    - Prepare a dimensioned drawing, to scale (suggest 1/2" = 1'0" or a ratio of 1 to 20 in metric using mm or cm), of the bathroom space. Be sure to include wall thickness. Double check each dimension and record your numbers carefully.
    - In a complex space, you may wish to prepare more than one dimensioned drawing. One drawing will note the correct dimensions of the space and additional drawings will be used to note other details, as noted below.
- Measure the ceiling height in several places.
    - Project an elevation of each bathroom wall, verifying the dimensions of each wall. You will use these elevations to note the location of architectural features, mechanical devices (Form 7), windows (Form 8), doors (Form 9), and fixtures to remain (Form 10).
- If needed, prepare a reflected ceiling plan to note features on the ceiling, such as heat registers, beams, or lighting.
- Locate each mechanical connection, such as the soil stack, plumbing supply pipes, and electrical receptacles. Locate these features on the floor plan or the elevations, as appropriate.
- Measure any architectural features in the space, such as columns, arches, or beams. Locate these features on the floor plan or the elevations, as appropriate.
- Measure the location and size of each heat register, radiator, or other mechanical device. Include items on the walls, floor, and ceiling. Record these measurements on Form 7, and locate these features on the floor plan and/or elevations.
- Measure each window. Measure the size of the window, frame, and overall size of the window including the trim. Measure the location of the window from the floor, ceiling, and corners of the room. Include the height of the sill (Form 8). Note the location of each window on the floor plan and elevations.
- Measure each door, similar to how you measured the window. Locate the height of the door handle. Note the location of doors on the floor plan and elevations. Indicate the door swings (Form 9).
- Measure the size of any fixtures to be removed. Include height, width, and depth. Note any potential problems with removal (see Form 10).
- Measure the size and location of any fixtures to remain. Include centerline dimensions to determine clearances (Form 10).

Form 7: Dimensions of Mechanical Devices

Measure and locate each heat register, radiator, or other mechanical devices. Note whether the location of these items are fixed.

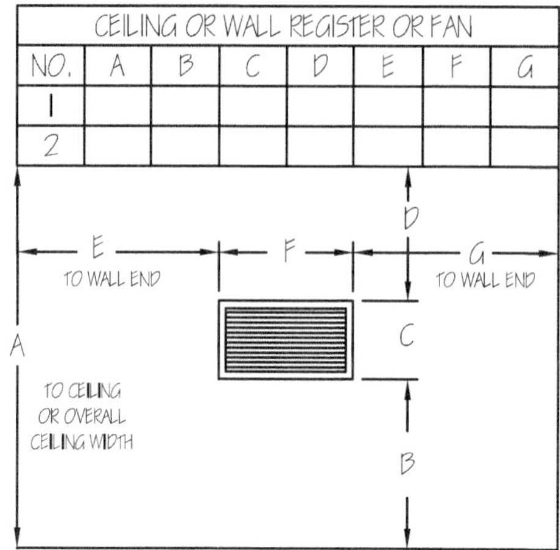

CEILING OR WALL REGISTER OR FAN							
NO.	A	B	C	D	E	F	G
1							
2							

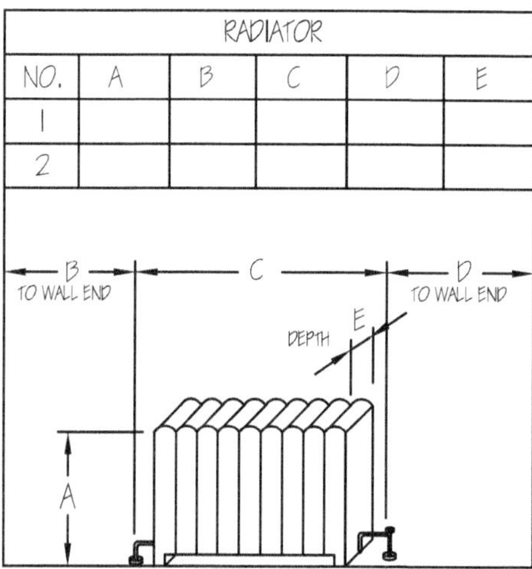

RADIATOR					
NO.	A	B	C	D	E
1					
2					

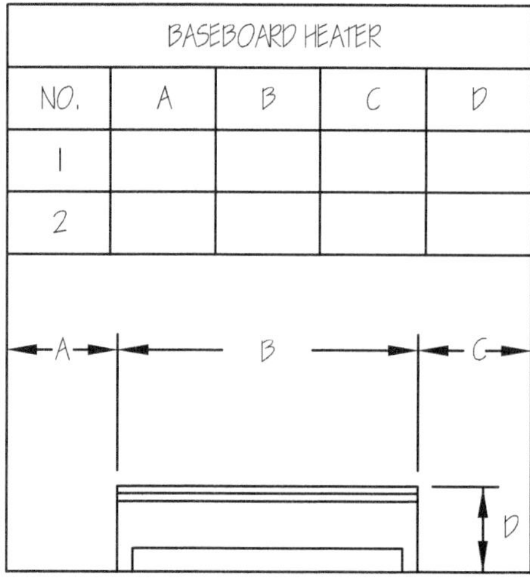

BASEBOARD HEATER				
NO.	A	B	C	D
1				
2				

FIGURE 5.4 Form 7

Form 8: Window Measurements

Note that the location of the window is determined in relation to the floor, ceiling, and both wall corners. Include the size of the window frame.

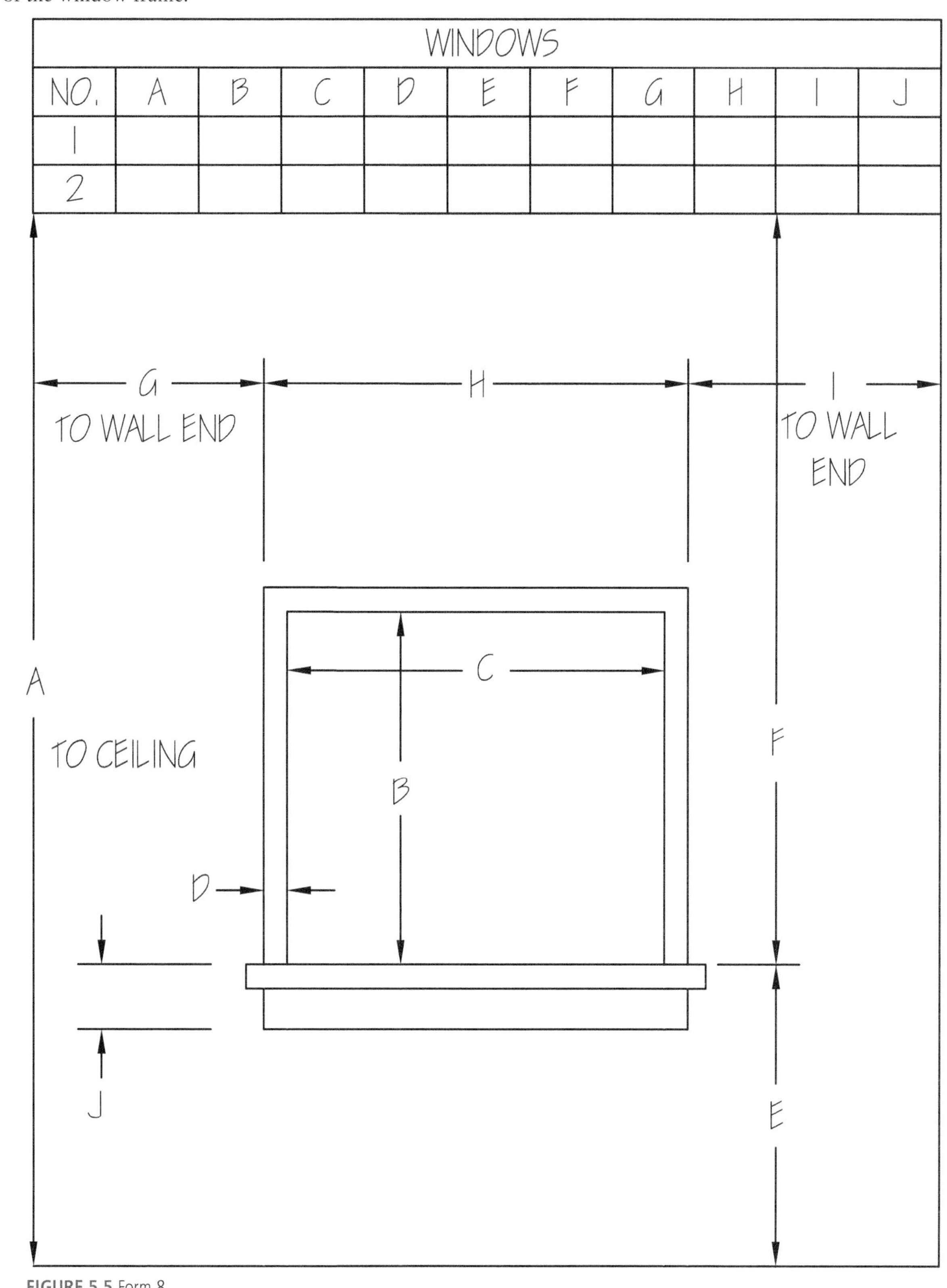

WINDOWS										
NO.	A	B	C	D	E	F	G	H	I	J
1										
2										

FIGURE 5.5 Form 8

Form 9: Door Measurements

Note the location of the door in relation to both wall corners and the ceiling. Include the size of the door and the casing. Note the location of the handle.

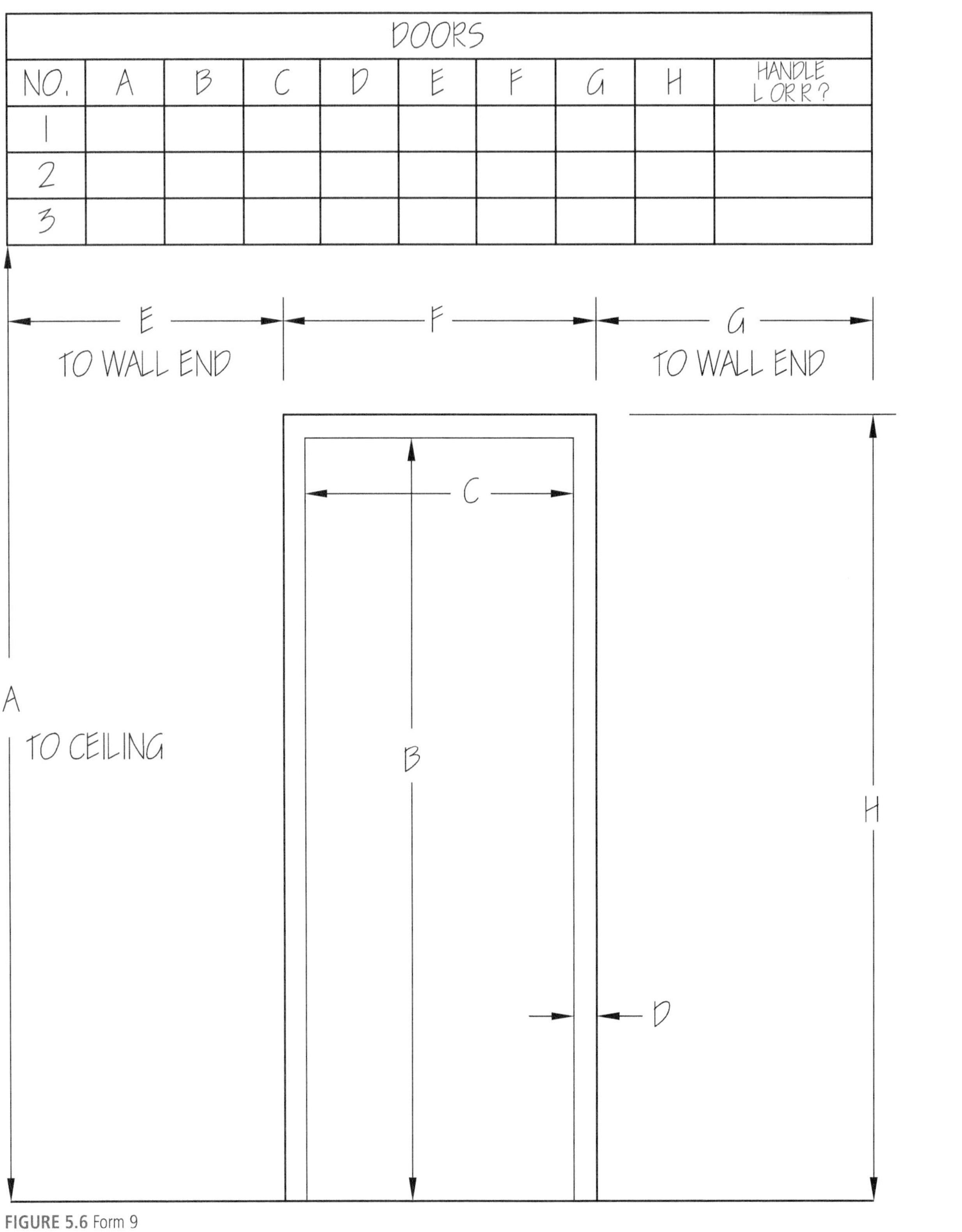

DOORS									
NO.	A	B	C	D	E	F	G	H	HANDLE L OR R?
1									
2									
3									

FIGURE 5.6 Form 9

Form 10: Fixture Measurements

Existing fixtures that will remain need to be measured carefully, including centerline dimensions.

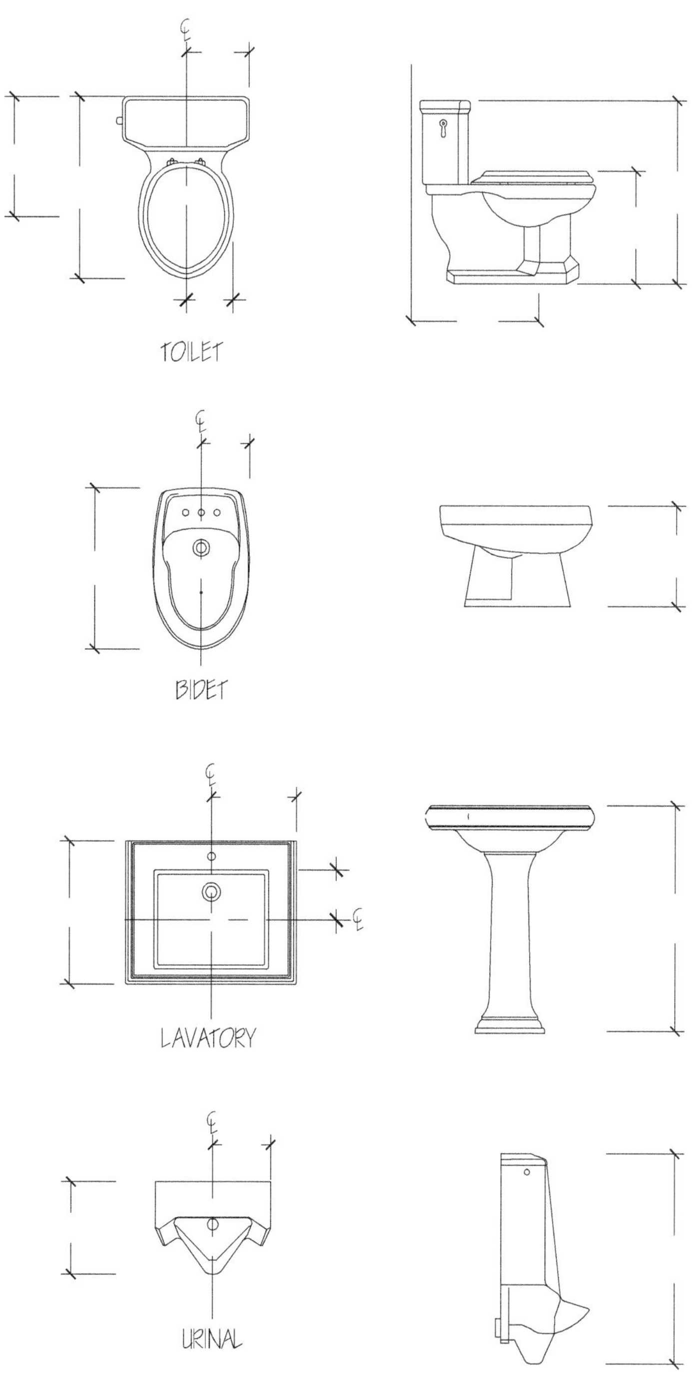

FIGURE 5.7 Form 10

PREPARE THE CLIENT

This chapter has detailed a process for assessing the needs of your client and gathering information necessary to design their bathroom. The process is extensive, but time spent on preparation will increase your success. Now that you are prepared, it's never too early to start preparing your client. At the end of the interview and/or jobsite inspection, or when you present your design proposal or contract, spend a few minutes discussing both the design process as well as the construction phase.

First, discuss the time frame of the project. Present a realistic plan for each phase of the project. Indicate to your client what factors may delay the project, and why. Discuss what you will do to keep the project on target. Suggest what your client can do to keep the project on time, such as minimizing change orders.

Talk to your client about what you will need from them. If they are going to do any of the work themselves, such as tearing out or painting, be very clear as to the time frame. At what point will they be needed to review plans and make color or design choices? When will they need to make decisions about fixtures and accessories? When will they need personal items removed from the workspace?

In a bathroom project that involves an addition or remodeling, there will be disruption in your client's home. Emphasize this with your client and reassure them you will do whatever you can to minimize that disruption. Preparing the client requires continuous communication, starting at the interview stage and continuing throughout the project.

READY FOR THE DESIGN PROGRAM?

After completing the needs assessment, you have a detailed picture of your client and their ideas about their new bathroom. In addition, you know about the users of the bathroom, activities in the bathroom, and storage needs. You have very specific information about the jobsite. It might be tempting to rush in and begin laying out your ideas. But first, you need to think about the next step in the design process. You need to develop a design program.

As you develop the design program, you clarify your client's priorities. The forms presented in this chapter, also available online for your use, can assist you in the process. What does your client need or require in the bathroom project? What do they want to have, and what would be desirable? Your goal is to provide all the needs and requirements, most of the "haves," and some of the "desirables." If you and your client are clear on priorities, then it is easier to make compromises or tradeoffs due to factors such as budget limitations, product availability, or structural problems.

Design Programming

Design programming is the translation of the information about the client into a plan to guide the design process. Developing the design program allows you to make sure you have gathered—and understand—all the information you need to complete the design. In addition, the design program should be reviewed with your client to ascertain that both you and your client agree on the plan for the bathroom project. A design program can even be the basis of your contract.

Design programming is discussed further in chapter 10, "Putting It All Together," as part of the design process, and a sample program is shown there. However, a brief review of the parts of a typical design program is included here to help emphasize the need for careful and complete client information gathering.

Elements of a Design Program

There are many ways to prepare a design program. Here is a suggested outline that has been effective for the authors and their students.

Goal or Purpose. A statement that describes the project and the client, and defines the scope and the parameters of the project.

Objectives and Priorities. A list of the specific features, items, materials, layout, or other details to be included in the design/project.

Activities and Relationships. A list of the different activities to be accommodated in the bathroom, and the fixtures, fittings, materials, cabinetry, lighting, furniture, storage, and other details needed to support the activities. Also included is an explanation of how the different spaces of the activities relate, in terms of access, circulation, or privacy. Some designers may include charts, matrices, or bubble diagrams in this section to visualize the different spaces and the relationships among them.

Consider the design program a working document. After you review the program with your client, you may need to make changes as you fine-tune the project plan. Once you and your client agree on the design program, you may ask the client to sign off on the program. This will give you a firm basis for negotiating any change orders as the bathroom project progresses.

You and your client are now prepared for a successful bathroom project.

SUMMARY

A needs assessment is the first step in the design process. The purpose is to gather detailed information about the client(s) and their home, how they will use the bathroom space, storage needs, and the requirements of the jobsite. Also included in the needs assessment are client preferences, including products, materials, fixtures, and design features. A variety of methods are used in a needs assessment, including client interview, checklists and assessment forms, photography, observation, and measurement.

A design program is a plan to guide the design process. The design program is based on the information gathered in the needs assessment. A typical design program includes the goal or purpose of the project, the objectives and priorities related to the project, the activities to be accommodated in the designed space, and the relationships or adjacencies among the activity spaces. A design program may be presented in various written or visual formats.

REVIEW QUESTIONS

1. What are the advantages of using a prepared interview format when interviewing a client as part of a needs assessment? (See "Needs Assessment Forms" page 112)
2. What is anthropometric information and why is it important to collect this information in a needs assessment? (See "Getting to Know Your Client [Form 1]" page 113)
3. How can the location of the home influence the design of the bathroom? (See "Your Client's Home: Location, Location, Location" page 117)
4. What are the special considerations when designing a bathroom in a multifamily structure? (See "What Type of Home?" page 117)

5. Why is a home tour an important part of the needs assessment? What can you learn from a home tour that will assist in the design process? (See "Getting to Know Your Client's Home [Form 2]" page 118)
6. When conducting a needs assessment, knowing the activities that will take place in the bathroom can provide an understanding of storage needs. Explain this relationship. (See "Storage in the Bathroom [Form 4]" page 125)
7. What is included in a detailed jobsite inspection? (See "Remodeling [Form 6]" page 134)
8. Describe the purpose and function of a design program. (See "Ready for the Design Program?" page 142)

Bathroom Planning

Planning a bathroom requires knowledge about many concepts related to people and their houses. The designer must draw on information about plumbing and electrical systems, bathroom fixtures, finishes, and the people who will be using the space.

This chapter presents background information about the type and location of bathrooms within the home, and gives key information about specific planning issues for various bathroom centers. Information about planning for different types of users is integrated into each section. The National Kitchen & Bath Association Bathroom Planning Guidelines and related Access Standards are presented as they relate to the bathroom centers. These Guidelines and Standards are presented in Appendix A in summary format.

Learning Objective 1: Identify the right bath type for your client and their home.

Learning Objective 2: Describe the various centers (grooming, bathing, toileting) and space planning considerations that combine to create the bathroom layout.

Learning Objective 3: Describe how the Bathroom Planning Guidelines and Access Standards can be used to design bathrooms that meet building code requirements and human factors recommendations.

TYPES AND LOCATIONS OF BATHROOMS

How the bathroom will be used affects the selection of fixtures and determines the type of bathroom needed. Following are brief descriptions of the types of bathrooms found in today's homes (see Figure 6.1):

- Half bathroom/powder room—includes only a lavatory and toilet. It is usually located close to a social area for guests or close to family activity areas, such as the kitchen or outdoors.
- Full bathroom—includes the lavatory, toilet, and a tub and/or shower. It is usually located close to privacy areas of the home.
- Compartmentalized bathroom—includes lavatory, toilet, and tub and/or shower, but one or more of these has been separated into its own compartment. This allows the bathroom to be

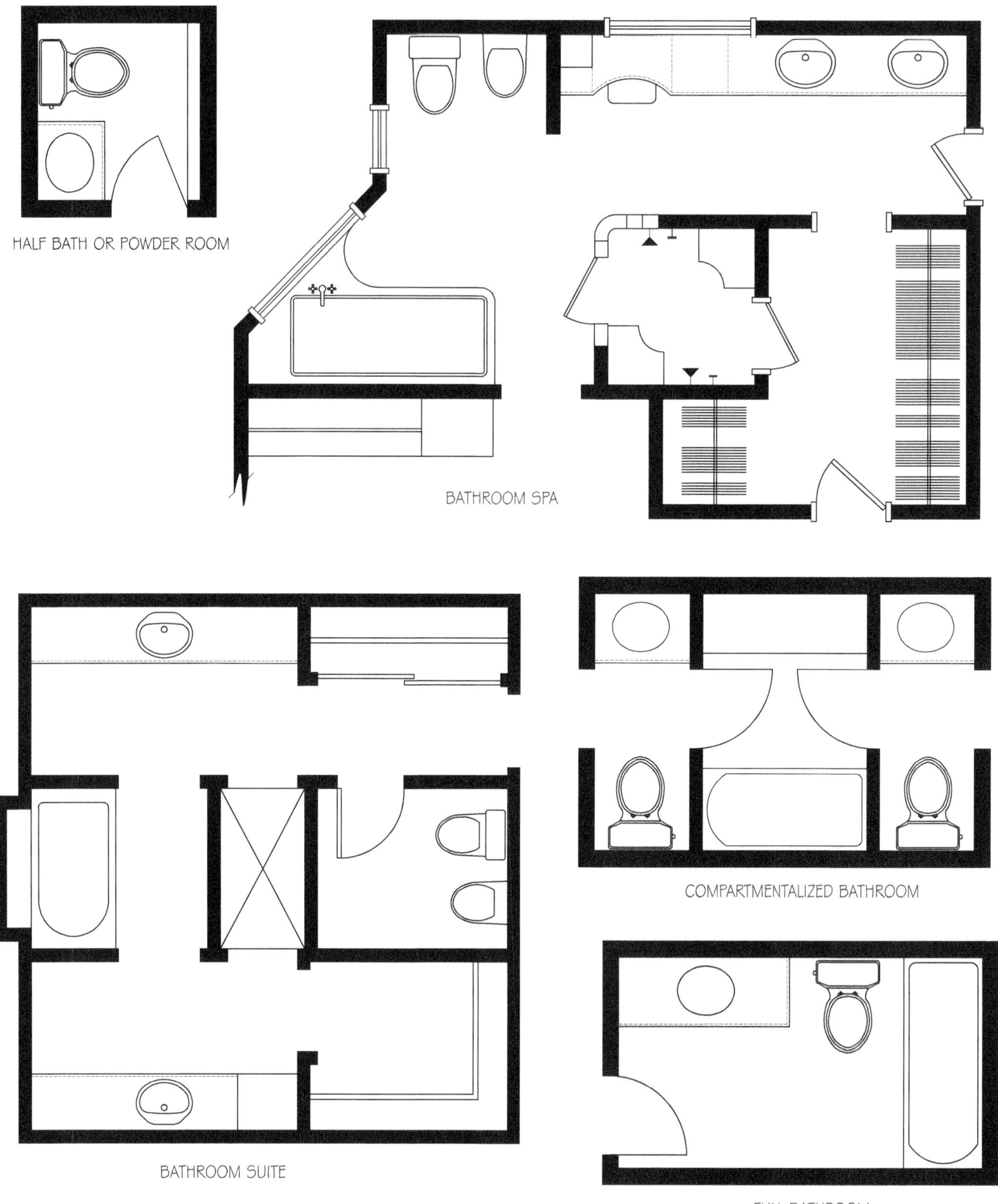

FIGURE 6.1 A variety of bathroom types are found in homes today.
NKBA

used simultaneously by more than one person. It can be located close to social and private areas or between two bedrooms.

- Bathroom suite—includes one or more lavatories, toilet, tub, shower, and various other fixtures and features such as a bidet, vanity, and dressing areas. It is located adjacent to a bedroom, such as the master or guest bedroom.
- Bathroom spa—includes fixtures similar to the bathroom suite as well as one or more spa fixtures, such as a whirlpool or jetted tub, soaking tub, spa tub, sauna, or steam bath.

Location in the Home

Using the bathroom is considered a private activity in the homes of most North Americans. Whether it is bathing or toileting, we often want these activities shielded from guests and other family members. Therefore, the bathroom is most commonly located in a private part of the home, usually close or adjacent to the bedrooms, which are also considered private spaces (see Figure 6.2).

Getting ready for a day of activities or a night's sleep requires some personal grooming and preparation, and locating the bathroom close to the sleep areas is convenient for the user and the rest of the household. In older homes, one bathroom centrally located to all the bedrooms may be typical, but today we often find multiple bedroom or privacy areas, such as master suites, guest suites, and children's areas. This suggests the need for bathrooms to be located in all of these areas.

Separating private and social areas can be handled in many different ways. In some homes, all social areas are on the first floor and all bedrooms are on the second floor. While this provides good separation of private and social activities, some difficulties may arise. A bathroom will still need to be planned on the first floor. A first floor bedroom, or room that can adapt to a bedroom, should be considered in order to provide private spaces for anyone finding stairs to be difficult or a barrier.

FIGURE 6.2 Today we often find bathrooms as part of master suites in the privacy area of the home.

Design by NKBA member: Holly Rickert

Another way to separate private and social areas is to locate bedrooms and bathrooms to one side of a social area. In some homes, all private spaces are together. In others there are separate primary (master suite) and secondary bedrooms, and even a third area (guest suite). All of these would have bathrooms. Plus, the home may have other bathrooms for special activity areas like pools and mudrooms.

Because guests may need to use the toilet and "freshen up," a small bath or powder room is often planned close to social spaces. It is particularly important that this bathroom be planned with universal design in mind so it can be used by any guest. Guest bathrooms may be located close to formal and informal living areas, outdoor social areas, and the kitchen. Sometimes these bathrooms will serve two purposes and be located near, or between, social areas and privacy areas, such as secondary bedrooms or guest rooms.

Wherever the bathroom is, consider the relationship between it and the adjacent spaces. Visual and auditory privacy should be maintained. A guest bath opening directly into a social area or kitchen may present a view of the toilet, making guests feel they are announcing their private activity to everyone, and causing them to feel uncomfortable. Going through a private bedroom to get to the only bathroom is also uncomfortable for guests, as well as the bedroom occupant. Even sharing a bathroom with doors opening into two bedrooms can leave overnight guests feeling uncomfortable about their privacy.

Private Areas

Within the private areas of the home, a bathroom that opens off a hallway is common in older homes. The hall is usually serving several bedrooms. However, if it is the only bathroom, or is also serving as the guest bathroom, it may also be close to social areas. In homes with more than one privacy area, the hall bathroom may serve the needs of occupants in secondary bedrooms. Traditionally, the hall bathroom includes a lavatory, a toilet, and a bathtub with shower. More recently, in homes with multiple bathrooms, this space may include a shower, but no tub.

Shared or compartmentalized bathrooms are also suitable for private spaces of the home. These bathrooms are divided so more than one person can use the space and still have privacy. In one version, the lavatory and toilet are in the same room, and the tub or shower is in a separate compartment. In another configuration, the lavatory is placed in the forward area, and the tub and toilet are placed together. These designs allow one person in the household to use the lavatory and/or toilet, while another is bathing. If visitors will also use the space, the lavatory and toilet compartment might be made available as a powder room.

Another version of the shared bathroom is one located between two bedrooms and only available for the bedroom occupants. This type of bathroom might have three compartments: a lavatory and toilet room on each side, with a tub and/or shower in the middle (see Figure 6.3).

All shared bathrooms provide the opportunity for more than one person to use the space at once, a real timesaver for families on a busy morning. The designer should determine the household's privacy comfort level with this type of arrangement, and be aware that extra space will be needed for circulation paths and doorways.

It may work better to provide two small bathrooms in the same area, so that each person has their own space. If guests and family members share a compartmentalized bathroom, it is best to have only one door in order to control access.

Private Bathrooms

Having a private bathroom for each bedroom is an option that offers the most privacy for occupants. Instead of one hall bathroom serving several bedrooms, each bedroom has a bathroom connected to it. In secondary bedrooms, this might be a small bathroom with a lavatory, toilet, and bathtub or shower. However, the primary or master bedroom often has a more expansive master bathroom.

The master bathroom is often part of the master suite, an area that can be envisioned as the retreat for the homeowners. In its simplest form, the master bathroom has a lavatory, toilet, and bathtub/

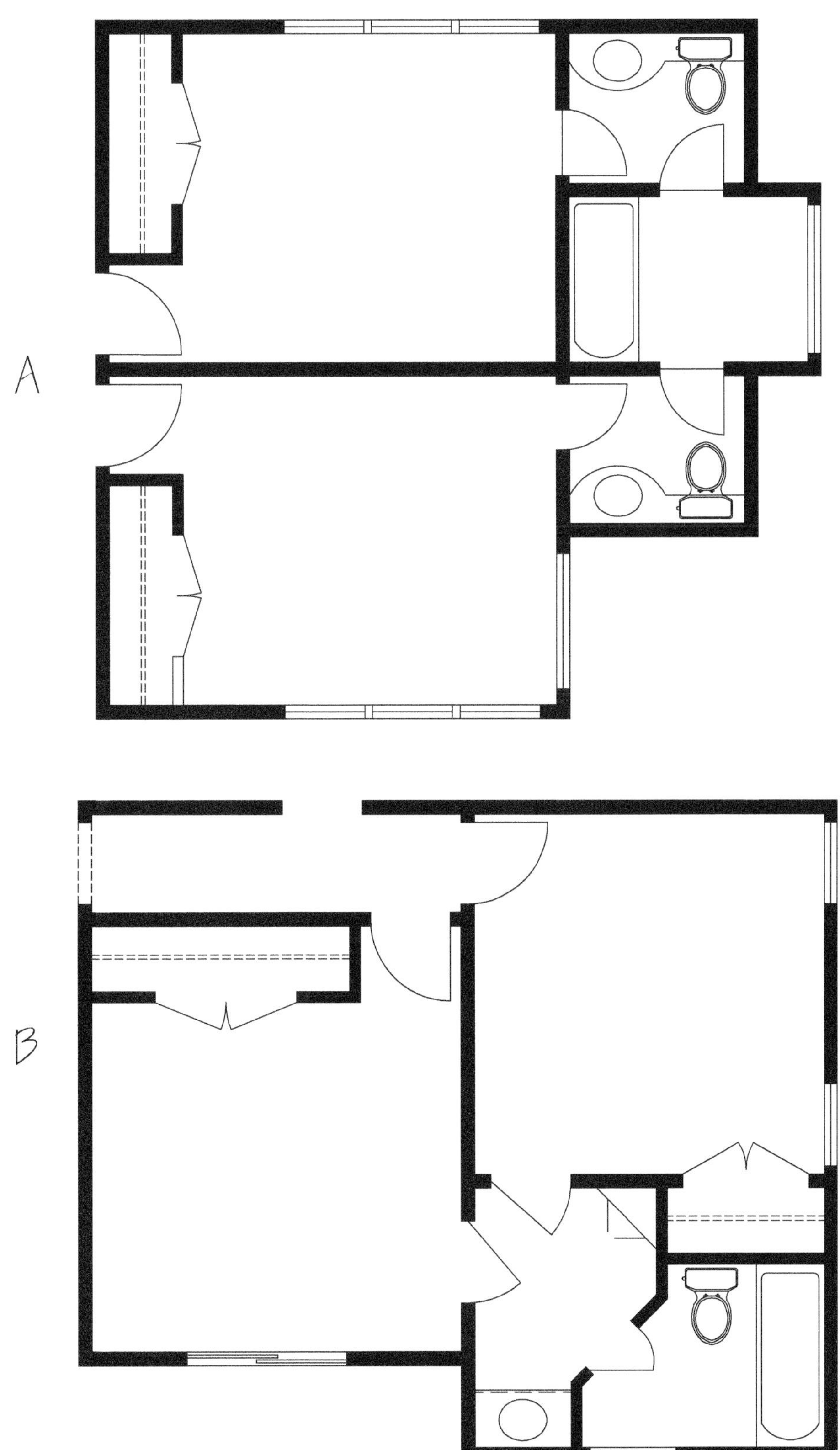

FIGURE 6.3 A bathroom shared between two bedrooms can provide privacy for one occupant to use a grooming area, while another can bathe or use the toilet.
NKBA

shower. However, more expansive options are often planned into the space: double lavatories, separate vanities, separate tub and shower, oversized showers, whirlpool tubs, compartmentalized toilets, bidets, dressing areas, and closets. Luxury master bathrooms might include exercise spaces and spa areas, discussed in detail in chapter 9, "More Than a Bathroom."

When planning a master suite, consider the relationship between the location of entry to the suite or bedroom and the location of the bathroom area. Circulation and visual focal point should be considered so that these spaces flow into one another (see Figure 6.4). From a task analysis perspective, clothes storage and dressing areas should be adjacent to the grooming and bathing areas of the bathroom and not separated by the bedroom. However, placing clothes storage too closely to the wet areas of the bathroom can create dampness and humidity in the area leading to mildew and mold. See the section on closet planning in chapter 9. Also, consider the issues of auditory privacy when placing the toilet adjacent to the bedroom.

Some couples prefer two separate bathrooms, so that each person has their own space. Depending on the size, the two spaces might have each of the basic fixtures. In some arrangements, a tub is in one bathroom and a shower in another. However, some have both fixtures in both bathrooms. These "his and her" bathrooms might be adjacent to separate closets and dressing areas, to provide complete grooming areas tailored to each individual. If the master bath is shared, then two lavatories in separate locations may be convenient and allow for each person to have their own space (see Figure 6.5).

Many homes have a guest room that is part of the secondary bedroom area. Guests are expected to use the hall bathroom or the private bathroom adjacent to their room. Occasionally, a separate suite with many of the features of the master bedroom and bathroom may be planned to provide guests with a more luxurious experience. This arrangement can be comfortable for short-term and long-term guests. It can also serve as a second master suite, should a family member find that differences in nighttime and sleep patterns indicate a need for separate sleeping areas. It can also serve as a caregiver's suite if the need arises.

Children's Bathroom

Bathrooms planned specifically for children require consideration of their ages and needs. This bathroom may be located in the hall of the secondary bedroom area or connected to the child's bedroom. A private bathroom may allow for the selection of fixtures and the design to most accurately reflect the age-specific needs of the child. But a hall bath that will be used by others may require consideration for both the child and other users. Lower, adjustable or tilting mirrors,

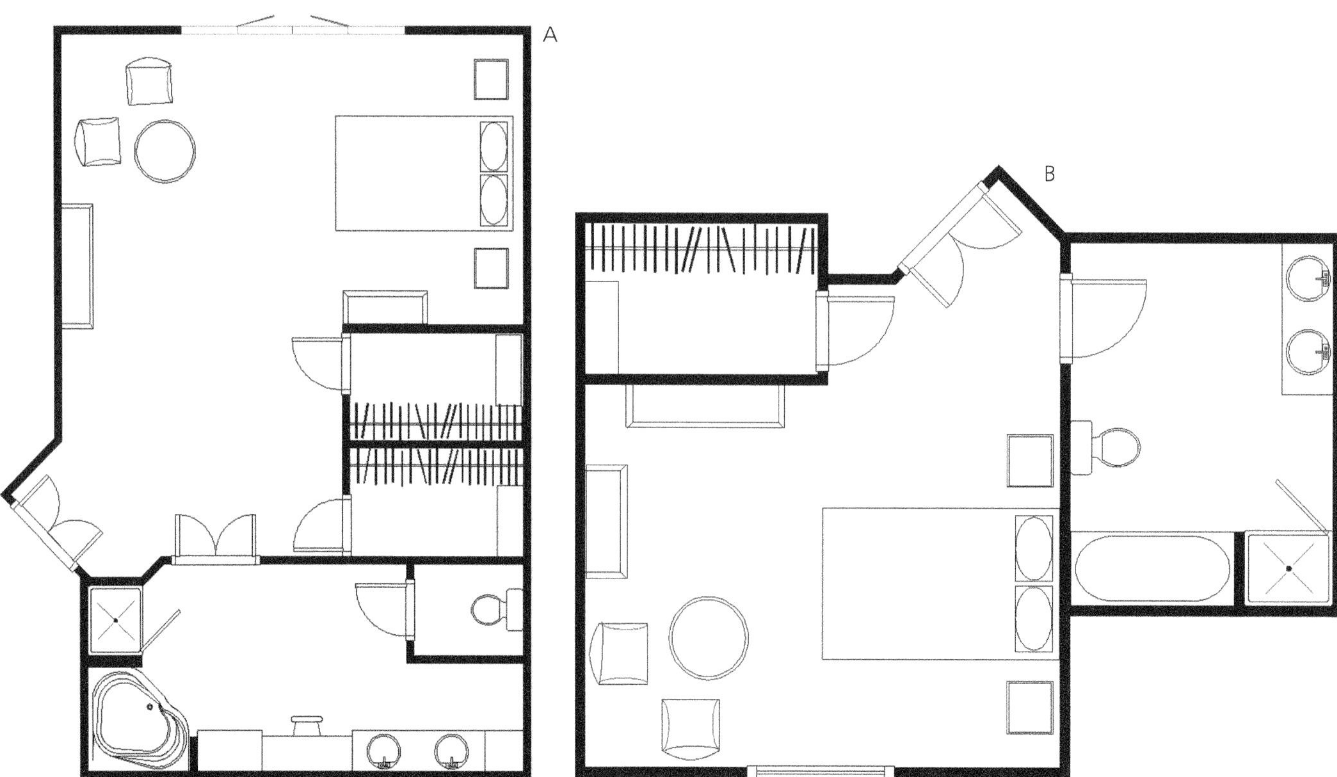

FIGURE 6.4 Consider the circulation, convenience, and the view of the entry to the bedroom suite in relation to the bathroom. In (A), the focus when entering the bedroom suite is the bedroom and the view to outside, while the closets and bathroom are located near each other. In (B), the entrance view is the toilet in the bathroom and the number of doors crowds the entrance.

Rendered in 20-20 by Michael R. Brgoch, CKD

FIGURE 6.5 In this shared bath, each person has their own vanity area so they can get ready in the morning at the same time and have plenty of room for their grooming items.

Design by NKBA member: Lynn David Monson CKD, CBD, Co-Designer: Sandy J. Monson

adjustable showerheads, and stepstools can help to make an adult-sized bath fit children. Remember that children grow quickly. Further information about designing for children is found in chapter 8, "Accessibility in Practice."

Public and Social Areas

Whenever possible, visitors to the home should be able to use the bathroom without having to invade the household's private spaces. Therefore, a bathroom should be planned within the social area of the home. However, placing the visitor bath at the front door or in the entry hall is not a good idea, since this is a very public location and does not provide for visual or auditory privacy.

In order to effectively plan guest or visitor bathrooms, it is important to understand the type and frequency of social activities that are typical of the client. The visitor bathroom should be consistent with the plan for the social areas. Is there formal sit-down dining? Informal open spaces? Basement recreation room? Outdoor living areas?

Considering the social activities and the spaces that accommodate them will help determine the location and type of the visitor bathroom. In some homes, one bathroom might accommodate all of these activities, but in others, several visitor bathrooms might be desired in the various social areas.

Social areas are usually planned on the first floor of the home. If no private spaces are planned on this level, then the visitor bathroom may be the only one convenient to guests and household members using the first floor spaces. As indicated previously, this might be a half-bathroom or powder room, with only lavatory and toilet fixtures (see Figure 6.1). If there are bedrooms that will also use the visitor bath, then a tub or shower should be included. Its placement should be convenient to the bedroom occupants as well as visitors.

Visitors' Needs

The needs of users are always critical to the decisions you will make in designing a bathroom. However, it is not always clear who the visitor in the home will be. Planning the visitor bathroom to be a universally designed space assures that most people will be able to use it.

Several communities and states are adopting visit-ability requirements for new homes. These indicate that as a minimum, there should be a doorway into the home that is accessible, and that doors and passage ways on the first floor should be wide enough for everyone to use. In addition to a door opening that is wide enough, the first floor bathroom should have adequate floor space and grab bars or reinforcement in the walls for future installation in case they are needed (see Figure 6.6).

Outdoor Baths

If a focus of social or household activities is on the outdoor living areas, then ideally there should be a bathroom adjacent to them. For example, a bathroom and dressing area adjacent to a pool or hot tub would provide a convenient space for toileting, showering, and changing without dripping water throughout the house. Some households enjoy an outdoor shower to rinse off beach sand or pool chlorine. Outdoor showers might also be part of a master bath with a private garden area.

Families who use outdoor play spaces for children, or who spend time outdoors gardening, find a bathroom or mudroom close to the backyard convenient for cleaning up before going into the house, or for using while outside. If outdoor kitchens and dining are part of the way the household entertains, then a bathroom close to this area provides a convenience to guests.

Sustainability Concerns

While we have identified numerous types of bathrooms and multiple locations where they can be placed in the home, every house does not need nor are they expected to have all of the variety of options available. Bathrooms require a great deal of water and substantial amounts of energy may be needed to heat the water and operate some of the luxury features that can be incorporated into these spaces. Just the size and use of materials in some large bathrooms diminish efforts to offer sustainable solutions to the built environment. While we as designers would love to create more and more bathrooms, consider reducing the size of a bathroom, maintaining the size of an existing small bathroom, specifying water efficient fixtures, and selecting materials that leave a light footprint on the environment, including repurposing items if possible.

THE CENTER CONCEPT

There are many different ways to approach designing bathrooms. This book focuses on the center concept. A center is an area where a particular task or function occurs. The user, space, fixtures, and other components are all analyzed in order to design a center for a particular task. The basic tasks and corresponding centers in the bathroom are grooming, bathing/showering and toileting.

Each bathroom center is described here separately, the tasks and activities are identified, and requirements associated with completing tasks safely and conveniently are detailed, followed by design recommendations. The Bathroom Planning Guidelines, important to the safe and comfortable use of the center, and some related Access Standards are discussed. For a quick reference, summary listings of the NKBA Bathroom Planning Guidelines, with the Access Standards, are presented in Appendix A.

Universal design concepts and ideas are presented and integrated throughout this chapter to encourage you to think about various user needs while planning the space. Thinking broadly about clients' needs, now and in the future, can help you develop a thoughtful design that anticipates changes that will occur over their lifespan. In chapter 8, "Accessibility in Practice," you will find

(a)

(b)

FIGURE 6.6 This powder room has a wide door and enough floor space that it would meet the criteria for a visit-able bathroom. Grab bars and a clear space under the lavatory would enhance its accessibility even more.
Design by NKBA member: Ines Hanl

expanded ideas and recommendations for designing for specific user groups and further discussion of the Bathroom Access Standards.

NKBA Guidelines and Access Standards

The National Kitchen & Bath Association has been providing information on the design of bathrooms since Ellen Cheever's book *The Basics of Bathroom Design. . .and Beyond* was published in 1989. The Bathroom Planning Guidelines, which first appeared in 1992, have always had a strong focus on safety and building code requirements. The Guidelines have been reviewed and updated periodically to include new information, such as universal design, and in 2003, an NKBA ad hoc committee developed the current Guidelines incorporated in this book. The Guidelines and Access Standards were reviewed in 2011 to assure they were consistent with current building codes and accessibility standards.

The 2003 update of the Guidelines incorporated a review of housing trends and an analysis of the International Residential Code (IRC). Space recommendations are based on documented ergonomic considerations, and code requirements are highlighted. The Guidelines incorporated into this book are consistent with the 2012 IRC. The IRC has been adopted by many states and localities, but designers should check the local building codes to make sure they are in compliance. The Bathroom Planning Guidelines are intended to serve as a reference tool for practicing designers and an evaluation tool for bathroom designs. Designers taking the Associate Kitchen and Bath Designer (AKBD) academic exam will be expected to know the Guidelines and designers taking the Certified Bathroom Design exam will be expected to apply the Guidelines to the designs they create for the exam.

NKBA has led the kitchen and bath industry in promoting universal design. Its 1996 Bathroom Planning Guidelines included recommendations that would make the bathroom universal and accessible, many based on ANSI 117.1 guidelines. Many of the universal design points included in the 1996 Guidelines continue to be incorporated in the current Guidelines.

In this book, Access Standards have been included as planning information that will improve a client's access to the bathroom. Because the International Building Code (IBC) references it, the 2009 Accessible and Useable Buildings and Facilities (ICC/ANSI 117.1) has been used as the basis for the Access Standards. As stated previously, designers should check local jurisdiction to ensure compliance. More information on accessibility standards are found in chapter 4 "Human Factors and Universal Design Foundations" and in chapter 8 "Accessibility in Practice."

An NKBA Access Standard follows each NKBA Bathroom Planning Guideline when appropriate. While these Access Standards and the ICC/ANSI 117.1 standards on which they are based provide a great starting point, designers should closely examine the needs of each individual client to assure that the bathroom is truly useable, not just meeting minimum requirements. The assessment forms presented in chapter 5, "Assessing Needs," should be used to gather information about the client's anthropometric information (Form 1: Getting to Know Your Client), the activities they perform in the bathroom (Form 3: Checklist for Bathroom Activities), and their storage needs (Form 4: Bathroom Storage Inventory).

GENERAL BATHROOM DESIGN

As you examine the space of an existing bathroom or the plans for a new one, there are several general things that should be assessed. Not only are the dimensions of the space important, but the form of the space needs to be considered. How will the space join to adjacent rooms or areas? Are there other openings, such as windows? Is the space a basic rectangle shape or are there curves or angles? How will the user(s) move about the space?

Design Recommendations

The Bathroom Planning Guidelines includes several recommendations that deal with the general layout and design of the bathroom. These include the entry, ceiling height, and circulation spaces within the bathroom.

Entry

One of the first decisions for the design is how to get into the bathroom. Door placement can make a real difference in the available space and in the circulation and sight lines to adjacent rooms. If a major remodeling or new construction is taking place, look carefully at the entry and examine all possibilities for its location. In more modest remodeling projects, there may not be space or budget to allow for a change in door location.

It is recommended that the entry to the bathroom have a 32-inch (813 mm) clear opening between the door jambs (see Figure 6.7). This can be accomplished by specifying at least a 2 foot, 10 inch (864 mm) door. While this is larger than what has been typical in the past, consumers are requesting this enhancement.

Not only will it make the bathroom more spacious, it will accommodate larger people, some people with assistive devices, and a large tub or shower installation. If a doorframe of a remodeled bathroom cannot be modified, NKBA allows a door as small as 2 feet, 0 inches (610 mm), but it will be difficult for many people to use and will not meet basic visit-ability or access standards. It will allow you to get a 21-inch (533 mm) deep vanity into the room, but not larger cabinetry or fixtures.

In many cases, a 3 foot, 0 inch (914 mm) door is preferred as it provides 34 inches (864 mm) of clear opening for even greater clearance. When the clear space of a door is less than desired, a swing-clear hinge may be used to gain clear passage by moving the door out of the opening. For a person using a wheelchair or mobility aid, a minimum of 18 inches (457 mm) on the pull side of the door is recommended to allow room for the person to maneuver around the swing of the door (see Figure 6.8). Actual clearances are impacted by a person's approach and the door configuration. Several of these are detailed in chapter 8, "Accessibility in Practice."

The IRC requires that entry doors and other cabinet doors not interfere with activity centers and circulation in the bathroom (see Figures 6.9 and 6.10). A poorly placed door could interfere with getting into the bathroom or shower to help someone who has fallen. An improperly placed door stop or door knob could interfere with a passage for a person with a vision or mobility impairment.

Traditionally, an interior door swings into the room it is serving, but in some cases it is recommended that the door swing out of the bathroom.

The benefit of this configuration is that someone could more easily enter the bathroom in the event a bather has fallen against the door and is injured. This would be a good safety measure,

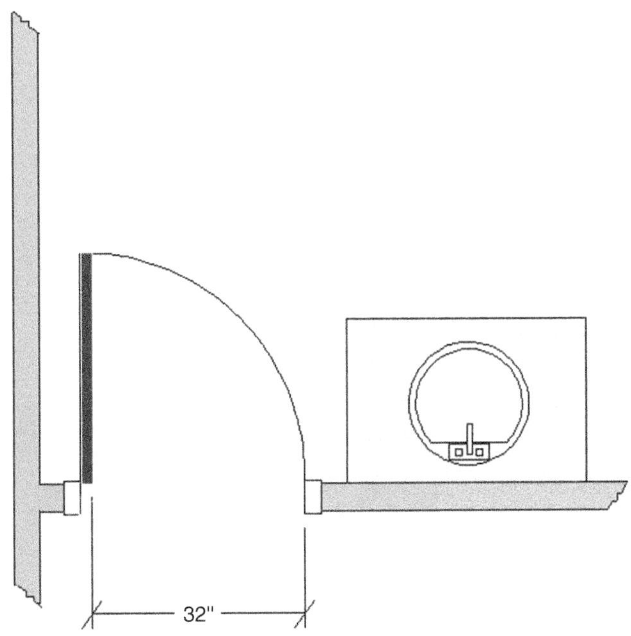

FIGURE 6.7 A 32-inch (813 mm) clear opening is recommended for bathroom entry (Bathroom Planning Guideline 1).
NKBA

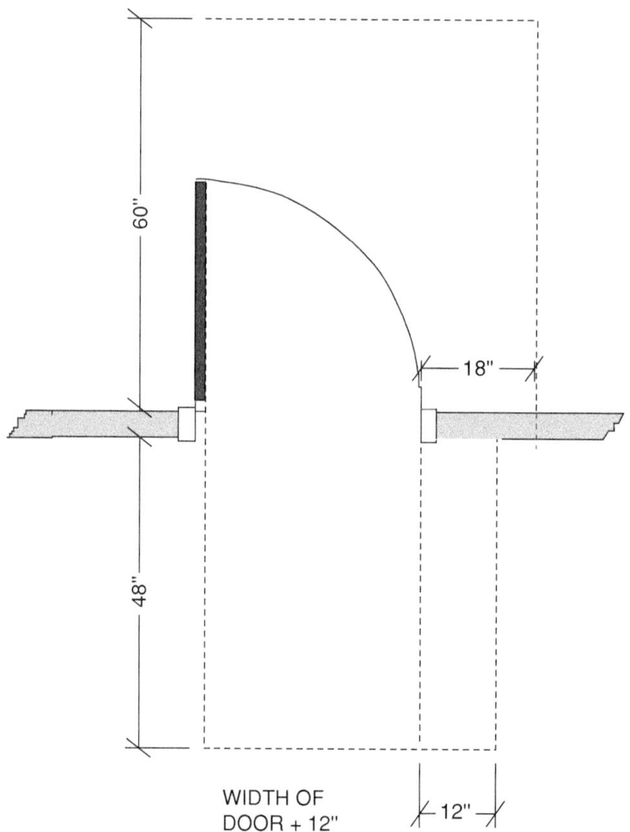

FIGURE 6.8 For a door to be useable by a person with a mobility aid there should be at least 18 inches (457 mm) of clear space on the pull side of the door and 12 inches (305 mm) on the push side of the door (Bathroom Access Standard 2).
NKBA

and it could create more useable room in the bathroom. Of course, the designer must look at the configuration of the adjacent space. Opening a bathroom door into a hallway could be a danger to a person walking down the hall.

Other options might include single or double pocket doors. Although attractive, these are typically higher in cost than a standard door and more challenging to install because they may interfere with the housing of plumbing. A sliding barn-style door may also be an option. In this installation track hardware is placed on the wall above the entry, and a door is hung on the track, allowing it to slide across the opening (see Figure 2.4 in chapter 2, "Infrastructure Considerations").

In private bathrooms, you may consider café doors, which are two doors hinged to the opposite door frames, meeting in the middle, thus reducing the amount of room needed for door clearances. The doors swing in both directions and close automatically once a person has passed beyond the door swing. Others may not need or want a door at all. A single user and certain family members may not feel the need for a full door to assure privacy.

Ceiling Height

Another factor to examine in planning a bathroom is the ceiling height. Most homes will have a ceiling height of at least 8 feet or 96 inches (2438 mm), which is adequate for most people. But occasionally, a bathroom may be planned into a space with a lower or sloped ceiling, for example, a half-bath under the hall stairs, or a bathroom that is part of a finished attic or bonus room.

In these situations, building codes require that there be at least 80 inches (2032 mm) from floor to ceiling over the bath fixture, to allow for use and standing room (see Figure 6.11). A floor-to-ceiling height of at least 80 inches is also required in a shower or a tub with a showerhead.

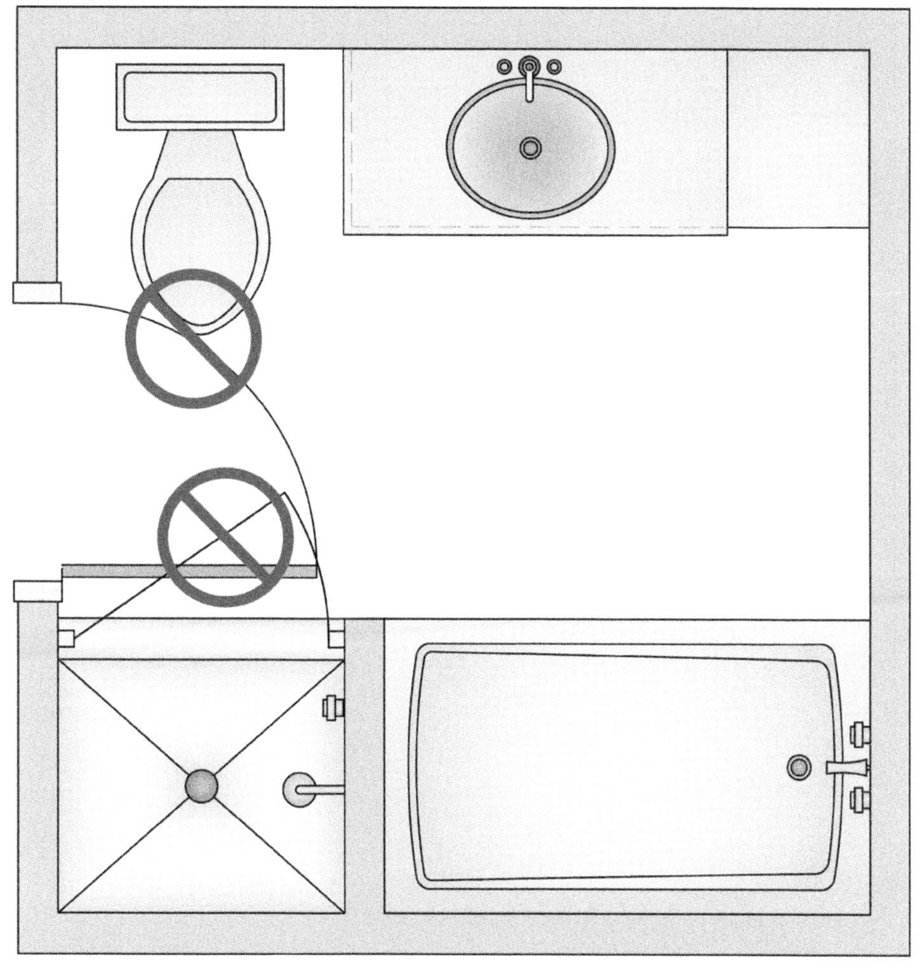

FIGURE 6.9 Doors and fixtures should be planned so that they do not interfere with one another (Bathroom Planning Guideline 2). *NKBA*

Many homes today have ceilings that are 9 feet (2743 mm), 10 feet (3048 mm), or 12 feet (3657 mm) high. These high ceilings can create wonderful spaces, but the designer should carefully consider the proportions of the bathroom space. Dropped ceilings, soffits, and moldings can help bring the volume into proportion.

Circulation

As you look at the options for placement of bathroom fixtures, you will use the information in the sections about the centers. In larger baths, maneuvering space is easier to attain, but careful planning is needed to arrange the fixtures so that they are convenient to use.

In very small bathrooms, the user can reach all fixtures with just a few steps, but clear space for maneuvering may be scarce. The designer has to weigh the needs of the client and the job parameters to reach the best solution.

Bathroom Planning Guideline 4 recommends that at least 30 inches (762 mm) of clear space is planned in front of each bathroom fixture. However, if more than one person will be using the bathroom at the same time, consider providing 48 inches (1219 mm) of clear space which allows for the minimum 30-inch (762 mm) clearance needed for one person to walk behind a person using the fixture (18 inches, or 457 mm) (see Figure 6.12)

If a person will be using a mobility aid, such as a wheelchair, plan a larger space for turning and maneuvering. A 60-inch (1524 mm) turning circle should be included somewhere in the bathroom. If this turning circle is not possible, a 36 inch by 60 inch by 36 inch (914 mm by 1524 mm by 914 mm) T-turn is a possible solution. See chapter 8, "Accessibility in Practice," for more details on planning circulation spaces.

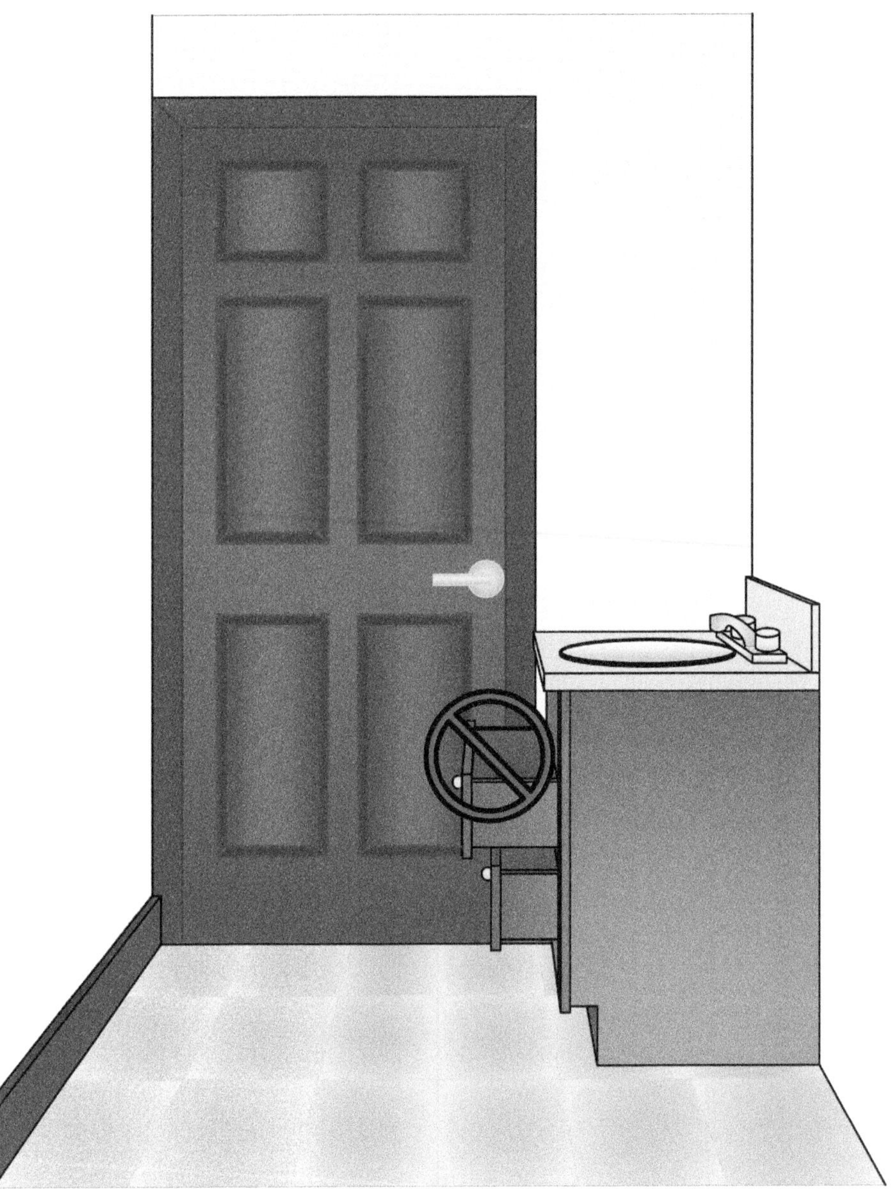

FIGURE 6.10 Avoid planning cabinets with drawers that would block the door when they are pulled out. If there is an emergency, a pulled-out drawer could prevent someone getting into the bathroom (Bathroom Planning Guideline 2).
NKBA

Guidelines and Access Standards

Bathroom Planning Guidelines and Access Standards that are important to the general design of the bathroom are 1, 2, 3, and 4. For the complete Guidelines and Access Standards, see Appendix A.

GROOMING CENTER

The grooming center should not be thought of as just the bathroom lavatory, the fixture with running water and a drainpipe, or the vanity, which is the cabinet that holds the lavatory. While a water source and basin are critical components, many activities occur in this center and it should be designed to accommodate as many client desires as the space and budget permit. The following are some of the key activities to consider when planning the grooming center.

- Washing hands after toileting is an important health measure and using soap is critical to assure that as many germs and bacteria are killed as possible. To effectively wash their hands, the user should be able to place their hands under the water spray while standing or sitting.

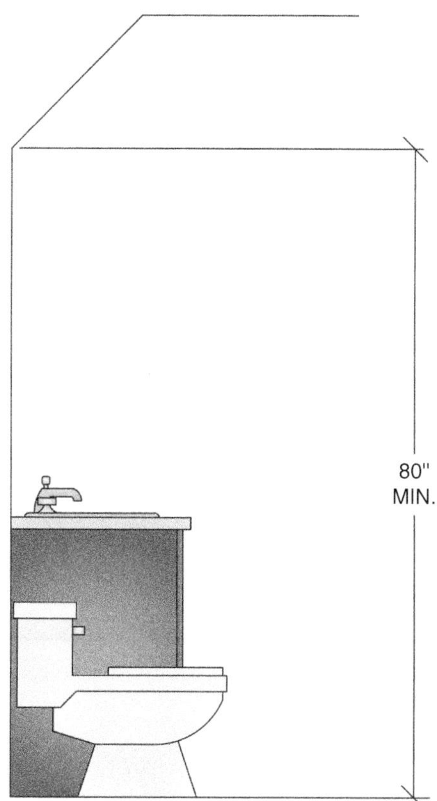

FIGURE 6.11 Allow at least 80 inches (2032 mm) from the floor to ceiling over each fixture (Bathroom Planning Guideline 3). *NKBA*

- Face washing is another important activity that occurs in this center. Usually people bend at the waist in order to place their face close to the water surface, especially if they wash by splashing water on their face. Other people may use a washcloth or cleansing pad and they may remain upright, wetting the cloth and bringing it to their face.
- Brushing teeth is another key activity, and people usually bend at the waist to rinse into the sink. They also stand upright and examine their teeth in the mirror. Other activities might be using mouthwash, flossing, and caring for dentures, braces, or other orthodontic devices. A water source is needed for cleansing brushes and a cup is needed for rinsing, as well as a power source for related appliances.
- Facial care and make-up applications are very important in the grooming routine. The number of products and the steps involved in cleansing and conditioning the skin, and in applying face, eye, and lip make-up, are staggering.

  This activity may require the user to be in the grooming center for some time. Although a water source may be needed, some facial care can and does occur at a seated vanity with water close by. A place to store and access products, good lighting, storage and power for any related appliances, and an appropriately placed mirror are important to successfully completing this task. Chapter 7, "Mechanical Planning," has more information about planning lighting.
- Facial shaving is a similar task. It may be completed with an electric razor (requiring an electric receptacle for use or when charging), or with a blade razor (requiring creams and a water source). As with other facial care, proper location of the mirror and good lighting will be important.
- Hair care may be as simple as combing or brushing hair in front of the mirror. More often, hair styling is done, using gels, mousse, crèmes, and sprays. Several electric appliances may be used to accomplish styling as well: blow dryers, curling irons, electric curlers, crimpers, and straighteners.

  Usually this activity will require an appropriately placed mirror, storage for the appliances, and electrical receptacles that can accommodate the requested appliances. Chapter 7, "Mechanical Planning," can provide information on planning for electrical receptacles.

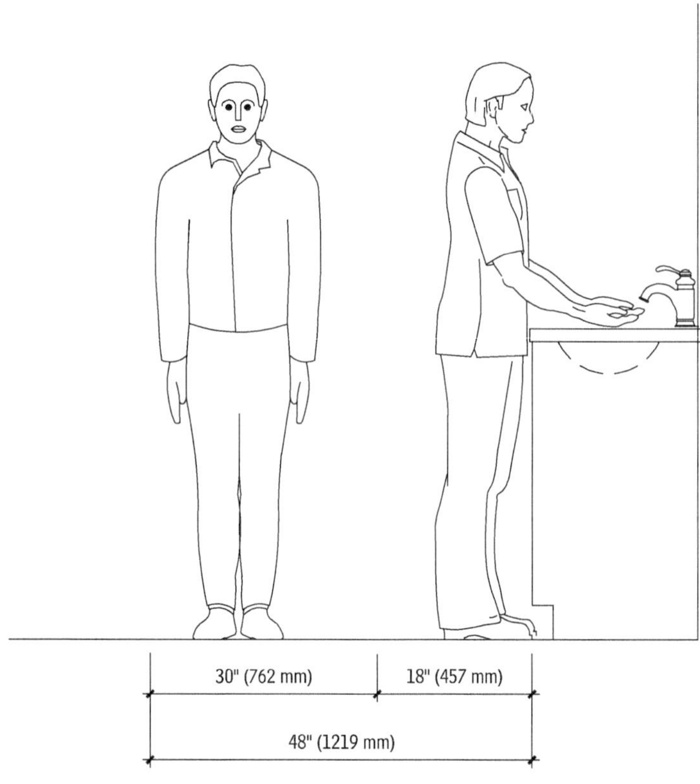

FIGURE 6.12 A walkway of 48 inches (1219 mm) allows 18 inches (457 mm) for a person using a fixture and 30 inches (762 mm) for a person to walk behind them.
NKBA

- Some people store and use medicines and first aid supplies in the bathroom. If medicines are taken first thing in the morning or last thing at night, this may be a good place for this activity.

  Because some medications require refrigeration or must be taken with food, people also take and store medicines in the kitchen.

  Some clients might be interested in having a small under-counter refrigerator in the bathroom, perhaps part of a small "morning" kitchen, to avoid a trip to the kitchen. Some medicines should not be stored in the moist and humid environment of the bathroom.

  First aid supplies might be stored in several places in the house, close to where they are needed, such as in the kitchen, hobby area, or a first-floor bathroom. Storage for these supplies is needed, as well as a sanitary way to dispose of them. The medicine cabinet is often used to store these items, although other storage may be more appropriate. Additional items needed for taking medicine might be good lighting, and a cup or glass.

- Nail care may be performed in the bathroom. Foot baths and massages might be undertaken. Manicures and pedicures require storage for supplies, good lighting, and ventilation, and a seat with a counter area.

Households may have a wide variety of other activities that they complete in the grooming center of the bathroom, so completing an analysis and inventory as provided in Form 3: Checklist for Bathroom Activities in chapter 5, "Assessing Needs," is important for planning.

Design Recommendations for Grooming Center

Considering all the possible activities, important planning considerations at the grooming center include clearance in front of and beside the lavatory; the height of the lavatory; amount and placement of storage; and mirror and towel placement. Lighting and ventilation will be important also, and are discussed in chapter 7, "Mechanical Planning." To plan the grooming center effectively, it is important to review the anthropometric measurements of the user. In the past, the dimensions

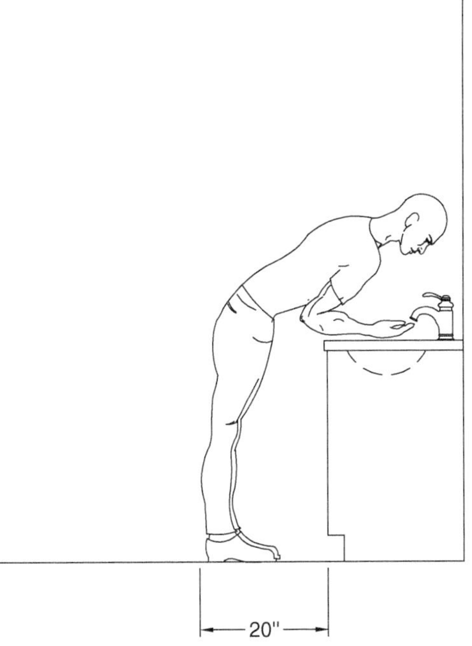

FIGURE 6.13 It takes about 18 inches (457 mm) of floor space for a person to stand to wash their hands, and about 20 inches (508 mm) for a person to bend to wash their face.
NKBA

of standard fixtures and cabinets have often determined this space, but as a designer working with individual clients, you should plan for the needs of the users.

Floor Clearance

The amount of space the human body requires to use the lavatory includes room to stand or sit in front of it. Anthropometric data indicates that about 18 inches (457 mm) of floor space is required to stand and face the lavatory (see Figure 6.12). It is also important to be able to bend at a comfortable angle when washing the hands or face which requires 20 inches (508 mm) (see Figure 6.13). Consideration of space needs for a person who is seated is also important. The space needed for a seated user at a vanity will depend on the chair and person (see Figure 6.14).

While 18 inches (457 mm) may allow some people to stand, it does not account for the movement of the standing user that might take place at the lavatory. NKBA Bathroom Planning Guidelines recommend 30 inches (762 mm) of clearance in front of the lavatory for a more comfortable space (Figure 6.15). This would even allow a person to place a seat at the lavatory. Building codes will permit 21 inches (533 mm) of floor clearance in front of the lavatory, but this will be very tight.

However, 30 inches (762 mm) does not provide adequate clearance for two people to use the space and move around each other, since the average shoulder width is 24 inches (610 mm). A floor space in front of the lavatory of 48 inches (1219 mm) will accommodate two users comfortably. A minimum

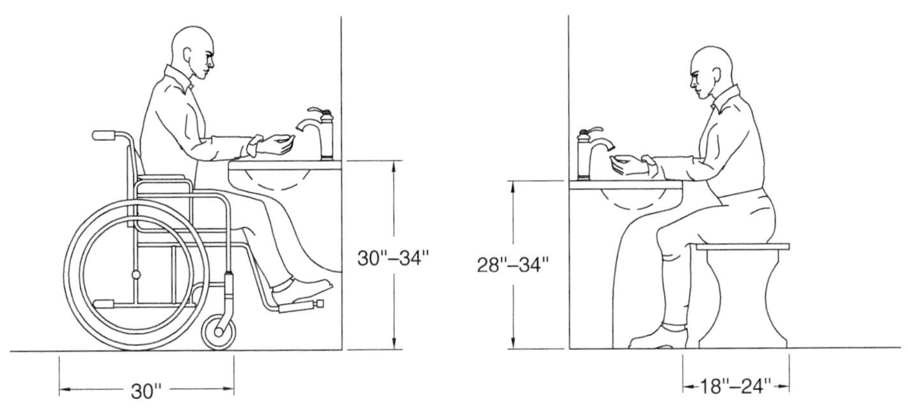

FIGURE 6.14 The space needed for a seated user at a vanity will depend on the chair and person. A wheelchair extends at least 30 inches (762 mm) beyond the vanity, while a small chair may require 18 inches (457 mm) to 24 inches (610 mm) beyond the vanity.
NKBA

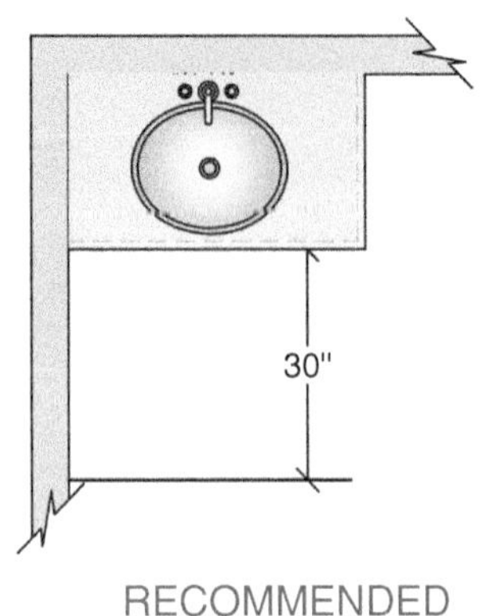

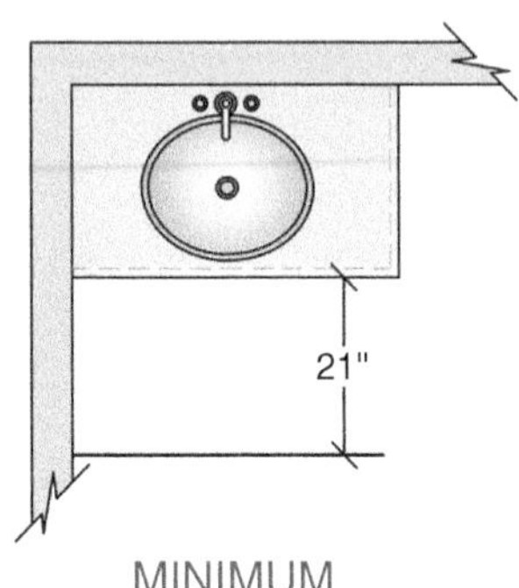

FIGURE 6.15 A clear space of 30 inches (762 mm) in front of the lavatory is recommended for comfortable use of the fixture. A minimum clearance allowed by code is 21 inches (533 mm) (Bathroom Planning Guideline 4).
NKBA

30 inch by 48 inch (762 mm by 1219 mm) space should be allowed in front of the lavatory for a user with an assistive device (Figure 6.16). Pedestal lavatories, wall-hung lavatories, and console lavatories can increase the clear floor space in front of, and under, the lavatory. Refer to chapter 8, "Accessibility in Practice," for more ideas on planning clearances in front of the lavatory.

Side Clearance

Body size affects how much room a person needs on either side of the lavatory. To complete typical grooming activities, a person needs to be able to raise hands and elbows. The recommended distance from the center of the lavatory to a wall or tall obstruction is 20 inches (508 mm) (Figure 6.17A). This provides about 6 inches (152 mm) of clear counter space from the edge of the average lavatory to the wall or obstruction, but even this may not be adequate. Consider the breadth of the user and items placed on the counter to determine if more counter area is needed.

If a wall-hung or pedestal lavatory is specified, allow at least 4 inches (102 mm) between the edge of the lavatory to the wall to be in compliance with the IRC building codes (Figure 6.17B). The minimum distance allowed by the IRC building code referenced in the NKBA Planning Guidelines is 15 inches (381 mm) from centerline of the lavatory to the wall, providing only about 2 inches (51 mm) from the edge of the average lavatory to the wall or obstruction (Figure 6.17C). If planning for an accessible clear floor space of 30 inches by 48 (762 mm by 1219 mm) inches in front of the lavatory, the center of the lavatory should be 24 inches (610 mm) from the wall (Figure 6.17D)

If two lavatories are being planned beside each other, 36 inches (914 mm) between the centerlines of the lavatories is recommended (Figure 6.18A). The code requirement for the centerline distance is 30 inches (762 mm) (Figure 6.18B). The IRC requires a 4-inch (102 mm) clearance between the edges of two freestanding or wall-hung lavatories (Figure 6.18C). These clearances also meet the Access Standards, but more generous spacing may be needed by many users.

Lavatory Height

Work surfaces in the bath, like those in the kitchen, should be about 3 inches (76 mm) below the users' elbow height. Subtracting 3 inches (76 mm) from the average female's elbow would place the comfortable height at 36 inches (914 mm).

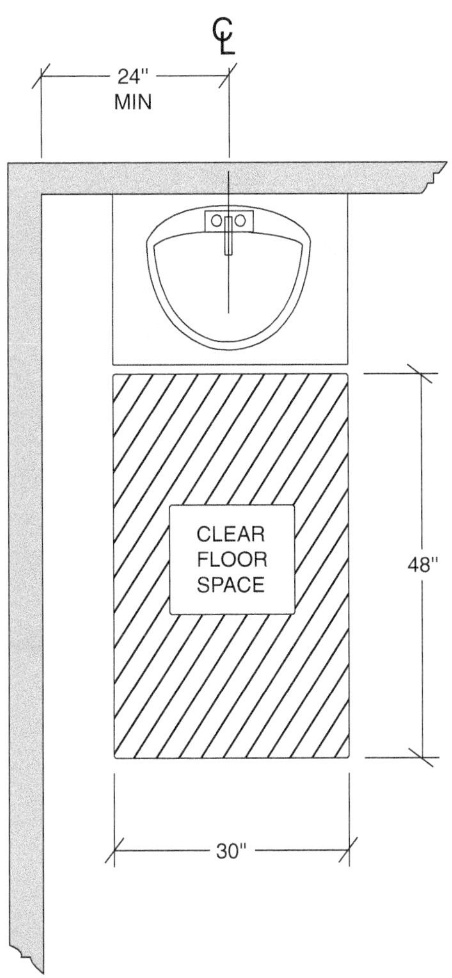

FIGURE 6.16 Accessibility standards require 30 inches by 48 inches (762 mm by 1219 mm) of clear space in front of the lavatory for a forward or parallel approach (Bathroom Access Standard 4).
NKBA

Panero and Zelnik (1979), whose work was discussed in chapters 1, "Bathroom History, Research, and Trends," and 4, "Human Factors and Universal Design Foundations," recommend a range of heights. For men it is 37 inches (940 mm) to 43 inches (1092 mm); for women, 32 inches (813 mm) to 36 inches (914 mm); and for children, 26 inches (660 mm) to 32 inches (813 mm). When a knee space is planned for a seated user at a vanity, the height of the front of the vanity may range from 28 inches (711 mm) to 34 inches (864 mm).

The recommended range of lavatory heights in the Bathroom Planning Guidelines reflects adult users and is 32 inches (813 mm) to 43 inches (1092 mm) (see Figure 6.19). Remember to plan the lavatory height so that the rim is about 3 inches (76 mm) below the elbow of the user.

If two users will use the same lavatory, a compromise will have to be made and discussions with the client will help determine which height is most comfortable. Two lavatories of different heights may be the best solution (see Figure 6.20).

There are many styles of lavatories, and the selection will impact how lavatory height is planned. Wall-mounted lavatories and those placed on wall-mounted counters offer flexibility in the height of the fixture.

Pedestal lavatories are available in a range of heights. In order to reach a height that is appropriate for an individual user the pedestal may need to be placed on a platform. Finish the platform at the baseboard height, and in the same material as the floor, so that it blends.

Several styles of lavatories can be placed in a counter: integral, self-rimming, under-mounted and rimmed. The height of these lavatories will depend on the height of the specified cabinet or counter. A vessel lavatory (see Figure 6.21) can be set on or cut into the counter. In all of these applications, it is important to estimate the actual height of the lavatory rim. A vessel lavatory will sit

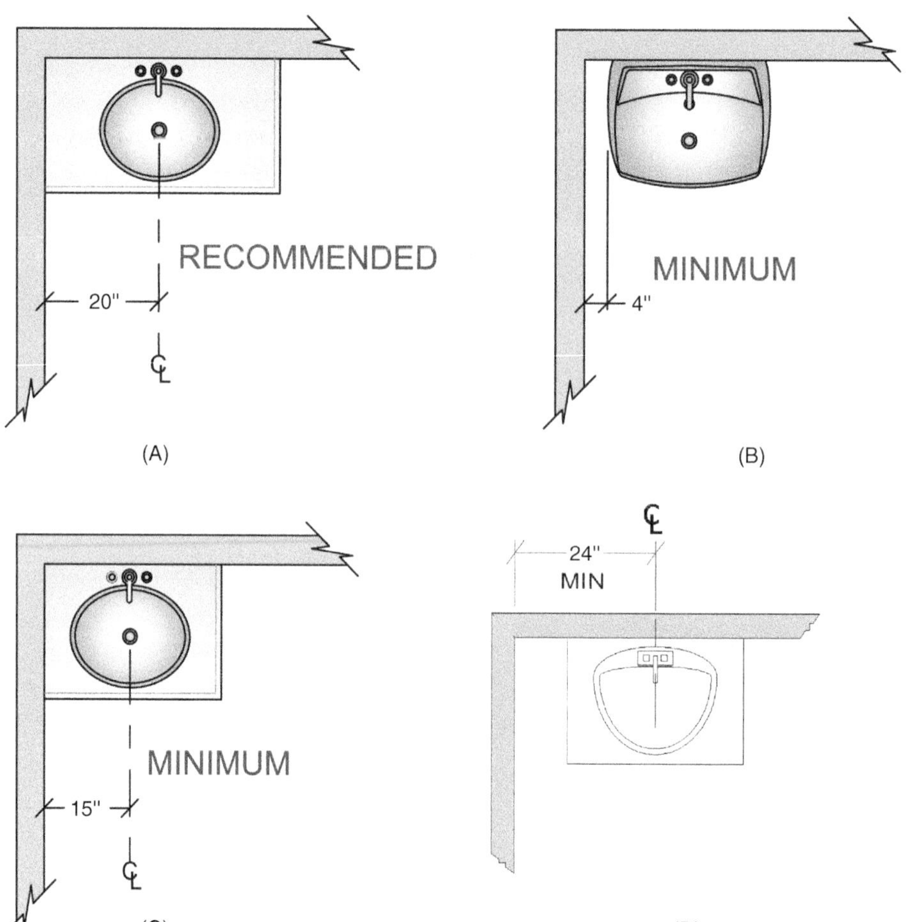

FIGURE 6.17 Placing the center of a single lavatory 20 inches (508 mm) from a wall or tall object provides about 6 inches of counter space (A). If a wall-hung or pedestal lavatory is used, make sure there is at least 4 inches (102 mm) from the edge of the lavatory to the wall to be in compliance with codes (B). The minimum distance allowed by code is 15 inches (381 mm) on center (C). Planning the lavatory 24 inches (610 mm) on center allows for an accessible approach (D) (Bathroom Planning Guideline and Access Standard 5).
NKBA

several inches above the counter, so add the height of the lavatory to the cabinet and counter heights, to get the finished height and make sure it meets the requirements of the client.

Because some vanity bases are low (30 inches to 32 inches; 762 mm to 813 mm), a cabinet or console may need to be adjusted to place the lavatory at an appropriate height. A 34 1/2-inch (876 mm) high cabinet with 1 1/2-inch (38 mm) countertop could be the appropriate height and bathroom cabinetry is available at this height. A standard kitchen cabinet is 34 1/2 inches (876 mm) high, but they also have a depth of 24-inch (610 mm), which may be out of proportion to a specified lavatory, since many lavatories have been designed to fit in the typical 21-inch (533 mm) deep vanity cabinet. The 21-inch (533 mm) deep cabinet also places the user closer to the mirror, allowing for closer examination of the face.

To get the cabinet at an appropriate height, specify a higher cabinet, or raise a standard cabinet by placing it on a deeper toe kick or mounting it on the wall and not using a toe kick. If the toe kick is raised, consider raising the baseboard dimension throughout the room for a clean line at the room base.

If the cabinet is raised, it creates a "floating" effect (see Figure 6.22), which can be enhanced by decorative lighting. Plus, it improves access by increasing clear floor space. The same flooring material used throughout the bathroom should be used beneath the cabinet.

Seated Vanity

A seated vanity can be a comfortable area for applying make-up (see Figure 6.23) and finishing accessorizing an outfit. Placing this feature in the bathroom allows for a nearby water source and therefore is part of the grooming center. However, this feature could be placed in the bedroom or dressing room.

People who wish to sit at a vanity or use the lavatory while seated can benefit from a knee space. The minimum dimensions for the opening under the counter are 30 inches (762 mm) wide by

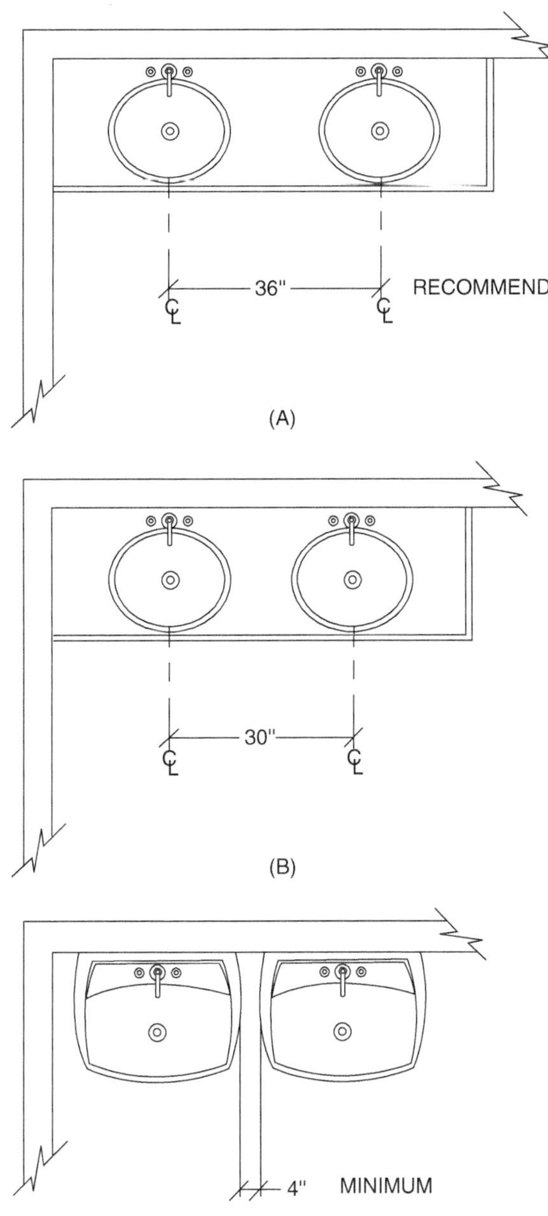

FIGURE 6.18 When planning a double lavatory configuration, it is recommended that the center of the fixtures be 36 inches (914 mm) apart (A). The minimum distance is 30 inches (762 mm) (B). If two pedestal or wall-hung fixtures are planned, make sure the edges are at least 4 inches (102 mm) apart (C) (Bathroom Planning Guideline 6).
NKBA

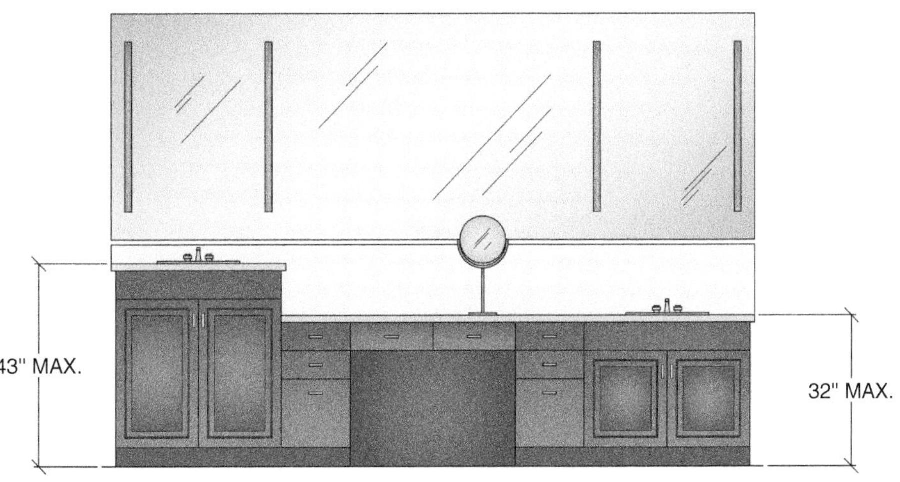

FIGURE 6.19 The height of the lavatory should fit the user. For adults, this could range from 32 inches (813 mm) to 43 inches 1092 mm) high depending on the user's height (Bathroom Planning Guideline 7).
NKBA

FIGURE 6.20 Lavatories at two heights can accommodate users with a wide range in their height.
Courtesy of Kohler Company

27 inches (686 mm) high by 19 inches (483 mm) deep, which would accommodate a seated user or a person in a wheelchair. However, a 36-inch (914 mm) wide knee space is recommended for a person using a wheelchair, since the opening can then be used as part of a T-turn. The exact knee space height for a specific client will be determined by the height of the client's knees, and for a person in a wheelchair, the height of the wheelchair arms. Bathroom Access Standard 7 states that the front of the lavatory should be no more than 34 inches (864 mm) (see Figure 8.12). When creating a knee space, support for the suspended counter should be planned.

Counter Edges

In order to remove sharp edges in the grooming center, counter edges should be rounded or clipped if the counter projects into the room (see Figure 6.24). This Bathroom Planning Guideline is a universal design recommendation that will help prevent injury if a person bumps into the edge or falls against it.

Faucet

The type and placement of the faucet used with a particular lavatory design are important, and they should be looked at together. First, select lavatory faucets that are water efficient, rated for above average water efficiency by the EPA WaterSense program, and contribute to sustainable housing. (For more information refer to chapter 3, "Environmental and Sustainability

FIGURE 6.21 A vessel lavatory sits above the counter, so add both the height of the cabinet and counter, and the height of the lavatory together, to get the total finished height.
Courtesy of Porcher

Considerations.") Also, the design of the faucet should have a water spray that stays in the lavatory and does not spray the user, the counter, or the floor.

Water will be less likely to splash out of a larger bowl. The faucet should be high enough for users to get their hands beneath the spray. The length of the faucet spout should be proportional to the size of the lavatory, to avoid overspray (see Figure 6.25).

Center-set, widespread, mini-widespread, and single-hole faucets require different specifications for the placement of holes on the lavatory or counter. A deck-mounting of the faucet may require a deeper counter and a longer neck on the spout.

FIGURE 6.22 A floating vanity can be dramatic and convenient.
Design by NKBA member: Michael Bright

Wall-mounted faucets require a more difficult installation, since they are plumbed through the wall. The designer will need to identify the height and location of these types of faucets. The spacing of the controls should be planned with consideration for the user's handedness. Consider the height of the faucet controls in a wall-mounted installation. Small children or persons in a seated position may have difficulty reaching the controls, since they must reach over the counter, thus reducing the height of their reach range.

Whenever the faucet controls are placed on the counter or wall, there may be excess water around the lavatory due to users turning off the controls with wet hands. The designer should assure that the counter material is not susceptible to standing water and work with clients on behaviors that could minimize any problems that the control placement creates.

Lever handles or controls that are easy to twist and maneuver are recommended. However, any design of the handles other than smooth round knobs will improve function, as will single controls.

FIGURE 6.23 A vanity near the lavatory can provide a place to apply make-up.
Design by NKBA member: Belva Johnson

(See Figure 6.26A, B, C, D, and E for examples of the varied types of faucets and their placement within the design.)

Storage

With all of the activities taking place at the grooming center, many items will need to be stored there. Many items will be used daily, while others will only be needed occasionally. Either way, plan according to the following storage principles:

- Store items at the first or last place of use. Soap should be beside the lavatory.
- Items used together should be stored or grouped together. An example is that all make-up should be stored in one place.
- Stored items should be easy to locate at a glance. Place items so labels are easy to read.
- Frequently used items should be within easy reach. Keep the toothbrush convenient to the lavatory.
- Store items in duplicate locations if needed. Towels will be needed at the lavatory, shower, and bidet.
- Store hazardous items out of the reach of children or others who might be harmed by them. Medicines and cleaning supplies should be put in high locations or behind locked cabinets.
- Store items in the appropriate environment. Some medicines should be stored away from light, heat, and/or humidity.

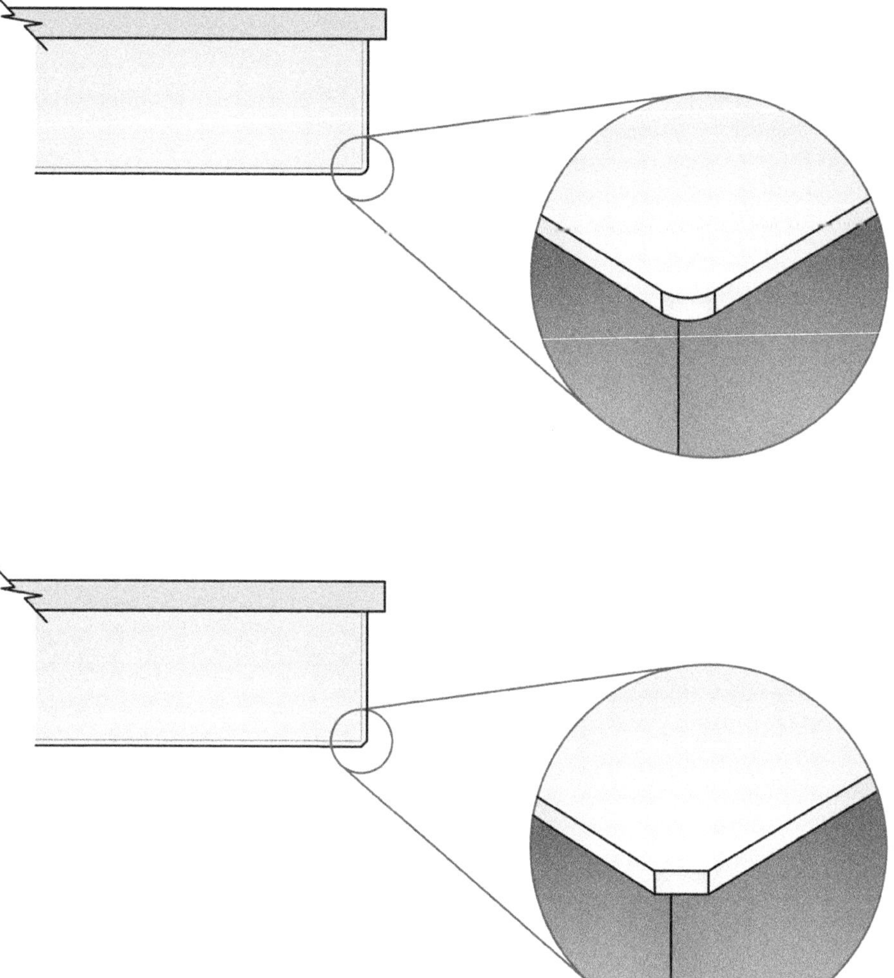

FIGURE 6.24 Counter edges should be rounded or clipped (Bathroom Planning Guideline 8).
NKBA

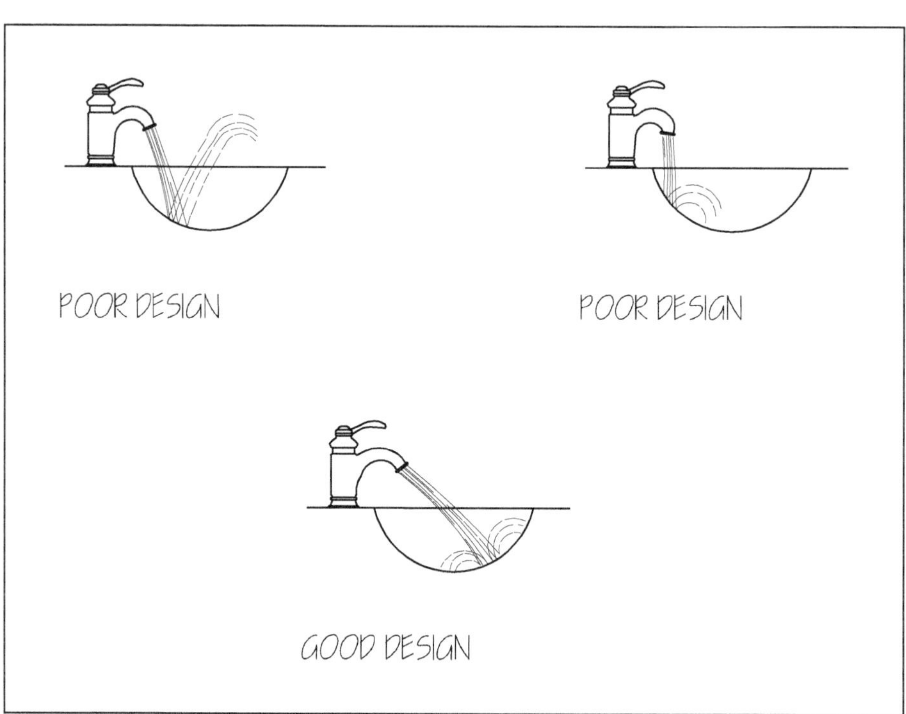

FIGURE 6.25 Plan the type and placement of lavatories and faucets so that the spray is accessible and stays within the sink bowl.
NKBA

FIGURE 6.26 Faucet types and placements vary and should be considered in conjunction with the lavatory design: (A) This undermounted lavatory has a faucet mounted in the counter; (B) A self-rimming lavatory has the faucet mounted on the rim; (C) This lavatory is integrated into the counter with the faucet on the counter; (D) The faucet for a vessel lavatory is often mounted on the wall; (E) This unique faucet delivers water from a glass dish and is mounted on the back of the console lavatory.

(A) Courtesy of Architectural Bath; (B) Courtesy of Danze; (C) Design by NKBA member: Lori W. Carroll, Co-Designer: Mary Roles; (D) Design by NKBA Member: John Sylvestre, CKD; (E) Courtesy of KWC

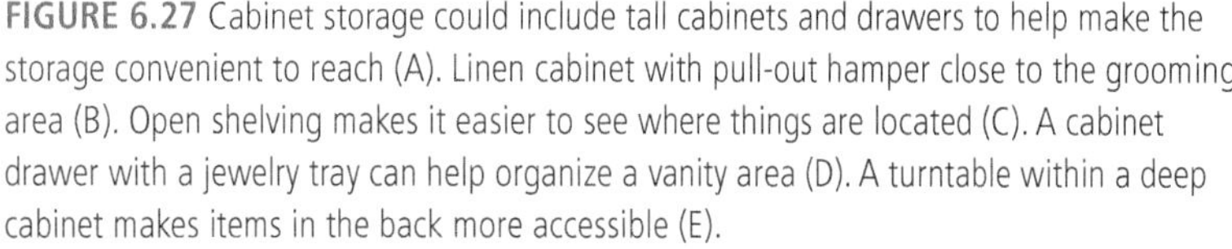

FIGURE 6.27 Cabinet storage could include tall cabinets and drawers to help make the storage convenient to reach (A). Linen cabinet with pull-out hamper close to the grooming area (B). Open shelving makes it easier to see where things are located (C). A cabinet drawer with a jewelry tray can help organize a vanity area (D). A turntable within a deep cabinet makes items in the back more accessible (E).

(A) Design by NKBA member: Ines Hanl; (B) Courtesy of Decora; (C) Courtesy of Kraftmaid; (D) Courtesy of Kraftmaid; (E) Courtesy of Kraftmaid

Use information gathered by completing Form 4: Bathroom Storage Inventory (see chapter 5, "Assessing Needs") with your client to determine the amount and type of storage needed in the bathroom design. Several storage options are available including stock and custom cabinetry, medicine cabinets, and furniture pieces.

Consider if storage should be open or closed. Closed storage hides clutter, provides privacy, and protects items from dust. But open storage is easier to see, reach, and remember. It can help people with cognitive impairments to see the item they need. Generous and appropriate lighting improves access to storage, particularly for the aging eye.

Storage should be flexible (adjustable shelves) and efficient (maximize the space). When spaces are too deep, items just get lost in the back. Also consider that the most comfortable reach range while standing is 26 inches (660 mm) to 59 inches (1499 mm) above the finished floor, and that the average maximum reach height for women is 69 inches (1753 mm).

Storage placed between 15 inches (381 mm) and 48 inches (1219 mm) above the floor is most accessible and within the universal reach range. D-pulls on cabinetry are better for a person with limited use of their hands, wrists, or fingers than other types of cabinet door hardware.

Cabinetry

When planning storage, you may want to specify cabinets in different areas of the bathroom. In order to plan this storage, it is important to understand what types of cabinets are available and how to plan the layout of the cabinets using nomenclature that will call out the selected cabinets. Many cabinet companies carry cabinetry that is particularly suited for the bathroom. These are available in both framed and frameless construction. Framed cabinets have a face frame at the opening of the cabinet box, offered in various door styles and configurations. Frameless cabinets, sometimes referred to as European cabinets, are constructed of panels and do not need a face frame. They are also offered in a variety of styles with full overlay doors.

Often framed cabinets use Imperial measurements and are specified using inches, with stock cabinets usually available in 3 inch increments in width. Bathroom cabinets vary in depth from 16 to 24 inches, with 21 inches being most common. The heights vary, typically from 28 1/2 inches to 34 1/2 inches high for a finished height of 30 inches to 36 inches, once the countertop is added. Cabinets are specified using a code of letters and numbers the manufacturer has determined represent their cabinet selections. Although the labeling is unique to each manufacturer, NKBA has provided generic nomenclature to help designers and design students plan bathrooms using the basic size and dimensions of cabinetry. Bathroom cabinetry is specified with the first letter V—for vanity. Other letters used with the V include B for base, W for wall, S for sink, D for drawer, and LC for linen closet, among others. The first one to two numbers reflect the width of the cabinet, the second two numbers reflect the depth, and the third indicates the height. For example a VSB362134 would be a vanity sink base 36 inches wide, 21 inches deep, and 34 inches high.

Frameless cabinetry is typically built on the metric system and is frequently specified in centimeters, which can result in variations in size from framed cabinets.

Other plumbing and cabinet companies sell cabinetry that is a combination of lavatory and cabinet. These furniture-like pieces come in a variety of styles from contemporary to traditional designs and are in depths, widths, and heights similar to cabinetry. Furniture pieces can also be used for storage in the bathroom. Figure 6.27 (6.27 A, B, C, D, and E) and Figure 6.28 (6.28 A, B, C, D, E) illustrate a variety of cabinet storage accessories and ideas for alternative storage features.

Medicine Cabinet

The medicine cabinet is the old standby for storage at the grooming center. Its shallow depth makes it suitable for many small grooming items. There are many sizes and styles available, and this type of storage can be useful. Medicine cabinets can be recessed into the wall, partially recessed, or surface-mounted. They can be placed centered over the lavatory, to the side, or on the returning wall, making contents easier to reach.

If the medicine cabinet is to be recessed, it is important to locate the studs as well as the plumbing, and place the cabinet within the framing. This decision must be made before construction begins.

FIGURE 6.28 Many creative and convenient storage options are available to meet recommendations for adequate storage (Bathroom Planning Guideline 22). These include furniture pieces (A), baskets (B), recessed shelves and niches (C), wall hooks (D), and a pole with adjustable shelves (E).

(A) Photography by Keller and Keller. Used with permission from Better Homes and Gardens® *magazine. Copyright © 2003 Meredith Corporation. All rights reserved; (B) Courtesy of American Woodmark; (C) Design by NKBA member: Anthony Binns; (D) Courtesy of Moen (E) Design by NKBA members: Tim Scott and Erica Westeroth, CKD*

A surface-mounted medicine cabinet can be placed anywhere, but may need to be secured into the studs to assure the weight does not pull it off the wall. The medicine cabinet can be moved to the side of the lavatory, which puts it within the reach of more users. Other items such as a large mirror, window, or decorative design can be placed above the lavatory.

Today medicine cabinets are available with features that can enhance the grooming experience by providing integrated televisions into the mirror and electrical and auxiliary outlets for grooming appliances, music, and other entertainment features. The placement of these cabinets should be at a height that is convenient for the height of the user's upper body and reach range.

Mirror

The mirror is an important feature of the grooming center. Several of the center's activities—applying make-up, hair care, and shaving—require users to view themselves in a mirror. This typically means a mirror is placed above the lavatory, but placing the mirror adjacent to the lavatory, in a vanity space, may also be convenient.

It is recommended that mirrors be placed with consideration for the users' eye height and line of sight (Bathroom Planning Guideline 23) (Figure 6.29).

Having the bottom edge of the mirror extend to the top of the counter allows for shorter people, seated people, and children to more easily see themselves. Access Standards state the bottom of the mirror should be a maximum 40 inches (1016 mm) above the finished floor. Don't forget to extend the height of the mirror so that it fits the taller user, as well.

Separate mirrors placed at each user's height can provide a custom fit, and an adjustable height or tilting mirror might also provide a solution. A full-length mirror in the bathroom is a universal design solution that can serve the needs of people of all heights, including children, and provide a final check after dressing.

To minimize glare, lighting should be selected and placed on either side of the mirror in a position that shields the light source from the naked eye. Refer to chapter 7, "Mechanical Planning," for more information on lighting placement.

FIGURE 6.29 The mirror at the vanity should be placed at the user's eye level (Bathroom Planning Guideline 23). This arrangement has counters and mirrors planned for a tall and short user with storage, including an appliance garage, separating the two areas.
NKBA

Towels

Towels need to be planned throughout the bathroom so that they are convenient to the user when needed (Bathroom Planning Guideline 23). At the grooming area, washcloths and hand towels are needed for face washing and hand drying. Guest towels might be stored and displayed in some powder rooms or guest baths.

Placement of all towels should be within the universal reach range of 15 inches (381 mm) to 48 inches (1219 mm) above the floor. Towel bars and towel rings are typical devices for storage and should be placed close to the lavatory so that water does not drip on the floor. Figure 6.30 illustrates sizes of hanging and folded towels that might be used in the bathroom.

Guidelines and Access Standards for Grooming Center

The Bathroom Planning Guidelines and Access Standards that are important to planning the grooming area are 4, 5, 6, 7, 8, 22, and 23. For the complete Guidelines and Access Standards, see Appendix A.

BATHING/SHOWERING CENTER

While the basic activity of the bathing/showering center is cleansing the body, there is a wide range of associated activities that take place in this area. The bathtub, shower, and tub/shower combination are the main fixtures, all of which have their own related planning considerations.

- Getting in and out of bathtubs is a serious safety issue, since falls can happen during transfer. Turning water on and off, and adjusting water temperature, are also key activities in bathing and showering. In addition to water and the fixture, soap and other cleansing products, washcloths, and sponges are used in cleansing.
- Washing hair also occurs in the bathtub or shower. A faucet spray, shampoos, conditioners, and a variety of other products will be needed for this activity.
- Shaving the face and legs might also take place in the tub or shower. A mirror may be needed to see the face, and a bench or ledge might make shaving legs safer and more convenient.
- The bathtub is also a place for relaxing, and is often therapeutic. Many people find that soaking in a warm bath can calm them and reduce stress. Tubs especially designed for relaxing might be deeper and jetted.

  Bubble baths, aromatic oils, bath salts, and fragrant additives can enhance the effect of the warm water. Special sponges and loofahs help exfoliate the skin, and pulsating hand sprays can enhance the spa experience. Candles, soft lighting, a lit fireplace, and music also add to the experience.
- Showering can also provide a sensual experience that goes beyond body cleansing. Pulsating showerheads and body sprays offer a variety of massaging actions that help to relax stiff muscles. Multiple showerheads from above, and jets from the side, can invigorate the body all over. Rain showerheads and waterfall heads may be more relaxing, offering a wide but gentle water flow from above. While these shower designs are luxurious, they also can use large amounts of water and the longer the user stays in the shower, the more water is used. Low-flow showerheads are available and should be considered. More information about water efficiency in bathrooms and selecting water efficient fixtures can be found in chapter 3, "Environmental and Sustainability Considerations."
- The amount of moisture created by bathing and showering will require specialized ventilation to remove some of the moisture and heat from the bathroom. Requirements for ventilation are covered in chapter 7, "Mechanical Planning."
- Clothing will be removed before bathing and showering, and replaced with more clothes or a robe. The designer should think about how dirty clothes will be handled in the bathroom, and how clean clothes or robes will be stored. Hampers, laundry chutes, and laundry rooms can help tackle the dirty clothes issue. Hooks, closets, and a nearby dressing center could make fresh clothes more accessible. More information on these topics is in chapter 9, "More Than a Bathroom."

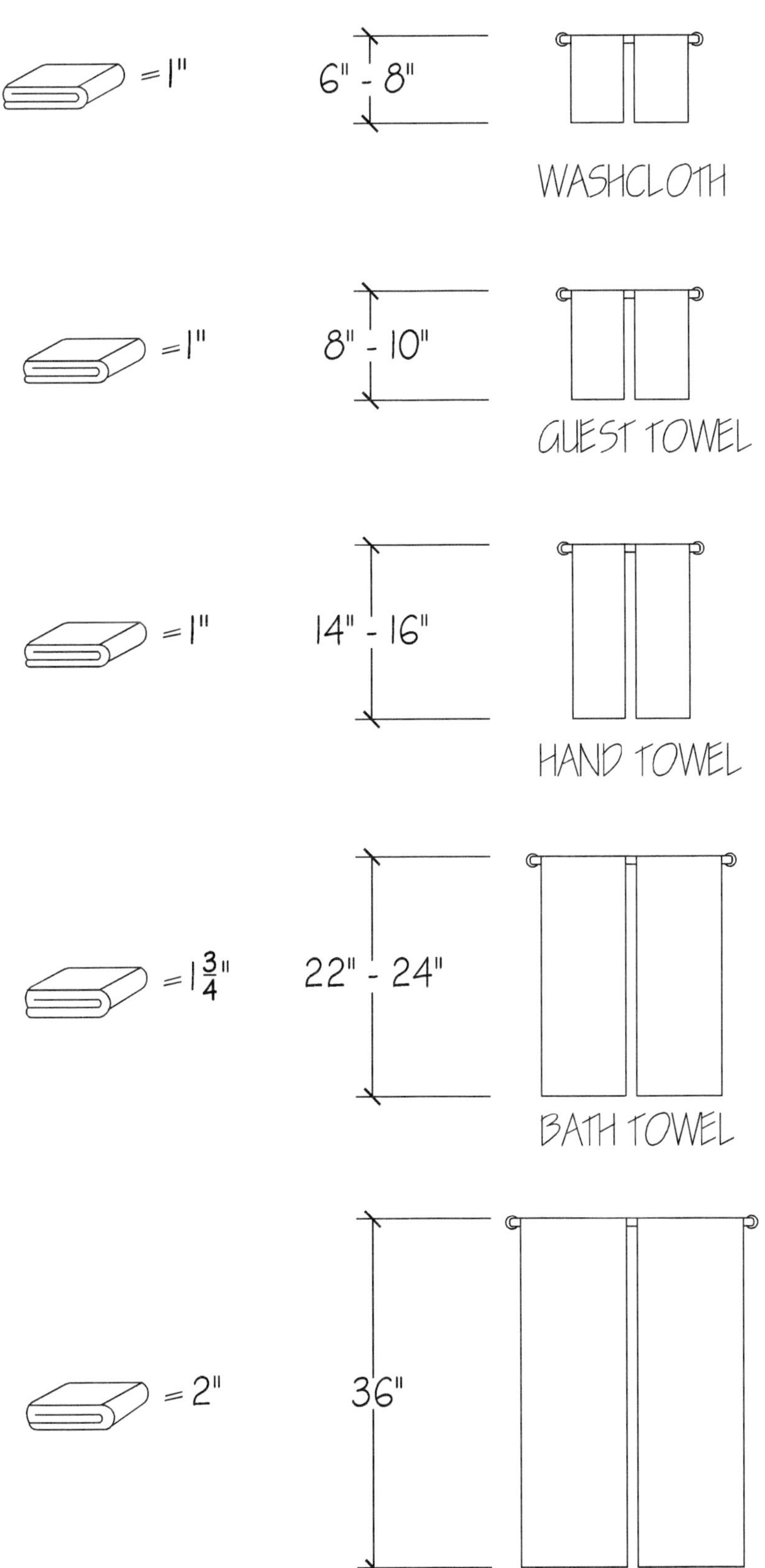

FIGURE 6.30 Towels should be placed where needed in the bathroom (Bathroom Planning Guideline 23). Make sure the hanging and folding space accommodates the size of towels used in an area.
NKBA

FIGURE 6.31 Bathtubs are available in several styles that reflect the way the tub will be installed, including: (A) a platform with a drop-in tub; (B) a freestanding tub;(C) a corner tub; (D) an alcove tub; and (E) a platform with an undermount tub.

A and C courtesy of Kohler; B, D, and E courtesy of Jacuzzi

Design Recommendations for Bathing

Bathtubs come in several installation styles and sizes (see Figure 6.31A, B, C, D, and E). A recessed tub style, sometimes called an alcove-style tub, is designed to fit into a space with walls on three sides so it is only finished on one side. A platform can be built up from the floor to hold a drop-in tub or the tub can be under-mounted beneath a cutout in the top of the platform. A corner tub is finished on three sides with two sides fitting against two walls. Tubs can also be freestanding and finished on all sides. This might be a traditional design, like the claw-foot tub, or a contemporary design.

The size of a traditional standard tub or tub/shower combination is 32 inches by 60 inches (813 mm by 1524 mm). This size will fit in most full bathrooms. However, it does not necessarily meet the needs of the user, so it is important to discuss tub size with the person(s) who will be bathing (see Figure 6.32).

A tub bath may be taken by simply sitting in the tub. Knees might be outstretched or bent at an angle, but the back is generally perpendicular to the bottom of the tub. Leaning back and relaxing in the tub requires an angled contour to support the user's back. The appropriate length of the tub should be determined by the leg length of the user. A short woman might slide under the water if her feet do not reach the end of the tub. A tall woman may never be able to lean back and relax without her bent knees raised out of the water.

Longer and shorter tubs are available, and tubs come in different depths that might make the bath more comfortable. Smaller square tubs might also be appropriate for shorter people. Tubs also come in various widths and depths that can accommodate people of different sizes. If there are multiple users at different times, a compromise in tub size will be needed.

Two people may want to use the tub at the same time. Longer and wider tubs are available for this purpose (see Figure 6.33). Sitting side-by-side requires a 42-inch (1067 mm) wide tub. Sitting opposite requires a 36-inch (914 mm) wide tub. Often these tubs will be jetted tubs and used sporadically. Soaking tubs which are often deeper may not be jetted. See chapter 9, "More Than a Bathroom," for more information about specialized tubs.

Because of its size, the tub is often a dominant feature in the bathroom (see Figure 6.34) and is placed as a focal point. It may be viewed from the entry or placed in the center of the room.

The IRC building codes used as a reference for NKBA Planning Guidelines also require that a tub with a showerhead fixture should be at least 80 inches (2032 mm) tall (Bathroom Planning Guideline 2).

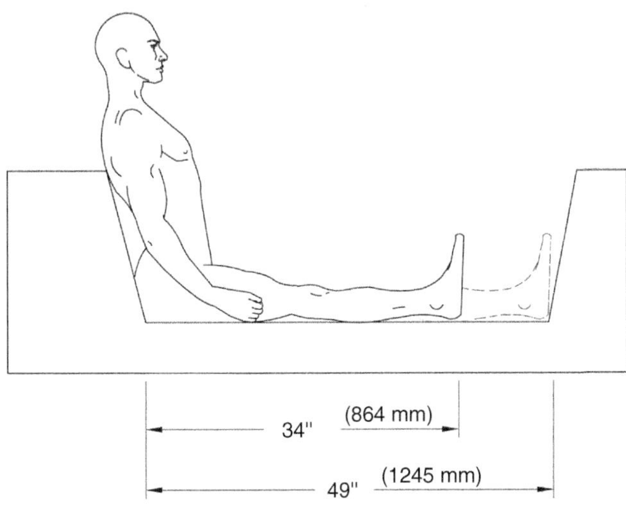

FIGURE 6.32 The buttock-to-heel measurement varies from 34 inches (864 mm) for small women to 49 inches (1245 mm) for tall men. When selecting a tub for a client, consider the interior dimension, the angle of the back, and the depth of the tub to achieve an appropriate fit.
NKBA

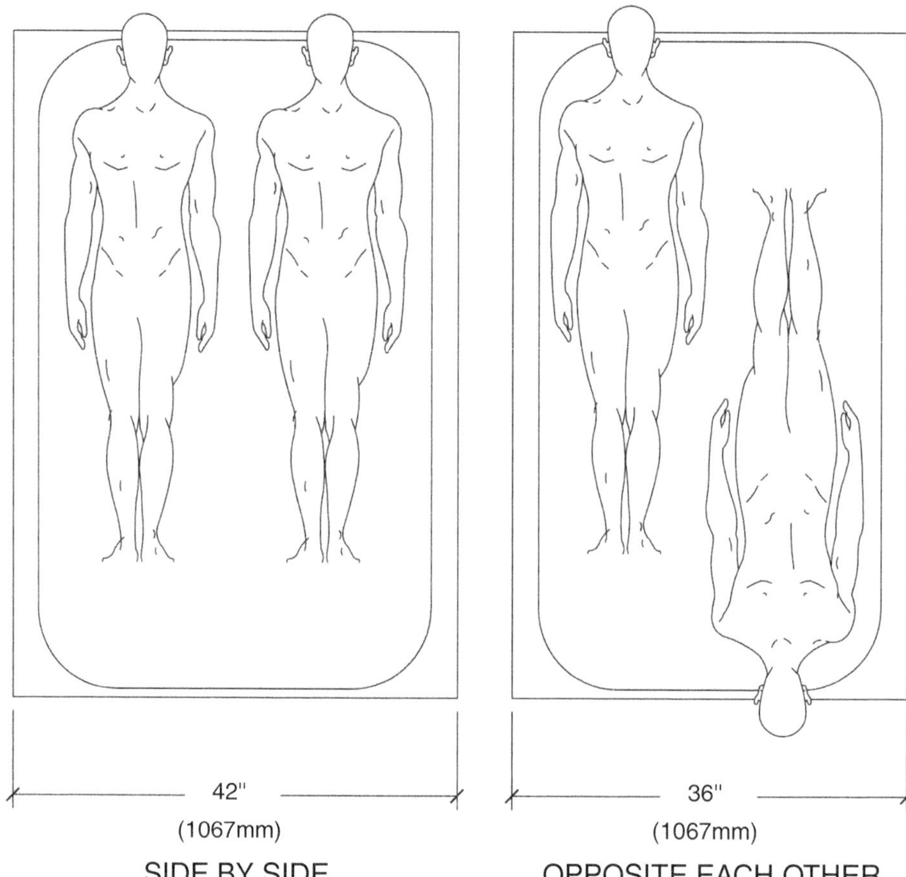

FIGURE 6.33 Bathtubs for two can accommodate side-by-side seating or an arrangement where bathers face each other.

FIGURE 6.34 Often the bathtub is the central feature in the bathroom.

Design by NKBA member: Holly Rickert

Floor Clearance

Wherever the tub is placed, it is recommended that at least a 30-inch (762 mm) clear space be planned along the side of it. If dressing occurs in front of the tub, more space is needed (see Figure 6.35). A 42-inch (1067 mm) to 48 inch (1219 mm) dressing circle will allow room to dry off and put on undergarments.

The IRC building codes allow a minimum of 21 inches (533 mm) in front of the tub, but this will be tight for many users. If a parent is helping bathe children, or a caregiver is assisting someone with a bath, extra floor space will be needed to accommodate them as well as the user.

If the bather will be transferring to the tub from a mobility aid or wheelchair, then 30 inches (762 mm) would be a minimum requirement, with more space preferred. When planning for a freestanding tub, consider which side(s) of the tub will be used for entering, exiting, and passage, and allow the proper clearances.

Getting in and out of the tub can be dangerous, but there are many things the designer can do to reduce the risks of falls. The typical method of entry is to stand on one foot and step over the side of the tub, which challenges anyone's balance. The danger is increased by wet and slippery surfaces, increased tub depth, and a tub bottom that is often not flat.

The ideal way to enter a tub is to sit on the edge, raise one leg at a time over the rim, and then ease into the water. Unfortunately, most standard tubs do not have an edge wide enough for most people to sit on.

With a standard tub, placing a seat at the head end provides a transfer seat. While 15 inches (381 mm) is the minimum recommended depth for a seat, even less depth can benefit some users. Attention must be given to the user's size and weight, so that the seat will support the intended use.

If a platform tub is placed on a frame, a seating edge can be designed. Some accessible tubs have doors that swing open to allow the user to step in before the tub is filled. Tubs with sides that drop down are placed on a platform making the bottom of the tub at seat height, resulting in a comfortable transfer into the tub.

When a platform deck cannot incorporate a seat, there are a variety of tubs that include integral or fold-away seats. Grab bars can be placed where they provide stability for entering and exiting the tub. For more details, see chapter 8, "Accessibility in Practice."

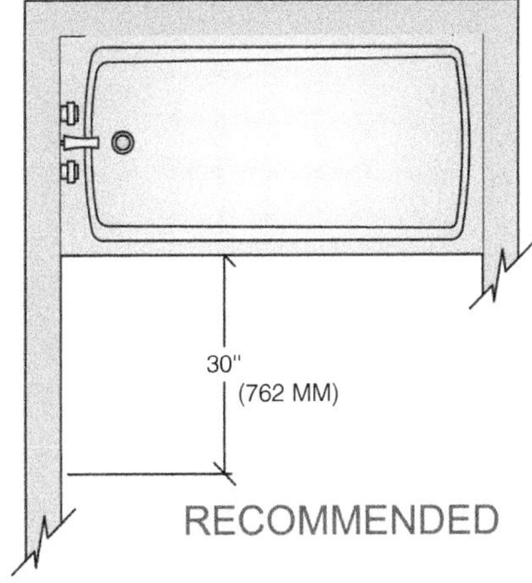

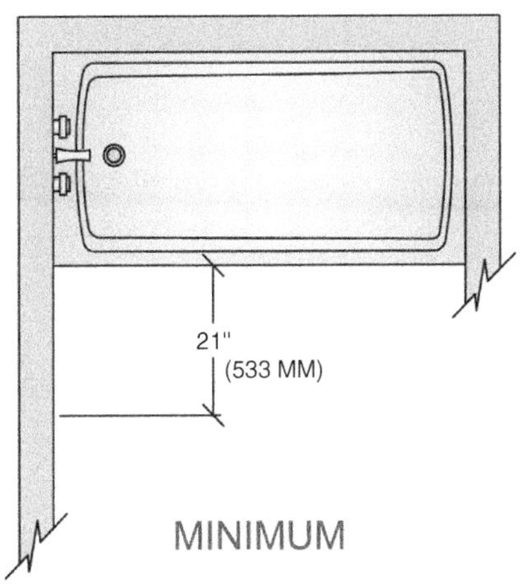

FIGURE 6.35 The recommended clearance in front of the tub is 30 inches (762 mm). A minimum distance would be 21 inches (533 mm) (Bathroom Planning Guideline 4).
NKBA

Flooring

While no floor is completely slip-resistant, especially when wet, to help prevent falls, use slip-resistant surfaces on the tub floor, as well as the bathroom floor (Bathroom Planning Guideline 18). Many tubs come with a slightly rough surface that helps the user grip the bottom of the tub.

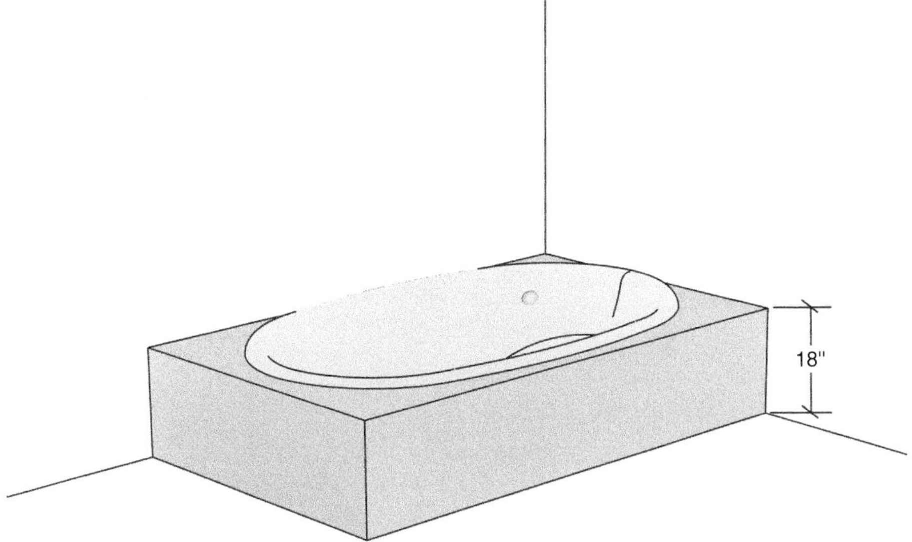

FIGURE 6.36 Plan the platform tub height so that no steps are needed to get into the tub with 18 inches (457 mm) being an ideal height for transfer (Bathroom Planning Guideline 17).
NKBA

No Steps

Tubs are most safely used if their floor is level with the bathroom floor, and the deck or top of the tub is approximately seat height (approximately 18 inches [457 mm]). Even one step into the tub creates a situation that can challenge balance and, therefore, is not recommended (Bathroom Planning Guideline 17) (Figure 6.36).

A tub placed directly into the floor is even worse since it creates a situation where the user will step down from the floor level to the tub level. Or the person will need to sit on the floor to get into the tub, which is difficult for many. The sunken tub may also create a hazard if one were to trip and fall into it.

A tub placed on a high platform can require several steps to get up to, creating the same problem as the sunken tub. When users reach the top of the steps, they have to step down onto the bottom of the tub, more than 15 inches (381 mm) below them.

Even though it is clear that steps can cause a hazard, a client may insist on them. If you have to compromise, try to design a step that is strictly decorative and not actually used for tub entry. Use only one step designed in compliance with local building codes, or at least 10 inches (254 mm) deep and 7-1/4 inches (184 mm) high. A grab bar or handrail must be included for safety.

FIGURE 6.37 The window next to this tub is diffused to provide privacy and a partial glass partition and door help keep water from showering in the tub area.

Design by NKBA members: Tim Scott, Co-Designers Erica Westeroth, CKD, and Sheena Hammond

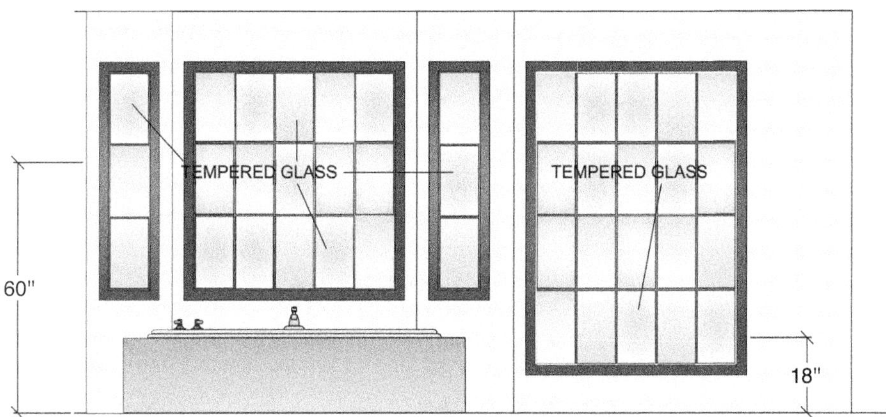

FIGURE 6.38 Tempered glass should be used in the bathroom wherever there is a chance that someone could fall against the glass, i.e., in tub and shower doors and surrounds. It should also be used in windows at the bathtub or shower that are below 60 inches (1524 mm), and in windows or doors below 18 inches (457 mm) (Bathroom Planning Guideline 15).

Access Panels

Plumbing equipment must be accessible for repairs. Whirlpool tubs and other equipment have motors and controls that need to be considered in the design of the bathroom space. Always follow manufacturers' specifications for installation. This equipment will need to be examined for maintenance and service, so it is important to plan for access. Removable panels should be easy to reach, and the equipment should be accessible for the installer and repair person.

A whirlpool tub is usually a drop-in style tub built into a platform. The electrical equipment is usually installed within the platform, so it is important to plan clearance for access to the equipment by incorporating a removable panel into the platform design. Building codes require this access and also require that information on any equipment be left with the homeowner (Bathroom Planning Guideline 19).

Glazing

Tubs that will be used for relaxing are sometimes placed next to a window that offers an interesting and calming view. (Caution: Looking into the neighbor's breakfast room may not be relaxing to the user or the neighbor.) A privacy garden adjacent to the tub area could create a relaxing atmosphere. If the window is placed so that privacy and view are compromised, a window treatment, a window of glass block, or a diffuser in the window, can be used to provide light without visual access (see Figure 6.37). Building codes require that a window next to the tub (bottom edge less than 60 inches [1524 mm] off the finished floor) be made of tempered glass (Bathroom Planning Guideline 15).

Bathtubs that are combined with a shower often have a glass door or enclosure to control the water. This glass should also be tempered to comply with building codes. See Figure 6.38 for code requirements for glazing.

Faucet Controls

Faucet controls should be accessible to the user before entering the tub. In an enclosed tub or tub/shower combination, the controls may be placed on the wall below 33 inches (838 mm) above the finished floor (see Figure 6.39).

Placing controls within 6 inches (152 mm) of the front wall makes them more accessible. For a freestanding tub, or one placed in a platform, controls should be on the front side. The user should not have to lean across the tub to turn on the water and check temperature. Place the faucet and controls so they do not conflict with the transfer area.

Besides faucet placement, the type and design should be considered. A faucet with a hand spray and 60-inch (1524 mm) hose allows a caregiver to assist with bathing and is recommended for a universally designed space. Controls should be easy to grasp and manipulate. Any design other than smooth round knobs improves function. A single control is easier to use than separate hot and cold controls. If a tub/shower combination is planned, the shower controls must be pressure balanced, have thermostatic mixing, or be a combination of both.

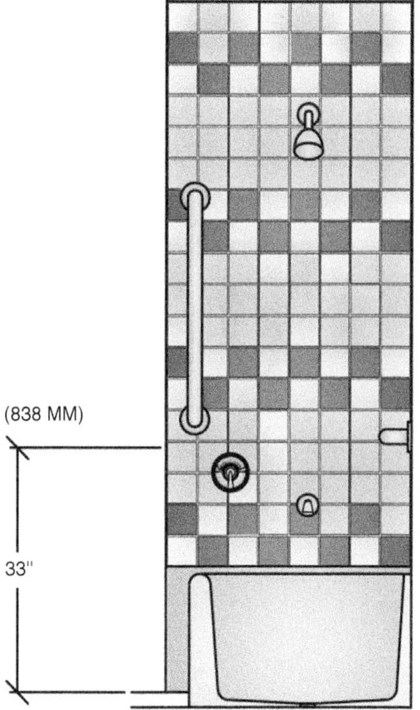

FIGURE 6.39 The centerline of the controls for the bathtub should be between the rim of the tub and 33 inches (838 mm) off the floor (Bathroom Planning Guideline 10). Offsetting the controls so that they are toward the front of the tub makes them accessible from both inside and outside of the tub (Bathroom Access Standard 10).
NKBA

FIGURE 6.40 The controls on a platform tub should be to the side to allow for easy access and space to get in and out of the tub.
Courtesy of Jacuzzi Company

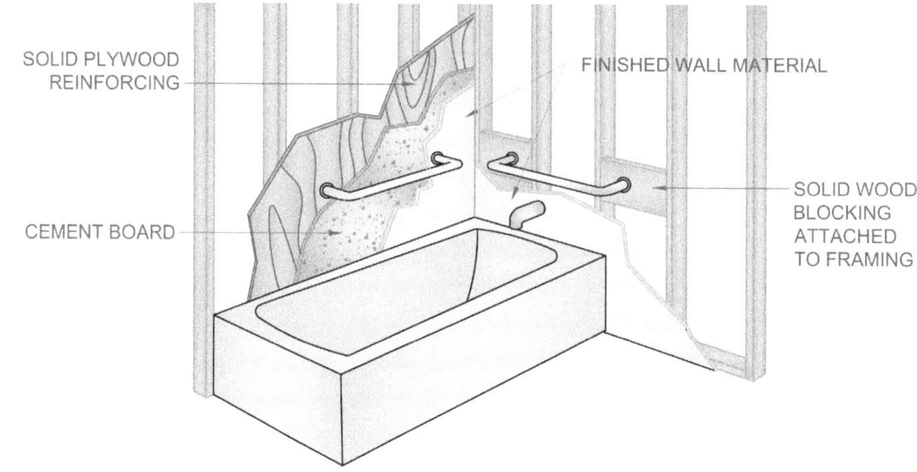

FIGURE 6.41 Providing blocking between studs or enclosing the entire tub surround with a solid plywood base will allow grab bars to be placed anywhere the user needs them (Bathroom Guideline 14).
NKBA

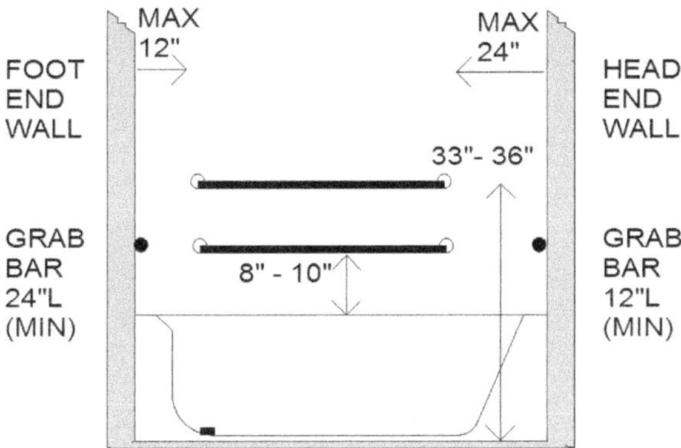

FIGURE 6.42 Grab bars should be placed according to user needs. A standard placement is along the back of the bathtub 33 inches (838 mm) to 36 inches (914 mm) high and vertically at the control end of the tub, 9 inches (229 mm) above the rim (Bathroom Planning Guideline 14).

NKBA

Grab Bars

Grab bars placed in the tub will give users something to hold onto as they enter and exit, thus alleviating some balance problems. NKBA recommends grab bars at the tub and shower to assist with this transfer. There are many decorative and attractive grab bars available to match other trim and accessories in the bathroom. It is critical that they be installed so they support at least 250 pounds (113 kg). Some clients may need more support.

The wall behind the tub and shower should be reinforced to support the grab bar. The placement of the bar should be planned where it best fits the user. Figure 6.41 indicates how walls can be reinforced around the tub. If a complete plywood surround is used as reinforcement, make sure

FIGURE 6.43 Shelving is recessed into the wall to the side of the whirlpool bathtub, creating a convenient place to store towels and bath accessories.

Design by NKBA member: Joan Descombes, CKD

the installation is water-tight, so that moisture does not seep into the plywood and create mold and deterioration of the membrane. This is also true when the grab bars are being installed into the membrane.

Besides bars placed at the back and ends of the tub, a vertical bar at the control end wall is also helpful. Figure 6.42 illustrates where grab bars should be placed in the tub. See NKBA Bathroom Planning Guideline and Access Standard 14 for more details on placement. Standard towel bars and soap dishes will not support someone in a fall and can be dangerous, since they protrude. Recessing soap dishes in the wall places them out of the bather's reach, while using attractive grab bars instead of towel bars will provide the stability needed if grabbed to prevent a fall.

Storage

Storage is needed at the tub for the activities occurring there (Bathroom Planning Guideline 22). Within the tub area, hair care products and shaving supplies may be needed regularly, and a shelf recessed within the wall to hold them would be a good option (see Figure 6.43).

Storage should be provided for occasionally used items that help with a relaxing bath. Bath salts and oils, candles, loofahs, and exfoliating sponges may be stored at the tub, on a shelf, or in a cabinet. Items used regularly in the tub (sponges, tub toys) should be placed where they can dry out, to avoid a mold problem.

Towels

Towels and washcloths should be stored close by the tub, and towel bars should be reachable from inside the tub (Bathroom Planning Guideline 23). Hanging bath towels require a 22-inch (559 mm) to 24-inch (610 mm) high space on the wall, while bath sheets require a 36-inch (914 mm) high space. Towel bars, towel rings, and hooks are all possible solutions in this area. Towel warmers or a warming drawer can be planned for a special drying experience.

Grab bars can be used in place of towel bars, but towel bars should not be placed where they will be used as grab bars. Towel bars have not been designed to withstand the weight of someone pulling on them. Accessible towel placement is between 15 inches (381 mm) and 48 inches (1219 mm) off the floor.

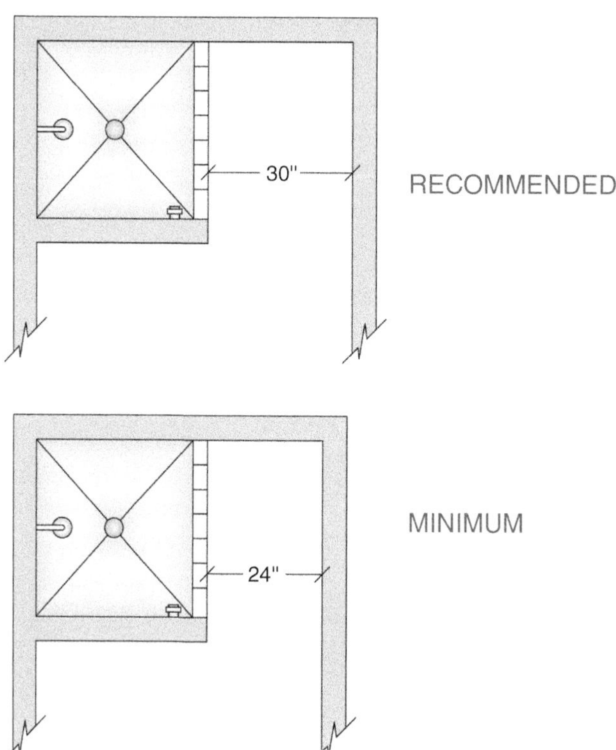

FIGURE 6.44 The recommended clearance in front of the shower is 30 inches (762 mm). The minimum clearance is 24 inches (610 mm) (Bathroom Planning Guideline 4).
NKBA

FIGURE 6.45 Slate and limestone tiles provide texture that can reduce slipping on the shower and bathroom floor.
Courtesy Arizona Tile

Design Recommendations for Showering

Showering is an increasingly common way to cleanse the body. The tub/shower combination is used in many simple bathrooms to provide both bathing and showering options. If the clients consistently take a shower, a larger shower may be preferred rather than a tub/shower combination. It is easier to get into than a tub/shower combination because the user will not have to step over the tub rim. In large bathrooms, a separate shower and bathtub may be specified. If the shower is separate, it may be placed adjacent to the bathtub, or in a separate area.

Floor Clearance

Bathroom Planning Guideline 4 recommends that at least 30 inches (762 mm) of clearance be in front of the shower for comfortable access (see Figure 6.44). The IRC building code requires 24 inches (610 mm) of clear space in front of the shower, but this will be a limited area. A dressing circle of 42 inches (1067 mm) to 48 inches (1219 mm) might be needed for drying off and changing into clothing. If the bather will be transferring from a wheelchair or other mobility aid to the shower, a 36 inch by 48 inch (914 mm by 1219 mm) space is a minimum requirement, with more space preferred.

Flooring

All flooring in the bathroom should be slip resistant and this is especially true in the area in and next to the shower (Bathroom Planning Guideline 18). Showers with tile floors can use a textured tile to create a slip-resistant surface (see Figure 6.45).

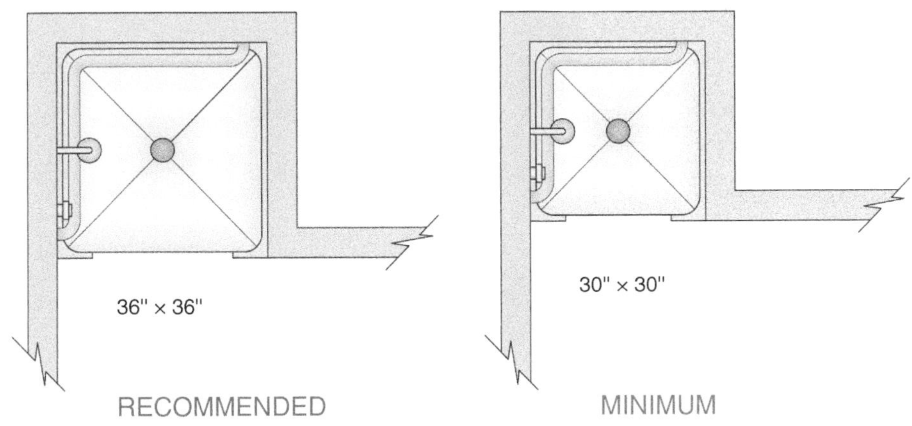

FIGURE 6.46 Plan a shower at least 36 inches by 36 inches (914 mm by 914 mm). The minimum sized shower is 30 inches by 30 inches (762 mm by 762 mm). If an angled or round shower is used, it should be large enough for a 30-inch (762 mm) disc to fit in the interior (Bathroom Planning Guideline 9).
NKBA

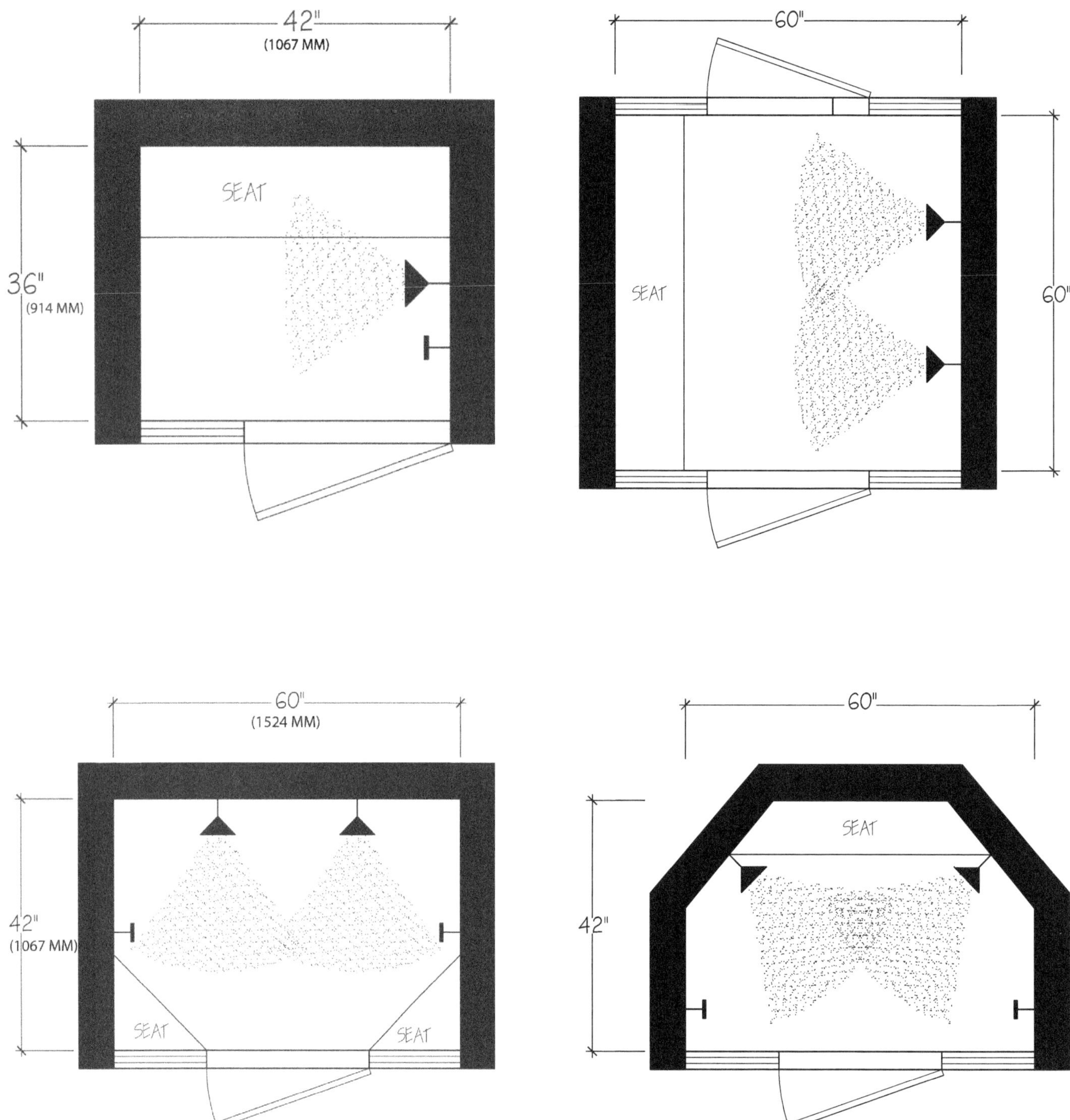

FIGURE 6.47 A shower at least 36 inches by 42 inches (914 mm by 1067 mm) allows one person to step out of the water spray (A). Showers at least 60 inches (1524 mm) wide can accommodate two shower sprays and two users comfortably (B–D).
NKBA

Shower Size

Most prefabricated showers come in standard sizes from 32 inches (813 mm) to 48 inches (1219 mm) square, but in recent years expanded options are becoming more common.

- The recommended interior shower size for one person is at least 36 inches by 36 inches (914 mm by 914 mm) (see Figure 6.46). This allows one person to comfortably stand in the shower with arms raised to wash their hair. The IRC building code states that the minimum interior shower size is 30 inches by 30 inches (762 mm by 762 mm), but this is a tight space for most adults.
- Check angled showers to make sure a 30-inch (762 mm) disc will fit into the shower floor. This will meet minimum code requirements. A larger disc area should be specified when user needs require more space.
- A 36 inch by 36 inch (914 mm by 914 mm) size is acceptable for a transfer shower to be used by a person transferring from a mobility aid. See chapter 8, "Accessibility in Practice," for more discussion.
- It is recommended that a roll-in shower used by a person with a bathing wheelchair should be at least 36 inches by 60 inches (914 mm by 1524 mm). Access Standards allow for a 30 inch (762 mm) minimum width, but 36 to 42 inches (914 to1067 mm) makes it easier to contain the water in the shower.

For a person to move out of the shower spray inside the shower, a 36 inch by 42 inch (914 mm by 1067 mm) shower should be considered (see Figure 6.47). Larger prefabricated showers are available, and custom showers can be designed to meet the needs of the user. (Check that any prefabricated shower will fit through the bathroom door.) In a shower at least 60 inches (1524 mm) deep, it is possible to control the spray within the shower. In a two-person shower, make sure there is room for both people.

Creating a Shower with No Threshold and/or Door

Curbless showers, showers with no thresholds, can be planned if the water spray can be controlled, drainage planned, and flooring outside the shower included in the wet area. When possible, eliminating the shower door and threshold makes for easy entry. It is a universal design that offers improved access and is popular in Europe.

While a roll-in shower should be 36 inches deep (914 mm), an even deeper shower would help control water spray into the bathroom area. The water spray can be controlled in several ways.

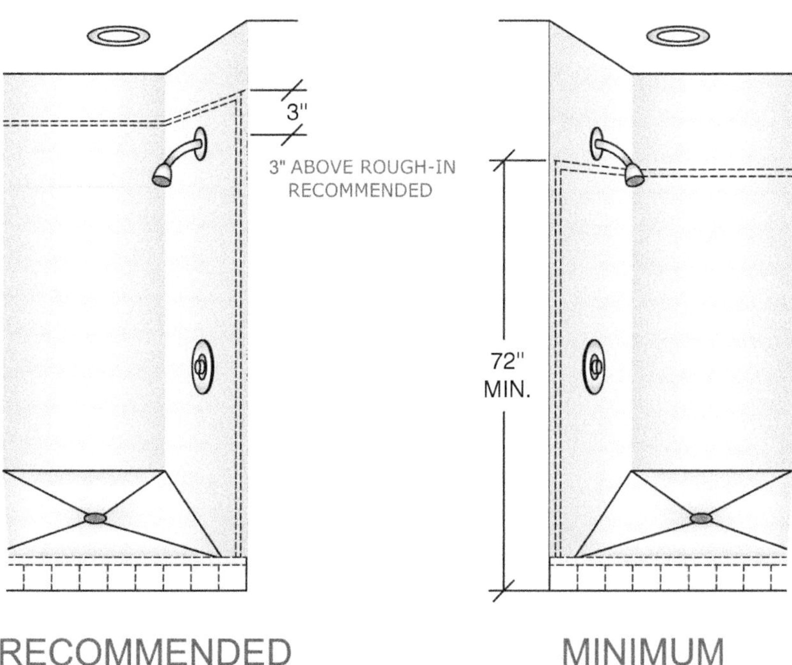

FIGURE 6.48 It is recommended that a shower surround be a waterproof material that extends 3 inches (76 mm) above the showerhead rough-in. A minimum surround should extend at least 72 inches (1823 mm) above the floor (Bathroom Planning Guideline 13).
NKBA

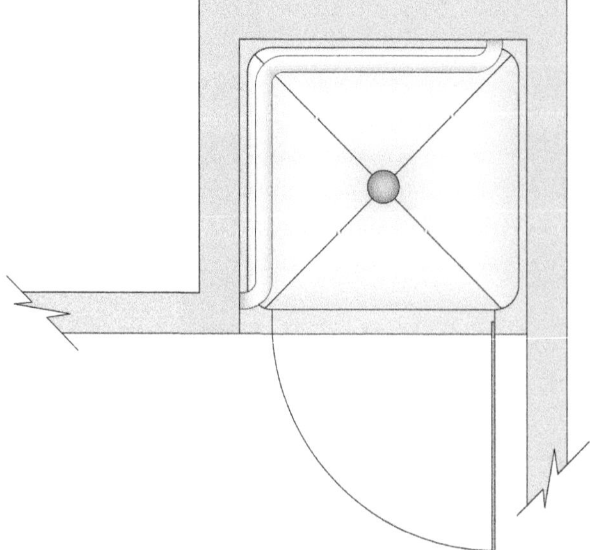

FIGURE 6.49 A shower door should open into the room, so that it can be opened even if the bather falls against it (Bathroom Planning Guideline 16).
NKBA

When a shower curtain is used, it will do a better job of water containment if it is made slightly longer than the height of the shower rod, and is weighted so that it drags. When not in use, the extra length can be draped using a tie-back to enhance the appearance and allow for proper drying. If a door is used on a shower with no threshold, consider the maneuvering space around the door swing.

Sloping the shower floor toward the drain is typical in any size shower and a shower pan that is raised off the floor helps direct water to the drain. With a no-threshold shower the slope should start at the front of the shower, which is even with the bathroom floor, and slope toward the back of the shower, and the waterproof membrane below the floor should be extended. This will typically require the floor in the shower to be lowered. A trough-style drain placed at the back of the shower will help remove the water from the shower and away from the bathroom. The trough drain can also be used to separate the shower from the bathroom, collecting any water that escapes. See chapter 8, "Accessibility in Practice," for more detail on designing a no-threshold shower.

Shower Surround

The shower is a wet space so water-resistant materials are critical. Remember that the IRC building code requires that the shower area be at least 80 inches (2032) high (Bathroom Planning Guideline 2). The surround of a shower or tub/shower combination should be of a waterproof material and extend a minimum of 3 inches (76 mm) above the showerhead rough-in (see Figure 6.48). A typical rough-in is 72 inches (1823 mm) to 78 inches (1981 mm) high. The IRC building code requires the waterproof wall materials extend at least 72 inches (1823 mm) above the finished floor.

Prefabricated shower surrounds may be one piece, or divided into multiple pieces to be assembled onsite. Check the size of the room entry to make sure an installer can get a prefabricated unit into the room.

Shower Doors

Keeping the water in the shower, and not on the floor outside, is often a challenge to designers and users. A shower curtain will be easier to maneuver around. However, in smaller showers, the spray often extends beyond the shower floor and a curtain may not easily contain the water.

Enclosures and shower doors help to further seal the shower area and contain the water spray. In the case of a steam shower, the door opening will be sealed to the ceiling with a transom or a fixed panel.

The shower door should slide or open out toward the bathroom, a safety precaution to allow someone to get into the shower if the user falls. It also permits more clear space within the shower (see Figure 6.49). However, a shower door that opens into the bathroom may drip water onto the

FIGURE 6.50 Tempered glass is used for the shower door and enclosure. The no threshold shower has a bench seat and drainage at the back of the shower.

Design by NKBA member: Elizabeth A. Rosensteel

bathroom floor as the user steps out of the shower, so consider the flooring and using mats that will absorb the extra water. Shower doors that swing both in and out, and curtains, can be easier for maneuvering. Ideally, door openings should be a minimum 32 inches (813 mm) wide to allow for easy circulation in and out of the shower.

Glazing

According to the IRC building code, if glass is used in the shower surround or enclosure (including the door) it must be tempered glass (Figure 6.50; see Figure 6.38 for guideline reference). When using glass in this area, consider the sight-lines of the end users. Windows in the shower area that are below 60 inches (1524 mm) must be of tempered glass. Other glass windows or doors in the bathroom that are below 18 inches (457 mm) must be of tempered glass or an equivalent (Bathroom Planning Guideline 15).

Shower Controls

The showerhead should be placed so it directs water toward the body, not the face or hair. A fixed showerhead, roughed-in at 72 inches (1823 mm) to 78 inches (1981 mm) off the floor, is typical in many showers and tub/shower combinations. Plan the shower rough-in so that the bottom of the showerhead will be 72 inches (1823 mm) off the finished floor or at a height appropriate to the user.

A showerhead on an adjustable bar, or a handheld showerhead, offers flexibility in a shower used by persons of different heights, or for different activities. Consider a lever or loop handle control for ease of use. A handheld shower may be used in place of, or in addition to, the fixed showerhead to offer the user flexibility. This may be especially nice if the user will sit to shower.

When the adjustable height shower/hand spray is used, its lowest position should always be within the universal reach range (15 inches [381 mm] to 48 inches [1219 mm] above finished floor).

The most convenient way for a plumber to install the shower control valves is to line them up under the showerhead. However, this is not most convenient for the user. Being able to reach the controls while standing outside of the shower spray is ideal. NKBA Bathroom Planning Guideline 10 recommends that the controls be placed out of the water spray and between 38 inches (965 mm) to 48 inches (1219 mm) above the floor (see Figure 6.51). An accessible location is 6 inches (152 mm) from the outside of the fixture.

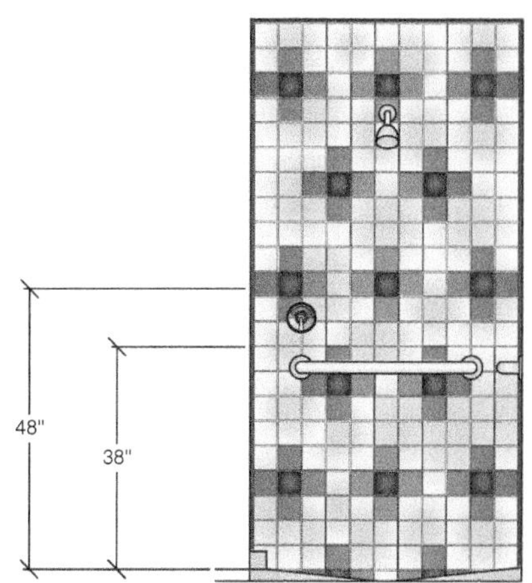

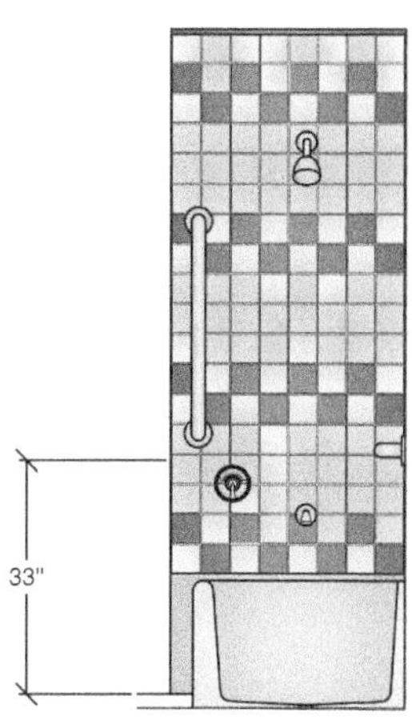

FIGURE 6.51 Shower controls should be placed 38 inches (965 mm) to 48 inches (1219 mm) off the floor (Bathroom Planning Guideline 10). Offsetting the controls toward the front of the shower will make them accessible both inside and outside the water spray.

NKBA

IRC building code requires that shower control valves must be either pressure balanced, have thermostatic mixing, or have a combination of both, to prevent scalding due to changes in water pressure (Bathroom Planning Guideline 11). Hot and cold water controls should be easily identified with red and blue indicators. If two people will be using the shower at the same time, there should be at least two showerheads, and each should be controlled separately. Design of the shower should take into account the number of body sprays, jets, control valves, and diverters needed. Consider the amount of water use these fixtures may require and select water-efficient shower fixtures whenever possible (see Figure 6.52). Refer to chapter 3, "Environmental and Sustainability Considerations," for more information on water use and the WaterSense program.

Access Panel

Plumbing fixtures in the shower must be accessible from an access panel. Furthermore, specialized showers may include mechanical equipment needed to provide steam, music, and lights. Access to this equipment should be planned as the shower is being designed so that it can be serviced (Bathroom Planning Guideline 19).

Grab Bars

Because most users stand in the shower, the risk of falling is great. Grab bars are recommended for the back and sides of the shower. Chapter 8, "Accessibility in Practice," provides more detail on placement. As in the bathtub, the grab bars in the shower should be able to support at least 250 pounds (113 kg).

The Guidelines and Access Standards recommend locations for grab bars. However, placing reinforcement throughout the shower walls allows clients to add supports when and where they will use them. Remember to maintain a water-tight seal to prevent water from seeping into these materials that are installed behind the finished wall.

Everyone is unique and their height and reach change as they age. A vertical bar at the shower entrance provides a helpful support when getting in and out. The surface and design of all grab bars should reduce the risk of a hand slipping on the bar.

Shower Seat

A seat or bench is very helpful to many people as they shower. A person, whose stamina is reduced due to age, pregnancy, injury, or too much physical activity, may not have the energy to stand throughout the shower. A woman may find a seated position the best position for shaving her legs. A seat or bench in the shower provides an opportunity to relax, assistance to people with limited strength or balance, and help with transfer.

NKBA recommends that a shower seat or bench be planned. It should be 17 inches (432 mm) to 19 inches (483 mm) high from the finished shower floor and at least 15 inches (381 mm) deep, finished (see Figure 6.53). Remember to allow for the thickness of the finishing material.

The seat or bench should not interfere with the recommended minimum shower size of 36 inches by 36 inches (914 mm by 914 mm) of floor area, although the IRC building code will allow the minimum 30 inch by 30 inch (762 mm by 762 mm) size to be maintained. Just as in the tub area, when less than 15 inches (381 mm) is available a narrower bench can benefit some users. Attention must be given to the user's size and weight so the seat will support the intended use.

Storage and Towels

Since the shower is a convenient place to wash hair and shave, it is likely that numerous products will be used there, and storage for items used daily will be important. A shelf built into the shower wall or surround at a convenient height to the user is a good solution.

Towels should be placed within reach of the person in the shower and 15 inches (381 mm) to 48 inches (1219 mm) above the floor. Extra towels will need to be stored close by. Refer to the previous section on towels and storage at the bathtub and to Bathroom Planning Guidelines 22 and 23 for guidance.

FIGURE 6.52 Water sprays and jets create a stress-relieving showering experience.
Courtesy of Grohe America

Guidelines and Access Standards for Bathing/Showering Center

The Bathroom Planning Guidelines and Access Standards important in planning the bathing and showering areas are 2, 4, 9, 10, 11, 12, 13, 14, 15, 16, 17, 18, 19, 22, and 23. For the complete Guidelines and Access Standards, review Appendix A.

TOILETING CENTER

Toileting is a universal activity of all bathrooms. It occurs in the master suite, as well as the powder room. In fact, "going to the bathroom" or "using the bathroom" often means using the toilet. But as with all the bath centers, there are many related activities to be considered in designing this area.

- The primary tasks taking place at the toilet are urination and defecation. Positions for urinating are culturally defined. A woman using a public toilet in Korea, for instance, may find that she is expected to stand over a receptacle in the floor. In North America, toilets have been designed so that women sit on the toilet and men stand when urinating, and both sit when defecating. Although Alexander Kira's research in the 1960s suggested that a squatting position is best for completing a bowel movement, this has not had an impact on the height of toilets in North America.

- The urinal is designed for a man to stand and urinate, and while common in commercial settings, it may also be a good idea in a house full of boys not known for accurate aim in using a toilet, and is becoming more common as a water-saving option.
- Another activity that can occur at the toilet is feminine hygiene, especially during the menstrual cycle. Having supplies of tampons and/or pads close by will assist in this activity. Sometimes medications must be used vaginally or anally and often this is done at, or close to, the toilet.
- All of the toilet area activities mentioned previously will require cleansing afterward. Having toilet paper close by is standard in the United States. Bidets are also being used by clients wishing a more thorough cleansing of the perineum area. The need for, and benefit of, the bidet increases as people age. Advanced toilet systems combine the toilet and bidet into one unit with automated controls.

A few other things might be considered when planning the toilet area. Some people read while sitting on the toilet, and having proper lighting and some reading materials stored in the area is helpful. Cleaning the toilet and surrounding areas should be done regularly to cut down on bacteria and odors, and having toilet brushes stored there will help make this easier. Ventilation should be planned in a toileting area to reduce odors.

The toilet is a major user of water in most households. Through changes in codes at the national, state, and local levels, manufacturers' design changes, and voluntary conservation programs, flushing systems have changed. Water use and flushing systems have become major considerations when selecting toilets for many clients concerned about sustainability. Chapter 3, "Environmental and Sustainability Considerations," has more information about these issues.

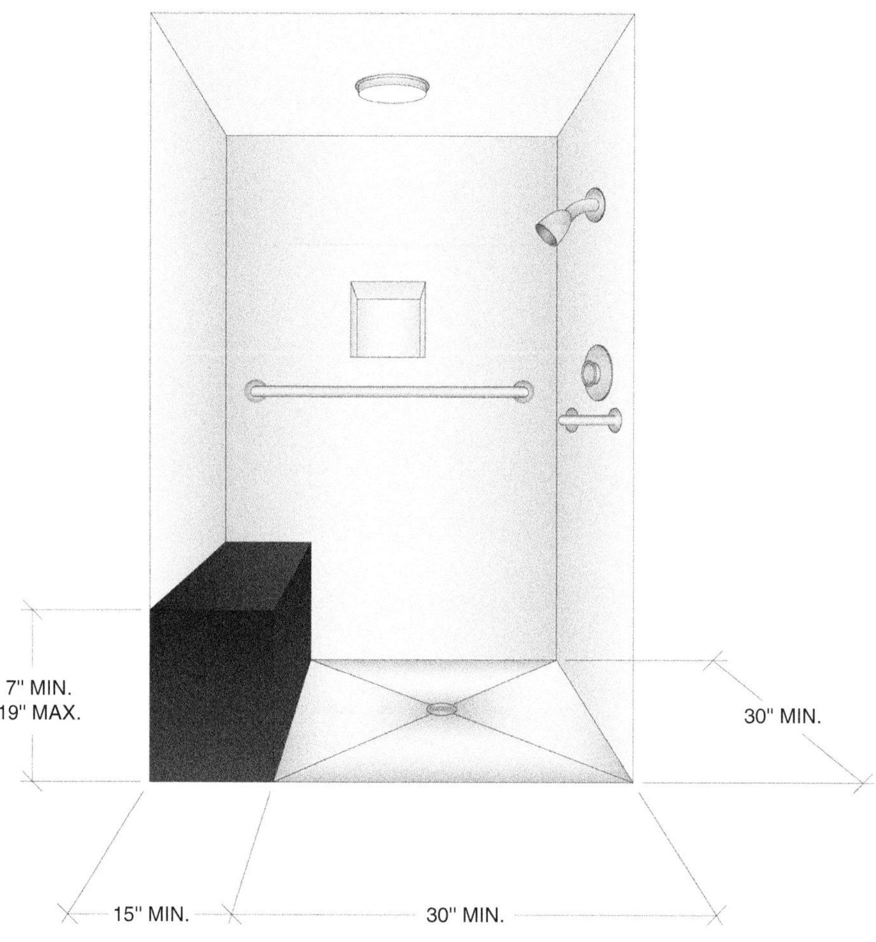

FIGURE 6.53 A shower seat or bench is recommended for the convenience and safety of all users (Bathroom Planning Guideline 12).
NKBA

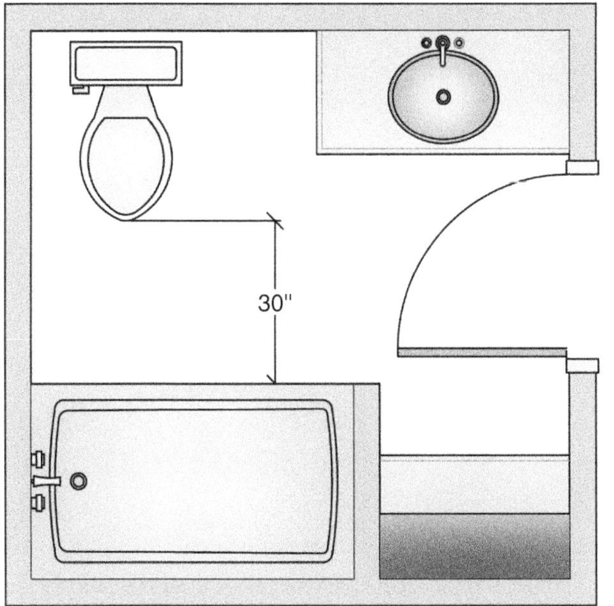

RECOMMENDED

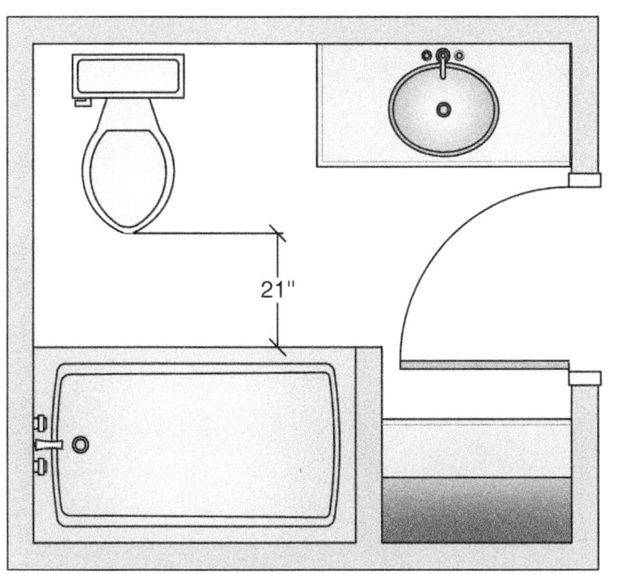

MINIMUM

FIGURE 6.54 Having at least 30 inches (762 mm) of clear floor space in front of the toilet allows for comfortable maneuverability. A minimum clearance of 21 inches (533 mm) is permitted (Bathroom Planning Guideline 4). *NKBA*

Design Recommendations for Toileting Center

The type and size of the toilet may affect the ability to meet some clearance recommendations, especially in small bathrooms. The two-piece toilet has a separate tank and bowl, while the one-piece toilet combines these and typically has a lower profile. The typical seat height of the toilet is between 14 inches (356 mm) and 17 inches (432 mm), although 17-inch (432 mm) to 19-inch-high (483 mm) toilets are growing in popularity, especially among aging baby boomers who have difficulty rising from a low seated position. For a person who transfers onto the toilet from a wheelchair, the best height for the toilet is to match the wheelchair height, with the average being plus or minus 18 inches (457 mm).

The toilet width ranges from 17 inches (432 mm) to 23 inches (584 mm). A toilet with a standard bowl is about 25 inches (635 mm) deep, while one with an elongated bowl is about 30 inches (762 mm). A wall-hung toilet with an in-wall tank will be about 22 inches (559 mm) deep. While not common, corner toilets are available for special applications. The fixture typically extends 33 inches (838 mm) from the corner and is about 15 inches (381 mm) wide.

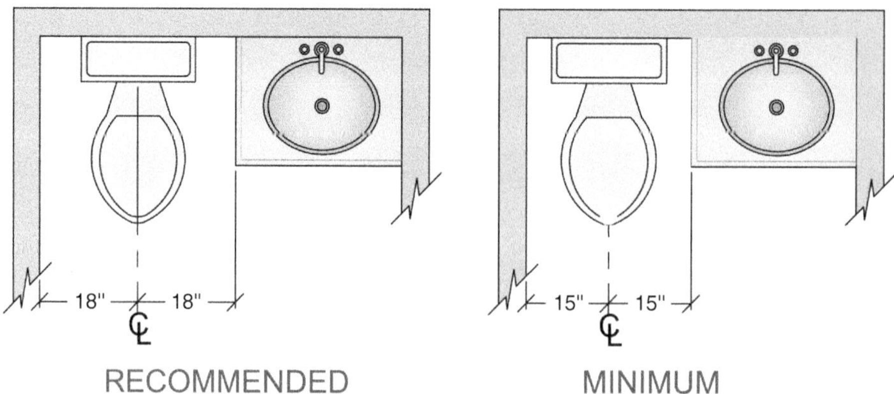

FIGURE 6.55 The toilet should be placed so that the center is 18 inches (457 mm) from a wall or other object. A minimum distance is 15 inches (381 mm) (Bathroom Planning Guideline 20).
NKBA

Floor Clearance

People using the toilet will need to stand, turn, sit, remove and replace parts of their clothing, and use nearby supplies like toilet paper. Bathroom Planning Guidelines recommend at least 30 inches (762 mm) of clear space in front of the toilet to allow for these activities, and perhaps more will be needed for larger people or persons needing assistance (see Figure 6.54). The IRC building code allows this space to be reduced to 21 inches (533 mm). This may allow leg room to sit on the toilet, but managing clothes will require moving to an area of the bathroom with more floor space.

For a person approaching the toilet with a mobility aid, or transferring from a wheelchair, 30 inches (762 mm) in front of the toilet is a minimum clear space, but more is better. For a person approaching and transferring from the side, plan a minimum 30 inches (762 mm) clear floor space to the side of the toilet. Wall-hung toilets improve the clear floor space, making it easier to maneuver at the toilet and to maintain the floor around it.

Plan reinforcement around the toilet area so that grab bars can be installed as needed or desired. Grab bars should be placed according to the user's requirements, including their method of transfer. Access Standards suggest that the grab bars be placed behind the toilet and on the wall beside

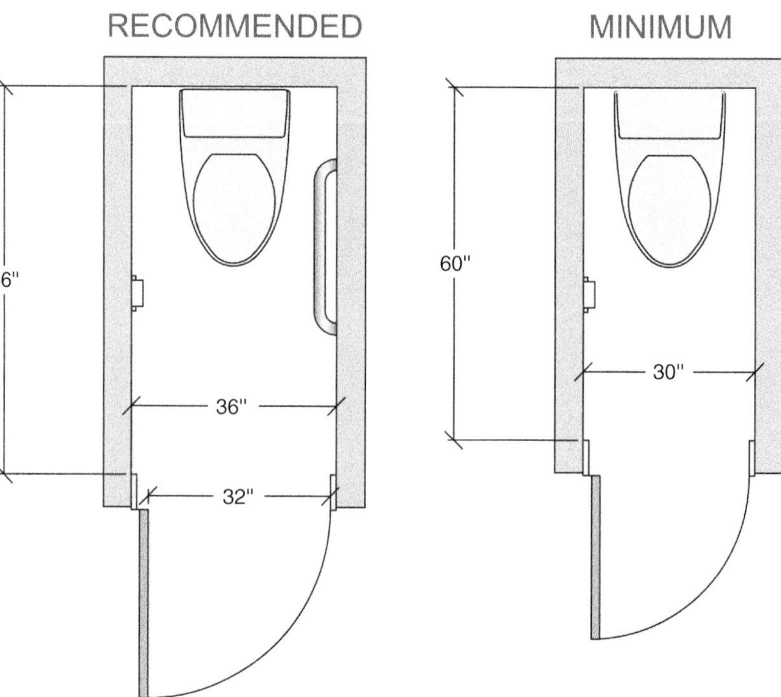

FIGURE 6.56 A toilet compartment that is 36 inches (914 mm) wide by 66 inches (1676 mm) deep allows for a 32 inch (813 mm) clear opening at the doorway and comfortable clearances around the toilet. A 30 inch by 60 inch (762 mm by 1524 mm) compartment will meet minimum building code requirements (Bathroom Planning Guideline 21).
NKBA

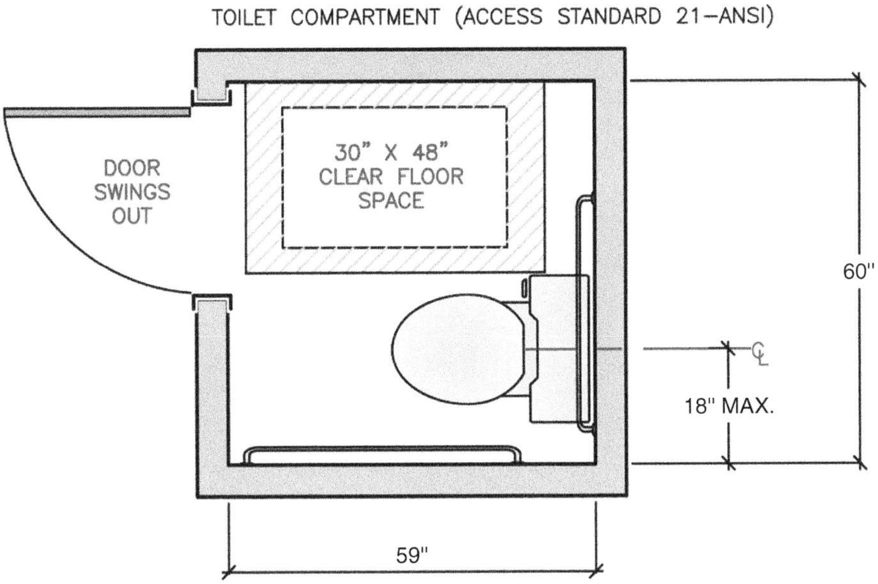

FIGURE 6.57 A toilet compartment that is 60 inches by 59 inches (1524 mm by 1499 mm) allows for a 30 inch by 48 inch (762 mm by 1219 mm) clear floor space beside the toilet (Bathroom Access Standard 21).
NKBA

it. See chapter 8, "Accessibility in Practice," for more information on transfers and grab bars at toilets.

Toilet Placement

The toilet can be in several places within the bathroom and may be within its own separate area or compartment if space allows. There should be clearances on both sides of the toilet to allow the user to be able to sit comfortably and to move the upper part of the body without bumping into a wall or counter.

Placing the toilet at least 18 inches (457 mm) on center from the nearest wall or obstacle is the recommended distance (see Figure 6.55). Building codes will typically allow the toilet to be placed 15 inches (381 mm) on center (Bathroom Planning Guideline 20). Remember that this should be

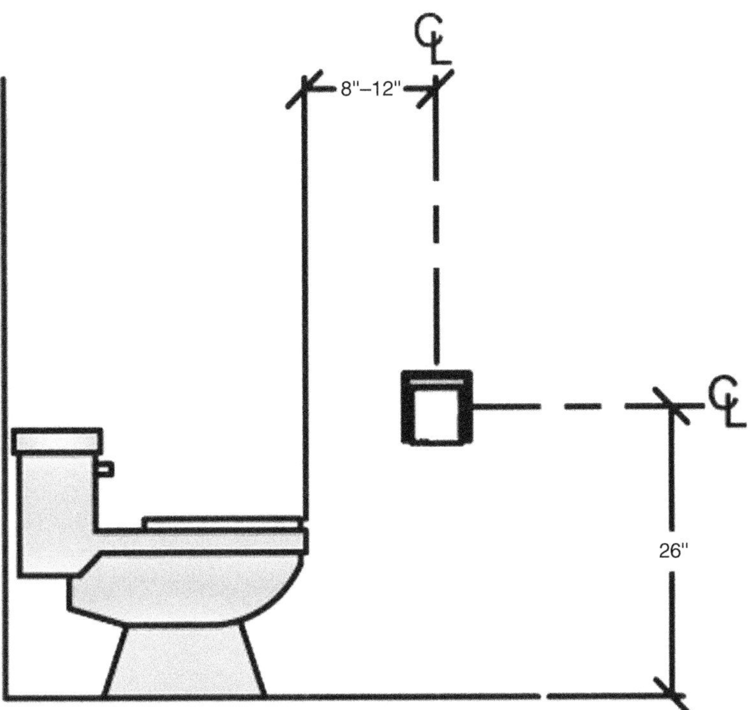

FIGURE 6.58 Place the toilet paper holder 8 inches (203 mm) to 12 inches (305 mm) in front of the toilet and 26 inches (660 mm) off the floor (Bathroom Planning Guideline 23).
NKBA

(*a*)

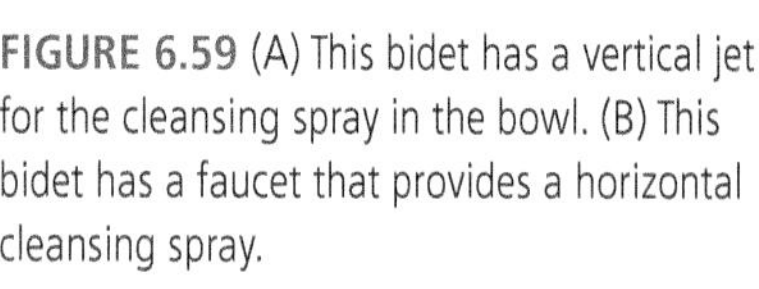

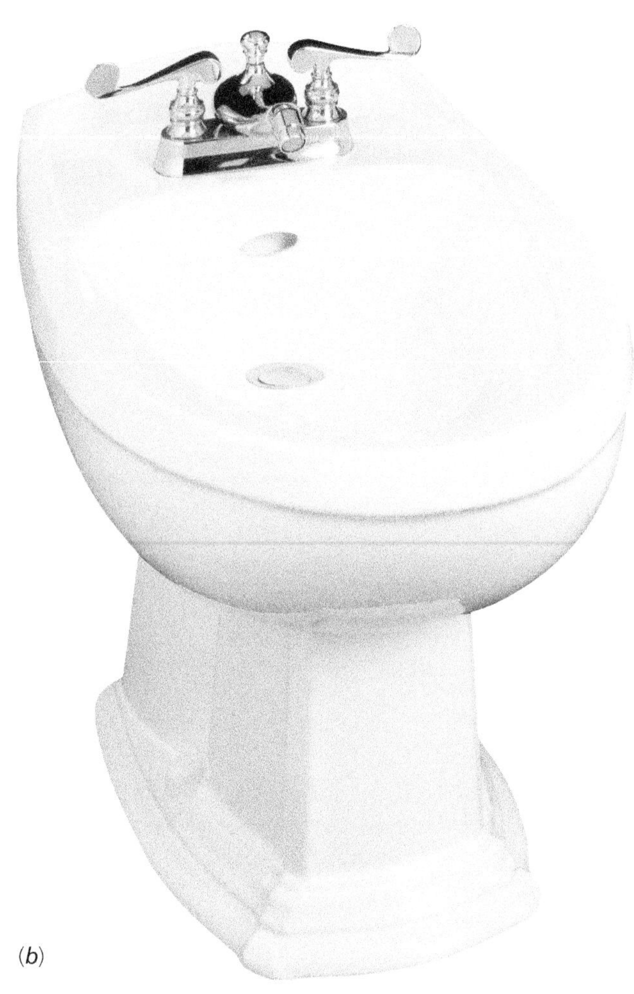

(*b*)

FIGURE 6.59 (A) This bidet has a vertical jet for the cleansing spray in the bowl. (B) This bidet has a faucet that provides a horizontal cleansing spray.
Courtesy of Kohler Company

a clear space. Placing another obstacle in the minimum space, such as a grab bar, towel bar, or toilet paper holder, will interfere with the clearance.

Toilet Compartment

Placing a toilet in a separate compartment can be accommodated by following the previously recommended clearances. A 36 inch by 66 inch (914 mm by 1676 mm) space measured from the inside walls will accommodate the recommended clearances. A 30 inch by 60 inch (762 mm by 1524 mm) space will comply with the IRC building code (see Figure 6.56).

In both applications, the door to the compartment should open out toward the adjacent room; otherwise the door swing will interfere with the clearance in front of the toilet. This size compartment is not recommended, because it limits options in transferring to a toilet, particularly for people using mobility aids. If one is used, it should be at least 60 inches by 59 inches (1524 mm by 1499 mm) (Bathroom Access Standard 21) (see Figure 6.57). An exception to this is the toilet area planned for a client with limited balance or stamina, as this client could benefit from a space with support within reach on both walls of the approach to the toilet.

Toilet Paper Placement

It is important that the toilet paper dispenser be convenient to the user. The best location is on a wall or partition to the side, and slightly to the front, of the toilet. This allows the user to reach the paper while seated. Locations behind the toilet or across from the toilet will be difficult to reach without bending or stretching. Bathroom Planning Guideline 23 recommends locating the toilet paper holder 8 inches (203 mm) to 12 inches (305 mm) in front of the toilet, centered 26 inches (660 mm) off the floor (Figure 6.58).

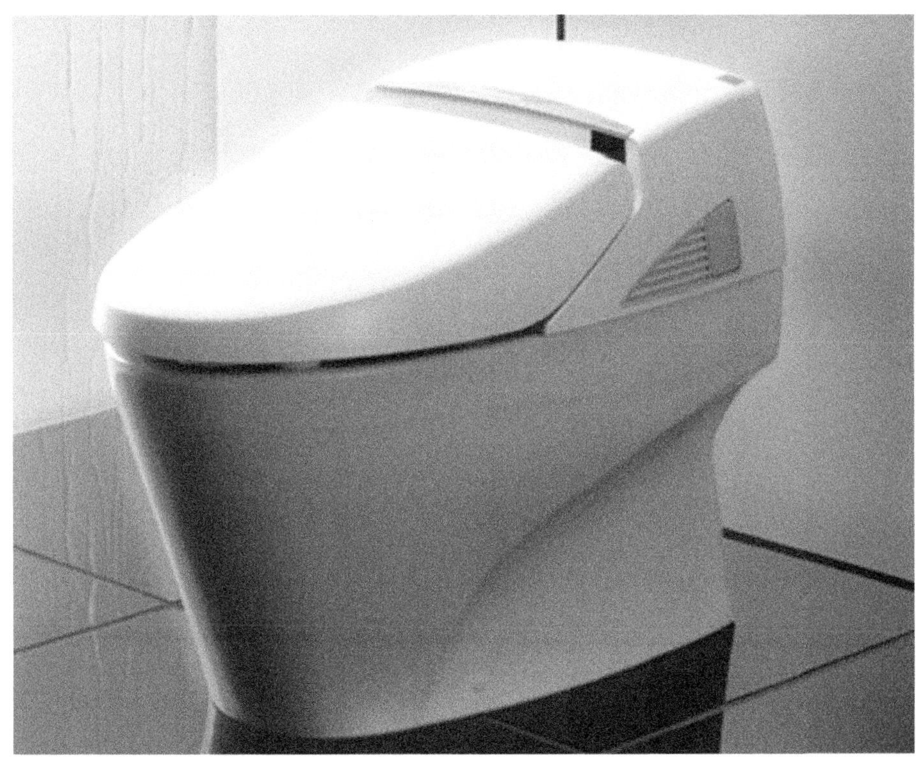

FIGURE 6.60 This toilet includes a washing system and uses sensors to control the toileting and cleansing actions.
Courtesy of TOTO

Storage

Bathroom Planning Guideline 22 also recommends locating storage close to, and accessible from, the toilet. Consider where extra toilet paper, feminine hygiene supplies, and medications are stored. Cabinets close by, and within reach of the person seated on the toilet, would assist them in performing whatever task needs to be completed in the toilet area.

Design Recommendations for Bidet

Bidets are used by straddling the bowl while facing the controls and the wall. Both hot and cold water must be provided. The bidet has a spray faucet spout (horizontal stream) or vertical spray in the center of the fixture (Figure 6.59). A pop-up stopper allows the bidet to be used more like a sink for a foot bath or hand washables. While the bidet looks similar to a toilet, it works like a sink.

The bidet provides cleansing for the pelvic area. Women may find the fixture particularly useful for douching and cleansing during their menstrual periods. The bidet also provides a cleansing for

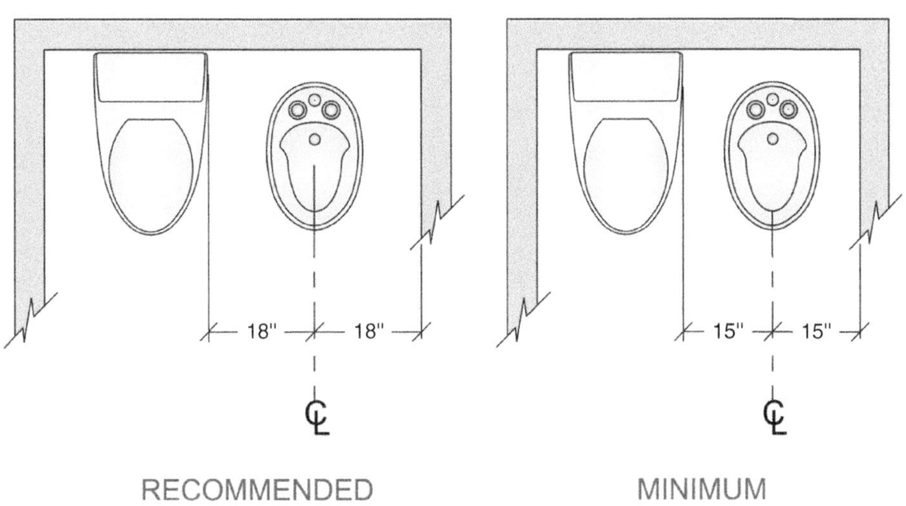

FIGURE 6.61 It is recommended that the bidet be placed 18 inches (457 mm) on center from a wall or other fixture and have a 30-inch (762 mm) clear floor space to the front of the fixture. Minimum clearances are 15 inches (381 mm) on center with a 21-inch (533 mm) clear floor space (Bathroom Planning Guidelines 4 and 20).
NKBA

both women and men that can help reduce irritation and heal rashes. The fixture may be especially useful for adults who have difficulty cleaning themselves. If a separate bidet cannot be included in the design, consider a toilet with an integrated bidet system or an add-on bidet system (Figure 6.60). These systems may have added features such as heated seats, lighting, air dryer, and air filters.

Clearances

The Bathroom Planning Guidelines 4 and 20 recommend clearances for the bidet that are the same as for the toilet (Figure 6.61). That is, 30 inches (762 mm) of clear space in front of the bidet, with the bidet placed 18 inches (457 mm) on center from the nearest wall, obstacle, or adjacent toilet. Minimum clearances are 21 inches (533 mm) of clear space in front of the bidet, with the bidet placed 15 inches (381 mm) on center from the nearest wall, obstacle, or adjacent toilet.

Storage and Towels

Some storage should be supplied close to the bidet. It is important to have towels and soaps located next to this fixture (Bathroom Planning Guideline 22).

Design Recommendations for Urinal

The urinal can be a very practical fixture in the home. The toilet is designed for seating. However, when men stand to urinate at the toilet, the urine spray may not stay in the bowl. Spray on the floor and around the toilet area can cause discoloration, staining, and odor. Men and boys of all ages can use the urinal with better control.

The height of the front lip of the bowl of the urinal off the floor should be 19 1/2 inches (495 mm) for children and 24 inches (610 mm) for adults. In a custom installation, plan the lip of the urinal at 3 inches (76 mm) below the man's pants inseam.

It is recommended that the urinal be placed 18 inches (457 mm) on center from a side obstacle, such as a toilet or wall. The minimum centerline distance is 15 inches (381 mm). Make sure at least 3 inches (76 mm) of clearance is allowed from the edge of the urinal to a side wall. A protective, durable wall surface material should cover at least 12 inches (305 mm) on either side of the urinal.

Flooring beneath, and in front of the urinal, should be of a durable material, as well.

The recommended clearance in front of the urinal is 30 inches (762 mm), the same as for other bath fixtures. The minimum clearance allowed is 21 inches (533 mm). Refer to chapter 3, "Environmental and Sustainability Considerations," to learn more about selecting water-efficient urinals.

Guidelines and Access Standards

The Bathroom Planning Guidelines and Access Standards that are important to the toileting area are 4, 14, 20, 21, 22, and 23. For the complete Guidelines and Access Standards, see Appendix A.

SUMMARY

The bathroom is an important part of any home and often a bathroom is located in both private and social areas. All bathrooms are composed of a combination of centers where the major activities of the bathroom occur: grooming, bathing/showering, and toileting. Planning a bathroom using the center concept encourages the designer to examine and use the NKBA Bathroom Planning Guidelines and Access Standards for each area. The Planning Guidelines are based on human factors and the 2012 International Residential Code. The Bathroom Access Standards are based on the 2009 International Code Council ANSI 1.117.

There are many decisions and details involved in creating a space plan for a bathroom that is functional and useable. Not only must the designer consider the client's needs and the physical space, the selection of products and materials in relation to the spatial requirements should also be considered. A certain style of lavatory or bathtub may be selected because of space and planning restrictions. On the other hand, the space may be arranged to accommodate the desired fixture or activity. There may be several ways that the bathroom could be planned depending on the choices that you make.

Budget, time, and space restrictions will influence how you incorporate the Guidelines within the parameters of each bathroom design. Of course, local building codes will have to be met and should be referenced during the design process. The Bathroom Planning Guidelines incorporate several building code requirements that must be followed when planning a bathroom: for instance, minimum space clearances, and requirements related to windows, doors, and access panels.

Beyond building codes, the Bathroom Planning Guidelines provide recommendations for space clearances at the entry and at each fixture. Universal design recommendations are also incorporated into the Planning Guidelines. Recommendations for slip-resistant flooring, rounded counter edges, grab bars at bathing and shower fixtures, and seating in the shower are helpful features that will make the bathroom safer.

Multiple Bathroom Access Standards also have been incorporated into this chapter's discussion of planning for a variety of users. Chapter 8, "Accessibility in Practice," provides a more detailed discussion of universal and accessible design concepts arranged according to user groups. This is a great place to look for ideas that might be useful if your client is older, has children, has a unique mobility or handedness requirement, or has sensory or cognitive impairments.

Remember that infrastructure requirements also must be considered. There are also decisions related to mechanical systems. Lighting, ventilation, heat, and placement of receptacles have been referred to in this chapter, but in chapter 7, "Mechanical Planning," there are more details (and Guidelines) related to these areas. Be sure you are familiar with these recommendations and requirements when you start to design a space.

Until you have mastered the planning criteria, be prepared to refer to the Bathroom Planning Guidelines and Access Standards. A quick reference for these Guidelines and Standards are in Appendix A.

REVIEW QUESTIONS

1. Describe the types of bathrooms in the privacy areas and in the social areas of the home. (See under "Types and Locations of Bathrooms" page 145)
2. List and discuss the Bathroom Planning Guidelines used to plan the entry, ceiling height, and circulation spaces of the bathroom. (See "Design Recommendations" page 154)
3. List and discuss the Bathroom Planning Guidelines used to design the grooming center of the bathroom. Identify which of these are building code requirements. (See "Design Recommendations for Grooming Center" page 201)
4. List and discuss the Bathroom Planning Guidelines used to design the bathing center of the bathroom. Identify which of these are building code requirements. (See "Design Recommendations for Bathing" page 179)
5. List and discuss the Bathroom Planning Guidelines used to design the showering center of the bathroom. Identify which of these are building code requirements. (See "Design Recommendations for Showering" page 187)
6. List and discuss the Bathroom Planning Guidelines used to design the toileting center of the bathroom. Identify which of these are building code requirements. (See "Design Recommendations for Toileting Center" page 195)

Mechanical Planning

Today's modern bathrooms are becoming multifunctional spaces that include an increasingly complex array of electrically powered devices. These electrical and mechanical components include the wiring for various electrical devices: entertainment equipment; heating, air conditioning, and ventilating equipment; and lighting. Consider the location and electrical needs of these items early in the project in order to assure the basic infrastructure is in place before the installation of finishes, cabinetry, and fixtures.

Learning Objective 1: Explain the mechanical systems that should be considered in bath planning.

Learning Objective 2: Describe important considerations for planning ventilation and lighting systems for a bathroom.

ELECTRICAL PLANNING

Whether building or remodeling, a careful evaluation of the space and planned components is extremely important. Use the Needs Assessment Forms provided in chapter 5, "Assessing Needs," to determine the planned electrical needs of the client. Then consult current codes to see what measures must be implemented in order to meet code approval. You might also suggest additional ideas for improving the system that the client may not have considered, especially those related to future needs or features they may not be able to afford at the current time.

Codes

The National Electric Code (NEC) and the Canadian Electric Code (CEC), which are almost identical, assure a safe electrical system which is a major consideration in the bathroom where water and electricity are in close proximity. To improve safety, these codes now require ground fault circuit interrupters (GFCI) (see Figure 7.1) in all bathroom receptacles. These devices reduce the hazards of electrical shock by cutting the electrical flow quickly when they detect that the flow going out to an appliance is different than the flow that returns. GFCI receptacles fit in the same space as the standard receptacles, but need to be appropriately wired.

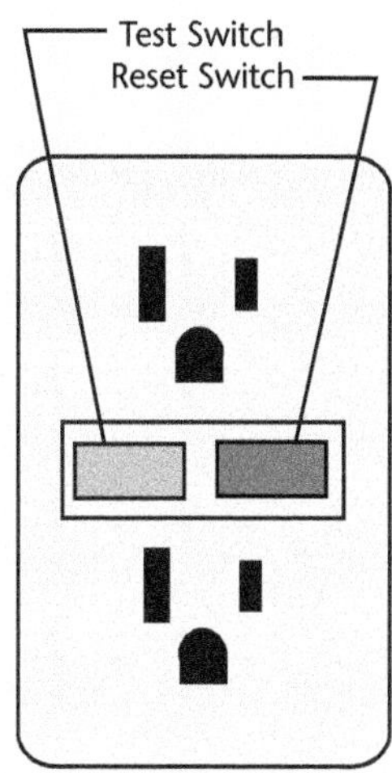

FIGURE 7.1 GFCIs are required in bathrooms by most local codes.
NKBA

Most local codes also require that at least one GFCI receptacle be installed within 36 inches (914 mm) of the outside edge of the lavatory (see Planning Guideline 24). These outlets shall be located on a wall or partition that is adjacent to the lavatory basin location, located on the countertop (but not in a face-up position on the countertop), or installed on the side or face of the basin cabinet not more than 12 inches (305 mm) below the countertop.

Furthermore, no receptacles can be placed within the tub or shower space. No switches can be located within wet locations, or within reach of a person standing in the tub or shower, unless the switches are part of a listed tub or shower assembly (see Planning Guideline 24).

Wiring

One component of older homes that is typically outdated is the wiring. Not only may the older wiring be in poor condition, it may also be made of unsafe materials like aluminum. In either case it should be replaced. Signs of inadequate or outdated wiring include:

- The home is over 30 years old and installed without a grounding system.
- A fuse box is present instead of a circuit breaker box.
- The wiring system has only two wires, and therefore is not grounded.
- Aluminum wire is present.
- No GFCIs are present.
- Fuses blow or circuit breakers trip often.
- Too few switches, receptacles, and lights are present.
- Extension cords are frequently used.
- The electrical supply at the entrance box or main entrance is 100 amps or less.

Aluminum wire, which has been found to develop fire hazards, was frequently used for new construction and remodeling from 1965 to 1973. Copper wire is now the wire of choice, so if aluminum wire is present, the entire home must be rewired as part of the remodeling project. Updating the wiring will ensure that the electrical system is safe and meets current electrical codes.

Adequate wiring for today's high-tech homes is as essential in the bathroom as in other rooms. Consumers are bringing more electrical devices into the bathroom, so plan ahead to ensure adequate wiring is available now and for future needs. Check to see if the room has an appropriate number of circuits. If not, can new circuits be added? Heaters for steam showers, saunas, and tubs will demand a large amount of electricity and may need 240-volt circuits, not commonly specified in older bathrooms. Be sure these new circuits are in place before the finishing work is completed.

Special Wiring Needs

With the addition of more equipment in the bathroom, especially in larger luxury bathrooms, plan for the wiring needs before walls are finished. Here are a few examples:

- Hard wire electric towel warmers or lighted magnifying mirrors to eliminate dangling cords.
- Incorporate wiring for towel warming drawers, antifogging mirrors, and heated toilet seats.
- Plan individual circuits for electric resistance heaters or electric floor heaters.
- Don't forget wiring for ceiling heaters and ventilation systems.
- Provide a line, and perhaps an individual circuit, to fixtures such as whirlpool tubs, steam showers, and some toilets and bidets.
- If a laundry area is being incorporated into the bathroom, plan a dedicated circuit for the clothes washer and/or clothes dryer. An electric clothes dryer will need a 240-volt circuit and some European clothes washers may also require a 240-volt circuit for heating water.
- If a television or a sound system is included, outlet receptacles will need to be located for their use as well as speakers that may be part of the system.

Receptacles

It seems that most rooms in the home never have enough receptacles to cover electrical needs, and the bathroom is no exception. Today's consumers are using an increasing number of appliances and electric devices for grooming and relaxation. In addition to the usual hair dryers and other hair care appliances, many families now have rechargeable appliances, like tooth brushes and shavers that are connected on a continuous basis. Additional dental care equipment or grooming equipment may also be present. Adding extra receptacles where these items are used would be advisable.

Consider including receptacles inside cabinets and on shelves for rechargeable appliances or other equipment like radios and televisions. It may also be a good idea to place a receptacle near the toilet for the possible addition of personal cleansing systems like a bidet or a fluid monitoring device. Some low-flush toilets and those with automated components like a pressure-activated toilet seat or other features may also require electricity.

Evaluate the receptacle needs in other areas of the bathroom (see Figure 7.2). Dressing areas may include space for ironing, clothes steamers, or the new clothes conditioning closets that steam and freshen clothing. Exercise and relaxation areas need receptacles for exercise equipment, video players, stereo systems, and televisions.

Communications

Communication devices are now coming to the bathroom, and the essential wiring for them should be considered in your design, especially in the luxury category. Linking the bathroom to the outside world and other parts of the house requires special wiring and planning. With new structured wiring bundles, many of the wires for communication are bundled together to make installation easier.

Internal home communication networks such as intercoms are becoming common, and bathrooms are logical components of these networks. Intercoms can be especially important if small children or older adults need assistance, but they must be easy to use and located where all users can easily access the controls. Wiring needs to be incorporated early in the project so that the speakers and controls for the system can be placed appropriately and wiring can be hidden behind walls. A telephone in the bathroom was once a luxury, but it can now be an easy addition. All it takes is extending another phone line. Although the phone is often found near the toilet, it can be located wherever the client finds it convenient to use, like near a sitting area. Help systems that use telephone lines for emergency calls may also be desired. Place the system where it can be easily accessed if someone needs help. A charging station for cell phones may also need to be located in the bathroom area.

As families include more activities in the bathroom, the television becomes a regular feature (see Figure 7.3). Linking the bathroom to the home cable or satellite system will allow family members to keep up with the news while they dress for work in the morning which might be a television screen as part of the mirror, view a program in the exercise area, and watch television as they relax in a spa or jetted tub. Some whirlpool and jetted tubs now come with the television built in. Connections for a DVD player and sound system are also part of the entertainment package. If the client does not want electronic equipment in the bathroom space, an alternative is to install speakers in the ceiling or in the wall which connect to equipment elsewhere.

Although Internet connections are not common in bathrooms at this time, there is no doubt they will be coming, especially as medical monitoring and security systems gain in popularity. Wiring for the Internet now, in anticipation of new uses, would be wise. Wireless systems could also be considered.

HEATING

Stepping out of a shower or tub with wet skin can be very chilling if the bathroom air is not at a comfortable temperature. There are many ways in which to add heat to the bathroom. The first step, however, is to take measures to reduce heat loss by sealing leaks, improving insulation in exterior walls, and upgrading the windows. Chapter 2, "Infrastructure Considerations," and chapter 3, "Environmental and Sustainability Considerations," provide more information on energy-efficiency considerations.

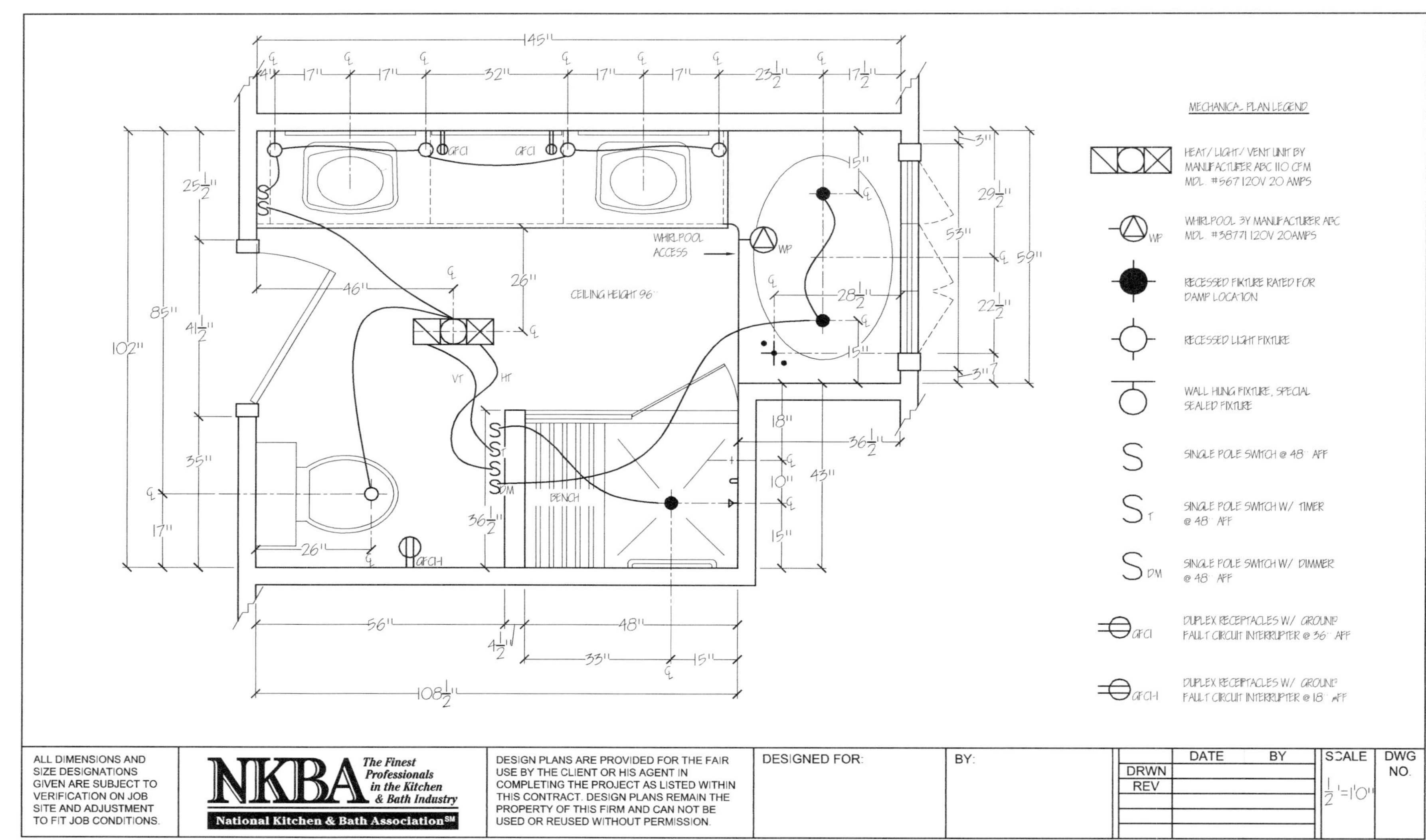

FIGURE 7.2 GFCI receptacles should be planned at each electrical point of use (Bathroom Planning Guideline 24). The correct electrical information on a mechanical plan will ensure that all electrical connections are included.

NKBA

FIGURE 7.3 Televisions and other entertainment and communications equipment are being incorporated into today's bathrooms.

Heating Considerations

When selecting a heating system for the bathroom, keep in mind the following:

- Even if the bathroom is part of the central heating system duct network, consider adding supplemental heat, especially if the bathroom is at the end of the duct run, or the client tends to keep the house cooler than they would like in the bathroom. Bathroom Planning Guideline 27 recommends a supplemental heat source and the IRC code (IRC R 303.8) states that all bathrooms should have an appropriate heat source to maintain a minimum room temperature of 68 degrees Fahrenheit (20 degrees Celsius).

- When ducting a central heating system into the bathroom, consider installing either a ceiling vent or a baseboard vent. Keeping the register off of the floor, especially in small bathrooms, will prevent users from stepping on the sharp vent with their bare feet.
- If converting a previously unheated area into a bathroom, or expanding a bathroom into an unheated area like a closet, be sure the central heating system can handle the additional load. If the new space is too far from a central heating system, a supplemental heater may be needed to deliver adequate heat.
- When multiple rooms need to be heated, use a zonal system that allows the flexibility to control the heating levels in each area separately.
- Strongly discourage the use of portable heaters as an option for supplemental heating. They are dangerous to use near water and can be a tripping hazard.
- If the shower is oversized or designed with a walk-in entry, additional heat may be necessary for comfortable use.
- If a tub/shower with a door is used, this enclosed area will also benefit from added heat.

Types of Supplemental Heaters

Heating systems for bathrooms come in a wide variety of types. They can vary as to installation needs, space requirement, responsiveness, comfort, and heating mode. Some of the most common choices are listed below.

- **Infrared heat lamp.** Recessed into the ceiling, these lamps are designed to heat what is directly below them. These heaters will do a decent job of warming your client up as they stand in one place, but because these heaters heat objects, they do not make good room heaters. As soon as someone moves from beneath the heater the air is cool. These lamps can be combined with a vent fan and light in a single ceiling fixture, or can be installed individually.
- **Ceiling-mounted convection heaters.** These units have a small heater and a fan that blows the warm air down onto the user and into the room. They may also be combined into a single ceiling unit with a vent fan and light. These units can heat a small bathroom area quite efficiently, but for larger bathrooms, multiple heaters or a more powerful unit would be needed.
- **Wall heaters.** Wall heaters are typically recessed into the wall and include a grate or screen over the heating elements. Most wall heaters are now electric, but some older homes may have gas wall heaters. Typically located on the lower portion of the wall, they can be somewhat dangerous because users can easily back into them and be burned.
- **Floor-mounted radiators.** In cases where hydronic heat is used throughout the home a client may have a radiator that must be incorporated into the plan. Protecting occupants from the hot radiator surface is an important consideration in a bathroom (see Figure 7.4).
- **Ceiling or wall panel heaters**. Electric heating coils can be installed in the ceiling or in walls behind the drywall. Ceiling units are especially welcome over a bathtub to keep the air warm. For wall applications, do not install the heaters higher than 48 inches (1219 mm) to avoid hammering a nail into the electric coils when hanging pictures.
- **Toe kick heater.** A small electric heater installed in the toe kick below the cabinet can provide comfortable supplemental heat to the feet and floor area (see Figure 7.5). Provision for this type of heater needs to be made when the cabinet is selected and installed.
- **Baseboard heaters.** Baseboard heaters are placed along the wall at floor level and can be either electric or hydronic. These are inexpensive to install and allow zonal control, but take up valuable floor space. Many small bathroom designs do not have enough wall space to accommodate this type of heater.
- **Floor heating systems.** Floor heating systems can be either electric or hydronic and will incorporate heating coils or tubes directly under the flooring materials. Floor heaters are popular in the bathroom because they give off an even heat that is comfortable to the feet. Stepping out of the tub or shower onto a warm floor is very soothing. Children especially like the warm floors because that is where they end up most of the time.

  Electric floor heating systems are typically easier to install during construction. Hydronic systems are a good choice if there is hot water heat in other parts of the home. Hydronic tubing

FIGURE 7.4 Framing over a radiator can protect occupants and be an attractive addition to the bathroom.

Design by NKBA Member Cindy McClure, CKD, MCR, CGP

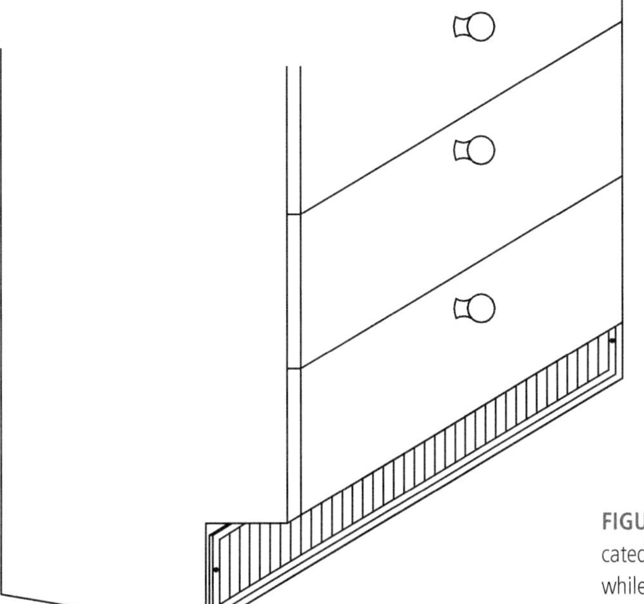

FIGURE 7.5 Small supplemental heaters located in the toe kick space can warm the feet while standing at the vanity.

NKBA

can also be placed behind mirrors to prevent fogging, or used as the heating system for a towel warmer.

Either type of floor heater will raise the height of the floor because of the heating elements being placed under the flooring material, so door clearances may need to be adjusted. In new construction the additional thickness can be easily incorporated into the plan, but when remodeling, an already established door may need to be trimmed in order to clear the new floor height. It is not advisable to install floor heating systems under wood floors that could be damaged by excessive heat, unless you use a product that is designed to be installed under wood flooring. There are also special products that are made to be installed under carpet.

Towel Warmers

Stepping out of the shower or bath and into a nice warm towel can be very inviting. Most towel warmers come in the form of a wall- or floor-mounted rack, and they are designed to heat and dry bath towels as they drape over the rods (see Figure 7.6). Some of these warmers, however, can also be used as the heater for the bathroom, serving two functions. Towel warmers come in both hydronic and electric models. The electric style can be either hard wired or plugged into a wall receptacle. To minimize the number of dangling cords, hard wiring is preferred. Hydronic styles can be used if there is already a hydronic system for other heating.

FIGURE 7.6 Electric or hydronic towel warmers can not only warm towels but heat the room as well.
Design by NKBA member: Stephanie Tozzo

Another type of towel warmer is the warming drawer. It is designed more for heating dry towels; a towel bar is still needed for drying wet towels. A warming drawer requires additional wiring in the back of the cabinet. If the drawer is to be integrated, specify the cabinet and doors to fit with the warming drawer unit.

COOLING

Bathroom comfort is important all year around. When warm weather arrives, your client will expect measures to be incorporated into the bathroom that will ensure a comfortable environment that is void of excess heat and extreme humidity. Although cool air can be chilling when stepping out of a shower or bathtub, it might be welcomed after a sauna or in an exercise or grooming area.

Climate will have a substantial impact on necessary cooling measures. In northern climates, little, if any, mechanical cooling may be necessary if summertime temperatures are not extreme. In warmer climates, mechanical cooling is essential for the most part.

In addition to cooling, some mechanical units can help remove excess humidity, which is important in the bathroom where so much extra moisture is added to the air during showering and bathing. If a closet or dressing area is part of the bathroom suite, less humid air in this area will help clothing slip on and off more easily. Air conditioning units are not, however, a replacement for good ventilation.

Home orientation is another factor that can affect cooling needs. If the bathroom is located on the east or west sides of the home, windows on these walls, especially large windows or those unprotected by landscaping, can allow a large amount of heat into the space. More cooling will be necessary during certain parts of the day. Northern windows and properly protected southern windows should not have heat gain problems from direct sunlight.

Lastly, cooling needs are affected by the home's level of insulation. Just as good insulation will help keep a home warmer in the winter, it will also benefit it in the summer, keeping the entire home cooler and requiring less mechanical cooling.

There are two main types of cooling methods you might plan into the bathroom project: natural and mechanical. Depending upon the climate, you may decide to incorporate one or both methods.

Natural Cooling

If you have operable windows, the most basic method of natural cooling is to open windows to let in fresh air during the cooler part of the day or night. Even on fairly warm days, allowing in cool night air and then closing windows during the heat of the day may be enough to keep a home or bathroom space comfortable. If you have windows on two sides of a room, opening these windows will set up cross ventilation to increase air circulation. Windows with low-e coatings can assist by reflecting the heat back out. Surface materials can also assist with cooling. Ceramic tile, stone, concrete, and other massive materials can provide a cool touch to the room. However, these materials will also feel cool in colder weather and may lead to discomfort during that time of year.

Mechanical Cooling

If natural cooling methods cannot give the comfort levels desired, then mechanical means are necessary. The most basic of mechanical devices is the fan. Although portable and window fans are available, they are not attractive and take up space in a room that may already be short on space. A ceiling fan may be a better option if the ceiling is high enough to accommodate one. Ceiling hugger fans are available for standard height ceilings, but taller clients may have an issue with whirling blades just a short distance above their heads. More information about fans is included in the section about ventilation.

Other mechanical cooling methods include refrigerated cooling and evaporative cooling. When incorporating either type, be aware of how the vent placement may affect the installation of fixtures, cabinetry, and other components. Also evaluate how the vent location will affect the occupants. Cool air blowing directly onto people will not be very comfortable.

VENTILATION

Ventilation is critical in a well-designed bathroom and is necessary for moisture control and healthy indoor air quality, as also discussed in chapter 3, "Environmental and Sustainability Considerations." The designer's responsibility is to plan a balanced and efficient system that does not compromise user comfort. Importantly, the designer needs to provide a ventilation system that will be used by the occupants.

Residential ventilation systems are generally designed with the assumption that indoor air is improved by mixing or replacing it with outside air. Air from outdoors is perceived to be fresher. Depending on the location of the home, this may not always be true. If the outside air is polluted, special ventilation systems may be needed that provide additional air filtration.

The minimum requirement for bathroom ventilation, as specified by the model 2012 International Residential Code (IRC), is an operable window of at least 3 square feet (0.3 square meters). One-half of the window area must be operable (1.5 square feet, .14 square meters). Within the IRC, an alternative to a window is an exhaust ventilation system (minimum 50 cfm, 23.6 liters per second), vented directly to the outside, provided adequate light is otherwise available.

Most experts recommend an exhaust system for bathrooms for more effective ventilation. NKBA Planning Guideline 26 states: "Plan a mechanical exhaust system, vented to the outside, for each enclosed area," of the bathroom, such as an enclosed toilet compartment (see Figure 7.7).

Windows

Although windows can be used to meet code requirements, relying on them for all bathroom ventilation can be a problem. It may not be practical or comfortable to open a window on cold or rainy days. An open window may compromise privacy or security. A single open window may not be enough to provide adequate air circulation to remove moisture.

Windows can be used in a bath not only for light and view, but also to supplement ventilation. If a window is being used for ventilation, place it high on the wall to take advantage of the natural

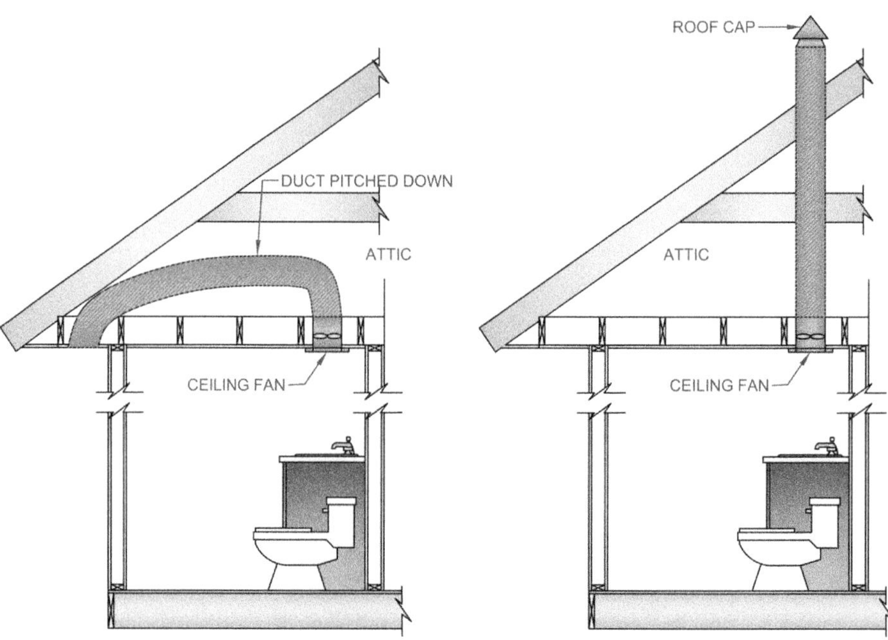

FIGURE 7.7 Plan a mechanical exhaust system, vented to the outside, for each enclosed area of the bathroom (Bathroom Planning Guideline 26).
NKBA

tendency of warm, moist air to rise. For example, operable skylights or roof windows can provide ventilation in nice weather. However, be aware that the placement of an operable skylight or roof window is dependent on maintaining building code requirements for a horizontal and vertical clearance from a plumbing vent.

Fan Systems

As stated, the most effective ventilation system for a bathroom is a mechanical one that exhausts air to the outside. This type of ventilation can be designed to remove moisture and control odors. Selecting the right fan is important, but only part of the decision. Bathroom ventilation must be considered as a system, including the fan, ducts, controls, and installation.

Many people resist using a bathroom fan because of the noise. A loud fan can be annoying, especially when using the bathroom as a stress-reducing retreat. The noise level of fans is rated in sones and fans vary in their sone rating. Generally, a fan rated less than 1.0 to 1.5 sones will be quiet enough to be considered background noise.

Choices in Bathroom Fans

Axial or propeller fans are common in bathrooms. This type of fan tends to be less expensive, but can be noisy. Centrifugal or "squirrel cage" fans are generally quieter, but can be more expensive (see Figure 7.8).

The Home Ventilating Institute (HVI) classifies bathroom fans according to the following types:

- **Ceiling-mounted fans**. Mounted in the ceiling between joists, this type of fan pushes air through ducts to the outside. Air can be exhausted vertically through the roof or horizontally out an exterior wall. If installing a fan in an insulated ceiling, specify a fan appropriate for this type of installation.
- **Fan lights**. This single fixture includes lights as well as the fan. If this type is selected, make sure that the location is optimal for both lighting and ventilation, and that the lighting is the type desired. Some fan lights may also include an infrared heater.
- **Exterior-mount fans**. This type of fan mounts outside the room, in either a ceiling or wall, and air is pulled through the ducts to the outside. Because the fan is mounted outside the room, these types of fans tend to be quieter.
- **Inline fans**. In this type of fan, the motor is mounted in the duct system. Often, inline fans are part of a whole-house ventilation system where exhaust vents are in more than one location. Keeping the fan motor out of the living space results in quieter operation.
- **Wall fans**. This type of fan is located on an exterior wall, and exhausts air directly to the outside without using any ducts.
- **Whole-house ventilation systems**. There are different types of systems that provide continuous ventilation of a house, exhausting air from it and bringing in outside air. A typical system will have an air intake in the bathroom and the fan will run continuously. More information on whole-house ventilation systems is provided below.

There are toilets on the market that are direct-vented to control odors and vapor spray from flushing. These are not likely to be adequate to control moisture from other bathroom sources. However, the exhaust venting capacity of the toilet needs to be considered in planning the total bathroom ventilation.

Fan Size

Bathroom fans are sized in cfm (cubic feet per minute) or L/s (Liters per second). These terms both describe the volume of air the fan can move in a period of time. The model 2012 IRC specifies a minimum of:

- 50 cubic feet per minute (23.6 L/s) intermittent exhaust capacity, or
- 20 cubic feet per minute (9.4 L/s) continuous exhaust capacity.

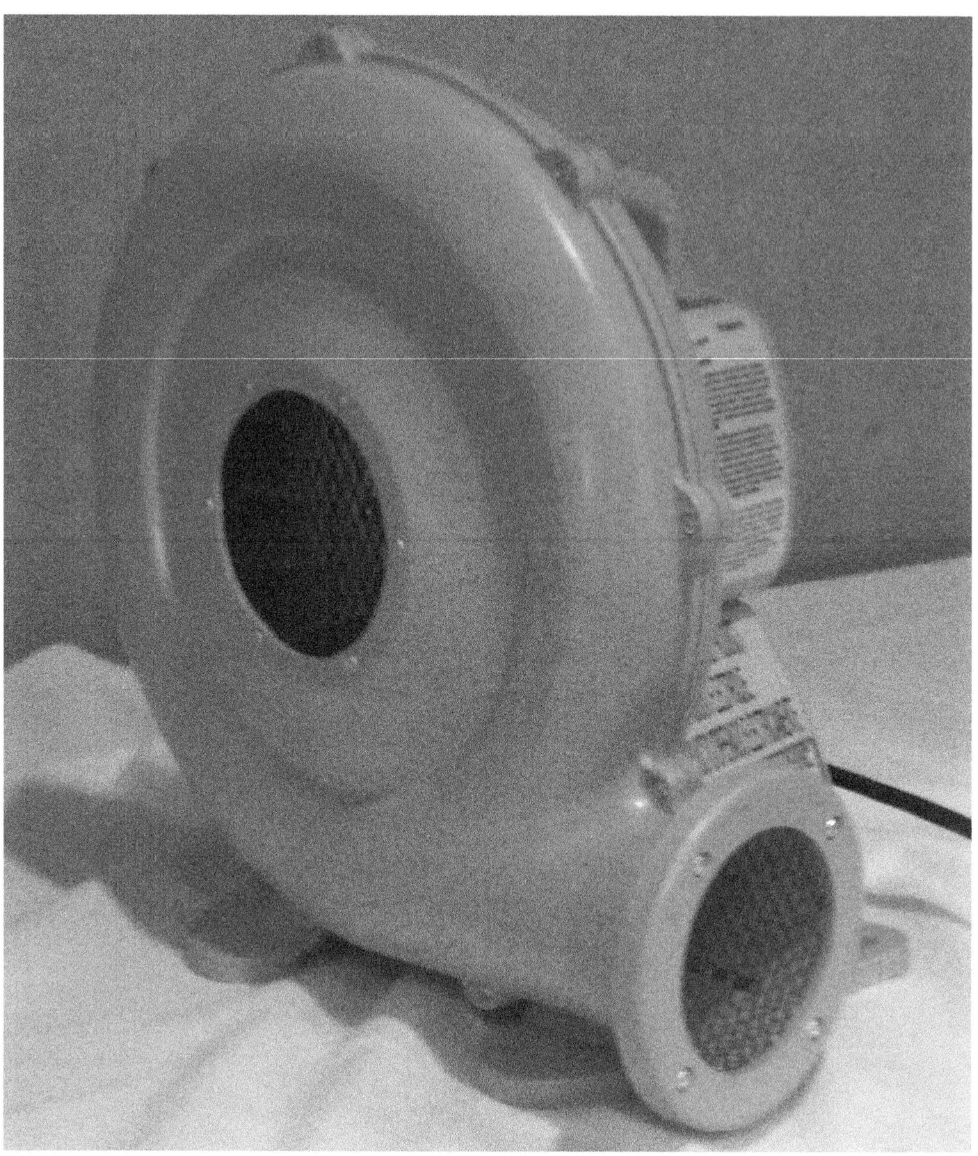

FIGURE 7.8 A centrifugal fan can provide quieter operation.

However, these IRC requirements are minimums and do not consider the size of the room, the amount of moisture produced, or the efficiency of the installation.

A more effective way to consider fan size is to look at ventilation needs and then size the fan accordingly. The Home Ventilating Institute recommends that the fan system should provide eight air changes per hour (ACH). This means that in one hour, the fan must be able to exhaust a volume equal to eight times the volume of the room. To determine what size fan is needed, follow this formula:

Step 1—Determine the volume of the room in cubic feet:
Length × width × height = volume of room

Step 2—Multiply the volume of the room by 8 ACH
Step 3—Divide by 60 minutes in an hour to get cfm

Example A: A bathroom is 8 feet 6 inches (8.5 feet) by 10 feet, with 8-foot ceilings

Step 1—8.5 × 10 × 8 = 680 cubic feet
Step 2—680 × 8 = 5440 cubic feet per hour
Step 3—5440/60 = 90.67 cubic feet per minute (cfm)

Example B (a metric example): A bathroom is 3 meters by 3.5 meters with a 2.5 meter ceiling.

Step 1—3 × 3.5 × 2.5 = 26.25 cubic meters
Step 2—26.25 × 8 = 210 cubic meters per hour
Step 3—210 × 1000 = 210,000 liters/hour
Step 4—210,000/60 = 3500 liters/minute
Step 5—3500/60 = 58.3 liters/second

A short-cut to this formula is to take the volume of the room (length × width × height) and divide by 7.5.

The fan size determined by the air change per hour method is effective fan capacity—or how much air the fan can actually move. Effective fan capacity is not the same as the mechanical size of the fan. The effective fan capacity will depend on a number of factors including:

- Length of duct runs from the intake vent to the exhaust vent. Generally, if the duct run is more than about 5 feet (1.5 meters), the size of the fan should be increased to compensate for the resistance of a longer duct run.
- Elbows or bends in the ducts. Generally, if there is more than one elbow or bend in the duct, the size of the fan should be increased to compensate for the greater resistance.

Size of the Bathroom

Larger bathrooms may have additional fixtures, especially jetted tubs or both a shower and bathtub, which produce more moisture and increase the need for ventilation. The Heating Ventilating Institute recommends that for larger bathrooms (over 100 square feet) (9.3 square meters), determine ventilation based on the fixtures. Add fan capacity as follows:

- Toilet: 50 cfm (23.6 liters per second)
- Shower: 50 cfm (23.6 liters per second)
- Bathtub: 50 cfm (23.6 liters per second)
- Jetted tub: 100 cfm (50 liters per second)

Fan Controls

Bathroom fans are available with different types of control systems. Whatever types of switches are chosen, make sure that they are easy to read and understand, and that clients can operate them.

Sensor controls are available that turn fans on and off based on humidity, and can provide excellent moisture control. Motion detectors turn a fan on when someone is in the bathroom, and then turn it off after they leave. However, motion detectors may not work effectively in some situations, such as when someone is soaking in a tub. Automatic timers can be convenient.

After showering or bathing, it may take time for moisture removal from the bathroom and ventilation system. The Home Ventilating Institute recommends that the ventilation system continues to operate for 20 minutes after use of the bathroom. A timer switch can help provide moisture control without wasting energy. Electronic timers can be easy to use, accurate, and offer many features. Variable speed controls allow the user to match the speed of the fan to the need for ventilation. The ability to run the fan at a slower (and quieter) speed may encourage more frequent use of ventilation.

Some fans are wired into the same switch as the bathroom light, so that the fan comes on with the light. This is a good way to ensure that ventilation is always provided. If this type of switching is selected, it is very important to use a quiet fan. Putting the light and fan on the same switch does have a drawback. To leave the fan running after bathing or showering, the light must also be left on—even if no one is in the bathroom.

Fan Location

Warm air tends to rise. In addition, the warmer the air, the more moisture it holds. Therefore, the warmest air, with the most moisture, tends to be near the ceiling. So the ceiling, or a high place on a wall, is the best place for a fan.

Another factor in fan location is having the air intake close to the source of air and moisture to be exhausted. Therefore, the best location for the fan is usually near the toilet, bathtub, and/or shower. Some fans are designed to be located in the shower or directly over a jetted tub. They are usually described as "vapor proof" or "moisture proof."

Consider the visual impact of the fan in placing it. The color and style of the fan grille, the choice of materials, and the relationship of the fan to other features such as lights that are mounted on the ceiling and wall should all be considered. In a larger bathroom, you may want to specify two exhaust fans, one over the toilet or near the floor, and one over the bathtub or shower. The size of these two fans can be added together to determine the total ventilation capacity of the bathroom. An advantage of using two smaller fans is that the smaller fans are usually quieter than one larger fan, which might encourage their use.

If the toilet is in a separate compartment, it will need its own ventilation fan. This can be sized using the eight ACH formula.

The relationship of the interior air intake (in the bathroom) and the exterior air exhaust (outside) needs to be considered in locating the fan. Minimizing the length of the duct run, as well as the number of elbows or bends, will increase the efficiency of the fan system.

Fan Installation

Smooth ducts with sealed joints will offer less resistance to air movement and provide quieter, more efficient operation. Any duct that must go through spaces that are not heated or cooled should be insulated to help prevent moisture condensation. The ducts should not terminate in the attic, but continue to the outside. Warm, moist air being exhausted into the attic can lead to condensation and eventual structural problems.

A back draft damper on the exhaust vent is important to the fan system. This prevents outside air from leaking back into the home when the fan is not operating. Also, the flap can prevent insects, birds, and other animals from getting into the fan duct.

A fan that is installed on rubber gaskets or similar cushioning material is less likely to vibrate and will operate more quietly.

Make-up Air

When a bathroom fan is operating, it is exhausting or removing air from the room. This creates a negative pressure in the room—and replacement air must come from somewhere. If replacement air is not provided, the effectiveness of the fan is reduced. A bathroom door should be undercut slightly to allow air to flow into the room, even with the door closed. A louvered door is sometimes used, although this may be unsatisfactory from a privacy concern.

The bathroom fan is not just exhausting air from the bathroom, but from the whole house. Some of the replacement air may come from open windows, or from people moving in and out of doors. Some replacement air may come from leaks and cracks in the building envelope. However, in well-constructed, energy-efficient homes, there are few places for replacement air to leak into the home.

If replacement air is not provided, negative pressure can become an issue. Problems can occur with the operation of appliances that need to exhaust to the outside, such as gas furnaces or water heaters. This situation is referred to as *back drafting*. When back drafting occurs, dangerous combustion pollutants, such as carbon monoxide, as well as excess moisture and radon can be pulled into the home.

A simple solution to back drafting problems, and to providing replacement air, can be opening a window when operating exhaust fans. However, this is not always practical. Other solutions include passive fresh air intake vents in the home and a whole-house mechanical ventilation system that balances airflow.

Whole-House Ventilation Systems

The 2012 International Energy Conservation Code, which has been incorporated into the 2012 International Residential Code (IRC) requires whole-house mechanical ventilation to provide adequate fresh air as well as moisture control into the tightly constructed, energy-efficient homes built to the code. With a whole-house mechanical ventilation system, the system operates continuously, providing a constant stream of fresh air to ventilate the home. Advantages to whole-house ventilation also include quiet operation, better moisture control, greater comfort, and less need for motivation to use ventilation fans.

There are different types of whole-house ventilation systems. In some cases, the design of the system needs to be matched to the type of climate—heating or cooling dominated. An effective and popular type of whole-house ventilation system is a balanced mechanical ventilation system. This type of system is available as a Heat Recovery Ventilation (HRV) system or Energy Recovery Ventilation (ERV) system. HRV and ERV systems work similarly and are effective in all types of climates.

In a balanced mechanical ventilation system (see Figure 7.9), fans are used to exhaust air from the home as well as to bring it into the home. Exhaust vents are located in areas of the home where moisture and pollutants are most likely to be generated, including bathrooms. Fresh air vents are centrally located but away from main living areas, such as in an entryway or closet. Exhaust and air pass through a heat exchanger. During the heating season, exhaust air preheats the incoming air. In the cooling season, the exhaust air is cooler than the air, so the reverse process occurs, and the incoming air is cooled. Thus, the house is ventilated and energy is conserved as well.

The HRV system transfers heat between incoming and outgoing air. The ERV system also provides moisture management by dehumidification or humidification, providing further energy savings.

FIGURE 7.9 A whole-house ventilation system provides controlled, uniform ventilation throughout the house
U. S. Environmental Protection Agency

WATER HEATING

Whether showering to prepare for a busy day or looking forward to a nice soak in the tub after a stressful day, an adequate supply of hot water is essential for the bathroom, as well as other rooms in the home. To ensure that hot water meets the demand and your client's satisfaction, plan the hot water needs carefully so that plenty of water will be available during peak use times.

Water Heater Location

How quickly hot water arrives to the bathroom fixtures can vary depending on the location of the water heater in relation to the bathroom. A somewhat common home design scenario is where the bathroom ends up on the opposite end of the house from, or two stories above, the home's water heater. Not only does this make for a long time lapse before hot water reaches the bathroom fixtures, but a large amount of water is wasted while waiting for the hot water to arrive.

If this appears to be an issue, a second water heater located near the bathrooms, would be a good idea. A second water heater may also be recommended if your client wants to install a whirlpool-type tub or multihead showers that require a large amount of hot water.

Selection Considerations

If after evaluating the hot water situation of your client you decide you either need to replace and/or upgrade the hot water source and delivery system, there are a number of factors to consider. These include fuel type, heater type, size, energy efficiency, and cost.

Water Heater Types

Water heaters can be of three basic types—tank, on-demand, and hybrid. The type best fits your client's needs depends on their hot water needs, storage space, and home size.

- **Tank.** Tank type units are what we commonly see in U.S. homes. This type of water heater keeps water hot on a 24-hour basis, adding more heat when the thermostat is below the set water temperature. Because these standard tank units keep water hot all the time they are more energy intensive than other types. Some larger households may have one tank located in the garage or basement and a second tank on the second floor or across the house. These tanks vary in size and fuel type and require a space large enough to store the tank.
- **On-demand.** On-demand water heaters, also called instantaneous water heaters, are becoming more popular and can also vary in size and fuel type. An on-demand water heater heats the water to a preset temperature as it is used and therefore does not require a storage tank. Smaller units are becoming popular in the kitchen as an instant source of near-boiling water for instant soups, coffee, tea, and other drinks. These units can be located in a cabinet under the sink or wherever the fixture is located. Whole-house units are large units that supply enough water for the entire home and are also wall mounted, typically in the garage or basement. Efficiency ratings of these units can vary. All whole-house units are limited in their capacity, especially the electric type, so be sure to carefully calculate the client's needs if you recommend this type of water heater.

Fuel Type

Water heaters can be fueled by a number of different sources and the type you choose depends on the client's preferences and where they live. Each has its advantages and disadvantages.

- **Electric.** Electric units are typically less expensive to buy but will generally cost more to operate, unless it is a heat pump water heater (HPWH). If a standard tank style electric water heater is your only option, it is very important that it be an energy-efficient model. Selecting an efficient model is discussed later in this section. Standard electric units contain two heating elements, one about a third of the way down inside the tank and the other closer to the bottom. If one of the elements burns out, the water heater will not supply hot water at the typical rate. The heat pump water heater is a tank style electric unit that works just like the heat pump home heating systems. It removes heat from the outside air and transfers it to the water to be heated.

These are more efficient than a standard electric element tank system but are expensive to buy. They also work best in climates where temperatures are between 40 and 90 degrees Fahrenheit (4.4 and 32.2 degrees Celsius) year-round.

Instantaneous or demand water heaters can also be electric. Smaller units are used for one specific usage. Whole-house electric units cost about the same as a standard electric tank unit but save on operating costs and last longer. Don't forget that they require an extra circuit for operation.

- **Gas.** Natural gas and propane (also called LP) water heaters are typically more expensive to buy but they cost less to operate. One drawback of the natural gas heater is that you need to have a natural gas pipeline nearby. Propane requires a tank placed in the backyard and is used when gas is desired but natural gas is not available. Gas tank water heaters have a gas burner at the bottom of the tank. The gas burner that heats the tank is ignited by a standing pilot light or a spark ignition. As the gas burns, it heats the water in the tank and releases carbon monoxide (CO) formed during the combustion process. These gas heaters vent out the CO through the center of the water heater to the outside, typically through the roof. This vent can be either a natural draft vent or a forced air vent which boosts the CO release with a fan.

  A more efficient style of tank gas water heater is the condensing heater. Condensing units differ in that they have a sealed combustion chamber inside the tank. As the combustion gases are exhausted they pass through a coiled steel tube within the water tank which is a secondary heat exchanger. The hot gases move through the heat exchanger, transferring additional heat to the water. When all of the heat is released the combustion gases cool to a point that water vapor is formed. The resulting vapor is now cool enough to be safely vented through inexpensive plastic plumbing pipe, far less expensive than the stainless steel flues needed for a standard gas water heater. These water heaters have an efficiency of 90 to 96 percent compared to the 60 percent for the average tank water heater.

  Most of the larger on-demand heating units are gas fueled. They require a vent to the outdoors and sometimes a large gas line. They are also more expensive to buy than a standard tank gas water heater, but can save money over time.
- **Solar.** Solar water heaters may be a good option if you live in a sunny climate. A typical solar water heating unit has a panel mounted to the roof. The ground is another mounting location but they are more prone to damage and shading in this location. The solar panels contain tubes where either the water or a heat transfer liquid passes. As the sun strikes the panel it heats the water or liquid in the tubes. The water would then go to a storage tank for use. The heat transfer liquid would pass through a heat exchanger where the heat would then be used to heat water in a tank.

Size

A properly sized water heating unit is essential to provide the necessary quantity of hot water and operate efficiently. Tank style heaters typically have a capacity of 30 to 70 gallons (113.56 to 264.97 liters) with about 70 percent of that as usable capacity. Most manufacturers have software that will help you calculate the proper size to install. Sizing will take into consideration the client's flow rate demand, the temperature of the water entering the tank, and the desired output temperature of the water.

The size of on-demand heaters is rated by the maximum temperature rise possible at a given flow rate. To properly size these units you need to know how much water is demanded from each fixture connected to the heater and the starting temperature of the water. Instructions on how to calculate this are on the Department of Energy's (DOE) website, energysavers.gov.

For tank style units use the water heater's first hour rating (FHR). The first hour rating is the amount of hot water in gallons the heater can supply per hour (starting with a tank full of hot water). It depends on the tank capacity, source of heat (burner or element), and the size of the burner or element. The FHR will be listed as "capacity" on the EnergyGuide label (or Canadian EnergyGuide label) for the product (see below for more information on energy labels). To determine your FHR you will need to select a time of day when the maximum amount of hot water is used and then calculate how much water is used during an hour within that time. The DOE's website, energysavers.gov, has more precise calculations for this FHR.

Energy Efficiency

The energy efficiency of a tank storage, demand (on-demand or instantaneous), or heat pump water heater can be determined through the use of an *energy factor* (EF). The energy factor indicates a water heater's overall energy efficiency based on the amount of hot water produced per unit of fuel consumed over a typical day. According to the DOE, this includes the following:

- Recovery efficiency—how efficiently the heat from the energy source is transferred to the water
- Standby losses—the percentage of heat loss per hour from the stored water compared to the heat content of the water (water heaters with storage tanks)
- Cycling losses—the loss of heat as the water circulates through a water heater tank, and/or inlet and outlet pipes

The standby losses can be minimized with better tank insulation and insulation on hot water pipes, especially those that run through unconditioned space. Heat traps, which allow water to flow into the water heater tank but prevent unwanted hot-water flow out of the tank, will eliminate cycling losses. Other water heater conservation measures, including lowering the water temperature, can be found on the DOE's Energy Savers website.

A couple of labels can assist you in finding the most energy-efficient water heater. The EnergyGuide is a black and yellow label established by the DOE and required on many products, including water heaters, to allow consumers to compare the average yearly operating costs of different water heaters, using the same criteria for all models tested. The EF is listed on the EnergyGuide label on the water heater. The other label to look for is the Energy Star logo. For more information about Energy Star, see chapter 3, "Environmental and Sustainability Considerations."

The Canadian EnergyGuide label is required by federal law in Canada, under Canada's *Energy Efficiency Regulations*, on all new electrical appliances manufactured in or imported into Canada. This black and white label includes the average annual energy consumption of the appliance in kilowatt hours (kWh), the energy efficiency of the appliance relative to similar models, the annual energy consumption range for models of this type and size, the type and size of the model, and the model number. This information is determined by standardized test procedures. A third-party agency verifies that an appliance meets Canada's minimum energy performance levels.

Cost

The cost of heating water will depend on the cost of the unit, installation costs, and the long-term operating cost. To calculate the most cost-efficient option, you need to consider all three. A unit may be inexpensive to buy, but will probably be the most expensive to operate in the long run. Calculating the yearly operating cost for a particular type of water heater will help you compare the "actual" cost over the life of the unit. The EnergyGuide label is one tool to help you compare energy costs.

LIGHTING

Modern bathrooms, especially larger luxury bathrooms, have a variety of lighting requirements for the many activities that take place in this room. It can be a personal retreat, a refuge to sooth the soul, a work place to prepare for the day, or a show place to enjoy. Lighting adds to the aesthetic appeal and can create a mood in the room. Many grooming tasks, including dressing, shaving, and applying make-up, take place in the bathroom and require a quality light source in order to be completed adequately. As more activities move into the bathroom area, lighting must be more varied and flexible to accommodate them all. For example, the lighting needed for vigorous exercise will not be the same as desired for relaxing in a tub or meditating.

Among the considerations for planning quality light is selecting sources that provide illumination that is flattering to skin tones and allows accurate matching of colors. In addition, the lighting should be comparable to the light where your client will spend their day.

Your client will be the main source of information for determining lighting needs. Once you have determined the client's bathroom activities using the forms in chapter 5, "Assessing Needs," and made note of any special vision needs or activities taking place in the bathroom space, you will

EnergyGuide Labels

The bright yellow EnergyGuide label (see Figure 7.10) is used to provide information on the comparative energy use and costs on a variety of many appliances. This is another tool that can be used to select an energy-efficient appliance. The EnergyGuide label provides the yearly estimated energy costs for an appliance (based on the national average energy cost) as well as the yearly estimated kilowatt hour usage. The label also provides a graph showing the range of energy costs to operate similar appliances and indicates how the labeled appliance compares to this range. If the appliance is Energy Star–certified, that information is included on the EnergyGuide label. EnergyGuide labels are found on those appliances where there is the most variation in energy use among models, including water heaters.

Based on standard U.S. Government tests

ENERGYGUIDE

Water Heater – Natural Gas
Capacity(first hour rating):
57 Gallons

GSW Water Heating Company
Model: JW540SNA
H4400

Compare the Energy Use of this Water Heater with Others Before You Buy.

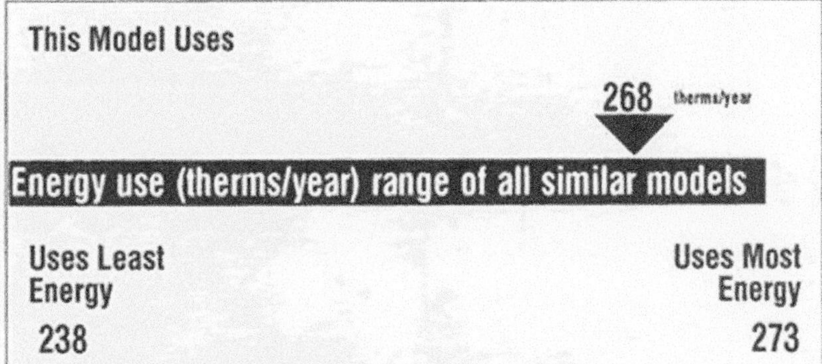
This Model Uses

268 therms/year

Energy use (therms/year) range of all similar models

Uses Least Energy 238

Uses Most Energy 273

Therms/year is a measure of energy use. Your utility company uses it to compute your bill. Only models with first hour ratings of 56 to 64 gallons are used in this scale.

Natural gas water heaters that use fewer therms/year cost less to operate. This model's estimated yearly operating cost is:

$162

Based on a 1994 U.S. Government national average cost of $0.604 per therm for natural gas. Your actual operating cost will vary depending on your local utility rates and your use of the product.

Important: Removal of this label before consumer purchase is a violation of Federal law (42 U.S.C. 6302) 73316

FIGURE 7.10 Use the EnergyGuide label to compare the efficiency of water heaters.
U.S. Department of Energy

have a better idea of where light sources will be needed and the type of lighting that will be most appropriate. For design concepts that improve visual access specifically, refer to chapter 8, "Accessibility in Practice." In addition to considerations for activities, the lighting plan should take into consideration the number and size of the windows, the ceiling height, the size of the room, and the room's style.

The focus of this chapter is on planning considerations. After you identify needs and research the options; consider the budget and then get creative with your lighting plan. A good lighting design does not rely on just one light source but uses light layering to incorporate all of the functions you would like the room's lighting to perform. You will be incorporating various levels of light in these layers. Begin by considering the basic types of lighting and how you might use them. These include daylighting, general or ambient, task, decorative, and accent lighting.

Natural or Daylighting

Daylighting is natural light from windows, doors and skylights that adds a warm, inviting quality to a room, as well as giving the room a feeling of openness. The following are tips for planning daylighting:

- Determine when the bathroom is used most. Emphasizing natural light when the bathroom is only used at night or in the early morning may not lead to logical or cost-effective planning.
- Too much natural light can also lead to glare. If the window area faces a sunny direction, incorporate window treatments that can help control the bright sunlight during certain times of the day. The bright sun could cause glare on mirrors if not properly placed.

FIGURE 7.11 Large windows provide an abundance of natural light.

Design by NKBA member: Peter Ross Salerno, CMKBD

FIGURE 7.12 Skylights can add quality daylight to a bathroom space.

Design by Candice Olson. Photography by Brandon Barre. Copyright © Fusion Television Sales Inc.

- Large windows and glass doors to the outside can provide adequate daytime lighting needs (see Figure 7.11), plus visually open the room to the outdoors.
- Windows and glass doors below 18 inches (457 mm) will need to be made of tempered glazing. Windows that surround a bathtub or shower should also be made of tempered glazing. See information in Bathroom Planning Guideline 15, discussed in chapter 6, "Bathroom Planning."
- Skylights (see Figure 7.12) can add natural light without sacrificing wall space, but be sure to select high-quality skylights and have them installed properly. Skylights provide about five times as much light as a comparably sized wall window.
- Select windows or skylights that have a high insulating value to keep the bathroom more comfortable year-round. Also study air leakage rates, and select windows or skylights that are rated as having low air leakage. More information on window ratings and selecting energy-efficient windows can be found in chapter 2, "Infrastructure Considerations," and chapter 3, "Environmental and Sustainability Considerations."

Privacy is another consideration when incorporating a large amount of glass in a bathroom. Privacy measures on the exterior of the windows, or adequate window treatments, are necessary to protect the privacy of the bathroom users. Some decorative fixed windows may look attractive but can also allow a view into the bathroom if not placed high on the wall. Covering decorative windows placed in the walking path of the room takes away from their aesthetic appeal. Glass block is a popular way to incorporate light without a need to be concerned about privacy.

Types of Artificial Lighting

The degree of natural light may not be adequate for the bathroom's activities so artificial lighting must be incorporated. When sizing artificial light, decide what is needed to supplement the natural light during the day and then consider the needs in the room after dark. No single type of fixture (luminaire) can produce the light needed for taking a relaxing soak in the tub, putting on make-up, or showering, so many different sources need to be considered. Artificial lighting should be thought of as light layers and these layers can be incorporated in a number of ways through ambient, task, accent, and decorative lighting sources. With the input of your client, decide if the light sources will be a prominent feature of the room or disappear into the background with only the effects of the lighting evident in the room.

FIGURE 7.13 A center fixture and recessed lights provide an abundance of varied lighting.
Design by NKBA Member: Sandra Steiner Houck, CKD

General or Ambient Lighting

Provisions for general or ambient lighting in each compartment or room of the bathroom are necessary, and can be accomplished through a variety of sources including: ceiling fixtures, vent/heater/light combination ceiling units, table lamps, wall fixtures, recessed lights, and indirect or cove lighting (see Figure 7.13). Keep these points in mind when adding ambient lighting to a bathroom:

- Recessed lights are less obtrusive and can distribute light in a wide, medium, or narrow spread, depending upon how the fixture is designed. Select the type that gives the desired effect.
- Adding dimmers to spa, exercise, or meditation areas will help set the desired light level or mood for the activity.
- Some types of lighting produce a lot of heat. The heat may feel comforting in the winter, but during the summer it will add to the cooling load and to the discomfort in exercise areas.
- Consider the surface finishes and colors when determining lighting. Shiny surfaces will produce glare and dark surfaces will absorb more light.
- Indirect or cove lighting adds a soft glow to the bathroom.
- Use gentle up-lighting, such as at the ceiling or in dark corners, to make the room feel larger.
- General lighting in powder rooms is probably sufficient to provide a softer, low level of light for general guest use. If the powder room is used by guests or family members as an extra bathroom for getting ready in the morning, then additional light will be needed for these activities.

Accent Lighting

In conjunction with general lighting, accent lighting can enhance many features in a bathroom. Highlight the visual texture of surfaces with wall washing lights. Focus lights onto art objects or interesting architectural features. Illuminate the floor as a night light with small linear lighting at the vanity toe kick. Accent lights for shelves, soffit areas, and glassed cabinets will add aesthetic appeal and interest. Small table lamps can add a soft touch to a corner of the vanity or other part of the bathroom, but be sure to keep them well away from a water source.

Task Lighting

Task lighting provides light at an area to help users see what they are doing. Task lighting should be provided for each functional area of the bathroom, such as grooming, showering, dressing, and bathing. Some points to remember:

- Most of the task lighting in the bathroom is needed for grooming. Place the lighting where your client typically performs grooming activities, which might be either standing or seated. Each bathroom user may perform grooming activities in a variety of locations, so include the proper task lighting for each.
- Plan for additional lighting at mirrors used for shaving and applying make-up (see Figure 7.14). Wall-mounted magnifying mirrors are often lighted, so a hard wire connection should be included to eliminate the cord.
- If you are incorporating a reading area into the bathroom, plan to add a quality reading light or a receptacle for a lamp in this area.
- Place focused lighting over the toilet to provide good lighting for readers.
- Dressing areas may include mirrors for dressing and some grooming. Good lighting at these mirrors will help the users be better able to perform such tasks as tying a tie, arranging jewelry, checking clothing for soiled spots or wrinkles, and combing hair.
- Placement of the mirrors and related lighting should consider people of various heights. A full-length mirror is appropriate for children and adults, standing and seated. Plan lighting that will illuminate the person in front of the long mirror.
- Include lights in closets and deep cabinets.
- If a pressing area is included in the dressing area, a light directly over the ironing table will aid the process.
- Lighting in the shower should be bright enough so that the person showering can see what they are doing.
- To avoid glare for those using a tub, aim the lighting to the outside edge of the tub.

FIGURE 7.14 Grooming lights placed along each side of the mirror prevent shadows from forming on the face. Floor lighting serves as a night light.

Design by NKBA Member: Yuko Matsumoto, CKD, CBD

Decorative Lighting

More clients are requesting decorative lighting in the bathroom. This lighting adds a little touch of sparkle to the room and enhances the ambience and feel of the room. Decorative lighting in a small space like a bathroom will most likely serve more than one purpose. For example, a chandelier is a very decorative fixture but it also provides ambient lighting to the space. A small table lamp may add a little sparkle as well as accent light for a corner.

Lamps

Light sources that we commonly call bulbs are referred to as "lamps" by the lighting industry. Choosing the correct lamp will depend on the fixture you select, the space it will light, and the effect you want to create or achieve. Even though you may consult a lighting designer to help you create a lighting plan for your client, having some knowledge of lighting terms and applications will give you a base for thinking through the possibilities.

Lamp Sizing

Lamps are sized in 1/8 inch intervals. For example, if you see a lamp labeled as PAR30, it means a lamp is 30 by 1/8 inches in diameter. An MR16 lamp is 16—1/8ths in diameter. Fluorescent tubes are also measured in 1/8ths of an inch. The original standard T12 (12—1/8ths) tube is being replace by T8 and T5 tubes, which are smaller in diameter. This sizing system will help you decide if a lamp will fit into a fixture. Lamps sold in Canada typically use the same measuring method.

Lighting Terms

The lighting industry uses many terms to describe various aspects of lighting related to lighting quantity, quality, and efficiency. Although not a complete list, discussion of the following terms will help you become familiar with some of the concepts used in lighting selection.

Quantity

Lumen is a measure of the lamp's light output. Most lamps are rated in lumens, and by comparing the lumen ratings of various lamps you can select the one that has the light level you desire.

Footcandles (fc) (or lux - one footcandle = about 10 lux) is a measure of the light levels on a surface or work plane, the place where activities needing light take place. A footcandle meter can be used to measure the light levels. Standard bathroom counter work planes are 2.5 to 3 feet(0.8 to 0.9 m) from the floor, and a reading work plane is typically 2.5 feet (0.8 m). Footcandle levels vary by activity. Footcandle levels for grooming in a bathroom are typically 20 to 50 fc (200-500 lux), but in other areas of the home they may be higher. The goal is to select lighting sources that will provide the appropriate level of lighting for the space.

Candelas or candle power. The intensity of the light beam in one direction is measured in candelas or candle power. This figure is taken into consideration when calculating the lamps needed to achieve a certain footcandle level onto a surface at a certain distance. If 10-foot (3.1 m) ceilings are present, for example, more intense light is needed than with 8-foot (2.4 m) ceilings.

Quality

Color temperature is the term used to specify the color of light coming from a lamp (see Figure 7.15). All lamps emit some color ranging from warm oranges to cool blues. Some lamps come close to neutral or white but may still have a small amount of color. The lamp color affects how the colors of objects appear in your room. Color temperature is rated in Kelvin and can range from 1500 to 9000; the higher the number, the bluer the light. Color temperatures in the 3000 to 3600 range are closer to neutral, which create little or no effect on the room colors. Warm lamps in a room with blue hues will make the blue color appear gray. Lamps placed in the same room or area should have the same color temperature to help them blend together. When selecting lamps for a bathroom you want colors that are pleasing to the face.

Color Rendering Index (CRI). Color rendering is the lamp's ability to accurately show the colors of objects illuminated by that lamp. CRI peaks at 100 and the higher the number, the more accurately the light will reproduce color—the more natural and normal colors appear. Daylight is very close to 100 and that is why many people will take fabrics over to a window to view them. Colors will appear differently under various lamps and is usually even more critical to color appearance than color temperature. Lamps may have the same color temperature but different CRI. Find lamps with the highest CRI as possible, and in most rooms a CRI of 85 to 90 is good. Incandescent lamps typically have the highest CRI but some newer fluorescent lamps are around 90.

Efficiency

Efficacy is a term typically used to quantify how efficiently a lamp turns electricity into light; the higher the efficacy, the more efficient the lamp. Calculate efficacy by dividing the lumen rating by the watts used to operate the lamp. Both figures are usually found on the lamp's package. Halogen lamps are more efficient than the standard A-type lamp, and fluorescent and LED lamps are more efficient than halogen.

Types of Lamps

Lamp choices have changed significantly in recent years with more variations in light quality, lamp shapes and sizes, voltage requirements, and efficiency. The lamps you select for your client's lighting needs will depend on the purpose of the light source, the effect you want to achieve, and the fixture in which the lamp will be placed. The following is a brief discussion of the most common lamp types used in the home.

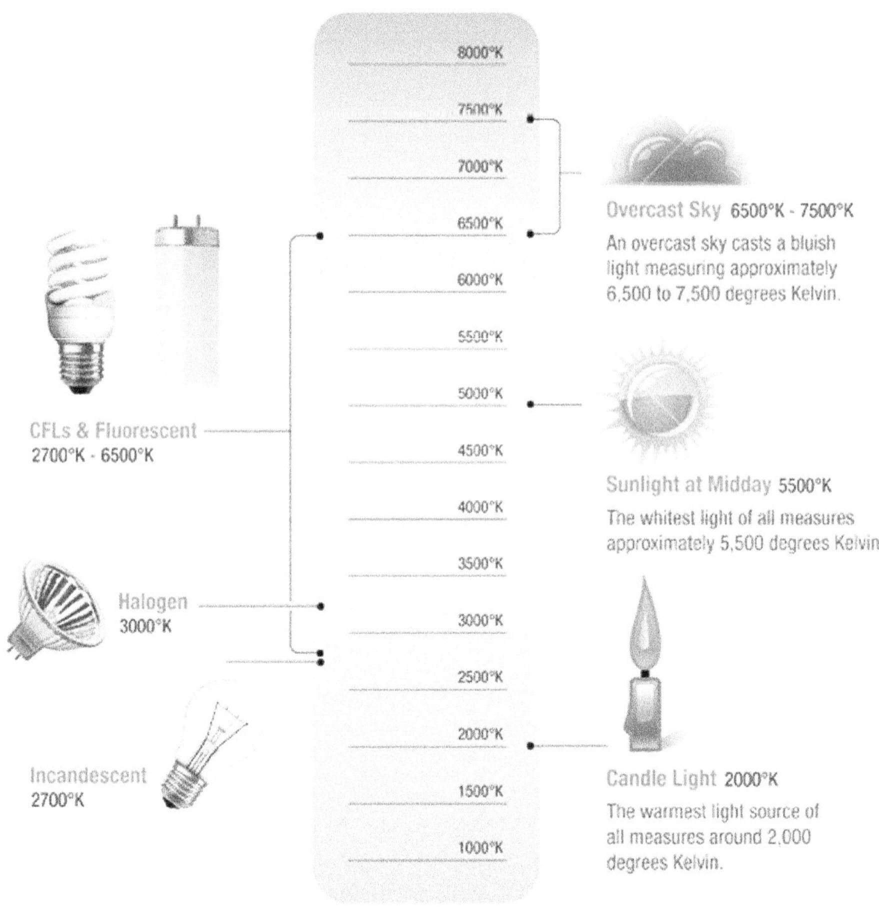

FIGURE 7.15 The color temperatures of various types of light.

Karlen, Mark. Lighting Design Basics, Second Edition. *New York: John Wiley & Sons, 2012.*

Incandescent

The incandescent lamp has been around since 1859 and most homes have used this type of lamp in a majority of their lighting fixtures. The most common type of incandescent lamp that most people think of as a "light bulb" is the A-bulb or "arbitrary" lamp. This lamp is very inexpensive to buy, but they are big heat producers with 90 percent of a standard A-bulb's energy used to produce heat. Because only 10 percent of the energy goes to light, these are very inefficient lamps, and the reason many of these lamps are being phased out. New energy standards do not ban incandescent use, but do require increased efficiency with the following schedule for the phasing out of the current most inefficient types of standard incandescent lamps as of this publication edition (see Table 7.1). Newer incandescent lamps will be rated by lumens rather than watts.

Incandescent lamps produce light by heating a tungsten filament and as it heats it glows, giving off light. These lamps give off a warm light and come in a wide variety of shapes and sizes. The life of these lamps is 750 to 1500 hours. They can be dimmed and their light becomes warmer as they are dimmed.

TABLE 7.1 Phase-Out Dates for the Current Standard Incandescent Lamps

Current Wattage	Phase-Out Date (no longer made)
100 Watt Incandescent	January 1, 2012
75 Watt Incandescent	January 1, 2013
60 and 40 Watt Incandescent	January 1, 2014

FIGURE 7.16 Examples of LED, compact fluorescent, and halogen lamps.
Clean Energy Resource Teams—www.cleanenergyresourceteams.org/lighting

Other types of more efficient incandescent lamps (see Figure 7.16), halogen and xenon, are now on the market. These can serve as replacements for the standard incandescent lamps and are available in the low-voltage type as well.

- **Halogen**—Halogen lamps were introduced in the 1950s and are 25 to 30 percent more efficient than standard incandescent lamps. A halogen is designed a little differently from the standard incandescent, and provides a soft, warm light but less warm than the standard incandescent. Halogen lamps are delicate to handle and emit ultraviolet rays (UV). Covers are available to filter out the UV. They come in a wide variety of shapes, sizes, and wattages, and the lamp life is closer to 3000 hours. These lamps cost more to purchase and become very hot with use.
- **Xenon**—Xenon lamps can be used interchangeably with halogen but they come in fewer varieties than the halogen. They are only low-voltage at this time. Xenon lamps have many advantages over the halogen in that they operate cooler, do not need special handling, and last about 5000 to 8000 hours. Xenon lamps may cost more than halogen and they do not emit UV rays.

Other styles of incandescent lamps:

- **Spot lamps**—These lamps focus the light energy into a narrow beam of concentrated light. They are often used as accent lighting.
- **Flood lamps**—Flood lamps spread the light beam and flood an area with a lower level of light.
- **PAR or parabolic aluminized reflector lamps**—These lamps have a heavy glass casing and reflective surface. They are often used for outdoor settings, and the low voltage MR-16 lamps can be PAR-style lamps as well.
- **Reflector lamps**—Reflector lamps are incandescent lamps with a reflective coating to reflect more of the light out the front of the lamp. These have been a popular source for recessed can lights but are being replaced by more efficient halogen, LED, and compact fluorescent lamps.

Fluorescent

Fluorescent lamps were introduced in the 1930s. They use a ballast to feed electricity through glass tubes filled with gas and a small amount of mercury, creating UV light that turns visible when it hits a phosphor coating on the inside of the tube. The newer electronic ballasts have replaced the magnetic ballasts, eliminating the former problems of slow startup, flickering, and humming. Fluorescent lamps, in general, are more efficient than incandescent lamps, last longer, and operate cooler. Fluorescent lamps contain a small amount of mercury so should be recycled properly. You will find three styles of fluorescent lamps on the market:

- **Tube**—This was the first style of fluorescent lamp and they now come in a variety of sizes. Tubes are excellent for ambient or some task lighting, they can be dimmed, and they last around 10,000 hours. For many locations, it is important to pay attention to the lamp's color temperature and CRI.
- **Compact fluorescent lamps (CFL)**—CFLs (see Figure 7.17) use the same fluorescent technology only the tube is designed into a compact style, the now familiar corkscrew style. This style has a screw-type base so they can be used in fixtures to replace some incandescent lamps. Dimmable lamps are available and compact fluorescents come in different color temperature and CRI ratings. The ballast for these lamps is contained in the lamp base and they last around 10,000 hours. Compact fluorescents are also available with a glass bulb around them to make them appear the same as incandescent lamps, which is a good alternative if your client does not like the appearance of the corkscrew lamp. Be aware that some compact fluorescent lamps take time to warm up so when they are first turned on they are very dim, but after a period of time achieve their full brightness. This too may not be popular with your client.

FIGURE 7.17 Different styles of compact fluorescent lamps.

- **Circline**—These fluorescent lamps are built with the tube forming a circle or ring. They operate like other fluorescent tubes and are designed to fit in many center room light fixtures for ambient lighting.

Light Emitting Diode (LED)

The LED lamp was developed in the 1960s and is fast becoming the energy-efficient lamp of choice. An LED lamp is a very small light source, 1/4 inch (6.35 mm) or smaller in size. In order to generate a large amount of light, these small dots are clustered together in various configurations. The light waves are only emitted in one direction so the configuration will determine how light is distributed. These lamps require a driver to operate and the color temperature and CRI depend on the lamps selected. LEDs can be either line voltage or low voltage and currently rated to last about 50,000 hours but the life expectancy is expected to increase far beyond that as more efficient LEDs are developed. LEDs come in an almost unlimited number of colors and they have recently been able to produce a white wavelength as well. They are temperature tolerant and durable, but currently carry a high cost. The applications for LED are increasing and the quality is improving. Many feel this will be the energy-efficient lamp of choice in the future.

Fiber Optics

Fiber optic lights send light along a glass fiber and are therefore very delicate. Fiber optic lights are quite expensive and are often used in decorative lighting to create a dramatic effect.

Table 7.2 is a comparison chart developed by the DOE and listed on their energysavers.gov website to show how the various types of lamps compare to one another.

TABLE 7.2 A Comparison of Lamp Types

Lighting Comparison Chart					
Lighting Type	**Efficacy (lumens/watt)**	**Lifetime (hours)**	**Color Rendition Index (CRI)**	**Color Temperature (K)**	**Indoors/ Outdoors**
Incandescent					
Standard A-type bulb	10–17	750–2500	98–100 (excellent)	2700–2800 (warm)	Indoors/ outdoors
Energy-Saving Incandescent Halogen	12–22	1,000–4,000	98–100 (excellent)	2900–3200 (warm to neutral)	Indoors/ outdoors
Reflector	12–19	2000–3000	98–100 (excellent)	2800 (warm)	Indoors/ outdoors
Fluorescent					
Straight tube	30–110	7000–24,000	50–90 (fair to good)	2700–6500 (warm to cold)	Indoors/ outdoors
Compact fluorescent lamp (CFL)	50–70	10,000	65–88 (good)	2700–6500 (warm to cold)	Indoors/ outdoors
Circline	40–50	12,000			Indoors
Light-Emitting Diodes					
Cool white LEDs	60–92	25,000–50,000	70–90 (fair to good)	5000 (cold)	Indoors/ outdoors
Warm White LEDs	27–54	25,000–50,000	70–90 (fair to good)	3300 (neutral)	Indoors/ outdoors

Lighting Fixtures

Lighting fixtures (luminaires) come in a wide variety of styles, mounting types, and sizes. When deciding which type to use in your bathroom, consider the size of the space you are lighting, the type of light you want emitted, the design theme of the space, and the tasks that must be illuminated. Following are a few important points to consider concerning light fixtures.

Location and Type

Locate the fixtures where they can deliver the maximum amount of light for their purpose. General lighting might involve one or two lights in the center of the room, or a number of lights around the perimeter. Provide enough light so that dark corners do not form. Do not use fixtures that can get into the way of the users. For example, wall sconces in the walkways of very small bathrooms, or central ceiling fan lights in average height ceilings, may be easily bumped by the user. General lighting can be provided by many types of fixtures. Center room fixtures can be ceiling mounted or hanging, such as a chandelier. A light may also be part of the ventilation system and provide general lighting in a small bathroom.

Don't forget to place some general lighting in all compartments of the bathroom, as well as in the shower and over the tub. According to Bathroom Planning Guideline 25 and most local building codes, hanging fixtures cannot be located within a zone of 3 feet (914.4 mm) horizontally and 8 feet (2439.4 mm) vertically from the top of the bathtub rim. Lights in the tub and shower areas should be "suitable for damp/wet locations."

When lighting a task area, the fixture should be mounted so it casts light onto the task area without creating a shadow or causing glare, and light the user's face and not the top of his/her head. For the best quality lighting while grooming, applying make-up, and shaving you would ideally want lights all around the mirror, such as with "Broadway" style lighting. This might not always be practical and may not fit the design plan of the client. The next best option for optimum lighting quality would be to place light fixtures to each side of the user's face. Fixtures located only above a mirror, like with "Hollywood" lights, cast shadows onto the user's face, whereas lamps at the sides of the mirror eliminate such shadows. Use the user's eye height measurement to guide where side lighting is placed and mount them at least 30 inches (762 mm) apart. These side lights could be wall-mounted sconces, pendants, or vertical fluorescent bars for good cross illumination. The fixture's lamps should be bright enough for the user to easily see what they are doing, but not be visible to the user so as to create glare.

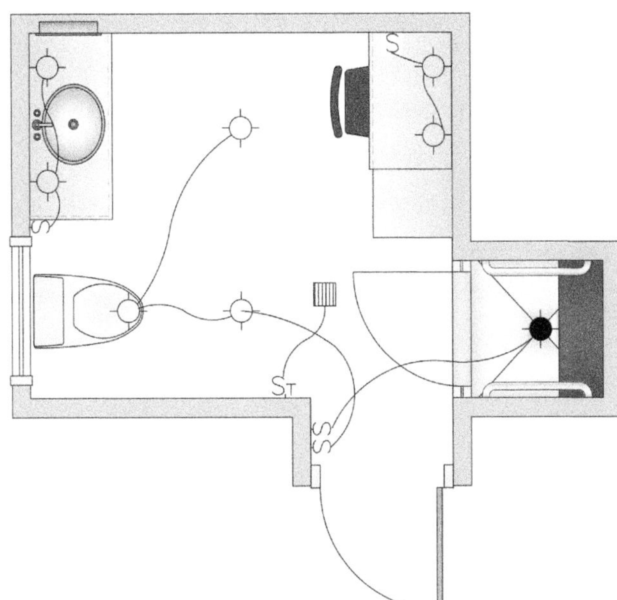

FIGURE 7.18 Bathrooms should include general and task lighting (Bathroom Planning Guideline 25). All of the bathroom's lighting needs should be illustrated on the mechanical plan.
NKBA

Place rope lighting behind ceiling moulding that is dropped a few inches from the ceiling to create a soft glow at the ceiling. Rope lighting in the toe-kick area makes a good night light. Recessed lights can be used for general lighting or lighting at individual fixtures.

Lighting Controls

Controls for general lighting should be located where a person enters the room, so they do not need to walk into a dark room to find the control. Place the light switch no higher than 48 inches (1.2 m) above the floor for ease of access (see Planning Guideline Access Standard 25). If a bathroom has two entrances, such as one door in the hall and one from a bedroom, use a three-way switch so that general lighting can be controlled at either door. Every bathroom has a number of lights that need switches, and some switches may be needed to control vent fans and heaters. Try to consolidate the switches into banks, as much as possible, to avoid having the wall dotted with switches. If you use banks of switches, three or four switches are perhaps all you would want together in one place and fewer would be better (see Figure 7.18).

Try to make it easy for your client to remember which switch controls which fixture. Try putting them in some logical order so that the light switch is nearest that light fixture. You can also mark them to avoid confusion. For example, if the two middle switches in a bank of four operate the vent fan and the overhead heater, a red marking on the heater switch will give the client a clue as to its use.

Additional compartments within the bathroom typically have the light controls at the compartment entrance rather than at the entrance to the main portion of the bathroom. Controls for other lights need to be close to where the light is being used.

Many different types of controls are now available for lighting. Select the type your client can use easily, as well as the style they prefer. The flip or rocker switches are perhaps the most common. You may also choose a toggle switch, or even a remote control switch for a light and/or fan on an elevated ceiling. Locate these controls in a convenient place for access by all users. Eliminate the need for controls by using motion-sensor light switches that do not require the use of hands in operation.

Controlling the amount of light is important in some areas of the bathroom. For spaces like the exercise area or near a spa tub, consider adding a dimmer switch so that the client has complete control over the light levels. Locate the controls, however, out of the reach of the bathers so they do not receive an electric shock if they touch the control while standing in water. Or, use remote lighting control devices.

Low-Voltage Lighting

Low-voltage systems use a transformer, either as a separate unit or built into the lighting fixture, to transform the 120-volt service to around 7 to 10 volts. The capacity needs to be matched to the lamp wattage, and the transformer should be in a central location. The very small low-voltage lamps have a separate transformer you will need to hide in or above a cabinet. Transformers incorporated into a fixture increase the size of the fixture, making the light source more difficult to hide.

Low-voltage lights come in a large variety of styles and offer many advantages. Low-voltage lights come with either halogen or xenon lamps, which last much longer (2000 to 3500 hours) than standard incandescent lamps. Halogen lights burn at a very high temperature, and even though the low-voltage lamps are small, added together they can still produce a significant amount of heat. Therefore, keep them out of reach of users and flammable objects. They are easy to wire for remodeling, and provide a very white and crisp light that can serve as an accent or create a sparkle.

In addition to small track and recessed lights for general lighting, low-voltage lamps can fit very small places providing light for cabinets, shelves, mirrors, floors, and artwork. Low-voltage lights can also make good night lights (see Figure 7.19). Drawbacks include high cost and limited availability in some areas.

FIGURE 7.19 Small lights placed under the bathroom vanity cabinet serve as a night light. Light behind the mirror is another way to light the mirror area.

Design by NKBA member: Leslie Lamarre, CKD, CID, Co-Designers: Erica Shjelflo & Casey Darcy

Lighting Safety

Although most lighting systems are generally tested and safe to use, following proper installation instructions and placing fixtures in locations away from contact with people, are extremely important steps to preventing light fixture hazards.

Safe installation is particularly important with recessed lights. If installed too close to construction members or smothered by insulation, these fixtures can reach very high temperatures and ignite materials around them. Many recessed fixtures are designed with built-in air spaces to help cool the bulbs.

Installing the incorrect lamp into a particular fixture can also increase the chances of a fire. Many times when a fixture is selected, it is difficult to tell how much light it may emit within a room. The size of the room, the colors used, and the textures present can all make a difference as to how much light is available.

If your client finds the fixture is not producing the amount of light they desired, they may increase the wattage of the lamps inside it. This will indeed provide more light, but in the meantime the larger lamps will give off more heat than the fixture can handle. The fixture can become hot to the point where it can crack or ignite. Think through the lighting needs carefully and select the appropriate lighting fixtures to avoid this.

Another safety precaution is to avoid contact with the light lamps. Many lamp types, like incandescent and halogen lamps, produce a significant amount of heat as they produce light. Be careful to locate these lamps where your client cannot easily come into contact with them, such as while walking through the room or reaching for something.

SUMMARY

Planning for electrical and mechanical equipment is more essential than ever. Changing lifestyles, a surge in technology, and an increase in the number of activities, fixtures, and electronic devices in the bathroom, all create a space that demands attention to the systems that form the structure for this equipment. Without a clear and detailed plan and an attention to local code requirements, necessary components of such a system can be easily overlooked, leading to disappointment on the part of the client, or added costs if features need to be redone.

Two features of a bathroom that require special consideration are the ventilation and lighting systems. Both features add to the bathroom's comfort, and adequate lighting is essential for a variety of tasks and activities that take place in the bathroom. Proper planning of these features will add to the client's satisfaction.

REVIEW QUESTIONS

1. What are the electric code requirement and guidelines for a bathroom? (See "Codes" pages 203)
2. What should be considered when selecting a heating system for a bathroom? (See "Heating Considerations" page 207)
3. What are the ventilation requirements for a bathroom and what factors are important for it to be efficient? (See "Ventilation" page 212)
4. What considerations are essential when selecting task lighting for a bathroom? (See "Task Lighting" page 225)
5. How are lighting, quality, quantity, and efficiency measured? (See "Lighting Terms" pages 227)
6. Describe some major differences between incandescent, fluorescent, and LED lamp choices. (See "Types of Lamps" page 227)

Accessibility in Practice

The goal of this chapter is to first clarify the differences and overlaps between universal design and design for accessibility, and then to provide examples for customizing the bathroom to your client, with respect for their sensory, cognitive, or physical abilities. To do this we will tie together chapter 4, "Universal Design and Human Factors," chapter 5, "Assessing Needs," and chapter 6, "Bathroom Design"; we will refer back to these three chapters often and repeatedly.

The tools presented in chapter 5, "Assessing Needs," give you a great start to gathering information that can help you identify and plan for each client's needs. When a specific chronic condition or disability is involved, the client will often be your best source of information regarding unique needs and solutions.

In addition, health professionals involved with your client, such as occupational or physical therapists make great team members. Their expertise is the human body and its workings, whereas yours is the space and its function and components. Keep in mind that when specific medical equipment is involved, your role as designer may be to provide appropriate space planning and to involve the equipment expert to execute the plan.

Learning Objective 1: Describe the differences between universal design and accessibility.

Learning Objective 2: Provide examples of the universal design principles that apply to variations in abilities, grouped as follows: sensory perception and cognitive and physical characteristics and needs.

Learning Objective 3: Identify design concepts for sensory perception and cognitive and physical characteristics and needs.

UNIVERSAL DESIGN VERSUS ACCESSIBILITY: FURTHER CLARIFICATION

These two categories of design certainly overlap, but they are not the same thing. By definition, universal design improves access and function for most people, with respect for differences in ability, size, or age, and as these concepts are tried and found successful, they are adopted into standard practice. For these reasons—that universal design works for most people and that the concepts are embraced as they are used—universal design has been included throughout the book. To the greatest extent possible, you will incorporate universal concepts into every bathroom you design in order to meet the needs of clients throughout their lifespan and the changes and variety in their physical condition.

In contrast, in some cases, you may be asked to create a bathroom design that responds to the particular requirements of a person with specific characteristics and needs—sometimes going beyond what would be considered universal design. This is accessible design. In response to demand, this chapter will expand on access issues and options, first by citing some of the variations in human factors and abilities that we may be called on to address. We'll go on to review the centers of the bathroom with a focus on design concepts that can respond to those variations and improve the bathroom experience. Finally, for each center, we will summarize the concepts according to the three categories previously used: sensory, cognitive/perception, and physical characteristics and needs. Where appropriate, concepts will be explored in more depth to broaden your understanding, or additional resources may be mentioned to enable you to go further in accessibility solutions.

The good news is that in the course of creating access solutions, we often find concepts that will work well for many types of people and they can be adopted into universal practice, such as the toilet that was first raised in height to support transfer from a wheelchair, and has been adopted as a comfortable height for those of us who are advancing in the aging process and who find it less comfortable bending low to the traditional height toilet.

A vanity designed to be accessible to a seated user might be lower in height with an open knee space, whereas a universally designed vanity area might have a second lavatory at a higher height for times when standing use is desired or necessary.

Universal Design

- It is an approach that accommodates a wide range of human performance characteristics.
- It is invisible.
- It is attractive.
- It has broad market appeal.
- It is flexible for ease of use with respect for the natural diversity in people.

Accessible Design

- It responds to the particular requirements of a person with specific characteristics and needs.
- While it can be attractive, it targets a narrow audience.

CHARACTERISTICS OF SPECIFIC USERS

According to some sources, we grow and change to our physical prime at around age 16 and then have a long period of gradual changes in our bodies and abilities. As we age, a broad range of environmental issues impact our abilities, such as broken bones and activity-related injuries, pregnancy, parenthood, increased responsibilities and related stresses, and caring for parents and children. During this time, many of us experience increased strength, stamina, balance and dexterity, with decreased time and conflicting demands for our attention.

Changes in vision, hearing, and memory are a common thread in our aging process. We reach a point in the growth process where a number of our abilities begin to change again, decreasing as we continue to age and grow. We adapt ourselves to the changes as we age and may not notice any difference until the environment is no longer enough to support us.

Better design for access related to these changes can alter our life experience, and the user groups and design recommendations listed here, while in no way complete, will provide a good start in this effort.

There is much overlap because, for example, the knee space that allows access at a vanity for a person using a wheelchair also provides for seated use by a pregnant woman experiencing fatigue. It can also function as a storage place for a step stool for a child. In some cases, information is repeated and in others, different sections of the chapter and book are referenced.

Sensory Characteristics

Hearing

Have you ever tried to have a conversation on a cell phone with background noise? Or tried to have a conversation in a noisy bar or restaurant?

In this user group are people who are fully or partially deaf, either from birth or from a loss of hearing resulting from illness, disease, blockages of the inner ear, damage from prolonged exposure to excessive noise, head injuries, stroke, or other causes. A common occurrence in aging is some level of hearing loss, usually beginning with difficulties with background or ambient noise and with high frequencies and progressing to lower frequencies. Ringing in the ears is also common. When these changes occur gradually, we may not recognize them until our ability to interact with our environment is affected. Hearing loss and the inability to communicate can cause significant emotional stress, and potential negative effects can be reduced through design.

Concerns with hearing impairments include both the social isolation and difficulty communicating, and also, the safety issues related to not hearing audio cues. Whether hearing loss is a congenital issue or one that occurs later in life, it frequently leads to keener development of the other senses, especially visual skills.

Pay attention to design concepts such as noise control, redundant cuing, and visual cuing on all equipment, sound-absorbing materials, quiet ventilation and whirlpool motors, good lighting, and safety. Because a person with hearing impairments relies more heavily on seeing what is happening and in many cases, on lip-reading, a clear line of sight is also important. These and other design considerations are detailed in the sections that follow.

Vision

Have you ever driven west into a setting sun, or struggled to focus when entering a dark theater from a bright lobby?

Because vision changes are a natural part of the aging process, many people would not consider themselves disabled, but would benefit from responsive design. This user group also includes anyone who is blind or who has partial vision loss due to cataracts, glaucoma, retinitis, macular degeneration, or eye injuries, as well as anyone with congenital vision impairments or those caused by other conditions. Depending on the condition, user needs will be different.

Physical changes in the eyes increase with age and can lead to vision impairment, such as difficulty seeing in dim light, increased light sensitivity, difficulty focusing on moving objects, and a decrease in peripheral vision. More time is needed for the eyes to adjust when transitioning between light and dark areas. Reading glasses become a common need beginning in the forties, and lenses begin to yellow, causing difficulty in distinguishing some colors.

A concern among people with vision impairments is their depth perception, and the ability to distinguish foreground from background. Their needs might also differ from day to night or summer to winter. As eyes age, difficulty differentiating colors with minimal contrast increases, such as navy, black, brown, or pastels and varying whites. Again, if a person has vision issues, he/she will rely more heavily on other senses, particularly auditory abilities.

Pay attention to design concepts such as redundant cuing, eliminating clutter, tactile indicators, intuitive operation, increased and adjustable general and task lighting, careful use of color, contrast, and pattern, and the selection of materials and lighting to reduce glare. These and other design considerations are detailed in the sections that follow.

Other Sensory Characteristics

We often will experience a general and gradual decline in other senses as we age. We may have a change in our ability to taste, including a decline in the recognition of sweet, sour, and salty foods, and a common complaint relates to a bitter taste in the mouth or food tasting bland. Many of us experience a decline in olfactory capacity, which affects our ability to recognize such odors as smoke and leaking gas. This decrease in our ability to smell what's cooking also directly affects our taste, negatively impacting our appetite. Our sensitivity to touch may decline as well; more specifically we may not feel the pain of a bump or burn as quickly, so our ability to recognize contact with something too hot or sharp is decreased. Add to this our slowing response time and there are definitely design decisions that will help us to function more safely and comfortably. Consider that we move more slowly, recover more slowly from changes in light levels or temperature in a space or in the water we are using and you'll begin to recognize appropriate design responses.

For a person with tactile or olfactory impairments, pay attention to design concepts such as rounded edges, temperature control that maintains a steady temperature, supplemental heat in the tub/shower area, anti-scald controls, and covered heating pipes or elements to prevent burning. These and other design considerations are detailed in the sections that follow.

Some key examples of the universal design principles in chapter 4, "Universal Design and Human Factors," that become more critical when responding to a client with sensory issues include:

- Provide effective prompting and feedback during and after task completion
- Provide adequate contrast between essential information and its surroundings
- Use multiple modes (pictorial, verbal, tactile, auditory) for redundant presentation of essential information
- Provide warnings of hazards and errors
- Provide a clear line of sight to important elements
- Maintain clear and well-lighted traffic and work areas

Perception and Cognition Characteristics

Have you ever been in a country where a language foreign to you is spoken and tried to use the phone or to get on the right train, or driven through the day and night and tried to follow oral directions to the nearest motel or gas station? Or have you ever arrived in a room and forgotten what you came to do, or stopped in the middle of a sentence because you have lost your train of thought? Or tried to assemble a new acquisition and found the instructions incomprehensible? How about using a new remote or computer?

This user group includes anyone with limited comprehension or memory, some confusion or reduced reasoning. A few of the contributing factors include injury, illness, learning disability, stroke, general aging, using a foreign language, or youth/limited vocabulary and reasoning skills. With a client who has cognitive impairments, safety is a primary concern, and involving caregivers in the design process is critical.

Some memory loss or occasional forgetfulness, as opposed to overall mental decline, is very common as we age. The ability to learn does not decrease with age, but stereotypes cause many to fear the loss of mental ability as one ages. Reaction time generally is longer. Reduced physical and reaction abilities cause many to prefer home where things are familiar, allowing for a sense of security.

At the other end of the age spectrum, children are in the process of developing cognitive skills, often having needs in common with those of us advancing in age, and deserve attention as well. A child's language and reasoning skills are only just beginning to develop. Children see the world differently than adults and often do not understand danger or the consequences of their actions. In addition, they have a short attention span and, occasionally, a lack of body function or control. In designing spaces they will inhabit, it is critical to acknowledge their limited awareness of risk/safety factors and lack of understanding.

A concern in planning for children arises when placing items within reach of an older child, which are still off-limits to a younger child or toddler. Detailed conversation with the supervising adult is needed to determine what responsible safety precautions must be taken. Children will be completing the same activities at the lavatory as adults. Small children will be learning to brush teeth, and wash hands and face, so it is important that the grooming center be planned to stimulate and enhance their learning experiences. Another concern in planning for any client with cognitive issues is clarification as to how involved the client will be in the design and use of the space. Will he/she use the space independently, and are there unique opportunities to enhance the living experience for the client? Or will a caregiver be involved at all times, and are there unique safety concerns? Are there aspects of the space that should be made more accessible and some that should be off-limits?

Pay attention to design concepts such as security, lock-out for off-limit medications, judicious use of contrast, provision for visual ordering of fixtures and items to be used, simple communication, preprogramming for controls or one-step operations, and creating familiar spaces. These and other design considerations are detailed in the sections that follow.

Some key examples of the universal design principles in chapter 4, "Universal Design and Human Factors," that become more critical when responding to a client with cognition issues include:

- Eliminate unnecessary complexity,
- Be consistent with user expectations and intuition,
- Accommodate a wide range of literacy and language skills,
- Arrange information consistent with its importance, and its order of use.
- Provide effective prompting and feedback during and after task completion.
- Use different modes (pictorial, verbal, tactile, auditory) for redundant presentation of essential information,
- Arrange elements to minimize hazards and errors.
- Provide fail-safe features.

Physical Characteristics

Mobility

Have you ever tried to walk a straight line on a moving airplane or train, or use steps that are slippery with water or ice? Have you ever tried to pass through a space not big enough to accommodate you?

Changes in mobility include body stiffness and rigidity, as well as diminished strength, stamina, balance, and range of motion, usually in the spine, legs, and/or lower body. This includes those who use a wheelchair, scooter, walker, crutches, braces, or other mobility aids. Less obvious, this group also includes those whose mobility is challenged, sometimes temporarily, by pregnancy, excess weight, cardiovascular or respiratory problems, injury, or fatigue. It also includes people who have difficulty bending or stooping.

Measurements used to plan the bathroom should include any assistive device the client uses. The wheelchair or mobility aid should be measured, just as you would document a client's height or body breadth. Standard dimensions for a person using a mobility aid are listed in chapter 4, "Universal Design and Human Factors," but in fact, each client and each mobility aid is unique. In the assessment tools in chapter 5, "Assessing Needs," you will find several diagrams to use when measuring people and their mobility aids.

Pay special attention to design concepts such as clear floor space for passage and storage of an assistive device, reach ranges, sight lines, selection of drawer pulls, supports, and controls for ease of use and safety. These and other design considerations are detailed in the section that follows.

Dexterity, Strength, Balance, and Stamina

Have you ever tried to lift a 20-pound (9 kg) box of laundry detergent and place it on a shelf above your head using only one arm? Or struggled to lift a wiggling and wet 25-pound (11 kg) child out of a bathtub?

Included in this user group are those who are fatigued or frail from illness or age, and the multitudes of people with limited upper body strength. Also included are individuals with pain, or limited joint or muscle motion, including the ability to grip or grasp, due to temporary or minor injuries and illness. Specific conditions include arthritis, carpel tunnel syndrome, asthma, allergies, chemical sensitivities, post-polio syndrome, stroke, Parkinson's disease, multiple sclerosis, ALS, cerebral palsy, and numerous additional unique physical conditions.

As we age, we experience a decrease in strength due to bone density and muscle loss, causing an increase in accidents and fractures. Decreased mobility can be caused by changes in joints, stooped posture, and/or decrease in height, and common disorders such as arthritis, osteoarthritis, and osteoporosis. As we "shrink" in height, our reach ranges become shorter than those of middle-aged people, moving closer to the range of children.

Changes in internal functions can cause increased incidence of high blood sugar, gallstones, diverticulitis, constipation, and loss of bowel control. Changes in kidney and bladder function can inhibit urinary control and cause dehydration. Changes in the nervous system result in slower movements, and decreased balance and coordination due to inefficiency of the nervous system and central brain processes. Many people experience a sleeping pattern change, requiring less sleep or experiencing less sound sleep.

A concern with this client is the prognosis, and how the condition will likely change, another critical issue that can be clarified by involved medical professionals. Strength and pace may vary throughout the day. If a cane, walker, or other mobility aid is needed, the ability to carry things is often compromised. Observe your client's balance, and how he/she lifts and moves his/her feet.

Pay special attention to design concepts such as clear floor space, options to sit or stand, reach ranges, design of supports, drawer pulls and controls for ease of use, particularly the strength/dexterity needed for operation and safety. These and other design considerations are detailed in the section that follows.

Stature

Do you remember, as a child, trying to reach the faucet at the lavatory? Children and others small in stature have reduced reach. A child's stature at age six is closer to that of a seated adult than it is to even the shortest of standing adult females (see Figure 8.1).

In contrast, those taller than average height can experience fatigue from operating in a stooped position at fixtures and fittings planned for the comfortable use of an average height person.

Pay special attention to design concepts such as reach ranges, whether unobstructed or over a counter or fixture, selection of supports including step stools, drawer pulls and controls for ease of use and safety, and sight lines. These and other design considerations are detailed in the section that follows.

Some key examples of the universal design principles in chapter 4, "Universal Design and Human Factors," that become more critical when responding to a client with physical issues include:

- Avoid segregating or stigmatizing any users.
- Make the reach to all frequently accessed components comfortable for any seating or standing user.
- Allow the user to maintain a neutral body position.
- Provide a clear line of sight to important elements for any seated or standing user.
- Provide space for the use of assistive devices or personal assistants.
- Use reasonable operating forces.
- Minimize necessary sustained physical effort.
- Accommodate variations in hand and grip size.

ACCESS DESIGN CONSIDERATIONS

Bathroom space planning considers the given parameters of the job, the NKBA Bathroom Planning Guidelines (referred to as Planning Guidelines) and the related Access Standards (referred to as Access Standards) found in Appendix A, and a client's preferences and budget. Although true in every bath design project, when a client has a unique condition, it becomes more critical to carefully consider clear floor space and support requirements for physical support, as well as features that offer sensory and cognitive support, based on the client's specific needs and abilities. For example, reverberation of noise off hard surfaces makes it more difficult for a person with limited hearing to perceive sound, so incorporation of sound-absorbing materials such as cork or fabrics to improve acoustics becomes more critical.

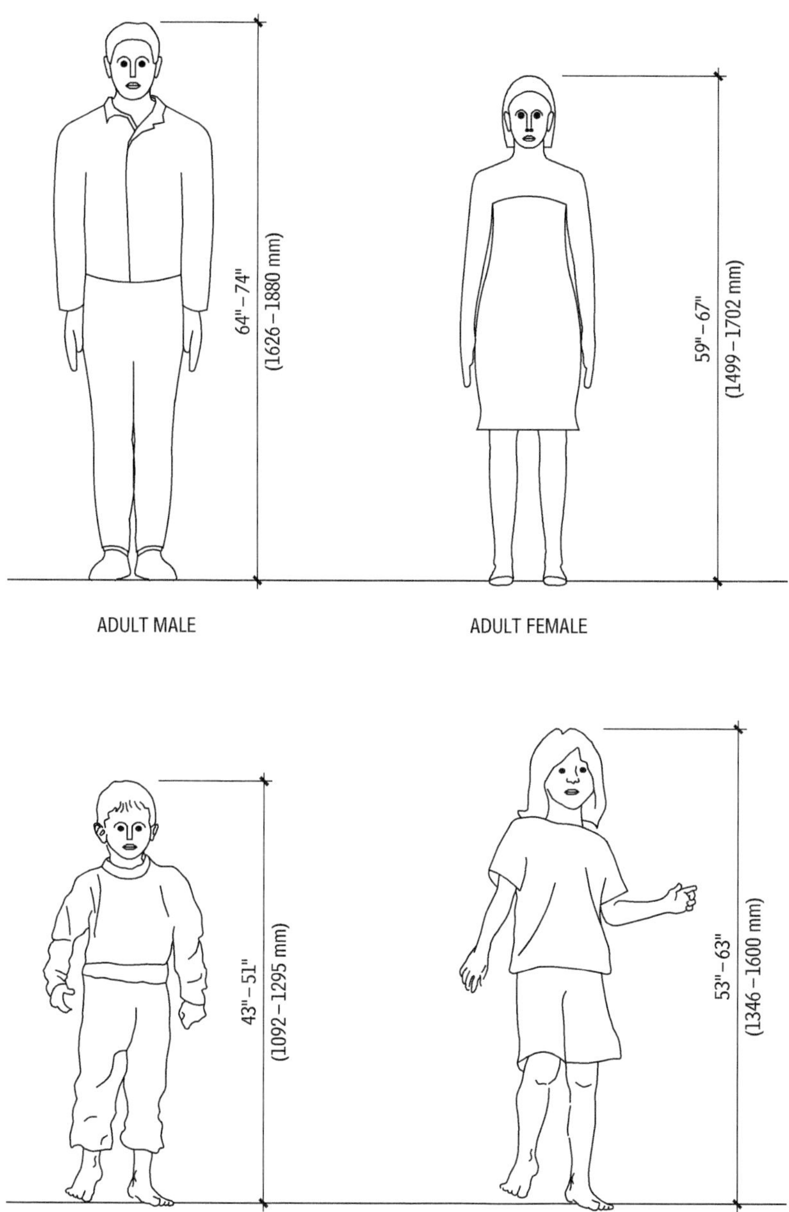

FIGURE 8.1 Differences between a child and even the smallest of adult females (5th percentile) require adjustments to the location of the adjustable showerhead, storage, controls, support, and more.
NKBA

The centers of the bathroom are reexamined here, with an emphasis on access modifications for a client with an injury, a disability, or abilities and characteristics that are otherwise unique. Design concepts will focus on three areas of human performance: sensory, perceptual/cognitive, and physical. To use this information successfully, it is imperative that you start with a full assessment of the person's current and future functional capabilities and again, this is where the OT (occupational therapist) or other medical professional will be useful.

Bathroom Entry and Circulation

In chapter 6, "Bathroom Design," design of the bathroom and its centers is discussed, including many references to design for the differences in people. The intent here is to supplement that chapter's discussion with only that information that is specific or unique to a client with exceptional needs. For a complete review of bath planning relating to entry and circulation, please refer to chapter 6.

Doorways to the Bathroom

Although most issues in designing the entry and doorway to the bath relate to physical characteristics and needs of the people who will use the space, there are considerations that relate to sensory and perceptual/cognitive aspects of the client.

The use of contrast to indicate the entry can help with way-finding, but this contrast must be used judiciously when perceptual/cognitive impairments are a concern, as the contrast that highlights the doorway can be perceived as a wall or an obstruction to those of us with cognitive issues. Another option to make the doorway leading to the bathroom safe is to plan responsive lighting concepts for nocturnal visits (see Figure 8.2), such as motion sensor lighting, night lighting that fades on and off rather than operating only in full on or off, or glow-in-the-dark grout.

In some cases, a door that swings out of the room will be desired as it will allow for an aide to enter the room if assistance is needed, and it can help to increase the clear floor space where needed in relation to the door swing. Planning so that the door swing and passage area can be

FIGURE 8.2 LED lights imbedded in the tiles guide the way for nocturnal bathroom visits. *Courtesy of Steuler-Fliesen Gmbh*

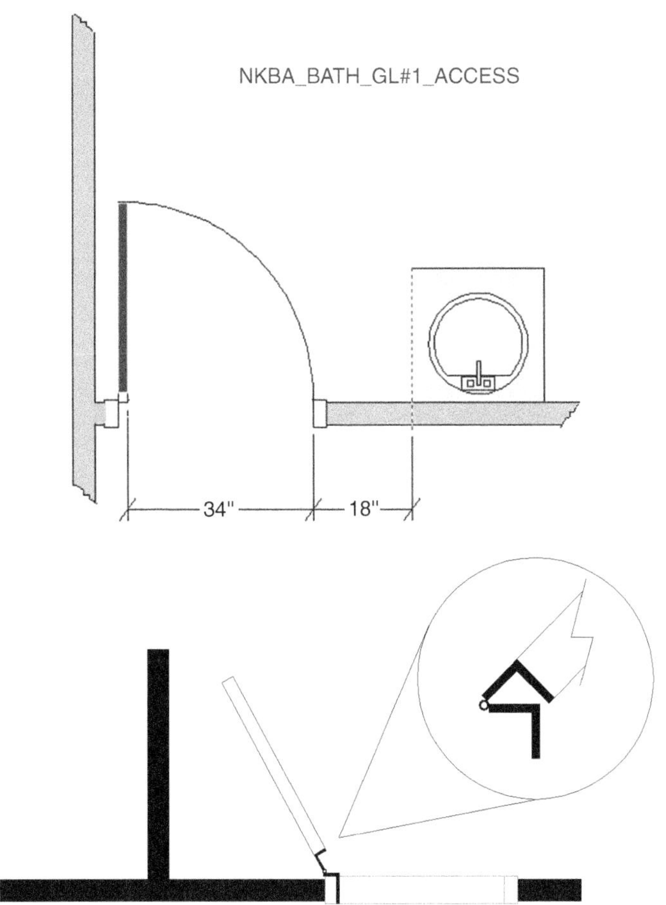

FIGURE 8.3 Access Standard 1: The clear opening of a doorway should be at least 34 inches (864 mm, requiring a 36-inch (914 mm) door to allow for passage by a person using a mobility aid.
NKBA

FIGURE 8.4 A swing-clear hinge swings the door out of the opening increasing the width of the opening by the width of the door.
Rendering by NKBA member: Michael Brgoch, CKD

clutter-free will also help. Repetition in the process and order of entry to the bathroom can make passage easier for those of us with perceptual/cognitive issues—in other words, if the way the door operates, the location of switches and controls at the door, and the order of things as one enters the room is similar to other spaces in the home, access will be improved.

Although a 32-inch (813 mm) clear door opening is allowed in the Planning Guidelines, entry doors into the bath should maintain a clearance of 34 inches (864 mm), which is the typical clearance of a 36-inch (914 mm) door minus the thickness of the door and doorstop (see Figure 8.3). When you consider the standard clear floor space for a person in a wheelchair is 30 inches (762 mm) wide, this seems a bare minimum.

Swing-away hinges allow the door to swing out of the door opening and increase the clear space by 1 inch to 1 1/2 inches (25 mm to 38mm), the thickness of the door (see Figure 8.4).

Guidance varies in the clearances required at a door or door opening, but several general guidelines can be helpful. First, a minimum clear floor space of the door width plus at least 18 inches (457 mm) beyond the latch by 60 inches (1524 mm) perpendicular to the door on the pull side of a standard door is called out as necessary to permit a person using a mobility aid to position themselves next to the door, beside the handle/lever, and out of the way of the door swing, in order to pull it open. In addition, on the push side of the door, a minimum clear floor space of the door width plus 12 inches (305 mm) beyond the latch by 48 inches (1219 mm) (when there is a closer and latch) is called out. This clear space is detailed in chapter 6 (Figure 6.8) and in Appendix A, the Access Standard 2,as shown in Figure 8.5. This dimension varies based on the type of door and the approach.

When planning a 36-inch (914 mm) wide door in a smaller bath, the challenge can be to bring the door into proper scale with the bath space. In these cases, options include pocket doors (see Figure 8.6), split or single, and barn doors(illustrated in chapter 2), both of which eliminate the

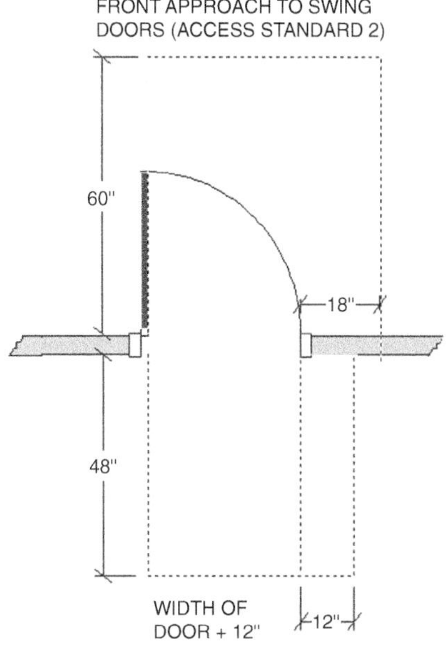

FIGURE 8.5 Access Standard 2: Minimum clearances on either side of a standard hinged door. Further clarification for clear spaces in other door configurations, including folding, pocket, or barn doors, is available in ICC A117.1-2009, section 404).
NKBA

FIGURE 8.6 Pocket door options have improved, including hardware that is easier for most to use.

Sources: A: Mary Jo Peterson, Inc.; B: Hafele America Co; C: Splash Galleries

door swing completely. The hardware used to operate these doors has been difficult to use, but research will reveal automated or otherwise easy-use options.

In older homes, hallways will sometimes be less than the 42 inches (1067 mm) minimum desired. When the width of the hallway cannot be changed, sometimes a creative solution can come from alternative door designs. Another alternative to be considered is angling the door opening, which eliminates the difficult 90-degree turn, as shown in Figure 8.7.

Clear Floor Space in the Bathroom

Although most issues in designing the circulation in the bath relate to physical characteristics and needs of the people who will use the space, there are considerations that relate to sensory and perceptual/cognitive aspects of the client.

For those of us with hearing impairments, a clear line of sight will make using the bathroom more comfortable. Increased and adjustable, nonglare lighting and tactile cuing, such as a change in texture around the door trim, will help those of us with vision impairments.

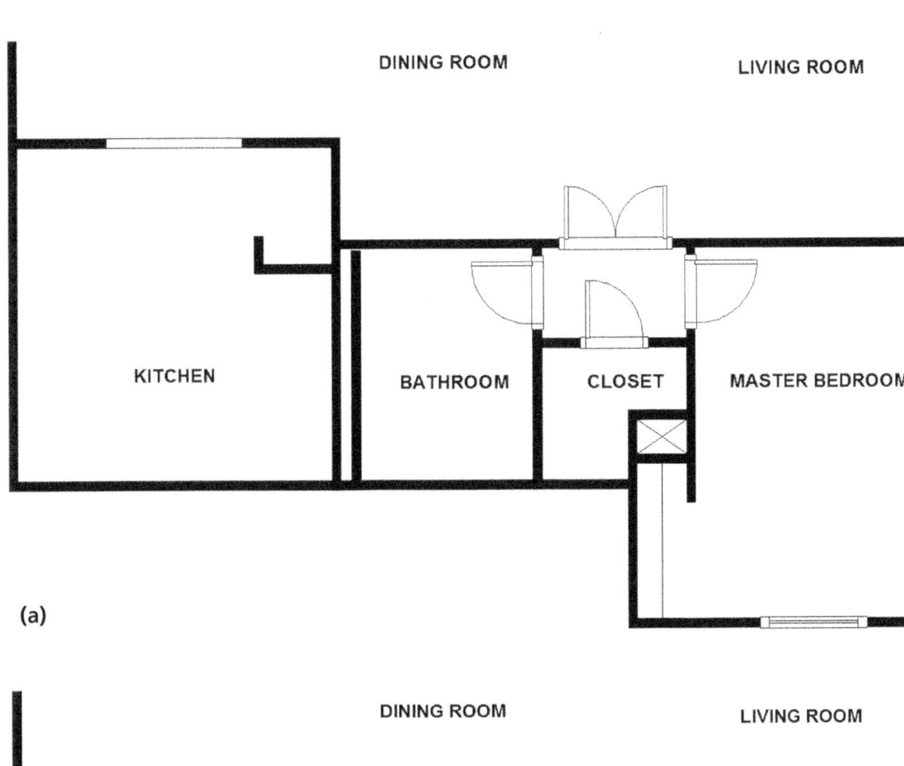

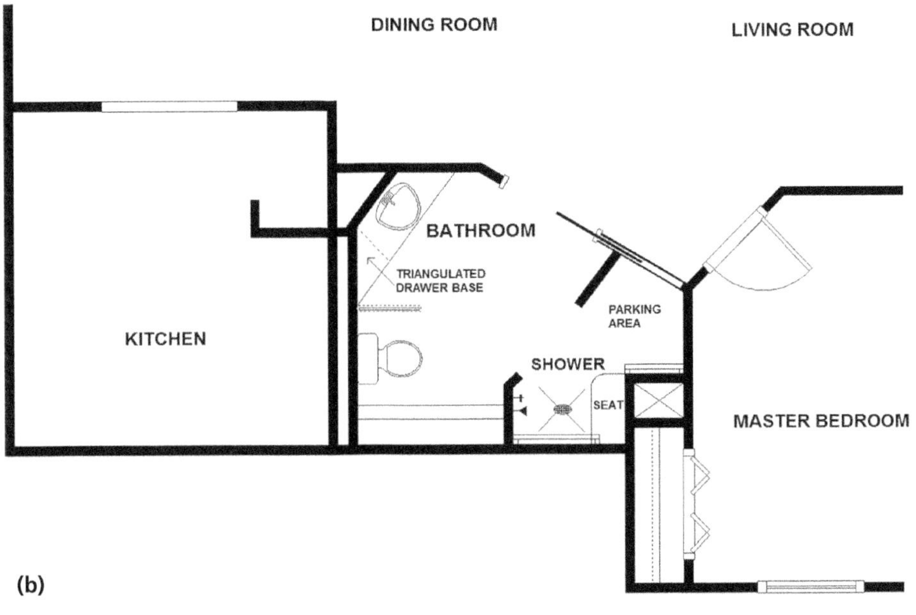

FIGURE 8.7 A 90-degree turn by a person using a wheelchair requires maneuvering space. Angling the door opening eliminates the need for the 90-degree turn.

Courtesy of Gracious Spaces by Irma Dobkin and Mary Jo Peterson

Colors and patterns should be chosen with consideration of the total room in terms of contrast and light. Color contrast can be used to highlight edges or borders, as in the edge of a counter or a border around the floor. Overuse of contrast, particularly on walls and floor borders, can block a person from maneuvering and must be carefully planned.

Use easy-to-maneuver flooring, such as slip-resistant tile or vinyl. Commercial quality resilient flooring resists wear, is easy to maintain and clean, and in some cases, has raised dots or granular materials to improve slip-resistance. Slip-resistant coatings can be applied to the floors.

Sufficient clear floor space for functional passage is a design challenge impacted mainly by physical characteristics and needs of the people who will use the bathroom and the space available. As strength, stamina, and balance decrease, minimal passage clearances can help to give people support as they move through a space. But with a mobility aid, more generous spaces are mandatory. As discussed in chapter 5, "Assessing Needs," if a client uses a mobility aid, the person and their aid must be measured to accurately design the space. Generous passage with integral options for support is one possible solution. The concept of adaptable design is another answer, as in a wall adjacent to a toilet that is built to be removable—or movable as in Figure 8.8— should a client's needs change.

Space in the bathroom for creature comforts, such as exercise, reading, or massage (see chapter 9, "More Than a Bathroom"), creates a sanctuary and private retreat away from the rest of the home, and in the case of a client with mobility impairments, it may serve more purposes. Space for physical therapy and storage of associated equipment/supplies may be needed. The "morning kitchen" or kitchen in/near the bedroom suite provides a place for coffee, and breakfast, or a late-night snack and it can also provide privacy and some

FIGURE 8.8 Moveable privacy wall.
Courtesy of AgingBeautifully.org.

independence, as well as serving as a station for a caregiver, keeping medication close to the bedroom. In some cases, the ability to shut down or lock away access to equipment may be desirable as a safety measure.

Once in the bathroom, space at each fixture for maneuvering is best planned around the 30 inch by 48 inch (762 mm by 1219 mm) clear floor space that is standard for a person using a wheelchair, although this dimension will vary with the client and their aid, so it is always best to measure your client, as outlined in chapter 5, "Assessing Needs." Remember that each wheelchair is unique, and that scooters and other mobility aids will measure differently. The suggestion is that either a parallel or front (perpendicular) approach is functional, but this varies tremendously from client to client and preferences and ability must be taken into account. Clearance recommendations will also be based on the fixture specified and will be detailed as the centers of the bath are discussed in the ensuing sections. In addition, a 60-inch (1524 mm) circle to allow for a person using a chair to make a 360-degree turn in place is advised.

It is often difficult to accomplish these clearances and there are some design approaches that will help. To begin with, clear floor spaces at the fixtures can overlap as long as there is sufficient space to operate the entry door (Figure 8.9). In addition, although a 60 inch (1524 mm) turning circle is preferred (Figure 8.10), it is possible to plan for a person using a chair to turn via a "T-turn," measuring a minimum 36 inches by 60 inches by 36 inches (914 mm by 1524 mm by 914 mm). This can sometimes be the better answer in a small bath, using the space under the vanity area for the stem of the turn.

Beyond this, reducing the number and depth of obstructions by planning shallow storage areas with open shelves or cabinetry suspended off the floor or a 9–12 inch high toekick, and tambour, sliding, up-lifting or other doors that will not protrude will increase and improve the clear floor space. It is good to remember that a person using a wheelchair needs the greatest amount of clear space at floor level (Figure 8.11), and that if storage or any obstruction can be planned off the floor, it will be easier to create that needed clear space.

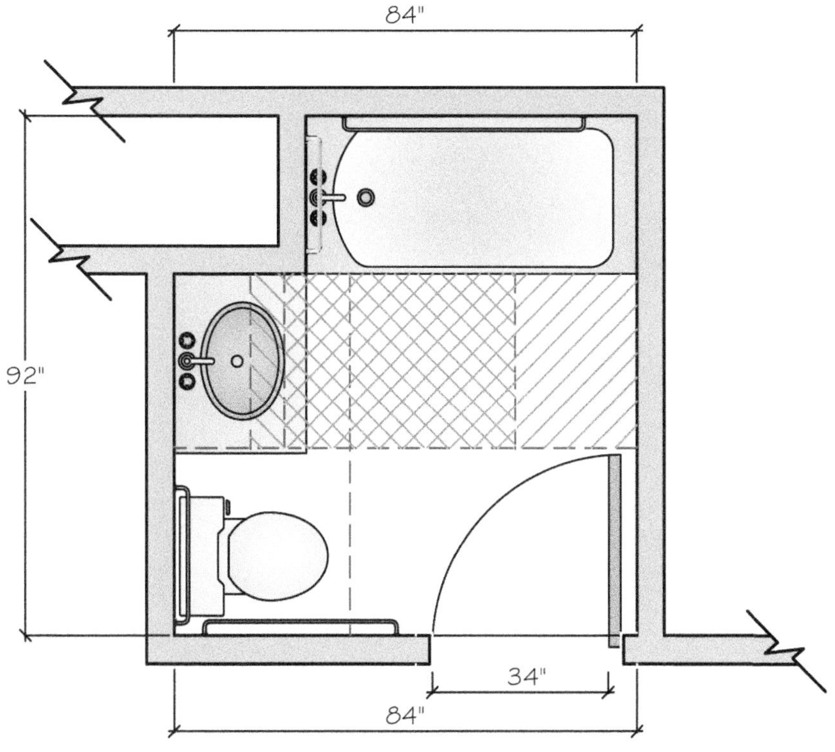

FIGURE 8.9 Access Standard 4: Overlapping clear floor space.
NKBA

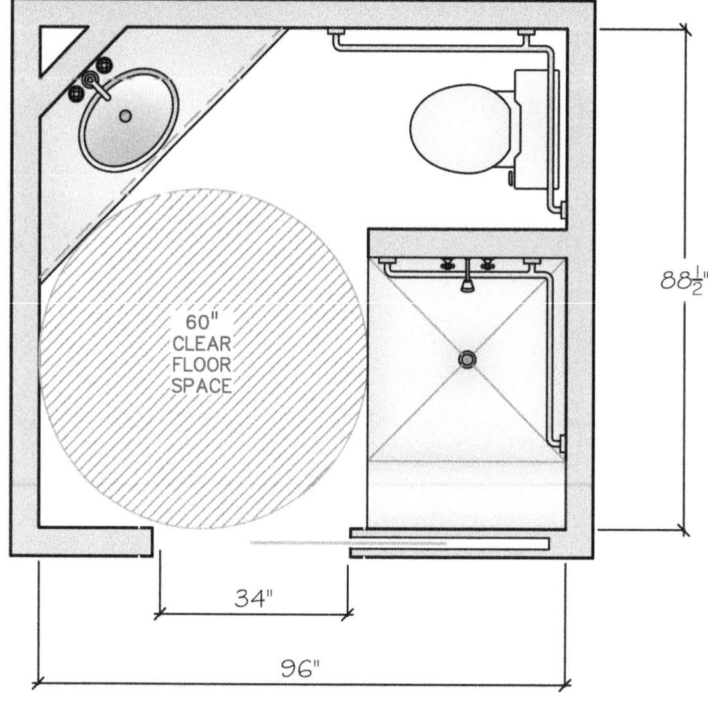

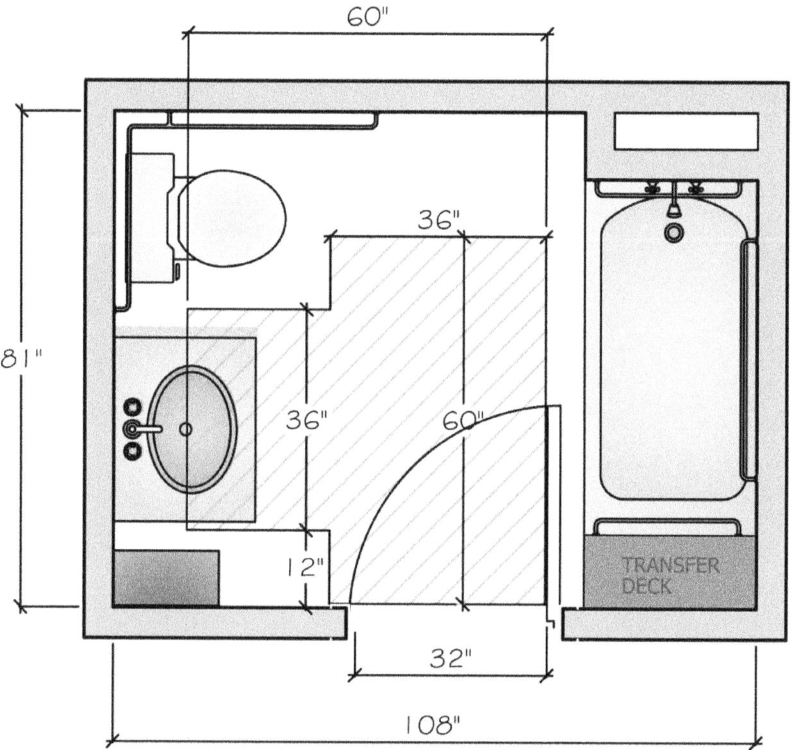

FIGURE 8.10 Access Standard 4: Wheelchair turning radius
NKBA

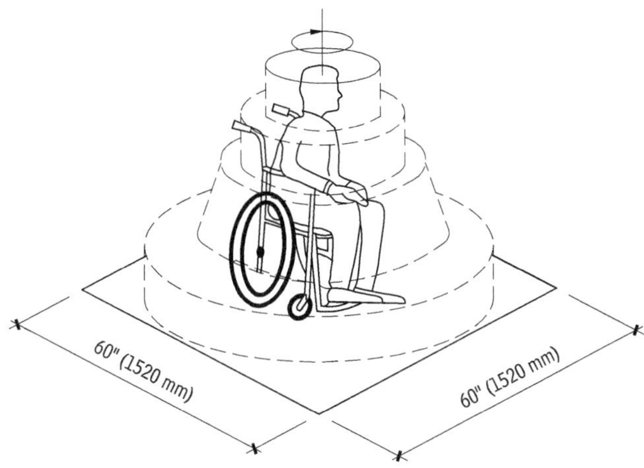

FIGURE 8.11 The clear space needed is greatest at the floor.
NKBA

Access Standards

The Guidelines and Access Standards that relate to the entry and circulation are 1, 2, 3, and 4.

Responsive Design Summary: Entry and Circulation

- Sensory
  - Universal recommendations
    - Increase tactile and audio cueing for way-finding, function, and warnings.
    - Carefully plan color contrast to highlight edges or borders, such as in the edge of a counter or a border around the floor.
    - Reduce the number and depth of obstructions that protrude into the passage space.
    - Provide clear sight lines for clients of various heights throughout the space (improves function for all, especially useful to those with hearing issues).
    - Plan lighting for nocturnal visits to the bathroom, such as motion sensor lighting, night lighting that fades on/off, or glow-in-the-dark grout.
  - Access recommendations
    - Plan needed allowance for a service dog or other service animal
    - Provide clear floor space according to the dimensions of the client, his/her assistive device and/or caregiver, and maneuvering needs.
- Cognitive
  - Universal design recommendations
    - Plan doors without locks.
    - Consider an out-swinging door to improve access and clear floor space.
    - Plan the entire bathroom as a wet area with a supplemental or second drain in the room to make maintenance easier and the space more flexible.
    - Do not overuse contrast, particularly on walls and floor borders, as it can confuse and inhibit a person's maneuvering and must be carefully planned.
  - Access recommendations
    - Repeat the arrangement of space among multiple bathrooms to reinforce order and function.
- Physical
  - Universal design recommendations
    - Reduce hallways and right-angle turns to provide easier maneuvering, particularly for a person using a wheelchair or other mobility aid.
    - Reduce/eliminate the number and depth of obstructions that protrude into the passage space.
    - Increase the range for sight lines, especially if the client is seated or exceptionally tall.
    - Consider a direct or quick route for egress in case of an emergency.
    - Organize space for minimum movement and reduced strength and bending.
    - Provide clear floor space/opportunities to operate from a seated position to preserve strength.
    - Include support for passing through a space to relieve demands on balance, stamina, and strength.

- Increase clear floor space to ease maneuvering, with particular attention to the door.
- Access recommendations
  - Door/entry: 34-inch (864 mm) clear doorways (Access Standard 1).
  - Plan a minimum 18 inches beyond the latch by 60 inches (305 mm by 1524 mm) clear floor space on pull side of door, and 12 inches beyond the latch by 48 inches on the push side of the door (305 mm by 1219 mm) (Access Standard 2).
  - Provide a minimum clear floor space of 48 inches by 30 inches (1219 mm by 762 mm) at each fixture (Access Standard 4).
  - When maneuvering space includes a knee space, especially useful at the vanity/lavatory, use these minimum dimensions: 36 inches wide by 27 inches high by 17 inches deep (914 mm by 686 mm by 432 mm (Access Standard 4).
  - Provide clear space for turning for a client using a mobility aid by measuring the client and the device, with minimum guidance being 60-inch (1524 mm) turning radius or 36 inch by 36 inch by 60 inch (914 mm by 914 mm by1524 mm) T-turn (Access Standard 4).
  - Include space to store and recharge mobility aid, with consideration to the associated noise.
  - Consider the strength and coordination of the client when choosing the door operating system.

Grooming Center

In chapter 6, "Bathroom Planning," the design of the grooming center is discussed in detail, including many references to design for the differences in people. The intent here is to supplement that chapter's discussion with only that information that is specific or unique to a client with exceptional needs. For a complete review of bath planning relating to the grooming center, please refer to chapter 6.

Clear Floor and Knee Space at Grooming Center

The minimum clear floor space, recommended 30 inches by 48 inches (762 mm by 1219 mm), should be centered on the lavatory. The recommended distance from the centerline of the lavatory to the side wall or obstruction is 20 inches (508 mm), which allows more than enough space for a front (perpendicular) approach. However, if you wish to allow for a parallel approach as well (48 inches by 30 inches (1219 mm by 762 mm), you will need to increase the distance from the centerline to the side wall to 24 inches (610 mm).

Keep in mind that clear floor spaces can overlap (Figure 8.9), so for example, when two lavatories are side by side, the original guideline might be enough. When possible, separate the lavatories so each one has its own clear floor space, and you have the opportunity to place them at different heights.

Raising toe kicks on vanity and storage cabinets 9 inches to 12 inches (228 mm to 305 mm) provides clearance for wheelchair footrests and other mobility aids, increasing functional clear floor space. Whenever possible, measure your client's foot in the footrest for specific clearance requirements.

To accommodate a client who will sit to use the lavatory, you will need to plan clear floor space for approach and clear knee space for approach and use (Figure 8.12). While a parallel approach is allowed by accessibility codes and standards, a perpendicular approach with an open knee space is much preferred.

When planning an open knee space it is best to measure the client in the chair that will be used, and when this is not possible, the recommended dimensions are cited in Access Guideline 4 (Figure 8.14). The width of an open knee space should be a minimum of 30 inches (762 mm), with the preference being 36 inches (914 mm) as this is the minimum needed to serve as one leg of a T-turn, (Figure 8.13).

The height of the counter, or the top of the sink should be designed to fit the user, usually between 27 inches and 34 inches (686 mm to 864 mm) for seated use. This dimension will best be determined by measuring the clearance needed in the knee space and considering the depth of the sink. With this in mind, a sink of no more than 6 1/2 inches (165 mm) depth is best, and it can be useful to consider dropping a vessel sink lower into the counter to bring the adjacent work surface closer to the height of the sink's edge. The height of the counter surface and sink is often a compromise as a seated user works well with the lowest height their lap will accommodate, but allowances must be made for the depth of the sink. Several products exist that allow for height

FIGURE 8.12 Knee space at lavatory.

(A): Design by NKBA member: John A Granato II, CKD (B): Courtesy of Louis Tenenbaum

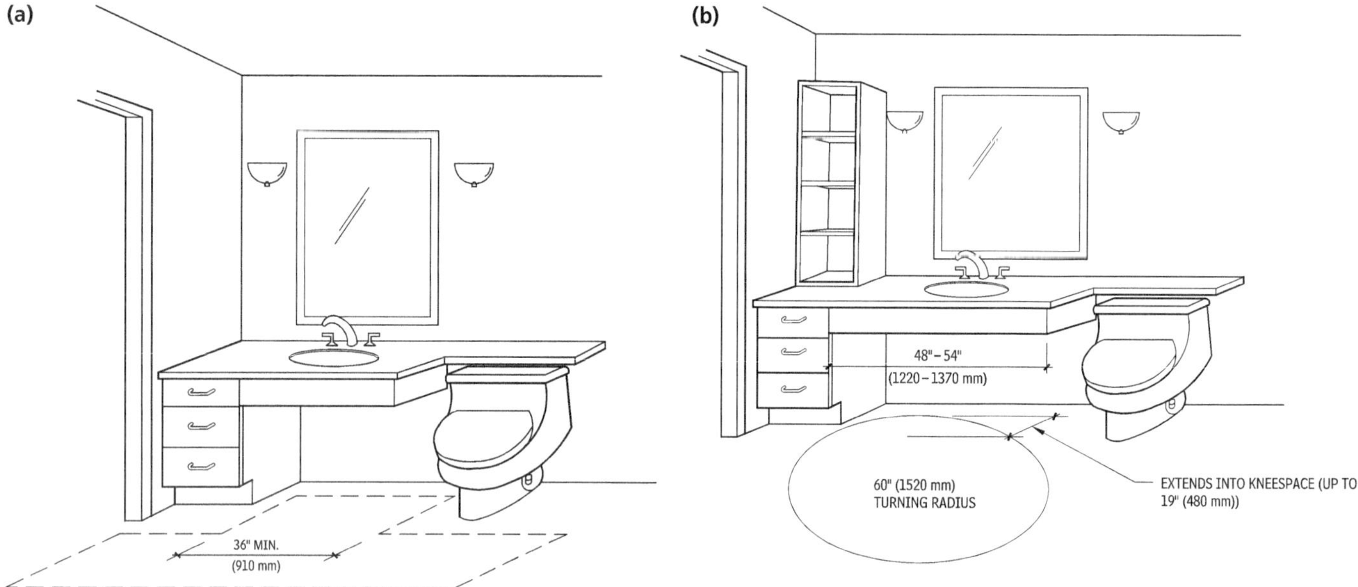

FIGURE 8.13 Knee spaces that provide clear floor space for turning.
NKBA

adjustment of the lavatory on a moment to moment basis (Figure 8.15). While this requires a flexible plumbing line and careful consideration and planning with the plumbing inspector, the system works well and can create the flexibility needed.

The depth of the knee space can vary from floor to counter with 19 inches (483 mm) being desirable. The greatest depth is needed at the floor where the feet of the seated user will be positioned, and often the clearance slopes back from the work surface to accommodate the lavatory depth. Today, drain fittings exist that bring the trap back towards the wall, making the depth of the knee space easier to achieve. The lavatory must be supported and the plumbing must be covered, with protective coverings including material to match surrounding cabinetry or the lavatory, or designed from custom railing systems to coordinate with the accessories. These coverings protect both the plumbing and the user and will need to be durable.

Although today's designs have a high level of comfort and beauty in the open knee space, there may be times when a client prefers or a design dictates concealing the open area, and this can be done in a variety of ways. Retractable doors are the most common, but the overall width of the knee space will need to grow to allow for the area the doors take up in the retracted position, and

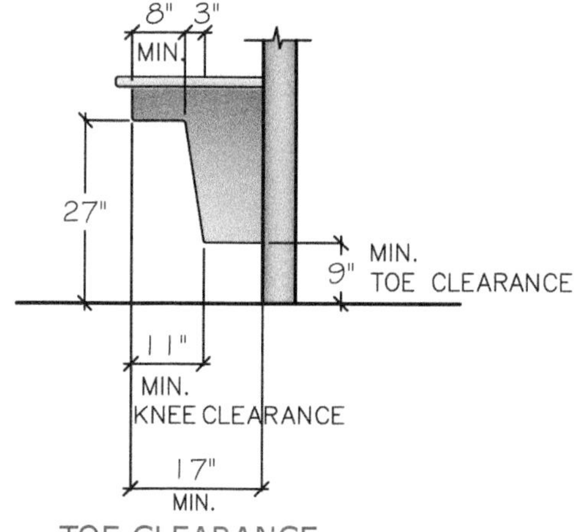

FIGURE 8.14 Access Standard 4: Recommended knee space dimensions.
NKBA

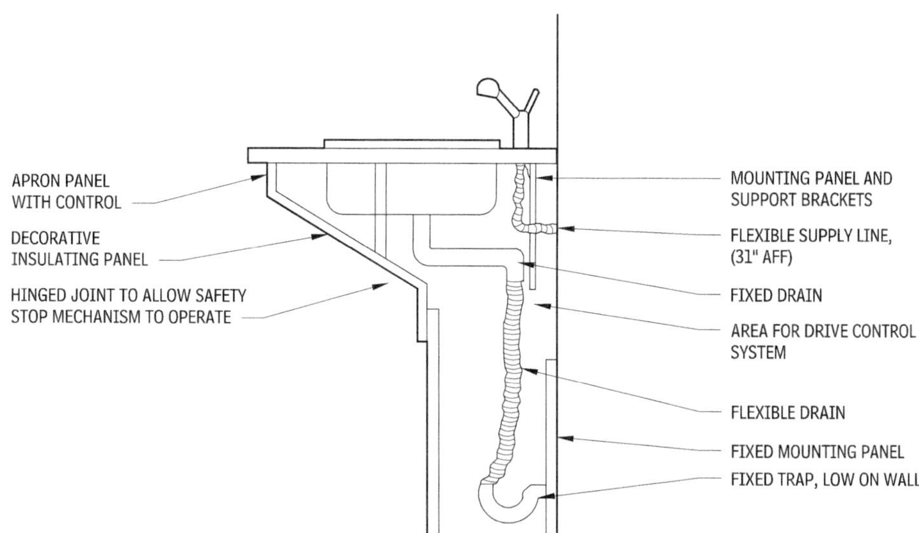

FIGURE 8.15 Adjustable height sinks solve flexibility challenges and must be carefully plumbed.
NKBA

this can be as much as 3 inches (76 mm) per side. Bi-fold doors are another option. Adaptable design might involve finishing the space as an open knee space and then installing a cabinet face frame and doors to be used until that point at which a client wishes to remove them and use the open knee space (see Figure 8.16).

Beyond simple comfort, being able to sit at the vanity area preserves strength and energy and it also improves balance, so this is a concept that suits many users. The open knee space can also provide flexibility as it allows a person to sit or stand, as well as providing storage for a waste bin, chair, or step stool for those not tall enough to comfortably reach the lavatory and controls.

As mentioned previously, adjustable-height vanities help accommodate a broad spectrum of users, but far more common is the use of two vanities. When possible, plan multiple-height vanities to accommodate the client in either a standing or seated position, and to further accommodate multiple clients using the same bathroom (see Figure 8.17). Consideration must also be given to the taller user, who might benefit from a higher than standard vanity.

Although it eliminates the open knee space, another design option is to plan an inverted vanity cabinet so the drawer at the bottom can be converted to a step stool (see Figure 8.18).

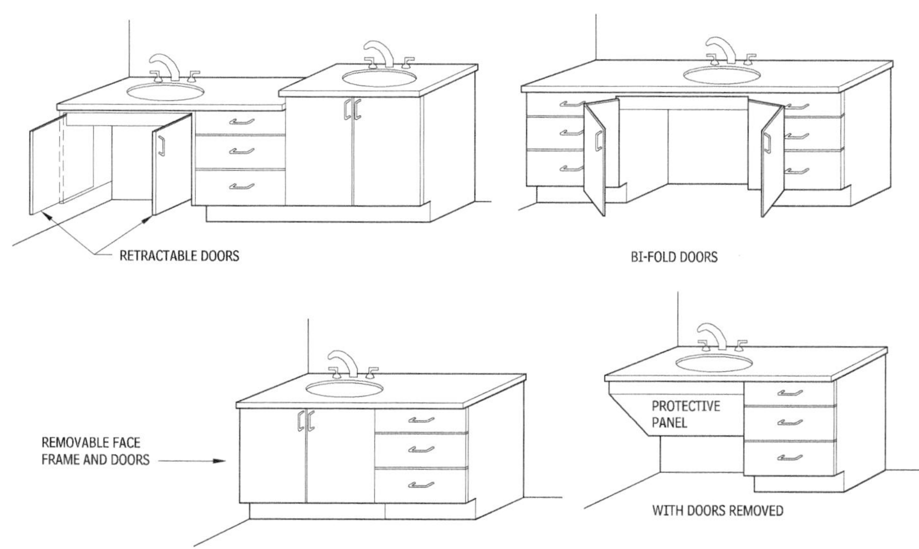

FIGURE 8.16 Some examples of adaptable lavatories include retractable doors, bi-fold doors, removable face frame, and removing doors.
NKBA

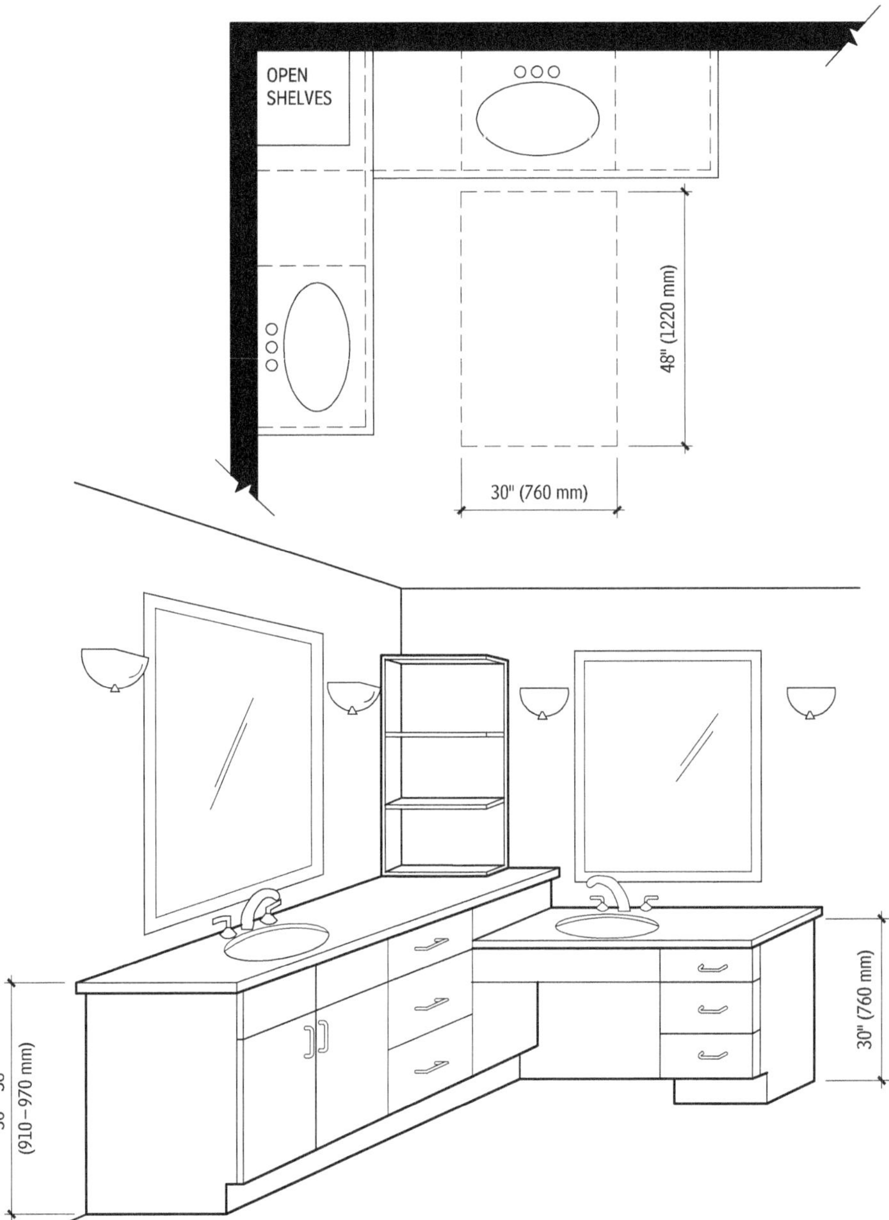

FIGURE 8.17 An example of two lavatories at different heights. The knee space can be storage for a step stool or waste bin, serving many purposes.
NKBA

Given the comfort and convenience of sitting at the vanity and the variety of tasks that take place at this center and could easily be done while sitting, there is another design option that sometimes comes into play. When the bathroom is adjacent to a dressing area or is part of a suite, the vanity and lavatory may be pulled out of the main wet area and placed in the dressing area, matching location and tasks, and freeing up often scarce clear floor space in the rest of the bathroom (see Figure 8.19).

Controls in the Grooming Center

Electronic sensor controls on faucets, lighting, and ventilation help ensure that things are shut off when the user is finished. Motion-sensor light switches eliminate the use of hands for operation.

In fittings, smooth, round handles should be avoided as they are difficult to grasp and operate. Lever or loop handles on faucets are easiest to use. An electronic or battery-operated motion-sensor faucet reduces the need to grip or grasp, as mentioned, the control and

FIGURE 8.18 A pull-out step stool at the vanity provides flexibility in access as a child grows. The lights placed on the side of the mirror assure that children can see.
Courtesy of Kohler Company

redundant cueing, such as using a blue color for cold and a red color for hot, helps to reinforce safe use (see Figure 8.20).

On cabinetry, touch latches eliminate the need for grasp or strength and the risk of anything being hooked by the hardware, but they may be confusing for someone with visual or cognitive impairments. Contrast can be used to visually highlight the controls. New systems that provide assisted automatic opening and soft closing have many access implications, freeing hands and requiring no coordination. Whatever the method, thought should be given to using it throughout to reduce confusion.

Storage in Grooming Center

Because much of what we store in the grooming center is small, thoughtful design can often result in storage right where it is needed. Storage should be placed at the point of use and within easy reach with as much as possible. When information specific to a client's reach range is not available, or in consideration of the varied users, apply the universal reach range of 15 to 48 inches (381 mm

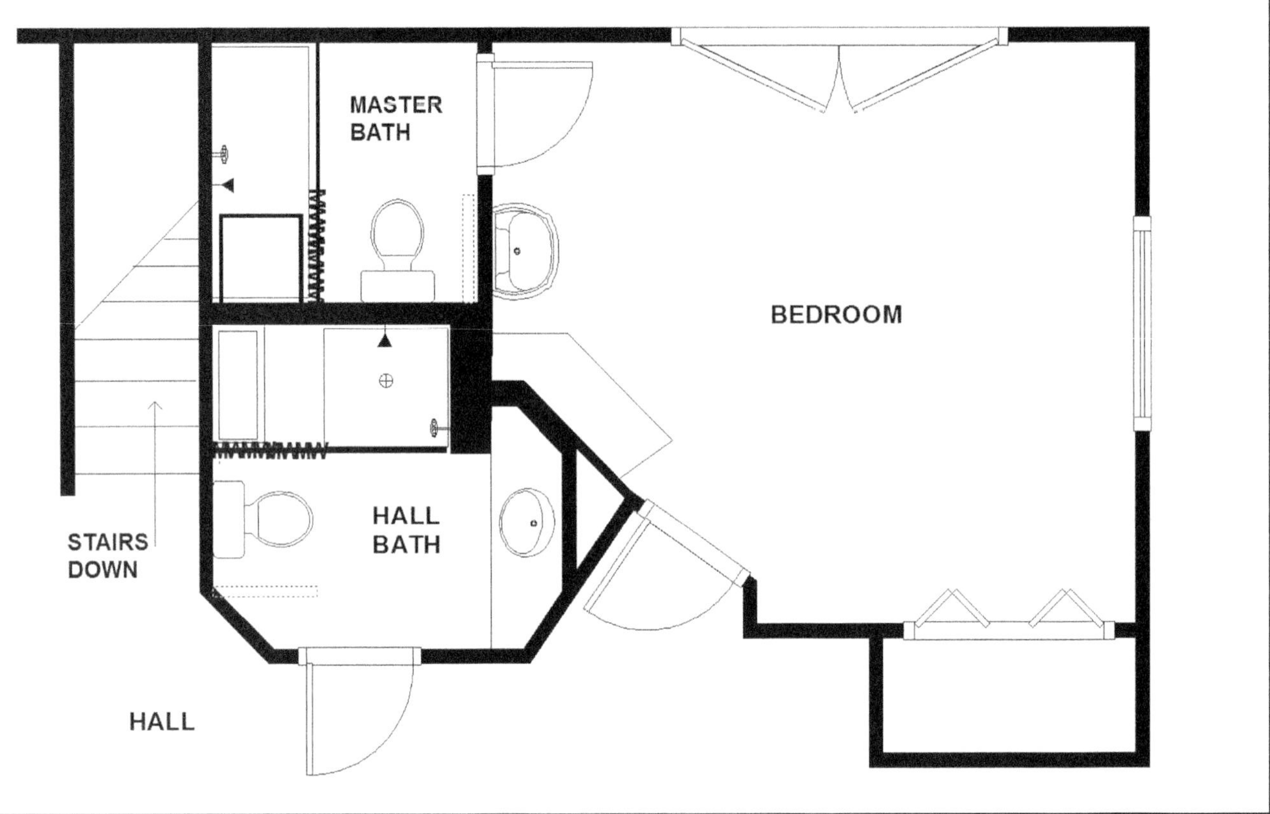

FIGURE 8.19 In a tight bathroom, the vanity can be pulled into the adjacent dressing area, matching task to location and freeing clear floor space.

Courtesy of Gracious Spaces *by Irma Dobkin and Mary Jo Peterson, Inc., Design rendered in 20-20 by Michael Brgoch, CKD*

to 1219 mm) When planning storage above the vanity or lavatory where reach is obstructed the high reach should be 44 inches (1118 mm) maximum (see Figure 8.21). Tall storage takes advantage of the full reach range.

A good approach is to measure a client's comfortable reach range and organize the needed storage for minimum movement, including storage of the heaviest items at no-bend and minimal lifting heights before designing the space (see chapter 5, "Assessing Needs," for needs assessment and chapter 6, "Bathroom Planning," for storage planning).

Storage in the accessible bath may be unique. Open shelves are easy to access and provide easy view of stored items—helpful when memory fails or vision is impaired. On the other hand, some items stored here might be private. If open storage is not possible or desired, lighting the interior of storage cabinets improves visibility. Storage of items in the order in which they will be used can be helpful to those of us with memory or other cognitive issues. Drawers on full extension glides and tambour doors make access easier. Because we may have begun this process with an open knee space, storage in the grooming center must be carefully designed into the available space. A rolling cart can be moved in and out of the knee space, and this can provide for the desired privacy when items are not in use, but planning must include an alternative location for the cart. An appliance garage or medicine cabinet placed on the returning wall adjacent to the vanity are additional options. Pull-out cabinetry adjacent to the knee space may include plug molding or other power sources to accommodate appliances, but safety shut-offs should be planned into them. Electrical appliances, such as hair dryers, should be stored "ready to use." Wall-mounted cabinets or toe kicks raised 9 inches to 12 inches (229 mm to 305 mm) provide clearance for wheelchair footrests and other mobility aids, increasing clear floor space (see Figure 8.22). Medications may be stored in this area and they will need to be secure, out of the hands of children or those of us with cognitive impairments.

FIGURE 8.20 Technology is helping in water conservation and intuitive use of faucets and fittings, shown here as an LED indicating red for hot water and blue for cold water and a faucet with touch control.

(A): Courtesy of Hansa; (B): courtesy of Delta Faucet

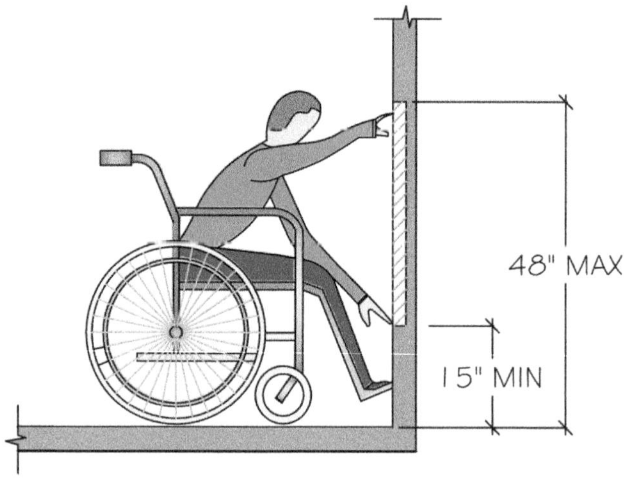

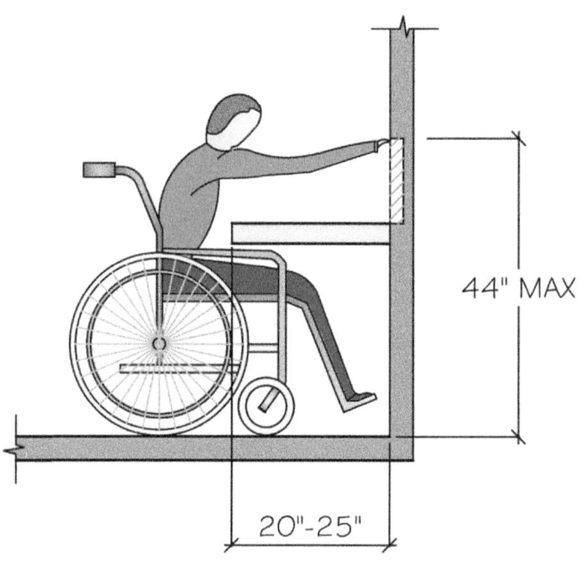

FIGURE 8.21 Access Standard 22: Unobstructed and obstructed forward reach.
NKBA

Accessories in the Grooming Center

Accessories such as towel rings and bars should be placed within reach of the lavatory and within the 15 inch to 48 inch (381 mm to 1219 mm) reach range. Keep in mind that for a person who needs a support for use or passage in the grooming center, anything within reach will be used, and consider specifying only those accessories that will hold the weight and function as grab bars if called on to do so (see Figure 8.23).

A waste container unit or hamper placed in cabinetry on full extension glides does not protrude into the clear floor space except when in use. If the knee space under the sink is flexible in use, the waste container can be placed there. Linen storage or towel warmers should be planned so the contents can be accessed within the 15 inch to 48 inch (381 mm to 1219 mm) reach range. Similar to the kitchen, a soap dispenser recessed into the counter will not move or fall over, and the client will always know its location.

Electrical appliances, such as hair dryers, can be installed in the wall or mounted for ease of use and storage, and to reduce the risk of a client relying on them for support they are not designed to offer.

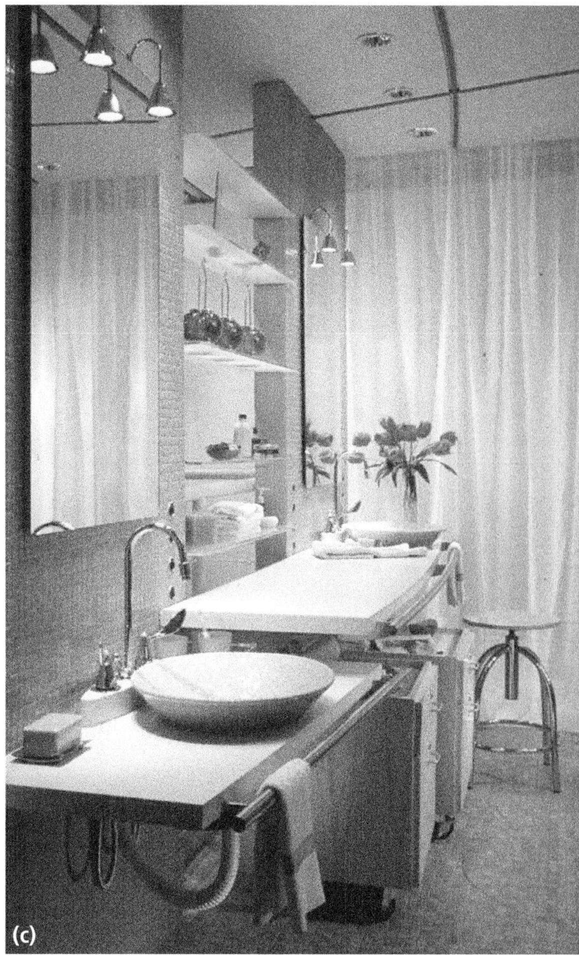

FIGURE 8.22 Storage suspended off floor in the grooming center.

(A): Design by NKBA member Beverley Leigh Binns; (B), (C), (D): courtesy of Kohler Company

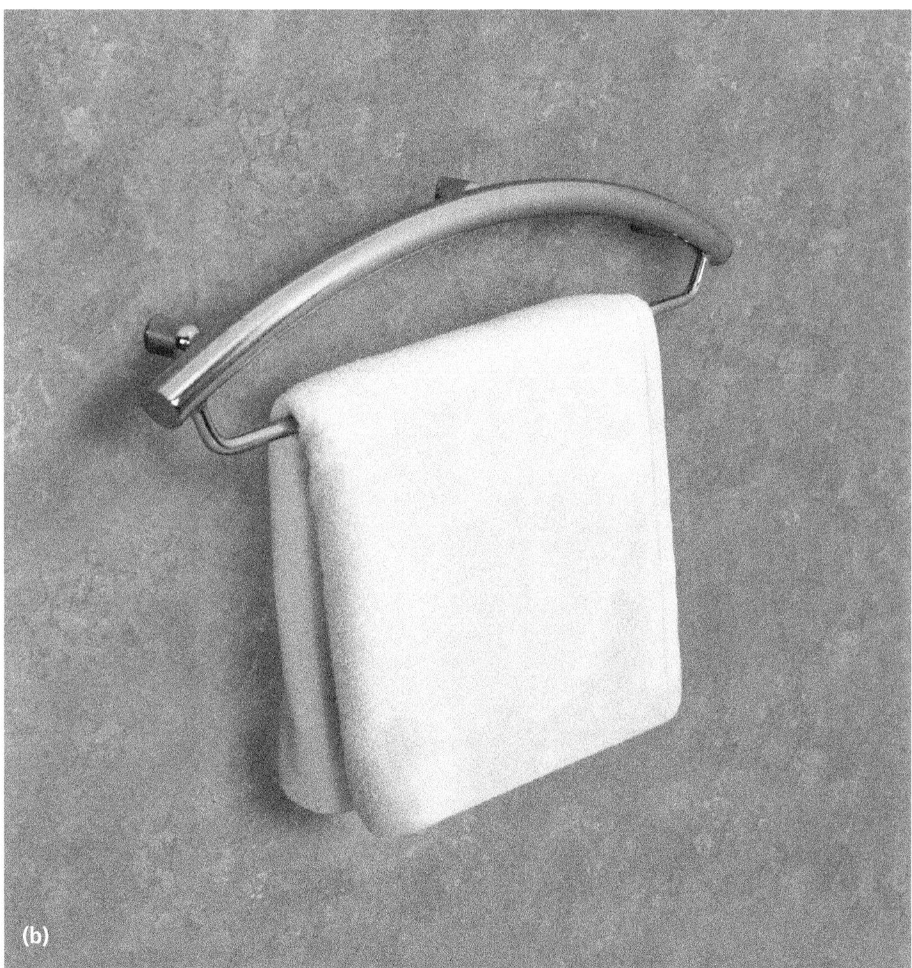

FIGURE 8.23 Consider accessories that incorporate support when possible.

(A): Courtesy of Moen; (B) Courtesy of Invisia by HealthCraft

Consider full-length mirrors that can be tilted and are adjustable to within the sight lines of a child, a seated user, or a taller user. In the case of the full length mirror, related storage and a bench may be planned to allow the client to sit while dressing, if this is to take place in the grooming center.

Lighting in the Grooming Center

In the grooming center, attention to lighting must be considered in relation to a client's sensory, cognitive, and physical characteristics. Natural light sources are best and should be generous, but attention must be paid to privacy and control of ambient light with the use of shades, blinds, or opaque surface treatments. Reducing glare and shadowing is especially important to those of us with aging eyes or impaired sight, so the location and direction of light as well as the amount of light is important. Increased light that is indirect, or at least diffusing the source will help with this. A lighted magnifying mirror can be another assistive addition to the lighting plan. While basic good design dictates that vanity lighting be placed at the height of the eyes of the user, lamps that run the length of the vanity mirror can provide light at varied heights for the wide spectrum of user heights in the space.

Better control of ambient and task lighting with dimmers will enable the user to adjust the lighting to his/her needs depending on the time of day and the task at hand, and also allows a variety of users to customize to suit their individual needs.

Selecting light-colored, matte surfaces for improved reflection of the light can be one way to avoid the shadows. As eyes age, it becomes difficult to differentiate colors with minimal contrast, such as navy, black, brown, or pastels. The contrast created by placing light objects against darker backgrounds, or vice versa, can be useful on controls, work surfaces, and storage. Our ability to place lighting precisely where it is needed through the use of LEDs is one way technology is helping the universal design/access cause.

Electrical in the Grooming Area

Consider the use of GFCI plug molding or other power sources both inside and outside cabinetry to accommodate appliances, with safety shut-offs planned into them. Be generous in the number of outlets provided and plan specific to your client's practices and needs.

Plan assistive devices with dual cueing that makes a sound and flashes a light when appliances, such as a curling iron, are left on. For safety, fire alarms with dual cueing should be included in or near the grooming area.

Supplemental heating and timed or sensor ventilation can be critical, especially to the older client, and these items are discussed in detail in chapter 7, "Mechanical Planning."

Access Standards

The Guidelines and Access Standards that relate to the grooming center are 4, 5, 6, 7, 8, 15, 22, 23, 25, and 36.

Responsive Design Summary: The Grooming Center

- Sensory
  - Universal design recommendations
    - Specify an anti-scald faucet device.
    - Specify eased counter edges and rounded corners, helpful and useful as a tactile guide (Guideline 8).
    - Use both visual and tactile cueing when possible to improve comprehension, such as to identify hot or cold water, or on the edge of a counter to aid in way-finding.
    - In addition to ambient lighting, task lighting should be provided (Guideline 25).
    - Provide the ability to adjust lighting levels (ambient down and task up).
    - Use contrast carefully to highlight edges or borders, as in the edge of a counter or a border around the floor.
    - Use reflective surfaces, pattern, and contrast judiciously to avoid visual confusion and issues with depth perception.

        - Plan shallow storage areas with open shelves, and tambour, sliding, up-lifting or other doors that will not protrude into the clear space.
        - Light storage interiors to improve visibility.
        - Consider the line of sight of user when planning height of bottom of mirrors and glazing (Access Standard 15). Task lighting should circle or be on either side of the mirror and at eye level, with the lamp not visible to the eye (Access Standard 25) to best illuminate the face and cut down on shadows.
    - Access recommendations
        - Include the appropriate assistive devices for redundant cueing for safe use of appliances and the space.
- Cognitive
    - Universal design recommendations
        - Specify electronic sensor controls on faucets to help ensure that things are shut off when the user is finished.
        - Look for the most intuitive cueing/operation, such as using a blue color for cold and a red color for hot, to insure ease of use.
        - Specify an anti-scald faucet device.
        - Use contrast carefully to avoid confusion.
        - Plan storage for medications that is out of the reach of children or others not able to use them as directed.
    - Access recommendations
        - Incorporate open storage and generous counters to allow for easy view and ordering of stored items, which may be helpful when memory fails.
- Physical
    - Universal recommendations
        - Plan multiple-height vanities with opportunities for flexible knee spaces below (Guideline 7).
        - Include a step stool at the vanity to eliminate the need to climb to use the sink or access storage, reducing safety risks.
        - Plan clipped or eased counter edges to reduce potential hazards for one's hip or head, particularly those at either extreme of the age spectrum.(Guideline 8).
        - Avoid any controls that are difficult to grasp or operate, particularly smooth, round knobs.
        - Consider an electronic or battery-operated motion-sensor faucet to reduce the dexterity required for operation and save water.
        - Place accessories and storage near fixtures (Guideline 23).
        - Task lighting should be beside the mirror and at eye level, with the lamp not visible to the eye (Access Standard 25).
        - Consider line of sight of user when planning height of bottom of glazing (Access Standard 15).
        - Provide storage of frequently used items, accessories, and controls at 15 inches to 48 inches (381 mm to 1219 mm) above floor (Access Standard 22).
    - Access recommendations
        - Plan a minimum clear floor space 48 inches by 30 inches (1219 mm by 762 mm) centered on the lavatory (Access Standard 4).
        - Plan the minimum size of a knee space to be 36 inches wide by 27 inches high by 17 inches deep (914 mm by 686 mm by 432 mm) (Access Standard 4).
        - Plan the height of at least one vanity in a bathroom to be no more than 34 inches (864 mm) above the floor (Access Standard 7).
        - Specify lavatory controls that are operable with one hand and do not require tight grasping, pinching, or twisting at the wrist (Access Standard 7).
        - Specify the mirrors above lavatories with the bottom edge no higher than 40 inches (1016 mm) above the floor (Access Standard 23).
        - Plan a full-height mirror to provide non-glare reflection at eye level, regardless of the users' height or stature (Access Standard 23).

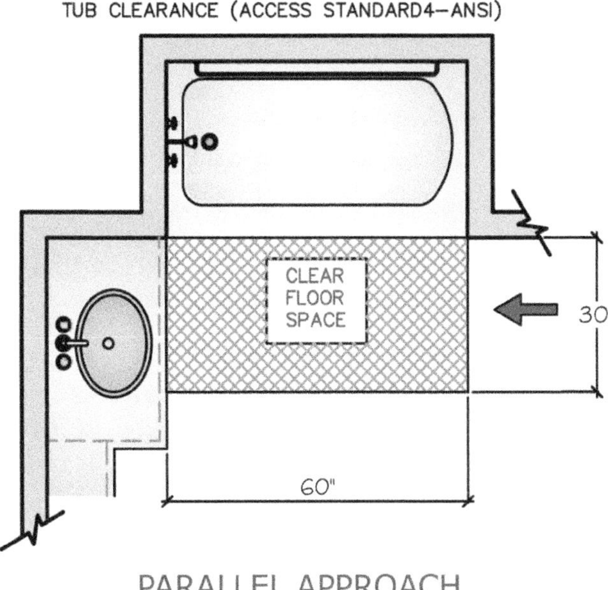

FIGURE 8.24 Access Standard 4: Basic clear floor space at tub.
NKBA

- Specify lighting controls between 15 inches and 48 inches (381 mm to 1219 mm) and operable with a closed fist and with minimal effort (Access Standard 25 and Code Reference).

Bathing and Showering Center

In chapter 6, "Bathroom Planning," the design of the bathing and shower center is discussed in detail, including many references to design for the differences in people. The intent here is to supplement that chapter's discussion with only the information that is specific or unique to a client with exceptional needs. For a complete review of bath planning relating to the bathing and showering center, please refer to chapter 6.

Clear Floor Space and Tub and Shower Dimensions

Bathtubs

As recommended in chapter 6, the clear floor space adjacent to a tub should be a minimum of 30 inches (762 mm) by the length of the tub, or the tub and transfer surface if the transfer surface is at the head of the tub (see Figure 8.24). If an aid will be assisting in bathing or if a person will be approaching using a mobility aid, the width of this clear floor space should increase, with 48 inches (1219 mm) being a good guide.

Beyond the control wall and beyond the head end an additional 12 inches to 18 inches (305 mm to 457 mm) of clear floor space improves access to the controls and to the transfer surface by a person using a wheelchair (see Figure 8.25). The Access Standard indicates that a minimum of 12 inches (305 mm) is needed at the head of the tub. It is worth noting that these clear floor spaces can challenge the proportions in the bathroom and there are several things that can help balance the open space in the room. A movable storage island can be an attractive and useful addition, and a design that integrates the adjacent shower or wet area can use the shower space as part of this clear floor space.

When selecting and specifying the tub fixture, there are several options to be considered to best meet a client's needs for entering/exiting the tub and bathing. Variations on the traditional tub that relate to improved access include built-in seats and transfer surfaces, and integral supports or grab bars. One tub may be deeper because it supports a person sitting upright to bathe, while another might be more traditional in size, supporting a person soaking or experiencing water-related therapy. In addition, tubs with doors are becoming more readily available. If considering a

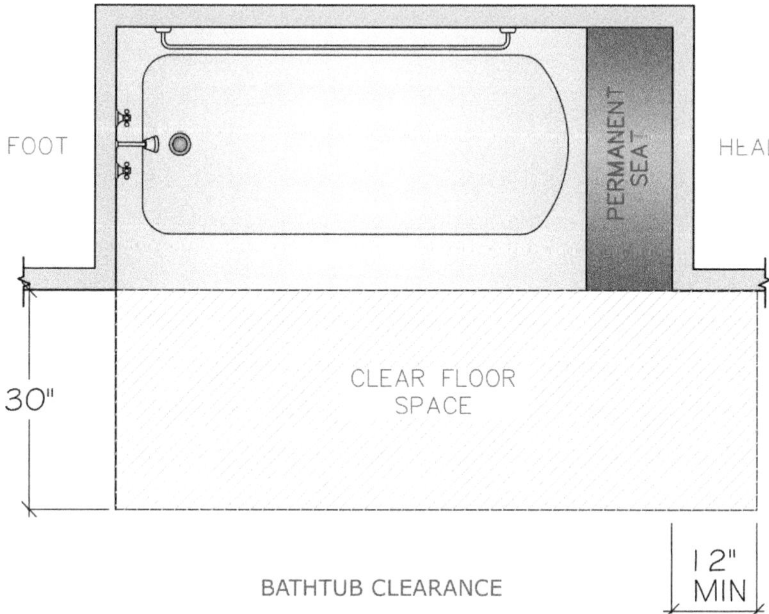

FIGURE 8.25 Access Standard 4: When possible, the clear floor space should extend at least 12 inches to 18 inches (305 mm to 457 mm) beyond the head wall of the tub to allow for positioning of the wheelchair in transfer. Similar clearance at the control wall improves access to the controls.
NKBA

tub with a door, the specific way in which a client is able to approach and enter the tub must be examined. When reviewing the fixture options, some of which are shown in Figure 8.26, the strength and clear space needed for the door to operate, the speed with which the tub can be filled with water and emptied, and the height of the threshold into the tub or the access to any built-in seat must be reviewed. Because the fixture specifications and the client's needs must be matched carefully, no general recommendations can be accurate in terms of matching the client with the tub. Keep in mind that the entry and exit from a tub can be challenging to the most agile among us and this is the most critical aspect in the design and specification of the appropriate fixture, as well as the surrounding space.

The Shower

The ease of entry and exit and the flexibility to sit or stand that can be designed into the shower probably contribute to the current preference for showering as our main method of personal hygiene. Based on size and design, there are two categories of showers relating to access, the transfer shower and the roll-in shower.

Transfer Shower The transfer shower must have a 36 inch by 36 inch (914 mm by 914 mm) finished interior dimension, with an L-shaped grab bar on the control and half of the back wall, a fold-up seat on the wall opposite the control wall, and a full 36-inch (914 mm) opening. These specifications must be precise to succeed at creating a space where anyone using the shower will have controls and support within reach at all times. It is important to note that, based on a client's needs, the transfer shower, although smaller, can be the better choice. When the clear floor space adjacent to the shower is sufficient, most standing or seated users will be able to use this shower independently. Access Standards suggest that the clear floor space adjacent to the transfer shower should be a minimum of 48 inches along the opening and extending beyond the opening on the seat wall, by 36 inches in depth(1219 mm by 914 mm) (see Figure 8.27).

However, a more generous clear space of 60 inches (1524 mm) in length will make showering easier for most people using a mobility aid, allowing for the positioning of the wheelchair to line up with the shower seat or to access the controls, and 60 inches (1524 mm)(see Figure 8.28) in depth would provide the turning clearance for that same bather.

Because the shower interior is so small, the transfer shower is not always designed as a no-threshold shower. When possible, making the area outside the shower a wet area by extending the waterproof membrane and sloping the floor gently toward the drain will make it possible to consider no threshold for this fixture (see Figure 8.29). With or without a raised threshold, care must

FIGURE 8.26 A sampling of available tub designs with door, seat, and deck.
Courtesy of (A): Delta Faucet; (B) Kohler Company; (C) MTI

FIGURE 8.26 *(continued) (D) MTI; (E) Kohler Company*

be taken to contain the water in a shower this size. Adding a second drain outside the shower, or using a trench-style drain can help with this, and there are many products available to streamline this process (see Figure 8.30). While a door will contain the water, it can be difficult to plan a door that will provide the 36-inch (914 mm) opening and still not interfere with maneuvering space. A shower curtain that is long enough to drop onto the floor and weighted to hold it down will help, and the curtain can be tied back when not in use, eliminating the obstruction.

Roll-in Shower A roll-in shower is a large waterproof area with no threshold or a flush threshold. This design is easier for children, those of us with balance issues and in general, most people

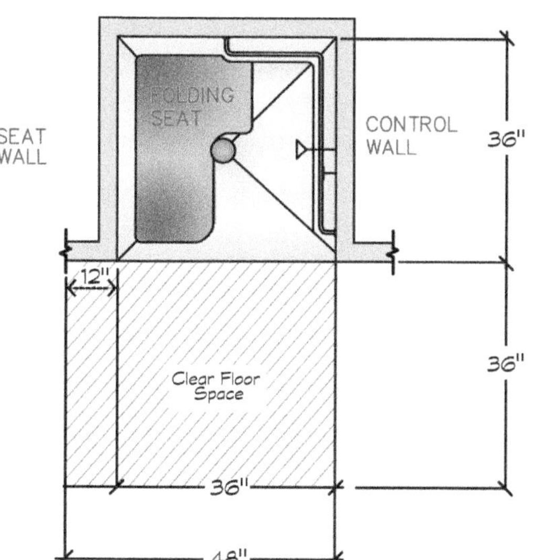

FIGURE 8.27 Access Standard 9: Minimum clear floor space at transfer shower.
NKBA

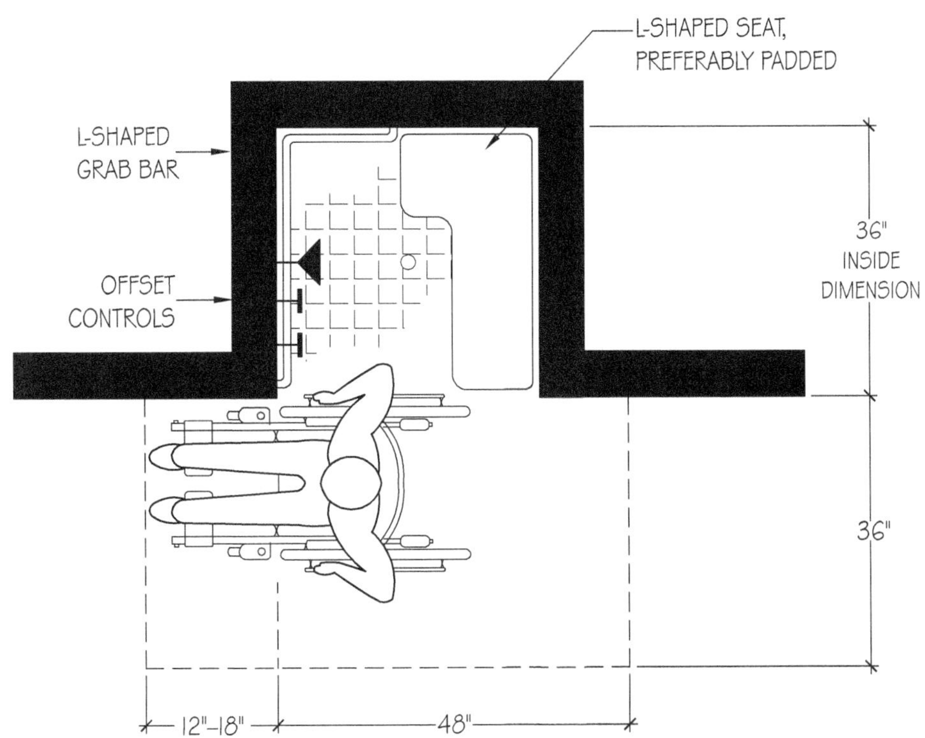

FIGURE 8.28 With the appropriate clear space beyond the control wall and the seat wall of the shower, some wheelchair users can more directly and independently transfer and use the space.
NKBA

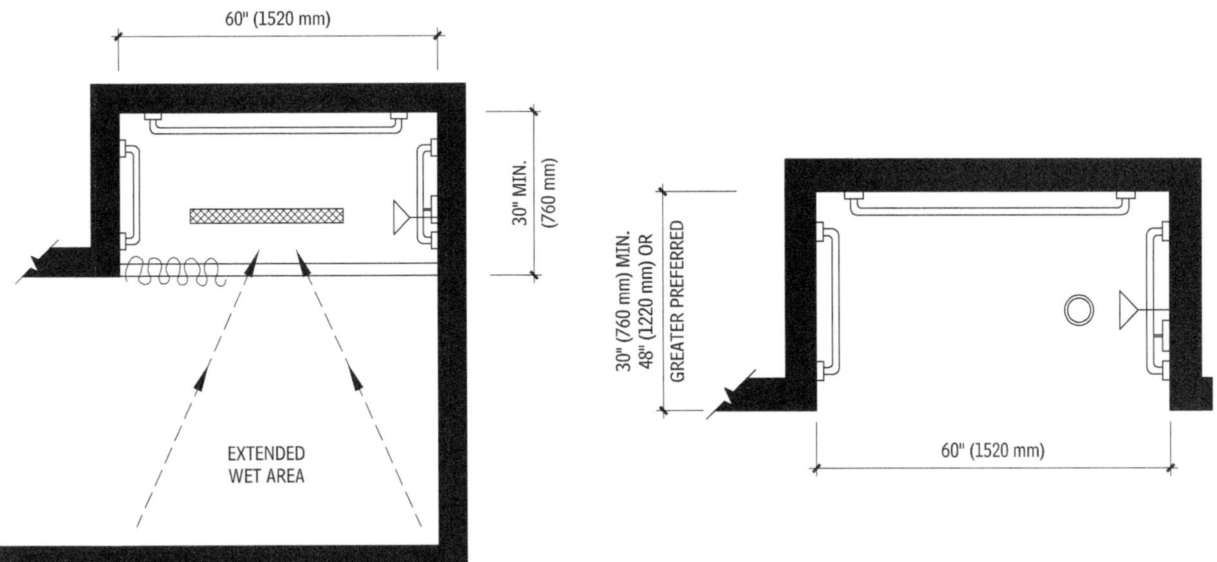

FIGURE 8.29 As shown with this roll-in shower, the incorporation of a wet area outside the shower can help with water containment
NKBA

to use, and it is particularly accommodating to a person using a wheelchair, as he/she is able to roll in and remain in the shower chair while showering. Most recommendations for access suggest a minimum 60 inches wide by 30 inches deep (1524 mm by 762 mm), which allows for conversion from a traditional bathtub to a shower in the existing space, but to help with water containment, a minimum depth of 36 inches to 42 inches (914 mm to 1067 mm) is preferred for a roll-in shower. Ideal dimensions are 60 inches wide by 48 to 60 inches deep (1524 mm by 1219 mm by1524 mm), (see Figure 6.50b in chapter 6) which makes entry and full turning easier for the bather using a wheelchair, and improves water containment. Given the current enthusiasm for generous size and Euro-style shower spaces, this is becoming a universal approach, with the

FIGURE 8.30 Trench-style drains make the no-threshold shower easier and more attractive.
Courtesy of Quick Drain

benefits expanding to include bathing pets, dual or multiple user showering, and more (refer to chapter 6, "Bathroom Planning").

The clear floor space in front of a roll-in shower compartment should be at least 60 inches (1524 mm) long next to the open face of the shower compartment and a minimum 30 inches wide (762 mm) (see Figure 8.31). As with the transfer shower, a more generous clear space will allow for easier maneuvering. To accommodate turning to enter the shower by a person using a wheelchair, the width of the entry opening must be considered. When using glass or other inflexible materials for the fixed panel and the door, the width of the door opening can be critical to the user who will roll in. If the shower is not more than 42 inches (1067 mm) deep, the door opening will need to be 36 inches (914 mm) to allow the seated bather to maneuver into the space, including

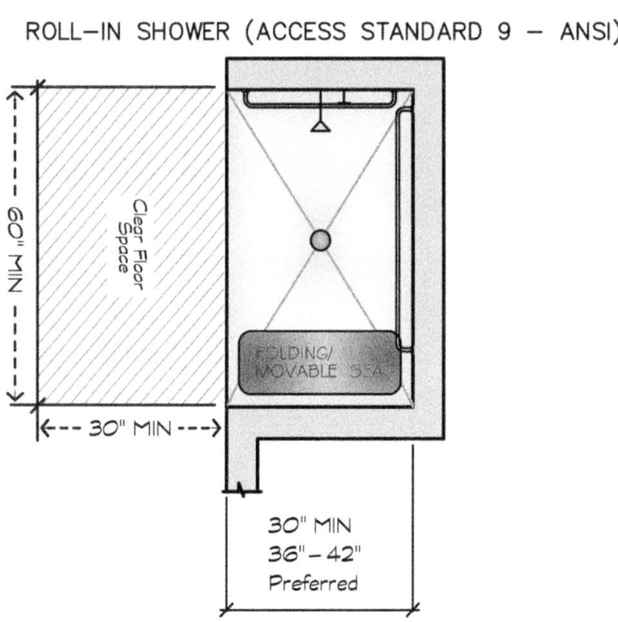

FIGURE 8.31 Access Standard 9, clear space and opening for roll-in shower entry.
NKBA

turning at the entry. If the shower is deeper, as shown at 60 inches (1524 mm), the opening can shrink to 32 inches (813 mm) as the bather can roll straight in before turning to the right position for showering (see Figure 8.32). The option of a seat in the shower is always good, and in a roll-in shower, it should be a folding type or designed not to interfere with the clear floor space. One location is on the wall adjacent to the controls. A second option presented in recent code updates is to have the seat on the end wall opposite the controls and when this is the case, care must be given to be sure the seated user will have access to the controls and the handheld spray.

Wet Room Planning the entire bathroom as a wet area, with a supplemental or second drain in the room and the waterproof membrane extended well beyond the shower or under the entire floor of the room, makes a very flexible space and easier water containment and maintenance. As mentioned above, this can be a good solution when working with a transfer

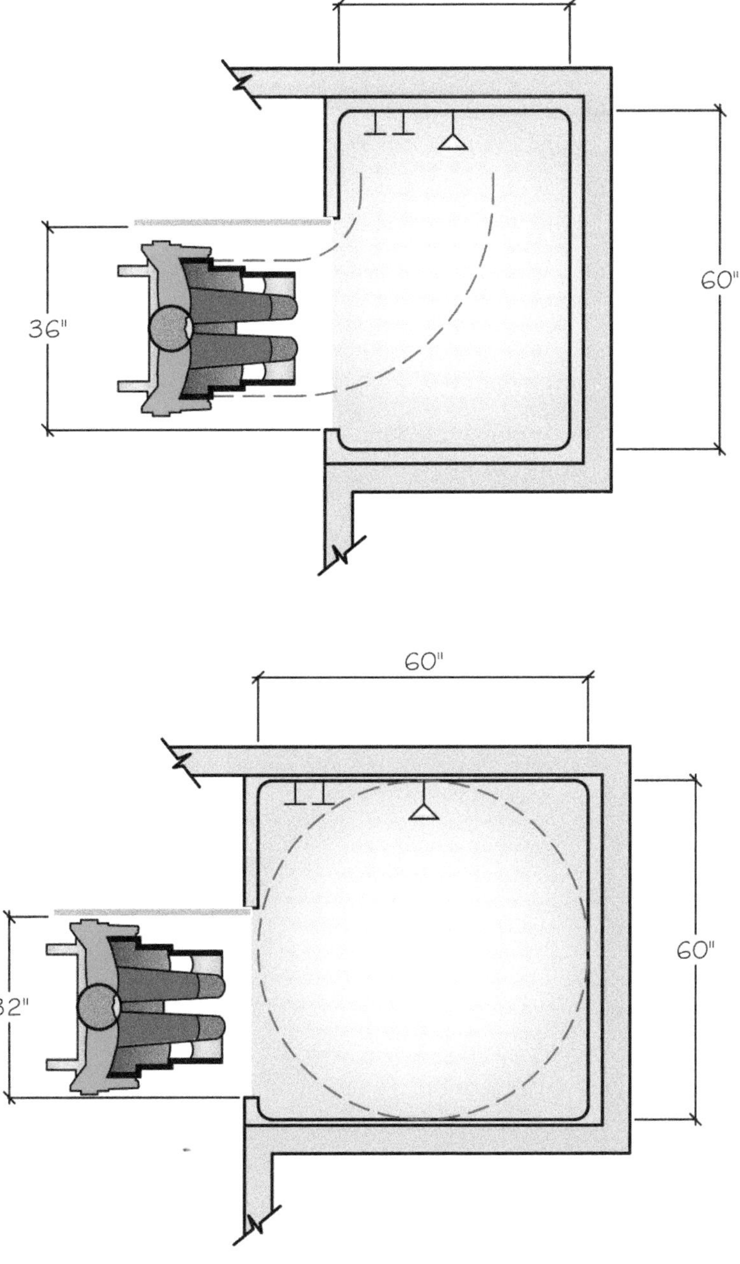

FIGURE 8.32 Access Standard 9: For a 60 inch (1524 mm) deep shower, a 32 inch (813 mm) opening is adequate, and for a 42 inch (1067 mm) deep shower, the opening must be at least 36 inches (914 mm) to allow for turning space. *NKBA*

shower and water containment. It is especially helpful when struggling to find sufficient clear floor space in a small bathroom, as the lack of thresholds makes the entire space available for maneuvering.

Controls in the Bathing and Showering Center

It's a natural consequence of aging that our tactile sensitivity decreases and thermoregulation becomes less efficient, and for those of us with cognitive impairments, the bathing experience can be intimidating. For clients with sensory and perceptual/cognitive issues, there is significant risk of injury from water that is too hot. In response, the bathing and shower center must first include controls that have temperature limits and are either pressure balanced or thermostatic mixing valves. This will help protect the user whose sensitivity to temperature has been compromised, as well as reducing the risk of error caused by confusion or distraction. Beyond this, pre-programmed controls can further reduce the guesswork in controlling flow and temperature of the water. Additional enhancements, including massage, chromatherapy, and aromatherapy can reduce anxiety and enhance the bathing experience.

Bath and shower controls should be offset toward the room for easy operation, within reach, at a height that works for the bather and does not interfere with grab bar installation (see Figure 8.33). Recent access code changes have added a fold-up seat to the roll-in shower and with it, a directive that the controls must be within reach of that seat, which may cause difficulty with keeping those controls accessible from outside the shower. In our privately owned, single-family residential work, we have the freedom to make this a matter of carefully matching clients' needs and preferences with the space parameters of the shower. Fittings with a lever control are easier to grasp and turn than smooth round knobs.

The controls should also be easy to understand. Although some feel color cueing takes away from the beauty of the fitting, it should be clear that red is for hot and blue is for cold. In addition, a visible arrow or line on the faucet that points to red or blue helps determine what direction to turn the control without scalding. Last, raised characters provide tactile cueing, and today LED enhancements send red light with the hot water and blue light with the cold.

In the Bathtub

As mentioned earlier, the controls should be offset toward the room for easy reach, and at a height within everyone's reach yet not interfering with the placement of grab bars, usually 33 to 36 inches

FIGURE 8.33 Access Standard 10: Control locations for the bath and shower.
NKBA

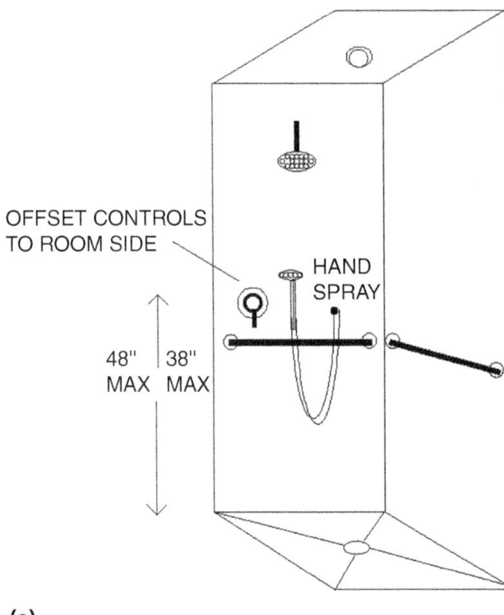

(a)

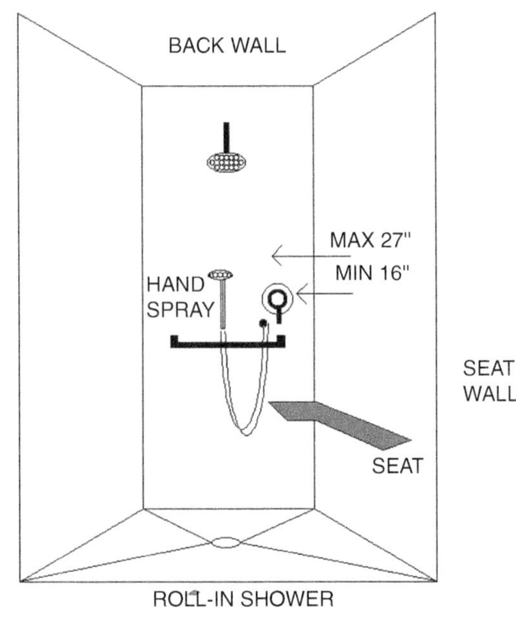

(b)

(838 mm to 914 mm) above the floor. A handheld spray, used as a showerhead or in addition to a showerhead, should be included, preferably with a trickle valve or control at the head for ease of use by a seated bather. To ensure that the spray reaches comfortably to the bather, the hose length should be increased to 72 inches (1829 mm) long, or the length you determine will be needed. If installed on a sliding bar to double as a showerhead, the lowest position should be no higher than 48 inches (1219 mm) and well within reach of the seat in the tub. The higher position should be 72 to 78 inches (1829 mm to 1981 mm) to serve as a showerhead. The diverter or separate control for the handheld spray will ideally be within reach of the bather when seated in the tub. Tub and shower fittings are available today with additional features that improve the user interface (see Figures 8.34 and 8.35).

In the Shower

Again, the controls should be offset to reduce reaching and bending and to allow the user to turn on the water before entering the shower. When a larger shower has a seat, care must be given to the placement of controls within the seated person's reach. One concept is to have one control for the overhead shower near the entry point and a second control or the diverter near the handheld spray, located near the seat.

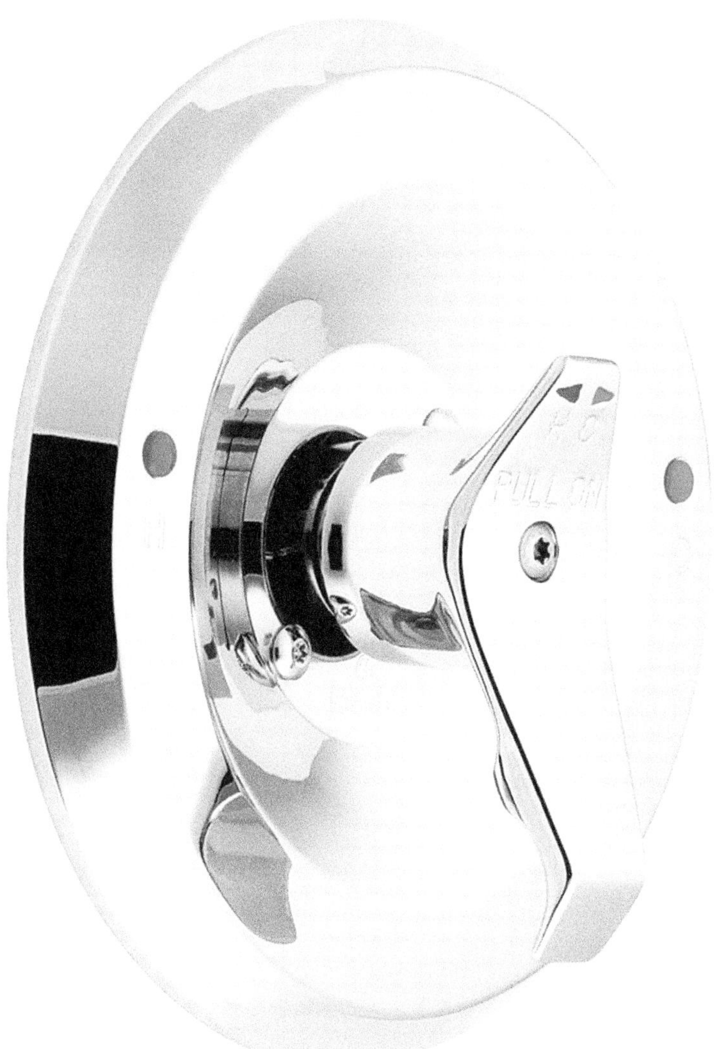

FIGURE 8.34 This single-lever faucet has arrows to indicate hot and cold for simple and intuitive use.
Courtesy of Moen

FIGURE 8.35 This showerhead displays the water temperature through LED lighting for simple and intuitive use, perceptual information, and tolerance for error.
Courtesy of KWC

In transfer type showers, the controls and showerhead, as well as the handheld spray, should be on the control wall within 15 inches (381 mm) of the centerline of the seat. If an adjustable height showerhead mounted on a vertical bar is used, the bar should not obstruct the use of the grab bars. Typically the height of the controls is between 36 inches and 48 inches (914 mm and 1219 mm) off the floor, within the reach range and not interfering with grab bar placement (see Figure 8.36). The use of a handheld spray as a showerhead on a sliding bar can provide for the various heights of users as well as functioning as a hand sprayer. With this concept, be sure to determine if the slide bar has the integrity to act as a support or grab bar.

Grab Bars in the Bathing and Showering Center

Grab bars benefit every client in this wet and slippery area and they become more critical when a client has issues with balance or strength. They are an aid to anyone who is transferring into the tub or shower, particularly the child or elder and the parent or caregiver assisting in the process.

Plan grab bars in bathtub and shower areas, to facilitate access to and maneuvering within the tub or shower, and place them to best fit the client. Begin by reinforcing the walls and enlist client input for actual locations of grab bars. Because this is not always possible, the basic locations called out in general recommendations for access can be helpful. In chapter 6, "Bathroom Planning," you'll find reinforcement and basic tub/shower recommendations. Beyond the basic fixtures, there are recommendations that relate to specific tub or shower configurations, which will be shown as the fixture is discussed below. It seems worth noting that while these locations are based on the ICC A117.1-2009, these numbers and configurations are not typically mandatory in privately owned single-family residential construction, and they are included here as guidance. While the purpose of each support in these drawings is clear, the use of multiple and stacked grab bars could be difficult to integrate visually. Given that the need for support in the bath or shower is without

FIGURE 8.36 This adjustable handheld shower is placed on a suspended column which leaves clear floor space for maneuvering.
Courtesy of KWC

question, it is the designer's responsibility to call out in the design recommended locations for support, and to specify and install the appropriate grab bars. With the incorporation of reinforcement throughout the surround in these areas, additional grab bars will be possible as needs and the desire for support changes.

In the Bathtub

Entering and exiting a bathtub can be physically challenging to the best of us, and the design and specification of the tub area deserves careful consideration (for transfer examples, see Figures 8.37 and 8.38). For those of us who wish to bathe in a tub, the size and features of the tub, its fittings and accessories, and the space around it can help to make the experience a safer one. First, as discussed in chapter 6, "Bathroom Planning," the tub should be sized to the user and the purpose. A tub used to bathe children will be smaller and shallower than the tub intended for soaking by a taller person, and to attempt either of these activities in the wrong sized tub would result in dissatisfaction and increased risks. Support, whether grab bars that are

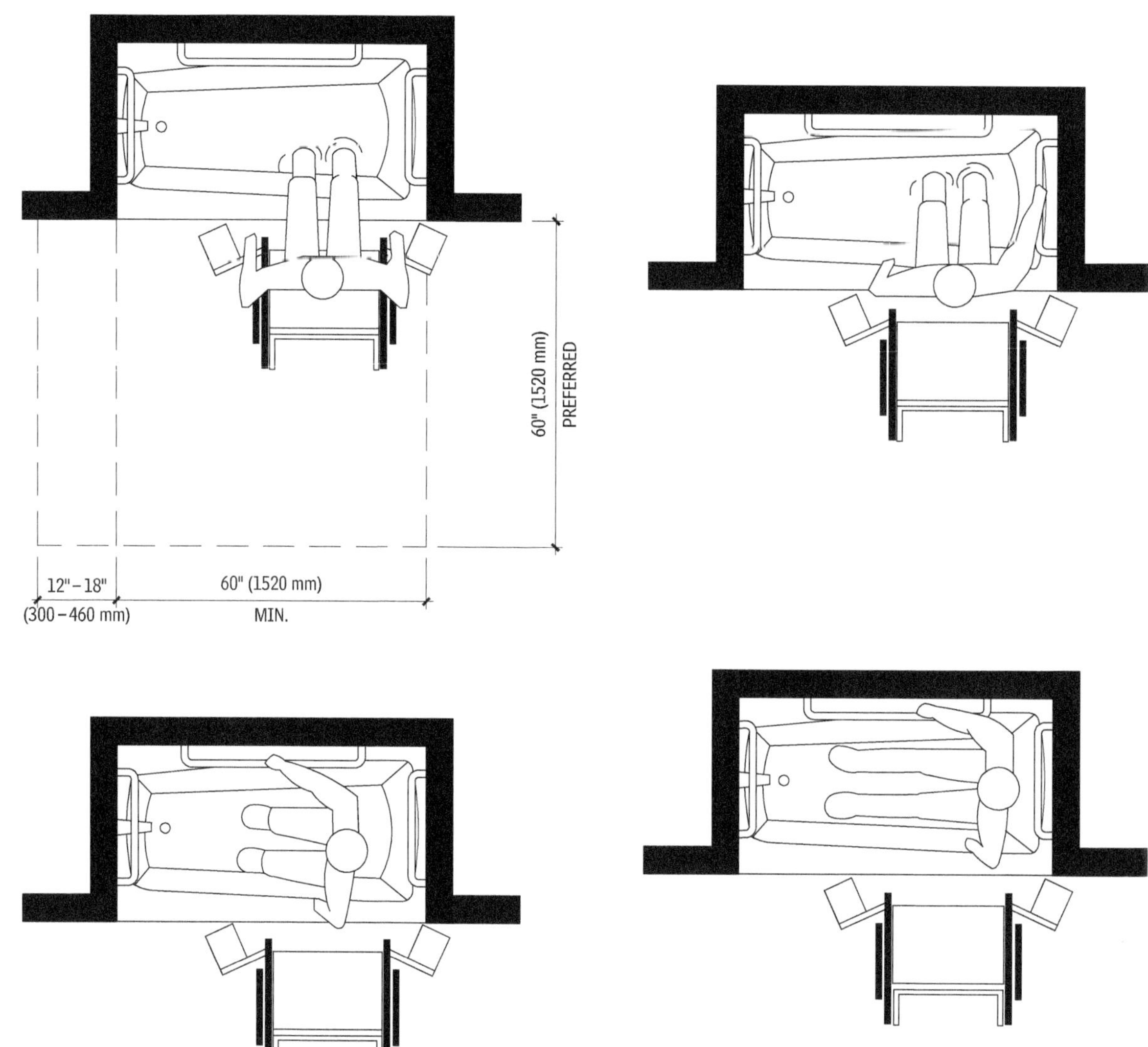

FIGURE 8.37 A typical forward approach and transfer to tub
NKBA

added or integral to the tub and its accessories should be included in every tub design, and there are several companies offering accessories with grips or supports built into their design, as shown in Figure 8.39.

While there are recommendations as to the placement of grab bars (see Figures 8.40 and 8.41); each client's approach and entry will be unique. When in doubt as to placement of the grab bars, as mentioned previously, the surrounding walls can be reinforced and the actual placement of the supports determined with a "dry run" by the client to identify where he/she will most use the support. In the case of a freestanding tub, there are limits to what can be done to improve the entry/exit experience, but J-shaped supports intended for pools can be used. For a client with more extreme impairments, a lift can be planned and this is an area where the appropriate professional should be consulted. In a project where the addition of a ceiling lift is likely, incorporating reinforcement in the ceiling and positioning framing and structural components such as door headers is important, so that it can be more easily added.

To further enable a safer entry to the tub, there are a number of products available, including tubs with integral grips and with doors to allow a bather to back up to the tub, sit on the raised floor or the integrated seat of the tub and swing their legs in, closing the door after this action. When this seat is at or close to comfortable seat height (18 inches [457 mm] is an average), this can provide an easier entry and exit for those of us who lack the strength and balance to step into and

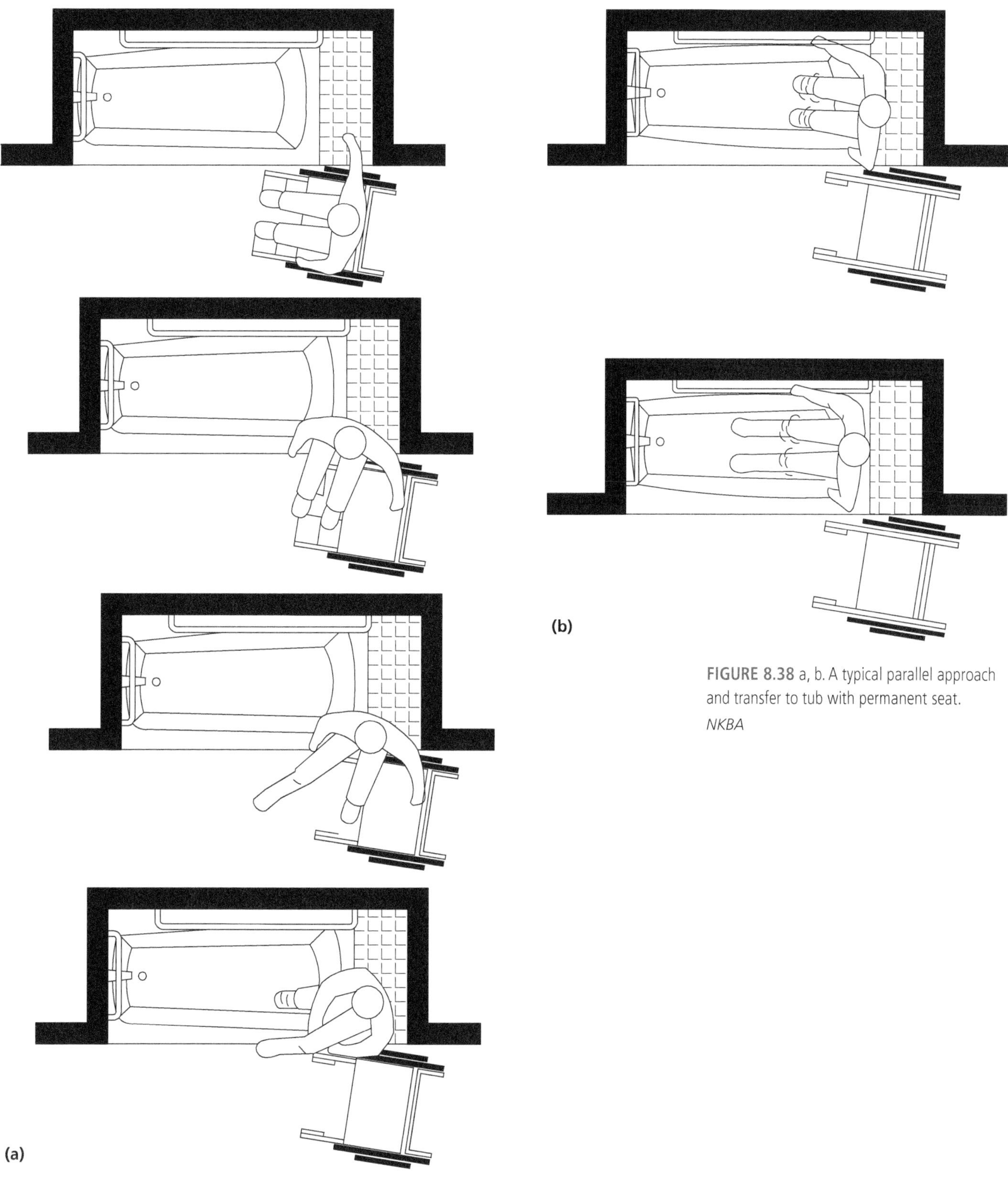

FIGURE 8.38 a, b. A typical parallel approach and transfer to tub with permanent seat.
NKBA

stand inside a traditional tub. There are also a variety of tubs with folding or permanent built-in seats as another option (see Figure 8.26, earlier in the bathing and showering section).

Historically, general recommendations for access have specified only horizontal grab bars, but this is now being altered because arguments can be made for specifying vertical and angled support

FIGURE 8.39 Accessories for the tub and shower with integral support.
Courtesy of HealthCraft Invisia Collection

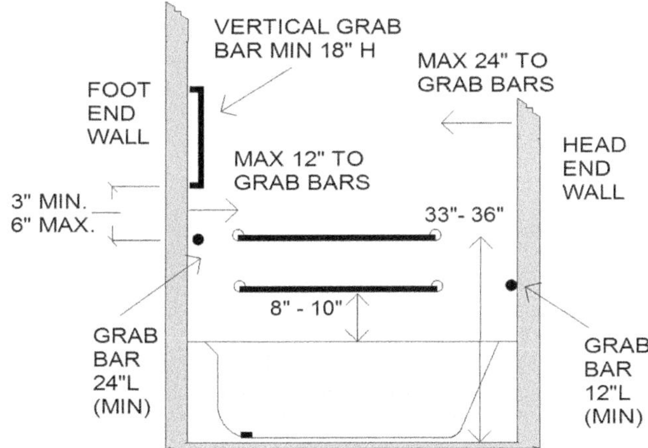

FIGURE 8.40 Access Standard 14: grab bars at tub.
NKBA

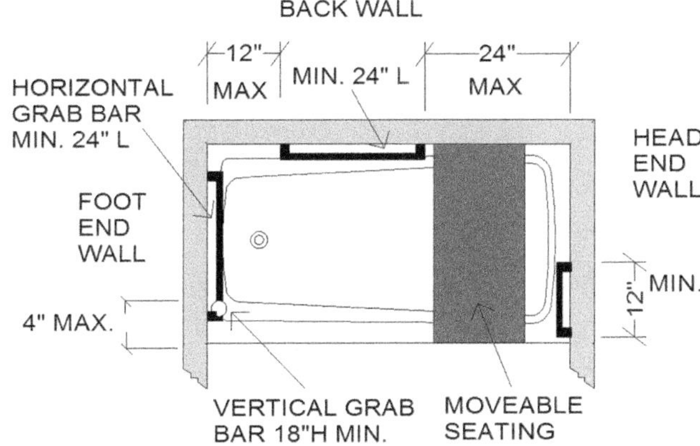

FIGURE 8.41 Access Standard 14: grab bars at tub with permanent seat and at tub with fold-down seat.
NKBA

for your client as well. Supports in the tub area are often specified in a horizontal position as this reduces the risk of slipping, but it is most natural for our wrist to be cocked, making an angled bar helpful in rising to step out of the tub. To reduce the risk of a slippery grab bar, specify those bars with a non-slip surface or shape. A vertical bar on the control wall can support the bather while reaching for the controls or if stepping to enter and this concept has been added as an Access Standard. With growing attention given to grab bars, the options have grown and improved (see Figure 8.42)

In the Shower

When choosing towel bars, soap holders, and even the bar on which a handheld spray slides, keep in mind that for a person who needs a support, anything within reach will be used, and consider specifying only those accessories that will hold the weight and function as grab bars if called on to do so. As previously illustrated, multiple manufacturers now offer accessories that incorporate the support into their design.

As with the tub, each client will approach and enter the shower differently (see Figure 8.43). While entering a roll-in shower is easier for many, it is still a wet area and support is impacted by the size of the shower and the location of the seat within the shower. Following are examples of suggested grab bar locations for several types of roll-in showers, with the priority being support within reach for the bather while operating the controls and entering, showering, and exiting (Figure 8.44).

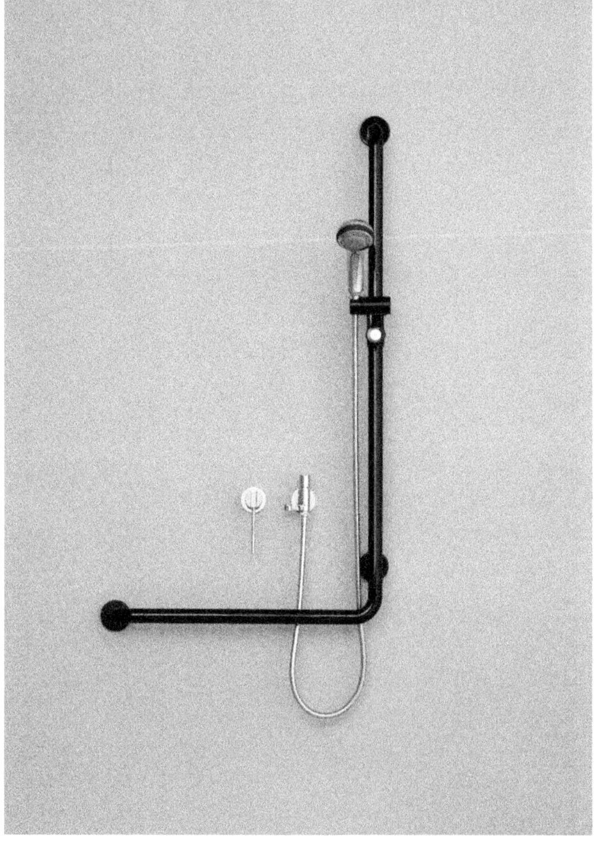

FIGURE 8.42 These examples illustrate just a few of the of grab bar applications, including attaching a showerhead to a bar.
Courtesy of Great Grabz

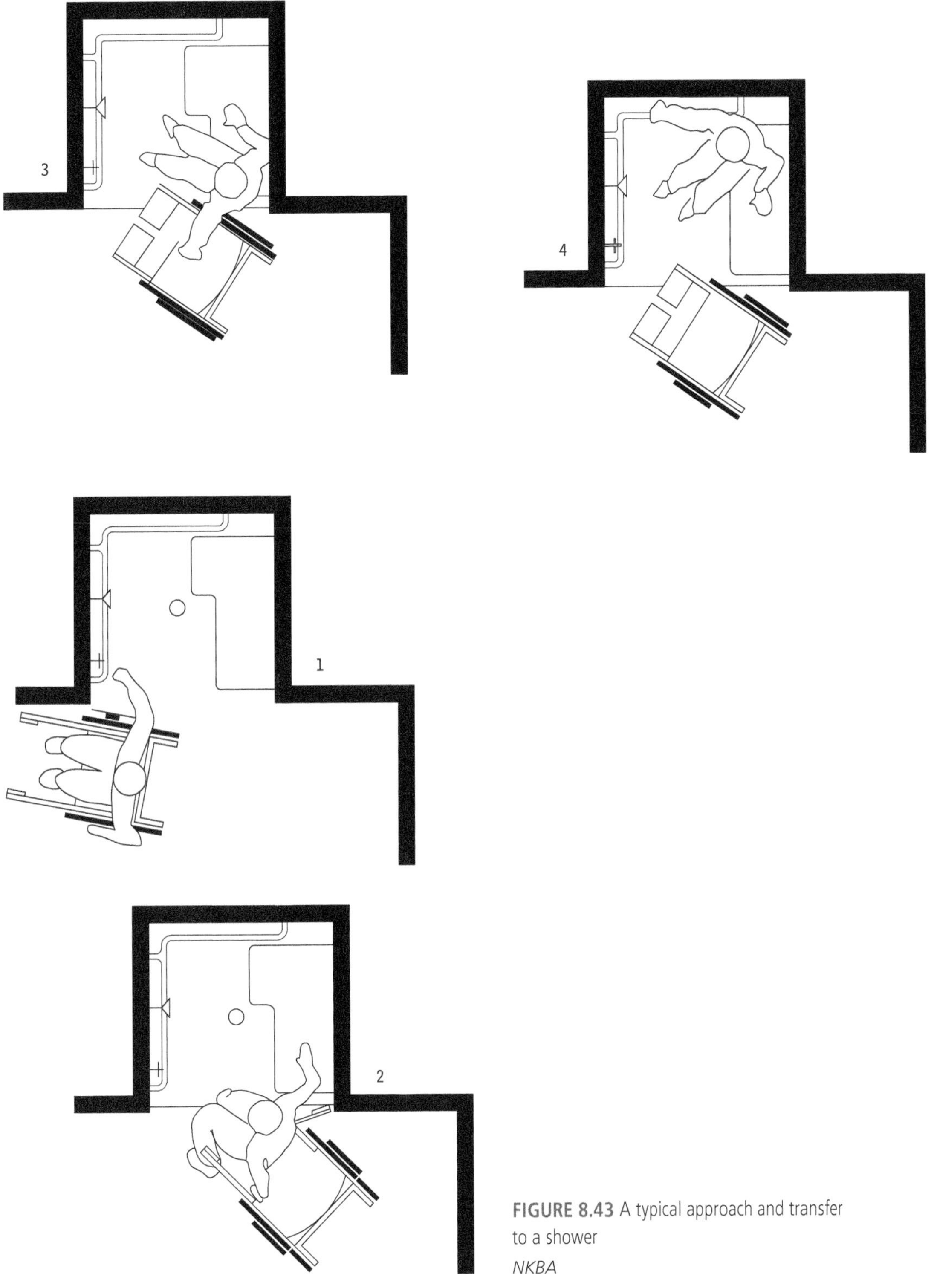

FIGURE 8.43 A typical approach and transfer to a shower
NKBA

Seats and Transfer Areas

Plan for the option of sitting in the shower and when entering and/or bathing in the tub. This can be done with an integrated design or as an added product, and there are guidelines for the planning and specification of the seat or surface.

Whether in a shower or tub, the recommended depth of the built-in seat is a minimum of 15 inches (381 mm), and a maximum of 16 inches (406 mm), with a preferred height of 17 inches

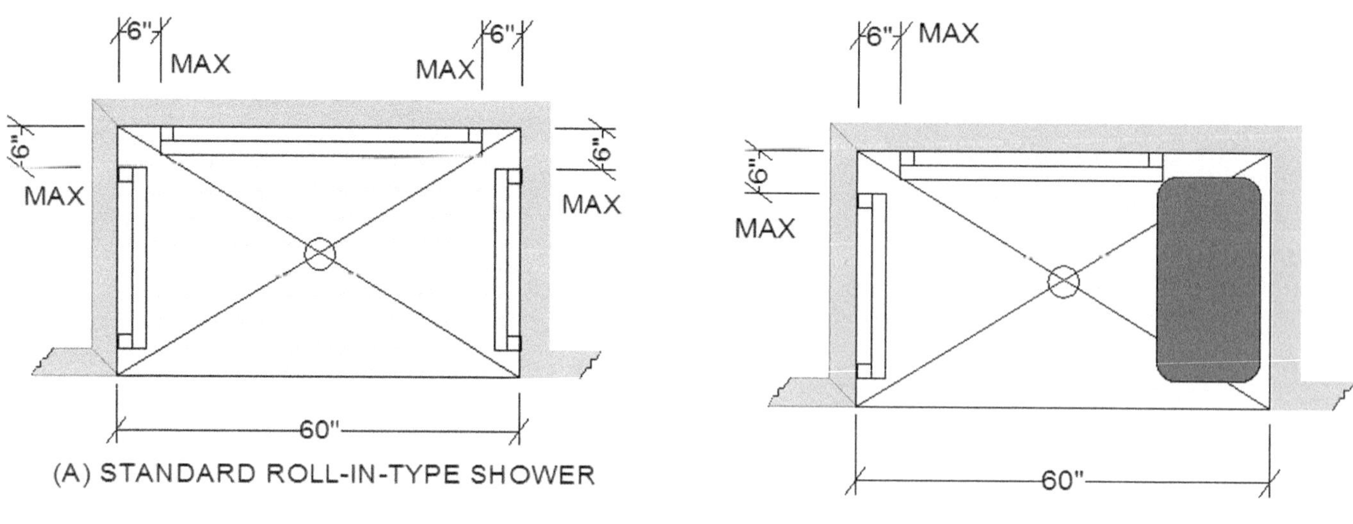

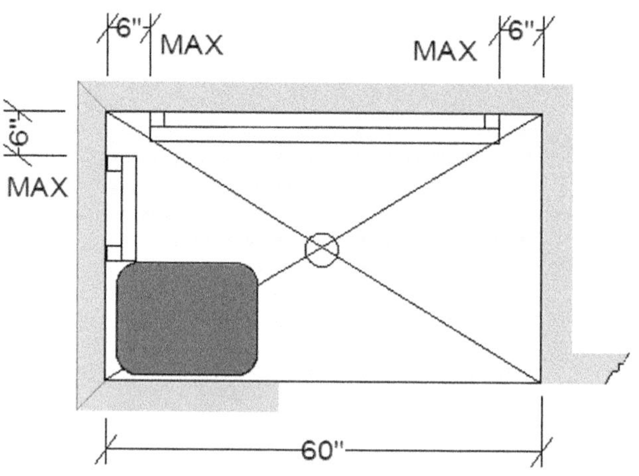

FIGURE 8.44 Access Standard 14: Grab bars for roll-in showers
NKBA

to 19 inches (432 mm to 483 mm), and it should gently slope toward the tub or shower base at not more than 1/4 inch per 12 inches (6 mm per 305 mm) to avoid standing water.

The deck of a drop-in, or preferably an undermount tub, can serve as a transfer seat for many. The tub deck surface needs to support a minimum load of 250 pounds (113 kg). If the tub is undermounted, the surface deck should overlap the tub flange to eliminate a permeable seam, again sloped slightly toward the tub.

When there is no room for a built-in transfer surface at the tub or shower, a removable seat can be used (see Figure 8.45). Separate bathtub and shower seats provide flexibility, but require storage space when not in use. Care must be given to ensure the stability of the seat. Fold-up shower seats do not interfere with the clear space of the shower when they are closed, and are desirable for those who wish to sit for part or all of a shower. When specifying or designing custom seats, plan for a user to put their feet under the seat for better leverage. Other features to consider in specifying the seat include a surface that is smooth for transfer and slots or an opening to provide for personal hygiene.

If using a shower curtain, the rod must extend over the seat, and a custom curtain (extra wide) or double curtains may be required. There are seats made with a slot to accommodate the shower curtain and an extension that can improve transfer.

As mentioned earlier, portable or ceiling-mounted lifting devices specified and installed by medical equipment professionals can be used to lower and lift a person in and out of the bathtub (see

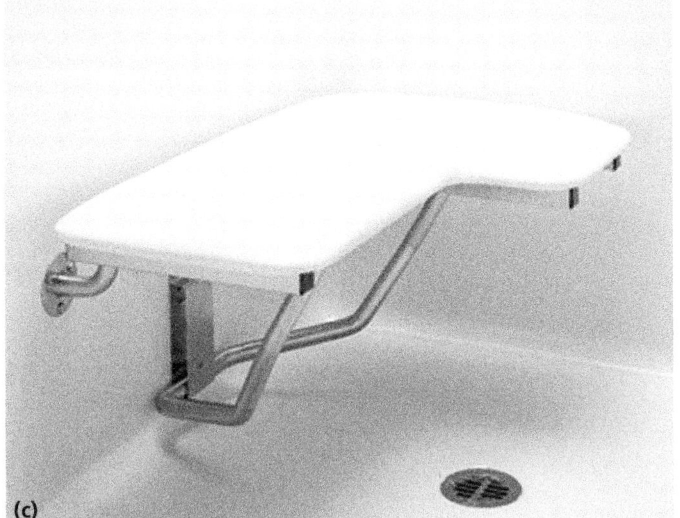

FIGURE 8.45 These seats are both flexible and solid in that they either fold-up out of the way or can be removed when not in use, but are attached securely to a wall support.

A and B courtesy of Signature Hardware Whittington Collection; C and D Hewi from Hafele

Figure 8.46). The space plan will need to accommodate the function of the lift and its storage when not in use. Structural adaptation for the lift may be required.

Surround

As eyes age, it becomes difficult to differentiate colors with minimal contrast, such as navy, black, brown, or pastels. Colors and patterns should be chosen with consideration of the total room in terms of contrast and light. Use matte or low-sheen surfaces that reduce glare. Contrast created by placing light objects against darker backgrounds, or vice versa, can be used to highlight edges, borders, or controls, however overuse of contrast, particularly on the floor, can block a person from maneuvering and must be carefully planned. Easy maintenance becomes more critical with the sensory changes that occur as we age, and today there are a number of products for the surround that can reduce bacterial growth risks.

Glazing, Doors, and More on No-Threshold Showers

For existing tubs and showers, a shower curtain is easier to maneuver and does not protrude into the clear floor space. Although all shower glass doors are tempered, there is still a safety concern that someone with visual or cognitive impairments will not recognize the glass. Textured and opaque glass can help with this confusion and reduce glare.

When the size and direction of flow of the water are right, thresholds can be omitted, with functional and aesthetic appeal (see Figure 8.47). While this European or no-threshold design is good for everyone, it becomes more critical for a person using a mobility aid, or a person who has trouble lifting a foot in walking. To function as a no-threshold passage, the height of the threshold at the shower should not be greater than 1/4 inch (6 mm) if square or 1/2 inch (12 mm) if beveled. A pitch in the level of the floor of not more than 1/4 inch per 12 inches (6 mm per 305 mm) will

FIGURE 8.46 A beautifully executed ceiling lift installation.
Courtesy of Kohler Company

aid in water containment. This pitch will decrease when the entire bath is built as a wet area. A trough drain placed where water is to be collected can further improve the design as it provides greater area and a smoother floor surface (see Figure 8.48). For more specific information on the concept of no-threshold showers, refer to "Curbless Shower, An Installation Guide," an online publication from the Center for Universal Design (www.design.ncsu.edu/cud).

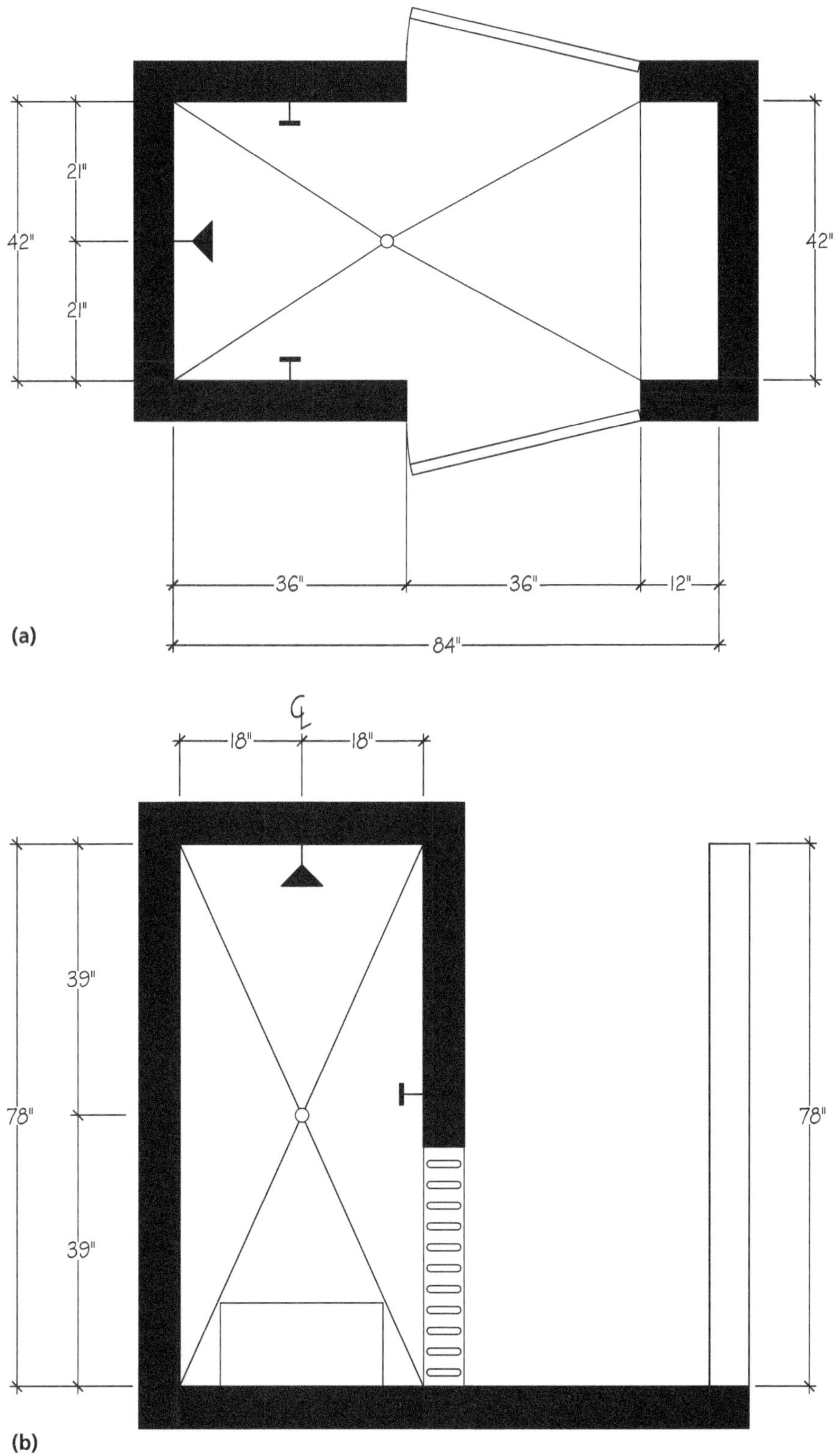

FIGURE 8.47 A, the thresholds have been eliminated in this shower with a double entry. B, doors and threshold have been eliminated in this serpentine shower with a trough drain at the entry.
Mary Jo Peterson, Inc

(a)

FIGURE 8.48 With the appropriate grill, a trough-style drain becomes an aesthetic and functional asset.

Courtesy of (A) QuARTz by Aco; (B) Infinity Drain; (C) Quick Drain

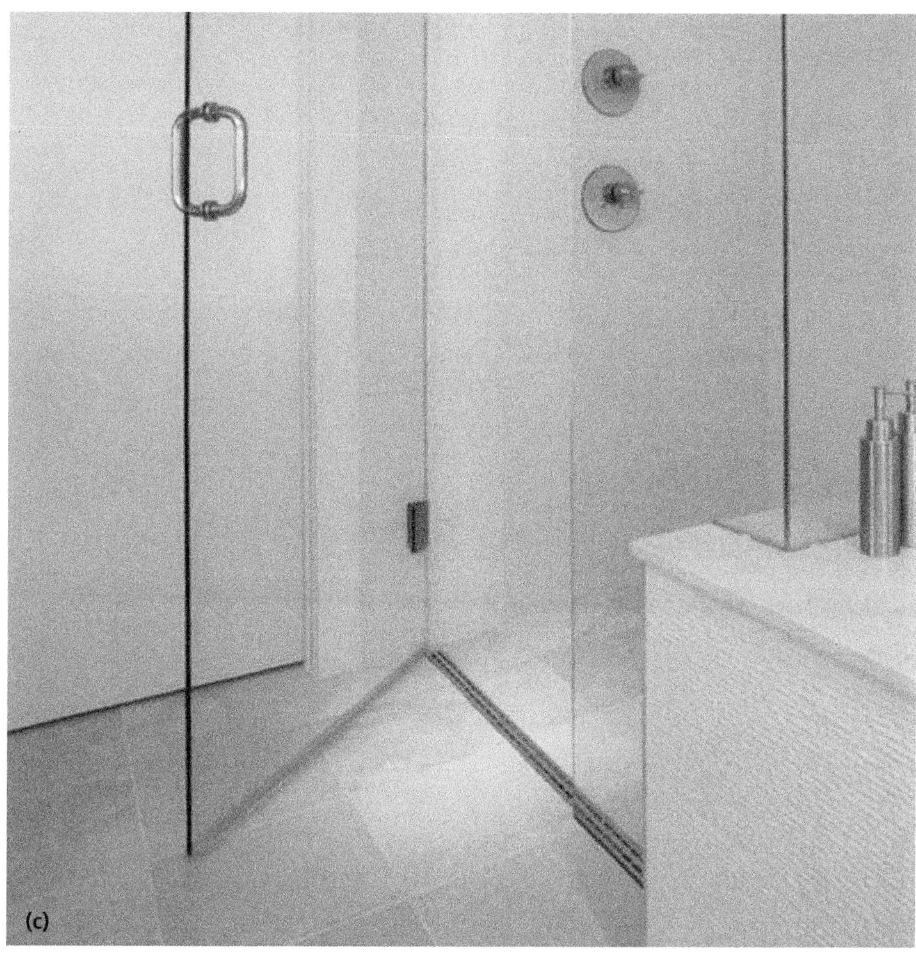

FIGURE 8.48 *(continued)*

Flooring in the Bathing and Showering Center

Use slip-resistant flooring inside and outside a bathing area to reduce falls. While no floor is slip-free when wet, some texture, whether inherent or applied to the floor surface can reduce the risk. In addition, the judicious use of contrast and texture can indicate wet versus dry areas, the edge or borders of the shower or tub, or a change in floor height. However, a combination of different flooring materials may have differing thicknesses, and installation should eliminate any uneven surfaces between materials. Colors and patterns should be chosen with consideration of the total room in terms of contrast and light. Use matte or low-sheen surfaces that reduce glare.

Storage and Accessories in the Bathing and Showering Center

Shampoo and soap dispensers, installed in the bathtub/shower within reach of the user, reduce strength and dexterity needed to squeeze shampoo out of the bottle and help eliminate items falling or being rearranged in an unknown order.

When choosing towel bars, soap holders and even the bar on which a handheld spray slides, keep in mind that for a person who needs a support, anything within reach will be used, and consider specifying only those accessories that will hold the weight and function as grab bars if called on to do so.

Storage outside the shower for back-up towels, shampoo, soap, and toiletries should be within the 15 inches to 48 inches (381 mm to 1219 mm) reach range and should not obstruct the shower door or protrude into the passage space.

Lighting, Ventilation, Electrical, and Heat in the Bathing and Showering Center

Ventilation and lighting controls should be placed 15 inches to 48 inches (381 mm to 1219 mm) above the floor, be operable with minimal effort, easy to read, and with visual and audible on/off indicators.

In addition to general lighting, task lighting that is suitable for wet locations should be included in the bathing and shower areas.

Specifying quiet ventilation will help to minimize background noise distortion, appealing to everyone and particularly helpful for those of us with hearing impairments.

Radiant heat or supplemental heat should be considered for those with thermoregulation issues, and in some cases, a blow-dryer can speed the drying process while maintaining body temperature for the bather.

Access Standards

The NKBA Guidelines and Access Standards that relate to the bathing and shower center are: 3, 4, 9, 10, 11, 12, 13, 14, 15, 16, 17, 18, 19, 22, 23, 25, 26, 27, and 36.

Responsive Design Summary: The Bathing and Shower Center

- Sensory
  - Universal design recommendations
    - Specify control valves with anti-scald capacity with a high limit stop of 120 degrees F (49 C) (Guideline 11)
    - Choose controls that incorporate indicator lights as an additional way to determine on/off or hot/cold
    - Consider a visible arrow or line on the faucet that points to red or blue to help determine what direction to turn the control
    - Use tactile cueing to identify hot or cold water.
    - Consider programmable controls to simplify operation
    - Select a shampoo and soap dispenser that can be installed in the bathtub/shower to help eliminate items falling or being rearranged in an unfamiliar order
    - Use visual and tactile contrast in the flooring between wet and dry areas
    - Consider supplemental heat or dryers (Guideline 27)
    - Choose quiet ventilation to minimize background noise distortion for those with partial hearing (Access Standard 26)
  - Access recommendations
    - None
- Cognitive
  - Universal recommendations
    - Specify control valves with anti-scald capacity with a high limit stop of 120 degrees (49 C) (Guideline 11)
    - Consider electronic sensor controls on faucets, and ventilation to help ensure that things are shut-off when the user is finished
    - Use intuitive cueing, such as using a blue color for cold and a red color for hot
    - Consider a visible arrow on the faucet that points to red or blue to help determine what direction to turn the control
    - Specifying programmable controls simplifies consistent operation and temperature of the water fill
    - Plan the entire bathroom as a wet area with a supplemental or second drain in the room to make water containment and maintenance easier
    - Specify slip-resistant surfaces in general bath flooring, shower floors, and tub/shower bottoms (Guideline 18)
  - Access recommendations
    - None

- Physical
  - Universal recommendations
    - Use the wet-room concept to improve generous clear floor space for maneuvering.
    - Specify slip-resistant surfaces in general bath flooring, shower floors, and tub/shower bottoms (Guideline 18).
    - Incorporate flexible equipment and assistive devices that can change as a child grows, or needs otherwise change.
    - Plan a seat in the shower and/or bathtub (Guideline and Access Standard 12).
    - Consider a bathtub design that allows the parent or caregiver to comfortably sit while bathing a child or other bather, and also allows the bather to sit to enter/exit the tub.
    - Walls should be reinforced at time of construction to allow for installation of grab bars (Guideline 14).
    - Plan grab bars to support safe entry/exit, to assist those with balance issues, and to support caregivers in bathing children or others.
    - Specify grab bars to be placed according to the needs and height of the user, with a general guide being 33 to 36 inches (838 mm to 914 mm) above the floor (Access Standard 14).
    - Shampoo and soap dispensers, installed in the bathtub/shower within reach of the user, reduce strength and dexterity needed to squeeze shampoo out of the bottle.
  - Access recommendations
    - Include additional clear floor space of 12 to 18 inches (305 to 457 mm) on the control side of shower/bath fixture to improve seated access to the controls
    - Plan clear floor space in front of a roll-in shower of 60 inches by a minimum 30 inches (1524 mm by 762 mm (Access Standard 4)
    - Plan a roll-in shower a minimum 60 inches by 36 to 42 inches (1524 mm by 914 mm to 1067 mm) to better contain water (Access Standard 9).
    - When possible, plan a roll-in shower 60 inches by 48 to 60 inches deep (1524 mm by 1219 mm by 1524 mm),to allow for easier maneuvering by a person using a mobility aid (Access Standard 9).
    - Plan a minimum clear floor space in front of a transfer shower of 48 inches wide, extending beyond the seat wall, by 36 inches deep (1219 mm by 914 mm) (Access Standards 4)
    - Increase the clear floor space at a transfer shower to a minimum 60 inches wide, with the clear space extending beyond both the control wall and the seat wall, by a minimum 36 inches deep (1524 mm by 914 mm) to improve access to both controls and the transfer seat
    - The dimensions of a transfer shower should be 36 inches wide by 36 inches deep (914 mm by 914 mm) and should include a seat, preferably a fold-up style, to place support and control within the reach of most any user (Access Standard 9)
    - Specify controls to be offset toward the room and easy to grasp, as with lever or loop handles (Access Standard 10)
    - Plan the handheld spray at a height accessible to the user (Access Standard 10)
    - Specify tub/shower controls that are operable with one hand and do not require tight grasping (Access Standard10)
    - Minimize thresholds at the shower entry to no more than 1/2 inch (13 mm) (Access Standard 16)

Toileting Center

Clear Floor Space in the Toileting Center

Clear floor space around the toilet is a changing need at all ages. Learning to use the toilet is a major development in early childhood. Often temporary solutions are found to make a standard toilet the appropriate size for young children. The clear floor space that is used for step stools, seats, and potty chairs that are helpful during the progression of toilet training can also be used for storage of mobility aids and transfer, or for a care provider later in life.

Transfer also impacts the amount of clear floor space at the toilet, depending on how a person transfers onto the fixture and whether or not an aide is involved. Two common approaches are illustrated in Figure 8.49, but transfer is unique to each user and should be discussed with your client.

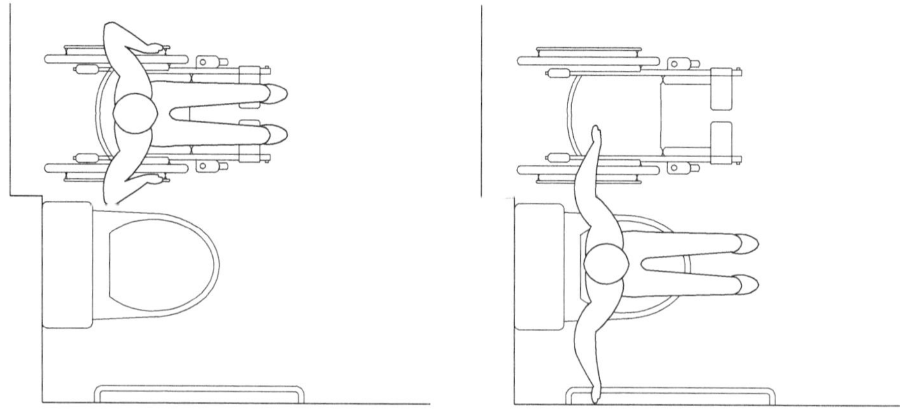

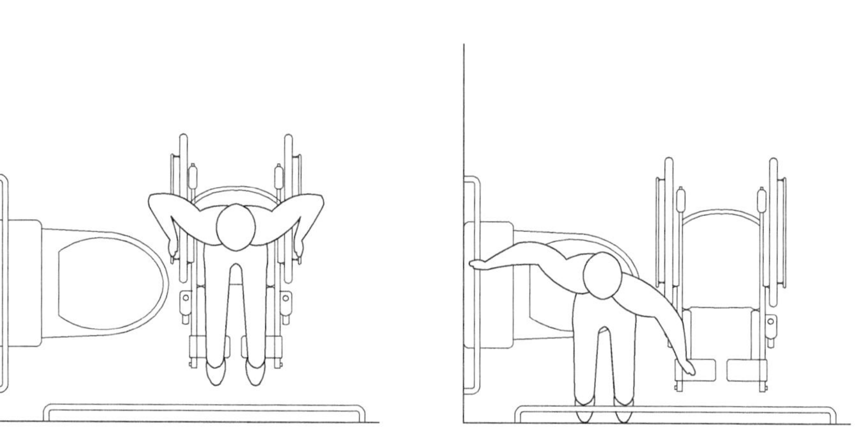

FIGURE 8.49 Planning space at the toilet becomes more complex because a person needs space not just to approach, but to transfer. (A) Parallel or diagonal approach requires more space to the side of the toilet. (B) A perpendicular or forward approach requires clearance in front of the toilet.
NKBA

The 30 inch by 48 inch (762 mm by 1219 mm) clear floor space in front of the toilet is a minimum, and greater clearance in front of the toilet will be required for a true forward approach or to the side of the toilet for a parallel transfer (see Figure 8.50). The ICC A117.1-2009 suggests 56 inches (1422 mm) measured perpendicular from the rear wall, and 60 inches (1524 mm) measured perpendicular from the sidewall for residential spaces, a good guide for most bathrooms or private toileting areas (see Figure 8.51).

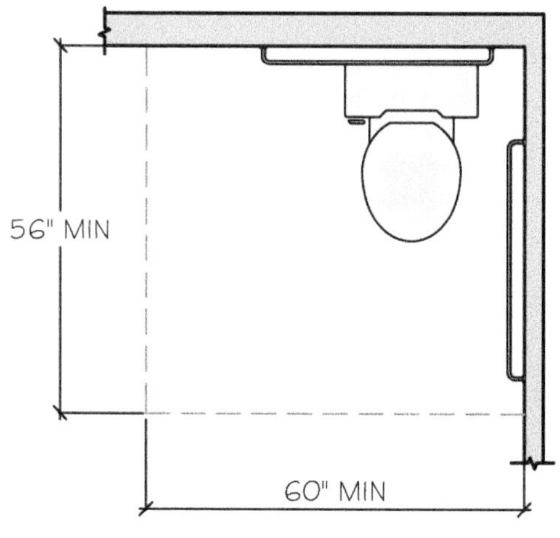

FIGURE 8.50 Access Standard 4: clear floor space at toilet.
NKBA

FIGURE 8.51 Clear floor space adjacent to the toilet.

Courtesy of Universal Designers & Consultants, Inc.

Achieving this clear floor space can be a challenge, particularly if a private toileting room is desired, a concept discussed in detail in chapter 6, "Bathroom Planning." The use of a wall-hung toilet can save as much as 5 inches (127 mm) which can greatly improve the available clear floor space.

Fixture Selection

There are great advances in the design of toilets, allowing for specification of a fixture that better supports transfer and ease of use.

The complexities of transfer onto and off of the toilet make this a space where each situation may have a different "best practice."

Transfer from a wheelchair to a toilet seat relies on the height of both seats being equal (see Figure 8.52). The elongated bowl and raised-height toilet at 17 to 19 inches (432 mm to 483 mm) that was first created to facilitate transfer from a wheelchair has become popular as "comfort height" or "right height" because it is often more comfortable than the traditional toilet height of 15 inches (381 mm) for a person with back strain, reduced strength, or joint conditions that make sitting and standing more difficult (see Figure 8.53).

In reality, the chair height can change over a client's lifetime, and it is sometimes best to plan flexibility in the height of the toilet. The addition of a thick toilet seat or spacers may look institutional,

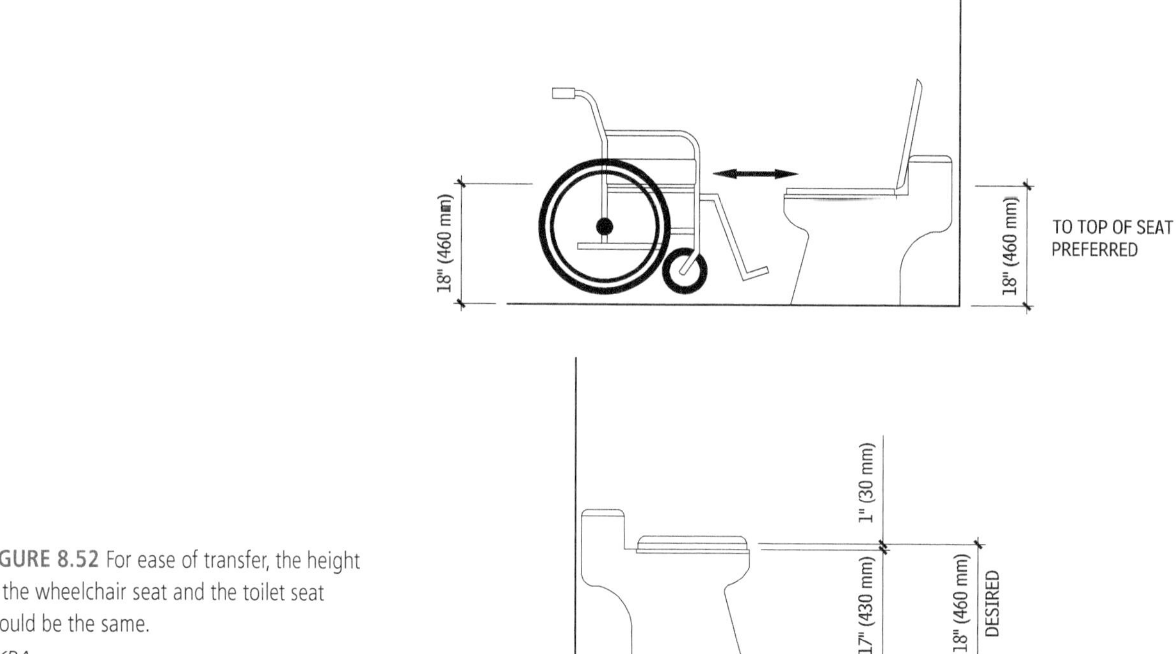

FIGURE 8.52 For ease of transfer, the height of the wheelchair seat and the toilet seat should be the same.
NKBA

FIGURE 8.53 Comfort height toilets have become both beautiful and mainstream.
Courtesy of Kohler Company

but they are flexible in that they can be changed as needs change. Be sure to consider your client's specific needs when determining toilet seat heights, and when planning more than one bathroom, consider specifying variable heights.

The mainstream adoption of comfort or right-height toilets is enhanced by the added features, including heated seats, automatic flushing, remote controls, integral washing systems, and recently the addition of an LED light source within the fixture to guide the way for nocturnal visits (see Figure 8.54).

FIGURE 8.54 LED offers gentle lighting to guide the way for nocturnal visits.

(A): Courtesy of TOTO; (B) Courtesy of Kohler Company

A wall-mounted toilet with the tankless flushing system concealed in the wall can be a beautiful choice that improves access and use of the fixture, provided the cost of changing the waste connection is realistic. To begin with, the toilet can be placed at the exact height that will be most effective for the client, and as mentioned earlier, the clear floor space increases as up to 5 inches (127 mm) is saved in the depth of the fixture. The open space below the toilet makes rising from a seated position easier as the user can position his/her feet farther under his/her body weight. This open space also provides for much easier maintenance. The flush plate is easy to use for most because it can be pushed with a closed fist and does not require grasping, and in some cases, a remote control is available (see Figure 8.55). Another feature that contributes to the youngest among us is the integral child seat that is built into the cover of the traditional standard seat (see Figure 8.56).

The inclusion of a bidet, or a washing system, that is incorporated into the toilet can be a solution to personal hygiene challenges when reaching and bending are difficult, and to cut down on constipation, a condition that can become more common with age (see Figure 8.57). An electrical connection is required for the systems that are integrated into the toilet, so as a minimum, a GFCI receptacle should be planned near the toilet. If the system is not installed, the receptacle near the toilet will allow for the easy addition of such a system at a later date. Consider features available as technology changes, including heated seats, self-closing covers, automatic flushing, bacteria and odor ventilation, and health monitoring systems.

FIGURE 8.55 The wall-hung toilet.
Courtesy of TOTO

FIGURE 8.56 Integrated child seat.
Courtesy of Kohler Company

Grab Bars in the Toileting Center

Grab bars should be planned at the toilet area. Grab bars can be used to assist with balance and limited strength when sitting down and standing up; and aid in transferring onto the toilet from a wheelchair. Attention should be given to visual cueing in the selection of grab bars. For example, white grab bars on a white wall can be difficult to see.

Like the shower, the walls around the toilet should be reinforced so grab bar installations can be customized for the user. There are common practices for locations for grab bars (see Figure 8.58), yet it is best to place the support where it will work best for the client.

Access Standards recommend grab bars should be provided on the rear wall and on the side wall that is closest to the toilet. The side-wall grab bar should be at least 42 inches (1067 mm) long and

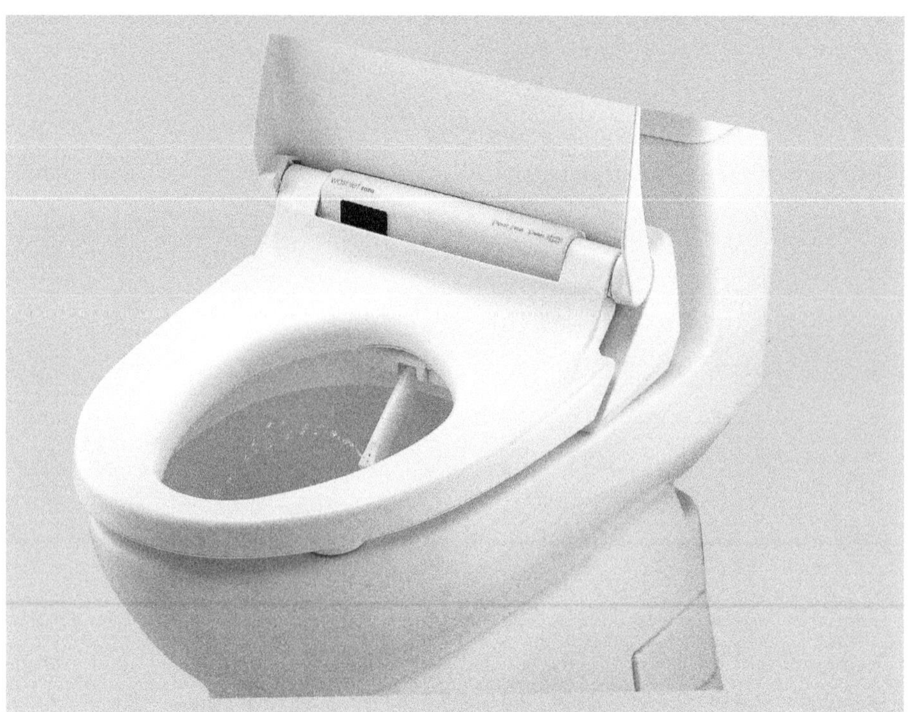

FIGURE 8.57 Integral washing systems.
Courtesy of TOTO

FIGURE 8.58 Grab bars in the toileting center.
Courtesy of Great Grabz

located between 12 inches and 54 inches (305 mm and 1372 mm) from the rear wall. The rear grab bar should be at least 24 inches (610 mm) long, centered on the toilet. Where space permits, the bar should be at least 36 inches (914 mm) long, with the additional length provided on the transfer side of the toilet (see Figure 8.59).

If the side wall is not long enough for the 42-inch (1067 mm) long grab bar, consider a fold-down grab bar off the back wall or a seat with integrated bars or hand-holds (see Figure 8.60).

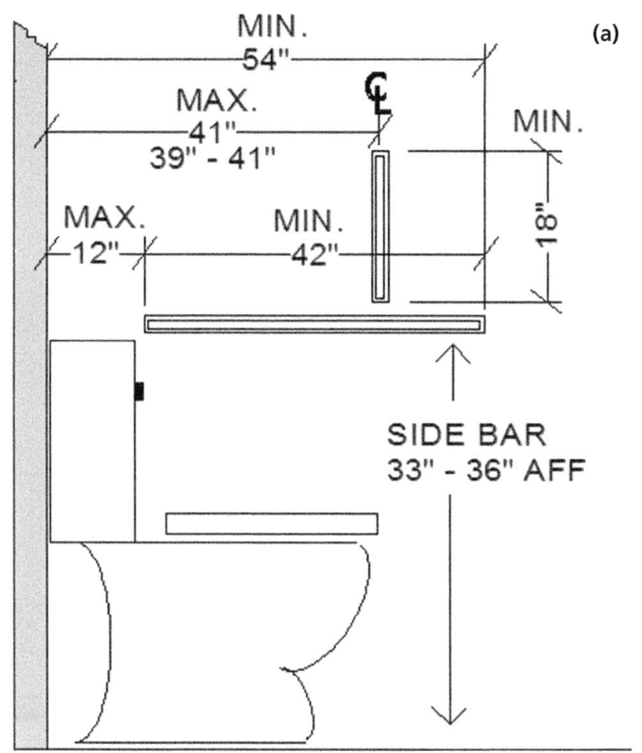

FIGURE 8.59 Access Standard 14, Standard grab bar positions at toilet center.
NKBA

Controls in the Toileting Center

Toilets with the push lever centered on the top of the tank are a great universal concept in that they are easy to use with equal access from either side, however, the unique location my confuse some people with cognitive or visual impairments. Standard flushing levers should be on the approach side of the toilet, and a lever extension may be added to make flushing easier. Better yet, toilets with an automatic flush will improve sanitation and odor control.

In summary, it is worth noting that technology and design are changing the toileting experience and access to it (see Figure 8.61), and the market should be explored each time a toilet is to be specified.

Privacy at the Toilet

To maximize access, provide privacy in the toileting area without using a separate compartment. For example, a cabinet, 18 inches wide by 12 inches deep by 48 inches (457 mm by 305 mm by 1219 mm) or higher, facing toward the toilet provides a visual barrier of the toilet. Drawers, tambour, or open shelves should not interfere with the toilet fixture. Continue the finished flooring under the cabinet so it can be removed if additional clear floor space is needed around the toilet.

If the space allows, accessible compartments should be at least 60 inches wide, measured perpendicular to the side wall, and 56 inches deep (1524 mm by 1422 mm) for a wall-hung toilet and at least 59 inches deep (1499 mm) for a floor-mounted toilet measured perpendicular to the rear wall.

Another concept that can be used in the accessible bathroom is to plan the toilet and shower in a combined wet area (see "Bathing and Shower Center, Doors and No-Thresholds," above) (see Figure 8.62). This concept allows turning and clear floor spaces to overlap; and access to the shower fixtures can improve personal hygiene and maintenance to the room.

Storage and Accessories in the Toileting Center

Storage near the toilet for back-up tissue rolls, towels, equipment, personal toiletries, and cleaning supplies should be within the 15 inches to 48 inches (381 mm to 1219 mm) reach

FIGURE 8.60 An option can be grab bars that drop down on either side of the toilet.
Courtesy of Cynthia Liebrock/Kohler Co.

range and should not obstruct or protrude into the clear floor space (see Figure 8.63). Recessed shelves between studs provide storage that does not protrude, and holds a surprising amount of the items needed in this area. Rolling storage allows items to be placed within reach, and is flexible and can be moved out of the toilet center for clear floor space. Waste containers should also be planned out of the clear floor space. A child or a person needing a foot brace at the toilet will also have a step stool which must be stored out of the clear floor space as well.

FIGURE 8.61 The Numi includes a touch screen control for seat heating, music, and lighting, among other features.
Courtesy of Kohler Company

Keep in mind that for a person who needs a support in the toilet area, anything within reach will be used, and consider specifying only those accessories that will hold the weight and function as grab bars if called on to do so (see Figure 8.64).

When planning grab bars, placement of the toilet paper holder can be tricky. According to NKBA Planning Guideline 23, it should be 8 inches to 12 inches (203 mm to 305 mm) in front of the toilet bowl and centered 26 inches (660 mm)(Planning Guideline 23). When working with a client, it is best to determine the placement based on his/her reach, and it can either be a minimum 1 1/2 inches (25 mm) below or up to 12 inches (305 mm) above the grab bar. For a more detailed

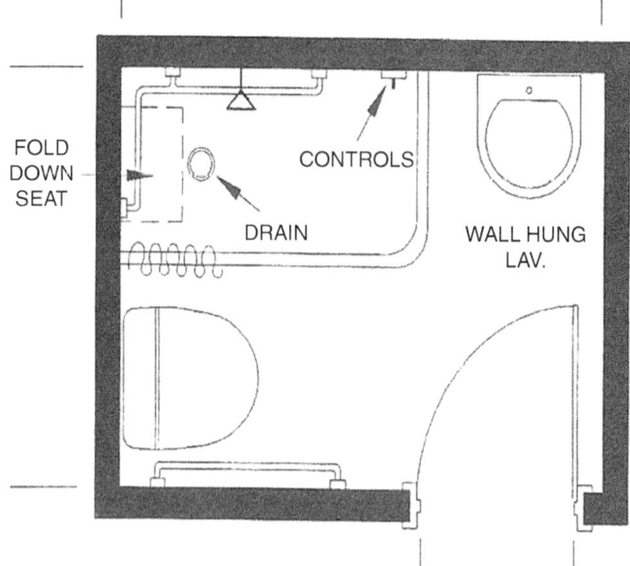

FIGURE 8.62 The entire floor is waterproof and slopes to the shower drain in this wet-room concept.
NKBA

FIGURE 8.63 Storage next to the toilet with sliding doors in the upper section.
Design by NKBA member: Adel Visser, CKD, CBD, CID

FIGURE 8.64 This toilet paper holder with integrated support should not replace a grab bar, but can support weight if needed.
Courtesy of HealthCraft Invisia Collection

discussion of the best location, reference the ICC (ANSI) A117.1- 2009, chapter 6. A recessed toilet paper holder will not protrude into the clear floor space, and it prohibits someone using it for support.

A towel bar or ring within reach of the toilet may be necessary for some clients, and it should typically be placed below the grab bar.

Electrical, Lighting, and Ventilation in the Toileting Center

Responsive lighting concepts for nocturnal visits to the bathroom include motion-sensor lighting and night lighting that fades on and off. In addition, recognize that task lighting appropriate to the activities of the user must be planned. For example, if this is to be a reading station, plan the lighting for it.

Ventilation and lighting controls should be placed 15 inches to 48 inches (381 mm to 1219 mm) above the floor, operable with minimal effort, easy to read, and with visual and audible on/off indicators. Electronic sensor controls on ventilation help ensure that things are shut off at the appropriate time after the user is finished. As previously noted, quiet ventilation will minimize background noise distortion, good for all and especially beneficial for those of us with hearing impairments.

For added security, consider planning for a security system, safety alarm, or hard-wired phone and/or an intercom in the toileting center.

Access Standards

The NKBA Guidelines and Access Standards that relate to the toileting center are: 4, 11, 14, 20, 21, 22, 23, 24, and 26.

Responsive Design Summary: the Toileting Center

- Sensory
  - Universal design recommendations
    - Plan responsive lighting concepts for typical activities and nocturnal visits to the bathroom
    - Choose quiet ventilation to minimize background noise distortion (Access Guideline 26)
  - Access recommendations
    - Incorporate redundant cueing for the controls to respond to vision and hearing issues
    - Plan storage that does not protrude into the clear floor space
- Cognitive
  - Universal design recommendations
    - Consider planning the entire bathroom as a wet area to reduce problems with water containment.
    - Consider toilets with an automatic flush to improve sanitation and odor control
    - Specify electronic sensor controls lighting and on ventilation to help ensure it is shut off after the user is finished
  - Access recommendations
    - Plan storage of any step stool or toilet training accessories out of the clear floor space and pathways around the toilet (Access Guideline 4)
- Physical
  - Universal design recommendations
    - Plan according to the client's transfer methods
    - Respect the need for private storage of medical/hygiene equipment and products
    - Plan a GFCI receptacle (Guideline 24) near the toilet for addition of a personal hygiene system or other features requiring an electrical connection
    - Specify that walls be reinforced at time of construction to allow for installation of grab bars (Guideline 14) as and where needed
  - Access recommendations
    - Plan a minimum clear floor space of 30 inches by 48 inches (762 mm by 1219 mm) centered at each fixture, plus space for maneuvering including approach and turning for a person using a wheelchair (Access Standard 4)
    - Design the space for transfer according to client needs, or plan for both a parallel and a forward approach to the toilet by providing clearance of at least 56 inches (1422 mm) measured perpendicular from the rear wall, and 60 inches (1524 mm) measured perpendicular from the side wall. No other fixture or obstruction should be within the clearance area
    - Plan grab bars according to the needs and height of the user, with 33 to 36 inches (838 mm to 914 mm) above the floor as a general guide (Guideline 14).
    - Consider users' height and ability when selecting toilet height and features. A standard is between 15 and 19 inches (381 mm to 483 mm) above the floor (Access Standard 20)

SUMMARY

In this chapter, you have been presented with information on various sensory, cognitive, and physical characteristics of people, and related design concepts to help stimulate and streamline your process when working on a space that is to accommodate a client with a specific disability. It is worth repeating that just as there is no average person, no two people with disabilities are alike. These general groups have been formed simply to help pull together and further explore the design concepts discussed throughout the book and particularly in chapter 6, "Bathroom Planning." You will have noticed repeated concepts and concepts that might fall into either the universal design list or the Access Standards list. As time passes and we embrace more and more of the Access solutions, more concepts will be moved from the access to the universal category, creating true equity in our design. Hopefully, you will continue to build on the lists and grow your library of access-related design. As you do, you'll discover that most of the access solutions are better for everyone and you'll be experiencing that "Aha" of universal design.

REVIEW QUESTIONS

1. Design that responds to the particular requirements of a person with specific characteristics and needs is (See under "Universal Design versus Accessibility: Further Clarification" page 235)
   a. Universal design
   b. Accessible design
   c. Barrier-free design
   d. Lifespan design
2. What are three bath design concepts or practices that will improve the function of the space for a client with hearing issues? (See under "Sensory Characteristics: Hearing" page 237)
3. What are three design concepts or practices that will improve the function of the space for a person with vision impairments? (See under "Sensory Characteristics: Vision" page 237)
4. What are three concepts or practices that will improve the function of the space for a person with tactile or olfactory issues? (See under "Other Sensory Characteristics" page 237)
5. What are three concepts or practices that will improve the function of the space for a person with cognitive impairments? (See under "Perception and Cognition Characteristics" page 238)

More Than a Bathroom

Often a bathroom design or renovation may include the opportunity to plan and design other activity spaces in the home. Typically, these spaces are still located in the private area of the home, and are often within the bathroom or adjacent to it. Designers may need to help the client rethink such functional spaces as clothes storage and laundry areas that are being incorporated into the new design.

Clients may also be looking for space within, or next to, the bathroom to address their interest in health and wellness. Exercise spaces and luxury home spas may be requested by clients who see these areas as important to their ability to take care of themselves or to pamper their mind and body. This chapter provides guidance to consider and plan closets, laundry, and health and wellness areas, so you can offer the client functional and beautiful spaces.

> ***Learning Objective: Discuss auxiliary spaces that are adjacent to or within the bathroom that include: clothes closet, dressing area, linen closet, laundry area, exercise area, and home spa.***

CLOTHES CLOSETS

Given that a bathroom is a place for people to take off—and put on—clothing, then including a clothes closet in or near it makes a lot of sense. As a bathroom designer, you are likely to be involved in designing clothes storage of some type. This may range from temporary clothes storage during bathing or showering to a complete walk-in closet. You may design an area for hanging clothes, or include drawers and shelves for all types of clothing.

During your initial client interview and needs assessment (see chapter 5, "Assessing Needs"), you will want to discuss clothes storage requirements with your client. This chapter focuses on designing a full clothes closet, but also includes useful information on all types of clothes storage. You can adapt the information to the situation of your particular client.

Moving Clothes

Start designing a clothes closet by thinking about how clothes are moved from one place to the next. For example, they are moved from the laundry area to storage, such as in a closet. Then they are removed from the closet when a person gets dressed. Sometimes clothes need to be moved from the closet to the dressing area, or to a temporary place (like a clothes hook) while a person is bathing, showering, or grooming. Another example is when a person gets undressed, clothes may move to another temporary storage place such as a "dirty clothes" container or go directly to the laundry area. Sometimes clothes are taken outside the home to a dry cleaner or laundry.

Placement of the closet needs to consider this movement of clothes and its relationship to clothes-related activities. Where will dressing and undressing occur? Does your client want centralized storage of all clothes in one area? Or will clothes be stored in several areas? For example, a decentralized option might be to keep only underwear or nightclothes near the bathing/showering area, and other clothes in the bedroom.

If more than one person regularly uses the bathroom area, access to both clothes storage and bathroom fixtures needs to be considered. Adequate room for multiple activities and users is needed. What is the desired privacy for both bathroom and/or dressing activities? Will one closet area be provided or will there be individual clothes storage for each user?

Closet Placement

The movement of clothes, the dressing/undressing activities, and circulation through the space are important determinants of the location of clothes storage in relation to other parts of the bathroom. There are other factors to consider as well.

Moisture is produced in the bathroom, and excess humidity can be damaging to stored clothes. The clothes storage area should be separated from damp areas of the bathroom by a door or partition. Good ventilation in the closet area reduces moisture problems and helps keep clothes fresher.

Consider what is on the other side of the closet wall. A closet on an interior wall can be used to advantage by providing sound insulation. For example, a bedroom closet can reduce sound transmission from other parts of the house, keeping peace among late-night television watchers, early risers, and late sleepers in the household.

If the closet will be on an outside wall, it is important to determine that the wall is well insulated. The clothes in the closet will act as insulation from the room air, and the closet could be cooler in winter and warmer in summer. This could lead to condensation problems and even mildew on clothes. Ventilation and air circulation will be especially important to prevent these problems.

A Place for Everything

A well-planned and organized clothes closet begins with an inventory of everything that will be stored in it. The storage inventory in chapter 5, "Assessing Needs," is a place to start. However, if you are designing a complete or custom closet, you will probably want to get more detail on clothes storage. Start by thinking about how clothes will be stored: put on hangers on rods; folded or rolled in drawers or on shelves; or on hooks. Think about all types of clothes from underwear to suits and include shoes, belts, scarves, ties, and other accessories.

Form 11: Clothes Storage Inventory for Hanging Clothes, and Form 12: Clothes Storage Inventory for Folded, Rolled, and Other Types of Clothes, are inventories that you can use with your client to determine what needs to be stored in the closet. These inventory checklists can be given to your client to complete and return to you, or you can complete them with the client. Form 11 and Form 12 are presented below, and are available online at: www.wiley.com/go/bathplanning.

The storage inventories group clothing by type of storage and similar size. This is an example of application of an important storage principle: like items should be stored together.

Form 11: Clothes Storage Inventory for Hanging Clothes

Instructions: Use this inventory checklist to determine the number of items to be stored in the closet on hangers. Items are grouped by the typical rod height. You may not have each item listed, or you may not store it on hangers. There are blank lines to add clothing items that you have which are not listed.

Clothing Item				
✓		Number of clothing items		
		Women	Men	Children
	Rod height*: 68"–72"			
	Floor-length gowns/evening dresses			
	Jumpsuits			
	Night gowns			
	Robes			
	Other:			
	Other:			
	Rod height: 54"– 63"			
	Coats			
	Dresses			
	Night gowns			
	Slacks, pants, jeans			
	Other:			
	Other:			
	Rod Height: 45"– 48"			
	Jackets			
	Skirts			
	Slacks, pants, jeans (folded over)			
	Sweaters			
	Suits			
	Other:			
	Other:			
	Rod height: 36"–45"			
	Blouses or shirts			
	Jackets			
	Shorts			
	Sweaters			
	Other:			
	Other:			

* Rod height is the length of the clothing item plus 10" (4" for the hanger and 6" floor clearance).

Form 12: Clothes Storage Inventory for Folded, Rolled, and Other Types of Clothes

Instructions: Use this inventory checklist to determine the number of items to be stored in the closet using built-in shelves, drawers, hooks, or other methods. Do not include items that will be stored on hangers, in furniture, such as dressers, or in other places besides the closet. You will probably not have each item listed. There are blank lines to add clothing items that you have which are not listed. There are two lists, one for women and girls, and another for men and boys.

Women's and Girl's Clothing

		Type of Storage				
✓	Clothing Item	Shelf	Drawer	Hook	Box	Other (describe)
	Belts					
	Boots					
	Bras					
	Blouses					
	Camisoles					
	Gloves, mittens					
	Handkerchiefs					
	Hats					
	Leggings, leotards					
	Jeans					
	Jewelry					
	Night gowns					
	Pajamas					
	Panty hose, stockings					
	Scarves					
	Shirts, dress					
	Shirts, knit (e.g., polo, rugby)					
	Shoes					
	Shorts					
	Slips, full, half					
	Socks					
	Sweaters					
	Sweatshirts					
	Swimsuits					
	Ties, ascots					
	T-shirts					
	Undershirts					
	Underwear					
	Additional items:					

(*continued*)

Men's and Boy's Clothing						
		Type of Storage				
✓	Clothing Item	Shelf	Drawer	Hook	Box	Other (describe)
	Belts					
	Boots					
	Gloves, mittens					
	Handkerchiefs					
	Hats					
	Jeans					
	Jewelry					
	Pajamas					
	Scarves					
	Shirts, dress					
	Shirts, knit (e.g., polo, rugby)					
	Shoes					
	Shorts					
	Socks					
	Sweaters					
	Sweatshirts					
	Swimsuits					
	Ties, ascots					
	T-shirts					
	Undershirts					
	Underwear					
	Additional items:					

Clothes Planning Dimensions

There are a number of commonly accepted planning dimensions that will be helpful as you design clothing storage. Keep in mind, however, that you may need to adapt these recommendations to allow for users of different sizes, ages, or abilities.

Hanging Clothes Storage

Depth. A typical closet is 24 inches (610 mm) deep, with the rod placed 12 inches (305 mm) from the wall. However, suit coats or jackets are bulkier and need 26 inches (660 mm) to 28 inches (711 mm) to hang perpendicular to the rod. Outerwear, such as winter coats, may need 30 inches (762 mm) of depth. If closet rod depth is inadequate, clothes will hang at an angle, and additional rod storage will be needed. If a closet is too shallow, clothes may get jammed and wrinkled in storage (see Figure 9.1).

Length. Recommendations for the length of rod storage vary, from as little as 36 inches (914 mm) to as much as 72 inches (1823 mm) per person. A more accurate way to determine rod length, for custom design, is to calculate the amount based on the number of items to be stored on hangers. Allow about 2 inches (51 mm) per item for women's clothing, and about 2 1/2 inches (64 mm) per item for men's clothing (see Figure 9.2). Some items, such as heavy coats or formal gowns, may take up more space [4 to 5 inches (102 to 127 mm), or more].

Use Form 11: Clothes Storage Inventory for Hanging Clothes to determine the number of items to be stored in the closet. Multiply the number of items by the appropriate size recommendation to get a minimum rod length recommendation. Increase this amount to allow extra rod space for ease of access to hangers, and to increase ventilation around clothing and minimize wrinkling. Extra rod space is also needed to allow for new items.

FIGURE 9.1 A generous depth of closet rod storage will allow clothes to hang perpendicular to the rod, maximizing storage space, and will prevent wrinkling of clothing.
Courtesy of Closet Maid

Height. Rod height is dependent on the length of the item to be stored and the reach of the user. Grouping similar length clothing and providing rods at more than one height can maximize the efficiency of closet storage (see Figure 9.3). Form 11: Clothes Storage Inventory for Hanging Clothes has already grouped clothing of similar lengths to make this process easier.

The rod needs to be reachable by the user. If the household for which you are designing includes a person who uses a wheelchair or mobility aid, a person with limited reach, or a shorter person, lower rods will be appropriate.

Children cannot reach a full-height closet rod. However, every parent wants to teach their children to hang up their own clothes! Lower rods that can be raised as children grow and their clothes get bigger, provide an option. After the age of 16, most children can reach rods as high as most adults.

Rod Span. The closet rod span, the distance between supports or brackets, typically depends on the diameter and material of the rod. Follow the spans for wood and metal rods that manufacturers of closet rod systems recommend to support the weight of hanging clothing. Depending on the style and design of the closet rod, support brackets may take up rod space. This will need to be considered in the calculation of rod length.

Access and Clearances. Adequate space to access hanging clothes is important to a well-planned closet area. Floor clearance of 36 to 38 inches (914 to 965 mm) is recommended in front of hangers (see Figure 9.4). This clearance gives room for activities such as turning, holding up clothes, or removing clothes from a hanger. If a shelf is placed above the rod, a clearance of 2 to 3 inches (51 to 76 mm) is needed to allow space to remove the hangers from the rod.

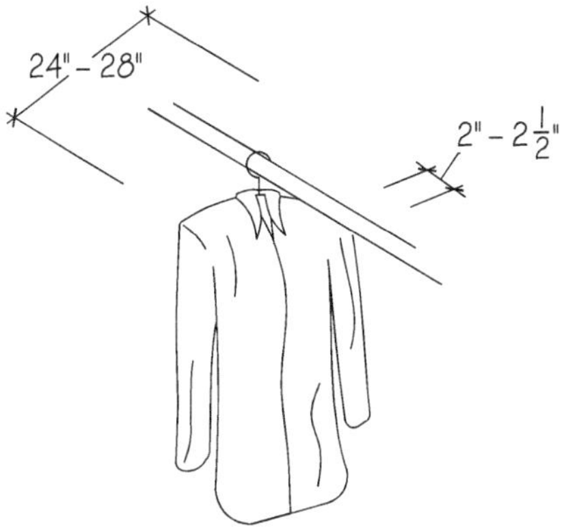

FIGURE 9.2 Women's clothes average about 2 inches (51 mm) of rod length per item and men's clothes need about 2 1/2 inches (64 mm). Bulkier items, such as overcoats, will require more rod space.

Closet Layouts

Closet layouts are often described in three different ways, based on the clearance for access to the hangers: reach-in, edge-in, and walk-in. Figure 9.5 shows examples of these closet layouts. The dimensions shown are minimum access space. However, these minimums are very tight, and more generous clearances are recommended. For example, although a 24-inch (610 mm) opening is shown as the minimum, an opening of 60 inches (1524 mm) to 72 inches (1823 mm) is desirable for a clear view of, and access to, a closet. For a roll-in closet, include a 60-inch (1524 mm) diameter clear space, which can extend 12 inches (305 mm) under one side, or 6 inches (152 mm) on both sides, of the hanging clothes (Figure 9.5d).

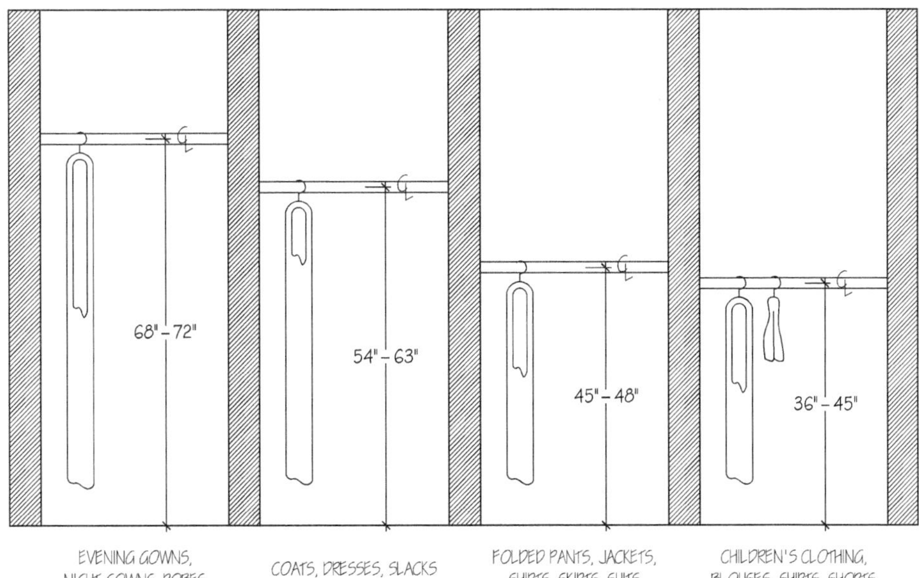

FIGURE 9.3 Most hanging clothing can be grouped into four rod heights.
NKBA

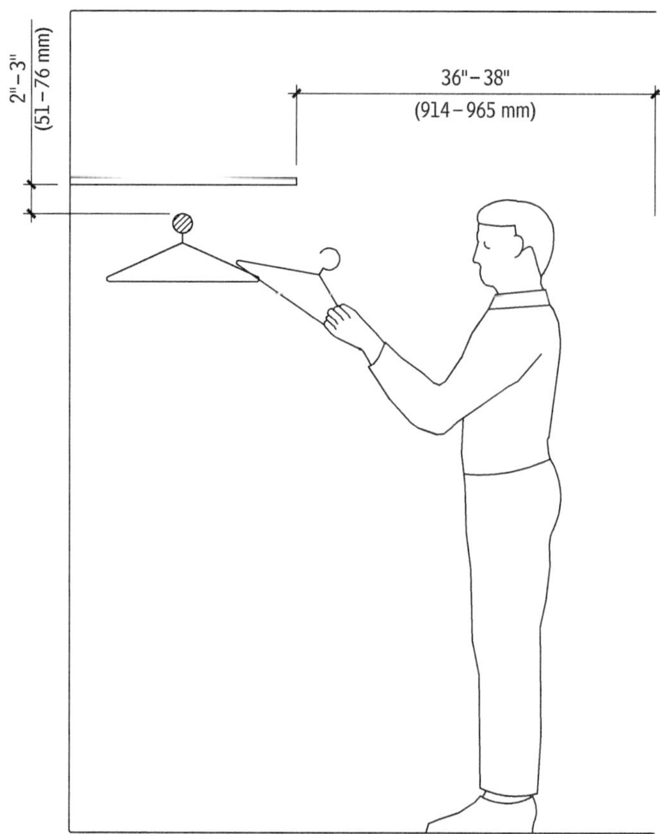

FIGURE 9.4 Adequate clearance space allows access to hangers.
NKBA

Other Types of Closet Storage

A clothes closet can hold much more than hanging clothes. A well-designed clothes storage area can include shelves, drawers, hooks, bins, and other devices for storing clothes, shoes, and accessories. The inventory checklist, Form 12: Clothes Storage Inventory for Folded, Rolled, and Other Types of Clothes, collects information about the number of other clothing items to be stored, as well as your client's preferred type of storage.

Shelf and Drawer Space. How much shelf and drawer space is needed? That can be a hard question to answer, depending on what items a person has to store in the closet, how they are

Storage Principles

Storage principles were introduced in chapter 6, "Bathroom Planning." As you plan shelves, drawers, and other types of storage in a closet, keep in mind the following storage principles:

- Items used together should be stored together. For instance, bras, underwear, socks, and stockings might be stored near each other.
- Like articles should be stored or grouped together. For example, store all sweaters together.
- Stored items should be easy to locate at a glance. Deep shelves might violate this principle because items stored behind others could be "forgotten."
- Frequently used items should be within easy reach. An example is that T-shirts might be stored just below shoulder height, while an evening purse might be put on an upper shelf.

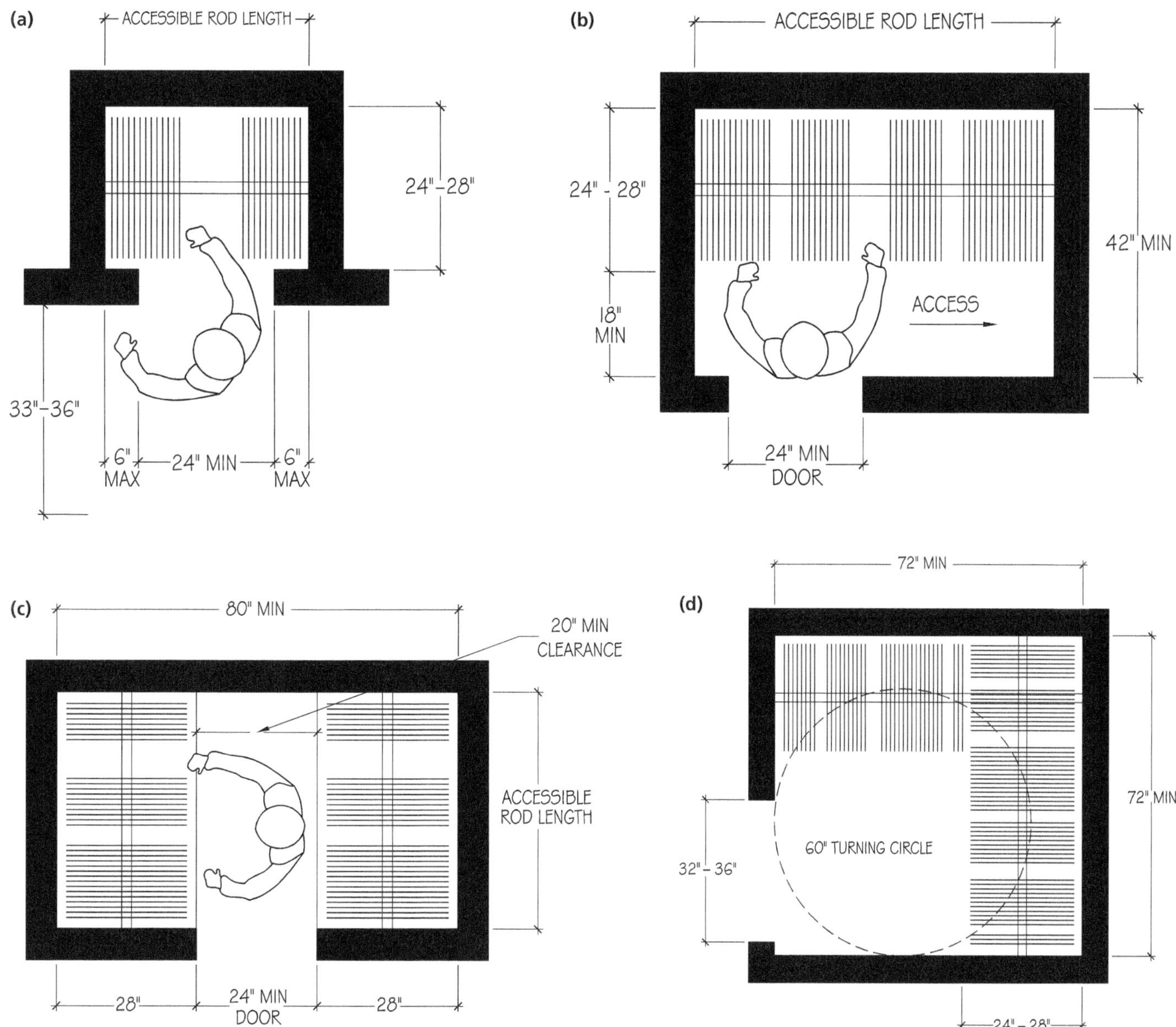

FIGURE 9.5 Minimum dimensions are shown for different closet layouts, but more generous clearances are recommended. (A) is a reach-in closet. (B) is an edge-in closet. (C) is a walk-in closet. (D) is an alternative design for a walk-in closet, which has been adapted to work as a roll-in closet.
NKBA

folded or rolled, and how they are stacked. Recommendations vary from 8 square feet (0.74square meters) to 20 square feet (1.86 square meters) of space per person. These recommendations assume a typical drawer depth or shelf clearance of at least 6 inches (152 mm).

For a custom installation, you may want to count the number of garments and the amount of space they will need. Use Form 12: Clothes Storage Inventory for Folded, Rolled, and Other Types of Clothes, to get a complete inventory of the items to be stored on shelves or drawers. Discuss with your client how things will be organized. What items will be stored together? Then take some sample measurements of the amount of space the stored items require.

Form 13: Worksheet for Folded or Rolled Clothing can be used to determine how much drawer and shelf space is needed. Using the worksheet, you can determine the size of the various stacks of garments, which can then be grouped into requirements for drawer and shelf space. Be sure to allow room for expansion!

Form 13: Worksheet for Folded or Rolled Clothing

Use the information from Form 12: Clothes Storage Inventory for Folded, Rolled and Other Types of Clothes to determine the number of garments. The number per stack is typically two to six items, depending on the number of garments and client preference. Determine the size of each stack. This information is then used to determine the total amount of shelf and/or drawer space that is needed.

Items Stored in Drawers

				Dimensions in Inches, per Stack		
✓	Garment	Number of garments	Number per stack	Frontage	Depth	Stack Height
	Example:					
	T-shirts	18	6	12	16	5

(continued)

Items Stored on Shelves						
				Dimensions in Inches, per Stack		
✓	Garment	Number of garments	Number per stack	Frontage	Depth	Stack Height
	Example:					
	T-shirts	18	6	12	16	5

Access and Clearance Space. When shelves or drawers are added to a closet, there needs to be adequate space for access. There are several concerns:

- Maximum reach to upper shelves (see Figure 9.6).
- Bending or kneeling space to reach lower shelves (see Figure 9.7).
- Depth of an open drawer added to bending or kneeling space (see Figure 9.8).

To accommodate clients who are shorter or who use a mobility aid, lower the storage reach to 48 inches (1219 mm), particularly for items used regularly, and increase the clear floor space. Alternatively, refer to the Reach and Grasp Profile and Mobility Aids information that is part of Form 1: Getting to Know Your Client which is discussed in Chapter 5, "Assessing Needs."

Hooks. Hooks work well to store frequently used items such as nightgowns, pajamas, robes, or belts. They also work well for items that are awkward to fold, such as scarves or ties. Put hooks within easy reach, but not in a passageway or other location where someone might bump into them. A minimum height for a hook is the length of the garment or item to store, plus 6 inches (152 mm) of clearance beneath. Space multiple hooks 3 to 12 inches (76 to 305 mm) apart, depending on the bulkiness of the items to be stored.

More Than Clothes?

A well-designed closet with plenty of rod, shelf, drawer, and hook storage may be just the beginning for your client. There may be other items or activities to be accommodated in the clothes storage and/or dressing area.

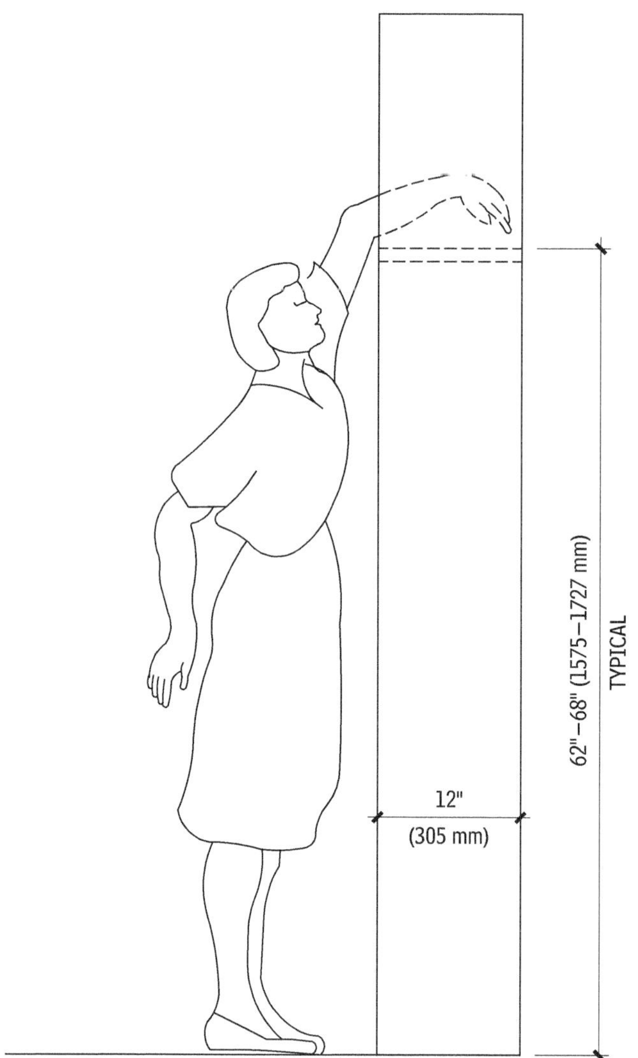

FIGURE 9.6 The typical maximum reach for a 12-inch (305 mm) shelf is illustrated here. A deeper shelf or obstruction (such as hanging clothes) will decrease the maximum shelf height.
NKBA

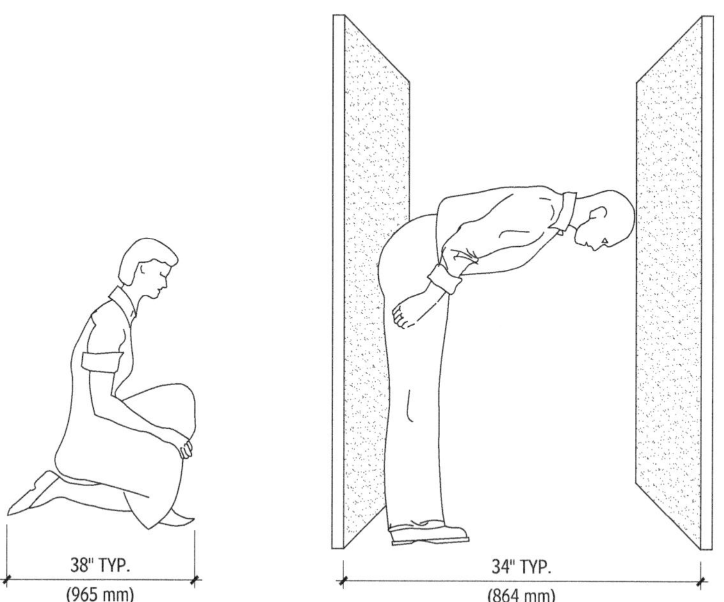

FIGURE 9.7 Minimum space allowances to bend or kneel, as if accessing a lower closet shelf, are shown.
NKBA

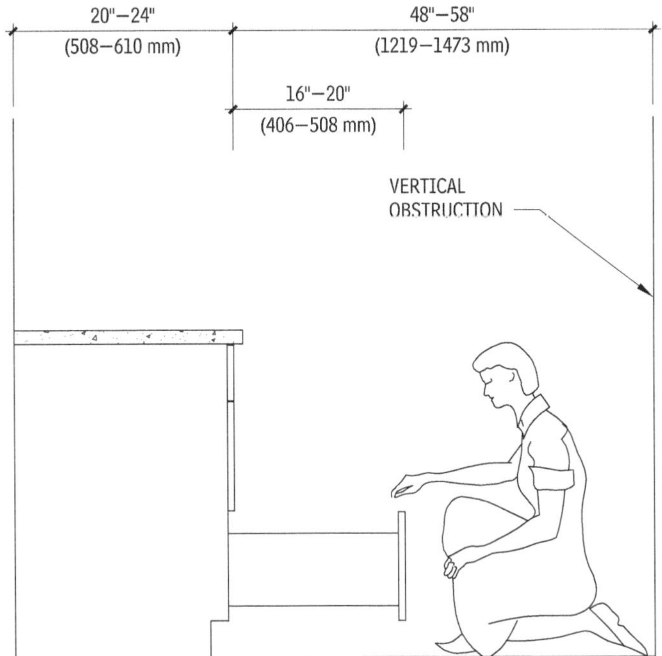

FIGURE 9.8 Bending or kneeling at an angle to the drawer will reduce the space needed for drawer access, but larger or deeper drawers will require more space.
NKBA

Does your client have a dresser, chest of drawers, armoire, or other piece of furniture that they would like to move into the closet area? Putting clothes storage furniture into the closet/dressing area can free up floor space in the bedroom and centralize clothes storage into one area. Measure the piece of furniture to know how much space will be needed. Allow for access to furniture pieces, just as for built-in storage.

A clothes storage area can also become a clothes care and maintenance area. Laundry areas as part of the bathroom are discussed later in this chapter. A closet may be the preferred area for a clothes hamper or a laundry chute. Perhaps an ironing or pressing area would be desirable (see Figure 9.9). A space for a sewing machine or mending supplies would be another extra feature.

FIGURE 9.9 A built-in ironing board is convenient for quick touch-ups when dressing.
Courtesy of Hafele

FIGURE 9.10 These are examples of closet storage accessories available today.
Courtesy of Closet Maid & Easy Track

Design Decisions

In our discussion about clothes storage, we have focused on capacity and clearances, for both clothes and the activities, such as dressing, that might occur in or near the closet area. Now it is time to make some design decisions.

Putting all the clothes storage requirements together, the goal is to maximize storage capacity, provide convenience of access and use, but minimize the total area devoted to clothes storage. Many storage accessories available today can help achieve this goal (see Figure 9.10).

Closet storage systems provide double rods to increase storage capacity in the same floor space. Shelves, drawers, bins, turntables, pull-out or swing-out racks, and other storage devices can be put above, below, or next to hanging rods to make sure every space is used while increasing the visibility of, and ease of access to, stored items. Mechanized systems, such as carousel rods and sliding racks, can increase storage capacity by increasing access to items stored in what would otherwise be dead space.

New materials used in closet systems can increase storage function. For example, plastic covered wire mesh drawers, shelves, and bins provide good ventilation and visibility of stored items. Other systems that incorporate chrome wire or slatted wooden shelves offer similar benefits.

Think about adjustability. Wardrobes change with the seasons, and as fashions and lifestyles change. The mix of clothing may vary. Therefore, think about adjustability of rod height, and the ability to increase or decrease hanging rod space. Adjustable height shelves are another plus.

Closet accessories may be desirable as well. Extra features can include a mirror, a place to sit while dressing, storage for luggage, or a place to rest a suitcase while packing.

Doors

Closet doors are an important part of the design. Think about the width of the door in relation to access. Although many experts recommend a 24 inch (610 mm) minimum, a 32 inch (813 mm) clear doorway (2 foot,10 inch door; 864 mm) is better to allow for universal access. Wider doors provide better visual access.

For any type of closet door, select good-quality, durable hardware, handles, latches, tracks, and/or hinges. Closet doors get daily use, and lots of wear and tear.

If a hinged door is used, consider where the door swing will be, and the potential for interference with circulation through the space. Bypass sliding doors eliminate the problem of accommodating the door swing. However, one panel of a bypass sliding door always covers the closet opening. Triple-panel sliding doors are available. Pocket doors are similar to by-pass sliding doors, except that they slide into the wall. This type of door can provide good access to a closet, as long as there is adequate space in the wall cavity for installation. Verify the placement of plumbing and electrical connections if a pocket door is considered.

"Barn style" sliding doors slide on an exterior track above the door opening and outside the closet. This style door would provide full access to the closet doorway and no limitations from door swing. However, there needs to be adequate wall space for the door to slide out of the way.

Bi-fold doors come in different widths and styles. Because the door panel is hinged and folds out of the way, the space for a door swing is reduced. Accordion doors have multiple folds to move out of the way of the door opening without blocking the walkway in front of the closet door. With both bi-fold and accordion doors, some space in the door opening is lost to the stacked door in the open position.

A louvered door provides ventilation. Mirrored closet doors can provide a dressing area mirror and visual expansion of the space. Another common door, a flush door, permits storage accessories to be hung on it. However, a hollow-core flush door may not be adequate to support accessories, and reinforcing strips or a solid-core door may be needed. In addition, heavy-duty hinges may be needed to help support the weight of items hanging on the door.

Lighting

A closet will need to be well lit with convenient switching. The lighting can be switched to come on when the closet door is opened or to respond to a motion sensor. It is important that the light sources give an excellent color rendition to facilitate coordinating of clothes. Some people like to have lighting in a closet area similar to their work place to assure color matches.

Open, exposed, or pendant lamps are generally prohibited in closets by building codes. The distance between the light fixture (luminaire) and the storage area is determined by the type of light source (such as incandescent, LED, or fluorescent) and the mounting or installation. Verify the lighting design with the specific local code. Consult chapter 7, "Mechanical Planning," for more information about lighting.

DRESSING AREAS

A closet is a place to store clothes, but where will the owners of those clothes get dressed? This is an important question to ask. Designers often refer to the dressing circle, which is the amount of space needed for someone to raise their arms, turn, or bend to put on an item of clothing. The dressing circle is 42 inches (1067 mm) to 48 inches (1219 mm). You may need to plan one in, or near, the clothes storage area.

The dressing circle can overlap with other space clearances, such as drawer access. However, be sure to allow a full circle of clearance. A closet designed for more than one user needs multiple dressing circle areas.

A bench or chair is a welcome addition to a closet or dressing area, particularly as user's age or balance is compromised. Socks, shoes, and pants are among the items that might be put on while seated. Allow a minimum of about 16 to 18 inches (406 to 457 mm) in width and depth for seating. Since most people using a seat for dressing will be bending toward the floor, keep the seat low, 18 to 20 inches (457 to 508 mm) or less.

A mirror, especially a full-length mirror, is a welcome addition to a dressing area. Another is counter space for temporary deposit of items used during the day, but not at night, such as wallets, coins, watches, cell phones, or hearing aids. A charging area for cell phones and other electronic devices may be desired. A counter is also a good location for jewelry boxes, small storage containers, and other personal items.

LINEN CLOSETS

Storage for household linens is often integrated into, or near, a bathroom. This can be as basic as storage for extra towels in the bathroom, or may include full storage for all household linens near the bathroom or bedroom area.

When designing a linen closet or storage area, start with an inventory of items to be stored. Will the closet be used for bath linens only? Will bedding be included (Figure 9.11)? What about kitchen linens? Will additional space be needed for nonlinen items such as soaps, grooming products, toilet paper, or cleaning products?

Use Form 14: Linen Closet Storage Inventory to gather information about items stored in the linen closet. As with the other checklists, Form 14 can be given to your client to complete, or you can use it at an interview. You may want to compare the information in Form 14 against Form 4: Bathroom Storage Inventory, discussed in Chapter 5, "Assessing Needs," to see that there is no duplication.

As you plan the linen closet, review the storage principles presented in this chapter. Think about how your client will organize and group the items to be stored. The ones used most frequently should be easiest to see and reach. Heavy or bulky items may be stored on lower shelves for convenience.

FIGURE 9.11 Both bath and bedroom items may need to be located in a linen closet.
Courtesy of Easy Track

Just as with the clothes closet, take advantage of storage accessories such as pullout shelves and bins, drawers, and turntables. Perhaps your client will want to roll some items for storage, such as towels. Some household linens, such as table cloths or placemats, may be stored on hangers to minimize wrinkling.

Think about whether the linen storage is for short or long term. Some items like extra towels and bedding may only be used occasionally, such as for holiday guests. Enclosed, dust-proof, moisture-proof storage may be desirable. Other items such as everyday towels may be accessed regularly, and well-ventilated, easy-access storage may be the priority.

Form 14: Linen Closet Storage Inventory

Use this form to inventory how many items will be stored in the linen closet, and how much space will be needed.

The example shows an inventory where there are 18 wash cloths, which can be divided into stacks with a maximum of 6 per stack, for a total of 3 stacks. Each stack is 6 inches by 6 inches and 5 inches (152 mm by 152 mm by 127 mm) high. This information can then be used in planning the layout of the linen closet.

Linen							
					Dimensions in Inches, per Stack		
✓	Example:	Number of Items	Items per Stack	Number of Stacks	Frontage	Depth	Stack Height
	Wash Cloths	18	6	3	6	6	5
	Bathroom Linens:						
	Bath mats						
	Towels, face or wash cloths						
	Towels, hand						
	Towels, bath						
	Towels, bath sheets						
	Towels, guest						
	Bedding:						
	Bed spreads						
	Blankets						
	Pillows						
	Pillowcases						
	Quilts						
	Sheets, twin						
	Sheets, double						
	Sheets, queen						
	Sheets, king						
	Kitchen Linens:						
	Coasters						
	Dish cloths						
	Dish towels						
	Hand towels						
	Hot mats						
	Napkins						
	Place mats						
	Table cloths						
	Table runners						
	Additional items to store in linen closet:						

LAUNDRY AREAS

A lot of laundry is generated in the vicinity of the bathroom, from dirty clothes to towels and wash cloths. Plus, there are likely to be bedrooms nearby, with sheets and pillowcases.

Planning a laundry area in or near the bathroom makes a lot of sense. It is a time- and work-saver as dirty clothes, towels, and bed linens do not need to be carried to another part of the house for washing and drying, and then carried back to their area of use and/or storage. In addition, a laundry requires plumbing, which is already in the bathroom. For these reasons, your client may be considering incorporating a laundry in or near the bathroom.

What Type of Laundry?

Some people like the idea of having a complete laundry area centrally located near the bedrooms and bathrooms for convenience. Others may choose a "mini-laundry" area right in the bathroom for washing towels or doing quick loads of laundry while bathing, grooming, or dressing. Still other people may want to use the bathroom to rinse out or hand-wash single items, and then hang them up to drip-dry.

The client needs assessment (chapter 5) should reveal what type of laundry area your client might like, in or near the bathroom. In addition, the checklists will help determine what type of laundry activities, equipment, and supplies will need to be accommodated in the design. This section gives some specific information about planning a laundry area.

A laundry area in or near the bathroom can be convenient, but there are some factors to consider first.

- Who will use the laundry area?

A laundry area used by different members of the household needs to be centrally located for easy access. A personal or "mini-laundry" in the master suite might make sense for individual use, but not for the whole family. A laundry area near the bathroom might save hauling laundry to and from different parts of the house. However, a laundry area near the kitchen or family room might actually be more centrally located to family activities and thus more convenient to use.

- Is there adequate space for a laundry area?

A laundry area is more than a washing machine. A well-designed complete laundry includes storage, hanging and folding space, a sink, and adequate clearance to move and complete tasks. A mini-laundry may only be a combination or stacked washer and dryer. Will the laundry area interfere with other activities and space needs associated with the bathroom?

- What about access to the laundry?

All users need access to the laundry without invading the private space of bathroom users. Another factor is door and hall width clearance for carrying laundry baskets and hanging clothes. If an outside clothesline is used, there needs to be a direct route to the outdoors.

- What about noise associated with laundry equipment?

Many busy households put in loads of laundry late at night. This might be a problem when the laundry equipment is adjacent to the sleeping space.

- Is it feasible to provide the infrastructure for a laundry area in or near the bathroom?

Water supply and drainage for the washing machine and electrical or gas connections, as well as exhaust ventilation for the dryer all need to be considered. The floor structure may need reinforcing for the weight or vibration of laundry equipment. A floor drain is good protection in the event of a leak or other water problem. These features may be easy to provide in new construction, but more of a problem in a remodeling project.

- What about the mess of the laundry area?

Laundry areas can be messy. Laundry areas seem to collect clothes waiting for special treatment, or to be folded, ironed, or repaired. This is a utility area of the home, and many people prefer to close it off from other areas.

Laundry Equipment

A washing machine and automatic dryer will anchor most laundry areas. Washers and dryers vary in size. A typical American model washer or dryer is 27 to 29 inches (686 to 737 mm) wide (across the front) and 25 to 32 inches (635 to 813 mm) deep. Most are about 36 inches high (914 mm), but some are as high as 45 inches (1143 mm). European models tend to be smaller. Always check the exact size of the equipment in the manufacturer's specifications, or by measuring the actual equipment.

A washer can either be a front-loading or top-loading model. Most dryers are front-loading. Washer doors can be hinged on either side, depending on the model. Some top-loading models may have the door hinged at the back. Dryer doors can also be hinged on either side and some models are hinged on the bottom. Front-loading laundry appliances with front controls are desirable to improve access within the universal reach range.

Knowing the size, location, and swing of the door is important to efficient placement of laundry equipment. It should be convenient to remove wet laundry from the washer and place it in the dryer without interference from the open door of either piece of equipment. This movement of laundry between appliances should determine how the appliances are placed in relationship to each other.

If you will be placing laundry equipment in a closet, cabinet, or under a counter, check the manufacturer's specifications. Typically there are requirements for clearances on the sides, front, back, and top of the equipment to allow for ventilation and equipment connections. Doors to closets and cabinets must have a specified area and location of ventilation screening or be louvered for air circulation.

Front-loading washers and dryers may require the user to bend down to load and unload. Some models of front-loading washers and dryers are available with a 12 to 15 inch (305 to 381 mm) pedestal, for easier access. The pedestal also provides storage. An alternative is to install the equipment on a raised platform so that the door is easier to access (see Figure 9.12). Planning the equipment at this height cuts down on bending and allows the door to swing open clear of the armrest or lap of a person using a wheelchair. If the equipment is raised, be sure that the user can still reach and read the controls. Also, consider that the top of the equipment may not be convenient to use as a work surface for folding clothes or storage.

Laundry and the Environment

Everyone wants laundry equipment that is high performance, easy to use, and quiet in operation. However, today we also want laundry equipment that contributes to our goals of sustainability and "green" design. If you are designing a laundry area, recommending a high-efficiency washer results in a laundry system that minimizes the use of both energy and water.

- **Energy Star–qualified washer**—Energy Star–qualified equipment is more efficient, uses less energy, saves money, and helps protect the environment.
  - **The modified energy factor** (MEF) is a performance factor based on washer capacity, electricity use, energy to heat the water, and energy to remove the water from the clothes (dry the clothes). The higher the MEF, the more efficient the washer.
  - **The water factor** (WF) measures water per cycle. The lower the water factor, the more water-conserving the washer.
- **CEE (Consortium for Energy Efficiency) Tier rankings**—The CEE uses the MEF and WF performance factors to rate clothes washers. A Tier I ranking is equivalent to an Energy Star–qualified washer. Tier II and Tier III rankings result in a more efficient appliance.
- **Equipment capacity**—Match the capacity of the washer and dryer to the size and frequency of the household laundry needs to encourage the efficient use of energy and water.

FIGURE 9.12 Raising a front-loading washer or dryer, as much as 15 inches (381 mm), reduces bending and makes access easier, but still allows most people to reach the controls.

Courtesy of GE

Stacked Washer and Dryer

If space is limited, a stacked washer and dryer can be a good choice (see Figure 9.13). A stacked washer and dryer can take up about the same floor space as a single washing machine [(approximately 30 inches by 30 inches (762 mm by 762 mm)], yet provides the capacity for full loads of laundry. While stacked equipment saves floor space, the height of the equipment precludes locating any accessible storage above it.

If a stacked washer and dryer are selected, be sure that all controls and door openings can be accessed by the user. Check model specifications to make sure that stacking is an option. Careful planning of water connections, shut-offs, and dryer venting will be required.

Smaller-capacity stacked washers and dryers are available, with integrated controls. There are also combination laundry machines which are both washer and dryer in one unit. These smaller machines are good choices for a mini-laundry area or a smaller household.

FIGURE 9.13 A stacked washer and dryer can save floor space, and be a good choice for a laundry area in a bathroom.
Courtesy of GE

Other Laundry Equipment

A laundry area may include other equipment for clothes maintenance, including irons and steamers. Your client may also want a sewing machine in the laundry area. Be sure to provide adequate space to use and store these additional appliances, as well as for utility connections.

Utility Service

Utility service requirements for laundry equipment are specified by the manufacturer, and may be controlled by local building codes. Consult the product specifications and installation information for accurate information. Listed below are typical requirements.

- Washing Machine
  - Hot and cold water supply
    - Check distance from water supply to washer.
    - Check that water pressure is adequate.
  - Vented drain
  - 120 volt, 15 or 20 ampere dedicated electrical circuit
    - Some European style washers require a 240 volt circuit
- Electric Dryer
  - 240 volt, 50 ampere dedicated electrical circuit
  - Exterior ventilation for dryer exhaust outlet; distance from dryer to outside is dependent on number of elbows
  - Cold water supply if dryer has steam feature
- Gas Dryer
  - Natural or LP gas connection
  - 120 volt, 15 or 20 ampere dedicated electrical circuit (may be able to share electrical circuit with the washer if a 30 ampere circuit is used)
  - Exterior ventilation for dryer exhaust outlet; distance from dryer to outside is dependent on number of elbows
  - Cold water supply if dryer has steam feature

One or more additional electrical circuits and receptacles are recommended in the laundry area, to use additional clothes care equipment, such as irons, sewing machines, or clothes steamers. An electrical circuit for lighting is also needed. A sink in the laundry area is desirable, and water supply and drain are needed for this.

Dryer Venting

Exterior ventilation of the dryer is important, even though there is sometimes consideration of venting dryers to the inside. The thought behind venting a dryer to the inside is that heat is retained, which is seen as an advantage in cold climates in the winter. However, the problems with this practice far outweigh the energy savings. The excess moisture can lead to serious condensation and mold problems in the home (see chapter 3, "Environmental and Sustainability Considerations").

Odors from laundry products can be a problem. Lint in the exhaust air presents maintenance problems. Gadgets are available to add to the dryer exhaust vent to filter lint. However, these filters require regular maintenance, and failure to do so clogs the exhaust vent, leading to a fire hazard.

If venting is a problem, condensing dryers that do not require an outside vent are available. A condensing dryer may require a drain.

Manufacturers' product specifications typically require vinyl, rubber, or other moisture- resistant flooring under laundry equipment. A level floor is important, particularly for front-loading washers which spin at high speeds. A floor drain near the washing machine is a desirable feature, to minimize the problems with water leaks. If this cannot be provided, the washer can be installed in a floor pan that would contain leaks and overflows.

Space Planning in the Laundry Area

Adequate space is needed in the laundry area to move, turn, bend, and twist, while moving laundry in and out of the equipment. Space for a laundry basket or cart is also needed. A clearance of 42 inches (1067 mm) in front of a washer, dryer, or stacked washer and dryer, is recommended (see Figure 9.14a). This will give adequate space to access either front- or top-loading machines, allowing space for door swings and a person to kneel or bend (see also Figure 9.8).

When the washer and dryer are placed side by side, the 42-inch (1067 mm) clearance space should be 66 inches wide (1676 mm) (see Figure 9.14b). If front-loading appliances are being used, check to see that this dimension allows adequate clearance for a door swing. If appliances are placed at right angles or across from each other, the clearance spaces for each machine overlap (see Figure 9.14c and Figure 9.14d).

If the person doing the laundry uses a mobility aid, such as a wheelchair or cane, these clearances will need to be increased. Refer back to Form 1, discussed in chapter 5, "Assessing Needs," for information on collecting clearances for mobility aids your client might use.

Laundry in Transition

Designing a laundry area is more than installing equipment with clearance space. The flow of laundry—mostly clothes—in and out of the space needs to be considered. Dirty laundry is brought into the area, clean laundry is moved out. During the transition, clothes, towels, bed linens, and other items may spend time "hanging out" in the laundry area. To help organize the laundry area, smooth the flow of laundry, and minimize clutter, consider the following ideas.

- **Dirty laundry needs to be collected.** Hampers, bins, or baskets in the laundry area can be used for short-term storage of dirty laundry (see Figure 9.15). Good ventilation of the dirty laundry containers is necessary to dispel dampness and odors.

Several containers might be used to pre-sort laundry. For example, white socks, t-shirts, and underwear might go into one container, jeans into another. (The effectiveness of this system depends on cooperation of everyone in the household!) Or, if several members of the household do laundry separately, each person can have their own container, using it to accumulate enough laundry for a washer load.

- **Dirty laundry needs to be sorted before washing**. Table or counter surface works well for this task, and then can later be used for folding and sorting clean laundry (see Figure 9.15). A work surface 24 to 36 inches (610 to 914 mm) deep and 32 to 36 inches (813 to 914 mm) high would work for most people. The length of work surface depends on how much laundry is typically sorted and how much space is available. The work surface should be smooth so it will not snag fabrics, durable, nonabsorbent, resistant to damage if laundry products such as detergent are spilled on it, and easy to clean and sanitize.

Several bins or baskets might be used to sort laundry. These items might rest on a work counter, pull out from underneath a counter, or store inside a cabinet.

- **Hanging up items removed from the dryer minimizes wrinkles.** Provide a space to hang shirts, blouses, skirts, dresses, and similar items. This hanging space should be convenient to the dryer. Garments on hangers should not block work areas or passages. Good ventilation is needed to allow garments to cool without wrinkling.

Refer to Figures 9.1, 9.2, 9.3, and 9.6 for information on planning space and clearances for hanging clothes storage.

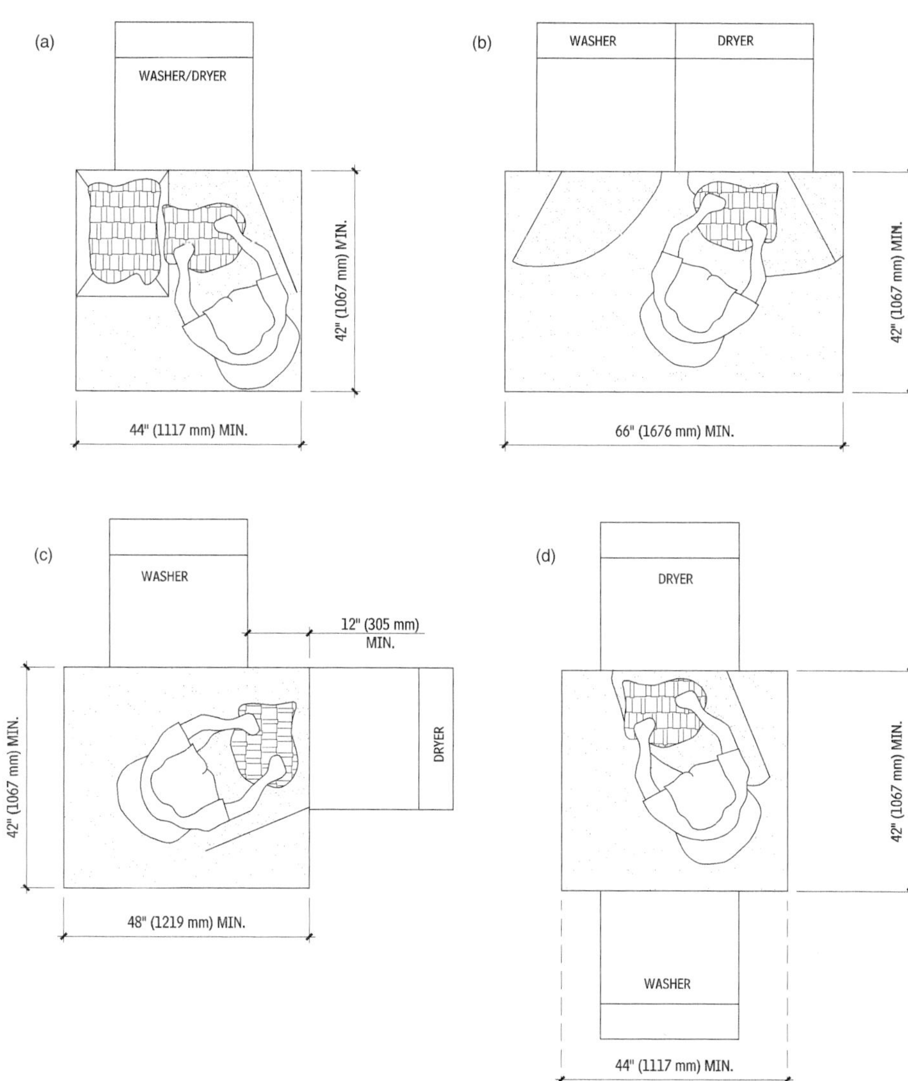

FIGURE 9.14a, b, c, d. Clearance in front of laundry equipment provides space for bending and kneeling, as well as door swings and space for a laundry basket or cart.
NKBA

- **Not everything goes into the dryer**. Some items, like sweaters, need to be laid flat, on a clean, smooth surface, to dry. Other items are hung up to drip-dry—and they may drip while drying—so a waterproof area is needed. Delicate items, like lingerie, may be put over a drying rack. The amount of space devoted to these activities will depend on your client.

If your client frequently air-dries laundry items, be sure that the area is adequately ventilated to prevent moisture problems.

- **Clean laundry needs to be folded**. A table or counter work surface, such as described above for sorting dirty laundry, will provide a space to fold clean laundry. Provide a knee-space for seated work when possible. If laundry is folded fresh from the dryer, wrinkles are minimized. Many people want space to sort clean laundry by type of garment or by its owner. Clean laundry may be stacked into a basket or cart for transport to storage areas in the home.

Several bins or baskets might be used to sort laundry by its owner. Household members can then come claim their own laundry.

- **A sink in the laundry area is a desirable feature** (see Figure 9.15). Some laundry products need to be diluted. Pre-rinsing may be helpful in removing stains. The sink can also be used for hand-washing items or soaking soiled items.

A laundry sink is typically placed next to or near the washer to facilitate plumbing connections, and for convenience of workflow. Unless your client does a lot of hand laundry, an extra-deep utility or

FIGURE 9.15 This laundry area includes many features, such as counter space for folding and sorting laundry, bins for sorting laundry, a sink, and generous storage
Courtesy of American Woodmark

laundry type sink may not be necessary. A small bar-type sink can work well. Select a gooseneck or pullout faucet for fitting bulky items under the water flow. Look for controls that are easy to operate, such as with one hand, one touch, or a foot pedal.

- The laundry area needs adequate lighting that is conveniently switched. Good color rendition in the light sources is important for noting stains and other problems on fabrics. See chapter 7, "Mechanical Planning," for more information about lighting.

Storage

Easily accessible storage is needed for laundry supplies. Items such as detergent and fabric softener are used almost every time something is washed, and need to be easily reached when using the laundry equipment. Other laundry supplies, such as stain removers, special detergents, bleaches, and fabric fresheners, may be used less frequently, but still need to be convenient to the laundry equipment. Most of these items will fit on 8- to 10-inch (203 to 254 mm) deep shelves.

Storage in laundry areas is often placed over the laundry equipment. However, the depth of the washer or dryer reduces the height of the user's reach. Bringing a shelf forward can make items more accessible, as long as they will not get lost at the back of extra-deep shelves.

Keep in mind that some laundry products, such as detergent, come in large containers that are heavy and/or awkward to lift. These items should not be stored above shoulder height (typically 52 to 57 inches; 1321 to 1448 mm). Finally, shelves above laundry equipment should not interfere with door openings or access to controls. For all these reasons, storage areas adjacent to, rather than above, laundry equipment may be more desirable for the most frequently used items.

Front-loading washers and dryers are available with pedestals that raise the machines 12 to 15 inches (305 to 381 mm) for easier access. Typically these pedestals are also drawers that provide additional storage (see Figure 9.14).

Other items may be stored in the laundry area, including hangers, clothespins, measuring cups for laundry products, stain removal guides, sponges, brushes, rags, and cleaning supplies. A divided drawer or small bins work well to collect items found in garment pockets or buttons that pop off. Some people keep basic sewing supplies in the laundry area so repairs can be made on the spot.

Open storage in the laundry area increases accessibility by making it easier to see stored items and eliminating cabinet doors that might not swing out of the way. However, the desirability of this depends on how open the laundry area is to view from other spaces in the home.

Laundry storage can be messy. Containers of detergents and other laundry products may drip when being used. Spills are inevitable. Storage areas, in fact all of the laundry area, should be made of durable, easily cleaned materials that are not damaged by exposure to water, detergents, and other laundry products. Vinyl, ceramic tiles, solid surface, and plastic laminates are popular materials used in laundry areas.

Ironing

Many people want a place to iron clothes and household linens. The laundry area is a logical place to put an ironing area. An ironing area might also be put in a closet, as discussed above. Built-in ironing boards (see Figure 9.9) fold down from wall cupboards or pull out from underneath a countertop, yet are out of the way when not in use. Many of these include storage space for the iron as well. Racks are available to hang freestanding ironing boards, or ironing boards can fold up to store in utility closets.

Adequate space needs to be included in the laundry area for using the iron and ironing board (see Figure 9.16). The amount of space may need to be increased if the user requires a mobility aid. Because an iron is very hot, the ironing area should not be in a passage or walkway. Most ironing boards adjust in height to allow a person to sit or stand to work and pull-out or drop-down versions create a full knee space.

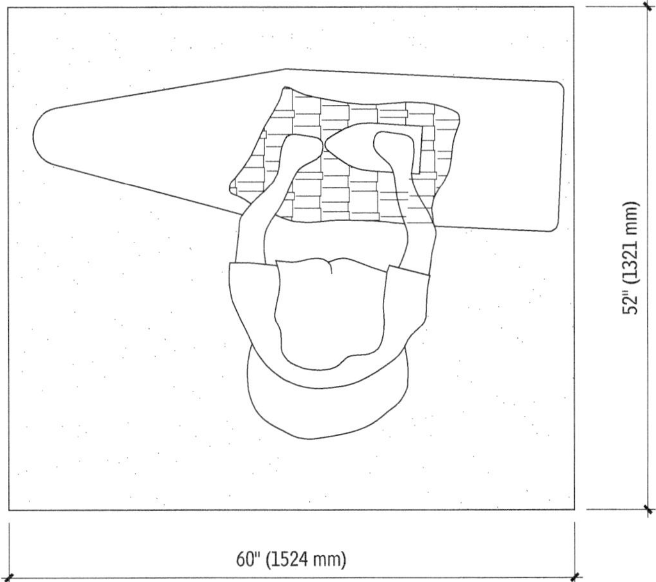

FIGURE 9.16 A typical ironing area would require a space that is 60 inches by 52 inches (1524 mm by 1231 mm).
NKBA

EXERCISE AREAS

An exercise space in or near the bathroom has many advantages and may be important to some clients.

Exercising at home can be more economical and more convenient than a membership to a health club. People are short on time, but can often spare 20 minutes if they can exercise in their home. The exercise area is accessible and does not require the motivation to drive to a health club. Home exercise equipment can be used in any weather, day or night. Some people will be more comfortable at home and prefer the privacy, rather than the more public health club or fitness center.

What Type of Exercise?

There are several things to be determined before planning an exercise space. Much of the information should be gathered during the client assessment discussed in chapter 5, "Assessing Needs." Form 15: Assessment for Exercise Area provides a checklist for recording information about exercise users, the type of exercise they participate in, and the type of equipment they may use. Find out about the client's fitness needs and exercise program. The client may have an established exercise program, but if they have not had the convenience of an exercise space at home, they need to think about how that space will impact their program. Here are some questions to consider.

- Who will be participating in the exercise program and using the space?

Is this just for a single user or will a couple or other family members be participating? It is possible that guests (either overnight or visitors) may also participate in an exercise program? Will a personal trainer be involved in the exercise program?

- How much time do the various users spend in their exercise program?

Do they spend 20 minutes on multiple exercise machines every evening or 30 minutes in an aerobic exercise program in the morning? Or do they just use the machine occasionally on a bad weather day when they cannot run or walk outside?

- What exercise activities do they do? This is critical in determining what equipment might be needed. Typical activities might be:

Flexibility exercise—stretches muscles. Includes yoga and warm-ups for other exercises.

Aerobic or cardiovascular exercise—increases heart rate, stimulates circulation, strengthens heart and lungs, and induces weight loss through fat burning. Programs may include dancing, walking, jump-roping, running, or swimming. Treadmills, bikes, stair climbers, and elliptical runners support cardiovascular exercise.

Strength training or weight conditioning programs—strengthens and tones muscles, burns fat, and improves posture. Programs may include situps and pushups, plyometrics or jump training, resistance training, and weight lifting.

- What are the resources available for designing the space?

Space will be needed for any equipment. Some programs can be completed in small areas, but some equipment requires a large amount of space.

- Is new equipment needed? If the client is selecting new equipment, they should try it out in a fitness center or equipment showroom.
- Will a personal trainer be used? A trainer may be an important partner in the selection of equipment and in planning the space.

Form 15: Assessment for Exercise Area

Record information about the users of the exercise area, the types of activities they prefer, equipment, and other requirements.

Exercise Users					
✓		Exercise Users			Notes and Special Requirements
	Users				
		Daily/weekly	Daily/weekly	Daily/weekly	
	Time Spent Exercising				
	Flexibility				
	Stretching				
	Yoga				
	Exercise Mat				
	Stability Balls				
	Other				
	Cardiovascular/Aerobic				
	Dancing				
	Walking				
	Running				
	Martial Arts				
	Boxing/Kickboxing				
	Punching bags				
	Jump-roping				
	Mats				
	Swimming				
	Aerobic Equipment				
	Sliders				
	Step benches				
	Treadmills				
	Bikes				
	Rowing machines				
	Stair climbers				
	Elliptical				
	Ski machines				
	Others				
	Strength training				
	Situps				
	Push-ups				
	Resistance training				
	Pilates				
	Reformer				

(continued)

Form 15: Assessment for Exercise Area (*continued*)

✓		Exercise Users			Notes and Special Requirements
	Users				
		Daily/weekly	Daily/weekly	Daily/weekly	
	Weight lifting				
	Free weights				
	Dumb bells				
	Weight bench				
	Single-station gym				
	Multistation gym				
	Other				

What else would you like to have in the exercise area?

- ☐ Clock
- ☐ Mirrors
- ☐ Television
- ☐ Extra fan and/or ventilation
- ☐ DVD/VCR
- ☐ Refreshment center
- ☐ Stereo/Music
- ☐ Seating or lounge area
- ☐ Game system
- ☐ Window view

Location

A common location for an exercise or fitness area is off the master bathroom. This is ideal for adults looking for privacy or retreat. An exercise program that takes place as part of the morning preparations might be well suited in a master bathroom suite. Being close to showers, grooming space, and clothing helps to make this a convenient activity that becomes readily incorporated into the daily routine.

If the exercise area is to be accessible to guests or other family members, then a space that is more centrally located may be more suitable than the master bathroom. This common area could be next to a hall bath, in a loft or attic space, basement, or a room off a living area. A room with an exterior entrance may be desirable for access to outdoor exercise areas. Being close to a bathroom will still be important for many people wanting to refresh themselves after exercising. The space may also have to be flexible to meet multiple users' needs and exercise programs. The space could allow for more than one person at a station, such as partners doing the same exercise at the same time, family fitness programs, or an instructor and student.

Exercise Equipment

Discussing the client's exercise program is critical in determining if the available space is adequate. The number and size of exercise equipment influences the space needed. To maximize the amount of exercise equipment in a limited space, fold-up models can be stored in a corner or closet.

- Some activities, such as aerobics, calisthenics, stretching, and yoga require no equipment other than a mat. Allow the space needed to safely perform the activity.
- Exercising or dancing with an instructional video may require a television and DVD, game system, or computer access.
- Stability balls are one of the most versatile pieces of exercise equipment. Sizes vary depending on the user. Common sizes are 18 inches (457 mm), 22 inches (559 mm), and 26 inches (660 mm).

- Sliders can be used for side-to-side or lateral exercises.
- Step benches are used for step-aerobic exercises.
- A punching or heavy bag is needed for kickboxing, boxing aerobics, or karate.
- Cardiovascular exercise equipment includes treadmills, bikes, rowing machines, stair climbers, elliptical runners, and ski machines.
- Strength training equipment includes free-weight sets with weights, bars, clips, and storage, as well as dumbbells and storage racks, single- and multistation gyms, and elastic tubes and bands. Benches are often used, including slant boards for weight lifting or situps. Reformers, including cables, pullers, springs, boxes, and sliding boards are used for Pilates.

Exercise equipment needs to be flexible if there will be multiple users of different heights, weights, and fitness goals. For multiple users, the equipment and finishes also need to be especially durable.

Other Equipment

Often other activities are taking place at the same time as exercising. Some of these are essential to the exercise experience, i.e., watching an aerobics video. Sometimes an activity to engage the mind is needed, i.e., watching the morning news. Be sure to record this information on Form 15. Some nonexercise equipment to consider:

- Equipment may be needed to play music for aerobics, dancing, or any exercise. Some people will use an MP3 player with head phones or ear buds to listen to music.
- A large easy-to-read clock may be needed for timing the exercise period or other activities. It should have a second hand, or count seconds.
- Mirrors on multiple walls can be used to ensure proper form.
- A juice bar, water cooler, beverage center, or small refrigerator could add to the exercise experience by providing refreshment.
- A massage table or massage area may also be required.

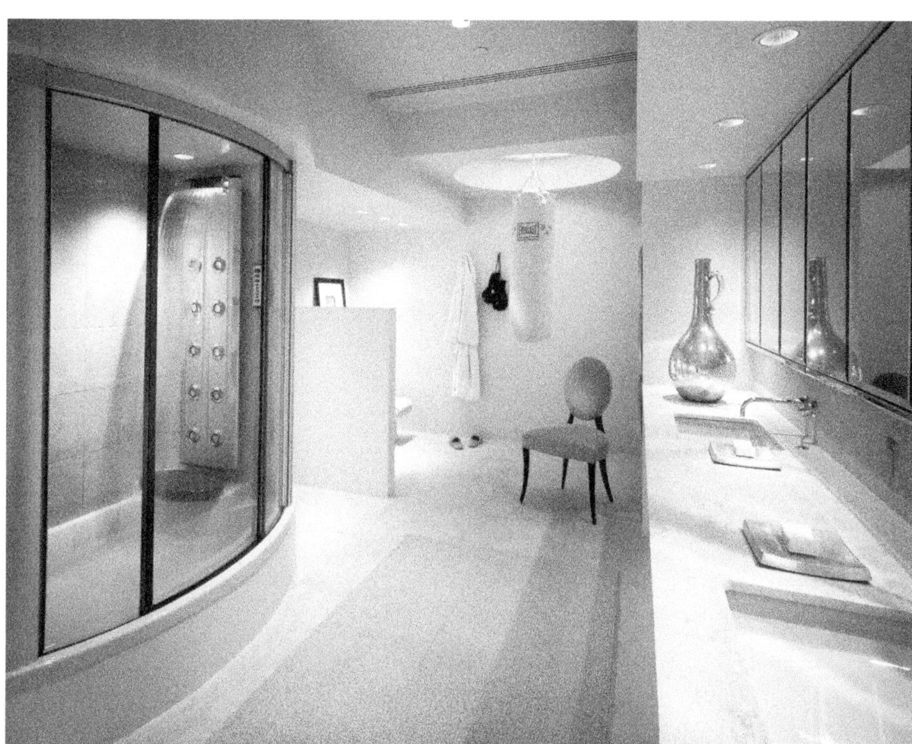

FIGURE 9.17 The luxury shower is conveniently located adjacent to this exercise area with punching bag.

Courtesy of Kohler Company

Mechanical and Structural Requirements

Some exercise equipment and audio visual equipment require electrical connections and wiring considerations. Most home equipment requires 120 volts and 20 amps, but some commercial equipment may require dedicated 240-volt receptacles. Floor receptacles may be desirable to reduce tripping hazards from cords. Some exercise equipment is oversized and the entry door needs to be planned to get the equipment in the room. Some exercise equipment is very heavy. Make sure the floor of the exercise area can handle the weight. In addition, the floor needs to be stiff enough to handle the stress of jumping and pounding from exercise activities.

Consider cushioning the entire floor with a dense mat to protect it and to help prevent transmission of sound to areas below, caused by jumping, loud music, or dropped weights. In addition, wall construction and/or treatment should be planned to limit sound transmission to adjacent rooms. See chapter 2, "Infrastructure Considerations" for more information on sound transmission through walls.

Use indirect lighting to avoid glare when the user is in a variety of positions. Fluorescent lamps do not put out as much heat as halogen or incandescent lamps. Avoid ceiling-mounted or hanging light fixtures or pendants that could accidentally be damaged during exercises. See chapter 7, "Mechanical Planning," for more information about lighting.

Plan for proper ventilation that will remove moisture and odor released into the air by exercising bodies. Information about ventilation is included in chapter 7.

Space Planning for Exercise

Use the anthropometric stature and body breadth measurements found in Chapter 4, "Human Factors and Universal Design Foundation," as a guideline when figuring minimum floor space for exercises such as situps and pushups. Form 1: Getting to Know Your Client can help you obtain information about your clients' measurements. The client's side arm reach, forward thumb tip reach, vertical grip reach, and buttocks-leg length should also be considered when planning for stretching or calisthenics. These are a minimum.

When possible, use human body measurements from the largest percentile. If more than one person is using the space, plan for clearance between people. *Human Dimension and Interior*

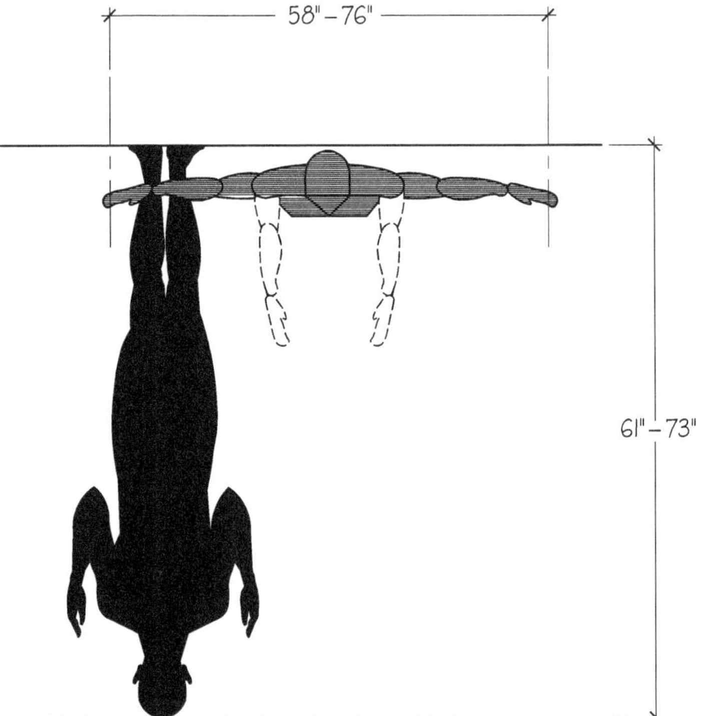

FIGURE 9.18 Consider the space needed to stretch out on the floor and to conduct exercise while standing. The range of measurements given is for small women to tall men.

Based on Human Dimension & Interior Space *by Julius Panero and Martin Zelnik, 1979, Watson-Guptill Publications.*

Space recommends 3 inches (76 mm) to 6 inches (152 mm) between two persons' arms extended to the side. Keep in mind that exercise implies movement, and someone who is exercising may not remain centered in the space. Be generous with clearances.

Ceiling Heights

In no other space in the home is ceiling height as critical as in the exercise area. This is especially true when an exercise program includes activities such as jumping jacks, jumping rope, or plyometrics, which may include jumping up and down on boxes or platforms. Dancing that includes lifts of another person requires a recommended ceiling height of 12 feet (144 inches; 3658 mm).

Equipment

Sizes: To develop the space plan and to determine if the space is adequate, measure the existing equipment or obtain manufacturer's specifications on new equipment, just as you would for other fixtures and appliances in a bathroom.

The American Council on Exercise (ACE) has guidelines that can quickly help determine the space needed for common exercise equipment.

- Treadmills: 30 square feet (2.9 square meters)
- Free weights: 20 to 50 square feet (1.9 to 4.6 square meters)
- Bikes, recumbent and upright: 10 square feet (0.9 square meters)
- Rowing machines: 20 square feet (1.9 square meters)
- Stair climbers: 10 to 20 square feet (0.9 to 1.9 square meters)
- Ski machines: 25 square feet (2,3 square meters)
- Single-station gym: 35 square feet (3.3 square meters)
- Multistation gym: 50 to 200 square feet (4.6 to 1.9 square meters)

Clearances: In addition to the dimension of the equipment, you must also provide a clear path of travel between each piece of equipment. There should be 30 inches (762 mm) minimum clearance or 36 inches (914 mm) if the client uses a mobility aid. Also consider how much additional space is needed for an exercise. For example, you may need to measure the length of the leg that extends past the bench during a leg extension strength exercise.

If a game system is used to provide instructions and feedback for exercise or dancing, generous clearance space should be provided for the space to work properly and for the movement involved in exercises. The user will need to be 3 feet (914 mm) to 10 feet (3048 mm) away from the sensor on the game system. Space in that area should also be large enough that the user can perform the movements promoted in the games. Also, these games are enjoyed by multiple users, requiring more space.

Storage

Like most activities, exercising requires "things" and they may need to be stored within, or close to, the exercise space. The section on closets provides some details for planning these spaces, but make sure you determine if the following are needed, and how they are being provided.

- Closets for equipment if it is stored after each use, or if an exercise area is to be used for a separate function
- A locker area for clothes, shoes, and accessories such as towels or water bottles
- A bench or place to sit for putting on shoes and socks
- A hamper for used clothes, socks, and towels
- Storage near exercise equipment for reading material such as books, magazines, or newspapers
- Storage for games, CDs, or DVDs

THE HOME SPA

The luxury of the spa experience is being captured in the homes of many clients seeking relaxation and pampering. The popularity of day spas and resort spas has many consumers seeking their own space for caring for mind, body, and soul. The home spa will be very individualized, depending on the client's desires. Different types of activities and equipment can be included, and the space can grow out of an existing bath or become a featured space in the home.

Some of the special features in a spa bath that provide hydrotherapy are a whirlpool tub, a soaking tub, a steam room, sauna, a massage table, and a chaise or sofa. Other spa activities could include chromatherapy and aromatherapy. Spaces for yoga and meditation might also be included in this space.

There are many considerations that must be addressed when designing a spa. Some of the information is gathered in the client assessment (chapter 5, "Assessing Needs"), but there may be some special questions such as:

- What type of spa activities would the client like to engage in? Clients may request activities that they have experienced in a resort or day spa, such as steam baths, massages, and saunas. Do they want to accommodate just one activity or multiple experiences?
- Who will be using the home spa? Will the spa be used by the adults or shared by family and guests? How many people will be using the spa at any one time? A soaking bath may be a private activity for one, while a spa tub might be used by a group. An assistant may come in to give a massage or pedicure.

Location

Often home spas are part of the master bathroom (Figure 9.19). It may already have a separate tub and shower, and upgrading or expanding the fixtures could create a spa space in the regularly used bathroom. Separating the spa area from the regularly used bath can create a space focused on the relaxing experience, not the day-to-day hassles of the morning rush to work.

FIGURE 9.19 This large master spa bathroom includes an elegant soaking tub.
Courtesy of Aquatic

FIGURE 9.20 This 60-inch (1524 mm) whirlpool tub will fit in many smaller bathrooms. *Courtesy of Kohler Company*

Whirlpool baths are increasingly being requested for guest and secondary baths, and smaller fixtures (Figure 9.20) can be fitted into tradeout installations. This allows all family members and guests to have a pampering bath.

A separate family spa close to the pool or outdoor hot tub might also be desirable in some homes. This location implies a social experience. Of course, a bathroom will be needed nearby for showers and dressing.

An outdoor component can add to the more traditional spa experience. An appropriate calming and beautiful view (Figure 9.21), or a privacy garden, can be important to meditation and relaxation. Sliding doors and windows can bring in fresh air and breezes. In addition, some spa activities can be conducted outside when the weather is appropriate.

Home Spa Activities

There are many activities, procedures, or therapies that a client may be interested in having in their home spa. Some require specialized equipment, discussed in the next section, along with space planning requirements. However, some can be accomplished with spa products and very little extra space, still providing the client with a luxury experience. The following section explains some terms your clients might use in describing the activities they would like to have.

Hydrotherapy

This is the most basic treatment that can be offered in a home spa. Hydrotherapy uses water as the primary facilitator to treat muscles and reduce stress. Different forms of hydrotherapy include jetted or whirlpool baths, jetted showers, underwater massage, Vichy showers, Swiss showers, Scotch hose (to provide water pressure to certain areas), foot or hand baths, and combining hot/cold water treatments (Figure 9.22).

FIGURE 9.21 A calming view and natural light add to the enjoyment of a bath.
Courtesy of Kohler Company

Thalassotherapy

This is a long-term treatment of seawater in baths, showers, and mud wraps. The premise is that the body absorbs the minerals from the seawater through osmosis. Thalassotherapy is supposed to help clear out the blood and keep the body in a balanced state. It might also be used as an inhalant to aid the upper respiratory tract. In a seawater bath (balenotherapy), the water is heated to 93°F (33.9°C) for optimal skin treatment.

Cleansing Steam

Steam baths offer a way to cleanse and relax at the same time. In a steam bath, the humidity reaches 100 percent and cleans out the body's pores. A lukewarm shower follows the steam bath to add to the relaxing experience. Or a cold shower can be invigorating. Clients might want a steam bath or shower, or may plan to use a steam tent over a massage table.

Heat

The sauna uses dry heat and humidity at 15 percent to warm and relax the body. The low humidity is created by pouring water on hot rocks. Users go into the sauna for 5 to 15 minutes after a short shower. They sit or lay on wooden (cedar) benches in the insulated sauna room. They follow this with another shower, or visit the pool or plunge bath and then rest for a few minutes. Finally, they return to the sauna for about 20 minutes and then rest for 20 minutes before a final shower and light snack.

Heat therapy rooms use infrared heaters to radiate heat to the body. Infrared rooms operate at a lower temperature than saunas, maintain normal room humidity, and take less time to heat up. Pre-built units have some similar features to a sauna: cedar or alder lining, cedar benches with

(a)

(b)

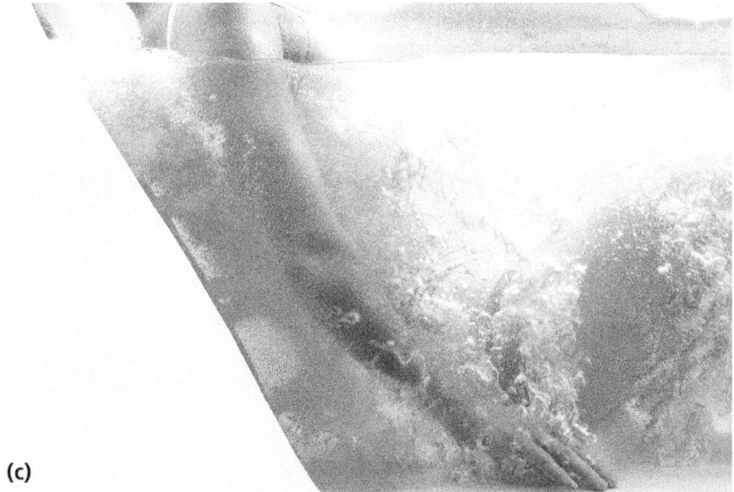

(c)

FIGURE 9.22 Hydrotherapy tubs can use jets, air, or a combination.
Courtesy of Aquatic

backrest, doors, controls, and lighting. Infrared heat can be used for warm-ups for athletes, physical therapy, or massages.

Chromatherapy

Color often has personal associations that lead to color preferences for certain spaces and activities. Various shades, tones, and intensities of blue and green are often considered soothing and are used in spa areas. Reds and yellows are considered warm and more active. It is important to talk to clients about their color preferences and associations.

Chromatherapy describes colored lights that are thought to influence the user's mood. Different colors have different effects. For example, to assist in relaxing, the bather turns off all room lighting and focuses on the colored light (many may choose blue) from the tub, while practicing deep breathing and visualization techniques. Red is considered a stimulating color which is supposed to activate blood flow and would help a person taking a shower to wake up and get ready for the day. Several manufacturers have incorporated light choices into plumbing fixtures that can be controlled by the user (Figure 9.23).

Facials, Exfoliation, and Body Wraps

These are several beauty treatments that can be conducted at home. A facial involves steaming and deep cleaning the face, followed by a massage, a mask, and moisturizer. Exfoliation is a way to remove dead skin from the entire body. It can be done simply by using a loofah with a graining paste in the shower. Body wraps might involve wrapping the body in a hot tea-soaked sheet. Another skin treatment is a body mask of mud.

Meditation and Yoga

Meditation has been suggested as a way to focus energy, reduce stress, and gain calm. Yoga is a specific technique for combining body movements, breathing, and meditation. Quiet spaces are needed. Shrines or focal points may be requested to focus thoughts during meditation.

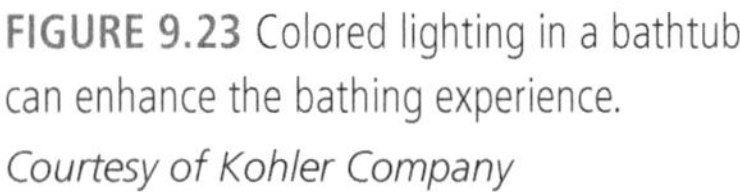

FIGURE 9.23 Colored lighting in a bathtub can enhance the bathing experience.
Courtesy of Kohler Company

Massage

There are many types of massage treatments and body works that are used to help clients to relax, reduce pain, and tone muscles. The specific type of massage will depend on the massage therapist and the needs of the client. Although the bath designer will not need to know all of the types of massage treatments, it might be helpful to be familiar with a few of the techniques.

- Cranio-sacral massages focus on the head and neck area to loosen tight neck muscles.
- Deep tissue massage releases tension in deeper muscle layers by using slow strokes and finger pressure on contracted muscle areas.
- Feldenkrais massage is a clothes-on massage that helps with sports injuries and tension.
- Reflexology is a massage based on a system of points or meridians in the hands and feet that correspond to organs in the body.
- Reike is a body work technique using subtle stationary hand positions on points of tension or injury.
- Shiatsu is a body work technique of acupressure used on pressure points to improve energy flow.
- Swedish massage uses long strokes, kneading, and friction techniques to relax muscles.
- Trager body work techniques help with joint movement.

Spa Supplies and Equipment

A home spa will need certain basic supplies and equipment, but it could be created in a bathroom with a bathtub and shower. The items depend on the treatments the client is using, but may well include candles, body brushes, loofahs, sponges, scrubbing mitts, oils, moisturizers, muds, towels, sheets, pillows, and a varied supply of nail care products. The more elaborate treatments require wet rooms and lounge chairs.

Whirlpools

Whirlpools or jetted bathtubs are one of the most requested items in new and remodeled baths and provide the client with a form of hydrotherapy. Many new homebuyers expect a whirlpool tub in the master suite, and whirlpools are frequently placed in remodeled bathrooms that contain a tub and shower. Small 60 inch by 32 inch (1524 mm by 813 mm) models are available and are more efficient with both water and energy used to heat. Deep two-person models are also available.

Consider who will be using the whirlpool and how much space they require. The shape of the seating, padding, and angled support determine the user's comfort while in the tub. Ideally the client will be able to sit in a working tub before selecting it, to see if it is comfortable and if the water action meets their expectations.

Whirlpools are filled with heated water each time they are used. They have different jetted actions that move the water in the tub. This is an important variable in design and selection of the units. Some may have jets that force the water out at certain locations. Other jet actions may move the water in a rotating pattern.

The number of jets and their location in relation to the bather (Figure 9.24) determine how effective they are as hydrotherapy. Air bubblers may line the bottom of the tub creating a soft massaging movement. The number of jets, and the integration of jets and air bubblers, will affect the quality of the whirlpool experience. The system should be integrated so that it works efficiently.

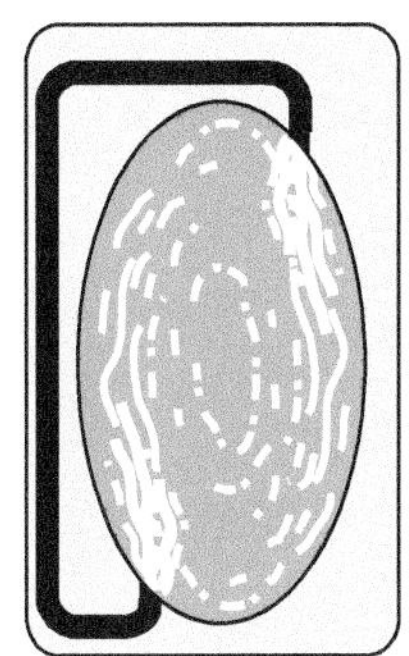
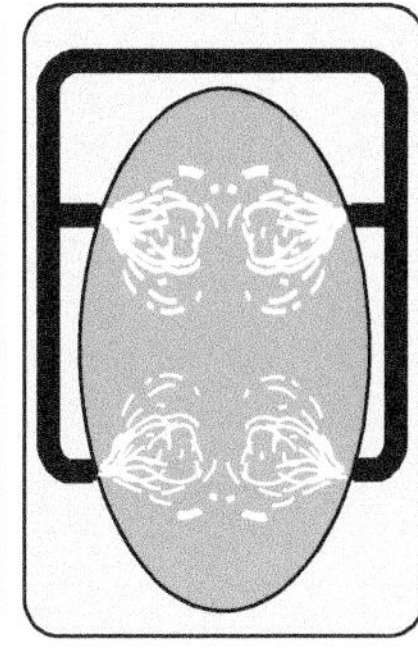

FIGURE 9.24 Whirlpool jets can be placed in different locations to create different patterns of water movement.
NKBA

Whirlpool users will sit in the warm water (103/104°F [39.4/40°C] for adults) for about 15 to 20 minutes. It is important to think about the user's view (Figure 9.25), which is why the tubs are often placed at a window. Some tubs come with DVD/CD/AM/FM stereo surround sound systems and plasma screen televisions, so the user can listen to relaxing music (or watch an action movie if desired). Tubs also may have different colored lights within the water to enhance chromatherapy.

Other features to consider in selecting a whirlpool are electronic touch pads and remote controls. Extra water heaters, such as an in-line water heater, may be needed to handle the demand of the larger tubs. The designer must plan for the location of the access panels, so that maintenance and repairs can be completed. Often a handheld shower is mounted on the whirlpool tub deck.

FIGURE 9.25 Consider the user's view when planning a whirlpool. Some users may want a view out a window; others may prefer a TV or other focal point, such as a fireplace.
Courtesy of Kohler Company

Spa Tubs

Spa tubs are often referred to as hot tubs. They offer some of the same relaxing options as the whirlpool, but the water remains in the tub and is re-used. The water is thermostatically controlled and stays heated. Skimmers and filters are essential to maintain water quality. An insulated cover keeps the moisture and heat in the tub.

Spa tubs are not used for bathing. Users should shower before entering the hot tub. Some larger hot tubs are more suited for a social area since they can handle up to ten people. Often these are placed outside and are accessible from the public parts of the house.

FIGURE 9.26 Built-in or freestanding soaking tubs are deep, allowing the user to submerge into deep warm water.
Courtesy of Aquatic

Soaking Tubs

Soaking tubs have become a popular option in the spa bathroom. They are deeper than standard tubs—25 inches (635 mm) instead of 15 inches (381 mm)—and they are often longer—as much as 78 inches (1981 mm). They relax the user by having them sink to their necks in warm water (Figure 9.26). Users should shower before entering, since soaps are not to be used in soaking.

Some of these tubs are freestanding and come in a variety of materials, such as copper, wood, acrylics, and marble. The form of the tub can be designed to support the back or legs. A Japanese soaking tub is smaller and deeper, with a seat that the bather uses to submerge into the water.

Often soaking tubs are designed for a wall- or floor-mounted faucet. A larger hot water tank will be needed and extra reinforcement in the floor is necessary to support the weight of the filled tub.

Steam Bathtubs or Showers

These bathtubs or showers can be freestanding, or a system can be added to a standard shower or tub/shower design. The same considerations presented in chapter 6, "Bathroom Planning," for designing a shower should be followed. However, the shower or bathtub must be sealed from the edge of the fixture to the ceiling to create the steam room. Seating is needed (Figure 9.27) and the controls must be placed within the steam room (Figure 9.28).

Saunas and Infrared Rooms

These are separate insulated rooms lined with cedar (Figure 9.29). In a sauna, a separate heater with rocks is placed in the room. Water can be sprinkled on the rocks occasionally to create steam at a low humidity to relieve the dryness in the sauna. In an infrared room, multiple infrared heaters are placed along the wall to provide direct heat on each user. The sauna or infrared room should allow at least 4 square feet (0.37 square meters) (6 square feet or 0.56 square meters is preferred) of space per person. The doors must swing out and should not lock. The sauna should be planned with the shower located nearby.

The bench in the sauna or infrared room should be 24 inches (610 mm) deep to allow for sitting and lying down. It should be about 18 to 20 inches (457 to 508 mm) high. A slanted back can also be provided to add a place to recline. Benches can be tiered to provide more seating, but a higher ceiling may be needed (Figure 9.30).

FIGURE 9.27 A steam shower should have good shower design features, such as a seat, storage, and a grab bar. It should be completely enclosed to seal in the steam.
Flikr

FIGURE 9.28 Controls are placed within the steam room.
Courtesy of Mr. Steam

FIGURE 9.29 Prefabricated saunas can fit into the home spa area.
Courtesy of Helo

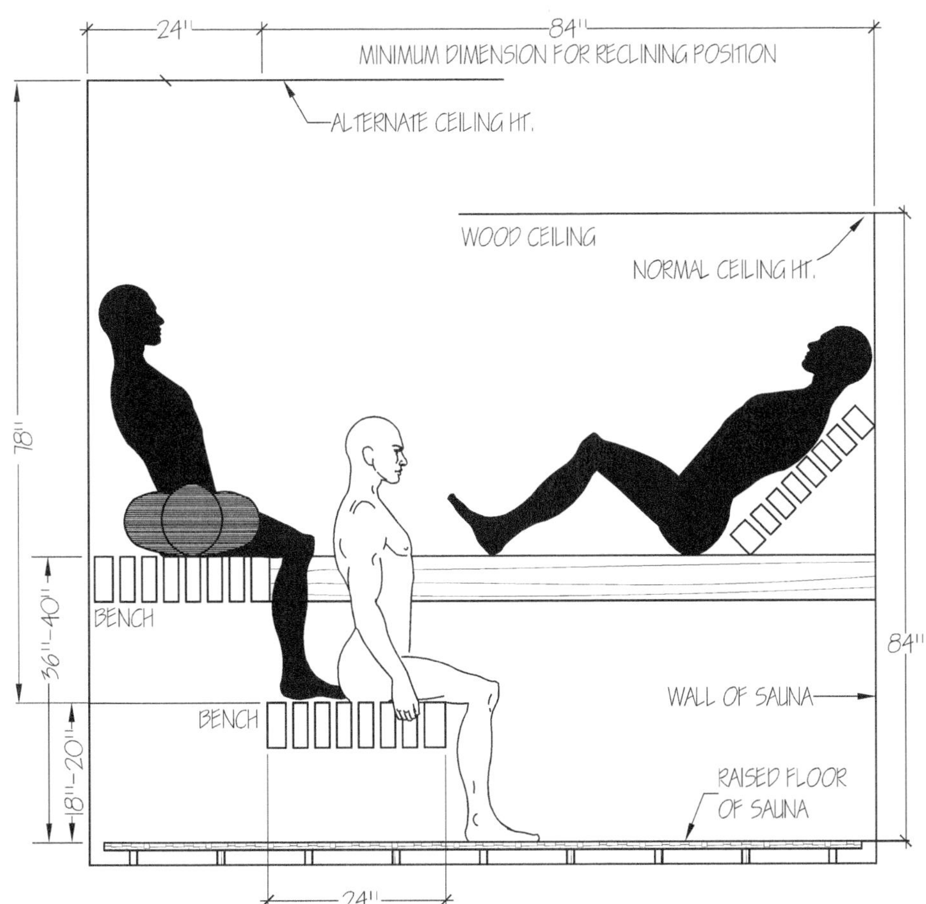

FIGURE 9.30 A sauna layout should consider bench height and depth, ceiling height, and floor clearance.
Based on Human Dimension & Interior Space *by Julius Panero and Martin Zelnik, 1979, Watson-Guptill Publications p. 254*

Vichy Shower

This system provides hydrotherapy from an overhead shower rainbar with several showerheads. The user lies in a wet spa bed while a therapist administers the shower treatment. Handheld showerheads might also be used to pin-point water pressure on specific areas of the body. The wet spa bed may have a drain or be incorporated onto a wet room that will drain the water.

Massage Tables

These tables can be portable or stationary, and electric lifts are available to adjust the height of the table. A standard size table ranges from 69 inches (1753 mm) to 73 inches (1854 mm) long and 26 inches (660 mm) to 37 inches 940 mm) wide, depending on manufacturer and model.

Utilities and Infrastructure

Several pieces of hydrotherapy equipment will require extra water heaters, either larger tanks or on-demand heaters. Extra support in the floor may be needed to handle the weight of the equipment, especially when filled with water. Electrical service will need to be planned to accommodate the heaters and pumps. Extra plumbing and electrical requirements may call for extra wall and floor space. Access panels for maintenance and servicing of equipment should be planned. These and other considerations are discussed in chapter 2, "Infrastructure Considerations" and chapter 7, "Mechanical Planning."

Lighting

A variety of lighting will be needed in the spa area to support different activities. General indirect lighting should be provided for the safe use of equipment and for dressing. Many treatments are accomplished under low lights which are calming and relaxing. Some people use candles for lighting and for the aromatic effect during a relaxing soaking bath.

More focused task lighting may be needed for facials, manicures, and pedicures. Other task lighting may be needed for preparing essential oils and other types of mixtures, reading, and some food preparation. Lighting is discussed in more detail in chapter 7, "Mechanical Planning."

Ventilation

Any hydrotherapy or steam treatment will put a great deal of moisture into the air, which must be removed with proper ventilation afterward. Special care should be given to indoor spas or hot tubs, since warm water remains in the tub and chemicals are used to treat it. Strong odors and candle soot may need to be removed through ventilation. Refer to the ventilation information in chapter 7, "Mechanical Planning," and the indoor air quality information in chapter 3, "Environmental and Sustainability Considerations."

Floor Space

The design recommendations for special spa fixtures are the same as those for bathtubs and showers presented in chapter 6, "Bathroom Planning." Check the measurements of the fixture or equipment specified and allow adequate clearance in front for access. Here are some key points:

- A recommended clear space of 30 inches (762 mm) is needed in front of any fixture.
- Space for larger dressing circles should be included (42 to 48 inches; 1067 to 1219 mm).
- At least 30 inches (762 mm) should be planned around massage tables or other equipment where an assistant or therapist might be applying treatment.
- Control valves should be reachable from both outside and within the fixture.
- Access panels should be easy to get to for repairs and maintenance.

Seating and Refreshments

A lounge area such as a chaise, or chair and ottoman, might provide another way to relax in the home spa along with storage for reading material.

Many spa activities suggest that the client have refreshments, especially something to drink, during or after, similar to exercise. A refreshment center may be needed in the spa area to store water, juice, and healthy snacks, and a water cooler or a refrigerator would be a helpful feature.

The refreshment center might expand to a mini-kitchen if more extensive food preparation is desired. Some aromatherapy treatments require that mixtures be cooked or distilled. Although these treatments may be prepared in the kitchen, a small cooktop in a spa area may not be out of the question.

Storage

The home spa will need some of the same items and thus, some of the same storage, as found in the more typical bathroom. For example:

- Towels will need to be located near the various fixtures, and a place to store extra towels will be needed. Often larger bath sheets are used as wraps. These require more space to hang and store.
- Robes and soft-soled shoes may be used and kept in this area. Plan hanging space or hooks for robes, and shelves for shoes.
- There may be several different types of bottles, jars, sponges, brushes, candles, foot massagers, portable steamers, and other items used in some treatments. Consider shelves and drawer storage for them.
- Several treatments require mixing ingredients, so bowls, measuring cups, and spoons may be needed.

Fireplace

A fireplace may be desired in a luxury bath or home spa (Figure 9.31). Although it might be considered a secondary heat source, it is more likely to be used for its ambience, to set a relaxing and romantic mood. Several types could be included such as masonry fireplaces, vented gas fireplaces, or direct vent fireplaces. Unvented gas fireplaces are available, but are not approved for use in some states.

FIGURE 9.31 A fireplace adds warmth and ambience to a spa area.
Courtesy of Kohler Company

The masonry fireplace is the traditional wood-burning fireplace. It will require a hearth and a chimney with flue. It will need to be planned by a professional to assure that it is properly sized to draw correctly. Wood will be needed, and the fireplace will have to be cleaned regularly.

A fireplace that uses vented gas logs also relies on the hearth and chimney with a flue. A direct vent system does not require a chimney and can be placed in many different locations. Ductwork from the outside provides air for the system and removes waste to the outside. Check local building codes for installation requirements.

Installing a fireplace will add to the space requirements. Check the clearance required between the fireplace and any combustible materials. Include adequate circulation space around any hot surfaces.

SUMMARY

There is so much that can be added to the bathroom. Determining the lifestyle needs of your client is an important step in the interview and assessment process. Do they need their life enhanced by an organized and expansive closet? Or does the convenience of having the laundry near the dirty clothes appeal to their efficiency? Are they concerned about their health, wanting to stay active and in shape? Or does the pampering and relaxation of spa treatments represent their desire to take care of themselves? Whatever the client might want, you should be able to assess their space and budget and look for ways to enhance their lifestyle.

REVIEW QUESTIONS

1. Why is good ventilation important in a closet or clothes storage area? (See under "Closet Placement" page 304)
2. What is the typical depth of a closet? What is the depth and height of the placement of the closet rod to accommodate most adult clothes? (See "Hanging Clothes Storage: Depth, Height" pages 308 and 309)
3. Access to storage, whether it is in a closet or laundry, needs to be designed with similar principles and considerations. What are these? (See "A Place for Everything," "Storage Principles," "Access and Clearance Space," "Design Decisions," "Storage," "Space Planning for Exercise" pages 304, 310, 313, 317, 328, and 334)
4. What criteria can be used to recommend energy- and water-efficient laundry appliances? (See "Laundry and the Environment" page 322)
5. Describe various types of exercise and the equipment that would be needed to perform each type. What are the implications for space planning with each of these? (See "Exercise Equipment" page 332)

Putting It All Together

Design is a process—but not a neat, tidy, linear process. Moving from the idea, or the wish, for a new bathroom to the finished product involves much going back and forth, checking and rechecking. A bathroom design involves a dose of inspiration, a spark of creativity, but mostly a lot of hard work.

This book has presented a considerable amount of information about bathrooms, what to include and how to arrange the space. It has emphasized how to gather information about your clients to help focus your design to meet their needs and desires. This chapter will help you figure out how to organize this wealth of information and translate it into an actual bathroom design.

The first part of this chapter discusses the overall *design process*, how to move from an idea to a complete design. The second part focuses on the *design program*, the part of the design process where you organize all your information and ideas into a plan for the bathroom design. The third part, the *design drawing*, presents a method to move from a conceptual design to an actual design layout. Throughout are examples of a simple bathroom design moving from program to drawing.

While the focus here is on developing a single design drawing through use of the design process, in reality, you will probably use this process to develop several alternative designs to present to your client. These alternatives will then be evaluated by you and your client in making the final selections for the bathroom design.

Learning Objective 1: Describe and explain the stages of the design process.

Learning Objective 2: Identify and describe the parts of a typical design program.

Learning Objective 3: Use a design program to develop a completed design drawing.

THE DESIGN PROCESS

There are many different ways to approach design, probably as many as there are designers. As you gain more experience, you will develop a method and unique style that is personally successful.

If you are a new designer, you can benefit by following a formal structure for the design process. This will help you become adept at sequencing the steps in developing a design and assure that

Summary of the Design Process

- Identify and describe the client.
- Organize the information.
- Identify the activity spaces.
- Visualize the activity spaces.
- Develop the visual diagram.
- Refine the visual diagram.
- Think in three dimensions.
- Evaluate the plan.
- Think about details, details, details.

no parts of the process are forgotten. If you are an experienced designer, by reviewing a formal design process, you may get a fresh approach and spark new creativity. What follows is a brief discussion of one approach to the design process that is used by the authors.

- **Identify the client**. Gather information about the client. This is both the tangible—such as anthropometric information and a list of items for storage—and intangible, such as ambience desired in the space or style preferences. Chapter 5, "Assessing Needs," provides a detailed guide to gathering information and assessing client needs. You may also want additional research at this stage, learning about things such as products or materials that the client wants. You also want to make sure that you are informed on issues that will influence design decisions, such as the need for accessible design, sustainable product choice, or multiculturalism.
- **Organize the information**. Develop the first part of your design program by determining the goals and objectives for the design. Prioritize the needs and wants of the client and identify the limitations of the project. (Design programming will be discussed in more detail later in this chapter.)
- **Identify the activity spaces**. Develop the second part of the design program by preparing the user analysis. The user analysis is a chart or table that groups design by the major activities that will take place in the bathroom space. (See Table 10.1 for an example of a user analysis.) In most cases, this will mean that you are organizing information by the activity centers described in Chapter 6, "Bathroom Planning."

  Check your user analysis against the client needs assessment information (chapter 5, "Assessing Needs") to make sure that you have accommodated the client's priority needs. You may even want to share the user analysis with the client as a double check.

- **Visualize the activity spaces.** This is the stage when you are moving from verbal and quantitative information to visual ideas. Many designers use bubble diagrams to represent activity spaces or various centers, and to explore the relationships of the different spaces. For example, you may have a bubble for the bathing center, another for the toilet area, and so on. (See Figure 10.1 for an example of a bubble diagram.)
- **Develop the visual diagram.** Select the best two or three bubble diagrams for refinement. Prepare a room outline, to scale (1/2 inch equals 1 foot or a ratio of 1 to 20 in metric with mm or cm as your base), and note project parameters, such as walls, windows, or doors that are fixed in location.

  Start using templates for each center or activity space, and place them on your room outline using the bubble diagrams as your guide. A template is a scale drawing representing the fixtures, cabinetry, and clearances for a center or activity space. (See Figures 10.2, 10.3, and 10.4 for examples of design templates.) Templates allow you to see how spaces fit together and how your design ideas will work in the actual bathroom space. Templates can be created by hand drafting or in computer-aided design software.

  Check your visual diagram against the user analysis. Have you included all the requirements?

- **Refine the visual diagram.** You will be moving from the bubble diagram to the arrangement of templates to a sketch of a floor plan. Work in scale! Evaluate your visual diagram against the project parameters.

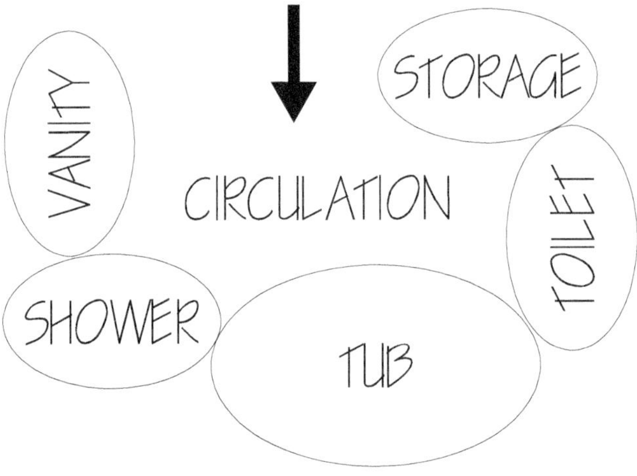

FIGURE 10.1 A bubble diagram is a simple sketch to show how different activity areas can be arranged in the bathroom space. Each "bubble" is an activity area. This bubble diagram is an example of one bathroom arrangement designed for clients Adia and Leroy. The same bathroom design will be carried through in Figures 10.4 to 10.11.
NKBA

- **Think in three dimensions.** Use elevation or perspective sketches to develop the vertical elements for your design. Changes in the floor plan may be required.
- **Evaluate the plan**. Check the preliminary design against the design program. Review the relationship of the centers. Evaluate zoning and circulation within the bathroom as well as in relationship to adjacent rooms. Evaluate your plan against the Bathroom Planning Guidelines (see Table 10.3) and, if appropriate, the Bathroom Access Standards (see Table 10.4). Check your plan against any additional building code requirements.

  Review the preliminary plan with the client. You may be working with more than one design option at this point, so gather feedback from the client.
- **Think about details, details, details.** Lay out the preferred design of the bathroom in dimensioned drawings. Select and specify the actual fixtures, cabinetry, materials, and other items in the space, so that you can verify sizes, installation requirements, clearances, and other details. Review product specifications against client priorities and realities as determined in the needs assessment and your research. Check dimensions to make sure that everything will fit as you envision.

  Review the final design with the client. Prepare the appropriate contract documents, such as needed for construction, code review, cost estimates, and bids.

The design process may not be complete at this point. For example, client review may require you to revise your plan. Or, products specified may, in fact, not be available. However, thinking through the parts of the design process does allow you to be thorough and careful, and results in a better design in the long run.

THE DESIGN PROGRAM

Let's imagine that you have just completed an exciting meeting with your client. Lots of ideas were shared back and forth. Enticing possibilities for a grand bathroom design were explored. You are eager to sketch, pull out material samples, and develop your thoughts into a new design. Ready to go? What, start by writing a design program? **No**, you say, let's just go straight to the design. You can incorporate the client's needs as you go along.

If you skip the design program, how will you know what to design? Design programming is an important and necessary part of successfully completing the design process. When we discussed the design process, did you note how often we recommended you check your developing design against the various parts of the design program? Think of the design program as the contract between you and your client. It is an organized directory of all the client's needs, wants, and wishes for the bathroom design, plus the important parameters of the total design.

Chapter 5, "Assessing Needs," talked about the design program as "both your guide through the design process and the inspiration to your creativity." Developing the design program allows you to make sure you have—and understand—all the information necessary for the bathroom design. A typical design program is in three parts:

- Goals and purpose
- Objectives and priorities
- Activities and relationships

Goals and Purpose

Can you briefly describe the goals of a design project? Think of this part of the design program as the overview. It should include a specific description of the client(s), the type and scope of the project, the budget, and your role and responsibilities in the project. Include the major criteria for the bathroom design and any unique aspects of the project. Most of the information can come from Form 1: Getting to Know Your Client and Form 5: Your Client's Bathroom Preferences found in chapter 5, "Assessing Needs."

You might want to share your goal statements with your client to determine that you have interpreted the project correctly. The statements could also be included in your contract.

Objectives

Objectives are used to operationalize your goals. If goals tell what you want to do, objectives tell how you are going to do it. Objectives are written with active verbs and the outcomes can be measured. Here is an example:

- **Goal:** The bathroom will have a relaxing atmosphere.
  - **Objective:** Install a soaking tub.
  - **Objective:** Put lights in tub area on a dimmer switch.
  - **Objective:** Specify a cabinet for a CD player.

Write objectives to identify the client's major wants and needs. Use the development of the objectives to sort out priorities—must have, should or want to have, and desire or would like to have.

To write objectives for the design program, you will want to focus on the information in Form 5: Your Client's Bathroom Preferences. It will also be important to review Form 3: Checklist for Bathroom Activities and Form 4: Bathroom Storage Inventory as these checklists may reveal priorities. For example, a frequent activity or a need for specialized storage should be reflected in the objectives for the design.

Activities and Relationships

This section is the crux of the design program. Focus on the various activities that will take place in the bathroom and what is needed in the design to support them. You may want to group activities together into centers. For example, teeth-brushing, hair-combing, and face-washing all have similar requirements and could be grouped together as part of the grooming center. Form 3: Checklist for Bathroom Activities and Form 4: Bathroom Storage Inventory are designed in sections by centers so that you can collect activity and storage information in an organized fashion.

Since the focus is on the activities taking place in the space, the emphasis is on who is doing what. Organize the activity information into a user analysis chart. (See Table 10.1 for a sample user analysis chart.) You might want to prepare a user analysis for each center in the bathroom or group of related activities. The user analysis can include the following information:

- Activities that take place in the space
- Who will be doing the activities; the users
- Frequency of activities
- Fixtures, fittings, furnishings, accessories, and any other physical items needed to support the activities, including special sizes or characteristics
- Storage to support the activities
- Amount of space for the activities including clearances, and relationships to other spaces
- Ambience requirements
- Special requirements, such as safety features
- Future changes to be accommodated
- Summary of Planning Guidelines or Access Standards relevant to the activities and requirements of the client and their bathroom

Preparing the user analysis as a chart or table helps to organize the information into an easily referenced format to which you can refer during the development of your design. Using a spreadsheet program or the table function in a word-processing program on your computer makes it easy to prepare a user analysis. However, it is a good idea to leave some open space for extra notes if changes are needed.

As you develop your user analysis, you will be relying on the client interview and needs assessment to determine what activities will take place in the bathroom. Using the prepared assessment forms can help assure that all activities are considered. However, you will want to review your user analysis to make sure that it is inclusive.

Some activities are so common and routine that we might not think about them. For example, your clients might tell you that they brush their teeth at the lavatory (affecting height of lavatory, and

TABLE 10.1 Sample User Analysis Chart*

Activity Space	Users	Frequency	Fixtures, Fittings, Furniture, etc.	Storage	Space and Relationships	Ambience	Special Needs	Future Needs	Guidelines
Shower area—full-body shower: Wash hair; Shave legs	Adia, Leroy	Daily	Tile shower, 48 "by 48" (1219 by 1219 mm) preferred; 42" by 42" (1067 by 1067 mm); minimum: Adjustable height showerhead; Interior seat	Interior shelf for toiletries; Towel rack adjacent	30" (762 mm) clear space for access and door swing; 6" (152 mm) wet wall; Adjacent to bathtub to share wet wall	Adjustable light level; Ventilation fan	Non-slip floor	None noted	Planning Guidelines 4, 9, 10, 11 12, 13, 14, 15, 16, 18, 26

*This will be used in the visual diagram shown in Figure 10.5 for clients Adia and Leroy.

storage for toothbrush and toothpaste), but assume you know that means they also rinse their mouth with water, and then use mouthwash (requiring storage for a drinking glass and the mouthwash).

As you develop the user analysis, it is a good time to review the Bathroom Planning Guidelines and Access Standards that apply to the space you are designing. You can note the number of the Guidelines, as in our example, or note detail, such as "pressure-balanced shower control." This also creates opportunities to determine if the design will meet both current and future accessibility needs of the client.

Reviewing the user analysis also gives you an opportunity to consider other aspects of the design that were not initially identified by the client. For example, for the shower area described in Table 10.1, Adia and Leroy (the clients) may not have considered water conservation. You, the designer, could then recommend WaterSense® showerheads (see chapter 3, "Environmental and Sustainability Considerations," for more information).

Relationship or Adjacency Matrix

The detail you include in your user analysis will depend on the complexity of the project. For a larger project, especially if it involves multiple spaces, you may want to use a *relationship* or *adjacency matrix* (Table 10.2). A relationship or adjacency matrix is a graphic method of organizing the

TABLE 10.2 This is an example of a matrix showing visual access. Similar matrices could be developed for physical access or auditory access. This matrix was used in developing the visual diagram shown in Figure 10.5.

Toilet				
3	Shower			
3	1	Bathtub		
3	2	2	Lavatory	
3	3	3	2	Bedroom

1. Direct visual access acceptable
2. Partial or indirect visual access acceptable
3. No visual access

To read the matrix: you read down a column and across a row from the right to the cell where the column and row meet. For example, the yellow highlighted cell is in the shower column and the lavatory row. There is a number 2 in the cell. That tells us that partial or indirect visual access is acceptable. However, if we look at the pink highlighted cell, in the shower column and the bedroom row, we see that there is a 3, which means that there should be no visual access.

relationships of multiple spaces. The matrix can help you more easily see the types of relationships among activity spaces, and assist in determining how you will group and separate activities into different centers and spaces.

The Four-Stage Interior Design Project

The discussion in this chapter is focused on the design process, from idea to product. We have emphasized the completed design. However, the design process can also include project management, including construction supervision and installation coordination.

A four-stage approach to the design process is commonly used by interior designers, who may also be bathroom designers. The four-stage interior design project includes both the development of the design and management of the project, and is similar in many ways to the discussion of the design process and design programming presented in this chapter. However, review of the four-stage interior design project is another way to examine and expand our understanding of the design process.

STAGE ONE

- Program design and analysis: The first designer-client meeting establishes the relationship and allows the designer to prepare a detailed *design analysis* of the project.
- Proposal: The *proposal* details the stages of the project, services, and products to be provided and fee structure.

STAGE TWO

- Survey and analysis: Stage two begins with a comprehensive *survey* and *measurement* of the space.
- Creativity and concept: A *creative concept* is developed, then analyzed, detailed, and evaluated.
- Space planning and design: Rough sketches of the design are explored until a *drafted presentation* and other visual material is prepared.
- Client presentation: A *professional presentation* is made to the client, supported by various visual materials of the proposed design.
- Client approval: The client provides *written approval* of the proposed design.

STAGE THREE

- Contract documents: *Working drawings* and all *contract documents* are prepared, including:
  - *Specifications* for all interior elements
  - Bids
  - Cost estimates
  - Contracts
- Permits: Designer obtains all necessary approvals for *codes and regulations*.

STAGE FOUR

- Project management: The designer may *manage the project*, or may coordinate with a project manager, to implement the design project. Responsibilities include:

(*continued*)

- Schedule
- Procurement
- Site supervision
- Construction management
- Installation planning
- Completion and client turnover

Reference: Gibbs, J (2005). *Interior Design: A Practical Guide.* New York, NY: Harry N. Abrams, Inc.

THE DESIGN DRAWING

Moving from the design program to the completed design solution is an exciting and creative process. It is also a process that requires accuracy and verification. In this section, we will discuss a process for moving from the design program to a dimensioned design drawing of your design solution. We will emphasize the importance of checking and rechecking dimensions to verify that your design solution will work in "real space." This section tells you how to manage the technical details—you supply the creativity!

Templates

We discussed moving, in the design process, from visualizing the activity spaces with a bubble diagram to developing a visual diagram. As you take your conceptual ideas, the bubble diagrams, and begin refining them, it is important to begin working to scale. First, this gives you a realistic picture of space relationships and possibilities—very important in the often-limited spaces of a bathroom. Second, it helps prevent you from making mistakes. If you work with the right proportions and sizes from the beginning, you tend to "see" the space relationships more clearly and are less likely to misjudge clearances and space needs.

A helpful way to develop your visual diagram is to use design templates (see Figures 10.2, 10.3, and 10.4). A design template is used to represent an activity space or a center, and includes any fixtures or equipment, plus the clearances needed.

For example, you can have a toilet center template, which would show the toilet, plus the recommended clearances in front and to the sides. A shower space template would include the shower, the thickness needed for the plumbing wall, the shower door swing, and clearance for access to the shower.

It is a good idea to prepare design templates in both plan and elevation view. This can be very useful as you evaluate your design in three dimensions.

Draw your design templates in a scale of 1/2 inch equals 1 foot (or in a ratio of 1 to 20 in metric with mm or cm as your base). Since these are the recommended scale for bathrooms drawings, starting in one of these scales will be a time saver.

Based on your design program, you will need to develop a number of design templates for a particular bathroom design. Consider special needs and requests of your client. You may develop alternative templates for the same activity space. For example, you may develop two design templates for different sized showers and then determine which will work best in the final design.

Label your design templates. This will facilitate using them to lay out the bathroom plan. It will also help you develop a timesaving file of design templates for future use. For example, if you have design templates for 36-inch (914 mm), 42-inch (1067 mm), and 48-inch (1219 mm) showers with clearances from one project, you can likely use them on many other bathroom designs. Depending on your preferred style of working, design templates can be saved in computer files or on sturdy paper.

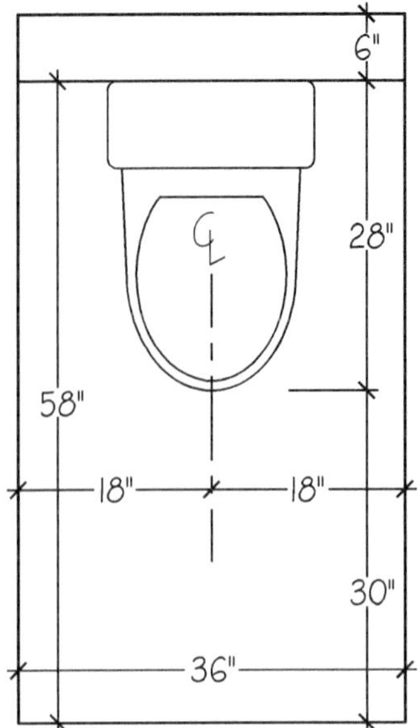

FIGURE 10.2 This drawing is a plan view design template with a standard size toilet, using recommended side (Planning Guideline 20) and front (Planning Guideline 4) clearances. Note that a 6-inch (152 mm) wet wall for plumbing is included in the template.
NKBA

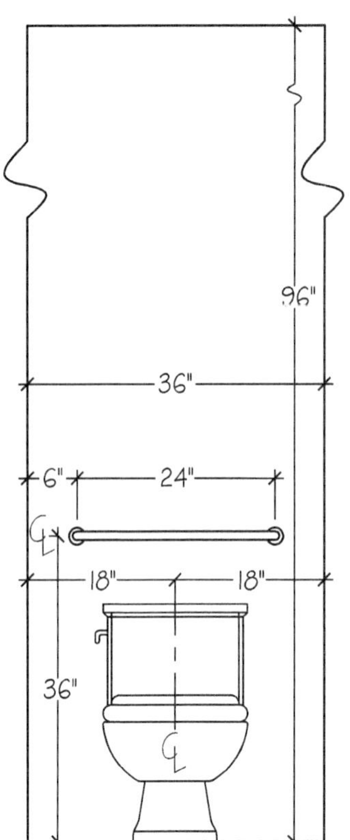

FIGURE 10.3 This elevation design template is a front elevation of a standard toilet with a grab bar on the back wall.
NKBA

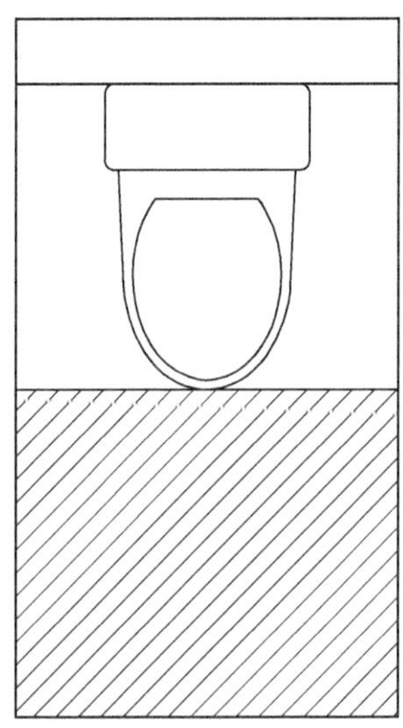

FIGURE 10.4 This illustration is a simplified design template in plan view, drawn to scale with clearance areas marked.
NKBA

ROOM OUTLINE

An important foundation for producing your visual diagram, and eventually your design drawing, is the room outline. The room outline is a scaled drawing of the perimeter of the bathroom space. Prepare a drawing of all walls and fixed structural or architectural features, such as windows and doors.

The information you need to complete the room outline should be found on the following needs assessment forms from chapter 5: Form 7: Dimensions of Mechanical Devices; Form 8: Window Measurements; Form 9: Door Measurements; and Form 10: Fixture Measurements.

In some bathroom design projects, walls, windows, doors, and other structural features are fixed, and cannot be moved or altered. For example, moving windows affects the exterior design of the home, and the client may not want to change this. In other projects, you may have some options to relocate some features or even expand the space. Perhaps a doorway can be moved or an interior wall removed. This is the type of information recorded on Form 6: Jobsite Inspection, and perhaps, Form 5: Your Client's Bathroom Preferences.

You may find it useful to prepare two room outlines. One shows the existing room space as it is. The second removes features that can be changed but retains the fixed features. The second drawing will help you see the possibilities of the space (see Figure 10.5).

You may have other limitations on your design that should be noted on your room outline. All structural, mechanical, electrical, and plumbing parameters need to be noted. For example, the location of one or more plumbing fixtures may be predetermined. Or, the location of heating and cooling vents may be fixed.

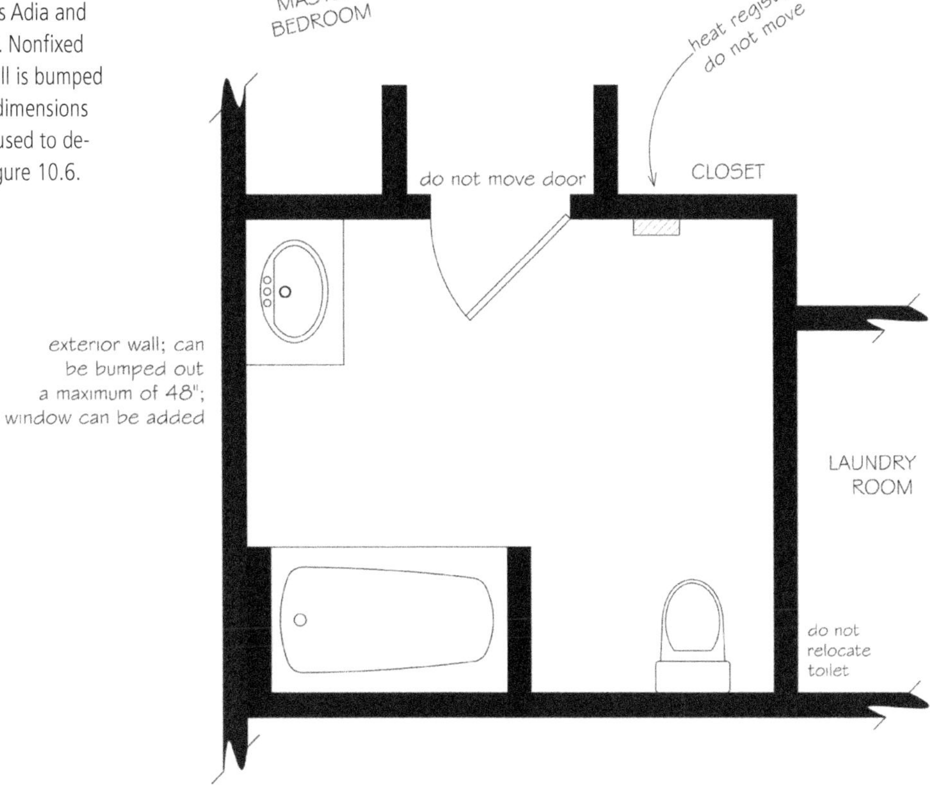

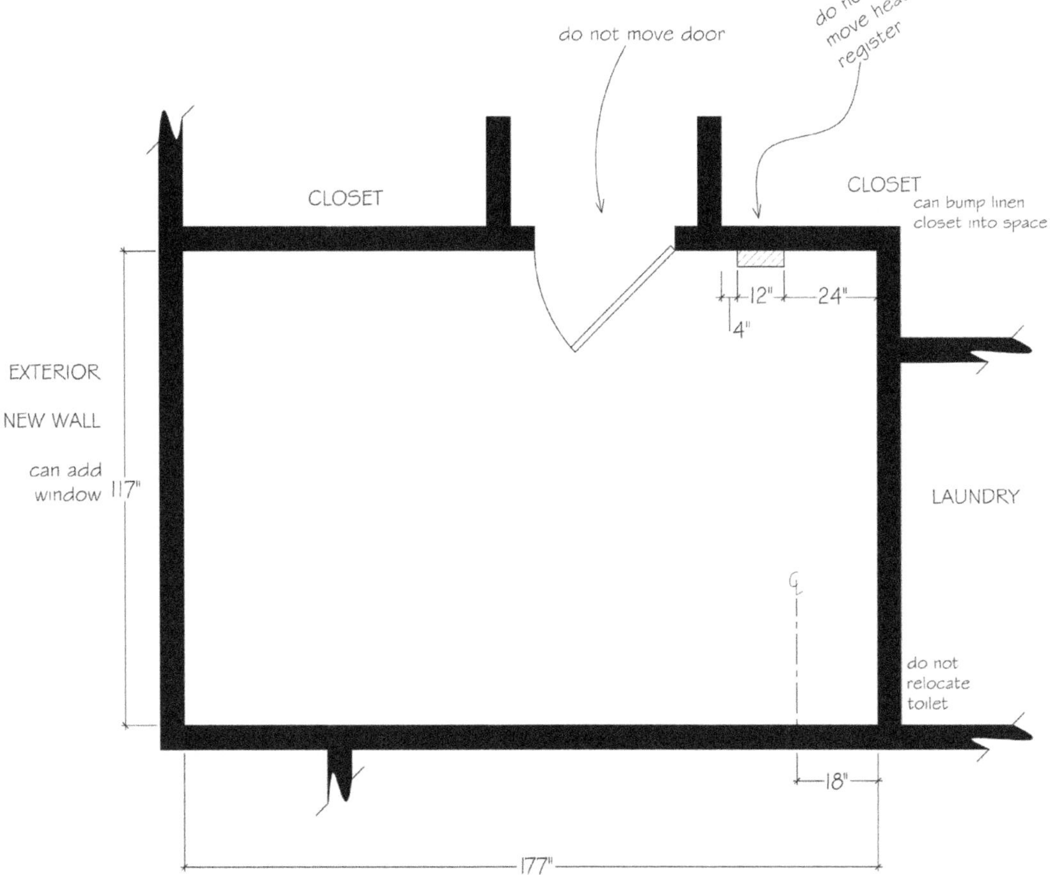

FIGURE 10.5 (A) The existing bathroom space with project parameters for our clients Adia and Leroy. (B) The room outline as altered. Nonfixed features are removed, the exterior wall is bumped out, fixed features are included, and dimensions are shown. This room outline will be used to develop the visual diagram shown in Figure 10.6. *NKBA*

Add any additional information to your drawing that will help in design decisions. Note what types of spaces surround the bathroom. Note interior and exterior walls. The height of windows or any fixed structural features will be useful to know. The location of existing walls (that can be changed) could be noted, if preferred, to allow economical planning of the design.

It is important to note all restraints and options on your room outline. Noting these features helps assure that your design will remain within the parameters of your project.

Verify all room measurements and check your room drawing. The room outline must accurately represent the space of the bathroom.

VISUAL DIAGRAMS

Bubble diagrams suggest ways to arrange spaces in the bathroom. Now it is time to see if these ideas can be translated into a design that will work in the actual space. This is the development of the visual diagram.

Using design templates, try multiple layouts in the room outline. Use the ideas generated by the bubble diagrams to guide your work. Refer to the information on the room outline to see if your design ideas are possible within the existing space.

You will want to try a number of different layouts before you achieve the best solution. As you consider a possible layout, review the information on your room outline that details project parameters. Refer back to the design program, especially the user analysis, to remind yourself what the design layout needs to accomplish.

If you are having trouble getting everything into the space, reconsider the templates you are using. Could space clearances overlap without compromising function or safety? Could a smaller fixture be used and still meet client needs?

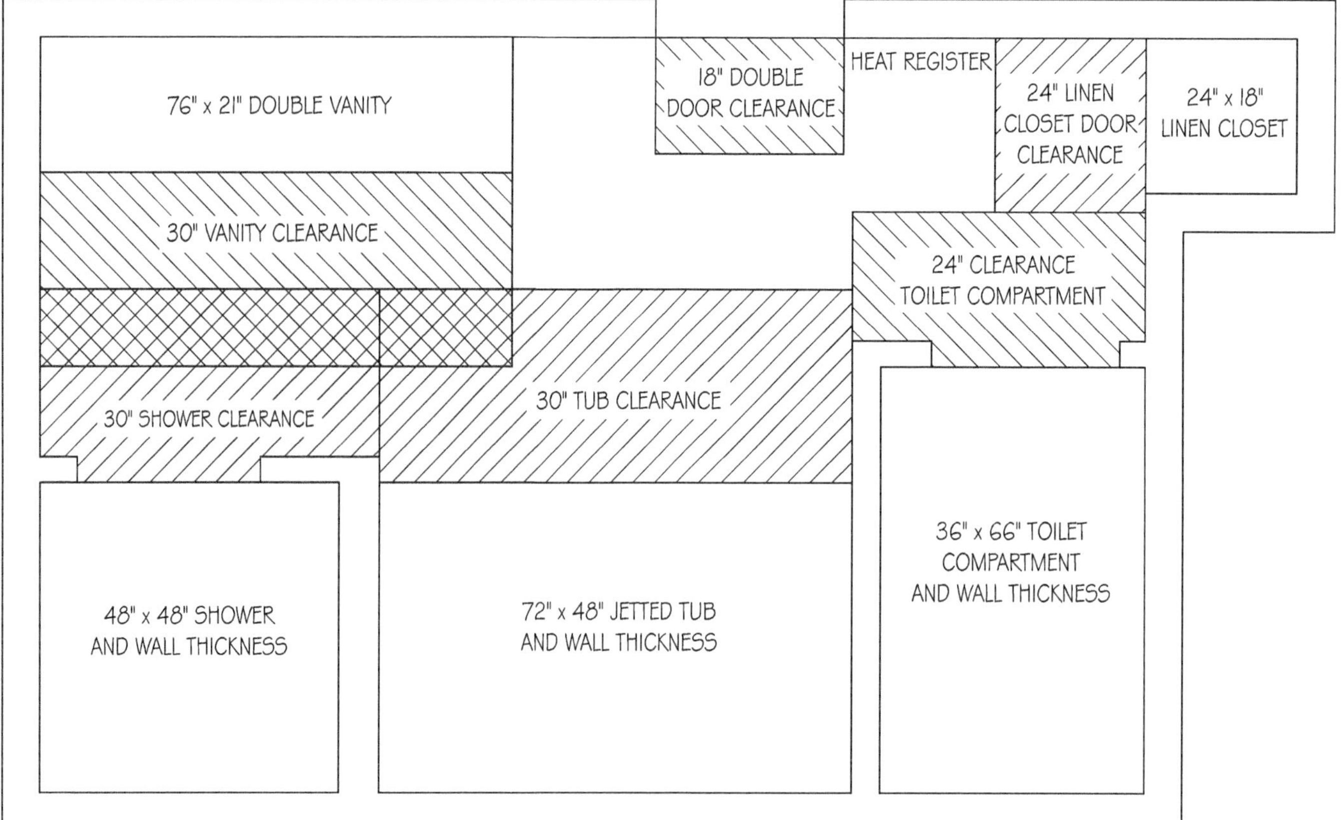

FIGURE 10.6 The visual diagram, for Adia's and Leroy's project, uses the room outline from Figure 10.5, and bubble diagram from Figure 10.1. Using design templates, the only area of overlap is in clearances in front of the lavatory, shower, and tub. However, this layout has adequate clear floor space to meet Planning Guideline 4.
NKBA

Three Dimensions and Vertical Diagrams

Very early in the design process, think in three dimensions. For example, placing the toilet next to the vanity may work fine in plan, but how will it look vertically? We experience space in multiple dimensions, so we must design for all perspectives.

After you have developed one or more visual diagrams that appear to work in plan, develop some three-dimensional sketches. Elevation sketches of a wall, to scale, are useful to evaluate spatial relationships of fixtures, cabinetry, and structural features. Design templates of elevation views can speed the process. You may wish to make notes on your elevations, as you did on the room outlines.

Many computer programs used in design drawing will generate perspective views. This technology is an excellent way to view your design from different angles and evaluate its effectiveness. Keep in mind, however, that these perspectives are interpretive—they give you a sense of the space but do not show all details.

After reviewing your visual diagrams, in plan and vertical views, select the best design layout. Review your design program to determine that the layout meets the goals and objectives. Verify that the design layout is appropriate to the structural and mechanical parameters of the project. For a renovation project, refer back to your onsite measurements of the existing space for verification. If you are working on new construction, consult project documents.

Now you are ready to detail your design solution in a complete dimensioned drawing.

PRIORITY AREAS

Start your dimensioned design drawing with the priority areas of the plan. These are the elements that are not moveable, demand the most space, or are most important to the client. For example, you might start your dimensioned drawing with the toilet area because plumbing connections dictate the location. Or you might start with a shower, because that is going to be the focal element.

Let's say you are going to start with the toilet area. Place the toilet, draw the centerline, and dimension the needed clearances on either side of the toilet. Planning Guideline 20 recommends 18 inches (457 mm) of clearance on either side of the toilet, so place the toilet (in its existing location) so that there is 18 inches (457 mm) of clearance from the centerline to the wall (see Figure 10.8). An additional 18 inches (457 mm) of clearance is needed on the other side of the toilet.

FIGURE 10.7 A rough elevation sketch, taken from the visual diagram in Figure 10.6, begins to show vertical relationships and encourages you to begin thinking about details such as the placement of plumbing fittings and door swings.
NKBA

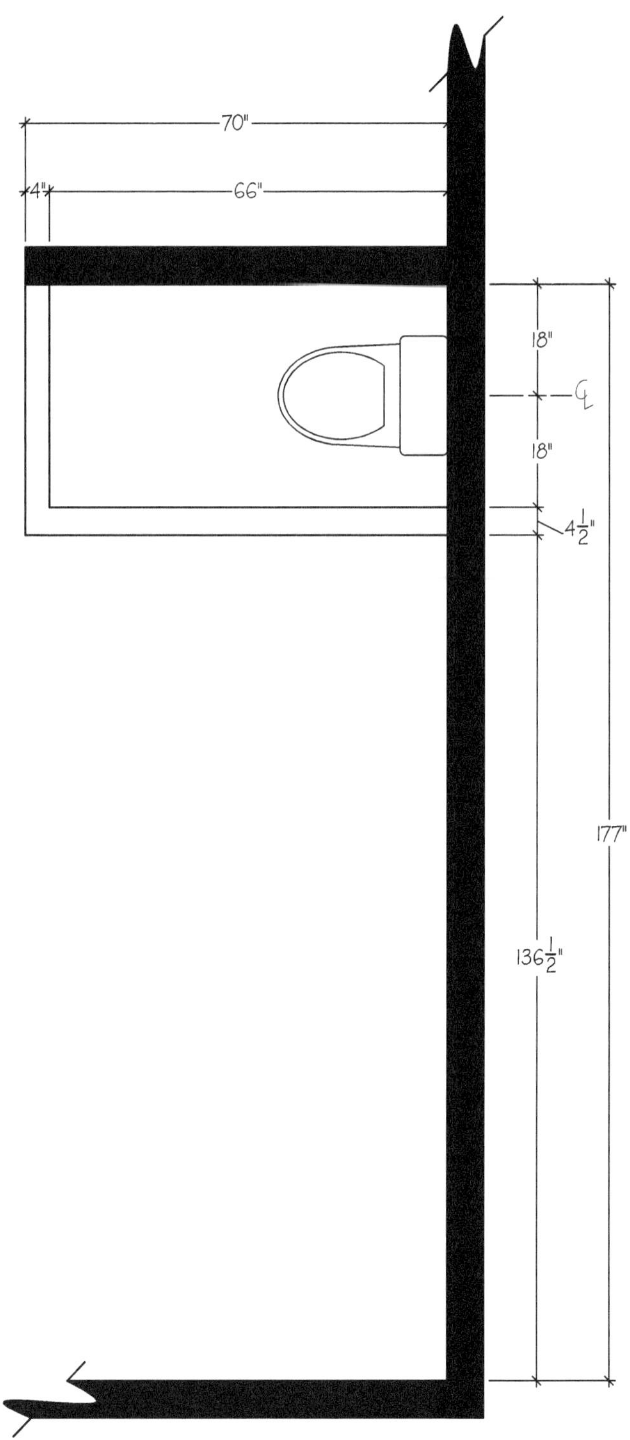

FIGURE 10.8 In this example, based on the visual diagram in Figure 10.6 for clients Adia and Leroy, the toilet compartment is placed first as this location is preferred by the client.
NKBA

In our example, the toilet and clearances take 36 inches (18 inches + 18 inches) (914 mm = 457 mm + 457 mm). Because the toilet will be in a compartment, an additional 4 1/2 inches (115 mm) of wall thickness must be included in our calculations (only one wall thickness is needed as the toilet compartment is against the room wall). Therefore, the toilet compartment uses 40 1/2 inches (1029 mm). The total dimension of the wall where the toilet is placed is 177 inches (4496 mm). So we can determine how much space is remaining for the placement of the jetted tub and custom shower, as is shown here and illustrated in Figure 10.8.

177 inches	4496 mm	total wall length
– 18 inches	– 457 mm	clearance from centerline of toilet to wall
159 inches	4039 mm	
– 18 inches	– 457 mm	needed clearance from centerline of toilet, on opposite side
141 inches	3582 mm	
– 4½ inches	– 115 mm	wall thickness for toilet compartment
136½ inches	3467 mm	available wall length for placement of jetted tub and custom shower

If there is a second priority area in your plan, follow the same procedure for placing the fixture, cabinetry, or other elements. Determine the needed clearances, and subtract from the overall wall dimension. For example, Figure 10.9 shows the placement of the custom shower in the bathroom, after the toilet has been located. In our example, we have allowed 6 1/2 inches (165 mm) for the wall between the shower and the bathtub, so that there is room for plumbing in the wall (wet wall) as well as the installation of ceramic tile—while maintaining a minimum clear dimension of 48 inches (1219 mm) in the shower interior.

After placing the custom shower, verify the remaining wall length, as follows:

136½ inches	3467 mm	wall length remaining
– 48 inches	–1219 mm	shower interior dimension
88½ inches	2248 mm	
– 6½ inches	–165 mm	wall thickness for shower
82 inches	2083 mm	available wall length for placement of jetted tub

Finishing the Floor Plan

After the priority areas are placed and dimensioned, add the other fixtures and features in the plan. Continue checking dimensions by subtracting the amount of clearances for each fixture from the remaining wall space. Be sure to verify dimensions in each direction, such as each side and in front of the fixture. Allow for door swings.

Sometimes, at this point, the dimensions do not work out. You may find that your total space, for fixtures, cabinetry, and clearances comes to more or less than the length of a wall. If this is the case, you may need to consider different alternatives.

If you have extra space, you may decide to increase the clearances around the fixtures. This is a good solution if you do not have a lot of extra space. For example, instead of the recommended 20 inches (508 mm) of clearance from the centerline of the lavatory to a wall, you could increase the clearance to 22 inches (559 mm).

Another alternative is to increase the size of a fixture, such as selecting a 42-inch (1067 mm) shower instead of a 36 inch (914 mm). The same idea could be implemented by selecting a 36-inch (914 mm) vanity cabinet instead of a 30 inch (762 mm). However, if you have a large amount of additional space, you might want to reconsider your design to determine if you have chosen the best solution.

In our example (Figures 10.8, 10.9, and 10.10), we have 82 inches (2083 mm) remaining after the toilet and shower are placed. The jetted tub needs 72 inches (1829 mm). No additional wall thickness is needed as we are placing the tub between two full-height walls. Therefore, we have 10 inches (82 inches – 72 inches = 10 inches) (2083 mm – 1829 mm = 254 mm extra space). We can solve this by adding 6 inches clearance to the toilet compartment (3 inches on each side) (152 mm clearance of 76 mm on each side), and lengthening the deck of the jetted tub by 4 inches (2 inches on each side) (102 mm or 51 mm on each side) (Figure 10.10).

If you are short on space, the solution can be more challenging. As you consider each alternative, review your design program to make sure that changes do not compromise important needs of the design. Think about design solutions that work best for your client. Some ideas for alternatives:

- Reduce the clearances around a fixture. If you have allowed generous clearances, you might reduce one or more of them. In the toilet area, for example, instead of the recommended 18 inches (457 mm) of clearance on either side of the centerline, you might use 17 inches

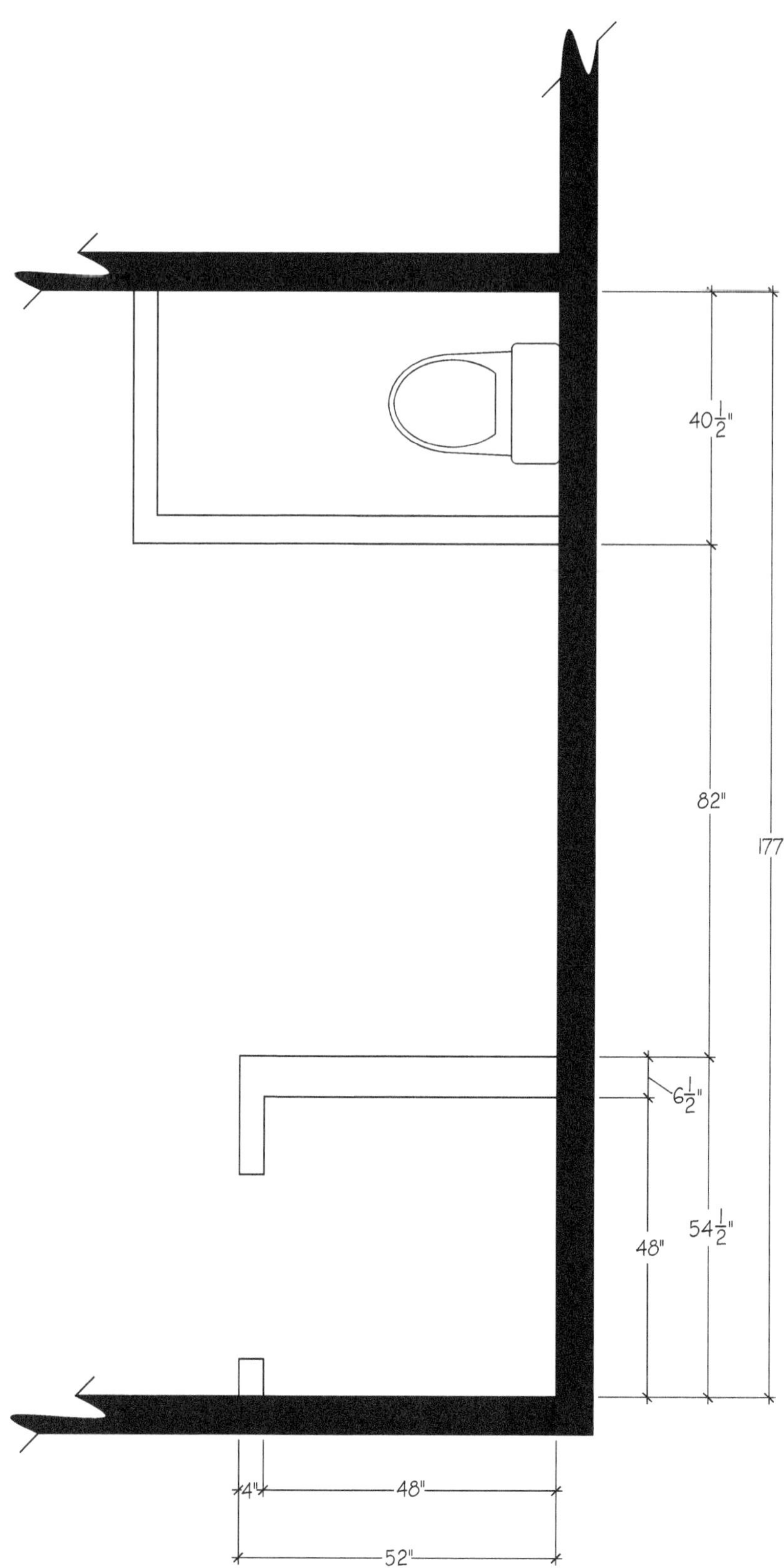

FIGURE 10.9 Continuing the drawing begun in Figure 10.8 for Adia's and Leroy's bathroom design, a 48-inch (1219 mm) custom shower is placed on the same wall as the toilet.
NKBA

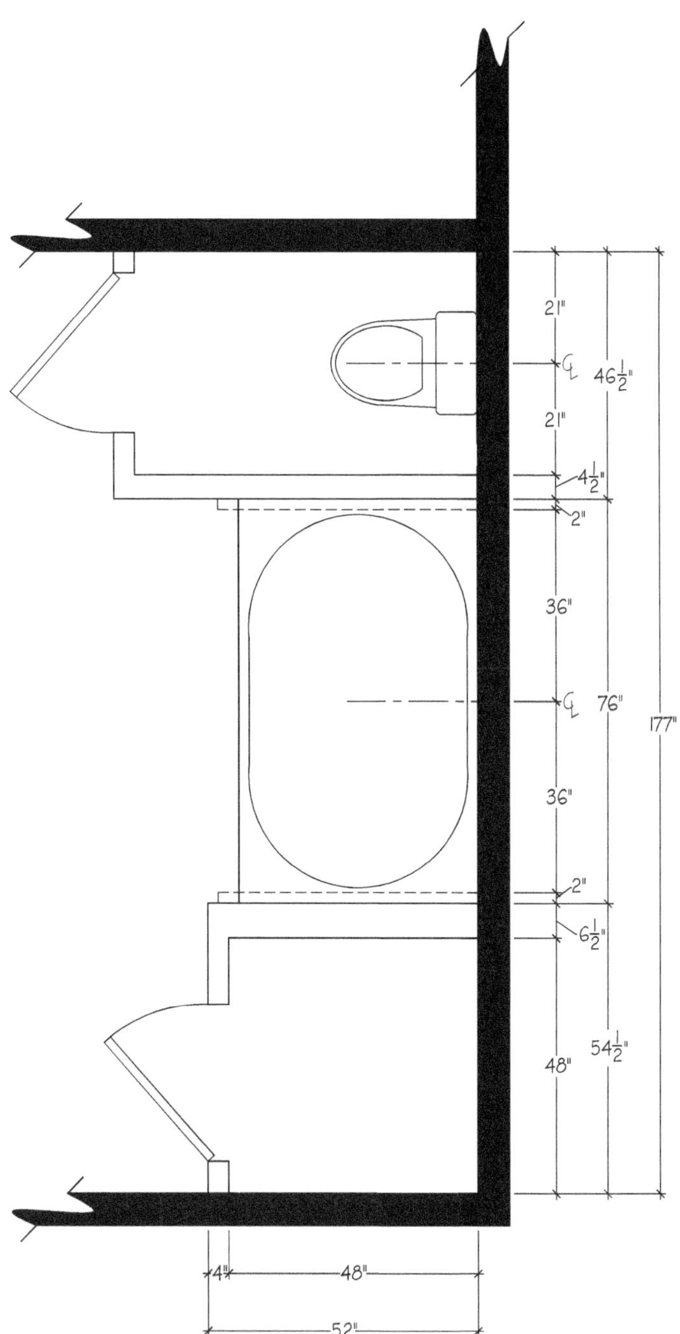

FIGURE 10.10 After adjustments, the drawing of the wall begun in Figure 10.8 is complete.
NKBA

(432 mm) or 16 inches (407 mm). Do not reduce clearances to less than the minimums identified in the Bathroom Planning Guidelines as code-based requirements.

- Use smaller fixtures or cabinetry. For example, instead of a 42 inch (1067 mm) square shower, consider a 42 inch by 36 inch (1067 mm by 914 mm), or 36 inch (914 mm) square shower. Again, make sure that you meet code-based minimums.
- Choose alternative fixtures or design elements. For example, instead of two, side-by-side vanities, each with a lavatory, choose one larger vanity cabinet with a single lavatory, which takes less total space. Or, choose a full-height, pantry-style cabinet to provide the same amount of storage as two vanity cabinets, but in less floor space.
- Choose cabinetry with smaller doors, to reduce door swings. This might be a smaller cabinet, such as going from a 24-inch (610 mm) cabinet to a 21-inch (533 mm) cabinet, or going from

a single-door 24-inch (610 mm) cabinet to a two-door cabinet. However, consider the functionality of the size of the door opening and the continuity of cabinet spacing when making size alterations.

You may need to try several alternatives to make sure your layout fits the actual space. As you are exploring alternatives, be sure that you are working with the actual dimensions of the various fixtures, cabinets, and other items to be placed in the bathroom. Do not depend on the size shown on a drawing template or a generic example in a computer program.

Verify the Dimensions

After you have placed each item on the dimensioned drawing, verify all your dimensions. Start at one corner and check your dimensions across the wall. In our example (Figures 10.8, 10.9, and 10.10), we can verify our dimensions as follows:

177 inches	4496 mm	total wall length
– 21 inches	– 533 mm	clearance from wall to centerline of toilet
156 inches	3963 mm	
– 21 inches	– 533 mm	clearance from centerline of toilet to wall
135 inches	3430 mm	
– 4½ inches	– 115 mm	wall thickness for toilet compartment
130½ inches	3315 mm	
– 2 inches	– 51 mm	extended tub deck
128½ inches	3264 mm	
– 72 inches	– 1829 mm	jetted tub
56½ inches	1435 mm	
– 2 inches	– 51 mm	extended tub deck
54½ inches	1384 mm	
– 6½ inches	– 165 mm	wall thickness for shower
48 inches	1219 mm	
– 48 inches	1219 mm	shower interior dimension
0 inches	0 mm	

Check your math! You can double-check your calculations by adding dimensions, working from the opposite corner from which you did the subtraction.

Vertical Relationships

Dimensioned elevation drawings of each wall of the bathroom are needed to determine the vertical relationships of the bathroom design. You may choose to place all items on the floor plan and verify the dimensions before drawing the elevations, and verifying vertical placement and dimensions. Or, you may choose to work with one wall at a time—place the fixtures, cabinets, clearances, and other elements on the floor plan, and then draw the elevation. If you are developing your design using computer software, you will likely find it easy to develop elevations as you go along.

Begin drawing the elevation of a wall by drawing an outline of the wall, showing the length and height of the wall. Include any architectural and structural features. Dimension these basic elements of the elevation.

Just as you did with the dimensioned drawing of the floor plan, start with the priority areas. For example, if you started with the toilet area, project the centerline and side clearances of the toilet onto the elevation. Sketch the toilet to show the approximate width of the fixture. Mark the height of the fixture—as determined from actual measurements or product specifications—and dimension this on the elevation (see Figure 10.11). Show other details, such as grab bars.

Continue drawing the elevation by adding items from the floor plan for which the height is known, such as cabinets and fixtures. Dimension the heights of each item. Detail items that are important

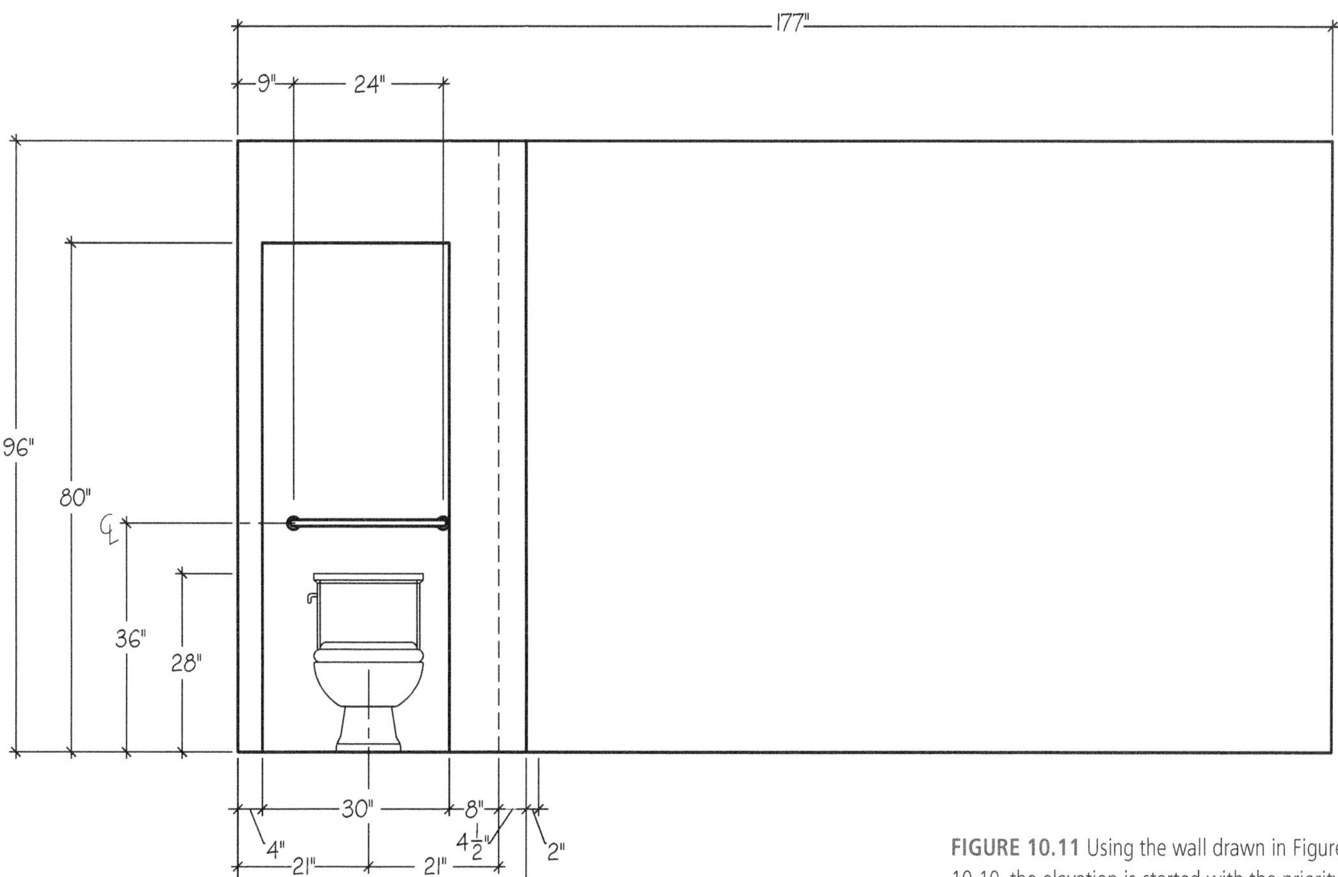

FIGURE 10.11 Using the wall drawn in Figure 10.10, the elevation is started with the priority area of the toilet compartment. This continues the development of Adia's and Leroy's bathroom design project.
NKBA

to the design and the visual continuity of the elevation design, such as cabinet doors and hardware placement.

Now, place items that were not identified in your dimensioned drawing of the floor plan, such as mirrors, towel racks, toilet paper holders, light fixtures, and mouldings. Review the elevation for both the vertical and horizontal relationships of line and shape.

Consider the functional placement of items, such as the relationship of a mirror to the user's eye height, and clearances below towel racks for hanging towels. You may need to do a detail drawing, such as an inside elevation of a shower.

Check all dimensions on the elevation drawing. Verify that individual items are dimensioned correctly and that all vertical dimensions are correctly added.

It is useful to develop all the wall elevations and then compare them together. Consider how your eye will be drawn across the room and the horizontal relationships from one wall to the next. Is there a unity to your design? What type of rhythm is established by the vertical and horizontal elements in the space? Are all the functional requirements of the design program being met?

Evaluating and Checking

Begin the evaluation of your plan by scoring your design against the Bathroom Planning Guidelines using the checklist in Table 10.3. This is an important step to make sure you have developed a design that is functional as well as safe.

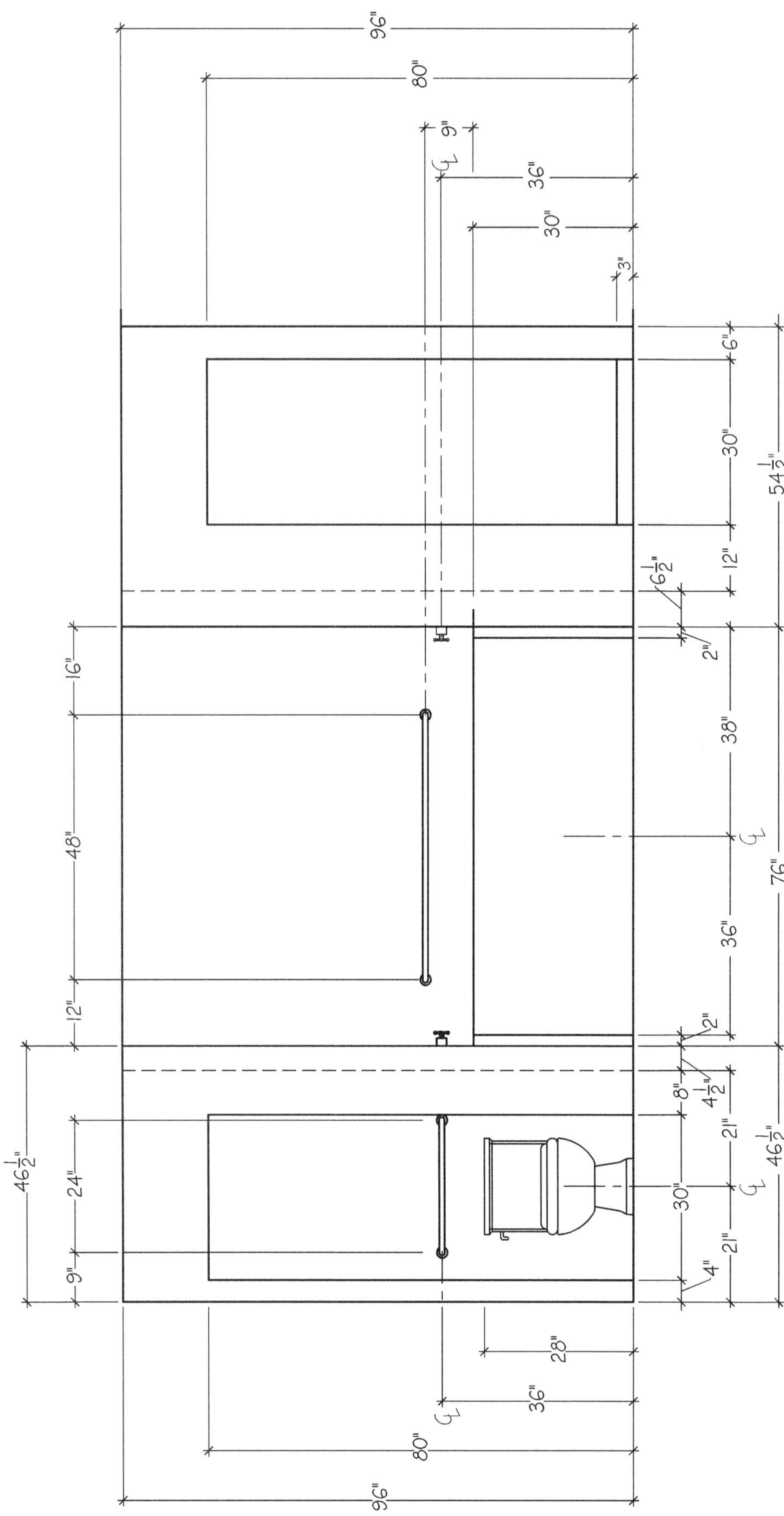

FIGURE 10.12 The custom shower and jetted tub are added to the elevation drawing started in Figure 10.11. Additional details, such as towel bars and plumbing fittings, can now be added to this drawing for clients Adia and Leroy.

NKBA

Review your plan against each Guideline on the checklist. Your design must meet or exceed all the code requirements and should meet the "Recommended" Planning Guidelines, unless there are extenuating circumstances that prevent this from happening.

Depending on your client and their needs, you will also want to review your plan against the Bathroom Planning Access Standards. In your user analysis, you will have noted the relevant Access Standards. Table 10.4 is a checklist to evaluate your plan using the Access Standards.

The final step in developing the design drawing is to check all dimensions and project details. Double-checking for accuracy is critical.

- Verify all jobsite or construction dimensions. If necessary, return to the jobsite and re-measure. The success of your final design is dependent on working from accurate information.
- Verify the construction constraints. Review all mechanical, electrical, and plumbing information for accuracy. Consult the plumber, electrician, or contractor, if needed. Review any structural limitations that impact your design, such as load-bearing walls.
- Verify that the actual dimensions of the space were transferred to the room outline that was the starting point of your dimensioned drawing.
- Verify the placement of all centerlines of fixtures. First, verify the sizes of all fixtures from actual measurements or product specifications, and determine that there is adequate space for all fixtures. Review the clearances for centerlines that are recommended and/or required in the Bathroom Planning Guidelines, and verify that you have met these.
- Verify the size of the cabinets, both vertically and horizontally. Check clearances for door swings.
- Check the dimensioned sizes on your drawing against the product literature for all new product specifications. Make sure you are using current literature and that the products will be available at the time of installation.
- Check the dimensioned sizes on your drawing for any cabinetry, fixtures, or other existing features that will remain in the space against the actual item.
- Verify the centerline placement for all accessories, such as towel bars, just as you did for the fixture centerlines.
- Verify all vertical relationships. Double-check the heights of fixtures and fittings, and review that there will be adequate clearance, as needed above or below items.

PUTTING IT ALL TOGETHER—A SAMPLE PROJECT

Meet Lily and Chen. Their bathroom remodeling project is an example of how to prepare a design program. We interviewed Lily and Chen at their home. We used the various forms and checklists from chapter 5, "Assessing Needs," to collect information for their design project. Then, we developed this design program.

After you read the design program, look at one of the designs that were prepared for Lily and Chen. Do you think the design meets their needs? Is the design solution functional, safe, and convenient? Use the Bathroom Planning Checklists (Table 10.3 and Table 10.4) to evaluate the plan.

This sample design program focuses on space planning, the emphasis in this book. If you were developing a design program, you will give more attention to color, style, and visual impact.

A Sample Design Program

Goals and Purpose

Client description: Lily and Chen are a couple in their early fifties. They are both employed full time as professionals. Chen has Parkinson's disease, which is expected to lead to mobility problems in the future.

Project description and goals: Lily and Chen have a spacious bathroom off their bedroom, which they would like to remodel to be more accessible in the event Chen needs to use mobility

TABLE 10.3 Bathroom Planning Checklist—Guidelines
Use this check sheet to determine that a bathroom design meets all code requirements and incorporates the recommended Planning Guidelines.

Guideline	Code Requirements	Planning Guidelines
1. Door entry is 32″ (813 mm) clear opening		
2. Door does not interfere with fixture		
Door does not interfere with cabinet		
3. Ceiling height over and in front of fixtures is 80″ (2032 mm)		
Showerhead must have 80″ (2032 mm) height clearance		
4. 30″ (762 mm) clear space at all fixtures		
21″ (533 mm) minimum clear space at lavatory, toilet/bidet, tub		
24″ (610 mm) minimum clear space at shower		
5. Single lavatory centered at 20″ (508 mm) or edge is 4″ (102 mm) from wall		
Single lavatory centered on 15″ (381 mm)		
6. Double lavatory centered on 36″ (914 mm) or edge is 4″ (102 mm) from wall		
Double lavatory centered on 30″ (762 mm)		
7. Lavatory between 32″ and 43″ (813 mm and 1092 mm) high		
8. Counter edges clipped or rounded		
9. Shower size at least 36″ x 36″ (914 mm x 914 mm)		
Shower size is 30″ x 30″ (762 mm x 762 mm)		
10. Shower controls 38″ to 48″ (965 mm to 1092 mm), useable inside and outside the spray		
Bathtub controls between tub rim and 33″ (838 mm) AFF		
11. Tub/shower controls pressure balanced and/or thermostatic mixing with temperature limit of 120°F (49°C) Bidets have temperature limit of 110°F (43°C)		
12. Shower includes seat 17″ to 19″ (432 mm to 483 mm) above shower floor, 15″ deep (381 mm)		
Shower seat does not infringe on shower size of 900 square inches (22,860 square mm)		
13.Waterproof material in shower 3″ (76 mm) above showerhead rough-in		
Waterproof material extends to 72″ (1829 mm) from finished floor		
14. Grab bars at tub/shower areas 33″ to 36″ (838 mm to 914 mm) from floor and hold 250 pounds (113 kg)		
Walls reinforced for grab bars at tub/shower		
15. Tempered glass used at tub/shower door, enclosure less than 60″ (1524 mm) AFF and at window and doors below 18″ (457 mm) from floor		
16. Shower door opens out or no shower door		
17. No steps at tub		
18. Slip-resistant flooring		
19. Access panels installed per manufacturers' instructions and instructions provided		
20. Toilet/bidet placed 18″ (457 mm) on center		
Toilet/bidet placed 15″ (381 mm) on center		
21. Toilet compartment is 36″ x 66″ (914 mm x 1676 mm)		
Toilet compartment is between 30″ x 60″ (762 mm x 1524 mm)		
22. Adequate storage is provided		

Guideline	Code Requirements	Planning Guidelines
23. Mirror placed at user height		
Toilet paper 8″ to 12″ (203 mm to 305 mm) to front of toilet, centered 26″ (660 mm) above the floor		
Other accessories located where needed		
24. GFCI receptacles located where needed		
At least one GFCI receptacle within 36″ (914 mm) of outside edge of lavatory		
No switches or receptacles within or accessible from tub/shower		
25. General and task lighting provided, at least one switch at entry		
Light in tub/shower suitable for damp location		
No hanging fixture over tub zone of 3′ (36″) x 8′ (96″) (914 mm x 2438 mm)		
26. Mechanical exhaust vented to the outside		
3 sq. ft (0.278 square meters) window, 50% operable or mechanical system of 50 cfm (1.42 cubic meters/minute or 24 liters/second)		
27. Supplemental heat source		
Room can be heated to 68°F (20°C)		

TABLE 10.4 Bathroom Planning Checklist—Access Standards. Use this check sheet to determine that a bathroom design meets all code requirements and incorporates the Access Standard appropriate to meet the client's needs.

Guideline and Access Standards	Code Requirements	Access Standards
1. Door entry is 34″ (864 mm) clear opening—36″ (914 mm) wide door		
2. Door does not interfere with fixture, cabinet		
18″ x 60″ (457 mm x 1524 mm) clear space on pull side of door		
12″ x 48″ (305 mm x 1219 mm) clear space on push side of door		
3. Code requirement meets Access Standard		
4. Minimum 30″ x 48″ (762 mm x 1219 mm) clear space at lavatory, tub, shower, toilet/bidet		
Minimum 36″x 27″ x 8″ (914 mm x 686 mm x 203 mm) wide knee space		
Transfer space at toilet		
5. Single lavatory centered at 24″ (610 mm) from wall		
6. Bathroom Planning Guideline meets Access Standard		
7. Lavatory controls no higher than 34″ (864 mm)		
Lavatory controls within user's reach, easy to operate		
8. Counter edges clipped or rounded		
9. Transfer shower (36″ x 36″; 914 mm x 914 mm) or		
Roll-in shower (30″ x 60″; 762 mm x 1524 mm)		
10. Shower controls 38″ to 48″ (965 mm to 1219 mm) AFF, offset toward the room, with minimal effort, identified with red and blue indicators		
Include handheld spray unit with minimum 59″ (1499 mm) hose		
11. Code requirement meets Access Standard		
12. Shower includes seat 17″ to 19″ (432 mm to 483 mm) above shower floor, 15″ (381 mm) deep		

(continued)

TABLE 10.4 (*Continued*)

Guideline and Access Standards	Code Requirements	Access Standards
13. Bathroom Planning Guideline meets Access Standard		
14. Grab bars at tub/shower and toilet areas 33" to 36" (838 mm to 914 mm) from floor		
Walls reinforced for grab bars at 250 lbs. (113 kg) throughout bathroom		
15. Bathroom Planning Guideline and code requirement meets Access Standard		
16. Thresholds should be no more than ½" (13 mm) high		
17. Bathroom Planning Guideline meets Access Standard		
18. Bathroom Planning Guideline meets Access Standard		
19. Access panels installed per manufacturers' instructions		
Equipment controls should be between 15" and 48" (381 mm and 1219 mm)		
20. Toilet/bidet placed 18" (457 mm) on center		
Toilet/bidet seat between 15" and 19" (381 mm and 483 mm) AFF		
21. Privacy created at toilet without needing compartment		
22. Storage 15" to 48" (381 mm and 1219 mm) AFF		
23. Full-height mirrors or placed at user height, maximum 40" above the floor		
Toilet paper 8" to 12" (203 mm to 305 mm) to front of toilet, centered 15" to 48" (381 mm to 1219 mm) AFF		
Accessories should be 15" to 48" (381 mm to 1219 mm) AFF		
24. GFCI receptacles located where needed, 15" to 48" (381 mm to 1219 mm) AFF		
25. General and task lighting provided, at least one switch at entry		
Switches 15" to 48" (381 mm to 1219 mm) AFF and operable with minimal effort		
Task lighting beside vanity mirror		
26. Mechanical exhaust vented to the outside, with control 15" to 48" (381 mm to 1219 mm) AFF, operable with minimal effort, easy to read, and with minimal noise pollution		
27. Supplemental heat source, with thermostats at 15" to 48" (381 mm to 1219 mm) AFF and operable with minimal effort		

aids in the future (Figure 10.13). In the existing bathroom, the toilet compartment may be limiting to accessibility. The door to the toilet compartment and access to the closet create a bottleneck in front of the vanity, especially in the morning. The jetted tub is seldom used, and can be removed to provide space for a larger shower. Only one vanity is needed in the bathroom, as a second vanity is going to be put into the adjoining bedroom. Storage is limited in the bathroom.

In their remodeled bathroom, Lily and Chen would like a large, accessible shower, more space around the toilet, a single vanity, water-efficient plumbing fixtures and fittings, improved traffic flow, generous storage, natural light, easy maintenance, and traditional, but simple styling. Lily and Chen want to emphasize sustainability in the choice of products for the bathroom project.

Scope of the Project

The designer will:

- Develop a design that meets the client needs
- Select all fixtures, fittings, and finish materials, considering the priorities of accessibility and sustainability

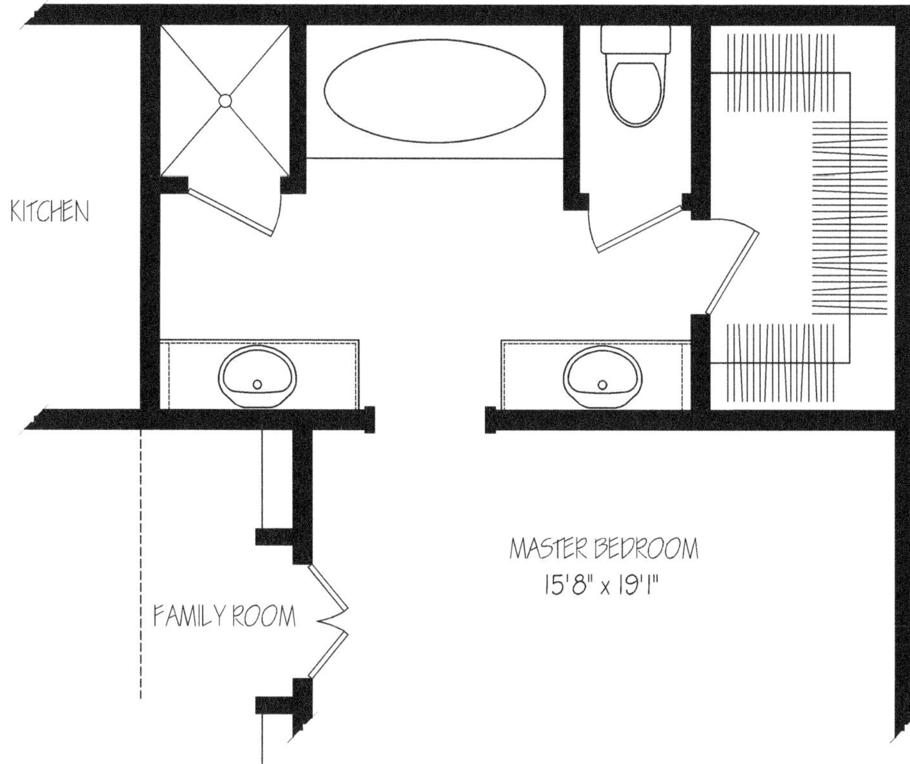

FIGURE 10.13 Lily's and Chen's existing bathroom is spacious but not planned to meet their current or future needs.
NKBA

- Prepare drawings and specifications for completion of the project
- Supervise construction and installation of the project

Objectives and Priorities

- Design a shower that is large enough to use with a mobility aid
- Design an open toilet area that would meet accessibility for a mobility aid if needed in the future
- Provide at least one tall cabinet with generous storage for towels, grooming products, and medicines
- Improve traffic flow to the closet by moving the adjacent vanity and enlarging the door
- Allow a turning circle of 60 inches (1524 mm) in the bathroom
- Design a vanity area with open access space below the lavatory for seated use
- Specify a window in the exterior wall
- Select easy maintenance materials that resist moisture and are simple to clean
- Specify water-efficient plumbing fixtures and fittings, including choosing WaterSense® certified products where available
- Specify sustainable products that are certified to meet standards to the material, including using recycled materials if possible
- Specify materials and products with traditional, but simple styling

Activities and Relationships

A user analysis was prepared for Lily's and Chen's remodeling project, and is presented in Table 10.5.

THE DESIGN SOLUTION

From Lily's and Chen's design program, we developed several bubble diagrams, all of which could be developed into designs. For our example, we drew design templates and laid out the templates

TABLE 10.5 User analysis for Lily's and Chen's Bathroom Design. Information for preparing the user analysis would come from the needs assessment forms. More information about sustainability, materials, color, and style could be added.

Activity Space	Users	Frequency	Fixtures, Fittings, Furniture, Etc.	Storage	Space and Relation-ships	Ambience	Special Needs	Future	Guidelines
Shower area-full body shower, wash hair, shave legs, relaxation	Lily, Chen	daily	tile shower, 60" x 60" (1524 mm x 1524 mm); no threshold, interior seat (flip-up); pressure balance control with on-hand operation & accessible from outside the shower and are water efficient; grab bars;	interior shelf for toiletries: 2 towel bars adjacent	30" x 60" (762 mm x1524 mm) clear space for access	Adjustable light level; ventilation fan	Non-slip floor	Replace shower door with curtain for easier access	Planning Guidelines: 4, 9, 10, 11, 12, 13, 14, 15, 16, 18, 19, 25, 26 Access Standards: 4, 9, 10, 12, 14, 16, 26
Vanity area-teeth brushing, face washing & shaving, hair combing, hand washing	Chen's needs will be primary concern, Lily will also use	daily	vanity counter at least 48" x 21" (1219 mm x 533 mm) and of sustainable material; lavatory 34" (864 mm) AFF integral to counter; fittings operate with one hand and are water efficient; large mirror maximum 40" (1016 mm) AFF; 4 receptacles; energy efficient light sources	drawer storage - minimum 2 15" (381 mm) drawers, more desirable	30" (762 mm) clear space in front; knee space under lavatory; out of path to closet	Adjustable light level; side placement preferred		Ability to sit at lavatory	Planning Guidelines: 2, 4, 5, 7, 8, 23, 24, 25, 26 Access Standards: 5, 7, 23, 24, 25
Toilet area-elimination, reading	Lily, Chen	daily	standard size toilet, low-profile, low-flush; grab bars	toilet paper holder; magazine basket	clear space 56" (1422 mm) from back wall and 60" (1524 mm) from side wall; 18" (457 mm) on centerline for fixture placement	Adjustable light level		Ability to transfer from front or right side	Planning Guidelines: 4, 20 Access Standards: 14, 20, 21, 23, 24
Storage area-towels, grooming supplies, cleaning products, personal hygiene, medicines	Lily will be primary user	daily	tall cabinet, minimum 18" (457 mm) deep and 48" (1219 mm) frontage with 50% pullout shelves		Clear space to include door swing		Hardware operable with one had; mirror on inside of one door	Adjustable height shelves	Planning Guidelines: 1, 22 Access Standards: 1, 22

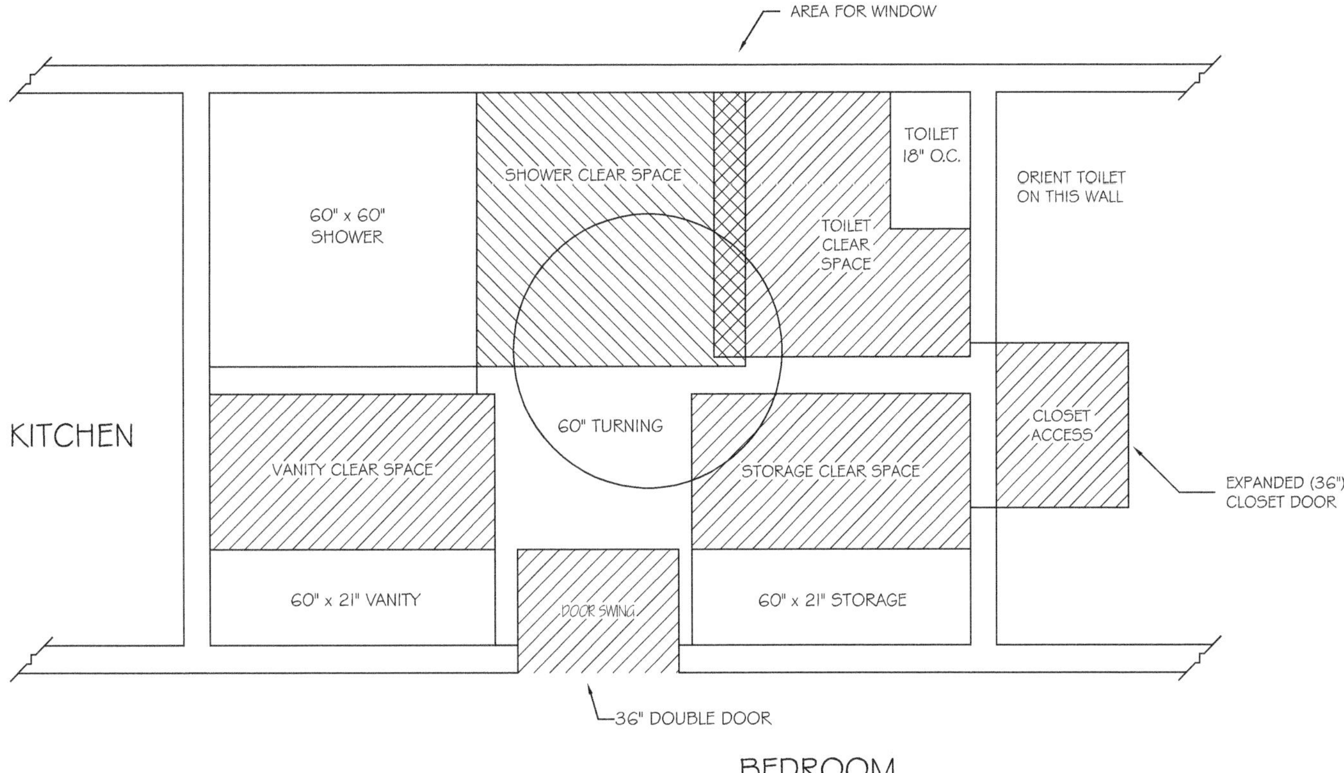

FIGURE 10.14 This visual diagram proposes a design solution for Lily and Chen that will meet their needs.
NKBA

within the room outline for one design. After choosing the best layout, we tried some elevation sketches and then refined the floor plan drawing. Finally, we carefully checked all our dimensions and clearances. Now it's time for you to evaluate our work.

Evaluating the Design

Lily's and Chen's bathroom appears to be a good solution to their objectives and priorities. The spacious shower and generous clearances around the toilet meet the Bathroom Planning Access Standards, and will be desirable in the event of future mobility problems. A window will bring in natural light. A generous amount of storage is provided. The closet can be accessed without interfering with someone using the bathroom fixtures.

However, the positioning of the vanity might be problematic. While the vanity is open for possible seated access or use, the 34-inch (864 mm) clearance between the vanity counter and shower wall might be limiting. Turning the vanity 90 degrees and placing it on the shower wall would provide better access with a mobility aid. This would mean a smaller vanity area (45 inches instead of 66 inches; 1143 mm instead of 1676 mm), but would not limit the overall success of the design in meeting our clients' needs.

Can you suggest other improvements? Perhaps you have ideas that would better meet Lily's and Chen's needs, create a more functional space, be more economical to build, or be easier to maintain? After all, this is where creativity is at work.

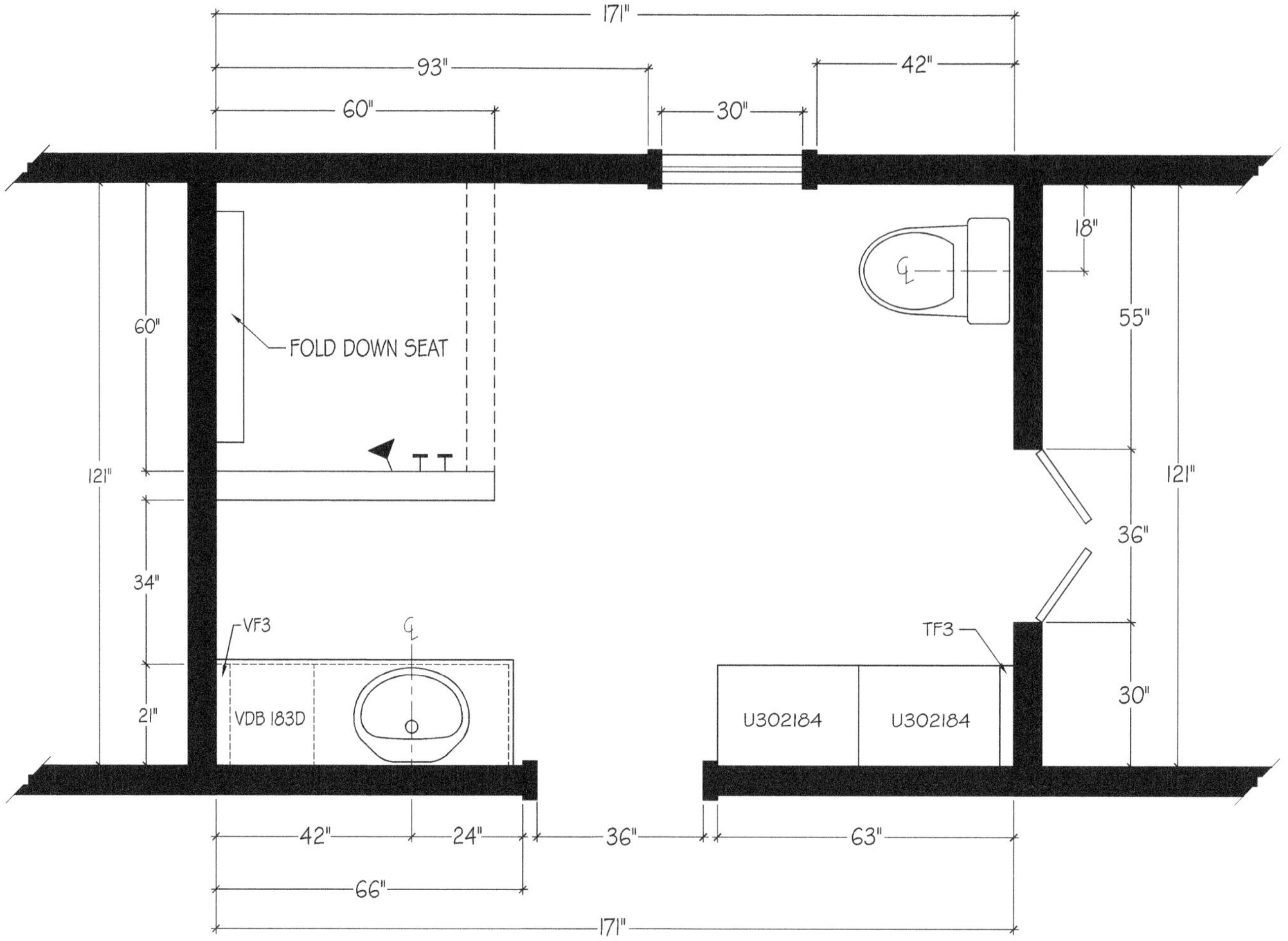

FIGURE 10.15 A large shower, adequate clear space in front of all fixtures, generous storage, a turning circle, and convenient traffic flow are included in the final design.
NKBA

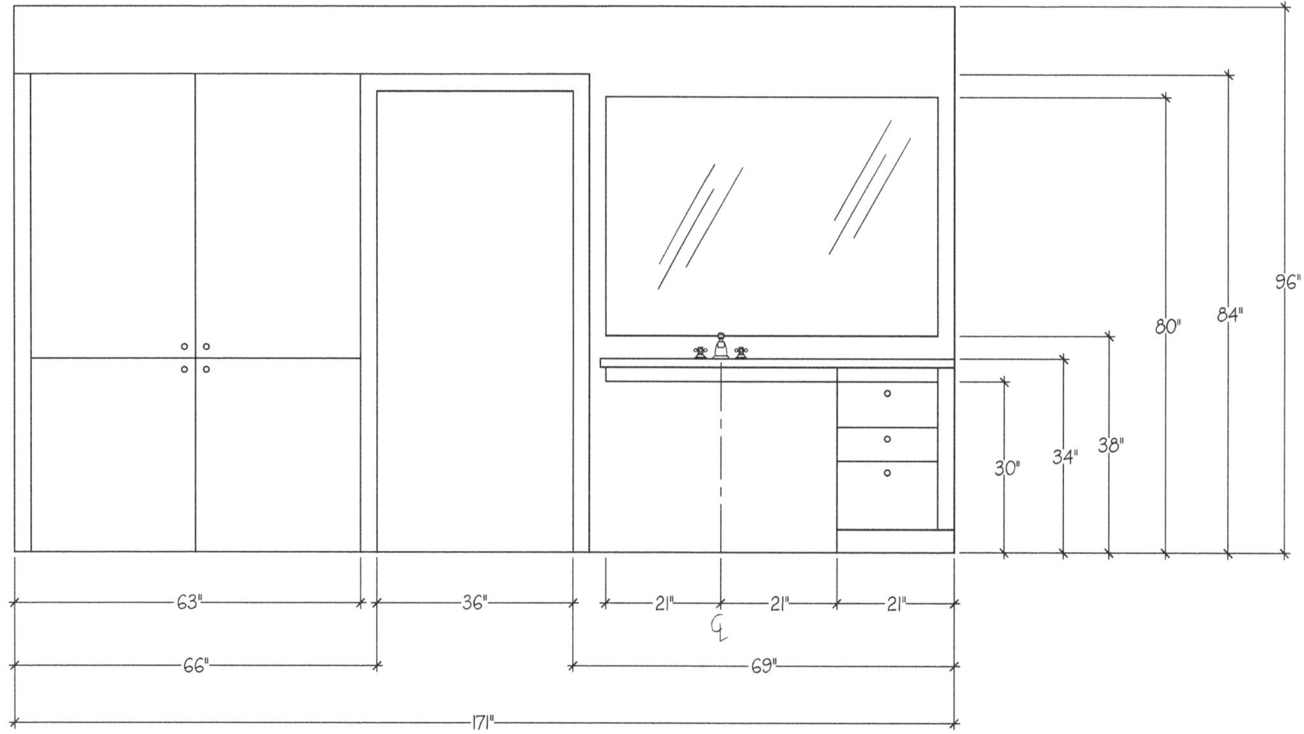

FIGURE 10.16 This elevation shows the vanity wall. Additional elevations should be developed to finalize the design.
NKBA

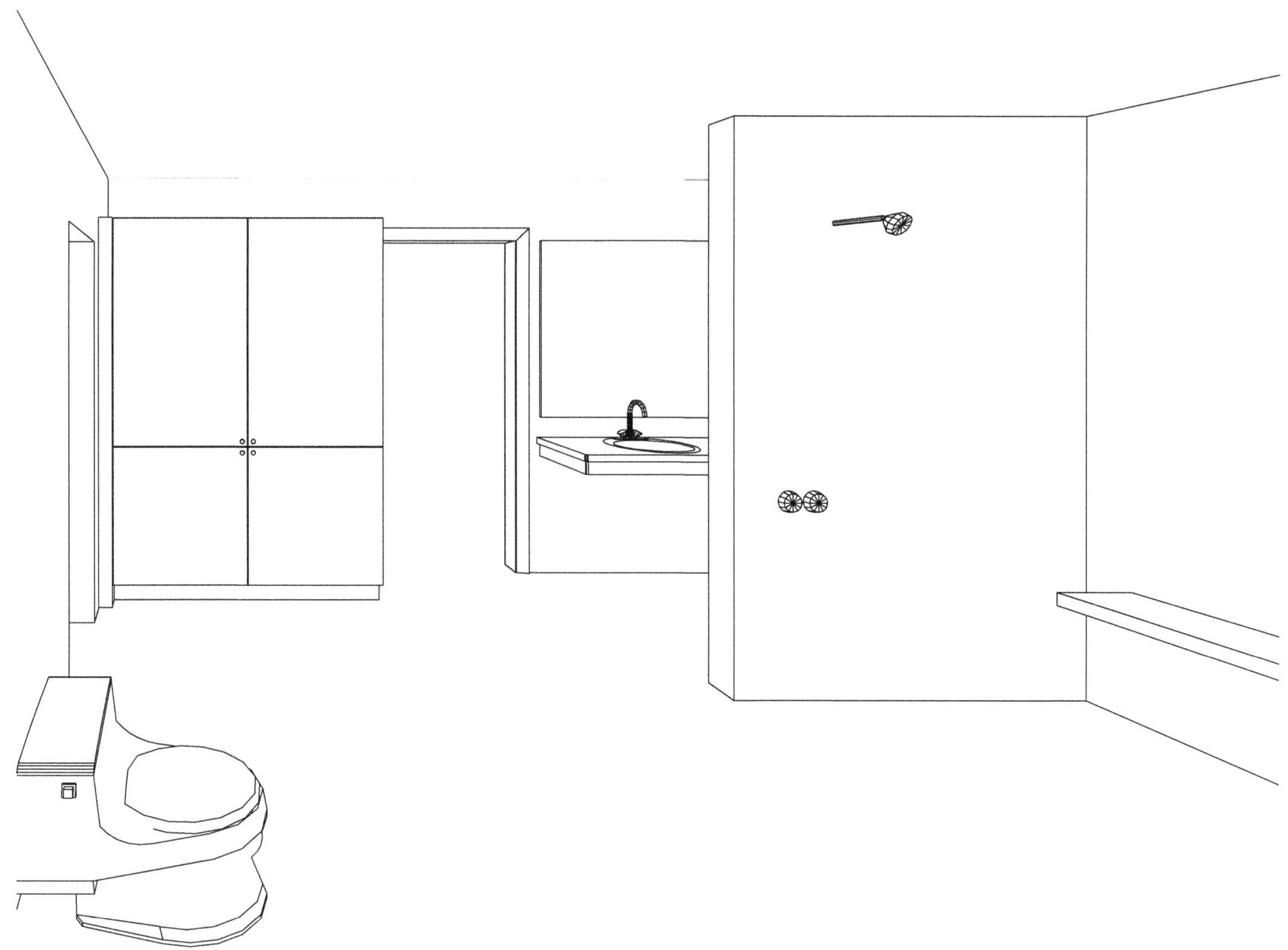

FIGURE 10.17 A perspective drawing gives the viewer a nice sense of the space.
NKBA

SUMMARY

Design is a process in which an idea is turned into a finished product. In order for this to happen, creativity and inspiration is needed. At the same time, organization, attention to detail, and hard work underlies the process. The design process involves gathering information about the client, the space to be designed, the activities that will occur in the space, and the materials that will be used to create the space. The design process also includes the translation of design information and ideas into visual and technical documents that communicate the design to the client and guide the construction and installation of the final product.

Keep in mind that you design for the client. Beauty and creativity does not succeed if you ignore the client's needs. A thorough understanding and mastery of the design process allows you to keep your goals in mind.

The design program is critically important documentation that defines what will be designed. Although a design program can take many formats, it is the basis for the creation of the design, the contract with the client, and the evaluation of the success of the final product.

The design drawings are the visual representations of the design. A variety of scale drawings are prepared as part of the design process, based on the design program, to communicate the details of the design. Attention to detail and accuracy are necessary in preparing design drawings that are part of the contract documents, including the basis of product specifications, bids, code compliance, construction decisions, and fee determination.

REVIEW QUESTIONS

1. Describe the steps of one example of a design process. (See "Summary of the Design Process" page 350)
2. What is a bubble diagram? (See under "The Design Process" page 349)
3. What is a user analysis and why is it an important part of a design program? Give several examples of the type of information found in a user analysis. (See under "Activities and Relationships" pages 352)
4. Describe a relationship matrix, and give an example of where you would find it useful to use one in preparing a bathroom design. (See under "Relationship or Adjacency Matrix" page 354)
5. What are design templates, and how can they be useful in preparing visual diagrams and drawings? Describe or sketch several types of templates. (See "Templates" page 355)
6. Sometimes, when laying out a design drawing, your dimensions do not work out correctly, and you have too much or too little space. What are some ideas for adjusting the space, to make your dimensions work accurately, without having to make major changes in the design? (See under "Finishing the Floor Plan" page 361)
7. Describe a process for checking your dimensions in a drawing to make sure you have placed everything correctly. (See "Verify the Dimensions" page 364)

APPENDIX

Bathroom Planning Guidelines with Access Standards

The National Kitchen & Bath Association developed the Bathroom Planning Guidelines with Access Standards to provide designers with good planning practices that consider the needs of a range of users.

The code references for the Bathroom Planning Guidelines are based on the analysis of the 2012 International Residential Code (IRC) and the International Plumbing Code.

The code references for the Access Standards are based on ICC A117.1-2009 Accessible and Usable Buildings and Facilities.

Be sure to check local, state, and national laws that apply to your design and follow those legal requirements.

BATHROOM PLANNING GUIDELINE 1

Door/Entry

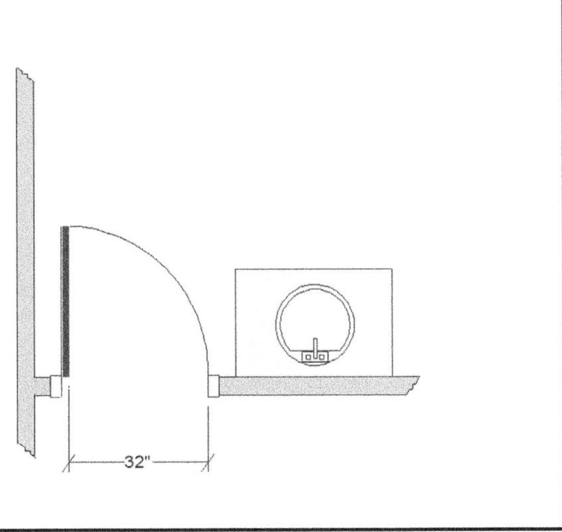

Recommended

- The clear opening of a doorway should be at least 32 inches" (813 mm). This would require a minimum 2 feet, 10 inches (864 mm) door.
- If the existing structure precludes changing the opening then a minimum 2-foot, 0-inch (610 mm) door is allowable.

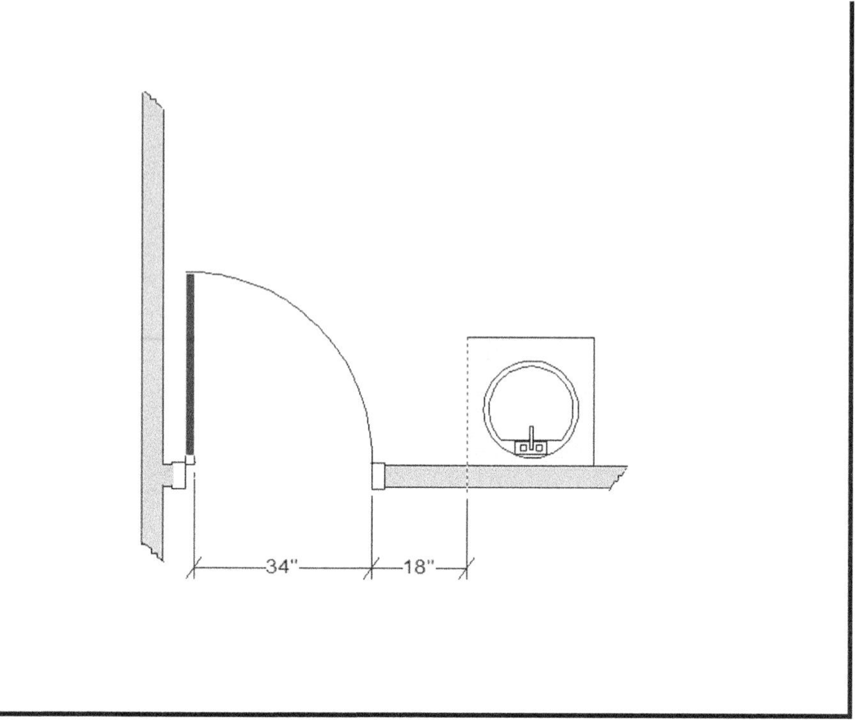

Code Requirement

- State or local codes may apply.

Access Standard

Recommended

- The clear opening of a doorway should be at least 34 inches (864 mm). This would require a minimum 3-foot, 0-inch (914 mm) door.

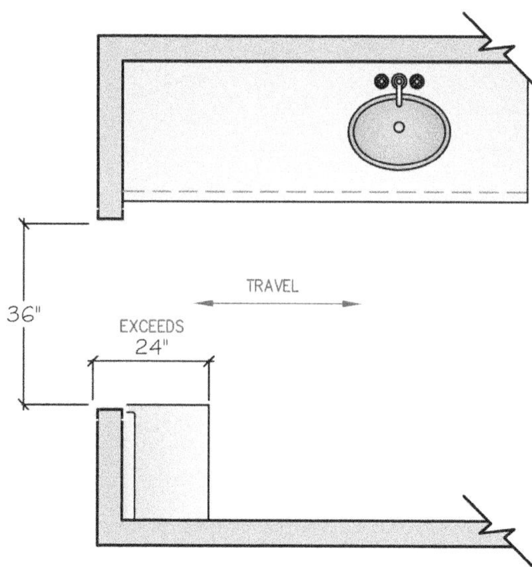

ICC A117.1–2009 Reference

- Clear openings of doorways with swinging doors shall be measured between the face of the door and stop, with the door open 90 degrees.
  - (404.2)
- When the depth of a passage exceeds 24 inches (610 mm), the minimum clear opening increases to 36 inches (914 mm).
  - (404.2.2)

BATHROOM PLANNING GUIDELINE 2

Door Interference

Recommended

- See Code Reference.

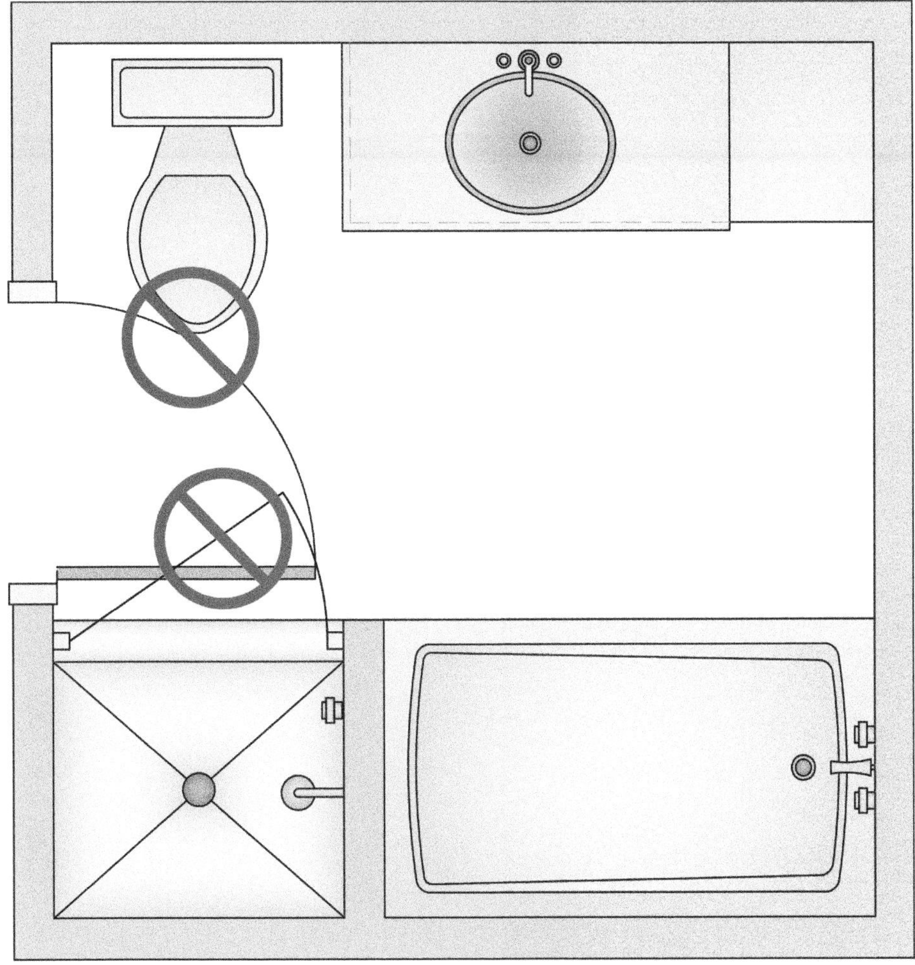

Code Requirement

- No entry or fixture doors should interfere with one another and/or the safe use of the fixtures or cabinets. (IRC P2705.1)

Access Standard

Recommended

- The door area should include clear floor space for maneuvering which varies according to the type of door and the direction of approach.

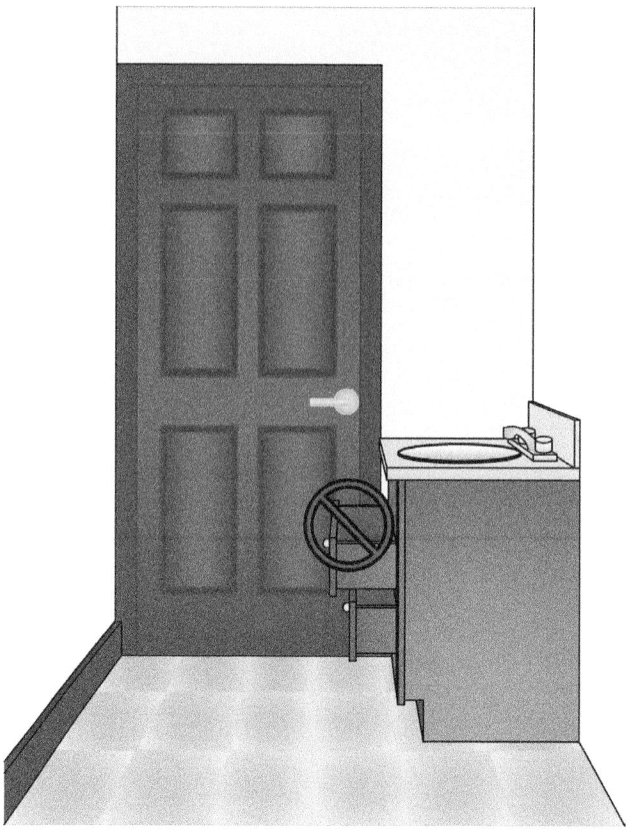

ICC A117.1–2009 Reference

- For a standard hinged door, the minimum clearance on the pull side of the door should be the width of the door plus 18 inches by 60 inches (457 mm by 1524 mm).
  - (404.2.3)
- The minimum clearance on the push side of the door should be the width of the door plus 12 inches by 48 inches (305 mm by 1219 mm).
  - (404.2.3)

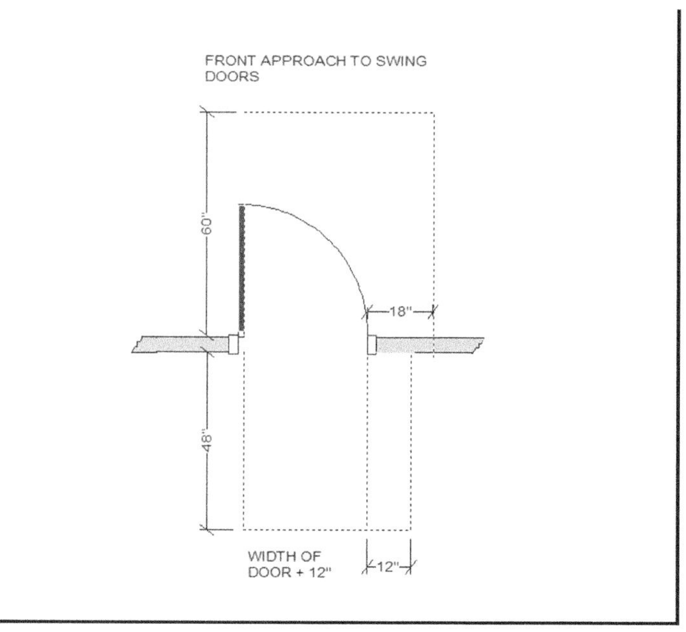

BATHROOM PLANNING GUIDELINE 3

Ceiling Height

Recommended

- See Code Requirement.

Code Requirement

- Bathrooms shall have a minimum floor to ceiling height of 80 inches (2032 mm) over the fixture and at the front clearance area for fixtures.
  - (IRC 305.1)

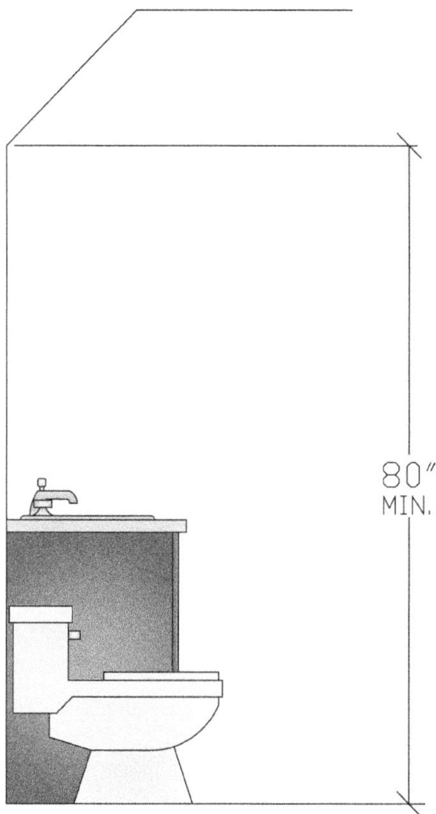

- A shower or tub equipped with a showerhead shall have a minimum floor to ceiling height of 80 inches (2032 mm) above a minimum area 30 inches by 30 inches (762 mm by 762 mm) at the showerhead.
  - (IRC 305.1)

Access Standard

Recommended

- Bathroom Guideline code requirement meets Access Standard.

BATHROOM PLANNING GUIDELINE 4

Clear Space

Recommended

- Plan a clear floor space of at least 30 inches (762 mm) from the front edge of all fixtures (e.g., lavatory, toilet, bidet, tub, and shower) to any opposite bath fixture, wall, or obstacle.

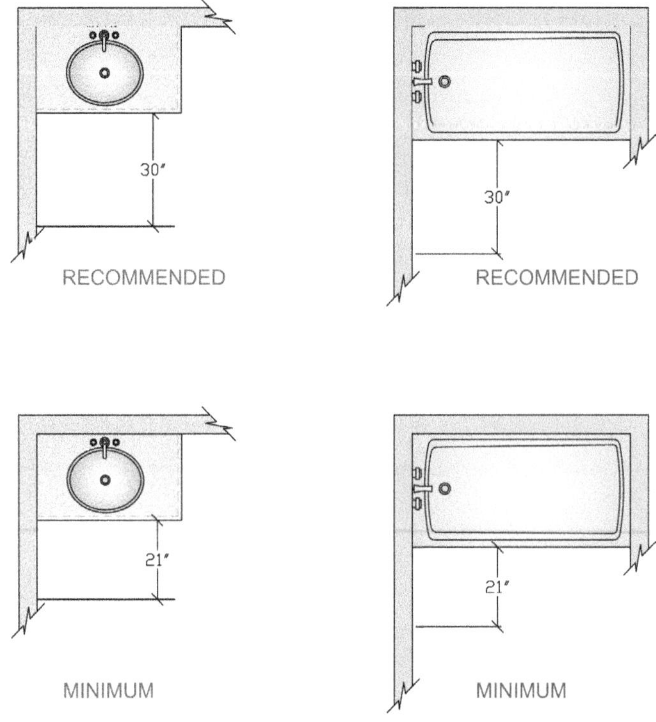

Code Requirement

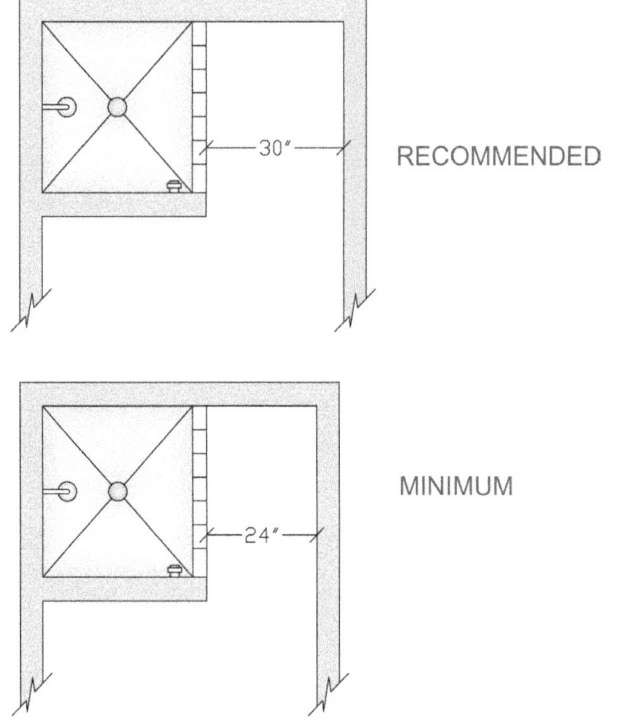

- A minimum space of at least 21 inches (533 mm) must be planned in front of the lavatory, toilet, bidet, and tub.
  - (IRC P2705.1.5)
  - (IRC R307.1)

- A minimum space of at least 24 inches (610 mm) must be planned in front of a shower entry.
  - (IRC R307.1)

Access Standard

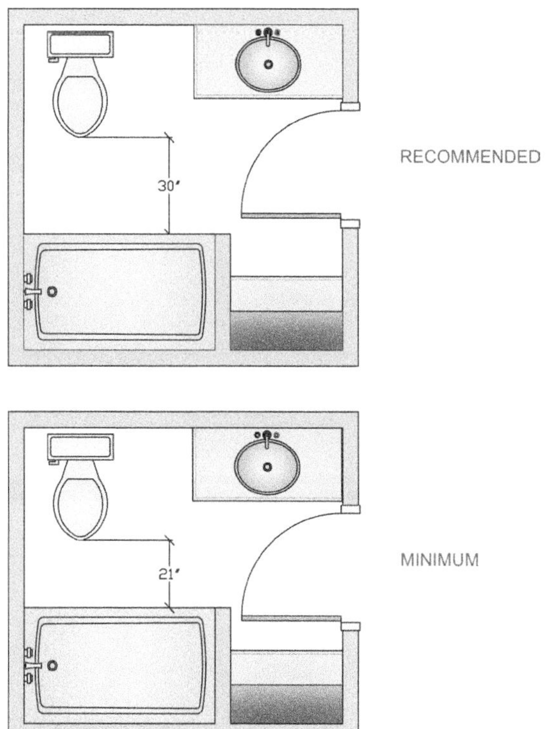

Recommended

- Plan a minimum clear floor space of 30 inches by 48 inches (762 mm by 1219 mm) centered at each fixture, plus space for maneuvering including approach and turning for a person using a wheelchair.
- Plan a knee space at the lavatory or workspace to allow for a front approach for a seated user. Recommended minimum size of a knee space is 36 inches wide by 27 inches high by 8 inches deep (914 mm by 686 mm by 203 mm), increasing to 17 inches (432 mm) deep in the toe space, which extends 9 inches (229 mm) from the floor. Insulation for exposed pipes should be provided.
- Consider the user's method of transfer to the toilet to plan a clear space to fit the user's needs.

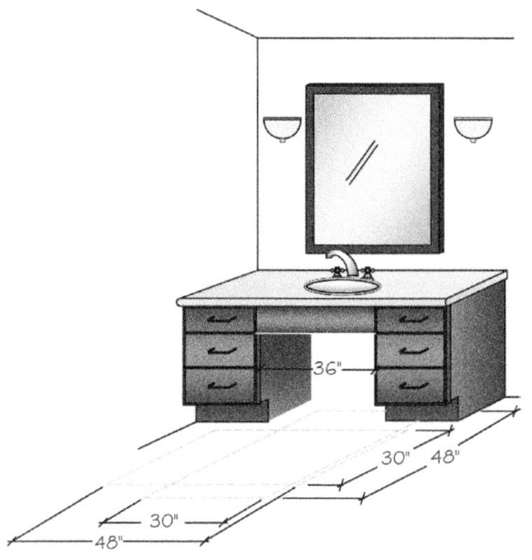

ICC A117.1–2009 Reference

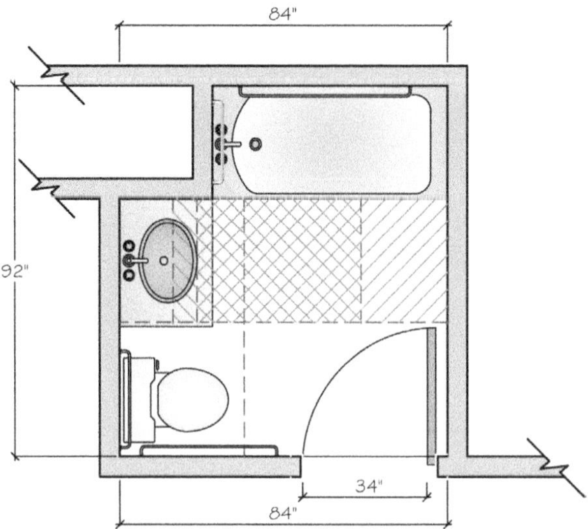

FIXTURE CLEAR FLOOR SPACE

- A clear floor space of at least 30 inches by 48 inches (762 mm by 1219 mm) must be provided at each fixture. Clear spaces can overlap.
  - (305.3)
- Include a wheelchair turning space with a diameter of at least 60 inches (1524 mm), which can include knee* and toe** clearances.
  - (304.3.0)
- A wheelchair turning space could utilize a T-shaped space, which is a 60-inch (1524 mm) square with two 12-inch wide by 24-inch deep (305 mm by 610 mm) areas removed from two corners of the square. This leaves a minimum 36-inch (914 mm) wide base and two 36-inch (914 mm) wide arms. T-shaped wheelchair turning spaces can include knee and toe clearances on one arm.
  - (304.3.2)

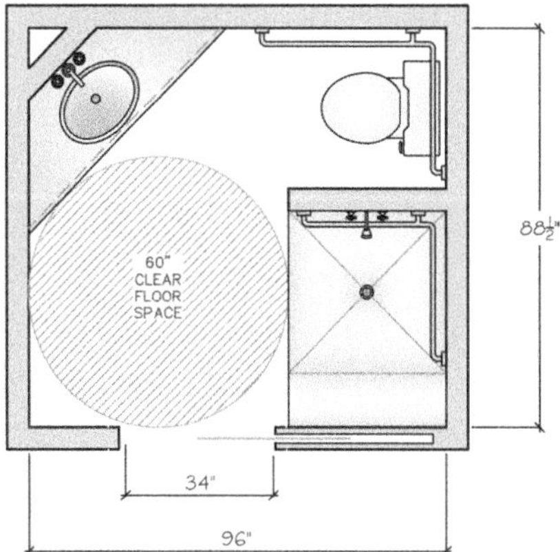

WHEELCHAIR TURNING SPACE

---

*Knee clearance must be a minimum 30 inches (762 mm) wide, 36 inches (914 mm) to use as part of the T-turn), and maintain a 27-inch (686 mm) high clear space under the cabinet, counter, or sink. At 27 inches (686 mm) above finished floor (AFF), the depth must be a minimum 8 inches (203 mm). At 9 inches (229 mm) AFF, the depth must be a minimum of 11 inches (279 mm). The space from 9 inches (229 mm) to the floor is considered toe clearance and must be a minimum of 17 inches (432 mm) and a maximum of 25 inches (635 mm).

**Toe clearance space under a cabinet or fixture is between the floor and 9 inches (635 mm) above the floor. Where toe clearance is required as part of a clear floor space, the toe clearance should extend 17 inches (432 mm) minimum beneath the element.

- (306.3)

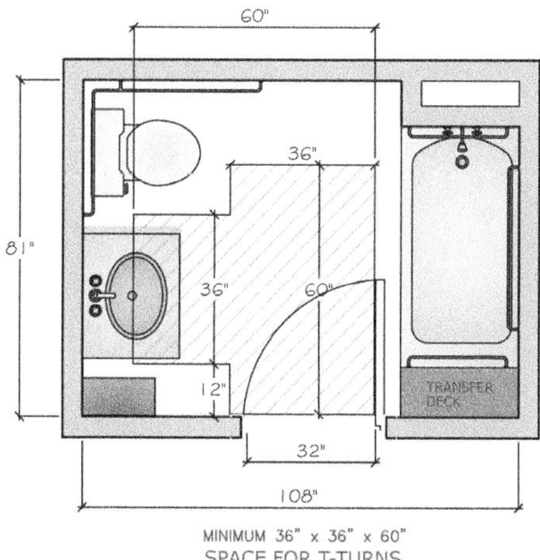

- (306.2.3)

KNEE STANDARD (ACCESS STANDARD 4—ANSI)

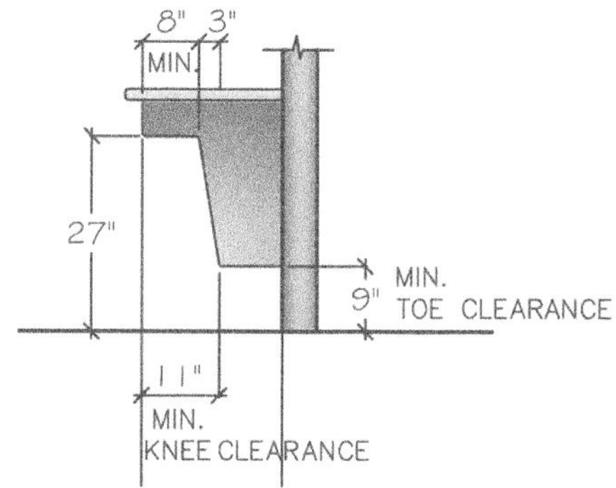

Grooming

- The clear 30-inch by 48-inch (762 mm by 1219 mm) floor space should be centered on the lavatory.
  - (606.2, 1004.11.3)

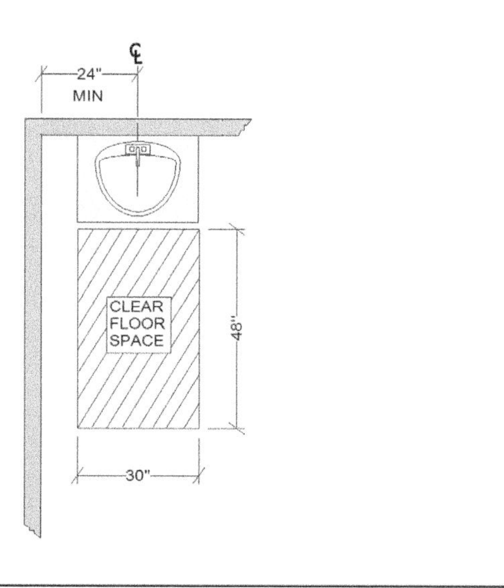

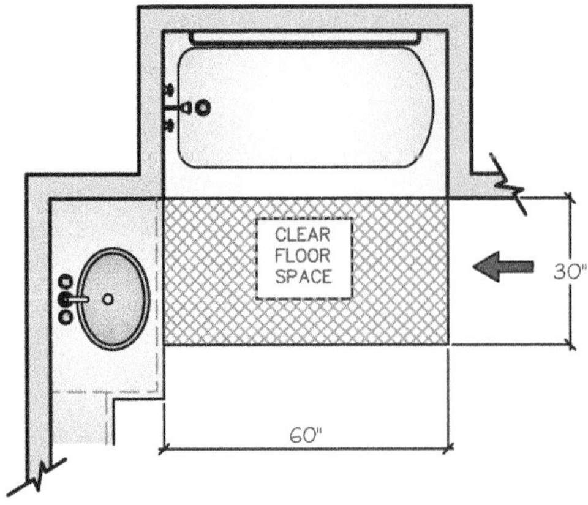

PARALLEL APPROACH

Bathing and Showering

- Clearance in front of bathtubs should extend the length of the bathtub and be at least 30 inches (762 mm) wide.
  - (607.2)
- When a permanent seat is provided at the head of the bathtub, the clearance should extend a minimum of 12 inches (305 mm) beyond the wall at the head end of the bathtub.
  - (607.2)

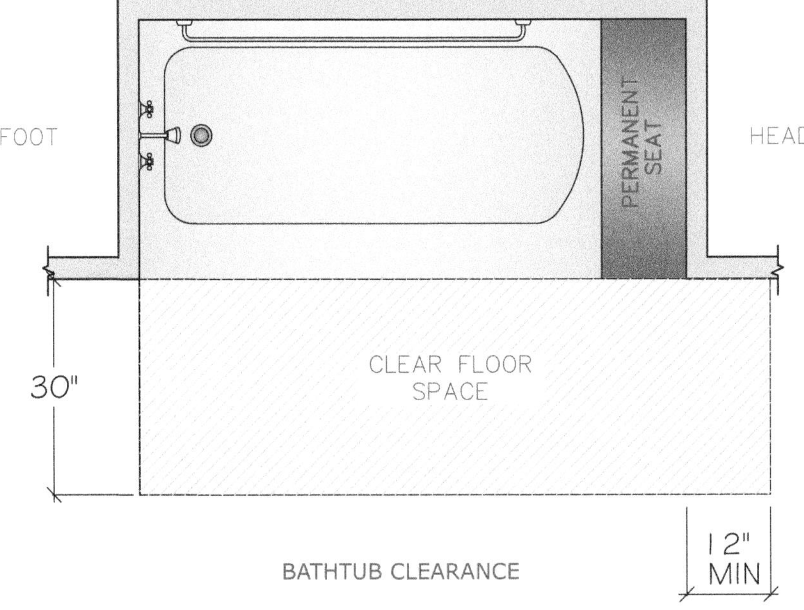

BATHTUB CLEARANCE

- The clearance in front of the transfer-type shower† compartment should be at least 48 inches (1219 mm) long measured from the control wall and 36 inches (914 mm) wide.
  - (608.2)
- The clearance in front of a roll-in-type shower†† compartment should be at least 60 inches (1524 mm) long next to the open face of the shower compartment and 30 inches (762 mm) wide.

††A roll-in shower is a waterproof area large enough for a person in a wheelchair to remain in the chair to shower. A preferred minimum size for a roll-in shower is 36 inches to 42 inches by 60 inches (914 mm to 1067 mm by 1524 mm).

  - (608.2.2)

---

†A transfer shower (36 inches by 36 inches) (914 mm by 914 mm) provides support to a standing person or one who can stand to transfer.

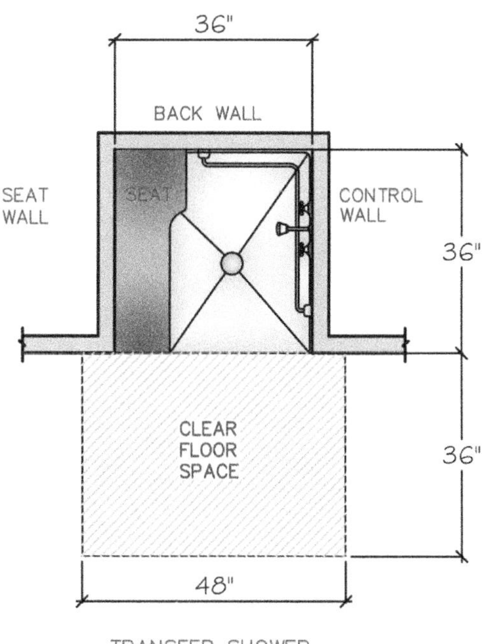

TRANSFER SHOWER

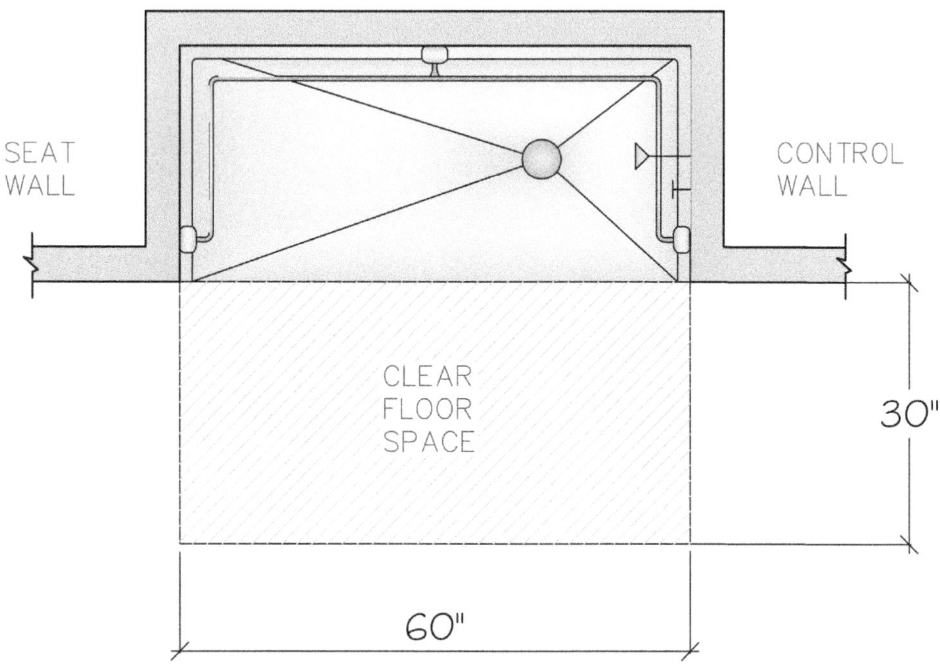

ROLL-IN SHOWER

Toileting

- When both a parallel and a forward approach to the toilet are provided, the clearance should be at least 56 inches (1422 mm) measured perpendicular from the rear wall, and 60 inches (1524 mm) measured perpendicular from the side wall. No other fixture or obstruction should be within the clearance area.
    - (604.3, 1002.11.2.4)

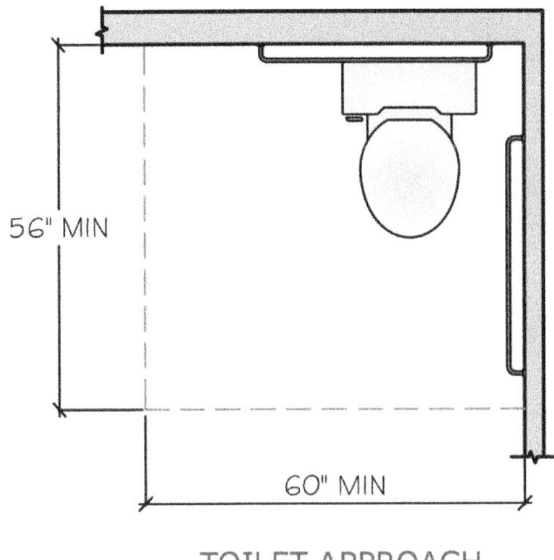

TOILET APPROACH

BATHROOM PLANNING GUIDELINE 5

single Lavatory Placement

Recommended

- The distance from the centerline of the lavatory to the side wall/tall obstacle should be at least 20 inches (508 mm).

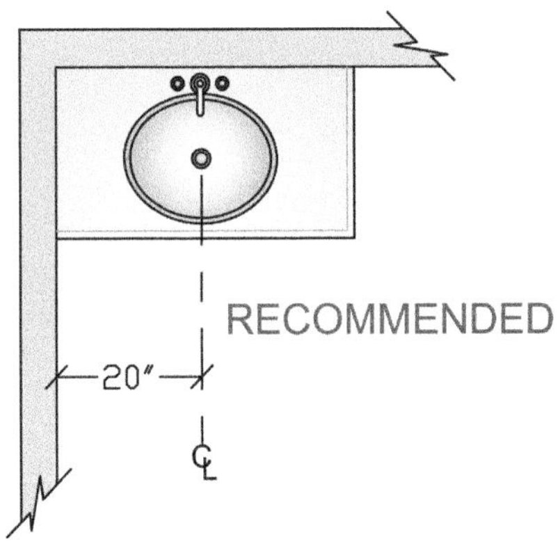

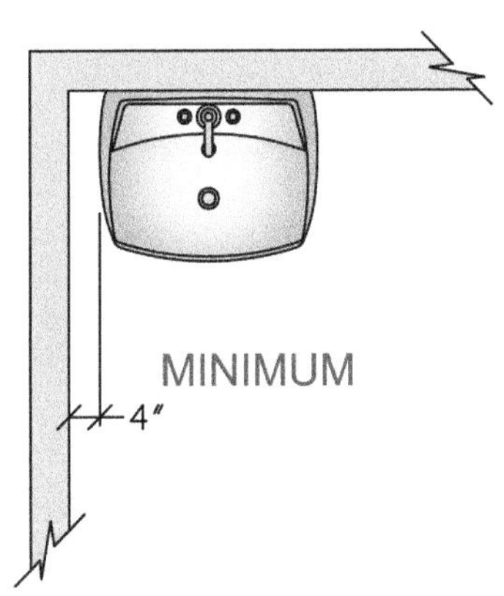

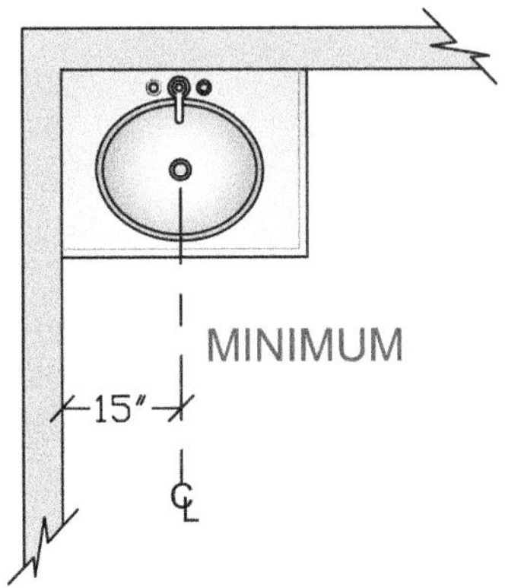

- The minimum distance between a wall and the edge of a freestanding or wall-hung lavatory is 4 inches (102 mm).

Code Requirement

- The minimum distance from the centerline of the lavatory to a wall is 15 inches (381 mm).
  - (IRC P2705)

Access Standard

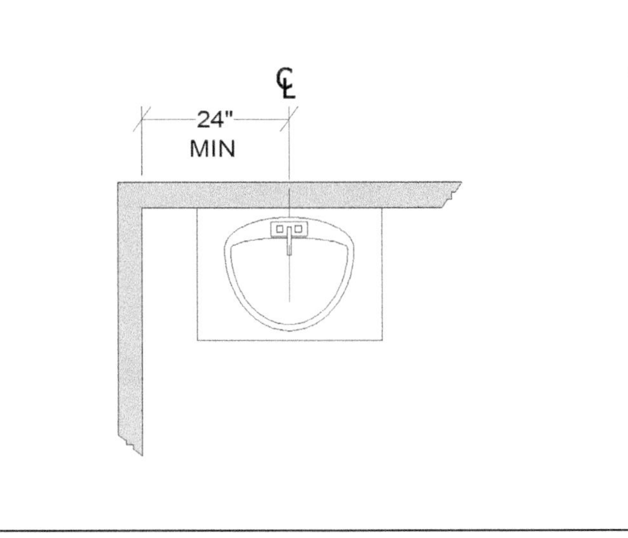

ICC A117.1–2009 Reference

- To assure a clear floor space (30 inches by 48 inches) (762 mm by 1219 mm) the lavatory must be a minimum 24 inches (610 mm) from the wall.
  - (A117.1, 1004.11.3)

BATHROOM PLANNING GUIDELINE 6

Double Lavatory Placement

Recommended

- The distance between the centerlines of two lavatories should be at least 36 inches (914 mm). The minimum distance between the edges of two freestanding or wall-hung lavatories is 4 inches (102 mm).

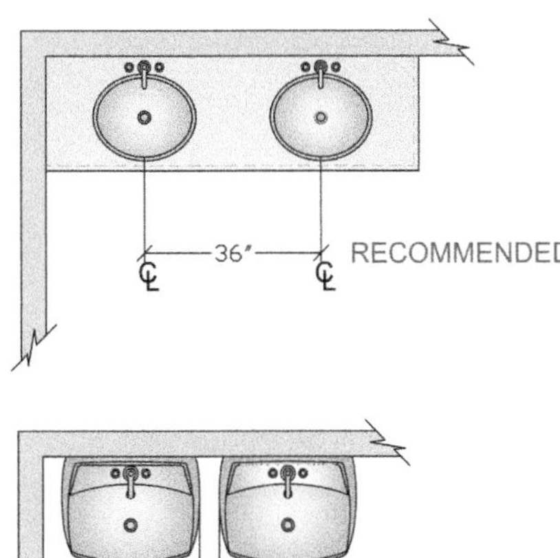

Code Requirement

- The minimum distance between the centerlines of two lavatories should be at least 30 inches (762 mm).
  - (IRC P2705)

Access Standard

Recommended

- Bathroom Guideline recommendation meets Access Standard.

BATHROOM PLANNING GUIDELINE 7

Lavatory/Vanity Height

Recommended

- The height for a lavatory varies between 32 inches and 43 inches (813 mm and 1092 mm) to fit the user.

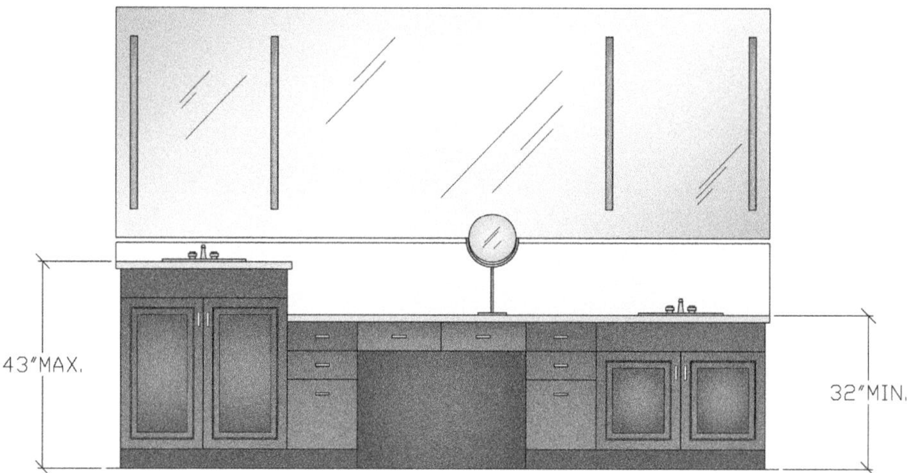

Code Requirement

- State or local codes may apply.

Access Standard

Recommended

- Lavatory controls should be within the user's reach and operable with minimal effort.

ICC A117.1–2009 Reference

- The front of the lavatory sink should be no more than 34 inches (864 mm) above the floor, measured to the higher of the fixture or counter surface.
  - (606.3)
- Lavatory controls should be operable with one hand and not require tight grasping, pinching, or twisting of the wrist.
  - (309.4)

BATHROOM PLANNING GUIDELINE 8

Counter

Recommended

- Specify clipped or round corners rather than sharp edges on all counters.

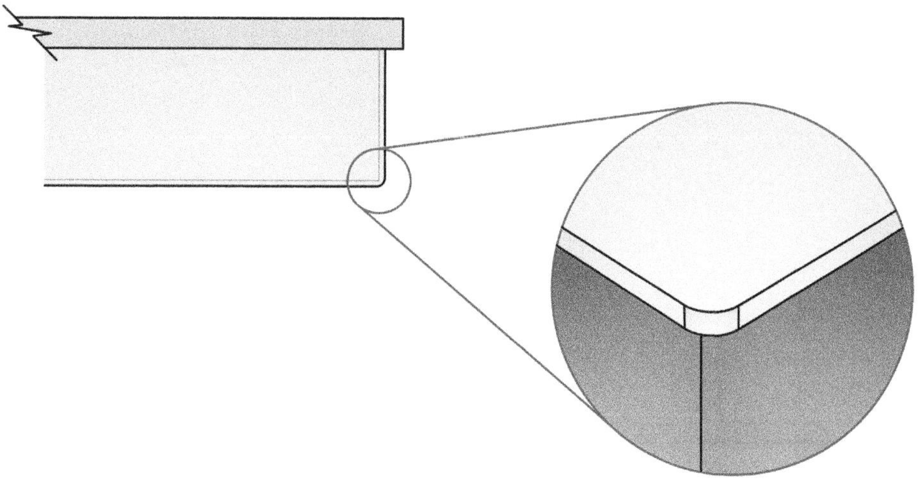

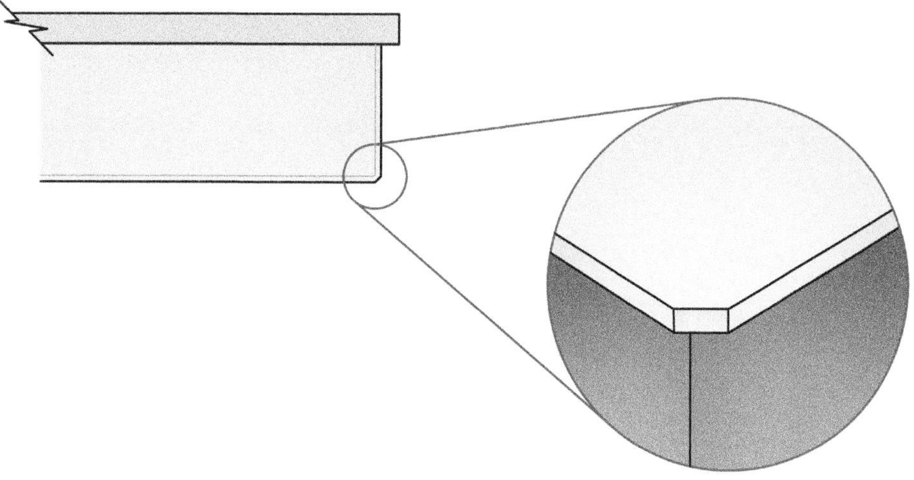

Code Requirements

- State or local codes may apply.

Access Standard

Recommended

- Bathroom Guideline recommendation meets Access Standard.

BATHROOM PLANNING GUIDELINE 9

Shower Size

Recommended

The interior shower size is at least 36 inches by 36 inches (914 mm by 914 mm).

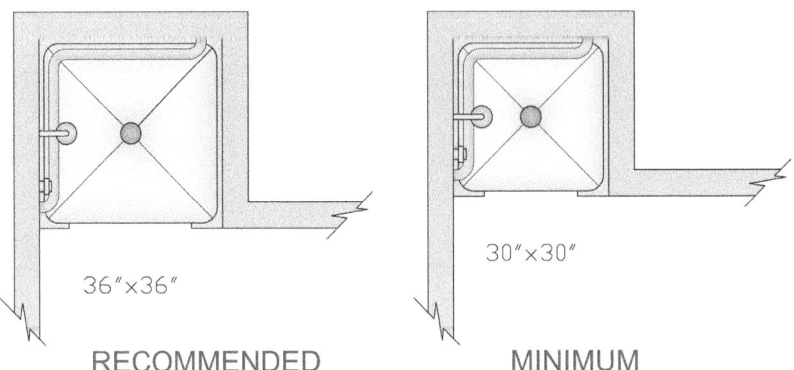

Code Requirement

- The minimum interior shower size is 30 inches by 30 inches (762 mm by 762 mm) or 900 square inches (22,860 square mm), in which a disc of 30 inches (762 mm) in diameter must fit.
  - (IRC P2708.1)

Access Standard

Recommended

- Plan either a transfer or a roll-in shower.
- Roll-in shower entries: For a 60-inch (1524 mm) deep shower, a 32- inch (813 mm) wide entry is adequate. For a 42-inch (1067 mm) deep shower, the entry must be at least 36 inches (914 mm) wide to allow for turning space.

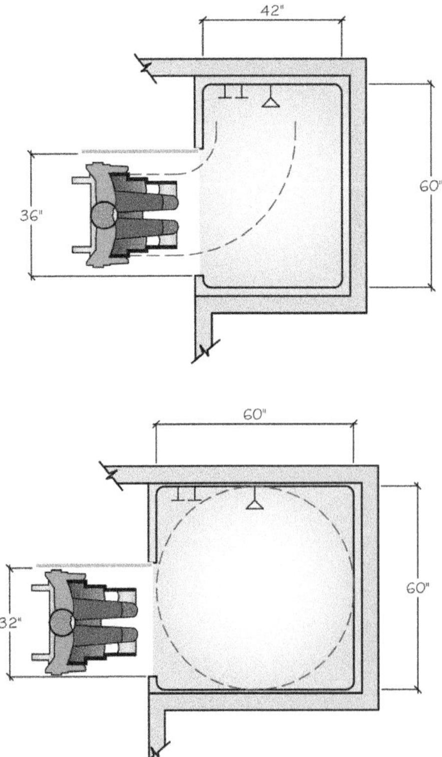

ICC A117.1–2009 Reference

TRANSFER TYPE SHOWER (ACCESS STANDARD 9–ANSI)

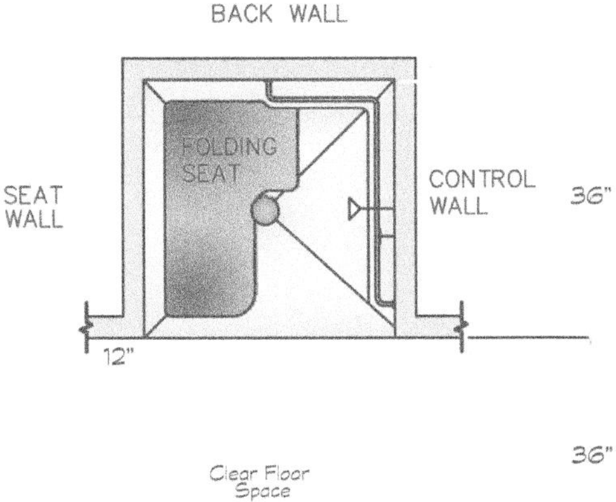

- Transfer-type shower compartments must have an inside finished dimension of 36 inches by 36 inches (914 mm by 914 mm), and have a minimum of a 36-inch (914 mm) wide entry on the face of the shower compartment. A sliding seat must be provided within the 36 inches by 36 inches (914 mm by 914 mm) area.
  - (608)

ROLL–IN SHOWER (ACCESS STANDARD 9 – ANSI)

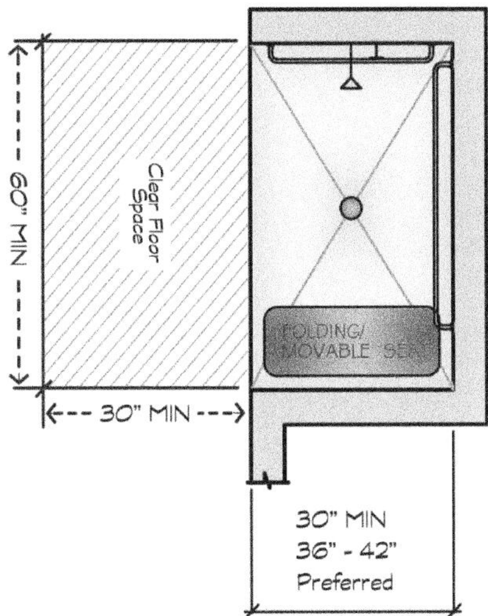

- Roll-in-type shower compartments should have a minimum inside finished dimension of at least 30 inches (762 mm) wide by 60 inches (1524 mm) deep, and have a minimum of a 60-inch (1524 mm) wide entry on the face of the shower compartment.
  - (608.2.2)

BATHROOM PLANNING GUIDELINE 10

Tub/Shower Controls

Recommended

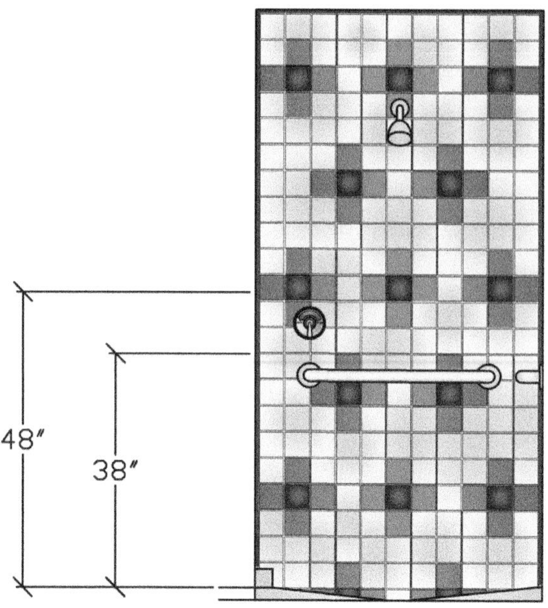

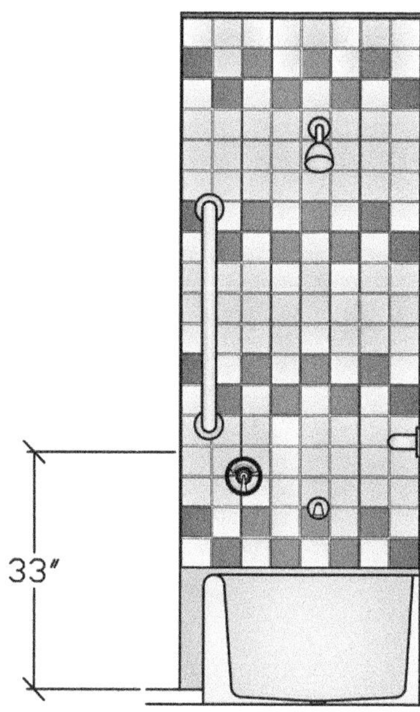

- The shower controls should be accessible from both inside and outside the shower spray and be located between 38 inches and 48 inches (965 mm and 1219 mm) above the floor depending on the user's height.
- The tub controls should be accessible from both inside and outside the tub and be located between the rim of the bathtub and 33 inches (838 mm) above the floor.

Code Requirement

- State or local codes may apply.

Access Standard

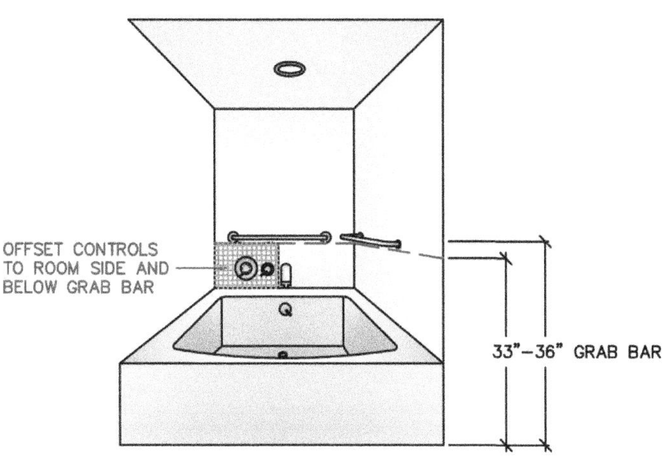

Recommended

- Controls should be offset toward the room and easy to grasp, as with lever or loop handles.
- Hot and cold should be identified with red and blue indicators.
- Provide a handheld spray at a height accessible to the user.

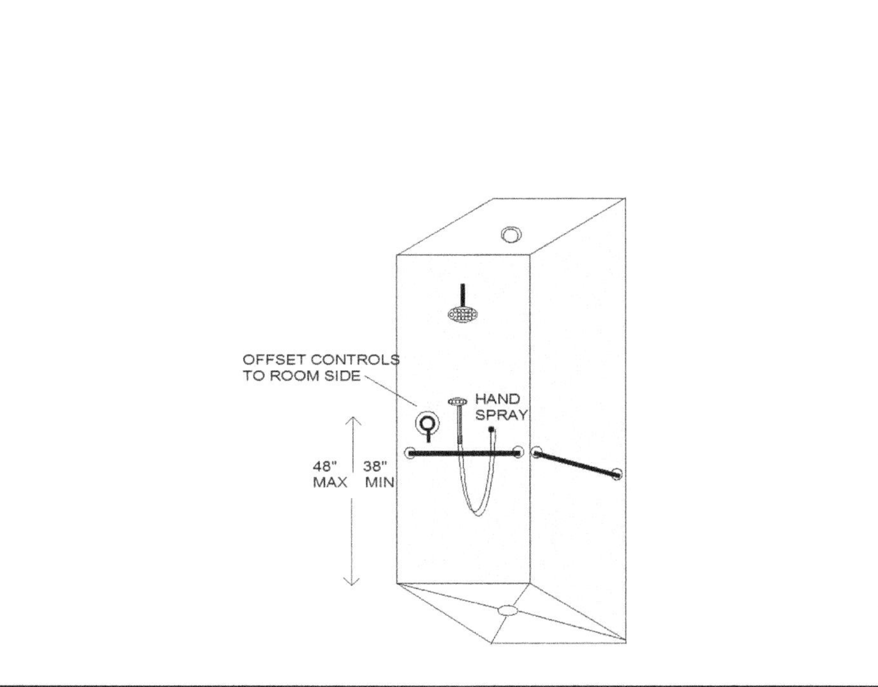

ICC A117.1–2009 Reference:

- Tub/shower controls must be operable with one hand and not require tight grasping.
  - (309.4)

- Controls must be on an end wall of the bathtub, between the rim and grab bar, and between the open side of the bathtub and the mid-point of the width of the tub.
  - (607.5) (a)

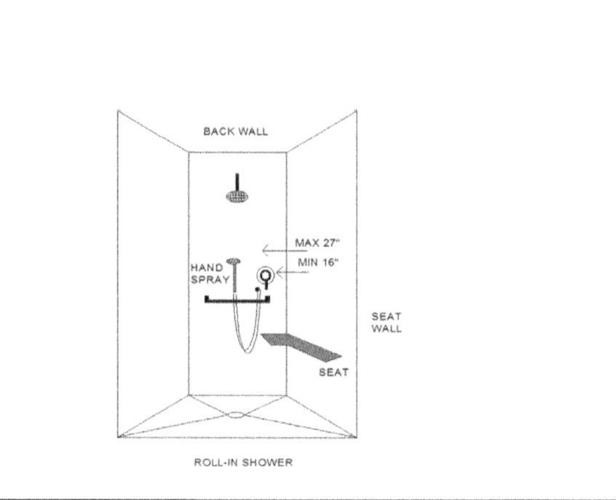

- In transfer-type shower compartments, controls and the showerhead should be on the side wall adjacent to the seat, between 38 inches and 48 inches (965 mm and 1219 mm) above the shower floor, within 15 inches (381 mm) of the centerline of the control wall toward the shower opening.
  - (608.4.1)
- Controls in roll-in showers should be above the grab bar, but no higher than 48 inches (1219 mm) above the shower floor and minimum 16 inches (406 mm), maximum 27 inches (686 mm) from the end wall behind the seat.
  - (608.4.2)
- A handheld spray unit must be provided with a hose at least 59 inches (1499 mm) long that can be used as a fixed showerhead and as a handheld shower. If an adjustable height showerhead mounted on a vertical bar is used, the bar should not obstruct the use of the grab bars.
  - (608.5)

BATHROOM PLANNING GUIDELINE 11

Water Temperature Safety

Recommended

- See below.

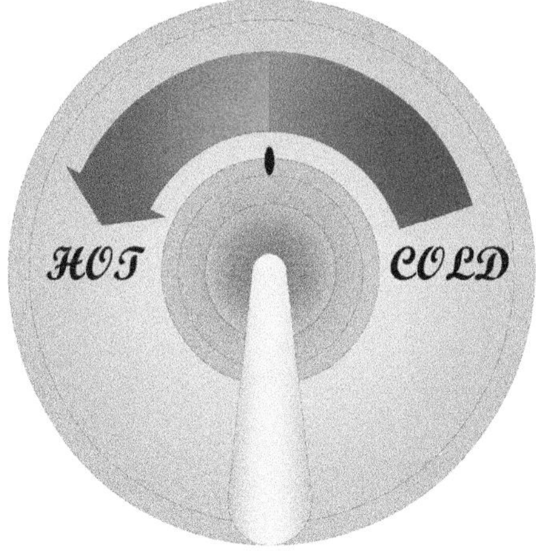

Code Requirement

Shower and tub/shower control valves must be one of the following:

- Pressure balanced
- Thermostatic mixing
- Combination pressure balance/thermostatic mixing valve types
  - (IRC P2708.3)
  - (IRC M1507.4)
- The valve must have a high limit stop to prevent water temperatures above 120°F (49°C).
  - (IRC P2708.3)
- Hot water delivered to bathtubs and whirlpool bathtubs shall be limited to a temperature of not more than 120°F (49°C).
  - (IRC P 2713.3)
- Hot water delivered to bidets shall be limited to no more than 110°F (43°C).
  - (IRC P2721.2)

Access Standard

Recommended

- Bathroom Guideline code requirement meets Access Standard.
  - (607.8, 608.8)

BATHROOM PLANNING GUIDELINE 12

Shower/Tub Seat

Recommended

- Plan a seat within the shower that is 17 inches to 19 inches (432 mm to 483 mm) above the shower floor and 15 inches (381 mm) deep.

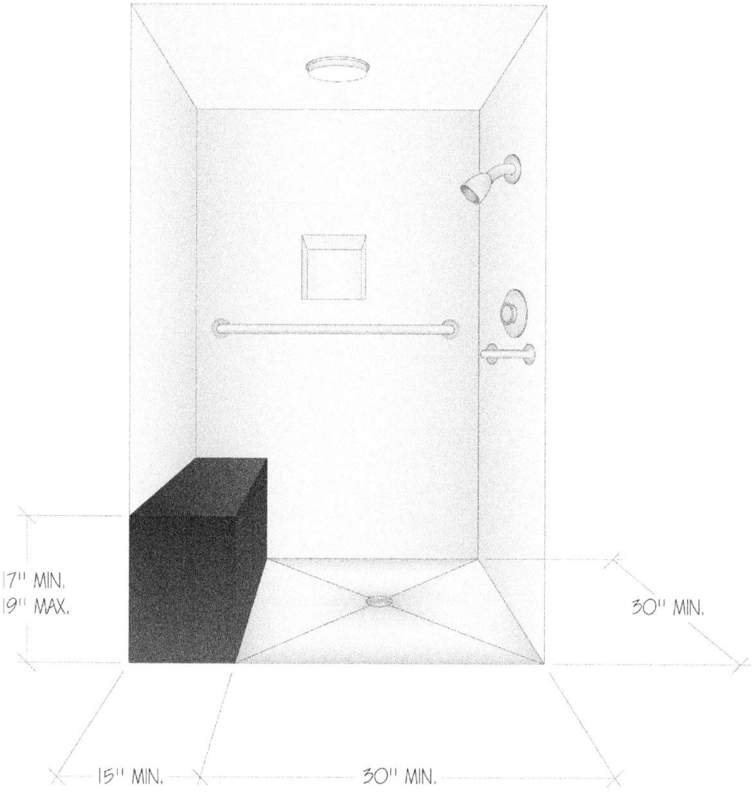

Code Requirement

- The shower seat must not infringe on the minimum interior size of the shower (900 square inches) (22860 square mm).
  - (IRC P2708.1)

Access Standard

Recommended

- Plan a seat in the shower and/or bathtub to fit the parameters of the space and the needs of the user.

ICC A117.1–2009 Reference

- A removable in-tub seat should be at least 15 inches to 16 inches (381 mm to 406 mm) deep and capable of secure placement.
  - (610.2)

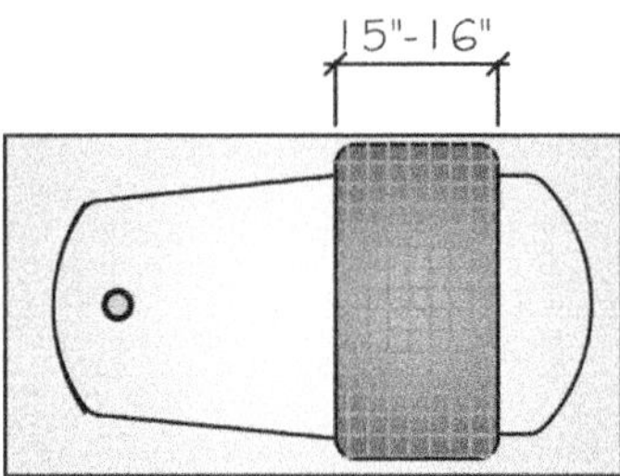

(a) REMOVEABLE IN–TUB SEAT

- A permanent tub seat should be at least 15 inches (381 mm) deep and positioned at the head end of the bathtub. The top of the seat should be between 17 inches and 19 inches (432 mm and 483 mm) above the bathroom floor.
  - (610.2)

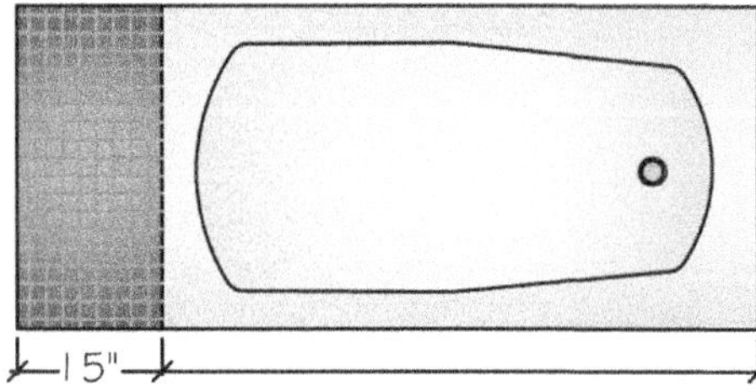

PERMANENT SEAT

- A shower seat should be 15 inches to 16 inches (381 mm to 406 mm) deep and 17 inches to 19 inches (432 mm to 483 mm) above the shower floor (to the top of the seat). The seat should extend from the back wall to a point within 3 inches (76 mm) of the entry. In a transfer shower, the seat should be on the wall opposite the control wall. In a roll-in shower, the seat should be on an end wall, extending from the control wall to the shower entry.
  - (ICC 608, 610)
- The materials and installation of the shower and/or bathtub seat must support a minimum of 250 pounds (113 kg) of pressure.
  - (610.4)

BATHROOM PLANNING GUIDELINE 13

Tub/Shower Surround

Recommended

- The wall area above a tub or shower pan should be covered in a waterproof material extending at least 3 inches (76 mm) above the showerhead rough-in.

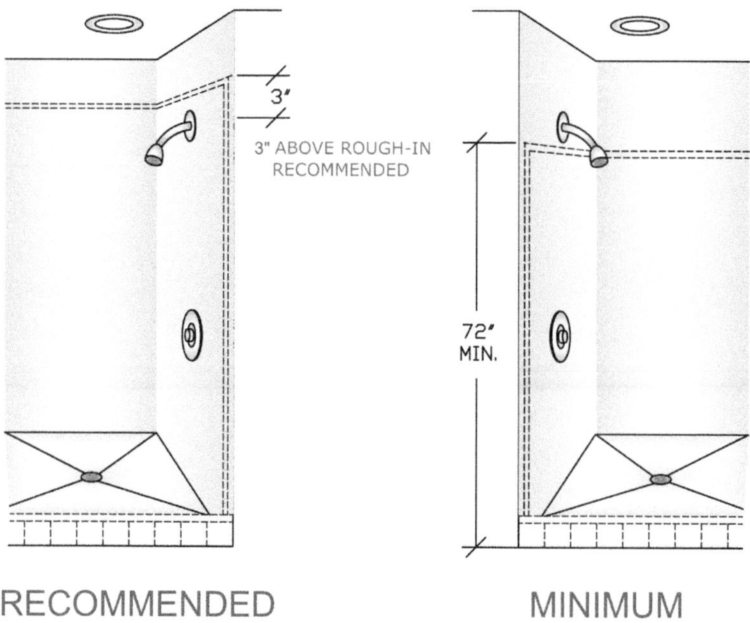

Code Requirement

- The wall area above a tub or shower pan must be covered in a waterproof material to a height of not less than 72 inches (1829 mm) above the finished floor.
    - (IRC R307.2)

Access Standard

Recommended

- Bathroom Guideline recommendation meets Access Standard.

BATHROOM PLANNING GUIDELINE 14

Grab Bars

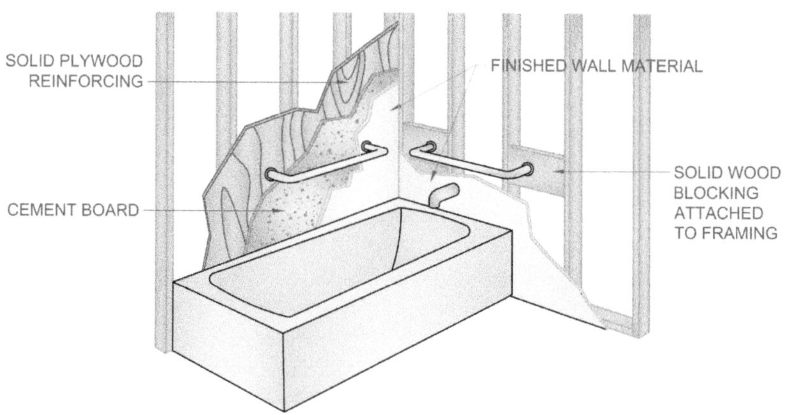

Recommended:

- Plan grab bars to facilitate access to and maneuvering within the tub and shower areas.
- Tub and shower walls should be prepared (reinforced) at time of construction to allow for installation of grab bars to support a static load of 250 pounds (113 kg).
- Grab bars should be placed at 33 inches to 36 inches (838 mm to 914 mm) above the floor.

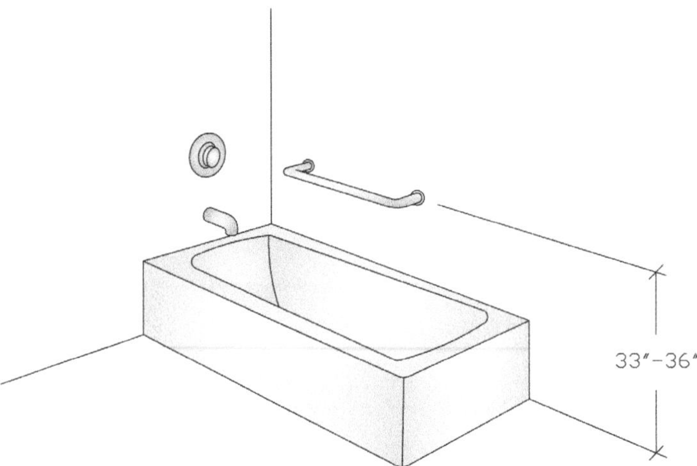

- Grab bars must be 1¼ inches to 2 inches (32 mm to 60 mm) in diameter and extend 1½ inches (38 mm) from the wall.

Access Standard

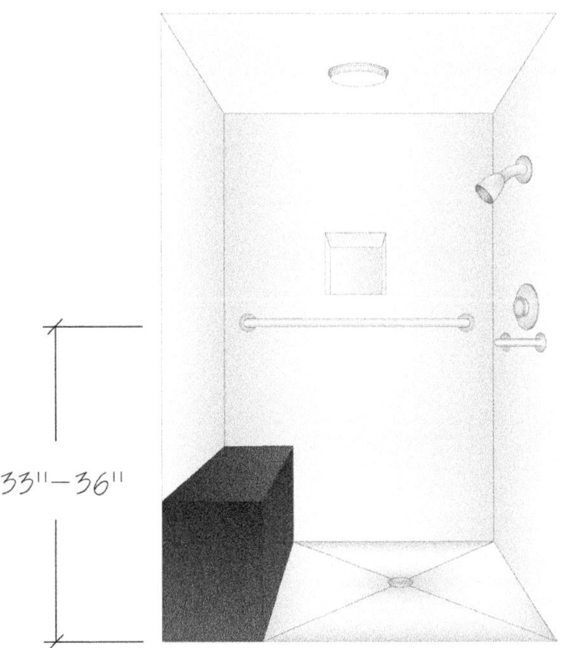

Recommended

- Walls throughout the bathroom should be prepared (reinforced) at time of construction to allow for installation of grab bars to support a minimum of 250 pounds (113 kg) of force in any direction.
- Grab bars should be placed according to the needs and height of the user, particularly near the tub/shower and the toilet.

ICC A117.1–2009 Reference

Grab bars should be installed at the tub, shower, and toilet according to the following:

- Bathtubs with permanent seats: Two horizontal grab bars should be provided on the back wall, one 33 inches to 36 inches (838 mm to 914 mm) above the floor and the other 8 inches to 10 inches (203 mm to 254 mm) above the rim of the bathtub. Each grab bar should be no more than 15 inches (381 mm) from the head end wall or 12 inches (305 mm) from the control end wall. A grab bar 24 inches (610 mm) long should be provided on the control end wall at the front edge of the bathtub. A vertical grab bar minimum 18 inches (457 mm) shall be placed 3 inches to 6 inches (76 mm to 152 mm) above and 4 inches (102 mm) maximum from the front edge of the horizontal bar.
  - (607.4.1)

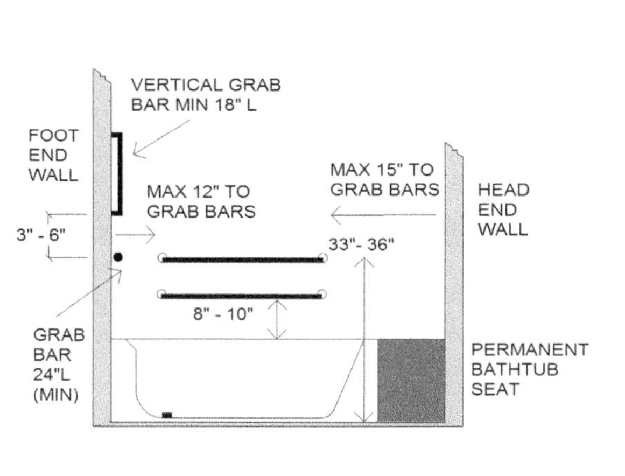

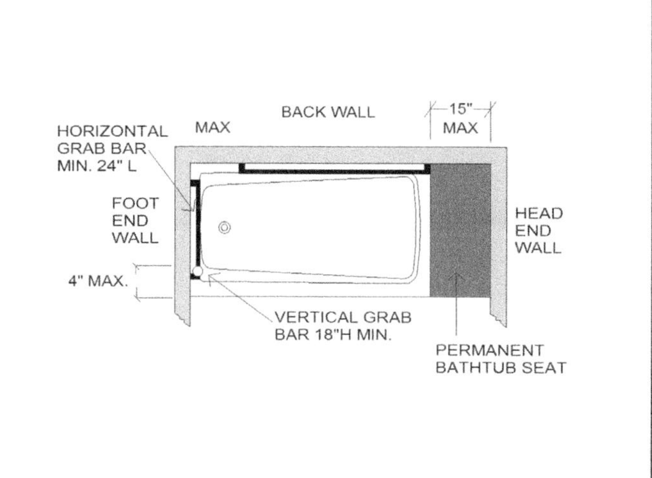

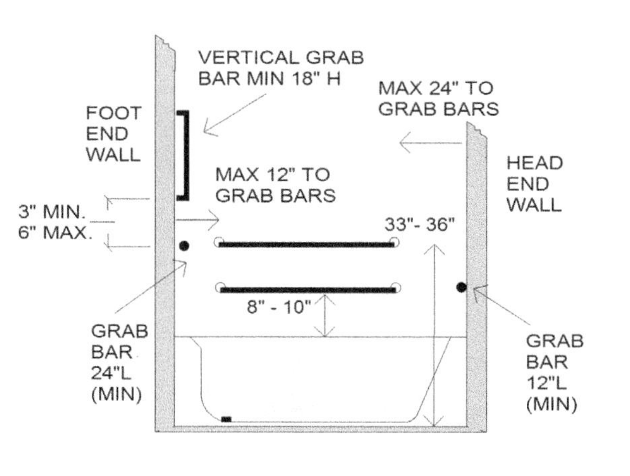

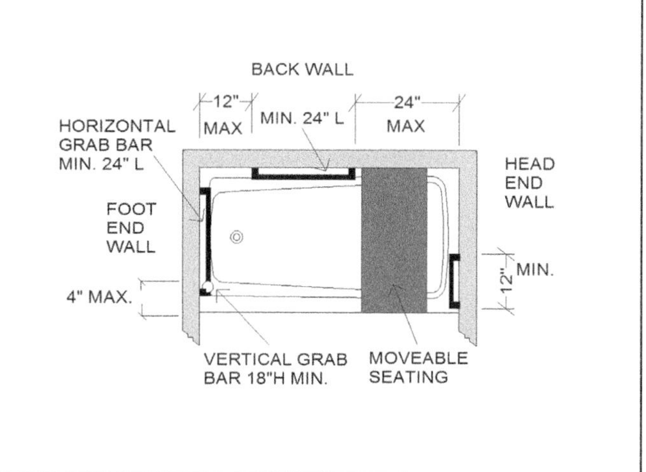

- Bathtubs without permanent seats: Two horizontal grab bars should be provided on the back wall, one 33 inches to 36 inches (838 mm to 914 mm) above the floor and the other 8 inches to 10 inches (203 mm to 254 mm) above the rim of the bathtub. Each grab bar should be at least 24 inches (610 mm) long and no more than 24 inches (610 mm) from the head end wall or 12 inches (305 mm) from the control end wall. A horizontal grab bar 24 inches (610 mm) long should be provided on the foot end wall at the front edge of the bathtub. On the control wall, a vertical grab bar minimum 18 inches (457 mm) shall be placed 3 inches to 6 inches (76 mm to 152 mm) above and 4 inches (102 mm) maximum from the front edge of the horizontal.
  - (607.4.2)

- Transfer-type showers: Grab bars should be mounted in a horizontal position, between 33 inches and 36 inches (838 mm and 914 mm) above the shower floor, across the control wall, and on the back wall to a point 18 inches (457 mm) from the seat wall. A vertical grab bar minimum 18 inches (457 mm) shall be placed 3 inches to 6 inches (76 mm to 152 mm) above the horizontal bar and 4 inches (102 mm) maximum from the front edge of the shower.
  - (608.3)

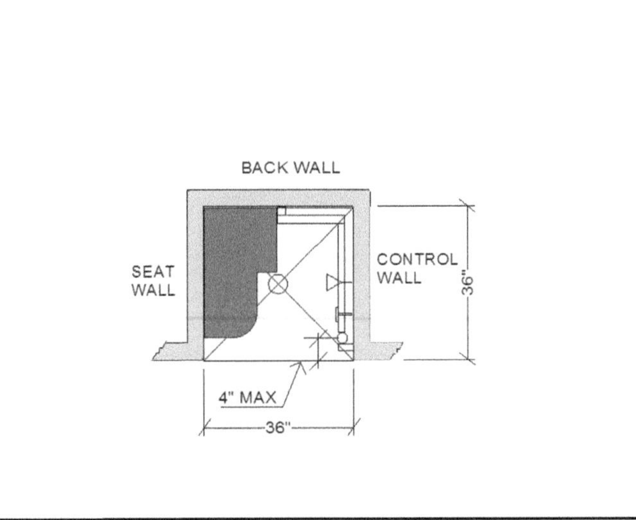

- Roll-in type shower: Grab bars should be mounted in a horizontal position, between 33 inches and 36 inches (838 mm and 914 mm) above the floor, on all three walls of the shower. An exception is that there be no grab bar on the length of wall behind and for the length of the seat. Grab bars should be no more than 6 inches (152 mm) from each adjacent wall.
  - (608.3.2)

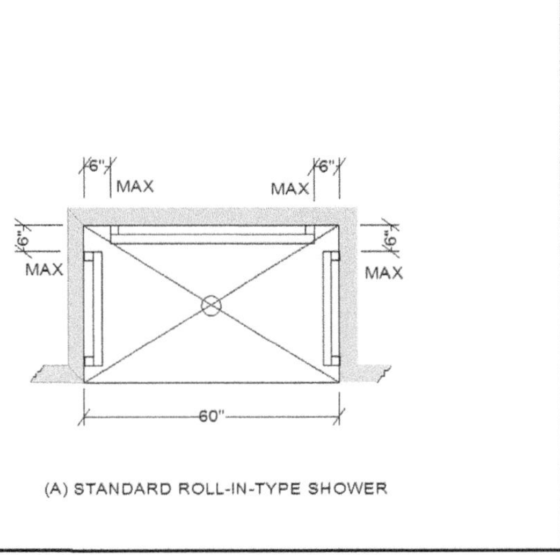

(A) STANDARD ROLL-IN-TYPE SHOWER

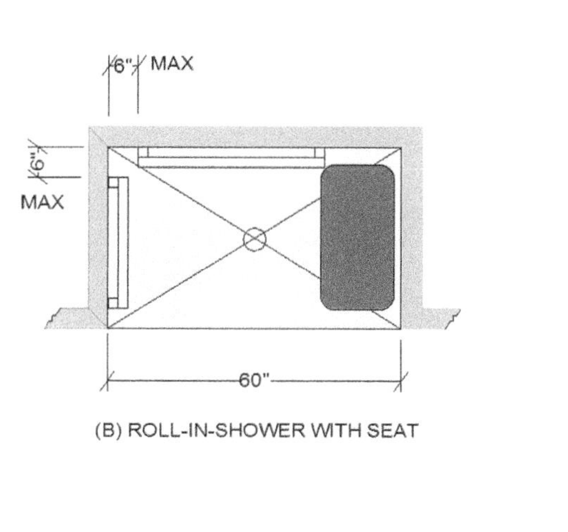

(B) ROLL-IN-SHOWER WITH SEAT

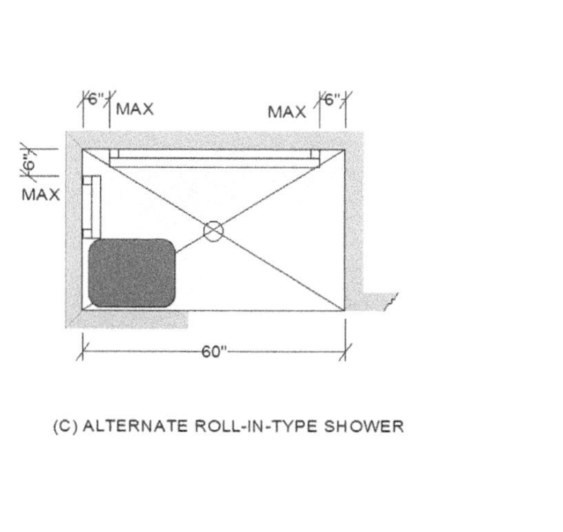

(C) ALTERNATE ROLL-IN-TYPE SHOWER

- Toilet: Grab bars should be provided on the rear wall and on the side wall closest to the toilet 33 inches to 36 inches (838 mm to 914 mm) high. Side wall grab bars should be at least 42 inches (1067 mm) long, located between 12 inches (305 mm) and 54 inches (1372 mm) from the rear wall. In addition, a vertical grab bar, 18 inches (457 mm) minimum length, shall be mounted with the bottom of the bar 39 inches to 41 inches (991 mm to 1041 mm) AFF and centerlined between 39 inches and 41 inches (991 mm and 1041 mm) from the rear wall. The rear grab bar should be at least 24 inches (610 mm) long, centered on the toilet. Where space permits, the bar should be at least 36 inches (914 mm) long, with the additional length provided on the transfer side of the toilet.
  - (604.5)

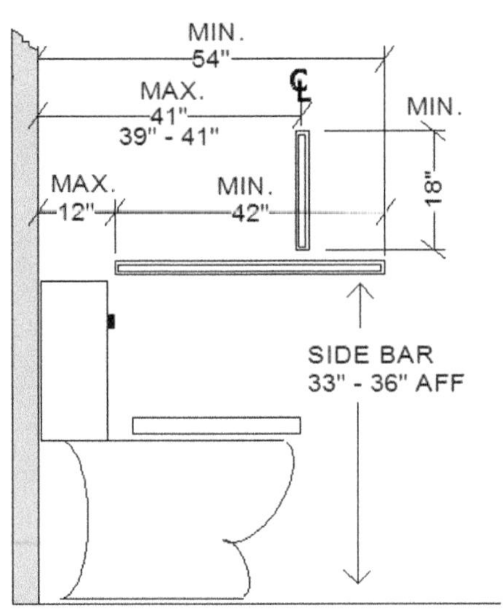

SIDE WALL GRAB BARS FOR TOILET

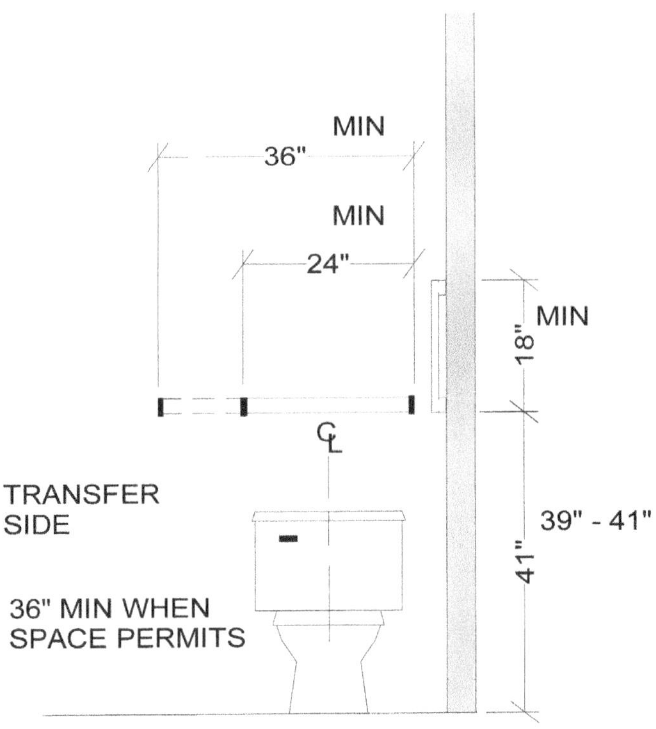

REAR WALL GRAB BAR FOR TOILET

BATHROOM PLANNING GUIDELINE 15

Glazing

Recommended

- See Code Requirement

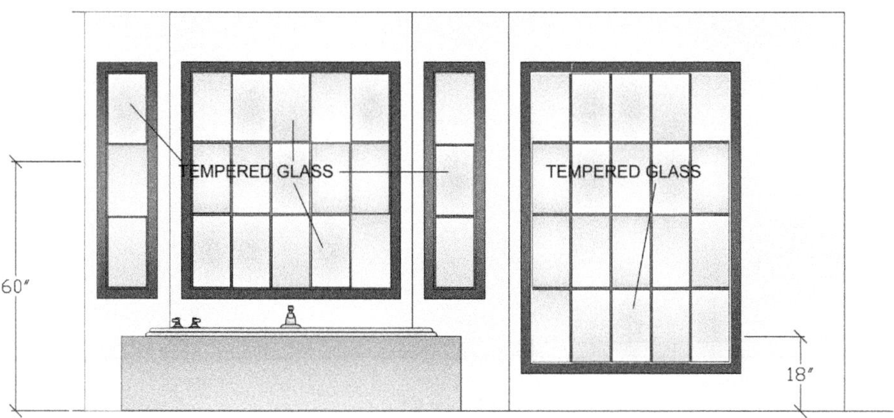

Code Requirement

- Glass used in tub or shower enclosures (e.g., tub or shower door) or partitions must be tempered or an approved equal and must be permanently marked as such.
  - (IRC R308.1)
- If the tub or shower surround has glass windows or walls, the glazing must be tempered glass or approved equal when the bottom edge of glazing is less than 60 inches (1524 mm) above any standing or walking surface.
  - (IRC R308.4)
- Any glazing (e.g., windows or doors) whose bottom edge is less than 18 inches (457 mm) above the floor must be tempered glass or approved equal.
  - (IRC R308.4)

Access Standard

Recommended:

- Consider line of sight of user when planning height of bottom of glazing.

BATHROOM PLANNING GUIDELINE 16

Tub/Shower Door

Recommended

- See Code Requirement.

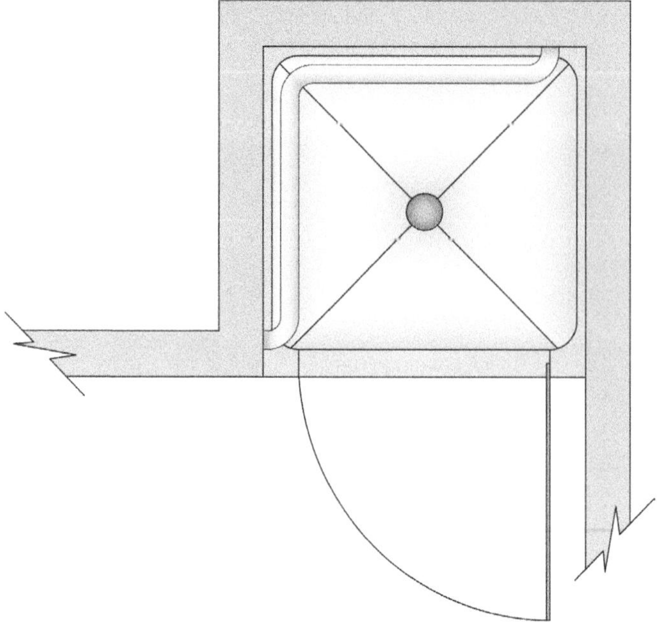

Code Requirement

- Hinged shower doors shall open outward.
    - (IRC P2708.1)

Access Standard

Recommended

- Minimize thresholds at the shower entry to no more than 1⁄2 inch (13 mm).

ICC A117.1–2009 Requirement

- Shower compartment thresholds should be no more than 1⁄4 inch to 1⁄2 inch(6 mm to 13 mm) high.
- Changes in level between 1⁄4 inch high and 1⁄2 inch (6 mm and 13 mm) high should be beveled with a slope not steeper than 1:2.
    - (608.6.303)

BATHROOM PLANNING GUIDELINE 17

Steps

Recommended

- Steps should not be placed outside a tub.

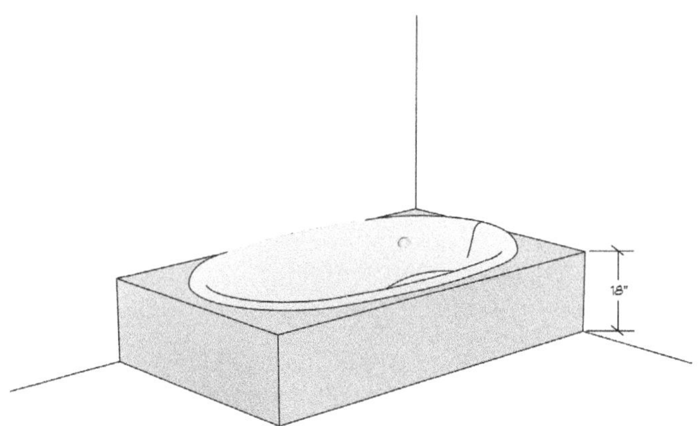

- If steps are used a grab bar/handrail is mandatory.

Access Standard

Recommended

- Bathroom Guideline recommendation meets Access Standard.

BATHROOM PLANNING GUIDELINE 18

Flooring

Recommended

- Slip-resistant surfaces should be specified for the general bath flooring, shower floors, and tub/shower bottoms.

Code Requirement

- State or local codes may apply.

Access Standard

Recommended

- Bathroom Guideline recommendation meets Access Standard.

BATHROOM PLANNING GUIDELINE 19

Equipment Access

Recommended

- See below.

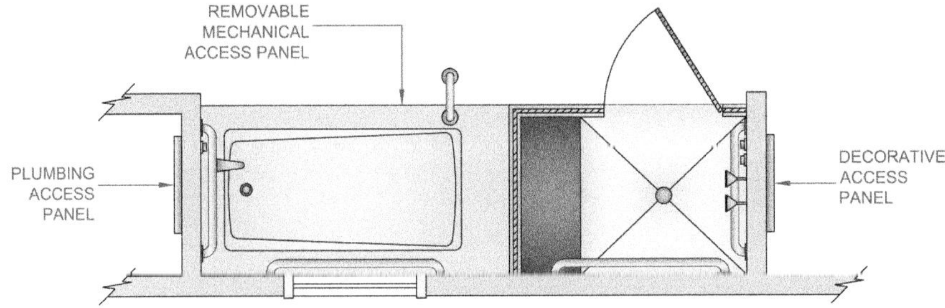

Code Requirement

- All equipment, including access panels, must be installed as per manufacturers' specifications.
  - (IRC P2720.1)
- All manufacturers' instructions must be available for installers and inspectors and left for homeowners.
  - (IRC P2720.4)

Access Standard

Recommended

Equipment controls should be placed between 15 inches and 48 inches (381 mm and 1219 mm) above the finished floor.

BATHROOM PLANNING GUIDELINE 20

Toilet/Bidet Placement

Recommended

- The distance from the centerline of toilet and/or bidet to any bath fixture, wall, or other obstacle should be at least 18 inches(457 mm).

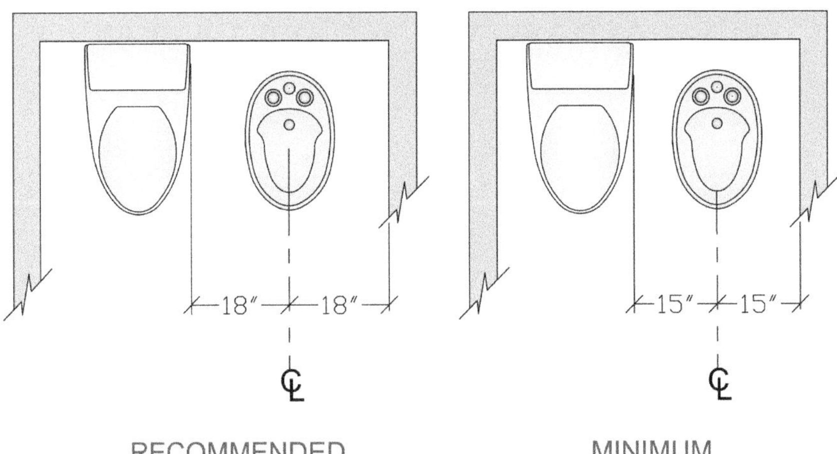

Code Requirement

- A minimum distance of 15 inches (381 mm) is required from the centerline of the toilet and/or bidet to any bath fixture, wall, or other obstacle.

  (IRC R307.1, IRC P2705.1)

Access Standard

Recommended

- Consider user height and ability when determining toilet height.

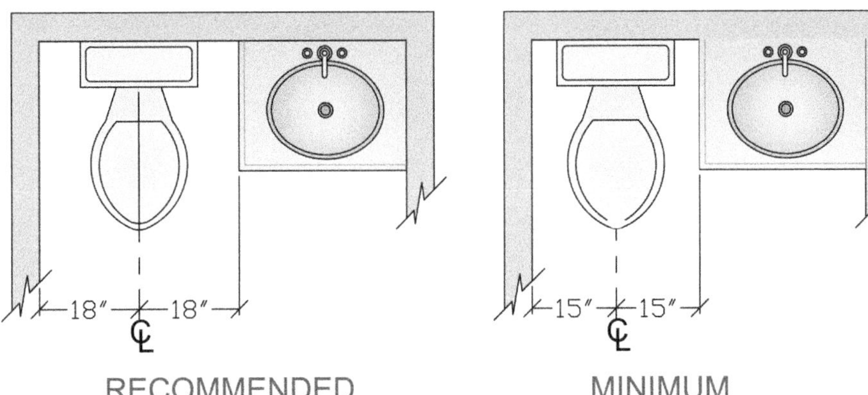

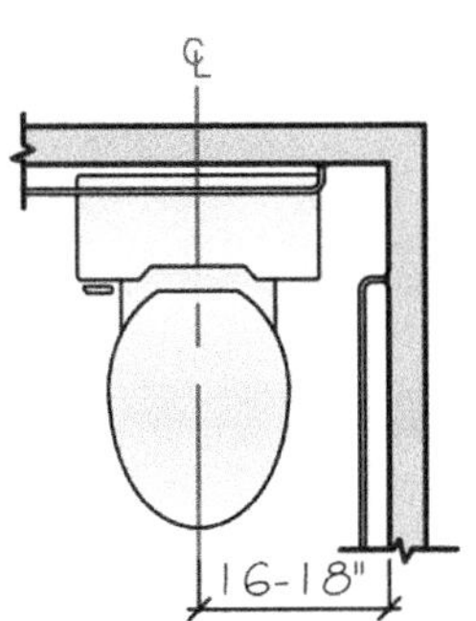

ICC A117.1–2009 Reference

- The toilet should be centered 16 inches to 18 inches (406 mm to 457 mm) from a side wall.
  - (1003.11.2.4)
- The toilet seat should be between 15 inches and 19 inches (381 mm and 483 mm) from the floor.
  - (1003.11.2.4.5)

BATHROOM PLANNING GUIDELINE 21

Toilet Compartment

RECOMMENDED

MINIMUM

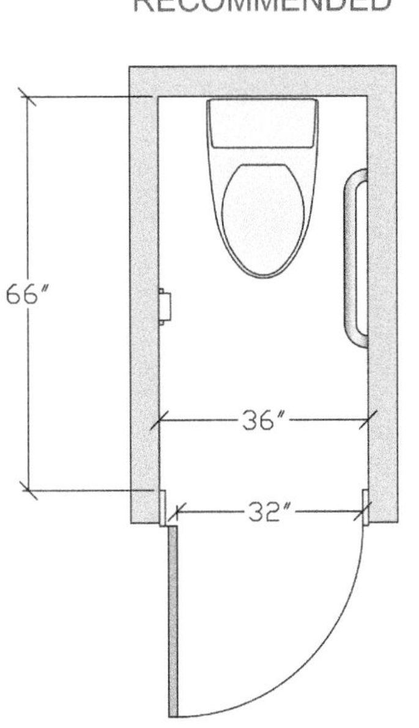

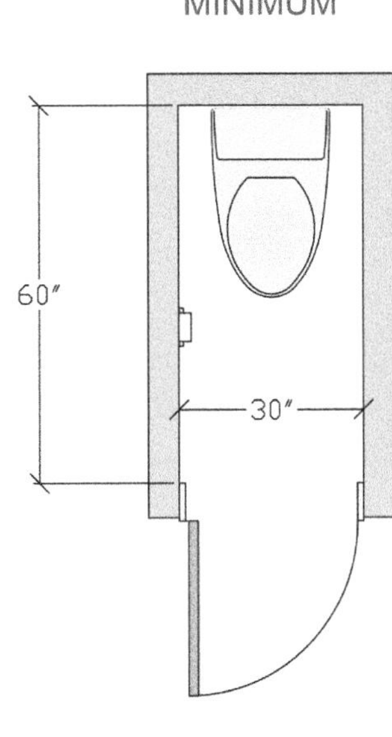

Recommended

- The size for a separate toilet compartment should be at least 36 inches by 66 inches (914 mm by 1676 mm) with a swing-out or pocket door.

Code Requirement

- The minimum size for a separate toilet compartment is 30 inches by 60 inches (762 mm by 1524 mm).
    - (IPC 405.3.1)

Access Standard

Recommended

- To maximize access, provide privacy in the toileting area without using a separate compartment.

ICC A117.1–2009 Reference

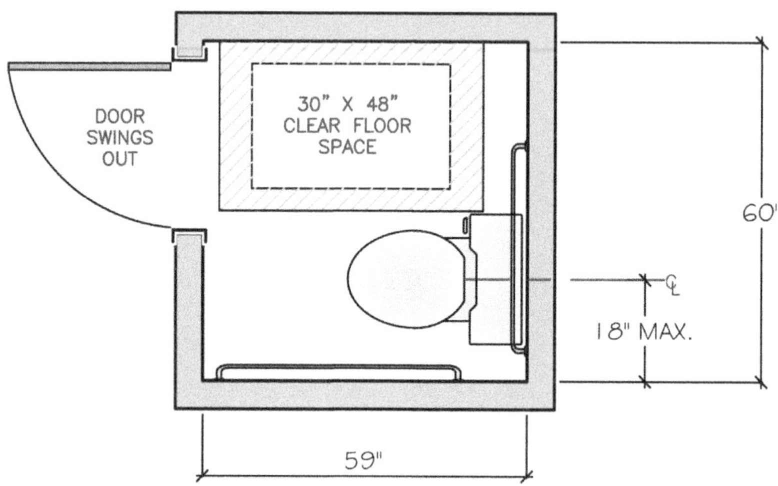

- Wheelchair accessible compartments should be at least 60 inches (1524 mm) wide, measured perpendicular to the side wall, and 56 inches (1422 mm) deep for a wall-hung toilet and 59 inches (1499 mm) deep for a floor-mounted toilet measured perpendicular to the rear wall.
    - (604.7)

BATHROOM PLANNING GUIDELINE 22

Storage

Recommended

- Provide adequate, accessible storage for toiletries, bath linens, grooming, and general bathroom supplies at point of use.

Code Requirement

- State or local codes may apply.

Access Standard

Recommended

- Plan storage of frequently used items between 15 v to 48 inches (381 mm to 1219 mm) above the finished floor.

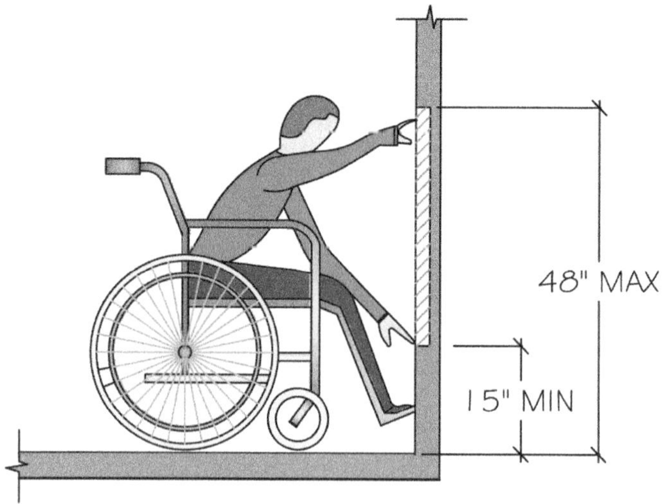

UNOBSTRUCTED FORWARD REACH

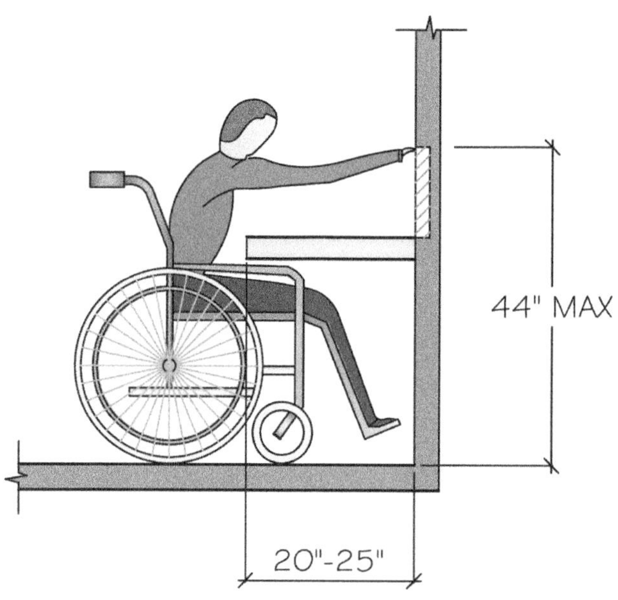

OBSTRUCTED HIGH FORWARD REACH

ICC A117.1–2009 Reference

- Where a forward or side reach is unobstructed, the high reach should be 48 inches (1219 mm) maximum and the low reach should be 15 inches (381 mm) minimum above the floor.
  - (308.2.1, 308.3.1)
- Where a forward or side reach is obstructed by a 20-inch to25-inch (508 mm to 635 mm) deep counter, the high reach should be 44 inches (1118 mm) maximum.
  - (308.2.2, 308.3.2)
- Door/drawer pulls should be operable with one hand, require only a minimal amount of strength for operation, and should not require tight grasping.
  - (309.4)

BATHROOM PLANNING GUIDELINE 23

Accessories

Recommended

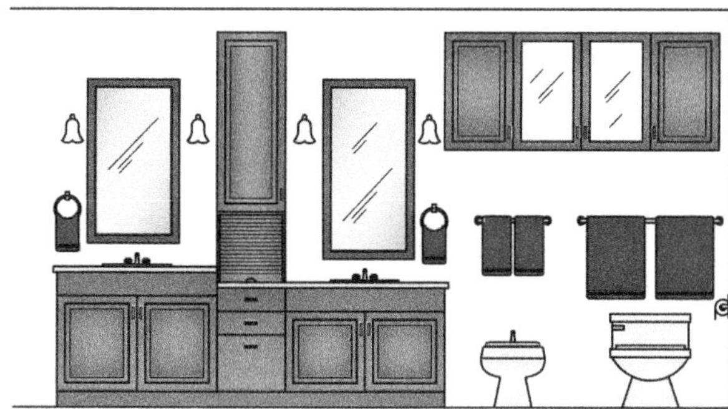

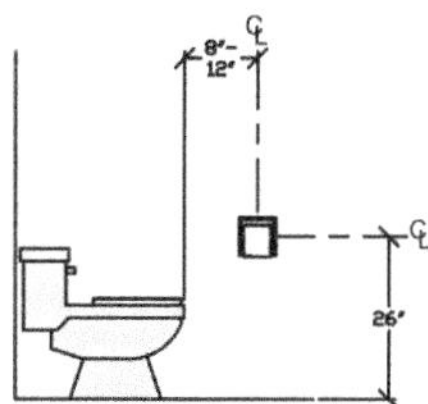

- Place a mirror above or near the lavatory at a height that takes the user's eye height into consideration.
- The toilet paper holder should be located 8 inches to 12 inches (203 mm to 305 mm) in front of the edge of the toilet bowl, centered at 26 inches (660 mm) above the floor.
- Additional accessories, such as towel holders, soap dishes, should be conveniently located near all bath fixtures.

Code Requirement

- State or local codes may apply.

Access Standard

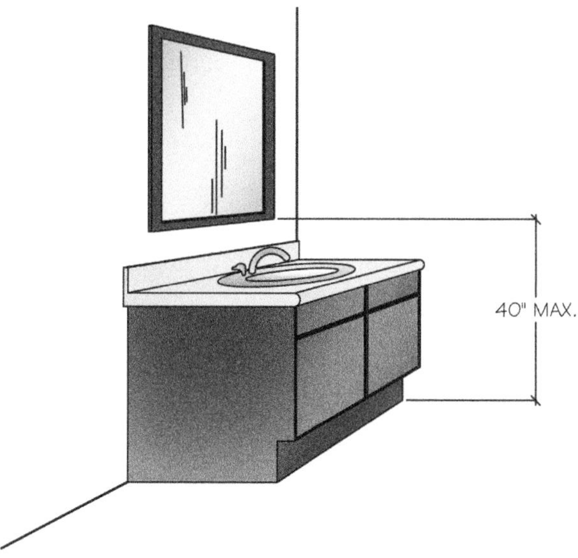

Recommended

- Plan a full-height mirror to provide reflection at eye level, regardless of the user's height or stature.
- See Code Reference on toilet paper placement.
- Accessories should be placed between 15 inches and 48 inches (381 mm and 1219 mm) above the floor, and operable with a closed fist and with minimal effort.

ICC A117.1–2009 Reference

- Mirrors above lavatories should have the bottom edge of the reflecting surface no more than 40 inches (1016 mm) above the floor.
  - (603.3)

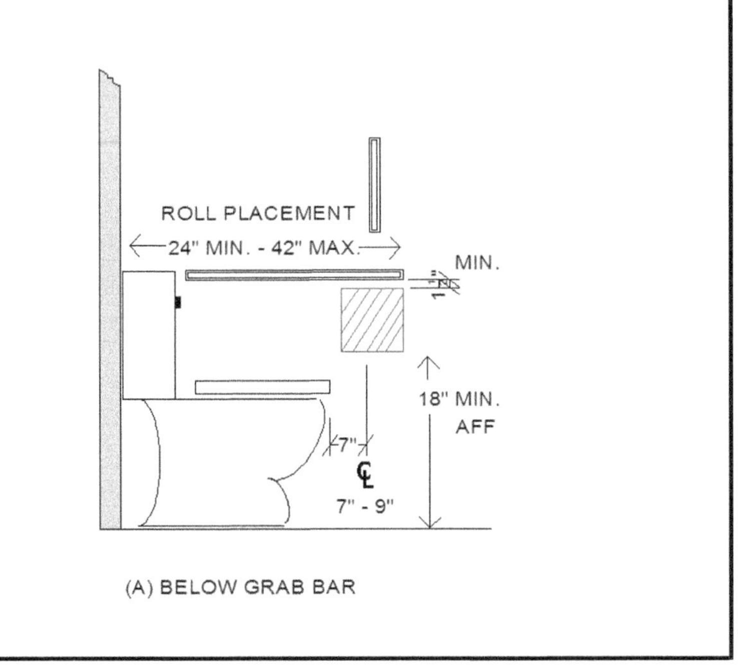

(A) BELOW GRAB BAR

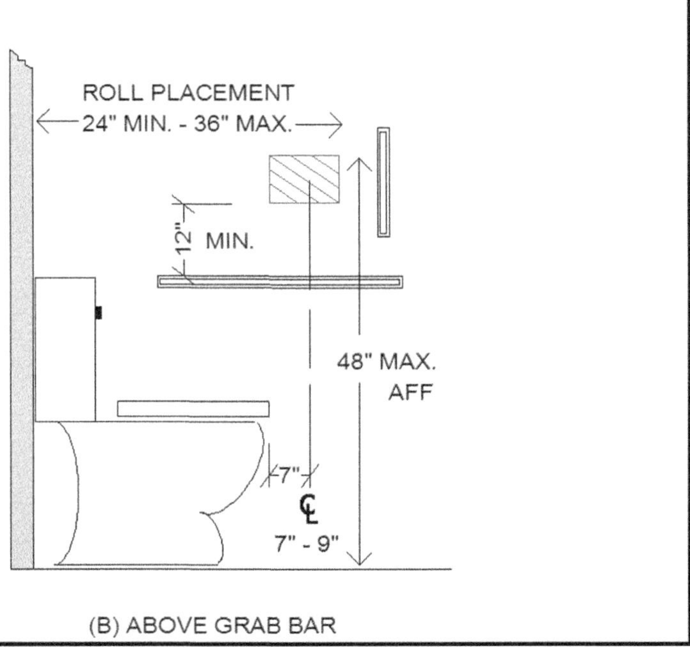

(B) ABOVE GRAB BAR

- The toilet paper holder should be 24 inches to 42 inches (610 mm to 1067 mm) off the rear wall and between 18 inches and 48 inches (457 mm and 1219 mm) above the floor with a clearance of at least 1½ inches (38 mm) below or 12 inches (305 mm) above the grab bar.
  - (604.7)
- See Access Standard 22 for reach specifications.

BATHROOM PLANNING GUIDELINE 24

Electrical Receptacles

Recommended

All GFCI receptacles should be located at electrical appliance points of use.

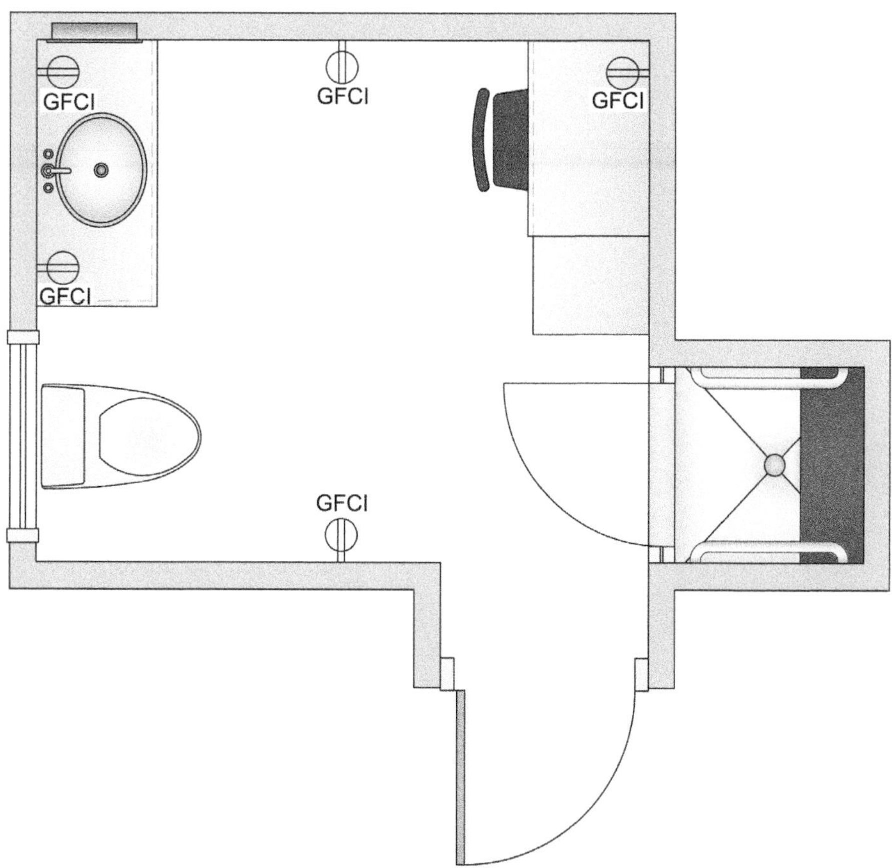

Code Requirement

- At least one GFCI-protected receptacle must be installed within 36 inches (914 mm) of the outside edge of the lavatory.
  - (IRC E3901.6)
- All receptacles must be protected by ground-fault circuit interrupters.
  - (IRC 3902.1)
- A receptacle shall not be installed within or directly over a bathtub or shower stall.
  - (IRC E4002.11)
- Switches shall not be installed within wet locations in the tub or shower spaces or within reach while standing in the tub or shower unless installed as part of the listed tub or shower assembly.
  - (IRC E4001.7)

Access Standard

Recommended

- See Code Reference.

ICC A117.1–2009 Reference

- See Access Standard 22 for specifications for placement within reach range.

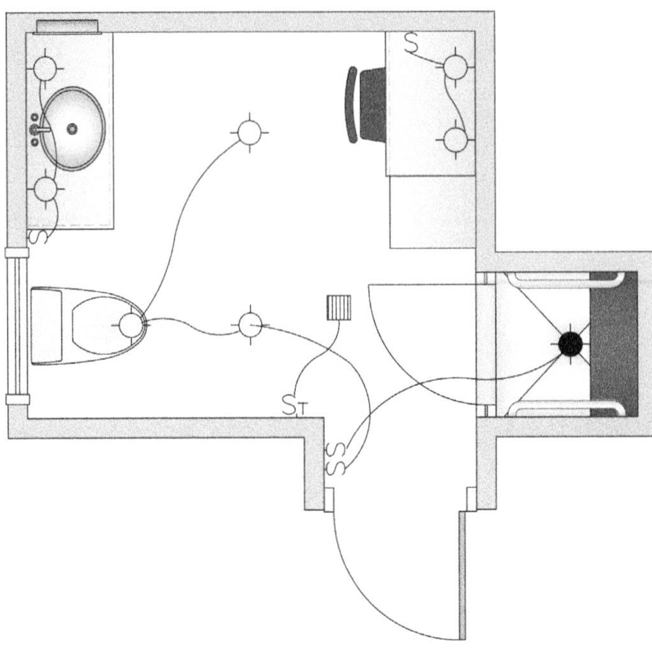

BATHROOM PLANNING GUIDELINE 25

Lighting

Recommended

- In addition to general lighting, task lighting should be provided for each functional area in the bathroom (e.g., grooming, showering).

Code Requirement

- At least one wall switch–controlled light must be provided. The switch must be placed at the entrance of the bathroom.
  - (IRC E3903.2)
- All light fixtures installed within tub and shower spaces should be marked "suitable for damp/wet locations."
  - (IRC E4003.9, 4003.10)
- Hanging fixtures cannot be located within a zone of 3 feet (914 mm) horizontally and 8 feet (2438 mm) vertically from the top of the bathtub rim or shower stall threshold.
  - (IRC E4003.11)

Access Standard

Recommended

- Task lighting at the vanity should be beside the mirror and at eye level, with the lamp not visible to the eye.
- Lighting controls should be between 15 inches and 48 inches (381 mm and 1219 mm) above the floor and operable with a closed fist and with minimal effort.

ICC A117.1–2009 Reference

- Operable parts should be operable with one hand and not require tight grasping, pinching, or twisting of the wrist. The force required to activate operable parts should be 5 pounds (2 kg) maximum.
  - (309.4)
- See Access Standard 22 for specifications for reach range for controls.

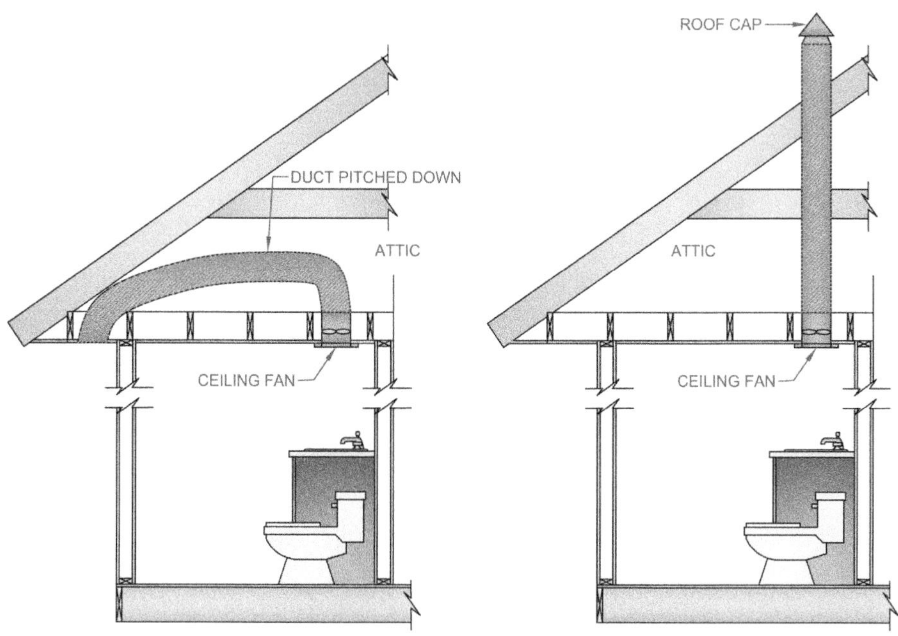

BATHROOM PLANNING GUIDELINE 26

Ventilation

Recommended

- Plan a mechanical exhaust system, vented to the outside, for each enclosed area.

Code Requirement

- Minimum ventilation for the bathroom is to be a window of at least 3 square feet (0.27 square meters) of which 50% is operable, or a mechanical ventilation system of at least 50 cubic feet (15,240 cubic mm) per minute (cfm) exhausted to the outside.
  - (IRC R303.3, IRC M1507.2, IRC M1507.3)

Access Standard

Recommended

- Ventilation controls should be placed 15 inches to 48 inches (381 mm to 1219 mm) above the floor, operable with minimal effort, easy to read, and with minimal noise pollution.

ICC A117.1–2009 Reference

- See Access Standard 25 for operable controls.
- See Access Standard 22 for reach range for controls.

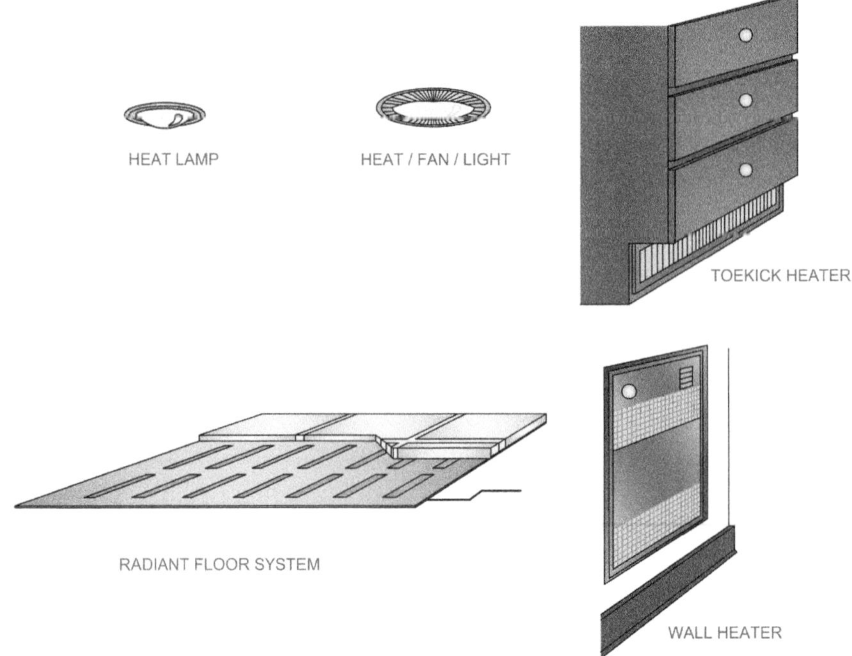

BATHROOM PLANNING GUIDELINE 27

Heat

Recommended

- A supplemental heat source, e.g., heat lamp, toe kick heater, or floor heat should be considered.

Code Requirement

- All bathrooms should have an appropriate heat source to maintain a minimum room temperature of 68° Fahrenheit (20° Celsius).

  (IRC R 303.8)

Access Standard

Recommended

- See Code Reference.

ICC A117.1–2009 Reference

- See Access Standard 25 for operable controls.
- See Access Standard 22 for reach range for controls.

APPENDIX

Measurement Conversions

Commonly Used Measurements for Landing Areas, Work Isles, and Preparation Centers

9 inches = 229 millimeters

12 inches = 305 millimeters

15 inches = 381 millimeters

18 inches = 457 millimeters

21 inches = 533 millimeters

24 inches = 610 millimeters

36 inches = 914 millimeters

42 inches = 1067 millimeters

48 inches = 1219 millimeters

Note: Millimeter measurements shown throughout this publication have been rounded to the nearest whole number when applicable.

Glossary

A

Accessibility and accessible design:
Characteristics of spaces or products that meet prescribed requirements for particular variations in ability, i.e., "wheelchair accessible."

Accordion door:
A door that folds into multiple sections.

Adjacency matrix:
Also called a relationship matrix, this is a graphic method of organizing relationships of multiple spaces, including various types of relationships, such as visual or auditory; a step in design programming.

Aging-in-place (design for):
Design that considers the changes that occur as one ages, supporting the ability to live in one's own home and community safely, independently, and comfortably, regardless of age, income, or ability level.

Air barrier:
Materials or products used to control air leakage out of, or air infiltration into a building.

Americans with Disabilities Act Accessibility Guidelines (ADAAG):
Guidelines for compliance with the accessibility requirements of the Americans with Disabilities Act (ADA) (1991).

Adaptable design:
Features that are either adjustable or capable of being easily added or removed to "adapt" the unit to individual needs or preferences.

ACH (Air changes per hour):
Used to measure the ventilation rate of a room or building; 1 ACH means that, in one hour, a volume of air equal to the volume of the room has been exhausted and replaced with outside air.

Aerobic exercise:
Exercise to increase heart rate; cardiovascular exercise.

Air leakage (AL):
Air leakage is the amount of heat loss or gain that occurs by infiltration through cracks and openings in the window assembly.

Ambient lighting:
General lighting diffused within an entire room.

Ambient noise:
The level of acoustic noise at a given location, such as in a room.

Amperes, amps:
Unit of electrical current. The current in amps equals the power in watts divided by the voltage in volts.

ANSI A117.1—Accessible and Useable Buildings and Facilities:
Original American National Standards Institute (ANSI) guidelines for accessible design in commercial and residential spaces. Now the International Code Council (ICC)/ANSI A117.1, the referenced technical standard for compliance with the accessibility requirements of International Building Code and many other state and local codes. Used as reference for NKBA Access Standards.

Anthropometry:
The study of human measurements, such as size and proportion, and parameters, such as reach range and visual range.

Antimicrobial finish:
A material that has an applied finish, or ingredient in the product, that inhibits the growth of microorganisms, such as bacteria or fungi.

Aromatherapy:
Using the scent from the essential oils of plants to affect mood and sense of well-being.

B

Back draft damper:
Placed within the duct work on the exhaust vent, this pivoting panel is important to the fan system. It opens when the fan is operating, but closes to prevent outside air from leaking back into the home when the fan is not operating. Also, the flap can prevent insects, birds and other animals from getting into the fan duct.

Back drafting:
Used to describe a situation where combustion byproducts, from furnaces, water heaters, fireplaces, stoves, and other fuel-burning appliances, are pulled back into the house instead of exhausting through the flue or chimney; the situation can occur when the air pressure inside the home is less than outside,

and is usually the result of running exhaust fans and appliances without providing adequate make-up air.

Ballast:
A device that controls the current in a fluorescent lamp.

Barrier-free design:
An older term for universal design, based on the concept of solutions that removed barriers in the environment.

Barn-style door:
A style of door with hardware that allows the door to slide along the wall. Useful when a pocket door is too costly or not possible.

Bidet:
A personal hygiene fixture with a hot and cold water supply that is designed for personal cleanliness; used to wash the perinea and genital area.

Bidet seat:
A toilet seat with integral bidet features, usually including personal hygiene, odor and bacteria venting, and heat.

Bi-fold door:
A door that is hinged in the center so that as the door opens, it folds in half; this reduces the floor area needed for a door swing. Most bi-fold doors are hung on a track.

Biological pollutants:
Indoor air pollutants that come from living sources, including molds, insects, and animals; more likely to be found in moist places.

Body spray shower head:
Body spray or body jet showerheads are a group of individual showerheads installed in a series of two or three along opposite walls of the shower.

Boudoir or console lavatory:
A lavatory supported by two cast metal legs which included a raised shelf and room for a dressing table bench under it. Body spray shower head: Body spray or body jet showerheads are a group of individual showerheads installed in a series of two or three along opposite walls of the shower.

Bubble diagram:
A simple visual or sketch where each "bubble" represents an activity area in the space to be designed; used to help organize activity and space relationships at an early stage of design programming.

Building code:
Community and state ordinances governing the manner in which a home may be constructed or modified.

Bypass sliding doors:
Two sliding doors of the same size, on parallel tracks, that can slide independently. No floor area is needed for a door swing, but only half of the door opening area is accessible.

C

Cabinet nomenclature:
A code of letters and numbers that designate a cabinet's size, use, and placement. Manufacturers typically have their own code for their products. The National Kitchen and Bath Association (NKBA) has developed a generic nomenclature for kitchen and bath cabinets.

CADR (Clean Air Delivery Rate):
A measure of the efficiency of a portable air cleaner, based on the percentage of particles removed from the air and the speed at which the particles are removed.

Café doors:
Two doors hinged to the opposite door frames, meeting in the middle, thus reducing the amount of room needed for door clearances. The doors swing in both directions and close automatically once a person has passed beyond the door swing .

Canadian Electric Code (CEC):
A code for electrical safety in Canada. It is almost identical to the National Electric Code (NEC) used in the United States.

Cardiovascular exercise:
Exercise to increase heart rate; aerobic exercise.

Casement window:
Panels are hinged at the side and crank open to a 90 degree angle, exposing almost all of the window area to the outside.

Center:
Area where a task occurs, including the fixture, clear space, storage, and other components that support the function of the task. In the bathroom the centers are grooming, bathing/showering, and toileting.

Ceiling-mounted convection heater:
These units have a small heater and a fan that blows the warm air down onto the user and into the room.

Ceiling or wall panel heater:
Electric heating coils installed in the ceiling or in walls behind the drywall.

Centrifugal or "squirrel cage" fan:
A type of fan that is circular with fins, resembling a hamster exercise wheel. These fans are generally quieter, but can be more expensive.

Certified Bath Designer (CBD):
NKBA designation for a bathroom designer who has passed the certification examination.

Chamber pot:
A small ceramic or metal pot, stored under the bed, in a cabinet, or stool (often called a commode or closestool), or it would sit out in the room if highly decorated. The pot was used until the nineteenth century as an indoor toilet when the weather was bad or during the night.

Chromatherapy:
Using color to affect mood and sense of well-being; using colored lights in a bathtub to set a specific mood.

Claw-foot tub:
A tub mounted off of the floor on four legs; the base of each leg is shaped like a claw foot.

Circuit breaker:
A device that is designed to protect electrical equipment and people from damage caused by overload or short circuit. It can be reset to resume operation.

Clear floor space:
Area which is free of obstruction within an overall space, typically used in reference to the recommendations for clearances at a center (i.e., the lavatory or the shower) or for a particular activity (i.e., bathing or exercising).

Closestool:
A piece of furniture like a chair, also called a night chair, which had the bottom enclosed to hide the chamber pot.

Color Rendering Index (CRI):
A method for describing the effect of a light source on the color appearance of objects compared to a reference source of the same color temperature.

Color temperature:
An index of how the light source, itself, looks to us, measured in degrees Kelvin (K).

Comfort zone:
A body buffer zone that we maintain between others and ourselves.

Compartmentalized bathroom:
A bathroom where individual activities, like toileting or showering, are separated by walls into individual compartments.

Composting toilet:
A fully self-contained toilet that requires no water inlet, or sewer connection, and uses chemicals in order to operate. It works like a septic tank with bacterial action breaking down the solid waste into a soil-type residue.

Condensation:
The process where water changes from a gaseous stage to a liquid stage; heat is released by condensation.

Condensation resistance (CR):
The CR measures how well a window resists the formation of condensation on the inside surface of the window and is expressed as a number between 1 and 100.

Console lavatory:
A lavatory basin supported by legs. The legs can be metal or wooden.

Corner bathtub:
A fixture for bathing with two sides at right angles that fit within the corner of the room.

Covenant:
Sometimes called a restrictive covenant, this is a legally binding clause in a property deed that imposes a limitation or requirement on the use of the property.

Cubic feet per minute (cfm):
Used as a measure of the amount of air a fan can move. See liters/second (l/s) for the metric equivalent.

Curbless or no-threshold shower:
A shower with an entry that is even with the floor in the bathroom.

Cycling losses:
The loss of heat as the water circulates through a water heater tank, and/or inlet and outlet pipes.

D

Daylighting:
Using light from the sun to illuminate the interior of a building.

Decorative fixed windows:
These windows use specially cut glass or design to give a decorative touch and also serve as a second source of light. A stained glass window is an example.

Dental lavatory:
A small sink used for brushing teeth that was typically located at a lower height for children to reach; promoted by the plumbing industry as a way to open the bathroom to multiple users.

Design process:
Multistage process where a designer moves from an idea to a completed product, usually with the help of a design program. The design process is both a verbal and visual process.

Design program:
Organized and documented information about a client and their proposed project that guides the design process. Design programming includes the various steps of gathering, organizing and analyzing the information to develop the plan of the design program, which is critical to the execution of the design.

Dew point:
The temperature at which water vapor condenses; the dew point temperature is a function of humidity; when the relative humidity is 100 percent, the air is saturated and can hold no more water vapor, therefore, if there is more water vapor, or the temperature drops below the dew point, condensation occurs.

Dressing circle:
Space needed to put clothes on and take clothes off, 42 to 48 inches (1069 to 1219 mm) in diameter.

Dual cueing:
Also called redundant cueing, refers to the use of different modes (pictorial, verbal, tactile) to communicate necessary information effectively to the user, regardless of ambient conditions or the user's sensory abilities.

E

Earth closet:
An indoor privy where dry soil was added to a reservoir below the seat after each use to absorb moisture and retain offensive odors; periodically the soil contents were removed and used as compost.

Efficacy:
The energy efficiency of a lighting source or lighting output per watt of power in lumens per watt (LPW).

Egress:
A path or opening for exiting a room or building.

Ejector toilet:
A typical ejector toilet has a pedestal made of polyethylene, which acts as a base for mounting the toilet. Inside the unit is a set of impellors and a sewage ejector pump, which processes the waste and pushes it up to the main sewer line.

Ergonomic design:
The application of human factor data or anthropometric data to the design of products and spaces to improve function and efficiency.

Ergonomic fit or ergofitting:
Focuses on the anthropometric aspects of, and the application of the data to the design of interior spaces where people work, play, or live.

Exfoliate:
To remove layers of dry, flaking skin.

F

Fair Housing Accessibility Guidelines (FHAG):
Accessibility regulations affecting the design of multifamily housing built since 1991. FHAG make up the technical guidance for compliance with the accessibility requirements of the Fair Housing Amendments Act of 1988.

Fenestration:
The arrangement of windows in a building.

Feng Shui:
The Chinese art or practice of positioning objects based on a belief in patterns of yin and yang and the flow of chi that have positive and negative effects.

Fitting:
A term used for a device that controls water entering or leaving a fixture. Faucets, spouts, drain, controls, water supply lines, and diverter valves are all considered fittings.

Fixture (lighting):
The assembly that includes the mounting base or socket and any features that reflect or dispense the light from a lamp fitted into the fixture.

Fixture (plumbing):
Any fixed part of the structural design, such as tubs, bidets, toilets, and lavatories.

Floating cabinets:
Cabinets take on a "floating look" when they are attached to a wall instead of grounded on the floor.

Floor heating systems:
Floor heating systems can be either electric or hydronic and will incorporate heating coils or tubes directly under the flooring materials.

Floor mounted radiators:
In homes where hydronic heat is used throughout the home, radiators are used to circulate hot water and from the water is dispersed to the room.

Flush door:
A slab door, with a smooth surface, as opposed to a panel door with panels and moldings.

Footcandle (fc):
A measurement in the American System (AS) for the amount of light that falls on a surface. One footcandle is the amount of light that falls on a surface one foot square, placed one foot from the source.

Framed cabinets:
Cabinets constructed with a face frame which provides the primary support for the cabinet. Doors and drawers fit in one of three ways: flush with the frame, partially overlying the frame, or completely overlaying the frame.

Frameless cabinets:
The case part of the cabinet does not need a front frame for stability. Doors and drawers cover the entire face of the cabinet.

Free-standing tub:
A fixture for bathing that is finished on all sides and suitable for placing in the middle of the bathroom.

Functional anthropometry:
The measurements of the body in motion.

Fuse:
A device that can interrupt the flow of electrical current when a circuit is overloaded.

G

GFCI (ground fault circuit interrupter):
A device that monitors the electric current on a circuit to make sure the amount of current going out is the same as that returning to the electric receptacle. Serving as a safety device, the slightest difference in current will shut off the current.

Graywater:
Water that has been used in the household that has the potential to be reused or recycled. Graywater may come from bathtubs, showers, sinks, lavatories, and washing machines, and does not contain sewage (black water).

Grab bars:
Safety bars installed as needed, particularly in bathtubs and showers and in the toileting area, to prevent falls. A device, usually installed on a wall, that provide support while rising from, sitting in, entering, or exiting a bathtub or shower, or using the toilet.

H

Hand-held showerhead:
The shower head is attached to a long flexible hose that allows the user to spray water directly onto parts of the body. It can be useful when showering people of various heights and people sitting to shower or bathe. They are often attached to a mounting pipe so they can also serve as an adjustable wall shower when in place.

Hard water:
Water with a high content of minerals, usually calcium and magnesium; often leads to plumbing problems from mineral deposits.

Hard-wired:
A permanent electrical connection for an appliance or device (as opposed to a cord with a plug).

Heat pump water heater (HPWH):
A heat pump adapted to heat water for domestic use.

Hollow-core door:
A flush door in which the surface material is nailed and/or glued over a skeleton framework, as opposed to a solid-core door where inner material is solid, usually wood.

Homeowner's association:
An organization of the property owners in a specific housing development or neighborhood. Responsibilities of the association will vary, but often include management of common area and oversight of requirements affecting the community as a whole; requirements for membership and dues may be a condition of property ownership.

Hopper and awning windows:
Hopper windows are hinged at the bottom and open inward and awning windows are hinged at the top and open outwards.

Hot tub:
A large container of heated water used for soaking. The original hot tub resembled a barrel. They usually did not have moving water. Currently similar to a spa tub—a large tub holding warm water, with whirlpool action and seating for multiple users.

Humidity:
The amount of water vapor in the air.

Hydronic systems:
A heating system that uses circulating hot water as the heat source; the water is distributed through tubes in the floor or freestanding radiators.

Hydrotherapy:
Refers to a variety of bathing options that use hot water, water movement, and/or pressure to stimulate or relax the body.

I

Infrared heat lamp:
Recessed into the ceiling, these lamps are designed to heat what is directly below them.

Inline fans:
In this type of fan, the motor is mounted in the duct system.

Integral lavatory:
A fixture fabricated from the same piece of material as the countertop material.

International Residential Code (IRC):
Building code developed by the International Code Council for single-family housing. Used as reference for NKBA Kitchen & Bathroom Planning Guidelines.

J

Jetted bathtub:
A large basin of hot water with air jets around the perimeter to create a pulsing action on the bather; whirlpool tub.

Joists:
A level or nearly level member used in a series to frame a floor or ceiling structure.

L

Lamp:
Industry term for a light bulb. An interchangeable bulb or tube that constitutes the lighting source in a fixture.

Latrine:
A pit dug in the ground used for disposing of and decomposing human waste. Also a communal toilet, often used in camps and military barracks.

Lavatory:
A fixture with running water and drainpipe, for washing hands and face, shaving, and the like. *See also* individual lavatory types. *See also* individual lavatory types.

Life cycle analysis:
An assessment or perspective that looks at a product from a long term or life cycle view. This perspective considers all the costs (purchase, energy, maintenance, disposal, etc.) as well as all the impacts (type of energy, pollution, disposal, etc.) of the product.

Lifespan design:
The aspect of universal design that provides for changes that occur in the lifespan of the home and its owners.

Liters per second (l/s):
Metric measurement used to rate the capacity of a ventilation fan.

Load-bearing wall:
Exterior and interior walls of the home that support the structure vertically. Openings in any load-bearing wall must be reinforced to carry the live and dead weight of the structural load.

Louvered door:
A door with horizontal slats (louvers) to provide ventilation.

Low-e coating:
A low-emissivity coating consisting of a thin, virtually invisible metal or metal oxide layer deposited on a window-glazing surface primarily to reduce the U-factor by suppressing radiant heat flow.

Lumen:
The amount of light, measured at the lighting source.

Luminaire:
See "Fixture (lighting)".

Lux:
A measurement in the International system (IS) for the amount of light that falls on a surface. One lux is the amount of light that falls on one square meter placed one meter from the source.

M

Massage:
A rubbing or kneading of the body to stimulate circulation and make muscles or joints supple. Several techniques focus on various parts of the body.

Maximum performance testing (MaP):
A test of the minimum solid waste flushing of a toilet.

Medicine cabinet:
A shallow storage unit typically planned for the Grooming Center in the bathroom. It is often is covered with a mirror and placed over, on, or into a wall next to the vanity.

Milk glass:
Opaque white glass, blown or pressed into a wide variety of shapes.

Modified energy factor (MEF):
A performance factor for clothes washing machines based on capacity, electricity usage, energy to heat the water and energy to remove water from the clothes. A higher MEF is more efficient.

Mold:
Fungi that grow in moist environments and organic materials, especially cellulosic building materials as a food source.

Monel:
A corrosive-resistant, lightweight white metal containing a mix of copper and nickel.

N

National Electric Code (NEC):
A code for electrical safety adopted by states and local jurisdictions.

Needs assessment:
The part of the design process where information is gathered about the client, their home and the parameters of the design project.

O

Off-gas:
A term used to describe the release or evaporation of chemicals into the air from building materials as they dry, cure, or age; the process can be more rapid if temperature and/or humidity are increased.

On-demand/instantaneous water heater:
A gas or electric unit that heats water, with no waiting as it is needed by the user; sometimes called a tankless water heater.

Overhead showerheads:
Showerheads that are mounted on the ceiling either in tiles or in a fixture such as the rain showerhead.

P

Pedestal lavatory:
A free-standing fixture with a wide top and narrow base that conceals the plumbing.

Pendant:
A lighting fixture containing one or more lamps and hung from the ceiling.

Peripheral vision:
Scope of vision on both sides of the eyes. Range often diminishes with age.

pH:
A scale used to measure the acidity or alkalinity of water, with values from 1 to 14; neutral is 7; decreasing numbers below 7 mean greater acidity and increasing numbers above 7 mean greater alkalinity.

Platform tub:
A fixture for bathing that is placed within a built platform. The tub is not finished on the sides and is designed to be placed within a cut-out at the top of the platform.

Pocket door:
A door that slides horizontally on a track and is typically moved inside a wall for storage.

Popliteal:
A human body measurement relating to the back part of the leg behind the knee.

Pounds per square inch (psi):
A standard measurement of water pressure in the American system; see kilopascals (kPa) for the metric equivalent.

Powder room:
A small bathroom for guests near the public areas of the home. Consists of a sink and toilet.

Primary Drinking Water Standards:
Federally mandated standards for acceptable levels of certain pollutants in water; used to assure that water is safe to drink or ingest.

Privatus:
From the Latin word meaning "secret," not publicly known; used to form the word *privy*.

Privy:
An English word used during the seventeenth and eighteenth centuries to describe what is commonly known as the outhouse, a toileting facility located outside the house and consisting of a seat over an opening placed in a small building.

Public bath house:
The center of social activities and a form of recreation for many ancient Roman citizens with some including courts for playing ball, a gymnasium, libraries, shops, tennis courts, and snack bars.

R

Radon:
A naturally occurring radioactive gas found in soil and groundwater; tasteless, odorless, and colorless and detectable only through testing equipment; can seep into homes and build to levels that can be a health threat; long-term exposure can lead to lung cancer.

Rain showerhead:
A large overhead showerhead that dispenses water in larger droplets that simulate rain drops.

Recessed bathtub:
A fixture for bathing that is unfinished on three sides and slides into an alcove or two end walls and a side wall. The fourth side of the tub is finished and exposed to the bathroom.

Redundant cuing:
Also referred to as "dual cueing," repetition of a message in more than one sensory mode, such as a smoke alarm that flashes a light, sounds a buzzer, and vibrates to alert in case of fire or smoke.

Relative humidity:
A ratio, usually expressed as a percent, of the actual amount of water vapor in the air to the maximum amount (saturation) of water vapor the air could hold at the current temperature.

Repurpose:
Use a material, product, or item for a new purpose in a project.

Rimmed lavatory:
A fixture with the top edge sitting flush with the countertop. The joint between the lavatory and the counter is concealed with a metal rim.

Rough-in:
Where the showerhead or other plumbing fitting will be placed in the wall or floor.

R-value:
A measure of the resistance to heat conductivity of a material; the higher the R-value, the more the materials resists heat conduction, or the better it acts as an insulator.

S

Salvage:
Generally used to describe materials that are reused in a building project, typically for a purposed similar to their original use; may also be described as reclaimed.

Safe harbors:
Standards that are legally recognized as compliance with the requirements of a code or guideline.

Sauna:
A Finnish steam bath. A room that uses dry heat and steam to cleanse and relax the user. Steam is produced by pouring water over heated rocks.

Sconce:
A light fixture that is fixed to a wall.

Secondary Drinking Water Standards:
Voluntary standards for acceptable levels of certain pollutants in water; used to assure that water is functional and aesthetic for typical household uses, such as bathing and laundry.

Self-rimming lavatory:
A fixture with the top edge sitting above the counter. A hole is cut into the counter surface and the lavatory is dropped into the whole. Caulking seals the edge of the lavatory to the counter.

Septic tank:
A large tank where solid matter or sewage from a home is disintegrated by bacteria.

Shut-off valve:
A valve control that allows the user to shut off the water entering a fixture. These valves are usually located close to the fixture.

Sight lines:
The range or visual field in direct line with a person's eyes, impacted by the position a person will be in when the space or product is being used. This is useful in planning heights of fixtures, fittings, lighting, windows, and more.

Single- and double-sliding windows:
Both sashes slide horizontally in a double-sliding window and only one sash slides in a single-sliding window.

Single or double hung windows:
In double-hung both sashes slide vertically whereas only the bottom sash slides upward in the single-hung window.

Siphon action water closet:
A vacuum action creates pressure to more efficiently flush away the waste and use less water in the process; this action is used in most modern toilets today.

Sitz bath:
A warm water bath used for healing or cleansing purposes. The individual sits in the bath that only covers the hips and buttocks.

Soaking tub:
Extra deep tub that allows the user to submerge to their neck.

Sone:
A unit of loudness, which is a subjective characteristic of a sound; the sone scale is based on data from people judging the loudness of pure tones; as an example, a noise at four sones is perceived to be four times as loud as a noise of one sone.

Solar heat gain coefficient (SHGC):
A measure of how much solar heat passes through glass, used in matching window glass to climate and location of the windows.

Sound transmission class (STC):
A measure of the absorption of sound as it passes through building materials (transmission loss); a higher STC will reduce the transmission of sound.

Spa tub:
A large tub holding warm water having whirlpool action and seating for multiple users; hot tub.

Skylight:
Typically located on the roof area and bring in natural light, usually eliminating the need for artificial light during the daylight hours.

Square or plumb:
Plumb means straight up or down: vertically. A wall, for example, is plumb when it is perpendicular to the floor. The sides of a door or window frame must be plumb (at a 90-degree angle) with the floor to function properly. When the horizontal surfaces are level and the vertical surfaces are plumb, the structure is said to be square on the vertical plane.

Standby losses:
For water heaters with a storage tank, it is the percentage of heat loss per hour from the stored water compared to the heat content of the water.

Static or structural anthropometry:
The study of the measurements of the body at rest.

Storage principles:
A series of recommendations, developed through research, to increase both the efficiency of storage space and the ease of use.

Subflooring:
The flooring applied directly to the floor joists on top of which the finished floor rests.

Sustainability, sustainable design:
As used in this book, sustainability is a philosophical approach to the built environment that emphasizes balance, thinking of the future, and minimizing the impact today.

T

Tactile cueing:
Using textural elements to communicate necessary information through touch to the user.

Tank water heater:
Tank type units are commonly used in U.S. and Canadian homes. This type of water heater keeps water hot on a 24 hours basis, adding more heat when the thermostat is below the set water temperature.

Task lighting:
Added lighting for specific tasks, like grooming, dressing, reading, and the like.

Thalassotherapy:
A form of hydrotherapy that uses seawater in baths, showers, or mud baths.

Thermal envelope:
In a house, the thermal envelope includes the boundary between the conditioned (heated and/or cooled) space and the non-conditioned spaces. For example, the bathroom is part of the thermal envelope, but a garage or attic is usually not.

Third-party verification:
A practice used in many certification and accreditation programs in which an independent organization or qualified professional evaluates compliance with program requirements.

Tempered glazing:
Tempered glass is a type of safety glass regularly used in applications in which standard glass could pose a potential danger. Tempered glass is four to five times stronger than standard glass and does not break into sharp shards when it fails.

Toe kick:
An indented space in cabinetry near the floor to accommodate the feet while standing next to a cabinet.

Toe kick heater:
A small electric heater installed in the toe kick below the cabinet.

Towel warmers:
Towel warmers can be either a wall- or floor-mounted rack. They are designed to heat and dry bath towels as they drape over the rods. Warming drawers are also available but they are typically used for warming only.

Transfer shower:
A shower open on one side with a seat adjacent to the opening, and grab bars on all three sides that allows for a person to transfer from a wheelchair to the seat.

Transformer:
An electrical device by which alternating current of one voltage is changed to another voltage.

Transgenerational design:
Another term for universal design, referring to design that acknowledges and supports the multiple generations more commonly living in a home.

Truss:
A framework of beams forming a rigid structure such as a roof truss.

Tubular daylight devices (TDD):
This type of skylight is a tube that extend from the roof down through the roof /attic to the interior space.

Turkish bath:
A steam bath that is followed by a shower and massage; developed when Roman bathing customs were combined with those of the nomadic people, such as the Byzantines.

U

U-factor:
U-factor is a measurement of heat conductivity or thermal transfer.

Ultraviolet:
An invisible portion of the light spectrum that fades fabrics.

Undermounted lavatory:
A fixture mounted under the countertop.

Uniform Federal Accessibility Standards (UFAS):
The technical standard referenced by two federal mandates for accessibility for federal buildings: the Architectural Barriers Act (ABA) and Section 504 of the Rehabilitation Act of 1973 (Section 504).

Universal design:
The design of products and environments to be useable by all people to the greatest extent possible.

User analysis:
A chart or table that groups design requirements by major activity spaces; an organizational tool used in design programming or as part of the design process.

V

Vanity:
Bathroom cabinet with the lavatory on the top.

Vanity base cabinets:
These cabinets are usually 21 inches (533 mm) deep and available in several heights ranging from 28 1/2 inches to 34 1/2 inches (724 mm to 877 mm). They may contain the lavatory(ies) as well as other storage in the bathroom.

Vapor retarder:
A building material that limits the flow of moisture. They are especially important in the construction of the building envelope to prevent moisture condensation within the building structure.

Vernacular housing:
Housing styles that are typical or common to a region and have developed over time in

response to factors such as available building materials, climate, and cultural heritage.

Vessel lavatory:
A lavatory bowl or basin that sits on top of the counter or ledge.

Vichy shower:
A seven headed rain bar with pressure spray treatment used to apply water and warmed essential oils to relax and stimulate the mind and body.

Visible transmittance (VT):
VT indicates the amount of visible light transmitted through the glass.

Visit-ability:
The condition of a home that has been planned to allow for a guest with accessibility needs. Includes a level entry, wide doorways, and an accessible bathroom on the first floor.

Vitreous china:
A ceramic material fired at high temperatures to form a nonporous, glass-like material.

Volatile organic compounds (VOCs):
A class of organic compounds that are easily evaporated into the air and used in the manufacturing, installation, and maintenance of many building products; many VOCs are toxic, and may contribute to urban smog, the greenhouse effect, and global warming.

Voltage, volts:
Voltage is the electrical force, or pressure that pushes the current over the conductors. Volts are the measurement units.

W

Wall cabinets:
Cabinets that are typically 12 inches to 18 inches (305 mm to 457 mm) deep and placed on the wall 15 inches to 18 inches (381 mm to 457 mm) above a base cabinet.

Wall-mounted lavatory:
A self-contained fixture that is mounted on the wall.

Wall-mounted showerhead:
A plumbing fixture mounted on the shower wall above the bather that dispenses water through a perforated surface. The wall-mounted showerhead is the most commonly used showerhead.

Waste pipe:
The pipe that carries water and waste away from a water-using fixture.

Water closet:
A term for an indoor privy where water was used to wash down human waste.

Water factor:
Measures water used per cycle in a clothes washing machine. The lower the water factor, the more efficient the machine.

Waterfall showerhead:
This type of showerhead dispenses water in sheets that resemble a waterfall.

WaterSense®:
A public-private partnership, led by the United States Environmental Protection Agency to provide independently tested and certified products that are 20% more water efficient than the market norm.

Water vapor:
Water in a gaseous form.

Wet spa bed:
A massage table with a shallow pool that holds water and drains.

Wet wall:
A wall containing supply lines and soil and waste lines.

Whirlpool:
A bath with jets that move warm water into a swirling motion; jetted bathtub.

X

Xenon:
Xenon lamps are similar to halogen lamps in their characteristics and are made with electrodes in a small tube filled with an inert gas. These lamps do not burn as hot as halogen lamps and are not as fragile. They operate at a lower voltage than the standard 120 volts, and thus require a transformer.

Z

Zen- or Spa-like theme:
A room design that provides a calm and quiet environment. It considers a focus that incorporates a togetherness of mind and body.

Resources

CHAPTER 2

National Association of Home Builders
1201 15th Street NW
Washington, DC 20005
www.nahb.com/

National Fenestration Rating Council
6305 Ivy Lane, Suite 140
Greenbelt, MD 20770
www.nfrc.org/about.aspx

CHAPTER 3

American Lung Association
1301 Pennsylvania Avenue NW
Washington, DC 20004
www.lung.org

American National Standards Institute
1899 L Street NW, 11th Floor
Washington, DC 20036
www.ansi.org

American Society of Heating, Refrigeration and Air-conditioning Engineers
1791 Tullie Circle N.E.
Atlanta, GA 30329
www.ashrae.org

American Tree Farm System®
1111 Nineteenth Street NW, Suite 780
Washington, DC 20036
www.treefarmsystem.org

Association of Home Appliance Manufacturers
1111 19th Street NW, Suite 402
Washington, DC 20036
www.aham.org

Austin Energy Green Building
721 Barton Springs Road
Austin, TX, 78704
www.austinenergy.com

Canada Mortgage and Housing Corp.
Housing Information Center
700 Montreal Road
Ottawa, ON, Canada K1A 0P7
www.cmhc-schl.gc.ca

Children's Environmental Health Network
110 Maryland Avenue NE, Suite 402
Washington, DC 20002
www.cehn.org

Cradle to Cradle Certification Program
MBDC, 1001 E. Market Street, Suite 200
Charlottesville, VA 22902
www.mbdc.com

Earth Advantage Institute
Director Building
808 SW 3rd Avenue, Suite 800
Portland, OR 97204
www.earthadvantage.org

Ecolabel
www.ecolabel.eu

Energy Star (see also: U. S. Environmental Protection Agency)
www.energystar.gov

Health Canada
Address Locator 0900C2,
Ottawa, ON, Canada K1A 0K9
www.hc-sc.gc.ca/

Forest Stewardship Council
www.fsc.org

Greenguard Environmental Institute
2211 Newmarket Parkway, Suite 110
Marietta, GA 30067
www.greenguard.org

International Code Council
500 New Jersey Avenue NW, 6th Floor
Washington, DC 20001
www.icc.org

National Green Building Program
www.nahbgreen.org

NAHB (National Association of Home Builders) Research Center
400 Prince George's Blvd.
Upper Marlboro, MD 20774
www.nahbrc.com

National Center for Environmental Health
Centers for Disease Control
1600 Clifton Road
Atlanta, GA 30333
www.cdc.gov/nceh

National Institute of Environmental Health Sciences
111 T.W. Alexander Drive
Research Triangle Park, NC 27709
www.niehs.nih.gov

Natural Resources Canada
www.oee.nrcan.gc.ca

Programme for the Endorsement of Forest Certification
www.pefc.org

Rocky Mountain Institute
2317 Snowmass Creek Roadd
Snowmass, CO 81654
www.rmi.org

Scientific Certification Systems
2000 Powell Street, Suite 600
Emeryville, CA 94608
www.sccscertified.com

Southface Energy Institute
241 Pine Street NE
Atlanta, GA 30308
www.southface.org

U.S. Environmental Protection Agency
Ariel Rios Building
1200 Pennsylvania Avenue NW
Washington, DC 20460
www.epa.gov

U.S. Green Building Council
2101 L Street, NW, Suite 500
Washington, DC 20037
www.usgbc.org

Water Quality Association
4151 Naperville Road
Lisle, IL 60532–3696
www.wqa.org

CHAPTER 4

Accessible and Usable Buildings and Facilities, ICC A117.1-2009
International Code Council
500 New Jersey Avenue NW, 6th Floor
Washington, DC 20001
www.iccsafe.org

American National Standards Institute
www.ansi.org (see chapter 3)

Barrier Free Architecturals, Inc.
2700 Dufferin Street, Unit 24
Toronto, ON, Canada M6B 4J3
www.barrierfree.org

Center for Inclusive Design and Environmental Access (IDEA Center)
School of Architecture and Planning
University of Buffalo
378 Hayes Hall
Buffalo, NY 14214-8030
www.ap.buffalo.edu/idea

Concrete Change-Visitability
600 Dancing Fox Road
Decatur, GA 30032
www.concretechange.org

Fair Housing Accessibility First
(see also U. S. Department of Housing and Urban Development)
www.fairhousingfirst.org

Institute on Human Centered Design (Adaptive Environments)
200 Portland Street
Boston, MA 02114
www.adaptenv.org
www.humancentereddesign.org

Mace Universal Design Institute
410 Yorktown Drive
Chapel Hill, NC 27516
www.udinstitute.org

National Resource Center on Supportive Housing and Home Modifications
Andrus Gerontology Center
University of Southern California
Los Angeles, CA 90089-0191
www.homemods.org

U.S. Access Board
1331 F. Street, NW, Suite 1000
Washington, DC 20004–1111
www.access-board.gov

U.S. Department of Housing and Urban Development
Tech. Assistance on Section 504 & Fair Housing: 800–827–5005
Publications Center: 800–767–7468
www.hud.gov/

CHAPTER 8

American Association of Retired Persons (AARP)
601 E Street NW
Washington, DC 20049
www.aarp.org

Abledata
8630 Fenton Street, Suite 930
Silver Spring, MD 20910
www.abledata.com

Access One
25679 Gramford Avenue
Wyoming, MN 55092
www.beyondbarriers.com

Alzheimer's Association
225 North Michigan Avenue, Suite 1700
Chicago, IL 60601–7633
www.alz.org

Alzheimer's Disease Education & Referral Center
ADEAR Center
P.O. Box 8250
Silver Spring, MD 20907–8250
www.alzheimers.org

American Foundation for the Blind
11 Penn Plaza, Suite 300
New York, NY 10001
www.afb.org

American Heart Association National Center
7272 Greenville Avenue
Dallas, TX 75231
www.americanheart.org

American National Standards Institute
1819 L Street, NW, 6th Floor
Washington, DC, 20036
www.ansi.org

American Occupational Therapy Association
4720 Montgomery Lane
P.O. Box 31220
Bethesda, MD 20850
www.aota.org

American Stroke Association
National Center
7272 Greenville Avenue
Dallas, TX 75231
www.strokeassociation.org

Amputee Coalition of America
900 East Hill Avenue, Suite 285
Knoxville, TN 37915–2568
www.amputee-coalition.org

Area Agencies on Aging
www.aoa.dhhs.gov/agingsites/state.html

Arthritis Foundation
1330 West Peachtree Street
P.O. Box 7669
Atlanta, GA 30309
www.arthritis.org

Barrier Free Architecturals, Inc.
2700 Dufferin Street, Unit 24
Toronto, ON, Canada M6B 4J3
www.barrierfree.org

Center for Inclusive Design and
Environmental Access (IDEA Center)
School of Architecture and Planning
University of Buffalo
3435 Main Street
114 Diefendorf Hall
Buffalo, NY 14214–3087
www.ap.buffalo.edu/idea/

The Center for Universal Design
North Carolina State University
50 Pullen Road
Brooks Hall, Room 104
Campus Box 8613
Raleigh, NC 27695
www.ncsu.edu/project/design-projects/udi/

Council for Exceptional Children
1110 North Glebe Road, Suite 300
Arlington, VA 22201
www.cec.sped.org

Cystic Fibrosis Foundation
6931 Arlington Road
Bethesda, MD 20814
www.cff.org

Disability Rights Education Defense Fund
1730 M Street NW, Suite 801
Washington, DC 20036
www.dredf.org

Disabled American Veterans
807 Maine Avenue SW
Washington, DC 20024
www.dav.org

Easter Seal Society
230 West Monroe Street, Suite 1800
Chicago, IL 60606
www.easter-seals.org

Eldercare Locator
c/o Administration on Aging
220 Independence Avenue SW
Washington, DC 20201
www.eldercare.gov

Harris Communications, Inc.
15155 Technology Drive
Eden Prairie, MN 55344–2277
www.harriscomm.com

Home Modification List Serve
Homemodification-list@listserv.acsu.buffalo.edu
Independent Living Research
Utilization Project
2323 South Shepard Street, Suite 1000
Houston, TX 77019
www.ilru.org

Institute for Human Centered Design
(Adaptive Environments) see Chapter 4)
Lifease Inc.
2451 15th Street NW, Suite D
New Brighton, MN 55112
www.lifease.com

Lighthouse International
111 East 59th Street
New York, NY 10022–1202
www.lighthouse.org

Mace Universal Design Institute (see Chapter 4)
Muscular Dystrophy Association
3300 East Sunrise Drive
Tucson, AZ 85718
www.mdausa.org

National Association of the Deaf
814 Thayer Avenue
Silver Spring, MD 20910–4500
www.nad.org

National Council on Independent Living
1916 Wilson Boulevard, Suite 209
Arlington, VA 22201
www.ncil.org

National Institute on Aging
Building 31, Room 5C27
31 Center Drive, MSC 2292
Bethesda, MD 20892
www.nia.nih.gov/

National Institute on Deafness and Other
Communication Disorders
National Institutes of Health
31 Center Drive, MSC 2320
Bethesda, MD USA 20892–2320
www.nidcd.nih.gov

National Institute on Disability and
Rehabilitation Research
US Department of Education
400 Maryland Avenue SW
Washington, DC 20202–2572
www.ed.gov/about/offices/list/osers/nidrr/
index.html? src=mr

National Kitchen & Bath Association
687 Willow Grove Street
Hackettstown, NJ 07840
www.nkba.org

National Rehabilitation Information Center
4200 Forbes Boulevard, Suite 202
Lanham, MD 20706
www.naric.com

National Resource Center on Supportive
Housing and Home Modifications
Andrus Gerontology Center
University of Southern California
3715 McClintock Avenue
Los Angeles, CA 90089–0191
www.homemods.org

Paralyzed Veterans of America
801 Eighteenth Street NW
Washington, DC 20006–3517
www.pva.org

ProMatura Group, LLC
142 Highway 30 E
Oxford, MS 38655
www.promatura.com\

Rehabilitation Engineering and Assistive
Technology Society of North America
(RESNA)
1700 North Moore Street, Suite 1540
Arlington, VA 22209–1903
www.resna.org

Trace Research and Development Center
University of Wisconsin
2107 Engineering Centers Bldg.
1500 Highland Avenue
Madison, WI 53706
www.trace.wisc.edu

U.S. Dept. of Justice Tech. Assist. on ADA
950 Pennsylvania Avenue NW
Civil Rights Division
Disability Rights Section—NYAV
Washington, DC 20530
www.usdoj.gov/crt/ada/adahom1.htm

Visitability List Serve
visitability-list@ACSU.buffalo.edu
Volunteers for Medical Engineering
2301 Argonne Drive
Baltimore, MD 21218
www.toad.net/~vme

CHAPTER 9

Consortium for Energy Efficiency, Inc.
98 North Washington Street, Suite 101
Boston, MA 02114-1918
www.cee1.org

Index